Essentials of Life-Span Development

THIRD EDITION

John W. Santrock

University of Texas at Dallas

Connect
Learn
Succeed™

ESSENTIALS OF LIFE-SPAN DEVELOPMENT, THIRD EDITION

Published by McGraw-Hill, a business unit of The McGraw-Hill Companies, Inc., 1221 Avenue of the Americas, New York, NY 10020. Copyright © 2014 by The McGraw-Hill Companies, Inc. All rights reserved. Printed in the United States of America. Previous editions © 2012 and 2008. No part of this publication may be reproduced or distributed in any form or by any means, or stored in a database or retrieval system, without the prior written consent of The McGraw-Hill Companies, Inc., including, but not limited to, in any network or other electronic storage or transmission, or broadcast for distance learning.

Some ancillaries, including electronic and print components, may not be available to customers outside the United States.

This book is printed on acid-free paper.

1 2 3 4 5 6 7 8 9 0 QDB/QDB 1 0 9 8 7 6 5 4 3

ISBN: 978-0-07-803542-5
MHID: 0-07-803542-2

Senior Vice President, Products & Markets: *Kurt L. Strand*
Vice President, General Manager, Products & Markets: *Michael Ryan*
Vice President, Content Production & Technology Services: *Kimberly Meriwether David*
Managing Director: *William Glass*
Director: *Mike Sugarman*
Brand Manager: *Allison McNamara*
Senior Director of Development: *Dawn Groundwater*
Editorial Coordinator: *Sarah Kiefer*
Marketing Manager: *Ann Helgerson*
Director, Content Production: *Terri Schiesi*
Lead Project Manager: *Sheila M. Frank*
Senior Buyer: *Sandy Ludovissy*
Designer: *Trevor Goodman*
Cover Images: **LEFT to RIGHT   First row:** *Jose Luis Pelaez Inc/Blend Images LLC, KidStock/Getty Images, Purestock/SuperStock;* **Second Row:** *Corbis, Drew Myers/Corbis;* **Third Row:** *Royalty-Free/Corbis, Purestock/SuperStock, Image Source/Corbis;* **Fourth Row:** *Fancy Collection/SuperStock, Purestock/SuperStock;* **Fifth Row:** *Fancy Collection/SuperStock, Bananastock/PictureQuest, Photodisc/Getty Images;* **Sixth Row:** *Tom Merton/OJO Images/Getty Images, Jose Luis Pelaez Inc/Getty Images;* **Seventh Row:** *Terry Vine/Blend Images LLC, Dave and Les Jacobs/Blend Images LLC, Royalty-Free/Corbis;* **Eighth Row:** *Liza McCorkle/Getty Images, Amos Morgan;* **Ninth Row:** *Getty Images, Ariel Skelley/Blend Images LLC, Gary John Norman/Getty Images;* **Tenth Row:** *Getty Images*
Lead Content Licensing Specialist: *Carrie K. Burger*
Photo Research: *Jennifer Blankenship*
Compositor: *Aptara®, Inc.*
Typeface: *10/12 Janson Text LT*
Printer: *Quad/Graphics*

Library of Congress Cataloging-in-Publication Data

Santrock, John W.
    Essentials of life-span development / John W. Santrock. – 3rd ed.
        p. cm.
    Includes index.
    ISBN 978–0–07–803542–5 — ISBN 0–07–803542–2 (hard copy : alk. paper)
    1. Developmental psychology. I. Title.
BF713.S256 2014
155–dc23

2012039919

The Internet addresses listed in the text were accurate at the time of publication. The inclusion of a website does not indicate an endorsement by the authors or McGraw-Hill, and McGraw-Hill does not guarantee the accuracy of the information presented at these sites.

www.mhhe.com

With special appreciation to my wife, Mary Jo

About the Author

John W. Santrock received his Ph.D. from the University of Minnesota in 1973. He taught at the University of Charleston and the University of Georgia before joining the Program in Psychology and Human Development at the University of Texas at Dallas, where he currently teaches a number of undergraduate courses and was given the University's Effective Teaching Award in 2006.

John has been a member of the editorial boards of *Child Development* and *Developmental Psychology*. His research on father custody is widely cited and used in expert witness testimony to promote flexibility and alternative considerations in custody disputes. John also has authored these exceptional McGraw-Hill texts: *Children* (12th edition), *Adolescence* (14th edition), *Life-Span Development* (14th edition), *A Topical Approach to Life-Span Development* (6th edition), and *Educational Psychology* (5th edition).

John Santrock, teaching in his undergraduate course in life-span development.

For many years, John was involved in tennis as a player, teaching professional, and coach of professional tennis players. At the University of Miami (Fl), the tennis team on which he played still holds the NCAA Division I record for most consecutive wins (137) in any sport. His wife, Mary Jo, has a master's degree in special education and has worked as a teacher and a Realtor. He has two daughters—Tracy, who also is a Realtor, and Jennifer, who is a medical sales specialist. He has one granddaughter, Jordan, age 21, currently an undergraduate student at Southern Methodist University, and two grandsons, Alex, age 8, and Luke, age 6. In the last decade, John also has spent time painting expressionist art.

Brief Contents

v

Contents

How Would You?

Health Care Professions

Family Studies Professions

McGraw-Hill Connect Life-Span Development

adaptive learning system

McGraw-Hill Connect® Life-Span Development is our response to today's student. The groundbreaking adaptive learning system helps students "know what they know" while helping them learn what they don't know through engaging interactive exercises, click/drag activities, the Milestones program, and video clips. Instructors using Connect are reporting that their students' performance is improving by a letter grade or more. Through this unique tool, *Essentials of Life-Span Development* gives instructors the ability to identify struggling students quickly and easily, *before* the first exam.

Connect Life-Span Development's adaptive diagnostic tool develops an individualized learning plan for every student. Confidence levels tailor the next question to each individual, helping students to identify what they don't know. If a student is doing well, the adaptive diagnostic tool will challenge the student with more applied and conceptual questions. If the student is struggling, the system identifies problem areas and directs the student to the exact page they need to read. In doing so, it works like a GPS, helping students master key concepts efficiently and effectively.

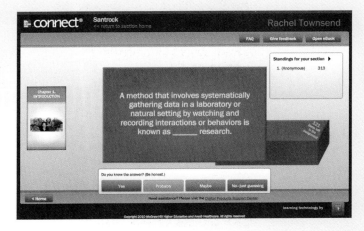

Regardless of individual study habits, preparation, and approaches to the course, students will find that *Essentials of Life-Span Development* connects with them on a personal, individual basis and provides a road map for success in the course.

milestones

Experience life as it unfolds

- Engage with real children developing over time.
- Test your ability to apply course content to real children, adolescents, and adults.

McGraw-Hill's Milestones is a powerful tool that allows students to experience life as it unfolds, from infancy to late adulthood.

Milestones consists of two essential components that work together to capture key changes throughout the life span—**Milestones of Child Development** and **Milestones: Transitions**.

In **Milestones of Child Development,** students track the early stages of physical, social, and emotional development. By watching one child over time or comparing various children, Milestones provides a unique, experiential learning environment that can only be achieved by watching real human development as it happens—all in pre-, transitional, and post-milestone segments.

In **Milestones: Transitions,** students meet a series of people—from teenagers to individuals in late adulthood—to hear individual perspectives on changes that occur throughout the life span. Through a series of interviews, students are given the opportunity to think critically while exploring the differences in attitudes on everything from body image to changes in emotion, sexuality, cognitive processes, and death and dying.

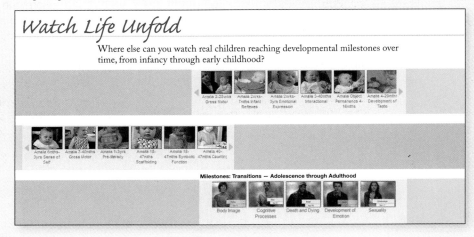

Watch Life Unfold

Where else can you watch real children reaching developmental milestones over time, from infancy through early childhood?

Easy to use course management allows you to **spend less time administering and more time teaching.**

MCGRAW-HILL/BB/DO MORE

Through McGraw-Hill's partnership with Blackboard®, *Essentials of LifeSpan Development* offers a seamless integration of content and tools:

- Seamless gradebook between Blackboard and Connect
- Single sign-on providing seamless integration between McGraw-Hill content and Blackboard
- Simplicity in assigning and engaging your students with course materials

create

Craft your teaching resources to match the way you teach! With McGraw-Hill Create™, **www.mcgrawhillcreate .com,** you can easily rearrange chapters, combine material from other content sources, and quickly upload content you have written, such as your course syllabus or teaching notes. Find the content you need in Create by searching through thousands of leading McGraw-Hill textbooks. Arrange your book to fit your teaching style. Create even allows you to personalize your book's appearance by selecting the cover and adding your name, school, and course information. Order a Create book and you'll receive a complimentary print review copy in three to five business days or a complimentary electronic review copy (eComp) via e-mail in about an hour. Go to **www.mcgrawhillcreate.com** today and register. Experience how McGraw-Hill Create empowers you to teach *your* students *your* way.

tegrity

McGraw-Hill Tegrity® is a service that makes class time available all the time by automatically capturing every lecture in a searchable format for students to review when they study and complete assignments. With a simple one-click start and stop process, users capture all computer screens and corresponding audio. Students replay any part of any class with easy-to-use browser-based viewing on a PC or Mac. Educators know that the more students can see, hear, and experience class resources, the better they learn. With Tegrity, students quickly recall key moments by using Tegrity's unique search feature. This search helps students efficiently find what they need, when they need it, across an entire semester of class recordings. Help turn all your students' study time into learning moments immediately supported by your lecture.

coursesmart

This text is available as a CourseSmart eTextbook at **www.CourseSmart.com.** At CourseSmart your students can take advantage of significant savings off the cost of a print textbook, reduce their impact on the environment, and gain access to powerful Web tools for learning. CourseSmart eTextbooks can be viewed online or downloaded to a computer. The eTextbooks allow students to do full text searches, add highlighting and notes, and share notes with classmates. CourseSmart has the largest selection of eTextbooks available anywhere. Visit **www.CourseSmart.com** to learn more and to try a sample chapter.

Preface

The Essential Approach

In the view of many instructors who teach the life-span development course, the biggest challenge they face is covering all periods of human development within one academic term. My own teaching experience bears this out. I have had to skip over much of the material in a comprehensive life-span development text in order to focus on key topics and concepts that students find difficult and to fit in applications that are relevant to students' lives. I wrote *Essentials of Life-Span Development* to respond to the need for a shorter text that covers core content in a way that is meaningful to diverse students.

This third edition continues my commitment to a brief introduction to life-span development—with an exciting difference. Recognizing that most of today's students have grown up in a digital world, I take very seriously the need for communicating content in different ways, online as well as in print. Consequently, I'm enthusiastic about McGraw-Hill's new online assignment and assessment platform, **Connect Life-Span Development,** which incorporates this text and the captivating **Milestones** video modules. Together, these resources give students and instructors the essential coverage, applications, and course tools they need to tailor the life-span course to meet their specific needs.

The Essential Teaching and Learning Environment

Research shows that students today learn in multiple modalities. Not only do their work preferences tend to be more visual and more interactive, but their reading and study sessions often occur in short bursts. With shorter chapters and innovative interactive study modules, *Essentials of Life-Span Development* allows students to study whenever, wherever, and however they choose. Regardless of individual study habits, preparation, and approaches to the course, *Essentials* connects with students on a personal, individual basis and provides a road map for success in the course.

Essential Coverage

The challenge in writing *Essentials of Life-Span Development* was determining what comprises the core content of the course. With the help of consultants and instructors who responded to surveys and reviewed the content at different stages of development, I have been able to present all of the core topics, key ideas, and most important research in life-span development that students need to know in a brief format that stands on its own merits.

The 17 brief chapters of *Essentials* are organized chronologically and cover all periods of the human life span, from the prenatal period through late adulthood and death. Providing a broad overview of life-span development, this edition also especially gives attention to the theories and concepts that students seem to have difficulty mastering.

Essential Applications

Applied examples give students a sense that the field of life-span development has personal meaning for them. In this edition of *Essentials* are numerous real-life applications as well as research applications for each period of the life span.

In addition to applied examples, *Essentials of Life-Span Development* offers applications for students in a variety of majors and career paths.

- *How Would You . . . ?* questions. Given that students enrolled in the life-span course have diverse majors, *Essentials* includes applications that appeal to different interests. The most prevalent areas of specialization are education, human development and family studies, health professions, psychology, and social work. To engage these students and ensure that *Essentials* orients them to concepts that are key to their understanding of life-span development, I asked instructors specializing in these fields to contribute *How Would You . . . ?* questions for each chapter. Strategically placed in the margin next to relevant topics, these questions highlight the essential takeaway ideas for these students.

How Would You...?

As a psychologist, how would you advise a 25-year-old mother who is concerned about the possibility of birth defects but has no genetic history of these types of problems?

point, NIPD has mainly focused on brain imaging techniques and the isolation and examination of fetal cells circulating in the mother's blood and analysis of cell-free fetal DNA in maternal plasma (Geaghan, 2012; Zugazaga Cortazar, & Martin Martinez, 2012).

Researchers already have used NIPD to successfully test for genes inherited from a father that cause cystic fibrosis and Huntington's disease. They also are exploring the potential for using NIPD very early in fetal development to diagnose a baby's sex and detect Down syndrome (Fernandez-Martinez & others, 2012; Miura & others, 2011).

- *Careers in Life-Span Development.* This feature personalizes life-span development by describing an individual working in a career related to the chapter's focus. Chapter 2, for example, profiles Holly Ishmael, a genetic counselor. The feature describes Ms. Ishmael's education and work setting, includes a direct quote from Ms. Ishmael, discusses various employment options for genetic counselors, and provides resources for students who want to find out more about careers in genetic counseling.

Careers in life-span development

Holly Ishmael, Genetic Counselor

Holly Ishmael is a genetic counselor at Children's Mercy Hospital in Kansas City. She obtained an undergraduate degree in psychology and then a master's degree in genetic counseling from Sarah Lawrence College.

Genetic counselors work as members of a health-care team, providing information and support to families with birth defects or genetic disorders. They identify families at risk by analyzing inheritance patterns and explore options with the family. Some genetic counselors, like Holly, become specialists in prenatal and pediatric genetics; others might specialize in cancer genetics or psychiatric genetic disorders.

Holly says, "Genetic counseling is a perfect combination for people who want to do something science-oriented, but need human contact and don't want to spend all of their time in a lab or have their nose in a book" (Rizzo, 1999, p. 5).

Genetic counselors have specialized graduate degrees in the areas of medical genetics and counseling. They enter graduate school with undergraduate backgrounds from a

Holly Ishmael (*left*) in a genetic counseling session.

variety of disciplines, including biology, genetics, psychology, public health, and social work. There are approximately 30 graduate genetic counseling programs in the United States. If you are interested in this profession, you can obtain further information from the National Society of Genetic Counselors at www.nsgc.org.

New in This Edition

I have extensively updated both the research and applied content for this edition of *Essentials of Life-Span Development*. In addition to presenting the latest, most contemporary research in each period of human development, including more than 1,000 citations from 2010, 2011, 2012, and 2013 alone, I made the following revisions.

Chapter 1: Introduction

- Update on life expectancy in the United States (U.S. Census Bureau, 2011)
- Expanded discussion of poverty and children, including updated statistics on the percentage of U.S. children under 18 years of age living in poverty (U.S. Census Bureau, 2012)
- Important new section, Age and Happiness
- Description of a study in which it was revealed that the oldest adults in the study—in their eighties—were the happiest of all the ages studied (Yang, 2008)
- New Figure 1.5, How Satisfied Am I with My Life? that gives students an opportunity to evaluate their life satisfaction on the most widely used measure in research on life satisfaction (Diener, 2012; Diener & others, 1985)
- Revised and updated commentary about social age and its links to happiness and longevity (Carstensen & others, 2011)
- Inclusion of recent research and commentary on Millennials involving ethnic diversity and technology, based on a recent national survey by the Pew Research Center (2010)
- New Figure 1.14 describing various generations, their historical period, and their characteristics

Chapter 2: Biological Beginnings

- Editing and updating of chapter based on detailed reviews by leading experts Kirby Deater-Deckard and David Moore
- New discussion of the genome-wide association study that is increasingly used to identify genetic variations in individuals who have a disease compared to those who don't (National Human Genome Research Institute, 2012)
- New coverage of some diseases for which genome-wide association studies recently have been conducted: child obesity (Early Growth Genetics Consortium & others, 2012), Alzheimer disease (Raj & others, 2012), and cardiovascular disease (Lusis, 2012)
- Expanded and updated material on modifications in DNA expression as a result of stress, radiation, and temperature (Georgakilas, 2011)
- Description of a recent study that found exposure to radiation changes the rate of DNA synthesis (Lee & others, 2011)

- New section on gene-gene interaction to include recent studies of immune system functioning (Reijmerink & others, 2011), asthma (Su & others, 2012), cancer (Bushel & others, 2012), cardiovascular disease (Xiao & others, 2012), and arthritis (Ronninger & others, 2012)
- Addition of information about epigenetic mechanisms involving the actual molecular modification of the DNA strand as a result of environmental inputs in ways that alter gene functioning (Feil & Fraga, 2012; Meaney, 2010)
- Updated coverage of the concept of $G \times E$, which involves the interaction of a specific measured variation in the DNA sequence and a specific measured aspect of the environment (Bihagi & others, 2012; Petersen & others, 2012; Zannas & others, 2012)
- Description of recent research indicating that variations in dopamine-related genes interact with supportive or unsupportive environments to influence children's development (Bakermans-Kranenburg & van IJzendoorn, 2011)
- Updated material on noninvasive prenatal diagnosis (NIPD) (Chiu & Lo, 2012; Geaghan, 2012)
- New information about being able to determine the sex of the fetus at an earlier point in pregnancy through new noninvasive procedures (Kolialexi & others, 2012)
- Discussion of a recent meta-analysis indicating that a baby's sex can be determined as early as seven weeks into pregnancy (Devaney & others, 2011)
- Coverage of recent research that found deficiencies in the brain pathways involved in the working memory of children with FASD (Diwadkar & others, 2012)
- Coverage of a recent study that found cigarette smoke weakened and increased oxidative stress in the fetal membranes from which the placenta develops (Menon & others, 2011)
- Information about a recent study that found environmental tobacco smoke exposure during pregnancy was linked to diminished ovarian functioning in female offspring (Kilic & others, 2012)
- Description of recent research that found deregulation of gene expression in 114 fetal cells of offspring was linked to pregnant women's exposure to environmental smoke (Votavova & others, 2012)
- Coverage of a recent research review that concluded cocaine quickly crosses the placenta to reach the fetus (De Giovanni & Marchetti, 2012)

- Update on the most consistent negative outcomes of cocaine use during pregnancy (Gouin & others, 2011)

- Description of recent research on the negative effects of cocaine exposure prenatally on children's attention and externalizing problems (Minnes & others, 2010; Richardson & others, 2011)

- Coverage of a recent study that found prenatal meth exposure was associated with smaller head circumference, neonatal intensive care unit (NICU) admission, and referral to child protective services (Shah & others, 2012)

- Discussion of prenatal methamphetamine exposure and decreased brain activation, especially in the frontal lobes, in 7- to 15-year-olds (Roussotte & others, 2011)

- Coverage of a recent research review that linked maternal depression to preterm birth (Dunkel Schetter, 2011)

- Description of a recent study that revealed paternal smoking around the time of the child's conception was linked to an increased risk of the child developing leukemia (Milne & others, 2012)

- Coverage of a recent research review indicating an increased risk of spontaneous abortion, autism, and schizophrenic disorders in offspring born when the father was 40 years of age and older (Reproductive Endocrinology and Infertility Committee & others, 2011)

- Coverage of a recent experimental study of the effects of a CenteringPregnancy Plus program on high-stress pregnant women (Ickovics & others, 2011)

- Inclusion of recent research indicating that exercise during pregnancy improved mothers' perception of their health (Barakat & others, 2011)

- Discussion of a recent study that revealed yoga and massage therapy sessions resulted in decreased levels of depression, anxiety, and back and leg pain (Field & others, 2012)

- Discussion of a recent study that found waterbirth was linked with a shorter second stage of labor (Cortes, Basra, & Kelleher, 2011)

- Discussion of the results of two recent research reviews that indicated massage therapy reduces pain during labor (Jones & others, 2012; Smith & others, 2012)

- Updated coverage of increased evidence that acupuncture can have positive effects on labor and delivery (Citkovitz, Schnyer, & Hoskins, 2011)

- Updated description of the percentage of infants born preterm in the United States, including the overall rate and ethnic variations in 2009 (National Center for Health Statistics, 2011)

- Updated data about the percentage of infants born with low birth weight in the United States (U.S. Census Bureau, 2012)

- Description of recent research that found low birth weight was associated with childhood autism (Lampl & others, 2012)

- Information from a recent research review that concluded kangaroo care reduced the risk of mortality in low birth weight infants (Conde-Aguedelo, Belizan, & Diaz-Rossello, 2011)

- Coverage of a recent study that revealed the mechanisms responsible for weight gain in massaged preterm infants (Field, Diego, & Hernandez-Reif, 2011)

Chapter 3: Physical and Cognitive Development in Infancy

- Inclusion of changes in the coverage of the development of the brain based on leading expert consultant Martha Ann Bell's comments

- Description of a recent analysis indicating the most frequent perpetrators of shaken baby syndrome (National Center on Shaken Baby Syndrome, 2012)

- Update on the role of myelination in providing energy for neurons (Fancy & others, 2012; Harris & Atwell, 2012)

- New section, The Neuroconstructivist View, that describes an increasingly popular perspective on the brain's development (Diamond, 2013; Johnson, 2011; Westerman, Thomas, & Karmiloff-Smith, 2011; Peltzer-Karpf, 2012)

- Description of a recent research review of sleep patterns in infancy (Galland & others, 2012)

- Inclusion of information about a recent study that revealed by 6 months of age, a majority of infants slept through the night, awakening their mothers only once or twice a week (Weinraub & others, 2012)

- Discussion of a recent study that revealed nighttime wakings at 12 months of age predicted a lower level of sleep efficiency at 4 years of age (Tikotzky & Shaashua, 2012)

- Description of a recent meta-analysis linking breast-feeding to a lower incidence of SIDS (Hauck & others, 2011)

- New material on recent research indicating that as many as 10 to 15 percent of SIDS cases are linked to heart arrhythmias with gene mutations being involved in the arrhythmias (Brion & others, 2012; Van Norstrand & others, 2012)

- Description of recent research that found low maternal sensitivity when infants were 15 and 24 months of age was linked to a higher risk of obesity in adolescence (Anderson & others, 2012)

- Inclusion of the American Academy of Pediatrics Section on Breastfeeding's (2012) reconfirmation of its recommendation of exclusive breast feeding in the first six months, followed by continued breast feeding as complementary foods are introduced, and further breast feeding for one year or longer as mutually desired by the mother and infant

- A number of changes made in the material on motor development based on leading expert Karen Adolph's feedback

- Description of a recent study by Karen Adolph and her colleagues (2012) that found 12- to 19-month-olds took 2,368 steps and fell 17 times an hour during free play, suggesting the extensiveness of locomotor experience

- Updated discussion of reflexes with the new look in infant reflexes arguing that reflexes are not exclusively inborn, genetic mechanisms but rather that infants can deliberately control such movements (Adolph & Berger, 2013; Adolph & Robinson, 2013)

- A number of changes in the discussion of perceptual development based on feedback from leading expert Scott Johnson

- Much expanded and updated coverage of the dramatic increase in the use of sophisticated eye-tracking equipment in the study of infant perception (Aslin, 2012; Oakes, 2012)

- Description of a recent eye-tracking study in which 1-year-old infants showed less efficient looking at an educational video than their older counterparts (Kirkorian, Anderson, & Keen, 2012)

- Coverage of a recent fMRI study that confirmed the fetus can hear at 33 to 34 months into the prenatal period by assessing fetal brain responses to auditory stimuli (Jardri & others, 2012)

- Added commentary that most perception is intermodal (Bahrick, 2010)

- Expanded conclusions about the themes of the current field of infant cognitive development to emphasize the substantial increase in interest in cognitive developmental neuroscience and links between brain processes and cognitive processes (Diamond, 2013; Morasch & others, 2013; Peltzer-Karpf, 2012)

- Updated coverage of concept formation, including a revised definition of concepts

- Added recent commentary about learning by infant research Alison Gopnik (2010) on the importance of putting things into the right categories

- Description of a recent study that revealed 6-month-old infants comprehend the names of parts of their body, such as "feet" and "hands" (Tincoff & Jusczyk, 2012)

- New coverage of Michael Tomasello's (2011) emphasis on the importance of specific contexts in learning language, especially in contexts involving joint attention

- New description of the increasing emphasis on the development of pointing in infancy as a key aspect of joint attention and an important index of the social aspects of language (Begus & Southgate, 2012; Goldin-Meadow & Alibali, 2013)

- Expanded discussion of strategies for effective communicating with infants (Gopnik, 2010)

- Increased emphasis on how important it is for children's optimal development that parents and teachers provide children with many opportunities to talk and be talked with (Hirsh-Pasek & Golinkoff, 2013)

Chapter 4: Socioemotional Development in Infancy

- Revision and updating of the functions of emotion in infancy to include its role in behavioral organization (social responding and adaptive behavior) (Easterbrooks & others, 2013; Thompson, 2013a)

- Discussion of a recent study that revealed the newborns of depressed mothers showed less vocal distress at the cries of another infant, reflecting emotional and physiological dysregulation (Jones, 2012)

- Description of a recent study that found mothers' emotional reactions (anxiety and anger) increased the risk of subsequent attachment insecurity (Leerkes, Parade, & Gudmundson, 2011)

- Inclusion of recent research indicating a link between problems in infant soothability at 6 months of age and insecure attachment at 12 months of age (Mills-Koonce, Propper, & Barnett, 2012)

- New coverage of how the development of temperament capabilities allows individual differences to emerge, including such factors as the development of the prefrontal cortex being necessary for effortful control to be achieved (Bates, 2012a, b)

- Description of a recent study that found infants of mothers who were stressed had a lower level of effortful control while infants of extraverted mothers showed a higher level of effortful control (Gartstein & others, 2012)

- Discussion of a recent study that revealed U.S. infants showed more temperamental fearfulness while Finnish infants engaged in more positive affect, especially effortful control (Gaias & others, 2012)

- Coverage of a recent study linking behavioral inhibition at 3 years of age with shyness 4 years later (Volbrecht & Goldsmith, 2010)

- Discussion of a recent longitudinal study linking shyness/inhibition in infancy/childhood to social anxiety at 21 years of age (Bohlin & Hagekull, 2009)

- Added information about research indicating that decreases in infants' negative emotionality are related to higher levels of parents' sensitivity, involvement, and responsivity (Bates, 2012a, b)

- New commentary about how too often the biological foundations of temperament are interpreted as meaning that temperament can develop and change. However, key dimensions (such as adaptability and soothability) of the self-regulatory aspect of temperament do develop and change as neurobiological and experiential processes develop and change (Easterbrooks & others, 2013)

- New discussion of decreases in negative emotionality in children when their parents are involved, responsive, and sensitive in interacting with them (Bates, 2012a, b; Penela & others, 2012)

- Coverage of a longitudinal study that found changes in attachment security/insecurity from infancy to adulthood were linked to stresses and supports in socioemotional contexts (Van Ryzin, Carlson, & Sroufe, 2011)

- New description of the developmental cascade model that is increasingly being used to study connections across domains over time that influence developmental pathways and outcomes (Cicchetti, 2013; Masten, 2013)

- Description of recent research linking disorganized attachment in infancy, a specific gene (5-HTTLPR), and levels of maternal responsiveness (Spangler & others, 2009)

- Inclusion of recent research studies on the transition to parenthood that involve negative changes in relationships for both married and cohabiting women with their partners, and violated expectations (Biehle & Mickelson, 2012; Mortensen & others, 2012)

- Discussion of recent research indicating that fathers with a college-level education engaged in more stimulating physical activities with their infants and that fathers in a conflicting couple relationship participated in less caregiving and physical play with their infants (Cabrera, Hofferth, & Chae, 2011)

- Inclusion of new information about the concept of transactions reflecting reciprocal socialization (Sameroff, 2009, 2012)

- New section, Managing and Guiding Infants' Behavior (Holden, Vittrup, & Rosen, 2011)

- New material on the percentage of parents who use various management and corrective methods in dealing with infants' undesirable behaviors, including new Figure 4.7 (Vittrup, Holden, & Buck, 2006)

- Description of a recent study that found marital intimacy and partner support during prenatal development were linked to father-infant attachment following childbirth (Yu & others, 2012)

- Coverage of a recent study that found depressed fathers focused more on their own needs than their infants' needs and engaged in more negative and critical speech toward their infants (Sethna, Murray, & Ramchandi, 2012)

- Description of a recent study using the NICHD SECCYD data indicating that the worst socioemotional outcomes for children occurred when both home and child care settings conferred risk (Watamura & others, 2011)

Chapter 5: Physical and Cognitive Development in Early Childhood

- Description of a recent study that found the most frequently consumed vegetable by 2- and 3-year-olds was French fries or other fried potatoes (Fox & others, 2010)

- Coverage of recent data on the increasing percentage of 2- to 5-year-old obese children in the United States, including trends from 1976–1980 through 2007–2010 (Ogden & others, 2012)

- Discussion of a recent study indicating that preschool children who were overweight had a significant risk of being overweight/obese at 11 years of age (Shankaran & others, 2011)

- Updated coverage of the WIC program to improve the nutrition, health, and well-being of infants, young children, and their mothers in low-income U.S. families (WIC New York, 2011)

- Expanded criticism of Vygotsky's theory (Goncu & Gauvain, 2011)

- New discussion of a recent literacy intervention program with Spanish-speaking families in the Los Angeles WIC program that increased literacy resources and activities in homes, which in turn led to a higher level of school readiness in children (Whaley & others, 2011)

- Description of a recent study that found parental smoking was a risk factor for higher blood pressure in children (Simonetti & others, 2011)

- Description of a recent fMRI study indicating brain locations that were linked to 9- and 10-year-olds' conservation success when compared with nonconserving 5- and 6-year-olds (Houde & others, 2011)

- Coverage of a recent research study linking television watching and video game playing to children's attention problems (Swing & others, 2010)

- New material on using computer exercises to improve children's attention, including a Web site (www. teach-the-brain.org/learn/attention/index.htm) about how to use the games with children (Jaeggi, Berman, & Jonides, 2009; Steiner & others, 2011; Tang & Posner, 2009)

- New discussion of the increasing interest in executive functioning, including the importance of its early development in the preschool years (Carlson & White, 2013; Zelazo & Muller, 2011)

- New description of Ann Masten and her colleagues' (Herbers & others, 2011; Masten, 2013; Masten & others, 2008) research that has found executive functioning and parenting skills are linked to school success in homeless children

- New commentary that whether infants have a theory of mind continues to be debated (Rakoczy, 2012)

- Expanded coverage of cognitive factors other than theory of mind that might be involved in autism, including eye gaze, face processing, memory, and language impairment (Boucher, 2012a, b; Boucher, Mayes, & Bigham, 2012)

- New material on Kathy Hirsh-Pasek and Roberta Golinkoff's (Harris, Golinkoff, & Hirsh-Pasek, 2011; Hirsh-Pasek & Golinkoff, 2013) six principles for optimal word learning in young children

- New material on strategies for using books with pre-schoolers (Galinsky, 2010)

- Description of a recent study indicating that Early Head Start had a protective effect on the risks children might experience in parenting, language development, and self-control (Ayoub, Vallotton, & Mastergeorge, 2011)

Chapter 6: Socioemotional Development in Early Childhood

- Description of the current debate about Ross Thompson's (2013c, d) view that young children are more socially sensitive and Susan Harter's (2012) view that they are more egocentric

- Coverage of a recent study that found fathers' emotion coaching was related to children's social competence (Baker, Fenning, & Crnic, 2011)

- Inclusion of recent research indicating that maternal emotional coping was linked to less oppositional behavior in children (Dunsmore, Booker, & Ollendick, 2012)

- Expanded material on the importance of emotion regulation in children's social competence, self-regulation, and executive functioning (Nelson & others, 2012; Thompson, 2013a, b)

- New description of recent research by Cybelle Raver and her colleagues (Raver & others, 2012; Zhai, Raver, & Jones, 2012) on links between increased caregiver emotional expression, self-regulation, and reduction of behavior problems in Head Start families

- Discussion of research indicating that mothers' knowledge about what distresses and comforts their children predicts children's coping, empathy, and prosocial behavior (Vinik, Almas, & Grusec, 2011)

- Updated and expanded coverage of criticisms of Piaget's view of young children's moral development based on research indicating that young children often show a non-egocentric awareness of others' intentions and know when someone violates a moral prohibition (Thompson, 2012)

- New commentary about recent research on Asian American parents and Confucian goals (Russell, Crockett, & Chao, 2010)

- Description of a recent study in six countries linking physical punishment to high rates of aggression in children (Gershoff & others, 2010)

- Expanded and updated discussion of the effects of punishment on children's development, including longitudinal studies that have linked early physical punishment to later aggression (Taylor & others, 2010), and cross-cultural studies that have found in countries in which physical punishment is considered normal and necessary for handling children's transgressions, the effects of punishment are less harmful (Lansford & others, 2005, 2012)

- Description of a recent study of father involvement and coparenting (Jia & Schoppe-Sullivan, 2011)

- Updated statistics on child maltreatment (U.S. Department of Health and Human Services, 2010)

- Expanded and updated coverage of family-related factors that can contribute to child maltreatment (Cicchetti, 2013; Laslett & others, 2012; Turner & others, 2012)

- Discussion of a study linking child maltreatment with financial and employment problems

- Added commentary about parental work's effect on children not being only a maternal employment issue, but often involving the father as well (Parke & Clarke-Stewart, 2011)

- Coverage of a recent study that revealed a significant increase in suicide attempts before age 18 when repeated child maltreatment occurred (Jonson-Reid, Kohl, & Drake, 2012)

- Description of recent research studies that linked child maltreatment to risk for various diseases and physical health problems, sexual problems, and depression as adults (Lacelle & others, 2012; Nanni, Uher, & Danese, 2012; Widom & others, 2012)

- Expanded and updated coverage of the relationship between divorced parents and its link to visitations by the non-custodial parent (Fabricius & others, 2010)

- Coverage of a recent study indicating that an intervention aimed at improving the mother-child relationship was linked to improvements in the coping skills of children of divorced parents (Velez & others, 2011)

- Added comment about father involvement dropping off more than mother involvement following a divorce, especially for fathers of girls

- Inclusion of information about joint custody working best for children when the divorced parents can get along with each other (Parke & Clarke-Stewart, 2011)

- New material on recent immigrants to the United States adopting a bicultural orientation and embracing the importance of education for their children (Cooper, 2011)

- Expanded and updated coverage of the stressful and difficult experiences that children in many immigrant families face, including children in undocumented families (Yoshikawa, 2011)

- Description of how many ethnic/immigrant families focus on issues associated with promoting children's ethnic pride, knowledge of their ethnic group, and awareness of discrimination (Rogers & others, 2012; Simpkins & others, 2012)

- Discussion of a recent study linking early and persistent poverty to lower cognitive functioning in 5-year-old children (Schoon & others, 2012)

- New discussion of Kathy Hirsh-Pasek, Roberta Golinkoff, & Dorothy Singer's (Hirsh-Pasek & others, 2009; Singer, Golinkoff, & Hirsh-Pasek, 2006) concerns about the decline of play in young children's lives and inclusion of the many positive cognitive and socioemotional outcomes that come from play

- New section, Media and Screen Time, that focuses on the increasing concern about the extensive time young children spend in media and screen time (De Decker & others, 2012; Zimmerman & others, 2012)

- Inclusion of recent research linking higher levels of screen time at 4 to 6 years of age with increased obesity and low physical activity from preschool through adolescence (te Velde & others, 2012)

Chapter 7: Physical and Cognitive Development in Middle and Late Childhood

- Inclusion of recent research focused on the connection between physical activity level of 9-year-olds and their risk of metabolic disease (Parrett & others, 2011)

- Description of recent data on the percentage of U.S. 6- to 11-year-olds who are overweight or obese, which in 2009–2010 was 50 percent higher than the percentage of 2- to 5-year-olds who were overweight (Ogden & others, 2012)

- Coverage of a recent study on the effectiveness of a school-based program for increasing children's physical activity (Kriemler & others, 2010).

- Description of a recent study that found having two overweight/obese parents significantly increased the likelihood that children would be overweight/obese (Xu & others, 2011)

- Inclusion of information from a recent research review that found obesity was linked to children's low self-esteem (Gomes & others, 2011)

- Inclusion of recent research that found both peers and family members teased overweight children more than normal-weight children (McCormack & others, 2011)

- Inclusion of information about a recent successful behavior modification program that increased overweight and obese children's exercise and reduced their TV viewing time (Goldfield, 2012)

- Coverage of recent intervention studies that indicate modifying parents' eating habits and increasing children's exercise can help overweight and obese children to lose weight (Collins & others, 2011)

- Updated material on childhood cancer, including improved survival rates for some childhood cancers (National Cancer Institute, 2012; Wayne, 2011)

- Updated statistics on the percentage of students with various disabilities who receive special education services in U.S. schools (Aud & others, 2011)

- Expanded discussion of possible misdiagnosis of ADHD, including details of a recent experimental study that found clinicians overdiagnosed ADHD symptoms, especially in boys (Bruchmiller, Margraf, & Schneider, 2012)

- New description of some developmental outcomes of children with ADHD, including increased risks for dropping out of school, adolescent pregnancy, substance abuse problems, and engaging in antisocial behavior (Chang, Lichtenstein, & Larsson, 2012; Von Polier, Vloet, & Herpertz-Dahlman, 2012)

- Coverage of a recent study indicating delayed development in the frontal lobes of children with ADHD, likely due to a delay or a decrease in myelination (Nagel & others, 2011)

- Description of a recent study that linked maternal cigarette smoking during pregnancy to ADHD in 6- to 7-year-old children (Sciberras, Ukoumunne, & Efron, 2011)

- New coverage of executive functioning deficits in children with ADHD and their links to brain functioning (Jacobson & others, 2011)

- New material on deficits in theory of mind in children with ADHD (Buhler & others, 2011)

- Inclusion of recent estimates indicating that in 2008 1 in 88 children had an autistic spectrum disorder, a dramatic increase since 2002 estimates (Centers for Disease Control & Prevention, 2012d)

- New discussion of the role that connectivity between different brain regions might play in the development of autism (Just & others, 2012; Philip & others, 2012)

- New section, Executive Functioning, that highlights the increased interest in children's executive functioning, including Adele Diamond's (2013; Diamond & Lee, 2011) view on the key dimensions of executive functioning in 4- to 11-year-old children and interventions that have been shown to improve executive functioning

- Description of a recent research review that concluded more than 1,000 genes may influence an individual's intelligence (Davies & others, 2011)

- New information about the environment's role in intelligence that is reflected in the 12- to 18-point IQ gain children make when they are adopted from lower-SES to middle-SES families (Nisbett & others, 2012)

- Coverage of recent research indicating that bilingual children have a lower vocabulary in each language than monolingual children (Bialystok, 2011)

Chapter 8: Socioemotional Development in Middle and Late Childhood

- Updating and expanded discussion of children's socioemotional development based on leading expert Ross Thompson's feedback
- New discussion of the role of executive functioning and children's perspective taking in socioemotional development (Galinsky, 2010)
- New information indicating that the foundations of self-esteem in middle and late childhood occur through the quality of relationships with parents in infancy and early childhood (Thompson, 2011, 2013a, b, c, d)
- New material on dose/response effects in the study of how disasters and traumatic events affect children's adjustment and adaptation (Masten, 2013; Masten & Narayan, 2012)
- Substantial updates based on feedback from leading experts Darcia Narvaez and Daniel Lapsley
- Coverage of a recent study that revealed links between a higher level of multicultural experience and a lower level of closed mindedness, a growth mindset, and higher moral judgment (Narvaez & Hill, 2010)
- New section on the domain theory of moral development and the distinction between moral, social conventional, and personal domains (Helwig & Turiel, 2011; Smetana, 2011a, b)
- Coverage of a recent gender stereotyping study of 6- to 10-year-olds who indicated that math is for boys (Cvencek, Meltzoff, & Greenwald, 2011)
- Inclusion of information about a recent meta-analysis that revealed no gender differences in math skills of adolescents (Lindberg & others, 2010)
- Description of a recent research review focused on girls' negative attitudes about math and the negative expectations that parents and teachers have for girls' math competence (Gunderson & others, 2012)
- Updated and expanded discussion of gender differences in emotion (Hertenstein & Keltner, 2011)
- New main section on attachment in middle and late childhood
- New discussion of Kathryn Kerns and her colleagues' (Brumariu, Kerns, & Seibert, 2012; Kerns & Seibert, 2012; Kerns, Siener, & Brumariu, 2011) research that focuses on the role of secure attachment in internalizing symptoms, anxiety, depression, and emotion regulation

- New discussion of cyberbullying (Donnerstein, 2012; Kowalsky, Limber, & Agatston, 2012)
- Coverage of a recent study that found having supportive friends was linked to a lower level of bullying and victimization (Kendrick, Jutengren, & Stattin, 2012)
- Inclusion of recent research on links between children's cyber aggression and negative peer relations outcomes (Schoffstall & Cohen, 2012)
- Discussion of recent research indicating higher levels of depression and suicide in children who are the victims of bullying (Fisher & others, 2012; Lemstra & others, 2012)
- Description of a recent longitudinal study of more than 6,000 children that found a link between bully victimization and suicide ideation (Winsper & others, 2012)
- Coverage of a recent study that found a link between victims of peer bullying and the development of borderline personality symptoms (Wolke & others, 2012)
- New Figure 8.6 involving Carol Dweck's (2013) Brainology program
- New discussion of the importance of parental involvement in children's learning, including the research of Eva Pomerantz and her colleagues (Cheung & Pomerantz, 2012; Pomerantz, Cheung, & Qin, 2012; Pomerantz, Kim, & Cheung, 2012) that especially focuses on comparisons of U.S. and Chinese children and their parents

Chapter 9: Physical and Cognitive Development in Adolescence

- New discussion of how social policy regarding adolescents needs to be changed
- New material on the work of Peter Benson and his colleagues (2010; Benson & Scales, 2011)
- Inclusion of information about a recent study of adolescents with the most positive body images, which was linked to their health-enhancing behavior, especially regular exercise (Frisen & Holmqvist, 2010)
- Description of a recent cross-cultural study in 29 countries that found childhood obesity was linked to early puberty in girls (Currie & others, 2012)
- Coverage of a recent study that found a linear increase in having a positive body image for both boys and girls as they moved from the beginning to the end of adolescence (Holsen, Carlson Jones, & Skogbrott Birkeland, 2012)
- Revised and updated data on the percentage of adolescents who reported having had sexual intercourse, including a recent gender reversal for twelfth-graders with a higher percentage of twelfth-grade girls reporting having had sex than twelfth-grade boys (Eaton & others, 2010)

- Updated percentage of U.S. adolescents who report that they are currently sexually active (Eaton & others, 2010)

- Discussion of a recent study that revealed a link between neighborhood poverty concentration and 15- to 17-year-old boys' and girls' sexual initiation (Cubbin & others, 2010)

- Updated information about trends in the percentage of sexually active adolescents who used a condom the last time they had sexual intercourse (Eaton & others, 2010)

- Discussion of recent research on U.S. 15- to 19-year-olds with unintended pregnancies resulting in live births: 50 percent of these adolescent girls were not using any type of birth control when they got pregnant and 34 percent believed they could not get pregnant at the time (Centers for Disease Control and Prevention, 2012f)

- Coverage of the recent decline in births to adolescent girls to a record low in 2009, including new Figure 9.3 (Ventura & Hamilton, 2011)

- Inclusion of information about some sex education programs that are now abstinence-plus sexuality, in which programs promote abstinence as well as contraceptive use (Realini & others, 2010)

- Updated data on trends in adolescent obesity from 1999–2000 to 2009–2010 with increased obesity rates in boys but not in girls during this time frame (Ogden & others, 2012)

- Inclusion of recent research linking obesity in adolescence with the development of severe obesity in emerging adulthood (The & others, 2010)

- Discussion of a recent longitudinal study of overweight and obesity from 14 years of age to 24 years of age (Patton & others, 2011)

- Description of recent research linking a higher level of exercise in adolescence with a lower level of alcohol, cigarette, and marijuana use (Terry-McElrath, O'Malley, & Johnston, 2011)

- New discussion of links between screen-based activity and physical exercise in adolescents, including recent research indicating that adolescents who combine low levels of physical activity with high screen-based activity are nearly twice as likely to be overweight (Sisson & others, 2010)

- Updated data on developmental changes in adolescent sleep patterns (Eaton & others, 2010)

- New coverage of sleep in emerging adulthood (Galambos, Howard, & Maggs, 2011)

- Discussion of a recent study of emerging adults' sleep patterns and indications that first-year college students have bedtimes and risetimes that are later than seniors in high school but that bedtimes and risetimes become earlier by the third and fourth year of college (Lund & others, 2010)

- Updated statistics on leading causes of death in adolescence (Eaton & others, 2010)

- Updated coverage of the Monitoring the Future study's assessment of drug use by secondary school students (Johnston & others, 2012)

- Description of research that found the onset of alcohol use before age 11 was linked to a higher risk of alcohol dependence in early adulthood (Guttmannova & others, 2012)

- Discussion of recent research that linked authoritative parenting with lower adolescent alcohol consumption (Piko & Balazs, 2012) and parent-adolescent conflict with higher consumption (Chaplin & others, 2012)

- Updated research on a confluence of peer factors that are linked to adolescent alcohol use (Patrick & Schulenberg, 2010; Tucker & others, 2012)

- New commentary about links between anorexia nervosa, obsessive thinking about weight, and compulsive exercise (Hildebrandt & others, 2012)

- New description of the perfectionistic tendencies of anorexics and bulimics (Lampard & others, 2012)

- New discussion of the likely brain changes in adolescents who are anorexic (Lock, 2012b)

- Extensively expanded and updated content on executive functioning in adolescence

- New section on the importance of controlling attention and reducing interfering thoughts

- New section on cognitive control, including new material on the importance of controlling attention and inhibiting distracting thoughts (Diamond, 2013; Galinsky, 2010)

- New discussion of Robert Crosnoe's (2011) recent book, *Fitting In, Standing Out*, which describes how the conformity demands of complex peer cultures in high school undermine students' academic achievement

- Updated coverage of school dropout rates, including new Figure 9.6 that shows dropout rates by gender and ethnicity, as well the significant decrease of Latino dropouts in the first decade of the twenty-first century (National Center for Education Statistics, 2010a, b)

- New discussion of the controversy in determining accurate school dropout rates

Chapter 10: Socioemotional Development in Adolescence

- Revised and updated information about diversity, especially ethnic identity and immigration, based on feedback from leading expert Diane Hughes

- New section, Parental Management and Monitoring, that provides recent information about the increasing interest in studying adolescents' management of their parents' access to information (Smetana, 2011a, b)

- Description of a recent analysis that concluded the most consistent outcomes of secure attachment in adolescence involve positive peer relations and the development of emotion regulation capacities (Allen & Miga, 2010)
- Updated and expanded coverage of the positive outcomes of positive friendship relationships in adolescence (Kendrick, Jutengren, & Stattin, 2012; Tucker & others, 2012; Way & Silverman, 2012)
- Coverage of a recent study that found romantic activity was associated with depression in early adolescent girls (Starr & others, 2012)
- Description of recent research on the negative outcomes of adolescent girls having an older romantic partner (Haydon & Halpern, 2010)
- Expanded and updated material on immigrant families and their bicultural orientation, including recent research by Ross Parke and his colleagues (2011)
- New discussion of immigrant adolescents as cultural brokers for their parents (Villanueva & Buriel, 2010)
- Substantial updating of media use based on the 2009 national survey of more than 2,000 U.S. adolescents, including comparisons with earlier national surveys to show trends in media use by adolescents (Rideout, Foehr, & Roberts, 2010)
- Description of a recent study of 8- to 12-year-old girls that found a higher level of media multitasking was linked to negative social well-being while a higher level of face-to-face communication was associated with a higher level of social well-being, such as social success, feeling normal, and having fewer friends whom parents perceived as a bad influence (Pea & others, 2012)
- Coverage of a recent national survey of trends in adolescents' use of social media, including dramatic increases in social networking and text messaging, and declines in tweeting and blogging (Lenhart & others, 2010)
- New commentary about text messaging now being the main way that adolescents prefer connecting with their friends (Lenhart & others, 2010)
- Inclusion of information that Facebook replaced Google as the most frequently visited Internet site in 2010
- Description of a recent study of parenting predictors of adolescent media use (Padilla-Walker & Coyne, 2011)
- Inclusion of recent research linking problematic mother-early adolescent relationships with negative peer relations on the Internet in emerging adulthood (Szwedo, Mikami, & Allen, 2011)
- Discussion of recent research on the role of parental monitoring and support during adolescence in reducing criminal behavior in emerging adulthood (Johnson & others, 2011)

- Description of a recent study that found repeated poverty was a high risk factor for delinquency (Najman & others, 2010)
- Discussion of a recent meta-analysis of five programs for reducing the recidivism of juvenile offenders, which found that family treatment was the only one that was effective (Schwalbe & others, 2012)
- Coverage of a recent study that revealed male Chinese adolescents and emerging adults experience more depression than their female counterparts (Sun & others, 2010)
- New discussion of the role of genes in adolescent depression and recent research that found the link between adolescent girls' perceived stress and depression occurred only when the girls had the short version of the serotonin-related gene—5HTTLPR (Beaver & others, 2012)
- Description of a recent study that found relational aggression was linked to depression in girls (Spieker & others, 2012)
- Coverage of a recent research review that found the most effective treatment for adolescent depression was combination of drug therapy and cognitive behavior therapy (Maalouf & Brent, 2012)
- Updated national data on the percentage of adolescents who seriously think about committing suicide (Eaton & others, 2010)
- Coverage of a recent study that found increased family support, peer support, and community connectedness was linked to a lower risk of suicidal tendencies (Matlin, Molock, & Tebes, 2011)
- Discussion of a recent study linking sexual victimization to suicide attempts in adolescence (Plener, Singer, & Goldbeck, 2011)
- Description of a recent study that found that the most common link between adolescent suicide attempts and drug use was any lifetime use of tranquilizers or sedatives (Kokkevi & others, 2012)

Chapter 11: Physical and Cognitive Development in Early Adulthood

- Expanded discussion of emerging adulthood, including material on whether it is likely to be universal or not, and its occurrence in European countries and Australia, as well as the United States (Kins & Beyers, 2010; Sirsch & others, 2009)
- Coverage of a recent Belgian study indicating that continued co-residence with parents during emerging adulthood slows down the process of becoming a self-sufficient and independent adult (Kins & Beyers, 2010)
- Inclusion of recent research indicating that the majority of 18- to 26-year-olds in India felt that they had achieved adulthood (Seiter & Nelson, 2010)

- Inclusion of criticism of the concept of emerging adulthood (Cote & Bynner, 2008)
- Updated and expanded information about the increase in health problems in emerging adulthood compared with adolescence (Fatusi & Hindin, 2010)
- Coverage of a recent study of emerging adulthood that found those from low-SES backgrounds engaged in less healthy exercise and food habits than their middle-SES counterparts (VanKim & Laska, 2012)
- Updated statistics on the percentage of U.S. 20- to 39-year-olds who are obese (National Center for Health Statistics, 2011a)
- New projection of the percentage of U.S. adults who will likely be obese in 2030 (Finkelstein & others, 2012)
- New coverage of the highest and lowest percentages of obese adults in 33 developed countries, including new Figure 4.12 (OECD, 2010)
- New material on the National Weight Control Registry, including research indicating that these individuals who have lost at least 30 pounds and kept it off for one year engage in a high level of physical activity (Catenacci & others, 2008; Ogden & others, 2012)
- Description of a recent study of gender differences in college students' motivation to exercise (Egli & others, 2011)
- Updated material on college students' drinking habits, including new data on extreme binge drinking and the recent decline in college drinking (Johnston & others, 2011)
- New commentary about the recent trend in "hooking up" to have casual sex in emerging adulthood (Holman & Sillars, 2011; Lewis & others, 2012)
- Inclusion of recent data from a study of sexual activity in 25- to 44-year-olds in the United States (Chandra, Mosher, Copen, & Sionean, 2011)
- Updated figures on the number of people in the United States who are living with an HIV infection (National Center for Health Statistics, 2011c)
- Inclusion of information about the recent significant drop in the rate of new HIV infections globally (UNAIDS, 2011)
- Inclusion of a recent survey on knowledge regarding contraception and HIV infection in low- and middle-income countries (UNAIDS, 2011)
- Description of a recent study on the significant underreporting of rape among college women (Wolitzky-Taylor & others, 2011)
- Revision of the definition of postformal thought to include the view of Labouvie-Vief and her colleagues (2010) on the role of emotion in cognitive changes
- Coverage of a recent study indicating that discussing purpose in life benefitted college students' goal direction (Bundick, 2011)

- New commentary about the increasing trend in the U.S. workforce of the disappearing long-term career with many young and older adults working at a series of jobs and/or short-term jobs (Hollister, 2011)
- Inclusion of recent information from the *Occupational Outlook Handbook* (2012) that includes job projections through 2020, including trends in the diversity of the workforce
- Updated statistics on the percentage of college students who work while going to college (National Center for Education Statistics, 2010a)
- Description of a recent study of unemployment and mortality risk at different point in an individual's career (Roelfs & others, 2011)

Chapter 12: Socioemotional Development in Early Adulthood

- Coverage of a longitudinal study that found securely attached infants were in more stable romantic relationships in adulthood (Salvatore & others, 2011)
- Inclusion of recent research on emerging adults' attachment security and the quality of their romantic relationships (Holland & Roisman, 2010)
- Description of recent research that found insecurely attached adults had a lower level of sexual satisfaction than securely attached adults (Brassard & others, 2012)
- Description of a recent study indicating that anxiously attached adults were more ambivalent about relationship commitment than their securely attached counterparts (Joel, MacDonald, & Shiomotomai, 2011)
- New research on adults with an avoidant attachment style being less resistant to the temptations of infidelity, which was linked to their lower level of relationship commitment (DeWall & others, 2011)
- Inclusion of recent research indicating that insecurely attached adults had higher levels of depressive and anxious symptoms than securely attached adults (Jinyao & others, 2012)
- Description of recent research confirming Erikson's theory that identity development in adolescence is a precursor of intimacy in romantic relationships in emerging adulthood (Beyers & Seiffge-Krenke, 2010)
- Coverage of a recent meta-analysis that found identity development was linked to intimacy, with the connection being stronger for men than women (Arseth & others, 2009)
- Inclusion of information from a recent meta-analysis in which males showed more avoidance and less anxiety about romantic love than females (Del Giudice, 2011)
- New coverage of Andrew Cherlin's (2009) recent analysis of how Americans move in and out of

relationship styles more than is the case in other countries

- Updated data on single adults in the United States—for the first time, in 2009 the number of U.S. single adults from 25 to 34 years of age surpassed the number of married adults (U.S. Census Bureau, 2010)
- Discussion of a recent large-scale study of U.S. singles that found women are now more likely than men to want to retain their independence in relationships (Match.com, 2011)
- Coverage of another large-scale survey that found many singles reported that they were looking for love, but either were ambivalent about getting married or did not want to get married (Match.com, 2012)
- New Coverage of Bella DePaulo's (2006, 2011) conclusion that there is widespread bias against unmarried adults
- Description of a recent study that found cohabiting relationships were characterized by more commitment, lower satisfaction, more negative communication, and more physical aggression than dating (noncohabiting) relationships (Rhoades, Stanley, & Markham, 2012)
- Inclusion of information from a recent study on the motivation for cohabiting, including gender differences regarding drawbacks in cohabiting (Huang & others, 2011)
- New commentary that recent research indicates that the link between premarital cohabitation and marital instability in first marriages has weakened in recent cohorts (Manning & Cohen, 2012; Reinhold, 2010)
- Updated coverage of the continuing decline in the rate of marriage in the United States from 2007 to 2010 (Pew Research Center, 2010a)
- Updated information about the percentage of individuals in the United States who have ever been married by age 40 (Pew Research Center, 2011)
- Revised and updated analysis of marriage trends, including recent research on the percentage of U.S. adults under 30 who think marriage is headed for extinction and the percentage of those young adults who still plan to get married (Pew Research Center, 2010a)
- Description of a recent large-scale analysis of a number of studies that concluded married individuals have a survival advantage over unmarried individuals, and that marriage gives men more of a longevity boost than it does women (Rendall & others, 2011)
- Revised discussion of remarried families in terms of some of these families being more adult-focused, while others are more child-focused (Anderson & Greene, 2011)
- Description of a recent study of stigma and same-sex relationships (Frost, 2011)

- Updated statistic on the age at which U.S. women give birth to a child for the first time (U.S. Census Bureau, 2011)

Chapter 13: Physical and Cognitive Development in Middle Adulthood

- Inclusion of recent ideas from Patricia Cohen's (2012) book, *In Our Prime: The Invention of Middle Age*, that provides an historical overview of the emergence of the concept of middle age in the nineteenth century
- New commentary about taking a balanced approach to middle age, acknowledging the physical declines that characterize middle age, but also recognizing that in recent decades an increasing number of middle-aged adults have engaged in healthier lifestyles
- Updated data on the percentage of middle-aged adults in the United States who are classified as obese (National Center for Health Statistics, 2011a)
- Description of a recent research review that concluded management of weight and resistance training were the best strategies for slowing down sarcopenia (Rolland & others, 2011)
- Added commentary about the health benefits of cholesterol-lowering and hypertension-lowering drugs being a major factor in improving the health of many middle-aged adults and increasing their life expectancy (de la Sierra & Barrios, 2012; Gadi & others, 2012)
- Description of a recent research review indicating a link between chronic stress exposure and metabolic syndrome (Tamashiro, 2011)
- Inclusion of recent research on physical activity, metabolic syndrome, and cardiovascular disease (Broekuizen & others, 2011)
- Discussion of a recent study that found several factors in adolescence were related to the development of metabolic syndrome in middle-aged women and men (Gustafsson, Persson, & Hammarstrom, 2011)
- Coverage of a recent study linking low cognitive ability in early adulthood to reduced lung functioning in middle age (Carroll & others, 2011)
- Description of a recent study that found middle aged adults who slept less than 6 hours a night on average had an increased risk of developing stroke symptoms (Ruiter & others, 2012)
- Coverage of a recent study that found links between changes in the number of hours of sleep and cognitive functioning in middle-aged adults (Ferrie & others, 2011).
- New discussion of the increase in sleep-disordered breathing and restless legs syndrome in middle age (Polo-Kantola, 2011)

- New description of David Almeida and his colleagues' (2011) view of chronic stress and how it can damage physiological functioning and increase disease

- Discussion of a recent study indicating that aerobic exercise was related to the presence of a lower level of senescent T cells (Spielmann & others 2011)

- New coverage of the roles that stress and negative emotions play in the course of cardiovascular disease (Dougall & Baum, 2012; Emery, Anderson, & Goodwin, 2013)

- Updated statistics on mortality causes in middle age (Kochanek & others, 2011)

- Description of a recent study indicating that increased estradiol and improved sleep, but not hot flashes, predicted enhanced mood during the menopausal transition (Joffe & others, 2011)

- Discussion of a recent research review indicating that there is no clear evidence that depressive disorders occur more frequently during menopause than at other times in a woman's reproductive life (Judd, Hickey, & Bryant, 2012)

- Description of the recent conclusion that reduction of cardiovascular disease occurs when HRT is initiated before 60 years of age and/or within 10 years of menopause and continued for 6 years or more (Hodis & others, 2012)

- Updated coverage of recent research studies in a number of countries indicating that coinciding with the decreased use of HRT in recent years, research is mixed regarding the incidence of breast cancer (Baber, 2011; Gompel & Santen, 2012; Howell & Evans, 2011)

- Update on the percentage of aging men who experience erectile dysfunction (Berookhim & Bar-Charma, 2011)

- Description of recent research that found how often middle-aged adults engaged in sexual intercourse, the quality of their sexual life, and their interest in sex was linked to how healthy they were (Lindau & Gavrilova, 2010)

- Recent update of Schaie's (2012) Seattle Longitudinal Study that includes data through 95 years of age and revised Figure 13.2

- Expanded and updated coverage of the causes of increases in intelligence in middle age in recent cohorts (Schaie, 2012)

- New discussion of the debate about when intellectual decline begins between K. Warner Schaie (2012) and Timothy Salthouse (2012)

- New discussion of whether there are differences between the job performance of young adults and middle-aged adults (Salthouse, 2012)

- Description of a recent study in which task persistence in early adolescence predicted career success in middle age (Andersson & Bergman, 2011)

- New commentary about the premature retirement of some middle-aged adults because of the recent economic downturn and recession (Lusardi, Mitchell, & Curto, 2012; Wang, 2012)

- New discussion of an analysis of research studies indicating a strong link between spirituality/religion and mortality (Lucchetti, Lucchetti, & Koenig, 2011)

- New discussion of links between having a higher sense of meaning in life and clearer guidelines for living one's life, enhanced motivation to take care of oneself and reach goals, a higher level of psychological well-being, and better health (Park, 2012b)

Chapter 14: Socioemotional Development in Middle Adulthood

- Description of a recent study of older adult women's daily stressors and negative affect (Charles & others, 2010)

- Expanded and updated coverage of personal control in middle age, including the importance of a sense of control in delaying the onset of disease in middle adulthood (Lachman, Neupert, & Agrigoroaei, 2011)

- New section, Stress and Gender, that focuses on how women and men differ in the way they experience and respond to stressors (Almeida & others, 2011)

- Coverage of a recent study on gender differences in depressive symptoms and the social contexts linked to those symptoms in middle-aged and older women (Lin & others, 2011)

- New discussion of Shelley Taylor and her colleagues' (2011c; Taylor & others, 2000) concept of tend and befriend that characterizes how women are likely to respond to stress

- Inclusion of a recent research study on stability and change in the Big Five personality factors indicating that the positive aspect of four of the five factors (such as emotional stability) peaked between 40 to 60 years of age, while being conscientious continued to increase from early through late adulthood (Specht, Egloff, & Shukle, 2011)

- New coverage of research on how the Big Five factors of personality are linked to important aspects of a person's life, such as health (Turiano & others, 2012) and intelligence (Sharp & others, 2010)

- New discussion of research on how the Big Five factors are related to historical changes (George, Helson, & John, 2011)

- Updated research indicating that the greatest change in personality occurs in early adulthood (Lucas & Donnellan, 2011)

- Updated data on the dramatic increase in the number of grandchildren who live with at least one grandparent (U.S. Census Bureau, 2011b)

- Description of two recent studies that found middle-aged parents provided more support for their children than for their aging parents (Fingerman & others, 2011a)

- Coverage of recent research that indicated affection and support, reflecting solidarity, were more prevalent in intergenerational relationships than ambivalence was (Hogerbrugge & Komter, 2012)

- New discussion of how more than 40 percent of middle-aged children (mainly daughters) provide care for their aging parents or parents-in-law (Blieszner & Roberto, 2012a; National Alliance for Caregiving, 2009)

- New coverage of the concept of the middle generation more often functioning as a "pivot" generation than as a "sandwich" generation (Fingerman & Birditt, 2011; Fingerman & others, 2011b)

Chapter 15: Physical and Cognitive Development in Late Adulthood

- New chapter opening story on the fascinating lifespan journey of 91-year-old Helen Small and her ongoing cognitive fitness, including publication of her first book, *Why not? My seventy year plan for a college degree* (Small, 2011)

- Updated statistics on life expectancy around the world, with Monaco having the highest estimated life expectancy at birth in 2011 (90 years of age) (Central Intelligence Agency, 2012)

- Updated statistics on life expectancy at birth and at 65 and 100 years of age (U.S. Census Bureau, 2011a)

- New commentary that the sex difference in longevity favoring women is still present but less pronounced in late adulthood and is especially linked to the higher level of cardiovascular disease in men than women (Yang & Kosloski, 2011)

- Updated information about the number of centenarians in the United States (U.S. Census Bureau, 2011)

- Coverage of a recent study indicating that the older the age group of centenarians (110 to 119 compared with 100 to 104, for example), the later the onset of diseases such as cancer and cardiovascular disease, as well as delayed functional decline (Andersen & others, 2012)

- Updated and expanded material on telomeres and telomerase, including the increasing role they might play in stem cell regeneration (Piper & others, 2012; Shay, Reddel, & Wright, 2012)

- Inclusion of information about recent research interest in the role that restricted diet and exercise might play in reducing oxidative damage in cells (Muthusamy & others, 2012)

- Discussion of a recent study that found a decrease in total brain volume and volume in key brain structures, such as the frontal lobes and hippocampus, from 22 to 88 years of age (Sherwood & others, 2011)

- Recent analysis indicating that the decrease in brain volume in healthy aging is likely due to neuron shrinkage, lower numbers of synapses, and reduced length of axons, but only to a minor extent to neuron loss (Fjell & Walhovd, 2010)

- New commentary about the increased interest in the role that neurogenesis might play in neurodegenerative diseases such as Alzheimer disease, Parkinson disease, and Huntington disease (Walton & others, 2012)

- New information about the percentage of older adults who have difficulty sleeping (Neikrug & Ancoli-Israel, 2010)

- Coverage of a recent study that found regular exercise improves the sleep profile of older adults (Lira & others, 2011)

- Coverage of a recent national study that found an increase in resistant hypertension in the United States in recent years, likely because of increases in obesity and the number of older adults (Roberie & Elliott, 2012)

- Description of a study linking macular degeneration to an increased risk of falls in older adults (Wood & others, 2011)

- Coverage of a recent national survey of the percentage of adults 70 years and older with hearing loss (Lin, Thorpe, & others, 2011)

- Discussion of recent research on developmental changes in the frontal and parietal lobes of the brain that are linked to attention and cognitive control (Campbell & others, 2012)

- New commentary about reductions in the number of older adults, especially the young old, with erectile dysfunction because of the recent development of drugs such as Viagra (Lowe & Costabile, 2012; Rubio-Aurioles & others, 2012)

- Description of a recent study of older adults that found total daily activity was linked to increased longevity across a 4-year period (Buchman & others, 2012)

- Description of a recent study that revealed exercise training increased the size of the hippocampus and improved the memory of older adults (Erickson & others, 2011)

- New discussion of a recent study of older adults that found the greater their variability in sustained attention, the more likely they were to experience falls (O'Halloran & others, 2012)

- New description of the tip of the tongue phenomena (TOT) and a recent study that found the most common memory errors reported by older adults in the last 24 hours involved TOT (Ossher, Flegal, & Lustig, 2012)

- Coverage of a recent study indicating that working memory continued to decline from 65 to 89 years of age (Elliott & others, 2011)

- New section on executive functioning and how it changes in older adults (Luszcz, 2011)

- Discussion of recent research across a 12-year period that found older adults who reduced their participation in lifestyle cognitive activities (using a computer and playing bridge, for example) showed subsequent poorer cognitive functioning (semantic memory, for example) (Small & others, 2012b). The poorer cognitive functioning was then linked to a lower level of engaging in social activities.

- Expanded, updated, and revised content on interventions in cognitive aging to include the views shared by leading experts at the Stanford University Center for Longevity (2011)

- New Figure 15.7 that shows an image of the prefrontal cortex

- Discussion of two recent neuroimaging studies that found older adults' memory was better the less lateralized their brain activity was (Angel & others, 2011; Manenti, Cotelli, & Miniussi, 2011)

- New coverage of Schaie's (2012) recent research regarding links between hippocampal and cognitive functioning from middle age to late adulthood

- Expanded commentary about older adults increasingly seeking a type of bridge employment that permits a gradual rather than a sudden movement out of the work context (Bowen, Noack, & Staudinger, 2011)

- New data on the average ages of retirement for men (64 years) and women (62 years) in 2011 in the United States (Munnell, 2011)

- Discussion of a 2012 survey that indicated confidence in having enough money to live comfortably in retirement had dropped to 14 percent (Helman, Copeland, & VanDerhei, 2012)

- New commentary about the two main retirement income concerns as individuals approach retirement: (1) drawing retirement income from savings, and (2) paying for health care expenses (Yakoboski, 2011)

- Coverage of a recent study that revealed different predictors for men's and women's psychological well-being after retirement (Kubicek & others, 2010)

- Description of a recent meta-analysis that found the following living conditions were associated with risk of depression in older adults: Living alone, in a nursing home, or in an institutionalized setting (Xiu-Ying & others, 2012)

- Expanded material on links between the ApoE4 gene and Alzheimer disease (Caselli, 2012; Ward & others, 2012)

- New discussion of K. Warner Schaie's (2012) recent research that found individuals who had the ApoE4 allele showed more cognitive decline beginning in middle age

- Coverage of a recent research study that found the ApoE4 gene creates a cascade of molecular signaling that causes blood vessels to become more porous and leak toxins into the brain and damage neurons (Bell & others, 2012)

- New material suggesting that one of the best strategies for preventing/intervening in people's lives who are at risk for Alzheimer disease is to improve their cardiac functioning (Gelber, Launer, & White, 2012; Wagner & others, 2012)

- Coverage of a recent study that compared the family caregivers' perceptions of caring for someone with Alzheimer disease, cancer, or schizophrenia; the highest perceived burden was for Alzheimer disease (Papastavrou & others, 2012)

Chapter 16: Socioemotional Development in Late Adulthood

- Expanded coverage of regrets in older adults, indicating that it is important for them not to dwell on such regrets, especially since opportunities to undo them decline with age (Suri & Gross, 2012)

- Inclusion of recent research that revealed an important factor in older adults who showed a higher level of emotion regulation and successful aging was reduced responsiveness to regrets (Brassen & others, 2012)

- Discussion of a recent meta-analysis of 128 studies of reminiscence interventions in older adults with positive effects on a number of dimensions (Pinquart & Frostmeier, 2012)

- Discussion of a recent study that found a life-review course titled "Looking for Meaning" reduced the depressive symptoms of middle-aged and older adults (Pot & others, 2010)

- Description of a recent study that found older adults were happiest when they combined effortful social, physical, cognitive, and household activities with restful activities (Oerlemans, Bakker, & Veenhoven, 2011)

- Coverage of research by Laura Carstensen and her colleagues (2011) on links between aging and emotional well-being, emotional stability, and longevity

- Expanded discussion of emotion and aging indicating that compared with younger adults, older adults react less to negative circumstances, are better at ignoring irrelevant negative information, and remember more positive than negative information (Mather, 2012)

- Description of a recent study that found positive emotion increased from 50 years of age through the mid-eighties while anger was highest in the early twenties (Stone & others, 2011)

- New coverage of the newly emerging field of developmental social neuroscience, which involves connecting changes in the aging brain and older adults' emotion (Kaszniak & Menchola, 2012; Samanez-Larkin & Carstensen, 2011)

- Inclusion of information about a recent study that found conscientiousness predicted greater longevity in older adults (Hill & others, 2011)

- Discussion of a recent study that revealed higher neuroticism was linked to older adults' medication non-adherence across a six-year time frame (Jerant & others, 2011)

- Description of a recent study indicating that elevated neuroticism, lower conscientiousness, and lower openness were related to increased risk of developing Alzheimer disease across a six-year period in older adults (Duberstein & others, 2011)

- New coverage of the role technology, including video games, might play in the cognitive functioning of older adults (Charness, Fox, & Mitchum, 2011)

- Discussion of recent research on frequency of computer use in older adults and cognitive functioning (Tun & Lachman, 2010)

- Coverage of a recent study that revealed when older adults played a brain training game about 15 minutes a day for 4 weeks, the experience improved their executive functioning and speed of processing information (Nouchi & others, 2012)

- Coverage of a recent study that found cohabiting older adults were less likely to receive partner care than married older adults (Noel-Miller, 2011)

- Description of research on marital satisfaction in octogenarians and its ability to protect their happiness from the effects of daily fluctuations in perceived health (Waldinger & Schulz, 2010)

- New material on how in late adulthood married individuals are more likely to find themselves having to care for a sick spouse with a limiting health condition (Blieszner & Roberto, 2012)

- Updated and expanded discussion of social support and aging, including recent research linking a higher level of social support with reduced cognitive decline (Dickinson & others, 2011)

- Discussion of a recent study that linked social isolation in late adulthood to a greater risk of being inactive, smoking, and engaging in other health-risk behaviors (Shankar & others, 2011)

- Description of three recent longitudinal studies that found feelings of loneliness were linked with an earlier death (Luo & others, 2012; Perissinotto, Stijacic Cenzer, & Covinsky, 2012)

- Inclusion of information from a recent study that found older adults who volunteered for other-oriented reasons had a lower mortality risk but those

who volunteered for self-oriented reasons had a mortality risk similar to nonvolunteers (Konrath & others, 2012)

- Discussion of a recent study that found the more older adults engaged in volunteering the happier they were (Dulin & others, 2012)

- New description of a research study that revealed maximizing one's psychological resources (self-efficacy and optimism) was linked to a higher level quality of life in the future for older adults (Bowling & Iliffe, 2011)

- Expanded discussion of successful aging, including information about the important agenda of continuing to improve our understanding of how people can live longer, healthier, more productive, and more satisfying lives (Beard & others, 2012)

Chapter 17: Death, Dying, and Grieving

- New discussion of Physician Orders for Life-Sustaining Treatment (POLST), a document that is more specific than other advance directives in translating treatment preferences into medical orders (Fromme & others, 2012; Hammes & others, 2012)

- Discussion of a recent Belgian study that found approximately 50 percent of the requests for euthanasia were granted (Van Wesemael & others, 2011)

- Description of a recent study in the Netherlands indicating that approximately 75 percent of the euthanasia requests came from cancer patients and the main reason for the requests was pain (van Alphen, Donker, & Marquet, 2010)

- Expanded and updated coverage of complicated grief or prolonged grief disorder, including a recent proposal for its inclusion in DSM-V (Shear, 2012a, b)

- Discussion of a recent study that found individuals who were depressed were more likely to have complicated grief (Sung & others, 2011)

- Inclusion of research that found complicated grief was more likely to be present in older adults when the grief occurred in response to the death of a child or spouse (Newsom & others, 2011)

- New information about the percentage of women and men 65 years of age and older who are widowed in the United States (U.S. Census Bureau, 2011a)

- Coverage of a recent large-scale study that found a link between loss of a spouse and risk of psychiatric visits as well as earlier death in individuals 75 years of age and older (Moller & others, 2011)

- Updated statistics and projections on the percentage of corpses being cremated in the United States (Cremation Association of North America, 2012)

Acknowledgments

The development and writing of the first, second, and third editions of *Essentials of Life-Span Development* were strongly influenced by a remarkable group of consultants, reviewers, and adopters.

Expert Consultants

In writing the third edition of *Essentials of Life-Span Development*, I benefitted considerably from the following leading experts who provided detailed feedback in their areas of expertise for *Life-Span Development*, Fourteenth Edition:

K. Warner Schaie, *Pennsylvania State University*

Diane Hughes, *New York University*

Ross Thompson, *University of California-Davis*

Maria Hernandez-Reif, *University of Alabama*

William Hoyer, *Syracuse University*

John Schulenberg, *University of Michigan*

Art Kramer, *University of Illinois*

Phyllis Moen, *University of Minnesota*

Kirby Deater-Deckard, *Virginia Tech University*

Crystal Park, *University of Connecticut*

David Almeida, *Pennsylvania State University*

Applications Contributors

I especially thank the contributors who helped develop the *How Would You . . . ?* questions for students in various majors who are taking the life-span development course:

Michael E. Barber, *Santa Fe Community College*

Maida Berenblatt, *Suffolk Community College*

Susan A. Greimel, *Santa Fe Community College*

Russell Isabella, *University of Utah*

Jean Mandernach, *University of Nebraska at Kearney*

General Reviewers

I gratefully acknowledge the comments and feedback from instructors around the nation who have reviewed *Essentials of Life-Span Development*. Recommendations from the following individuals helped shape *Essentials*:

Eileen Achorn, *University of Texas–San Antonio*

Michael E. Barber, *Santa Fe Community College*

Gabriel Batarseh, *Francis Marion University*

Troy E. Beckert, *Utah State University*

Stefanie Bell, *Pikes Peak Community College*

Maida Berenblatt, *Suffolk Community College*

Kathi Bivens, *Asheville Buncombe Technical Community College*

Alda Blakeney, *Kennesaw State University*

Candice L. Branson, *Kapiolani Community College*

Ken Brewer, *Northeast State Technical Community College*

Margaret M. Bushong, *Liberty University*

Krista Carter, *Colby Community College*

Stewart Cohen, *University of Rhode Island*

Rock Doddridge, *Asheville Buncombe Technical Community College*

Laura Duvall, *Heartland Community College*

Jenni Fauchier, *Metro Community College–Omaha*

Richard Ferraro, *University of North Dakota*

Terri Flowerday, *University of New Mexico–Albuquerque*

Laura Garofoli, *Fitchburg State College*

Sharon Ghazarian, *University of North Carolina–Greensboro*

Dan Grangaard, *Austin Community College*

Rodney J. Grisham, *Indian River Community College*

Rea Gubler, *Southern Utah University*

Myra M. Harville, *Holmes Community College*

Brett Heintz, *Delgado Community College*

Sandra Hellyer, *Butler University*

Randy Holley, *Liberty University*

Debra L. Hollister, *Valencia Community College*

Rosemary T. Hornack, *Meredith College*

Alycia Hund, *Illinois State University*

Rebecca Inkrott, *Sinclair Community College–Dayton*

Russell Isabella, *University of Utah*

Alisha Janowsky, *Florida Atlantic University*

Lisa Judd, *Western Technical College*

Tim Killian, *University of Arkansas–Fayetteville*

Shenan Kroupa, *Indiana University–Purdue University Indianapolis*

Pat Lefler, *Bluegrass Community and Technical College*

Jean Mandernach, *University of Nebraska–Kearney*

Carrie Margolin, *Evergreen State College*

Michael Jason McCoy, *Cape Fear Community College*

Carol Miller, *Anne Arundel Community College*

Gwynn Morris, *Meredith College*

Ron Mossler, *Los Angeles Community College*

Bob Pasnak, *George Mason University*

Curtis D. Proctor-Artz, *Wichita State University*

Janet Reis, *University of Illinois–Urbana*

Kimberly Renk, *University of Central Florida*

Vicki Ritts, *St. Louis Community College–Meramec*

Jeffrey Sargent, *Lee University*

James Schork, *Elizabethtown Community and Technical College*

Jason Scofield, *University of Alabama*

Christin E. Seifert, *Montana State University*

Elizabeth Sheehan, *Georgia State University*

Peggy Skinner, *South Plains College*

Christopher Stanley, *Winston-Salem State University*

Wayne Stein, *Brevard Community College–Melbourne*

Rose Suggett, *Southeast Community College*

Kevin Sumrall, *Montgomery College*

Joan Test, *Missouri State University*

Barbara VanHorn, *Indian River Community College*

John Wakefield, *University of North Alabama*

Laura Wasielewski, *St. Anselm College*

Lois Willoughby, *Miami Dade College–Kendall*

Paul Wills, *Kilgore College*

A. Claire Zaborowski, *San Jacinto College*

Pauline Davey Zeece, *University of Nebraska–Lincoln*

Design Reviewers

Cheryl Almeida, *Johnson and Wales University*

Candice L. Branson, *Kapiolani Community College*

Debra Hollister, *Valencia Community College*

Alycia Hund, *Illinois State University*

Jean Mandernach, *University of Nebraska–Kearney*

Michael Jason Scofield, *University of Alabama*

Christin Seifert, *Montana State University*

Life-Span Symposium

In the spring of 2010, McGraw-Hill held a symposium on life-span development for instructors from across the country. This event provided a forum for instructors to exchange ideas and experiences with colleagues they might not have met otherwise. It was also an opportunity for editors from McGraw-Hill to gather information about the needs and challenges of instructors of life-span development. The feedback we received has been invaluable and has contributed to the development of this edition of *Essentials of Life-Span Development.* We would like to thank the participants for their insights.

Mitchell Baker, *Moraine Valley Community College*

Chuck Calahan, *Purdue University*

Stephanie Ding, *Del Mar College*

Alycia Hund, *Illinois State University*

Gabriela Martorell, *Virginia Wesleyan College*

Daniel McConnell, *University of Southern Florida*

Jorge Milanes, *St. Johns River Community College*

Michael Miranda, *Kingsborough Community College*

Kaelin Olsen, *Utah State University*

Victoria Peeples, *University of Alabama*

Angi Semegon, *Santa Fe College*

The McGraw-Hill Team

A large number of outstanding professionals at McGraw-Hill helped me to produce this edition of *Essentials of Life-Span Development.* I especially want to thank Mike Sugarman, Dawn Groundwater, Sheryl Adams, Allison McNamara, and Sarah Kiefer for their extensive efforts in developing and publishing this book. Sheila Frank and Janet Tilden did superb work in the production and copyediting of the text.

Instructor and Student Resources

The resources listed here may accompany *Essentials of Life-Span Development*, Third Edition. Please contact your McGraw-Hill representative for details concerning policies, prices, and availability.

Instructor Resources

The instructor side of the Online Learning Center at http://www.mhhe.com/santrockessls3e contains the following instructor resources. Ask your local McGraw-Hill representative for your password.

- **Instructor's Manual**
- **Test Bank and Computerized Test Bank**
- **PowerPoint Slides**
- **McGraw-Hill's Visual Asset Database for Lifespan Development (VAD 2.0) www.mhhe.com/vad**

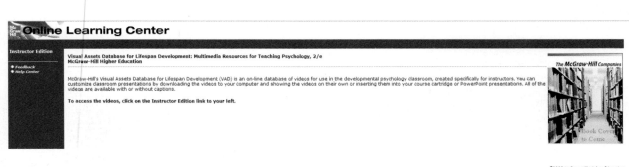

1

Introduction

Stories of Life-Span Development: How Did Ted Kaczynski Become Ted Kaczynski and Alice Walker Become Alice Walker?

Ted Kaczynski sprinted through high school, not bothering with his junior year and making only passing efforts at social contact. Off to Harvard at age 16, Kaczynski was a loner during his college years. One of his roommates at Harvard said that he avoided people by quickly shuffling by them and slamming the door behind him. After obtaining his Ph.D. in mathematics at the University of Michigan, Kaczynski became a professor at the University of California at Berkeley. His colleagues there remember him as hiding from social interaction—no friends, no allies, no networking.

After several years at Berkeley, Kaczynski resigned and moved to a rural area of Montana, where he lived as a hermit in a crude shack for 25 years. Town residents described him as a bearded eccentric. Kaczynski traced his own difficulties to growing up as a genius in a kid's body and sticking out like a sore thumb in his surroundings as a child. In 1996, he was arrested and charged as the notorious Unabomber, America's most wanted killer. Over the course of 17 years, Kaczynski had sent 16 mail bombs that left 23 people wounded or maimed and 3 people dead.

In 1998, he pleaded guilty to the offenses and was sentenced to life in prison.

A decade before Kaczynski mailed his first bomb, Alice Walker spent her days battling racism in Mississippi. She had recently won her first writing fellowship, but rather than use the money to follow her dream of moving to Senegal, Africa, she put herself into the heart and heat of the civil rights movement. Walker had grown up knowing the brutal effects of poverty and racism. Born in 1944, she was the eighth child of Georgia sharecroppers who earned $300 a year. When Walker

1

was 8, her brother accidentally shot her in the left eye with a BB gun. Since her parents had no car, it took them a week to get her to a hospital. By the time she received medical care, she was blind in that eye, and it had developed a disfiguring layer of scar tissue. Despite the counts against her, Walker overcame pain and anger and went on to win a Pulitzer Prize for her book *The Color Purple*. She became not only a novelist but also an essayist, a poet, a short-story writer, and a social activist. What leads one individual, so full of promise, to commit brutal acts of violence and another to turn poverty and trauma into a rich literary harvest? If you have ever wondered why people turn out the way they do, you have asked yourself the central question we will explore in this book.

This book is a window into the journey of human development—your own and that of every other member of the human species. Every life is distinct, a new biography in the world. Examining the shape of life-span development helps us to understand it better. In this first chapter, we explore what it means to take a life-span perspective on development, examine the nature of development, and outline how science helps us to understand it. ▪

Ted Kaczynski, the convicted Unabomber, traced his difficulties to growing up as a genius in a kid's body and not fitting in when he was a child.

Alice Walker won the Pulitzer Prize for her book *The Color Purple*. Like the characters in her book, Walker overcame pain and anger to triumph and celebrate the human spirit.

The Life-Span Perspective

Each of us develops partly like all other individuals, partly like some other individuals, and partly like no other individual. Most of the time we notice the qualities in an individual that make that person unique. But as humans, we have all traveled some common paths. Each of us—Leonardo da Vinci, Joan of Arc, George Washington, Martin Luther King, Jr., and you—walked at about 1 year, engaged in fantasy play as a young child, and became more independent as a youth. Each of us, if we live long enough, will experience hearing problems and the death of family members and friends. This is the general course of our **development,** the pattern of movement or change that begins at conception and continues through the human life span.

In this section we explore what is meant by the concept of development and why the study of life-span development is important. We outline the main characteristics of the life-span perspective and discuss various influences on development. In addition, we examine some contemporary concerns related to life-span development.

The Importance of Studying Life-Span Development

How might you benefit from studying life-span development? Perhaps you are, or will be, a parent or teacher. If so, responsibility for children is, or will be, a part of your everyday life. The more you learn about them, the better you can raise them or teach them. Perhaps you hope to gain some insight about your own history—as an infant, a child, an adolescent, or a young adult. Perhaps you want to know more about what your life will be like as you grow through the adult years—as a middle-aged adult, or as an adult in old age, for example. Or perhaps you just stumbled across this course, thinking that it sounded intriguing. Whatever your reasons, you will discover

development The pattern of movement or change that starts at conception and continues through the human life span.

that the study of life-span development addresses some provocative questions about who we are, how we came to be this way, and where our future will take us.

In our exploration of development, we will examine the life span from the point of conception until the time when life (at least, life as we know it) ends. You will see yourself as an infant, as a child, and as an adolescent, and you will learn about how those years influenced the kind of individual you are today. And you will see yourself as a young adult, as a middle-aged adult, and as an adult in old age, and you may be motivated to consider how your experiences will affect your development through the remainder of your adult years.

PEANUTS © United Features Syndicate, Inc.

Characteristics of the Life-Span Perspective

Growth and development are dramatic during the first two decades of life, but development is not something that happens only to children and adolescents. The traditional approach to the study of development emphasizes extensive change from birth to adolescence (especially during infancy), little or no change in adulthood, and decline in old age. Yet a great deal of change does occur in the decades after adolescence. The life-span approach emphasizes developmental change throughout adulthood as well as childhood (Bertrand, Graham, & Lachman, 2013; Schaie, 2012; Whitbourne & Sliwinski, 2012).

Recent increases in human life expectancy have contributed to greater interest in the life-span approach to development. The upper boundary of the human life span (based on the oldest age documented) is 122 years. The maximum life span of humans has not changed since the beginning of recorded history. What has changed is life expectancy, the average number of years that a person born in a particular year can expect to live. In the twentieth century alone, life expectancy increased by 30 years, thanks to improvements in sanitation, nutrition, and medicine (see Figure 1.1). At the beginning of the second decade of the twenty-first century, the life expectancy in the United States was 78 years of age (U.S. Census Bureau, 2011). Today, for most individuals in developed countries, childhood and adolescence represent only about one-fourth of their lives.

The belief that development occurs throughout life is central to the life-span perspective on human development, but this perspective

Average Life Expectancy (years)	Time Period
78	2011, USA
70	1954, USA
54	1915, USA
47	1900, USA
41	19th century, England
35	1620, Massachusetts Bay Colony
33	Middle Ages, England
20	Ancient Greece
18	Prehistoric times

Figure 1.1 Human Life Expectancy at Birth from Prehistoric to Contemporary Times
It took 5,000 years to extend human life expectancy from 18 to 41 years of age.

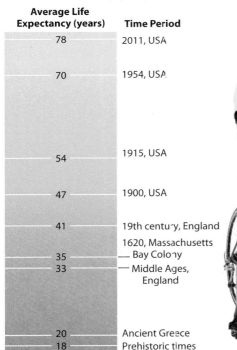

has other characteristics as well. According to life-span development expert Paul Baltes (1939–2006), the **life-span perspective** views development as lifelong, multidimensional, multidirectional, plastic, multidisciplinary, and contextual, and as a process that involves growth, maintenance, and regulation of loss (Baltes, 1987, 2003; Baltes, Lindenberger, & Staudinger, 2006). In this view, it is important to understand that development is constructed through biological, sociocultural, and individual factors working together (Baltes, Reuter-Lorenz, & Rösler, 2006). Let's look at each of these characteristics.

Development Is Lifelong

In the life-span perspective, early adulthood is not the endpoint of development; rather, no age period dominates development. Researchers increasingly study the experiences and psychological orientations of adults at different points in their lives. Later in this chapter we describe the age periods of development and their characteristics.

Development Is Multidimensional

Development consists of biological, cognitive, and socioemotional dimensions. Even within each of those dimensions, there are many components (Dixon & others, 2013). The cognitive dimension, for example, includes attention, memory, abstract thinking, speed of processing information, and social intelligence. At every age, changes occur in every dimension. Changes in one dimension also affect development in the other dimensions.

To get an idea of how interactions occur, consider the development of Ted Kaczynski, the so-called Unabomber discussed at the opening of the chapter. When he was 6 months old, he was hospitalized with a severe allergic reaction, and his parents were rarely allowed to visit him. According to his mother, the previously happy baby was never the same after his hospital stay. He became withdrawn and unresponsive. As Ted grew up, he had periodic "shutdowns" accompanied by rage. In his mother's view, a biological event in infancy warped the development of her son's mind and emotions.

Development Is Multidirectional

Throughout life, some dimensions or components of a dimension expand and others shrink. For example, when one language (such as English) is acquired early in development, the capacity for acquiring second and third languages (such as Spanish and Chinese) decreases later in development, especially after early childhood (Levelt, 1989). During adolescence, as individuals establish romantic relationships, their relationships with friends might decrease. During late adulthood, older adults might become wiser by being able to call on experience to guide their intellectual decision making (Dixon & others, 2013), but they perform more poorly on tasks that require speed in processing information (Salthouse, 2012, 2013).

Development Is Plastic

Even at 10 years old, Ted Kaczynski was extraordinarily shy. Was he destined to remain forever uncomfortable with people? Developmentalists debate how much plasticity people have in various dimensions at different points in their development (Lerner, Easterbrooks, & Mistry, 2013). Plasticity means the capacity for change. For example, can you still improve your intellectual skills when you are in your seventies or eighties? Or might these intellectual skills be fixed by the time you are in your thirties so that further improvement is impossible? Researchers have found that the cognitive skills of older adults can be improved through training and developing better strategies (Schaie, 2012). However, possibly we possess less capacity for change when we become old (Salthouse, 2012, 2013). The exploration of plasticity and its constraints is a key element on the contemporary agenda for developmental research (Depp, Vahia, & Jeste, 2012; Freund, Nikitin, & Riediger, 2013).

Developmental Science Is Multidisciplinary

Psychologists, sociologists, anthropologists, neuroscientists, and medical researchers all share an interest in unlocking the mysteries of development through the life span. How do your heredity and health limit your intelligence? Do intelligence and social relationships change with age in the same way around the world? How do families and schools influence intellectual development? These are examples of research questions that cut across disciplines.

Development Is Contextual

All development occurs within a **context**, or setting. Contexts include families, schools, peer groups, churches, cities, neighborhoods, university laboratories, countries, and so on. Each of these settings is influenced by historical, economic, social, and cultural factors (Lerner, Easterbrooks, & Mistry, 2013).

Contexts, like individuals, change (Antonucci, Birditt, & Ajrouch, 2013; Gerstorff & Ram, 2012; Schaie, 2012). Thus, individuals are changing beings in a changing world. As a result of these changes, contexts exert three types of influences (Baltes, 2003): (1) normative age-graded influences, (2) normative history-graded influences, and (3) nonnormative or highly individualized life events. Each of these types can have a biological or environmental impact on development. **Normative age-graded influences** are similar for individuals in a particular age group. These influences include biological processes such as puberty and menopause. They also include sociocultural, environmental processes such as beginning formal education (usually at about age 6 in most cultures) and retirement (which takes place in the fifties and sixties in most cultures).

Normative history-graded influences are common to people of a particular generation because of historical circumstances. For example, in their youth American baby boomers shared the experience of the Cuban missile crisis, the assassination of John F. Kennedy, and the Beatles invasion. Other examples of normative history-graded influences include economic, political, and social upheavals such as the Great Depression in the 1930s, World War II in the 1940s, the civil rights and women's rights movements of the 1960s and 1970s, the terrorist attacks of 9/11/2001, as well as the integration of computers and cell phones into everyday life during the 1990s (Schaie, 2012). Long-term changes in the genetic and cultural makeup of a population (due to immigration or changes in fertility rates) are also part of normative historical change.

Nonnormative life events are unusual occurrences that have a major impact on the individual's life. These events do not happen to all people, and when they do occur they can influence people in different ways. Examples include the death of a parent when a child is young, pregnancy in early adolescence, a fire that destroys a home, winning the lottery, or getting an unexpected career opportunity.

Non-normative life events, such as Hurricane Sandy, in October, 2012, are unusual circumstances that can have a major influence on a person's development.

How Would You...?
As a social worker, how would you explain the importance of considering nonnormative life events when working with a new client?

Development Involves Growth, Maintenance, and Regulation of Loss

Baltes and his colleagues (2006) assert that the mastery of life often involves conflicts and competition among three goals of human development: growth, maintenance, and regulation of loss. As individuals age into middle and late adulthood, the maintenance and regulation of loss in

context The setting in which development occurs, which is influenced by historical, economic, social, and cultural factors.

normative age-graded influences Biological and environmental influences that are similar for individuals in a particular age group.

normative history-graded influences Biological and environmental influences that are associated with history. These influences are common to people of a particular generation.

nonnormative life events Unusual occurrences that have a major impact on a person's life. The occurrence, pattern, and sequence of these events are not applicable to many individuals.

culture The behavior patterns, beliefs, and all other products of a group that are passed on from generation to generation.

cross-cultural studies Comparisons of one culture with one or more other cultures. These provide information about the degree to which children's development is similar, or universal, across cultures, and the degree to which it is culture-specific.

ethnicity A range of characteristics rooted in cultural heritage, including nationality, race, religion, and language.

their capacities takes center stage away from growth. Thus, a 75-year-old man might aim not to improve his memory or his golf swing but to maintain his independence and to continue playing golf. In Chapters 15 and 16, we will discuss these ideas about maintenance and regulation of loss in greater depth.

Development Is a Co-Construction of Biology, Culture, and the Individual

Development comes from biological, cultural, and individual factors influencing each other (Baltes, Reuter-Lorenz, & Rösler, 2006). For example, the brain shapes culture, but it is also shaped by culture and the experiences that individuals have or pursue. In terms of individual factors, we can go beyond what our genetic inheritance and environment give us. We can create a unique developmental path by actively choosing from the environment the things that optimize our lives (Rathunde & Csikszentmihalyi, 2006).

Contemporary Concerns in Life-Span Development

Pick up a newspaper or magazine and you might see headlines like these: "Political Leanings May Be Written in the Genes," "Mother Accused of Tossing Children into Bay," "Gender Gap Widens," "FDA Warns About ADHD Drug," "Heart Attack Deaths Higher in African American Patients," "Test May Predict Alzheimer Disease." Researchers using the life-span perspective explore these and many other topics of contemporary concern. The roles that health and well-being, parenting, education, and sociocultural contexts play in life-span development, as well as how social policy is related to these issues, are a particular focus of this textbook.

Health and Well-Being

Health professionals today recognize the power of lifestyles and psychological states in health and well-being (Hahn, Payne, & Lucas, 2013; Siegler & others, 2013). Clinical psychologists are among the health professionals who help people improve their well-being. Read about one clinical psychologist who helps adolescents who have become juvenile delinquents or substance abusers in the *Careers in Life-Span Development* profile.

Careers in life-span development

Luis Vargas, Child Clinical Psychologist

Luis Vargas is Director of the Clinical Child Psychology Internship Program and a professor in the Department of Psychiatry at the University of New Mexico Health Sciences Center. He also is Director of Psychology at the University of New Mexico Children's Psychiatric Hospital.

Luis obtained an undergraduate degree in psychology from St. Edward's University in Texas, a master's degree in psychology from Trinity University in Texas, and a Ph.D. in clinical psychology from the University of Nebraska–Lincoln.

Luis' main areas of interest are cultural issues and the assessment and treatment of children, adolescents, and families.

Luis Vargas (*left*) conducting a child therapy session.

Parenting and Education

Can two gay men raise a healthy family? Do children suffer if both parents work outside the home? Are U.S. schools failing to teach children how to read and write and calculate adequately? We hear many questions like these related to pressures on the contemporary family and the problems of U.S. schools (Grusec & others, 2013; Eccles & Roeser, 2013; McCombs, 2013). In later chapters, we analyze child care, the effects of divorce, parenting styles, intergenerational relationships, early childhood education, relationships between childhood poverty and education, bilingual education, new educational efforts to improve lifelong learning, and many other issues related to parenting and education (Squires & others, 2013; Taylor & Fratto, 2012).

Sociocultural Contexts and Diversity

Two Korean-born children on the day they became United States citizens. Asian American and Latino children are the fastest-growing immigrant groups in the United States. *How diverse are the students in your life-span development class? Are their experiences in growing up likely to have been similar to or different from yours?*

Health, parenting, and education—like development itself—are all shaped by their sociocultural context. To analyze this context, four concepts are especially useful: culture, ethnicity, socioeconomic status, and gender.

Culture encompasses the behavior patterns, beliefs, and all other products of a particular group of people that are passed on from generation to generation. Culture results from the interaction of people over many years (Matsumoto & Juang, 2012). A cultural group can be as large as the United States or as small as an isolated Appalachian town. Whatever its size, the group's culture influences the behavior of its members. **Cross-cultural studies** compare aspects of two or more cultures. The comparison provides information about the degree to which development is similar, or universal, across cultures, or is instead culture-specific (Mistry, Contreras, & Dutta, 2013; Postert & others, 2012).

Ethnicity (the word *ethnic* comes from the Greek word for "nation") is rooted in cultural heritage, nationality, race, religion, and language. African Americans,

How Would You...?

As a health-care professional, how would you explain the importance of examining cross-cultural research when searching for developmental trends in health and wellness?

He is motivated to find better ways to provide culturally responsive mental health services. One of his special interests is the treatment of Latino youth for delinquency and substance abuse.

Clinical psychologists like Luis Vargas seek to help people with psychological problems. They work in a variety of settings, including colleges and universities, clinics, medical schools, and private practice. Some clinical psychologists only conduct psychotherapy; others do psychological assessment and psychotherapy; some also do research. Clinical psychologists may specialize in a particular age group, such

as children (child clinical psychologist) or older adults (geropsychologist).

Clinical psychologists like Dr. Vargas have either a Ph.D. (which involves clinical and research training) or a Psy.D. degree (which only involves clinical training). This graduate training usually takes five to seven years and includes courses in clinical psychology and a one-year supervised internship in an accredited setting toward the end of the training. Most states require clinical psychologists to pass a test to become state licensed and to call themselves clinical psychologists.

socioeconomic status (SES)
Refers to the conceptual grouping of people with similar occupational, educational, and economic characteristics.

gender The psychological and sociocultural dimensions of being female or male.

social policy A national government's course of action designed to promote the welfare of its citizens.

Latinos, Asian Americans, Native Americans, European Americans, and Arab Americans are a few examples of broad ethnic groups in the United States. Diversity exists within each ethnic group (Gollnick & Chen, 2013; Kottak & Kozaitis, 2012).

Socioeconomic status (SES) refers to a person's position within society based on occupational, educational, and economic characteristics. Socioeconomic status implies certain inequalities. Differences in the ability to control resources and to participate in society's rewards produce unequal opportunities (Nieto & Bode, 2012).

Gender, the psychological and sociocultural dimensions of being female or male, is another important aspect of sociocultural contexts. Few aspects of our development are more central to our identity and social relationships than gender (Hyde & Else-Quest, 2013; Matlin, 2012). We discuss sociocultural contexts and diversity in each chapter.

The conditions in which many of the world's women live are a serious concern (UNICEF, 2012). Inadequate educational opportunities, violence, and lack of political access are just some of the problems faced by many women. One analysis found that a higher percentage of girls than boys around the world have never had any education (UNICEF, 2004) (see Figure 1.2). The countries with the highest percentages of uneducated females are in Africa. In contrast, Canada, the United States, and Russia have the highest percentages of educated women. In developing countries, 67 percent of women over the age of 25 (compared with 50 percent of men) have never been to school. At the beginning of the twenty-first century, 80 million more boys than girls were in primary and secondary educational settings around the world (United Nations, 2002).

Doly Akter, age 17, lives in a slum in Dhaka, Bangladesh, where sewers overflow, garbage rots in the streets, and children are undernourished. Nearly two-thirds of young women in Bangladesh get married before they are 18. Doly recently organized a club supported by UNICEF in which girls go door-to-door to monitor the hygiene habits of households in their neighborhood. The monitoring has led to improved hygiene and health in the families. Also, her group has managed to stop several child marriages by meeting with parents and convincing them that it is not in their daughter's best interests. When talking with parents in their neighborhoods, the girls in the club emphasize the importance of staying in school and how this will improve their daughters' future. Doly says that the girls in her UNICEF group are far more aware of their rights than their mothers ever were. (UNICEF, 2007).

Social Policy

Social policy is a government's course of action designed to promote the welfare of its citizens. Values, economics, and politics all shape a nation's social policy. Out of concern that policy makers are doing too little to protect the well-being of children and older adults, life-span researchers are increasingly undertaking studies that they hope will lead to effective social policy (Cross & others, 2012; Fisher & others, 2013).

Children who grow up in poverty represent a special concern of researchers who see social policy as a way of improving children's lives (Duncan & others, 2013). In 2009, 20.1 percent (an increase from 18.5 percent in 2008 and the highest rate since 1995) of U.S. children were living in families that had incomes below the poverty line (U.S. Census Bureau, 2012). As indicated in Figure 1.3, one study found that a higher percentage of children in poor families than in middle-income families were exposed to family turmoil, separation from a parent, violence, crowding, excessive noise, and poor housing (Evans & English, 2002).

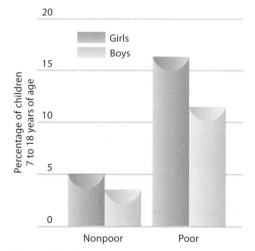

Figure 1.2 Percentages of Children 7 to 18 Years of Age Around the World Who Have Never Been to a School of Any Kind
When UNICEF (2004) surveyed the education that children around the world are receiving, it found that far more girls than boys receive no formal schooling at all.

How Would You...?
As a psychologist, how would you explain the importance of examining sociocultural factors in developmental research?

Developmental psychologists are seeking ways to help families living in poverty improve their well-being, and they have offered many suggestions for improving government policies. For example, the Minnesota Family Investment Program (MFIP) was designed in the 1990s primarily to influence the behavior of adults—specifically, to move adults off welfare rolls and into paid employment. A key element of the program was its guarantee that adults participating in the program would receive more income if they worked than if they did not. How did the increase in income affect their children? A study of the effects of MFIP found that higher incomes of working poor parents were linked with benefits for their children (Gennetian & Miller, 2002). The children's achievement in school improved, and their behavior problems decreased. A current MFIP study is examining the influence of specific services on low-income families at risk for child maltreatment and other negative outcomes for children (Minnesota Family Investment Program, 2009).

At the other end of the life span, older adults have health issues that social policy can address (Siegler, 2013). Key concerns are escalating health-care costs and the access of older adults to adequate health care (Dilworth-Anderson, Pierre, & Hilliard, 2012). One study found that the health-care system fails older adults in many areas (Wenger & others, 2003). For example, older adults received the recommended care for general medical conditions such as heart disease only 52 percent of the time; they received appropriate care for undernutrition and Alzheimer disease only 31 percent of the time.

Concerns about the well-being of older adults are heightened by two facts. First, the number of older adults in the United States is growing rapidly. Second, many of these older Americans are likely to need society's help (Viachantoni, 2012). Compared with earlier decades, U.S. adults today are less likely to be married, more likely to be childless, and more likely to live alone. As the older population continues to expand during the twenty-first century, an increasing number of older adults will be without either a spouse or children—traditionally the main sources of support for older adults (Ament & others, 2012). These individuals will need social relationships, networks, and supports (Antonucci, Birditt, & Ajrouch, 2013).

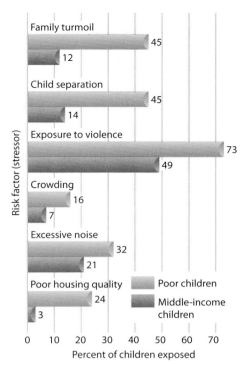

Figure 1.3 Exposure to Six Stressors Among Poor and Middle-Income Children One study analyzed the exposure to six stressors among poor children and middle-income children (Evans & English, 2002). Poor children were much more likely to face each of these stressors.

The Nature of Development

In this section we explore what is meant by developmental processes and periods, as well as variations in the way age is conceptualized. We examine some key developmental issues.

If you wanted to describe how and why Alice Walker or Ted Kaczynski developed during their lifetimes, how would you go about it? A chronicle of the events in any person's life can quickly become a confusing and tedious array of details. Two concepts help provide a framework for describing and understanding an individual's development: developmental processes and periods.

Biological, Cognitive, and Socioemotional Processes

At the beginning of this chapter, we defined development as the pattern of change that begins at conception and continues through the life span. The pattern is

biological processes Changes in
an individual's physical nature.

cognitive processes Changes in
an individual's thought, intelligence,
and language.

socioemotional processes
Changes in an individual's relationships with other people, emotions,
and personality.

complex because it is the product of biological, cognitive, and socioemotional processes.

Biological Processes

Biological processes produce changes in an individual's physical
nature. Genes inherited from parents, the development of the brain,
height and weight gains, changes in motor skills, nutrition, exercise,
the hormonal changes of puberty, and cardiovascular decline are all
examples of biological processes that affect development.

Cognitive Processes

Cognitive processes refer to changes in an individual's thinking, intelligence, and
language. Watching a colorful mobile swinging above the crib, putting together
a two-word sentence, memorizing a poem, imagining what it would be like to be
a movie star, and solving a crossword puzzle all involve cognitive processes.

Socioemotional Processes

Socioemotional processes involve changes in the individual's relationships with
other people, changes in emotions, and changes in personality. An infant's smile
in response to a parent's touch, a toddler's aggressive attack on a playmate, a
school-age child's development of assertiveness, an adolescent's joy at the senior
prom, and the affection of an elderly couple all reflect the role of socioemotional
processes in development.

Connecting Biological, Cognitive, and Socioemotional Processes

Biological, cognitive, and socioemotional processes are inextricably intertwined
(Diamond, 2013). Consider a baby smiling in response to a parent's touch. This
response depends on biological processes (the physical nature of touch and
responsiveness to it), cognitive processes (the ability to understand intentional
acts), and socioemotional processes (the act of smiling often reflects a positive
emotional feeling, and smiling helps to connect us in positive ways with other
human beings). Nowhere is the connection across biological, cognitive, and socioemotional processes more obvious than in two rapidly emerging fields:

- *developmental cognitive neuroscience*, which explores links between development,
  cognitive processes, and the brain (Diamond, 2013; Johnson & de Haan, 2012)
- *developmental social neuroscience*, which examines connections between socioemotional processes, development, and the brain (Pfeifer & Blakemore, 2012;
  Weir, Zakama, & Rao, 2012).

In many instances, biological, cognitive, and socioemotional processes are
bidirectional. For example, biological processes can influence cognitive processes
and vice versa. For the most part, we will study the different processes of development (biological, cognitive, and socioemotional) in separate chapters, but the
human being is an integrated individual with a mind and body that are interde-
pendent. Thus, in many places throughout the book we will call attention to the
connections between these processes.

Periods of Development

The interplay of biological, cognitive, and socioemotional processes (see Figure 1.4)
over time gives rise to the developmental periods of the human life span. A developmental period is a time frame in a person's life that is characterized by certain
features. The most widely used classification of developmental periods involves
an eight-period sequence. For the purposes of organization and understanding,
this book is structured according to these developmental periods.

The *prenatal period* is the time from conception to birth. It involves tremendous growth—from a single cell to a complete organism with a brain and behavioral capabilities—and takes place in approximately a nine-month period.

Infancy is the developmental period from birth to 18 or 24 months when humans are extremely dependent on adults. During this period, many psychological activities—language, symbolic thought, sensorimotor coordination, and social learning, for example—are just beginning.

Early childhood is the developmental period from the end of infancy to age 5 or 6. This period is sometimes called the "preschool years." During this time, young children learn to become more self-sufficient and to care for themselves. They also develop school readiness skills, such as the ability to follow instructions and identify letters, and they spend many hours playing with peers. First grade typically marks the end of early childhood.

Middle and late childhood is the developmental period from about 6 to 11 years of age, approximately corresponding to the elementary school years. During this period, children master the fundamental skills of reading, writing, and arithmetic. They are formally exposed to the world outside the family and to the prevailing culture. Achievement becomes a more central theme of the child's world, and self-control increases.

Adolescence encompasses the transition from childhood to early adulthood, entered at approximately 10 to 12 years of age and ending at 18 to 22 years of age. Adolescence begins with rapid physical changes—dramatic gains in height and weight, changes in body contour, and the development of sexual characteristics such as enlargement of the breasts, growth of pubic and facial hair, and deepening of the voice. At this point in development, the pursuit of independence and an identity are prominent themes. Thought is more logical, abstract, and idealistic. More time is spent outside the family.

Early adulthood is the developmental period that begins in the late teens or early twenties and lasts through the thirties. For young adults, this is a time for establishing personal and economic independence, becoming proficient in a career, and for many, selecting a mate, learning to live with that person in an intimate way, starting a family, and rearing children.

Middle adulthood is the developmental period from approximately 40 years of age to about 60. It is a time of expanding personal and social involvement and responsibility; of assisting the next generation in becoming competent, mature individuals; and of achieving and maintaining satisfaction in a career.

Late adulthood is the developmental period that begins in the sixties or seventies and lasts until death. It is a time of life review, retirement from the workforce, and adjustment to new social roles involving decreasing strength and health.

Late adulthood lasts longer than any other period of development. Because the number of people in this age group has been increasing dramatically, life-span developmentalists have been paying more attention to differences within late adulthood. According to Paul Baltes and Jacqui Smith (2003), a major change takes place in older adults' lives as they become the "oldest-old," at about 85 years of age. The "young-old" (classified as 65 through 84 in this analysis) have substantial potential for physical and cognitive fitness, retain much of their cognitive capacity, and can develop strategies to cope with the gains and losses of aging. In contrast, the oldest-old (85 and older) show considerable loss in cognitive skills, experience an increase

Figure 1.4 Processes Involved in Developmental Changes Biological, cognitive, and socioemotional processes interact as individuals develop.

"This is the path to adulthood. You're here."

© Robert Weber/The New Yorker Collection/www.cartoonbank.com

(*a*) Dawn Russel, competing in a recent Senior Olympics competition in Oregon. (*b*) A sedentary, overweight middle-aged man. *Even if Dawn Russel's chronological age is older, might her biological age be younger than the middle-aged man's?*

(a)   (b)

in chronic stress, and are more frail (Baltes & Smith, 2003). Nonetheless, considerable variation exists in how much of their capabilities the oldest-old retain.

Conceptions of Age

In our description of developmental periods, we attached an approximate age range to each period. But we also have noted that there are variations in the capabilities of individuals of the same age, and we have seen how age-related changes can be exaggerated. How important is age when we try to understand an individual?

According to some life-span experts, chronological age is not very relevant to understanding a person's psychological development (Hoyer & Roodin, 2009). Chronological age is the number of years that have elapsed since birth. But time is a crude index of experience, and it does not cause development. Chronological age, moreover, is not the only way of measuring age. Just as there are different domains of development, there are different ways of thinking about age.

Four Types of Age

Age has been conceptualized not just as chronological age but also as biological age, psychological age, and social age (Hoyer & Roodin, 2009). *Biological age* is a person's age in terms of biological health. Determining biological age involves knowing the functional capacities of a person's vital organs. One person's vital capacities may be better or worse than those of others of comparable chronological age. The younger the person's biological age, the longer the person is expected to live, regardless of chronological age.

Psychological age is an individual's adaptive capacities compared with those of other individuals of the same chronological age. Thus, older adults who continue to learn, remain flexible, are motivated, and think clearly are engaging in more adaptive behaviors than their chronological age-mates who do not do these things (Dixon & others, 2013).

Social age refers to connectedness with others and the social roles individuals adopt. Individuals who have better social relationships with others are happier and more likely to live longer than individuals who are lonely (Carstensen, 2011; Carstensen & others, 2011).

From a life-span perspective, an overall age profile of an individual involves not just chronological age but also biological age, psychological age, and social age. For example, a 70-year-old man (chronological age) might be in good physical health (biological age), but might be experiencing memory problems and having trouble coping with the demands placed on him by his wife's recent hospitalization (psychological age) and dealing with a lack of social support (social age).

Age and Happiness

Is there a best age to be? An increasing number of studies indicate that at least in the United States adults are happier as they age (Stone & others, 2010). Consider also a U.S. study of approximately 28,000 individuals from 18 to 88 that revealed happiness increased with age (Yang, 2008). For example, about 33 percent were very happy at 88 years of age compared with only about 24 percent in their late teens and early twenties. Why might older people report being happier and more satisfied with their lives than younger people? Despite the increase in physical problems and losses older adults experience, they are more content with what they have in their lives, have better relationships with the people who matter to them, are less pressured to achieve, have more time for leisurely pursuits, and have many years of experience that may help them adapt to their circumstances with greater wisdom than younger adults do.

Now that you have read about age variations in life satisfaction, think about how satisfied you are with your life. To help you answer this question, complete the items in Figure 1.5, which presents the most widely used measure in research on life satisfaction (Diener, 2012).

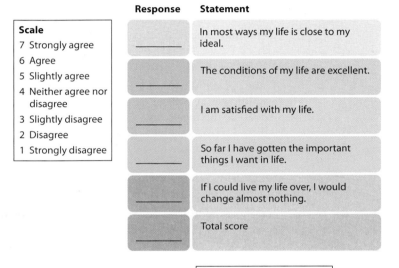

Below are five statements that you may agree or disagree with. Using the 1–7 scale below, indicate your agreement with each item by placing the appropriate number on the line preceding that item. Please be open and honest in your responding.

Response   Statement

Scale
7 Strongly agree
6 Agree
5 Slightly agree
4 Neither agree nor disagree
3 Slightly disagree
2 Disagree
1 Strongly disagree

_____ In most ways my life is close to my ideal.

_____ The conditions of my life are excellent.

_____ I am satisfied with my life.

_____ So far I have gotten the important things I want in life.

_____ If I could live my life over, I would change almost nothing.

_____ Total score

Scoring
31–35 Extremely satisfied
26–30 Satisfied
21–25 Slightly satisfied
20 Neutral
15–19 Slightly dissatisfied
10–14 Dissatisfied
5–9 Extremely dissatisfied

Figure 1.5 How Satisfied Am I With My Life?
Source: Diener, E., Emmons, R. A., Larson, R. J., & Griffin, S. (1985). The Satisfaction with Life Scale. *Journal of Personality Assessment, 49,* 71–75.

Developmental Issues

Was Ted Kaczynski born a killer, or did his life turn him into one? Kaczynski himself thought that his childhood was the root of his troubles. He grew up as a genius in a boy's body and never fit in with other children. Did his early experiences determine his later life? Is your own journey through life marked out ahead of time, or can your experiences change your path? Are the experiences you have early in your journey more important than later ones? Is your journey more like taking an elevator up a skyscraper with distinct stops along the way or more like a cruise down a river with smoother ebbs and flows? These questions point to three issues about the nature of development: the roles played by nature and nurture, stability and change, and continuity and discontinuity.

Nature and Nurture

The **nature-nurture issue** concerns the extent to which development is influenced by nature and by nurture. *Nature* refers to an organism's biological inheritance, *nurture* to its environmental experiences.

nature-nurture issue The debate about the extent to which development is influenced by nature and by nurture. Nature refers to an organism's biological inheritance, nurture to its environmental experiences.

According to those who emphasize the role of nature, just as a sunflower grows in an orderly way—unless flattened by an unfriendly environment—so too the human grows in an orderly way. An evolutionary and genetic foundation produces commonalities in growth and development (Buss, 2012; Durrant & Ellis, 2013). We walk before we talk, speak one word before two words, grow rapidly in infancy and less so in early childhood, experience a rush of sex hormones in puberty, reach the peak of our physical strength in late adolescence and early adulthood, and then physically decline. Proponents of the importance of nature acknowledge that extreme environments—those that are psychologically barren or hostile—can depress development. However, they believe that basic growth tendencies are genetically programmed into humans (Maxson, 2013).

By contrast, other psychologists emphasize the importance of nurture, or environmental experiences, in development (Grusec & others, 2013). Experiences run the gamut from the individual's biological environment (nutrition, medical care, drugs, and physical accidents) to the social environment (family, peers, schools, community, media, and culture).

Stability and Change

Is the shy child who hides behind the sofa when visitors arrive destined to become a wallflower at college dances, or might the child become a sociable, talkative individual? Is the fun-loving, carefree adolescent bound to have difficulty holding down a 9-to-5 job as an adult? These questions reflect the **stability-change issue**, involving the degree to which early traits and characteristics persist or change over time.

Many developmentalists who emphasize stability in development argue that stability is the result of heredity and possibly early experiences in life. For example, many argue that if an individual is shy throughout life (as Ted Kaczynski was), this stability is due to heredity and possibly early experiences in which the infant or young child encountered considerable stress when interacting with people. Some argue that unless infants experience warm, nurturant caregiving in the first year or so of life, their development will never be optimal (Cassidy & others, 2011).

Developmentalists who emphasize change take the more optimistic view that later experiences can produce change. Recall that in the life-span perspective, plasticity, the potential for change, exists throughout the life span (Lerner, Easterbrooks, & Mistry, 2013; Schaie, 2012). Experts such as Paul Baltes (2003) argue that older adults often show less capacity for learning new things than younger adults do. However, many older adults continue to be good at applying what they have learned in earlier times.

Continuity and Discontinuity

When developmental change occurs, is it gradual or abrupt? Think about your own development for a moment. Did you gradually become the person you are today? Or did you experience sudden, distinct changes in your growth? For the most part, developmentalists who emphasize nurture describe development as a gradual, continuous process. Those who emphasize nature often describe development as a series of distinct stages.

The **continuity-discontinuity issue** focuses on the degree to which development involves either gradual, cumulative change (continuity) or distinct stages (discontinuity). In terms of continuity, as the oak grows from a seedling to a giant tree, its development is continuous. Similarly, a child's first word, though seemingly an abrupt, discontinuous event, is actually the result of weeks and months of growth and practice. Puberty might seem abrupt, but it is a gradual process that occurs over several years.

In terms of discontinuity, as an insect grows from a caterpillar to a chrysalis to a butterfly, it passes through a sequence of stages in which change is qualitatively rather than quantitatively different. Similarly, at some point a child moves from not being able to think abstractly about the world to being able to do so. This is a qualitative,

stability-change issue The debate about the degree to which early traits and characteristics persist through life or change.

continuity-discontinuity issue The debate about the extent to which development involves gradual, cumulative change (continuity) or distinct stages (discontinuity).

discontinuous change in development rather than a quantitative, continuous change.

Evaluating the Developmental Issues

Developmentalists generally acknowledge that development is not all nature or all nurture, not all stability or all change, and not all continuity or all discontinuity. Nature and nurture, stability and change, continuity and discontinuity characterize development throughout the human life span.

Although most developmentalists do not take extreme positions on these three important issues, there is spirited debate regarding how strongly development is influenced by each of these factors (Buss, 2012; Kagan, 2013; Rutter, 2013; Schaie, 2012).

Theories of Development

How can we answer questions about the roles of nature and nurture, stability and change, and continuity and discontinuity in development? How can we determine, for example, whether memory declines in older adults can be prevented or whether special care can repair the harm inflicted by child neglect? The scientific method is the best tool we have to answer such questions (Smith & Davis, 2013).

The scientific method is essentially a four-step process: (1) conceptualize a process or problem to be studied, (2) collect research information (data), (3) analyze data, and (4) draw conclusions.

In step 1, when researchers are formulating a problem to study, they often draw on theories and develop hypotheses. A **theory** is an interrelated, coherent set of ideas that helps to explain phenomena and make predictions. It may suggest **hypotheses,** which are specific assertions and predictions that can be tested. For example, a theory on mentoring might state that sustained support and guidance from an adult makes a difference in the lives of children from impoverished backgrounds because the mentor gives the children opportunities to observe and imitate the behavior and strategies of the mentor.

This section outlines five theoretical orientations to development: psychoanalytic, cognitive, behavioral and social cognitive, ethological, and ecological. These theories look at development from different perspectives, and they disagree about certain aspects of development. But many of their ideas are complementary, and each contributes an important piece to the life-span development puzzle. Although the theories disagree about certain aspects of development, many of their ideas are complementary rather than contradictory. Together they let us see the total landscape of life-span development in all its richness.

Psychoanalytic Theories

Psychoanalytic theories describe development primarily in terms of unconscious (beyond awareness) processes that are heavily colored by emotion. Psychoanalytic theorists emphasize that behavior is merely a surface characteristic and that a true understanding of development requires analyzing the symbolic meanings of behavior and the deep inner workings of the mind. Psychoanalytic theorists also stress that early experiences with parents extensively shape development. These characteristics are highlighted in the main psychoanalytic theory, that of Sigmund Freud (1856–1939).

Freud's Theory

Freud was a pioneer in the treatment of psychological problems. Certain that by talking about their problems, his patients could be

theory A coherent set of ideas that helps to explain data and to make predictions.

hypotheses Assertions or predictions, often derived from theories, that can be tested.

psychoanalytic theories Theories holding that development depends primarily on the unconscious mind and is heavily couched in emotion, that behavior is merely a surface characteristic, that it is important to analyze the symbolic meanings of behavior, and that early experiences are important in development.

Oral Stage	Anal Stage	Phallic Stage	Latency Stage	Genital Stage
Infant's pleasure centers on the mouth.	Child's pleasure focuses on the anus.	Child's pleasure focuses on the genitals.	Child represses sexual interest and develops social and intellectual skills.	A time of sexual reawakening; source of sexual pleasure becomes someone outside the family.
Birth to 1 1/2 Years	**1 1/2 to 3 Years**	**3 to 6 Years**	**6 Years to Puberty**	**Puberty Onward**

Figure 1.6 Freudian Stages

Because Freud emphasized sexual motivation, his stages of development are known as psychosexual stages. In his view, if the need for pleasure at any stage is either undergratified or overgratified, an individual may become fixated, or locked in, at that stage of development.

restored to psychological health, Freud developed a technique called psychoanalysis. As he listened to, probed, and analyzed his patients, he became convinced that their problems were the result of experiences early in life. He thought that as children grow up, their focus of pleasure and sexual impulses shifts from the mouth to the anus and eventually to the genitals. Consequently, he determined, we pass through five stages of psychosexual development: oral, anal, phallic, latency, and genital (see Figure 1.6). Our adult personality, Freud (1917) claimed, is determined by the way we resolve conflicts between sources of pleasure at each stage and the demands of reality.

Freud's followers significantly revised his psychoanalytic theory. Many of today's psychoanalytic theorists believe that Freud overemphasized sexual instincts; they place more emphasis on cultural experiences as determinants of an individual's development. Unconscious thought remains a central theme, but conscious thought plays a greater role than Freud envisioned. Next, we will outline the ideas of an important revisionist of Freud's ideas—Erik Erikson.

Erikson's Psychosocial Theory

Erik Erikson recognized Freud's contributions but believed that Freud misjudged some important dimensions of human development. For one thing, Erikson (1950, 1968) said we develop in psychosocial stages, rather than in psychosexual stages, as Freud maintained. According to Freud, the primary motivation for human behavior is sexual in nature; according to Erikson, motivation is social and reflects a desire to affiliate with other people. According to Freud, our basic personality is shaped in the first five years of life; according to Erikson, developmental change occurs throughout the life span. Thus, Freud viewed early experiences as far more important than later experiences, whereas Erikson emphasized the importance of both early and later experiences.

In **Erikson's theory,** eight stages of development unfold as we go through life (see Figure 1.7). At each stage, a unique developmental task confronts individuals with a crisis that must be resolved. According to Erikson, this crisis is not a catastrophe but a turning point marked by both increased vulnerability and enhanced potential. The more successfully an individual resolves the crisis, the healthier development will be.

Trust versus mistrust is Erikson's first psychosocial stage, which is experienced in the first year of life. Trust in infancy sets the stage for a lifelong expectation that the world will be a good and pleasant place to live.

Autonomy versus shame and doubt is Erikson's second stage. This stage occurs in late infancy and toddlerhood (1 to 3 years). After gaining trust in their caregivers, infants begin to discover that their behavior is their own. They start to assert their sense of independence or autonomy. They realize their will. If infants and toddlers are restrained too much or punished too harshly, they are likely to develop a sense of shame and doubt.

Erikson's theory A psychoanalytic theory in which eight stages of psychosocial development unfold throughout the human life span. Each stage consists of a unique developmental task that confronts individuals with a crisis that must be faced.

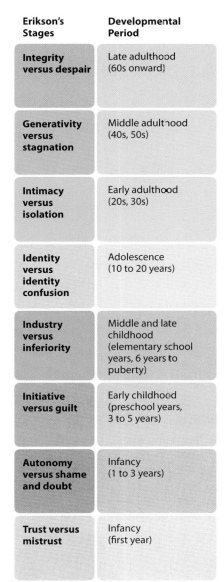

Erikson's Stages	Developmental Period
Integrity versus despair	Late adulthood (60s onward)
Generativity versus stagnation	Middle adulthood (40s, 50s)
Intimacy versus isolation	Early adulthood (20s, 30s)
Identity versus identity confusion	Adolescence (10 to 20 years)
Industry versus inferiority	Middle and late childhood (elementary school years, 6 years to puberty)
Initiative versus guilt	Early childhood (preschool years, 3 to 5 years)
Autonomy versus shame and doubt	Infancy (1 to 3 years)
Trust versus mistrust	Infancy (first year)

Figure 1.7 Erikson's Eight Life-Span Stages
Like Freud, Erikson proposed that individuals go through distinct, universal stages of development. In terms of the continuity-discontinuity issue, both favor the discontinuity side of the debate. Notice that the timing of Erikson's first four stages is similar to that of Freud's stages. *What are the implications of saying that people go through stages of development?*

Initiative versus guilt, Erikson's third stage of development, occurs during the preschool years. As preschool children encounter a widening social world, they face new challenges that require active, purposeful, responsible behavior. Feelings of guilt may arise, though, if the child is irresponsible and is made to feel too anxious.

Industry versus inferiority is Erikson's fourth developmental stage, occurring approximately in the elementary school years. Children now need to direct their energy toward mastering knowledge and intellectual skills. The negative outcome is that the child may develop a sense of inferiority—feeling incompetent and unproductive.

During the adolescent years individuals face finding out who they are, what they are all about, and where they are going in life. This is Erikson's fifth developmental stage, *identity versus identity confusion.* If adolescents explore roles in a healthy manner and arrive at a positive path to follow in life, then they achieve a positive identity; if not, then identity confusion reigns.

Intimacy versus isolation is Erikson's sixth developmental stage, which individuals experience during the early adulthood years. At this time, individuals face the developmental task of forming intimate relationships. If young adults form healthy friendships and an intimate relationship with another, intimacy will be achieved; if not, isolation will result.

Generativity versus stagnation, Erikson's seventh developmental stage, occurs during middle adulthood. By generativity, Erikson means primarily a concern for helping the younger generation to develop and lead useful lives. The feeling of having done nothing to help the next generation is stagnation.

Integrity versus despair is Erikson's eighth and final stage of development, which individuals experience in late adulthood. During this stage, a person reflects on the past. If the person's life review reveals a life well spent, integrity will be achieved; if not, the retrospective glances likely will yield doubt or gloom—the despair Erikson described.

Erik Erikson with his wife, Joan, an artist. Erikson generated one of the most important developmental theories of the twentieth century. *Which stage of Erikson's theory are you in? Does Erikson's description of this stage characterize you?*

Evaluating Psychoanalytic Theories

Contributions of psychoanalytic theories like Freud's and Erikson's to life-span development include an emphasis on a developmental framework, family relationships, and unconscious aspects of the mind. Criticisms include a lack of scientific support, too much emphasis on sexual underpinnings, and an image of people that is too negative.

Cognitive Theories

Whereas psychoanalytic theories stress the unconscious, cognitive theories emphasize conscious thoughts. Three important cognitive theories are Piaget's cognitive

Sensorimotor Stage	**Preoperational Stage**	**Concrete Operational Stage**	**Formal Operational Stage**
The infant constructs an understanding of the world by coordinating sensory experiences with physical actions. An infant progresses from reflexive, instinctual action at birth to the beginning of symbolic thought toward the end of the stage.	The child begins to represent the world with words and images. These words and images reflect increased symbolic thinking and go beyond the connection of sensory information and physical action.	The child can now reason logically about concrete events and classify objects into different sets.	The adolescent reasons in more abstract, idealistic, and logical ways.
Birth to 2 Years of Age	**2 to 7 Years of Age**	**7 to 11 Years of Age**	**11 Years of Age Through Adulthood**

Figure 1.8 **Piaget's Four Stages of Cognitive Development**
According to Piaget, how a child thinks—not how much the child knows—determines the child's stage of cognitive development.

developmental theory, Vygotsky's sociocultural cognitive theory, and information-processing theory. All three focus on the development of complex thinking skills.

Piaget's Cognitive Developmental Theory

Piaget's theory states that children go through four stages of cognitive development as they actively construct their understanding of the world. Two processes underlie this cognitive construction of the world: organization and adaptation. To make sense of our world, we organize our experiences. For example, we separate important ideas from less important ideas, and we connect one idea to another. In addition to organizing our observations and experiences, we must adjust to changing environmental demands (Miller, 2011).

Piaget (1954) argued that we go through four stages in understanding the world (see Figure 1.8). Each stage is age-related and consists of a distinct way of thinking, a different way of understanding the world. Thus, according to Piaget, the child's cognition is *qualitatively* different in one stage compared with another. What are Piaget's four stages of cognitive development?

The *sensorimotor stage*, which lasts from birth to about 2 years of age, is the first Piagetian stage. In this stage, infants construct an understanding of the world by coordinating sensory experiences (such as seeing and hearing) with physical, motor actions—hence the term *sensorimotor*.

The *preoperational stage*, which lasts from approximately 2 to 7 years of age, is Piaget's second stage. In this stage, children begin to go beyond simply connecting sensory information with physical action and represent the world with words, images, and drawings. However, according to Piaget, preschool children still lack the

Jean Piaget, the famous Swiss developmental psychologist, changed the way we think about the development of children's minds. *What are some key ideas in Piaget's theory?*

ability to perform what he calls *operations*, which are internalized mental actions that allow children to do mentally what they previously could only do physically. For example, if you imagine putting two sticks together to see whether they would be as long as another stick, without actually moving the sticks, you are performing a concrete operation.

The *concrete operational stage*, which lasts from approximately 7 to 11 years of age, is the third Piagetian stage. In this stage, children can perform operations that involve objects, and they can reason logically about specific or concrete examples. Concrete operational thinkers, however, cannot imagine the steps necessary to complete an algebraic equation because doing so would require a level of thinking that is too abstract for this stage of development.

The *formal operational stage*, which appears between the ages of 11 and 15 and continues through adulthood, is Piaget's fourth and final stage. In this stage, individuals move beyond concrete experiences and think in abstract and more logical terms. As part of thinking more abstractly, adolescents develop images of ideal circumstances. They might think about what an ideal parent is like and compare their parents to this ideal standard. They begin to entertain possibilities for the future and are fascinated with what they can be. In solving problems, they become more systematic, developing hypotheses about why something is happening the way it is and then testing these hypotheses. We will examine Piaget's cognitive developmental theory further in Chapters 3, 5, 7, and 9.

Vygotsky's Sociocultural Cognitive Theory

Like Piaget, the Russian developmentalist Lev Vygotsky (1896–1934) reasoned that children actively construct their knowledge. However, Vygotsky (1962) gave social interaction and culture far more important roles in cognitive development than Piaget did. **Vygotsky's theory** is a sociocultural cognitive theory that emphasizes how culture and social interaction guide cognitive development.

Vygotsky portrayed the child's development as inseparable from social and cultural activities (Gauvain, 2013; Mahn & John-Steiner, 2013). He stressed that cognitive development involves learning to use the inventions of society, such as language, mathematical systems, and memory strategies. Thus, in one culture children might learn to count with the help of a computer; in another they might learn by using beads. According to Vygotsky, children's social interaction with more-skilled adults and peers is indispensable to their cognitive development (Daniels, 2011). Through this interaction, they learn to use the tools that will help them adapt and be successful in their culture. In Chapter 5 we examine ideas about learning and teaching that are based on Vygotsky's theory.

Lev Vygotsky was born the same year as Piaget, but he died much earlier, at the age of 37. There is considerable interest today in Vygotsky's sociocultural cognitive theory of child development. *What are some key characteristics of Vygotsky's theory?*

Information-Processing Theory

Information-processing theory emphasizes that individuals manipulate information, monitor it, and strategize about it. Unlike Piaget's theory but like Vygotsky's theory, information-processing theory does not describe development as stage-like. Instead, according to this theory individuals develop a gradually increasing capacity for processing information, which allows them to acquire increasingly complex knowledge and skills (Robinson-Riegler & Robinson-Riegler, 2012).

Robert Siegler (2006, 2012a, b), a leading expert on children's information processing, states that thinking is information processing. In other words, when individuals perceive, encode, represent,

Vygotsky's theory A sociocultural cognitive theory that emphasizes how culture and social interaction guide cognitive development.

information-processing theory A theory that emphasizes that individuals manipulate information, monitor it, and strategize about it. The processes of memory and thinking are central.

behavioral and social cognitive
theories Theories holding that
development can be described in
terms of the behaviors learned
through interactions with the
environment.

store, and retrieve information, they are thinking. Siegler emphasizes that an important aspect of development is learning good strategies for processing information. For example, becoming a better reader might involve learning to monitor the key themes of the material being read.

Evaluating Cognitive Theories

Contributions of cognitive theories include a positive view of development and an emphasis on the active construction of understanding. Criticisms include skepticism about the pureness of Piaget's stages and too little attention to individual variations.

Behavioral and Social Cognitive Theories

Behavioral and social cognitive theories hold that development can be described in terms of behaviors learned through interactions with our surroundings. Behaviorism essentially holds that we can study scientifically only what can be directly observed and measured. Out of the behavioral tradition grew the belief that development is observable behavior that can be learned through experience with the environment (Miltenberger, 2012). In terms of the continuity-discontinuity issue discussed earlier in this chapter, the behavioral and social cognitive theories emphasize continuity in development and argue that development does not occur in stage-like fashion. Let's explore two versions of behaviorism: Skinner's operant conditioning and Bandura's social cognitive theory.

Skinner's Operant Conditioning

According to B. F. Skinner (1904–1990), through *operant conditioning* the consequences of a behavior produce changes in the probability of the behavior's recurrence. A behavior followed by a rewarding stimulus is more likely to recur, whereas a behavior followed by a punishing stimulus is less likely to recur. For example, when an adult smiles at a child after the child has done something, the child is more likely to engage in that behavior again than if the adult gives the child a disapproving look.

In Skinner's (1938) view, such rewards and punishments shape development. For Skinner the key aspect of development is behavior, not thoughts and feelings. He emphasized that development consists of the pattern of behavioral changes that are brought about by rewards and punishments. For example, Skinner would say that shy people learned to be shy as a result of experiences they had while growing up. It follows that modifications in an environment can help a shy person become more socially oriented.

Bandura's Social Cognitive Theory

Some psychologists agree with the behaviorists' notion that development is learned and is influenced strongly by environmental interactions. However, unlike Skinner, they also see cognition as important in understanding development. **Social cognitive theory** holds that behavior, environment, and person/cognition factors are the key factors in development.

American psychologist Albert Bandura (1925–) is the leading architect of social cognitive theory. Bandura (1986, 2004, 2009, 2010a, b, 2011, 2012) emphasizes that cognitive processes have important links with the environment and behavior. His early research program focused heavily on *observational learning* (also called *imitation* or *modeling*), which is learning that occurs through observing what others do. For example, a young boy might observe

social cognitive theory The
theory that behavior, environment,
and person/cognition factors
are important in understanding
development.

Albert Bandura has been one of the leading architects of social cognitive theory. *How does Bandura's theory differ from Skinner's?*

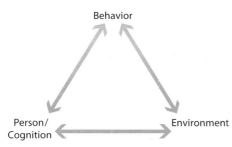

Figure 1.9 Bandura's Social Cognitive Model
The arrows illustrate how relations between behavior, person/cognition, and environment are reciprocal rather than one-way. Person/cognition refers to cognitive processes (for example, thinking and planning) and personal characteristics (for example, believing that you can control your experiences).

his father yelling in anger and treating other people with hostility; and then later with his peers, the young boy acts very aggressively, showing the same characteristics as his father's behavior. Social cognitive theorists stress that people acquire a wide range of behaviors, thoughts, and feelings through observing others' behavior and that these observations form an important part of life-span development.

What is *cognitive* about observational learning in Bandura's view? He proposes that people cognitively represent the behavior of others and then sometimes adopt this behavior themselves.

Bandura's (2004, 2009, 2010a, b, 2011, 2012) most recent model of learning and development includes three elements: behavior, the person/cognition, and the environment. An individual's confidence that he or she can control his or her success is an example of a person factor; strategies for achieving success are an example of a cognitive factor. As shown in Figure 1.9, behavior, person/cognitive, and environmental factors operate interactively.

Evaluating Behavioral and Social Cognitive Theories

Contributions of the behavioral and social cognitive theories include an emphasis on scientific research and environmental determinants of behavior. Criticisms include too little emphasis on cognition in Skinner's view and giving inadequate attention to developmental changes.

Ethological Theory

Ethology is the study of the behavior of animals in their natural habitat. Ethological theory stresses that behavior is strongly influenced by biology, is tied to evolution, and is characterized by critical or sensitive periods. These are specific time frames during which, according to ethologists, the presence or absence of certain experiences has a long-lasting influence on individuals.

Lorenz's Research with Greylag Geese

European zoologist Konrad Lorenz (1903–1989) helped bring ethology to prominence. In his best-known research, Lorenz (1965) studied the behavior of greylag geese, which follow their mothers as soon as they hatch. Lorenz separated the eggs laid by one goose into two groups. One group he returned to the goose to be hatched by her. The other group was hatched in an incubator. The goslings in the first group performed as predicted. They followed their mother as soon as they hatched. However, those in the second group, which saw Lorenz when they first hatched, followed him everywhere as though he were their mother. Lorenz marked the goslings and then placed both groups under a box. Mother goose and "mother" Lorenz stood aside as the box lifted. Each group of goslings went directly to its "mother." Lorenz called this process *imprinting*—the rapid, innate learning that involves attachment to the first moving object seen.

John Bowlby (1969, 1989) illustrated an important application of ethological theory to human development. Bowlby stressed that attachment to a caregiver over the first year of life has important consequences throughout the life span. In his view, if this attachment is positive and secure, the individual will likely develop positively in childhood and adulthood. If the attachment is negative and insecure, development will likely not be optimal. In Chapter 4, we explore the concept of infant attachment in much greater detail.

ethology An approach that stresses that behavior is strongly influenced by biology, tied to evolution, and characterized by critical or sensitive periods.

Konrad Lorenz, a pioneering student of animal behavior, is followed through the water by three imprinted greylag geese. Describe Lorenz's experiment with the geese. *Do you think his experiment would have the same results with human babies? Explain.*

In Lorenz's view, imprinting needs to take place at a specific, very early time in the life of the animal, or else it will not take place. This point in time is called a critical period. A related concept is that of a sensitive period, and an example is the time during infancy when, according to Bowlby, attachment should occur in order to promote optimal development of social relationships.

Another theory that emphasizes biological foundations of development—evolutionary psychology—is presented in Chapter 2, along with views on the role of heredity in development. In addition, we examine a number of biological theories of aging in Chapter 15.

Evaluating Ethological Theory

Contributions of ethological theory include a focus on the biological and evolutionary basis of development, and the use of careful observations in naturalistic settings. Criticisms include too much emphasis on biological foundations and a belief that the critical and sensitive period concepts might be too rigid.

Ecological Theory

While ethological theory stresses biological factors, ecological theory emphasizes environmental factors. One ecological theory that has important implications for understanding life-span development was created by Urie Bronfenbrenner (1917–2005).

Bronfenbrenner's Ecological Theory

Bronfenbrenner's ecological theory (1986, 2004; Bronfenbrenner & Morris, 2006) holds that development reflects the influence of several environmental systems. The theory identifies five environmental systems: microsystem, mesosystem, exosystem, macrosystem, and chronosystem (see Figure 1.10).

The *microsystem* is the setting in which the individual lives. These contexts include the person's family, peers, school, and neighborhood. It is in the microsystem that the most direct interactions with social agents take place—with parents, peers, and teachers, for example. The individual is not a passive recipient of experiences in these settings, but someone who helps to construct the settings.

The *mesosystem* involves relations between microsystems or connections between contexts. Examples are the relation of family experiences to school experiences, school experiences to church experiences, and family experiences to peer experiences. For example, children whose parents have rejected them may have difficulty developing positive relations with teachers.

The *exosystem* consists of links between a social setting in which the individual does not have an active role and the individual's immediate context. For example, a husband's or child's experience at home may be influenced by a mother's experiences at work. The mother might receive a promotion that requires more travel, which might increase conflict with the husband and change patterns of interaction with the child.

How Would You...?

If you were an educator, how might you explain a student's chronic failure to complete homework from the mesosystem level? From the exosystem level?

Bronfenbrenner's ecological theory Bronfenbrenner's environmental systems theory, which focuses on five environmental systems: microsystem, mesosystem, exosystem, macrosystem, and chronosystem.

The *macrosystem* involves the culture in which individuals live. Remember from earlier in the chapter that culture refers to the behavior patterns, beliefs, and all other products of a group of people that are passed on from generation to generation. Remember also that cross-cultural studies—the comparison of one culture with one or more other cultures—provide information about the generality of development.

The *chronosystem* consists of the patterning of environmental events and transitions over the life course, as well as sociohistorical circumstances. For example, divorce is one transition. Researchers have found that the negative effects of divorce on children often peak in the first year after the divorce (Hetherington, 2006). By two years after the divorce, family interaction has become more stable. As an example of sociohistorical circumstances, consider how the opportunities for women to pursue a career have increased since the 1960s.

Responding to growing interest in biological contributions to development, Bronfenbrenner (2004) added biological influences to his theory and relabeled it as a bioecological theory. Nonetheless, it is still dominated by ecological, environmental contexts (Gauvain & Parke, 2010).

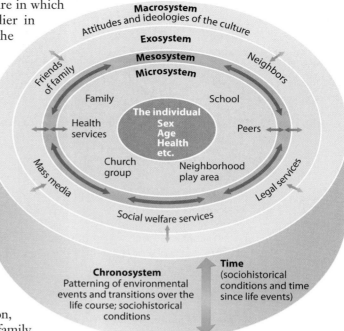

Figure 1.10 Bronfenbrenner's Ecological Theory of Development
Bronfenbrenner's ecological theory consists of five environmental systems: microsystem, mesosystem, exosystem, macrosystem, and chronosystem.

Urie Bronfenbrenner developed ecological theory, a perspective that is receiving increased attention today. His theory emphasizes the importance of both micro and macro dimensions of the environment in which the child lives.

Evaluating Ecological Theory

Contributions of the theory include a systematic examination of macro and micro dimensions of environmental systems, and attention to connections between environmental systems. A further contribution of Bronfenbrenner's theory is an emphasis on a range of social contexts beyond the family, such as neighborhood, religious, school, and workplace environments, as influential in children's development (Gauvain, 2013). Criticisms include giving inadequate attention to biological factors, as well as too little emphasis on cognitive factors.

An Eclectic Theoretical Orientation

No single theory described in this chapter can explain entirely the rich complexity of life-span development, but each has contributed to our understanding of development. Psychoanalytic theory highlights the importance of the unconscious mind. Erikson's theory best describes the changes that occur in adult development. Piaget's, Vygotsky's, and the information-processing views provide the most complete description of cognitive development. The behavioral and social cognitive and ecological theories have been the most adept at examining the environmental determinants of development. The ethological theories have drawn attention to biology's role and the importance of sensitive periods in development.

	Continuity/discontinuity, early versus later experiences	Biological and environmental factors
Psychoanalytic	Discontinuity between stages—continuity between early experiences and later development; early experiences very important; later changes in development emphasized in Erikson's theory	Freud's biological determination interacting with early family experiences; Erikson's more balanced biological-cultural interaction perspective
Cognitive	Discontinuity between stages in Piaget's theory; continuity between early experiences and later development in Piaget's and Vygotsky's theories; no stages in Vygotsky's theory or information-processing theory	Piaget's emphasis on interaction and adaptation; environment provides the setting for cognitive structures to develop; information-processing view has not addressed this issue extensively but mainly emphasizes biological-environmental interaction
Behavioral and social cognitive	Continuity (no stages); experience at all points of development important	Environment viewed as the cause of behavior in both views
Ethological	Discontinuity but no stages; critical or sensitive periods emphasized; early experiences very important	Strong biological view
Ecological	Little attention to continuity/discontinuity; change emphasized more than stability	Strong environmental view

Figure 1.11 Summary of Theories and Issues in Life-Span Development

eclectic theoretical orientation
An approach that selects and uses whatever is considered the best in many theories.

In short, although theories are helpful guides, relying on a single theory to explain development is probably a mistake. This book instead takes an **eclectic theoretical orientation,** which does not follow any one theoretical approach but rather presents what are considered the best features of each theory. In this way, it represents the study of development as it actually exists—with different theorists making different assumptions, stressing different problems, and using different strategies to discover information. Figure 1.11 compares the main theoretical perspectives in terms of how they view important issues in life-span development.

Research in Life-Span Development

How do scholars and researchers with an eclectic orientation determine that one theory is somehow better than a different theory? The scientific method discussed earlier in this chapter provides a guide. Through scientific research, theories are tested and refined (Graziano & Raulin, 2013; Rosnow & Rosenthal, 2013).

Generally, research in life-span development is designed to test hypotheses, which may be derived from the theories just described. Through research, theories are modified to reflect new data, and occasionally new theories arise. How are data about life-span development collected? What types of research designs are used to study life-span development? And what are some ethical considerations in conducting research on life-span development?

Methods for Collecting Data

Whether we are interested in studying attachment in infants, the cognitive skills of children, or social relationships in older adults, we can choose from several ways of collecting data. Here we outline the measures most often used, beginning with observation.

Observation

Scientific observation requires an important set of skills. For observations to be effective, they must be systematic (Gravetter & Forzano, 2012). We need to have some idea of what we are looking for. We have to know whom we are observing, when and where we will observe, how the observations will be made, and how they will be recorded.

laboratory A controlled setting in which research can take place.

Where should we make our observations? We have two choices: the laboratory and the everyday world.

When we observe scientifically, we often need to control certain factors that determine behavior but are not the focus of our inquiry (Rosnow & Rosenthal, 2013). For this reason, some research in life-span development is conducted in a **laboratory**, a controlled setting where many of the complex factors of the "real world" are absent. For example, suppose you want to observe how children react when they see other people behaving aggressively. If you observe children in their homes or schools, you have no control over how much aggression the children observe, what kind of aggression they see, which people they see acting aggressively, or how other people treat the children. In contrast, if you observe the children in a laboratory, you can control these and other factors and therefore have more confidence about how to interpret your observations.

Laboratory research does have some drawbacks, however, including the following concerns: (1) it is almost impossible to conduct research without the participants knowing they are being studied; (2) the laboratory setting is unnatural and therefore can cause the participants to behave unnaturally; (3) people who are willing to come to a university laboratory may not fairly represent groups from diverse cultural backgrounds; (4) people who are unfamiliar with university settings, and with the idea of "helping science," may be intimidated by the laboratory setting.

What are some important strategies in conducting observational research with children?

Naturalistic observation provides insights that we sometimes cannot attain in the laboratory. **Naturalistic observation** means observing behavior in real-world settings and making no effort to manipulate or control the situation. Life-span researchers conduct naturalistic observations at sporting events, child-care centers, work settings, malls, and other places people live in and frequent.

Naturalistic observation was used in one study that focused on conversations in a children's science museum (Crowley & others, 2001). When visiting exhibits at the museum with their children, parents were more than three times as likely to engage boys than girls in explanatory talk. The gender difference occurred regardless of whether the father, the mother, or both parents were with the child, although the gender difference was greatest for fathers' science explanations to sons and daughters. This finding suggests a gender bias that encourages boys more than girls to be interested in science.

Survey and Interview

Sometimes the best and quickest way to get information about people is to ask them for it. One technique is to interview them directly. A related method is administering a survey (sometimes referred to as a questionnaire) consisting of a standard set of questions designed to obtain peoples' self-reported attitudes or beliefs about a particular topic. Surveys are especially useful when information from many people is needed (Madill, 2012). In a good survey, the questions are clear and unbiased, allowing respondents to answer unambiguously.

Surveys and interviews can be used to study topics ranging from religious beliefs to sexual habits to attitudes about gun control to beliefs about how to improve schools. Surveys and interviews may

naturalistic observation Observation that occurs in a real-world setting without any attempt to manipulate the situation.

standardized test A test that is given with uniform procedures for administration and scoring.

case study An in-depth examination of an individual.

be conducted in person, over the telephone, by mail, and over the Internet.

One problem with surveys and interviews is the tendency of participants to answer questions in a way that they think is socially acceptable or desirable rather than to say what they truly think or feel (McMillan & Wergin, 2010). For example, on a survey or in an interview some individuals might say that they do not take drugs even though they do.

Standardized Test

A **standardized test** has uniform procedures for administration and scoring. Many standardized tests allow performance comparisons; they provide information about individual differences among people (Geisinger, 2012; Watson, 2012). One example is the Stanford-Binet intelligence test, which is described in Chapter 7. Your score on the Stanford-Binet test tells you how your performance compares with that of thousands of other people who have taken the test.

One criticism of standardized tests is that they assume a person's behavior is consistent and stable, yet personality and intelligence—two primary targets of standardized testing—can vary with the situation. For example, a person may perform poorly on a standardized intelligence test in an office setting but score much higher at home, where he or she is less anxious.

Case Study

A **case study** is an in-depth look at a single individual. Case studies are performed mainly by mental health professionals when, for either practical or ethical reasons, the unique aspects of an individual's life cannot be duplicated and tested in other individuals. A case study provides information about one person's experiences; it may focus on nearly any aspect of the subject's life that helps the researcher understand the person's mind, behavior, or other attributes. A researcher may gather information for a case study from interviews and medical records. In later chapters we discuss vivid case studies, such as that of Michael Rehbein, who had much of the left side of his brain removed at 7 years of age to end severe epileptic seizures.

A case study can provide a dramatic, in-depth portrayal of an individual's life, but we must be cautious when generalizing from this information. The subject of a case study is unique, with a genetic makeup and personal history that no one else shares. In addition, case studies involve judgments of unknown reliability. Researchers who conduct case studies rarely check to see if other professionals agree with their observations or findings (Yin, 2012).

Physiological Measures

Researchers are increasingly using physiological measures to study development at different points in the life span. For example, as puberty unfolds, the blood levels of certain hormones increase. To determine the nature of these hormonal changes, researchers analyze blood samples from adolescent volunteers (Susman & Dorn, 2013).

Another physiological measure that is increasingly being used is neuroimaging, especially *functional magnetic resonance imaging (fMRI)*, in which electromagnetic waves are used to construct images of a person's brain tissue and biochemical activity (Bauer & Dunn, 2013;

Mahatma Gandhi was the spiritual leader of India in the middle of the twentieth century. Erik Erikson conducted an extensive case study of Gandhi's life to determine what contributed to his identity development. *What are some limitations of the case study approach?*

Fletcher & Rapp, 2013). We will have much more to say about neuroimaging and other physiological measures in later chapters.

Research Designs

In addition to a method for collecting data, you also need a research design to study life-span development. There are three main types of research designs: descriptive, correlational, and experimental.

Descriptive Research

All of the data-collection methods that we have discussed can be used in **descriptive research,** which aims to observe and record behavior. For example, a researcher might observe the extent to which people are altruistic or aggressive toward each other. By itself, descriptive research cannot prove what causes some phenomenon, but it can reveal important information about people's behavior and provide a basis for more scientific studies (Leedy & Ormrod, 2013).

Correlational Research

In contrast to descriptive research, correlational research goes beyond describing phenomena by providing information that helps to predict how people will behave. In **correlational research,** the goal is to describe the strength of the relation between two or more events or characteristics. The more strongly the two events are correlated (or related or associated), the more effectively we can predict one event from the other (Aron, Aron, & Coups, 2013).

For example, to study if children of permissive parents have less self-control than other children, you would need to carefully record observations of parents' permissiveness and their children's self-control. You might observe that the higher a parent was in permissiveness, the lower the child was in self-control. You would then analyze these data statistically to yield a **correlation coefficient,** a number based on a statistical analysis that is used to describe the degree of association between two variables. Correlation coefficients range from −1.00 to +1.00. A negative number means an inverse relation. In the above example, you might find an inverse correlation between permissive parenting and children's self-control with a coefficient of, say, −.30, meaning that parents who are permissive with their children are likely to have children who have low self-control. By contrast, you might find a positive correlation of +.30 between parental monitoring of children and children's self-control, meaning that parents who monitor their children effectively have children with good self-control.

The higher the correlation coefficient (whether positive or negative), the stronger the association between the two variables. A correlation of 0 means that there is no association between the variables. A correlation of −.40 is stronger than a correlation of +.20 because we disregard whether the correlation is positive or negative in determining the strength of the correlation.

A word of caution is in order, however. Correlation does not equal causation (Heiman, 2012). The correlational finding just mentioned does not mean that permissive parenting necessarily causes low self-control in children. It could mean that, but it also could mean that a child's lack of self-control caused the parents to throw up their arms in despair and give up trying to control the child. It also could mean that other factors, such as heredity or poverty, caused the correlation between permissive parenting and low self-control in children. Figure 1.12 illustrates these possible interpretations of correlational data.

Experimental Research

To study causality, researchers turn to experimental research. An **experiment** is a carefully regulated procedure in which one or more

descriptive research Type of research that aims to observe and record behavior.

correlational research A type of research that focuses on describing the strength of the relation between two or more events or characteristics.

correlation coefficient A number based on statistical analysis that is used to describe the degree of association between two variables.

experiment A carefully regulated procedure in which one or more of the factors believed to influence the behavior being studied is manipulated and all other factors are held constant. Experimental research permits the determination of cause.

Possible explanations for this observed correlation

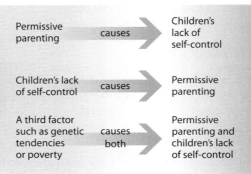

Permissive parenting	causes →	Children's lack of self-control
Children's lack of self-control	causes →	Permissive parenting
A third factor such as genetic tendencies or poverty	causes both →	Permissive parenting and children's lack of self-control

An observed correlation between two events cannot be used to conclude that one event causes the second event. Other possibilities are that the second event causes the first event or that a third event causes the correlation between the first two events.

Figure 1.12 **Possible Explanations for Correlational Data**

factors believed to influence the behavior being studied are manipulated while all other factors are held constant. If the behavior under study changes when a factor is manipulated, we say that the manipulated factor has caused the behavior to change. In other words, the experiment has demonstrated cause and effect. The cause is the factor that was manipulated. The effect is the behavior that changed because of the manipulation. Nonexperimental research methods (descriptive and correlational research) cannot establish cause and effect because they do not involve manipulating factors in a controlled way (Graziano & Raulin, 2013).

Independent and Dependent Variables Experiments include two types of changeable factors: independent and dependent variables. An *independent variable* is a manipulated, influential experimental factor. It is a potential cause. The label "independent" is used because this variable can be manipulated independently of other factors to determine its effect. An experiment may include one independent variable or several of them.

A *dependent variable* is a factor that can change in an experiment, in response to changes in the independent variable. As researchers manipulate the independent variable, they measure the dependent variable for any resulting effect.

For example, suppose that you wanted to study whether pregnant women could change the breathing and sleeping patterns of their newborn babies by meditating during pregnancy. You might require one group of pregnant women to engage in a certain amount and type of meditation each day, while another group would not meditate; the meditation is thus the independent variable. When the infants are born, you would observe and measure their breathing and sleeping patterns. These patterns are the dependent variable, the factor that changes as the result of your manipulation.

Experimental and Control Groups Experiments can involve one or more experimental groups and one or more control groups. An experimental group is a group whose experience is manipulated. A control group is a comparison group that is as much like the experimental group as possible and that is treated in every way like the experimental group except for the manipulated factor (independent variable). The control group serves as a baseline against which the effects of the manipulated condition can be compared.

Random assignment is an important principle for deciding whether each participant will be placed in the experimental group or in the control group. Random assignment means that researchers assign participants to experimental and control groups by chance. It reduces the likelihood that the experiment's results will be due to any preexisting differences between groups (Gravetter & Forzano, 2012). In the example of the effects of meditation by pregnant women on the breathing and sleeping patterns of their newborns, you would randomly assign half of the pregnant women to engage in meditation over a period of weeks (the experimental group) and the other half to not meditate over the same number of weeks (the control group). Figure 1.13 illustrates the nature of experimental research.

Time Span of Research

Researchers in life-span development have a special concern with the relation between age and some other variable. To explore these relations, researchers can study different individuals of different ages and compare them, or they can study the same individuals as they age over time.

Cross-Sectional Approach

The **cross-sectional approach** is a research strategy that simultaneously compares individuals of different ages. A typical cross-sectional study might include three groups of children: 5-year-olds, 8-year-olds, and 11-year-olds. Another study might include groups of 15-year-olds, 25-year-olds, and 45-year-olds. The groups can be compared with respect to a variety of dependent variables, such as IQ, memory, peer relations, attachment to parents, hormonal changes, and so on. All of this can be accomplished in a short time. In some studies data are collected in a single day. Even in large-scale cross-sectional studies with hundreds of subjects, data collection does not usually take longer than several months to complete.

The main advantage of the cross-sectional study is that the researcher does not have to wait for the individuals to grow up or become older. Despite its efficiency, though, the cross-sectional approach has its drawbacks. It gives no information about how individuals change or about the stability of their characteristics. It can obscure the hills and valleys of growth and development. For example, a cross-sectional study of life satisfaction might reveal average increases and decreases, but it would not show how the life satisfaction of individual adults waxed and waned over the years. It also would not tell us whether the same adults who had positive or negative perceptions of life satisfaction in early adulthood maintained their relative degree of life satisfaction as they became middle-aged or older adults.

Longitudinal Approach

The **longitudinal approach** is a research strategy in which the same individuals are studied over a period of time, usually several years or more. For example, in a longitudinal study of life satisfaction, the same adults might be assessed periodically over a 70-year time span—at the ages of 20, 35, 45, 65, and 90, for example.

Longitudinal studies provide a wealth of information about vital issues such as stability and change in development and the importance of early experience for later development, but they do have drawbacks (Sliwinski, 2011; Windle, 2012). They are expensive and time-consuming. The longer the study lasts, the more participants drop out—they move, get sick, lose interest, and so forth. The participants who remain may be dissimilar to those who drop out, biasing the outcome of the study. Those individuals who remain in a longitudinal study over a number of years may be more responsible and conformity-oriented than the ones who dropped out, for example, or they might have more stable lives.

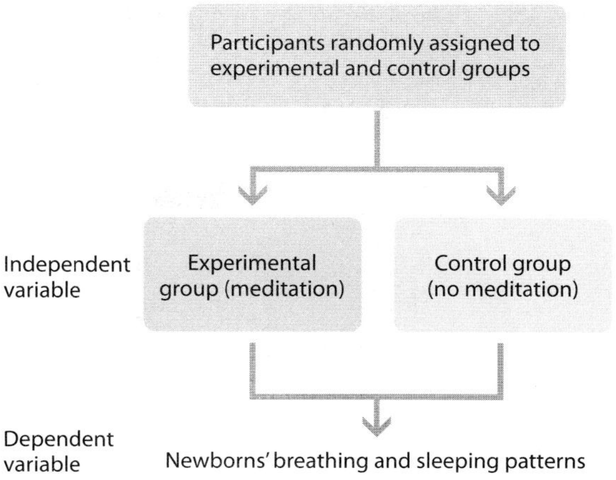

Figure 1.13 Principles of Experimental Research Imagine that you decide to conduct an experimental study of the effects of meditation by pregnant women on their newborns' breathing and sleeping patterns. You would randomly assign pregnant women to experimental and control groups. The experimental-group women would engage in meditation over a specified number of sessions and weeks. The control group would not. Then, when the infants are born, you would assess their breathing and sleeping patterns. If the breathing and sleeping patterns of newborns whose mothers were in the experimental group are more positive than those of the control group, you would conclude that meditation caused the positive effects.

cross-sectional approach A research strategy in which individuals of different ages are compared at one time.

longitudinal approach A research strategy in which the same individuals are studied over a period of time, usually several years or more.

cohort effects Effects that are due to a subject's time of birth or generation but not age.

Cohort Effects

A *cohort* is a group of people who are born at a similar point in history and share similar experiences as a result, such as living through the Vietnam war or growing up in the same city around the same time. These shared experiences may produce a range of differences among cohorts (Hofer, Rast, & Piccinin, 2012). For example, people who were teenagers during the Great Depression are likely to differ from people who were teenagers during the booming 1990s in their educational opportunities and economic status, in how they were raised, and in their attitudes toward sex and religion. In life-span development research, **cohort effects** are due to a person's time of birth, era, or generation but not to actual age.

Cohort effects are important because they can powerfully affect the dependent measures in a study ostensibly concerned with age. Researchers have shown it is especially important to be aware of cohort effects when assessing adult intelligence (Schaie, 2012). Individuals born at different points in time—such as 1920, 1940, and 1960—have had varying opportunities for education. Individuals born in earlier years had less access to education, and this fact may have a significant effect on how this cohort performs on intelligence tests.

How does the youth experienced by today's millennials differ from that of earlier generations?

Cross-sectional studies can show how different cohorts respond, but they can confuse age changes and cohort effects. Longitudinal studies are effective in studying age changes but only within one cohort.

Various generations have been given labels by the popular culture. Figure 1.14 describes the labels of various generations, their historical period, and the reasons for their labels. Consider the following description of the current generation of youth and think about how they differ from earlier youth generations:

They are history's first "always connected" generation. Steeped in digital technology and social media, they treat their multi-tasking hand-held gadgets almost like a body part—for better or worse. More than 8-in-10 say they sleep with a cell phone glowing by the bed, poised to disgorge texts, phone calls, e-mails, songs, news, videos, games, and wake-up jingles. But sometimes convenience yields to temptation. Nearly two-thirds admit to texting while driving (Pew Research Center, 2010, p. 1).

Generation	Historical Period	Reasons for Label
Millennials	Individuals born in 1980 and later	First generation to come of age and enter emerging adulthood (18 to 25 years of age) in the twenty-first century (the new millennium). Two main characteristics: (1) connection to technology, and (2) ethnic diversity.
Generation X	Individuals born between 1965 and 1980	Described as lacking an identity and savvy loners.
Baby Boomers	Individuals born between 1946 and 1964	Label used because this generation represents the spike in the number of babies born after World War II; the largest generation ever to enter late adulthood in the United States.
Silent Generation	Individuals born between 1928 and 1945	Children of the Great Depression and World War II; described as conformists and civic minded.

Figure 1.14 Generations, Their Historical Periods, and Characteristics

Conducting Ethical Research

Researchers who study human development and behavior confront many ethical issues. For example, a developmentalist who wanted to study aggression in children would have to design the study in such a way that no child would be harmed physically or psychologically and would need to get permission from the university to carry out the study. Then the researcher would have to explain the study to the children's parents and obtain consent for the children to participate. Ethics in research may affect you personally if you ever serve as a participant in a study. In that event, you need to know your rights as a participant and the responsibilities of researchers to ensure that these rights are safeguarded.

Today, proposed research at colleges and universities must pass the scrutiny of a research ethics committee before the research can begin. In addition, the American Psychological Association (APA) has developed ethics guidelines for its members. This code of ethics instructs psychologists to protect their research participants from mental and physical harm. The participants' best interests need to be kept foremost in the researcher's mind (Fried, 2012).

APA's guidelines address four important issues:

1. *Informed consent*—All participants must know what their research participation will involve and what risks might develop. Even after informed consent is given, participants must retain the right to withdraw from the study at any time and for any reason.

2. *Confidentiality*—Researchers are responsible for keeping all of the data they gather on individuals completely confidential and, when possible, completely anonymous.

3. *Debriefing*—After the study has been completed, participants should be informed of its purpose and the methods that were used. In most cases, the experimenter also can inform participants in a general manner beforehand about the purpose of the research without leading participants to behave in a way they think that the experimenter is expecting.

4. *Deception*—In some circumstances, telling the participants beforehand what the research study is about substantially alters the participants' behavior and invalidates the researcher's data. In all cases of deception, however, the psychologist must ensure that the deception will not harm the participants and that the participants will be *debriefed* (told the complete nature of the study) as soon as possible after the study is completed.

Summary

The Life-Span Perspective

- Development is the pattern of change that begins at conception and continues through the human life span. It includes both growth and decline.

- The life-span perspective includes these basic ideas: Development is lifelong, multidimensional, multidirectional, and plastic; its study is multidis-

ciplinary; it is embedded in contexts; it involves growth, maintenance, and regulation; and it is a co-construction of biological, sociocultural, and individual factors.

- Health and well-being, parenting, education, sociocultural contexts and diversity, and social policy are all areas of contemporary concern for those who study life-span development.

fingernails down to the nubs, had almost identical drinking and smoking habits, had hemorrhoids, put on 10 pounds at about the same point in development,

they were always making each other laugh. A thorough search of their adoptive families' histories revealed no gigglers. The giggle sisters ignored stress, avoided

investigate their lives. There the twins complete personality and intelligence tests, and provide detailed medical histories, including information about diet and smoking, exercise habits, chest

The Nature of Development

- Three key developmental processes are biological, cognitive, and socioemotional. Development is influenced by an interplay of these processes.

- The life span is commonly divided into the prenatal

- Behavioral and social cognitive theories emphasize the environment's role in development. Two key behavioral and social cognitive theories are Skinner's operant conditioning and Bandura's social cognitive theory.

X-rays, heart stress tests, and EEGs. The twins are asked more than 15,000 questions about their family and childhood, personal interests, vocational orientation, values, and aesthetic judgments (Bouchard & others, 1990).

When genetically identical twins who were separated as infants show such striking similarities in their tastes and habits and choices, can we conclude that their genes must have caused these similarities? Although genes play a role, we also need to consider other possible causes. The twins shared not only the same genes but also some similar experiences. Some of the separated twins lived together for several months prior to their adoption; some had been reunited prior to testing (in some cases, many years earlier); adoption agencies often place twins in similar homes; and even strangers who spend several hours together and start comparing their lives are likely to come up with some coincidental similarities (Joseph, 2006).

The Minnesota study of identical twins points to both the importance of the genetic basis of human development and the need for further research on genetic and environmental factors.

The examples of Jim and Jim and the giggle sisters stimulate us to think about our genetic heritage and the biological foundations of our existence. Organisms are not like billiard balls, moved by simple, external forces to predictable positions on life's pool table. Environmental experiences and biological foundations work together to make us who we are. Our coverage of life's biological beginnings and experiences will emphasize the evolutionary perspective; genetic foundations; the interaction of heredity and environment; and charting growth from conception through the prenatal period, the birth process itself, and the postpartum period that follows birth. ▪

Jim Lewis (*left*) and Jim Springer (*right*).

The Evolutionary Perspective

From the perspective of evolutionary time, humans are relative newcomers to Earth. As our earliest ancestors left the forest to feed on the savannahs and then to form hunting societies on the open plains, their minds and behaviors changed, and humans eventually became the dominant species on Earth. How did this evolution come about?

Natural Selection and Adaptive Behavior

Charles Darwin (1859) described *natural selection* as the evolutionary process by which those individuals of a species that are best *adapted* to their environment are the ones that are most likely to survive and reproduce. He reasoned that an intense, constant struggle for food, water, and resources must occur among the young of each generation, because many of them do not survive. Those that do survive and reproduce pass on their characteristics to the next generation (Hoefnagels, 2013). Darwin concluded that these survivors are better adapted to their world than are the nonsurvivors. The best-adapted individuals survive and leave the most offspring. Over the course of many generations, organisms with the characteristics needed for survival make up an increased percentage of the population (Mader & Windelspecht, 2013; Simon, Dickey, & Reece, 2013).

How Would You…?

As a health-care professional, how would you explain technology and medicine working against natural selection?

Evolutionary Psychology

evolutionary psychology Emphasizes the importance of adaptation, reproduction, and "survival of the fittest" in shaping behavior.

Although Darwin introduced the theory of evolution by natural selection in 1859, his ideas have only recently become a popular framework for explaining behavior. Psychology's newest approach, **evolutionary psychology,** emphasizes the importance of adaptation, reproduction, and "survival of the fittest" in shaping behavior. ("Fit" in this sense refers to the ability to bear offspring that survive long enough to bear offspring of their own.) In this view, natural selection favors behaviors that increase reproductive success—that is, the ability to pass your genes to the next generation (Cosmides, 2013; Durrant & Ellis, 2013).

David Buss (2008, 2012) argues that just as evolution has contributed to our physical features, such as body shape and height, it also pervasively influences how we make decisions, how aggressive we are, our fears, and our mating patterns. For example, assume that our ancestors were hunters and gatherers on the plains and that men did most of the hunting and women stayed close to home, gathering seeds and plants for food. If you have to travel some distance from your home to track and slay a fleeing animal, you need certain physical traits along with the capacity for certain types of spatial thinking. Men with these traits would be more likely than men without them to survive, to bring home lots of food, and to be considered attractive mates—and thus to reproduce and pass on these characteristics to their children. In other words, if their assumptions were correct, potentially these traits would provide a reproductive advantage for males, and over many generations, men with good spatial thinking skills might become more numerous in the population. Critics point out that this scenario might or might not have actually happened.

Evolutionary Developmental Psychology

There is growing interest in using the concepts of evolutionary psychology to understand human development (Bjorklund, 2007, 2012, 2013; Brune & others, 2012; Durrant & Ellis, 2013). Following are some ideas proposed by evolutionary developmental psychologists (Bjorklund & Pellegrini, 2002).

One important concept is that an extended childhood period might have evolved because humans require time to develop a large brain and learn the complexity of human societies. Humans take longer to become reproductively mature than any other mammal (see Figure 2.1). During this extended childhood period, they develop a large brain and have the experiences needed to become competent adults in a complex society.

Another key idea is that many of our evolved psychological mechanisms are *domain-specific*. That is, the mechanisms apply only to a specific aspect of a person's psychological makeup. According to evolutionary psychology, the mind is not a general-purpose device that can be applied equally to a vast array of problems. Instead, as our ancestors dealt with certain recurring problems such as hunting and finding shelter, specialized modules evolved that process information related to those problems: for example, such specialized modules might include a module for physical knowledge for tracking animals, a module for mathematical knowledge for trading, and a module for language.

Evolved mechanisms are not always adaptive in contemporary society. Some behaviors that were adaptive for our prehistoric ancestors may not serve us well today. For example, the food-scarce environment of our ancestors likely led to humans' propensity to gorge when food is available and to crave high-caloric foods, a trait that might lead to an epidemic of obesity when food is plentiful.

How Would You...?

As an educator, how would you apply the idea that psychological mechanisms are domain-specific to explain how a student with a learning disability in reading may perform exceptionally well in math?

Evaluating Evolutionary Psychology

Although the popular press gives a lot of attention to the ideas of evolutionary psychology, it remains just

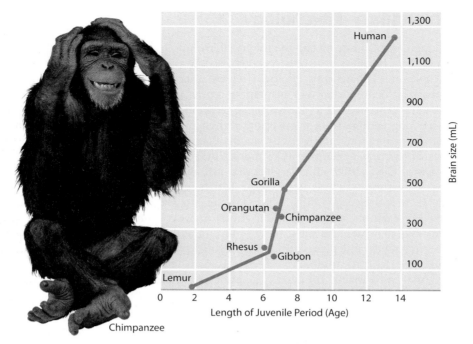

Chimpanzee

Figure 2.1 The Brain Sizes of Various Primates and Humans in Relation to the Length of the Juvenile Period
Compared with other primates, humans have both a larger brain and a longer childhood period. *What conclusions can you draw from the relationship indicated by this graph?*

Children in all cultures are interested in the tools that adults in their cultures use. For example, this 11-month-old boy from the Efe culture in the Democratic Republic of the Congo in Africa is trying to cut a papaya with an apopau (a smaller version of a machete). *Might the infant's behavior be evolutionary-based or be due to both biological and environmental conditions?*

one theoretical approach. Like the theories described in Chapter 1, it has limitations, weaknesses, and critics (Hyde & Else-Quest, 2013; Matlin, 2012). One criticism comes from Albert Bandura (1998), whose social cognitive theory was described in Chapter 1. Bandura acknowledges the important influence of evolution on human adaptation. However, he rejects what he calls "one-sided evolutionism," which sees social behavior as the product of evolved biological characteristics. An alternative is a *bidirectional view,* in which environmental and biological conditions influence each other. In this view, evolutionary pressures created changes in biological structures that allowed the use of tools, which enabled our ancestors to manipulate the environment, constructing new environmental conditions. In turn, environmental innovations produced new selection pressures that led to the evolution of specialized biological systems for consciousness, thought, and language.

In other words, evolution gave us bodily structures and biological potentialities, but it does not dictate behavior. People have used their biological capacities to produce diverse cultures—aggressive and pacific, egalitarian and autocratic. As American scientist Stephen Jay Gould (1981) concluded, in most domains of human functioning, biology allows a broad range of cultural possibilities.

The "big picture" idea of natural selection leading to the development of human traits and behaviors is difficult to refute or test because evolution occurs on a time scale that does not lend itself to empirical study. Thus, studying specific genes in humans and other species—and their links to traits and behaviors—may be the best approach for testing ideas coming out of the evolutionary psychology perspective.

Genetic Foundations of Development

Genetic influences on behavior evolved over time and across many species. Our many traits and characteristics that are genetically influenced have a long evolutionary history that is retained in our DNA. In other words, our DNA is not just inherited from our parents; it's also what we've inherited as a species from the species that came before us. Let's take a closer look at DNA and its role in human development.

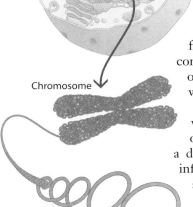

chromosomes Threadlike structures made up of deoxyribonucleic acid, or DNA.

DNA A complex molecule with a double helix shape that contains genetic information.

genes Units of hereditary information composed of DNA. Genes direct cells to reproduce themselves and manufacture the proteins that maintain life.

How are characteristics that suit a species for survival transmitted from one generation to the next?

Darwin did not know the answer to this question because genes and the principles of genetics had not yet been discovered. Each of us carries a human "genetic code" that we inherited from our parents. Because a fertilized egg carries this human code, a fertilized human egg cannot grow into an egret, eagle, or elephant.

Each of us began life as a single cell weighing about one twenty-millionth of an ounce. This tiny piece of matter housed our entire genetic code—instructions that orchestrated growth from that single cell to a person made of trillions of cells, each containing a replica of the original code. That code is carried by our genes. What are genes and what do they do? For the answer, we need to look into our cells.

The nucleus of each human cell contains **chromosomes,** which are threadlike structures made up of deoxyribonucleic acid, or DNA (see Figure 2.2). **DNA** is a complex molecule that has a double helix shape, like a spiral staircase, and contains genetic information. **Genes,** the units of hereditary information, are short segments of DNA. They help cells to reproduce themselves and to assemble proteins. Proteins, in turn, are the building blocks of cells as well as the regulators that direct the body's processes (Belk & Maier, 2013; Tortora, Funke, & Case, 2013).

Each gene has its own designated place on a particular chromosome. Today, there is a great deal of enthusiasm about efforts to discover the specific locations of genes that are linked to certain functions and developmental outcomes (Plomin, 2012; Starr & others, 2013). An important step in this direction was taken when the Human Genome Project and the Celera Corporation completed a preliminary map of the human *genome*—the complete set of developmental instructions for creating proteins that initiate the making of a human organism (Hughes & Rosen, 2012).

Completion of the Human Genome Project has led to use of the *genome-wide association method* to identify genetic variations linked to a particular disease, such as cancer, cardiovascular disease, or Alzheimer disease (National Human Genome Research Institute, 2012). To conduct a genome-wide association study, researchers obtain DNA from individuals who have the disease and those who don't have it. Then, each participant's complete set of DNA, or genome, is purified from the blood or cells and scanned on machines to determine markers of genetic variation. If the genetic variations occur more frequently in people who have the disease, the variations point to the region in the human genome where the disease-causing problem exists. Genome-wide association studies have recently been conducted for child obesity (Early Growth Genetics Consortium & others, 2012), cardiovascular disease (Lusis, 2012), Alzheimer disease

Figure 2.2 Cells, Chromosomes, DNA, and Genes
(*Top*) The body contains trillions of cells. Each cell contains a central structure, the nucleus. (*Middle*) Chromosomes are threadlike structures located in the nucleus of the cell. Chromosomes are composed of DNA. (*Bottom*) DNA has the structure of a spiral staircase. A gene is a segment of DNA.

Cell
Nucleus
Chromosome
DNA

(Raj & others, 2012), and depression (Major Depressive Disorder Working Group of the Psychiatric GWAS Consortium, 2012).

One of the big surprises of the Human Genome Project was a report indicating that humans have only about 30,000 genes (U.S. Department of Energy, 2001). More recently, the number of human genes has been revised further downward, to approximately 20,500 (Science Daily, 2008). Scientists had thought that humans had as many as 100,000 or more genes. They had also believed that each gene programmed just one protein. In fact, humans appear to have far more proteins than they have genes, so there cannot be a one-to-one correspondence between genes and proteins (Commoner, 2002). Each gene is not translated, in automaton-like fashion, into one and only one protein. A gene does not act independently, as developmental psychologist David Moore (2001) emphasized by titling his book *The Dependent Gene*. Rather than being a group of independent genes, the human genome consists of many genes that collaborate both with each other and with nongenetic factors inside and outside the body (Moore, 2013). The collaboration operates at many points. For example, the cellular "machinery" mixes, matches, and links small pieces of DNA to reproduce the genes, and that machinery is influenced by what is going on around it.

Whether a gene is turned "on"—that is, working to assemble proteins—is also a matter of collaboration. The activity of genes (*genetic expression*) is affected by their environment (Gottlieb, 2007). For example, hormones that circulate in the blood make their way into the cell, where they can turn genes "on" and "off." And the flow of hormones can be affected by environmental conditions such as light, day length, nutrition, and behavior. Numerous studies have shown that events outside of the cell and the person, as well as events inside the cell, can excite or inhibit gene expression (Gottlieb, 2007). Recent research has documented that factors such as stress, radiation, and temperature can influence gene expression (Georgakilas, 2011). For example, one study revealed that an increase in the concentration of stress hormones such as cortisol produced a fivefold increase in DNA damage (Flint & others, 2007). A recent study also found that exposure to radiation changed the rate of DNA synthesis in cells (Lee & others, 2011).

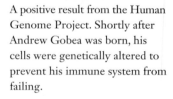

A positive result from the Human Genome Project. Shortly after Andrew Gobea was born, his cells were genetically altered to prevent his immune system from failing.

Genes and Chromosomes

Genes are not only collaborative; they are enduring. How do they get passed from generation to generation and end up in all of the trillion cells in the body? Three processes explain the heart of the story: mitosis, meiosis, and fertilization.

Mitosis, Meiosis, and Fertilization

All cells in your body, except the sperm and egg, have 46 chromosomes arranged in 23 pairs. These cells reproduce through a process called **mitosis.** During mitosis, the cell's nucleus—including the chromosomes—duplicates itself and the cell divides. Two new cells are formed, each containing the same DNA as the original cell, arranged in the same 23 pairs of chromosomes.

However, a different type of cell division—**meiosis**—forms eggs and sperm (which also are called *gametes*). During meiosis, a cell of the testes (in men) or ovaries (in women) duplicates its chromosomes but then divides *twice*, thus forming four cells, each of which has only half of the genetic material of the parent cell (Johnson, 2012). By the end of meiosis, each egg or sperm has 23 *unpaired* chromosomes.

During *fertilization*, an egg and a sperm fuse to create a single cell, called a *zygote*. In the zygote, the 23 unpaired chromosomes

mitosis Cellular reproduction in which the cell's nucleus duplicates itself with two new cells being formed, each containing the same DNA as the parent cell, arranged in the same 23 pairs of chromosomes.

meiosis A specialized form of cell division that occurs to form eggs and sperm (or gametes).

from the egg and the 23 unpaired chromosomes from the sperm combine to form one set of 23 paired chromosomes—one chromosome of each pair from the mother's egg and the other from the father's sperm. In this manner, each parent contributes half of the offspring's genetic material.

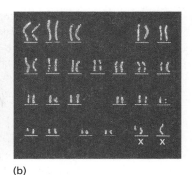

(a)   (b)

Figure 2.3 shows 23 paired chromosomes of a male and a female. The members of each pair of chromosomes are both similar and different: Each chromosome in the pair contains varying forms of the same genes, at the same location on the chromosome. A gene that influences hair color, for example, is located on both members of one pair of chromosomes, at the same location on each. However, one of those chromosomes might carry the gene associated with blond hair; the other might carry the gene associated with brown hair.

Do you notice any obvious differences between the chromosomes of the male and those of the female in Figure 2.3? The difference lies in the 23rd pair. Ordinarily, in females this pair consists of two chromosomes called *X chromosomes*; in males the 23rd pair consists of an X chromosome and a *Y chromosome*. The presence of a Y chromosome is one factor that makes a person male rather than female.

Figure 2.3 The Genetic Difference Between Males and Females
Set (*a*) shows the chromosome structure of a male, and set (*b*) shows the chromosome structure of a female. The last pair of 23 pairs of chromosomes is in the bottom right box of each set. Notice that the Y chromosome of the male is smaller than the X chromosome of the female. To obtain this kind of chromosomal picture, a cell is removed from a person's body, usually from the inside of the mouth. The chromosomes are stained by chemical treatment, magnified extensively, and then photographed.

Sources of Variability

Combining the genes of two parents in their offspring increases genetic variability in the population, which is valuable for a species because it provides more characteristics on which natural selection can operate (Lewis, 2012). In fact, the human genetic process creates several important sources of variability.

First, the chromosomes in the zygote are not exact copies of those in the mother's ovaries and the father's testes. During the formation of the sperm and egg in meiosis, the members of each pair of chromosomes are separated, but which chromosome in the pair goes to the gamete is a matter of chance. In addition, before the pairs separate, pieces of the two chromosomes in each pair are exchanged, creating a new combination of genes on each chromosome (Mader & Windelspecht, 2013). Thus, when chromosomes from the mother's egg and the father's sperm are brought together in the zygote, the result is a truly unique combination of genes.

Another source of variability comes from DNA (Brooker, 2012). Chance events, a mistake by the cellular machinery, or damage caused by an environmental agent such as radiation may produce a *mutated gene*, a permanently altered segment of DNA.

Even when their genes are identical, however, as for the identical twins described at the beginning of the chapter, people vary. The difference between *genotypes* and *phenotypes* helps us understand this source of variability. All of a person's genetic material makes up his or her **genotype.** There is increasing interest in studying *susceptibility genes* (Paquette & others, 2010), those that make an individual more vulnerable to specific diseases or acceleration of aging, and *longevity genes,* those that make an individual less vulnerable to certain diseases and more likely to live to an older age (Soerensen & others, 2012; Tabara, Kohara, & Miki, 2012); these are aspects of the individual's genotype. However, not all of the genetic material is apparent in an individual's observed and measurable characteristics. A **phenotype** consists of observable characteristics, including physical characteristics (such as

genotype A person's genetic heritage; the actual genetic material.

phenotype The way an individual's genotype is expressed in observed and measurable characteristics.

height, weight, and hair color) and psychological characteristics (such as personality and intelligence).

For each genotype, a range of phenotypes can be expressed, providing another source of variability (Miller & Spoolman, 2012; Rende, 2012). An individual can inherit the genetic potential to grow very large, for example, but good nutrition, among other things, will be essential to achieving that potential.

Genetic Principles

What determines how a genotype is expressed to create a particular phenotype? This question has not yet been fully answered (Starr, 2011). However, a number of genetic principles have been discovered, among them those of dominant and recessive genes, sex-linked genes, and polygenically determined characteristics.

Dominant and Recessive Genes

In some cases, one gene of a pair always exerts its effects; in other words, it is *dominant*, overriding the potential influence of the other gene, which is called the *recessive* gene. This is the *dominant-and-recessive genes principle*. A recessive gene exerts its influence only if the two genes of a pair are both recessive. If you inherit a recessive gene for a trait from each of your parents, you will show the trait. If you inherit a recessive gene from only one parent, you may never know that you carry the gene. Brown hair, farsightedness, and dimples override blond hair, near-sightedness, and freckles in the world of dominant and recessive genes. Can two brown-haired parents have a blond-haired child? Yes, they can. Suppose that each parent has a dominant gene for brown hair and a recessive gene for blond hair. Since dominant genes override recessive genes, the parents have brown hair, but both are *carriers* of blondness and pass on their recessive genes for blond hair. With no dominant gene to override them, the recessive genes can make the child's hair blond.

Sex-Linked Genes

Most mutated genes are recessive. When a mutated gene is carried on the X chromosome, the result is called *X-linked inheritance*. It may have implications for males that differ greatly from those for females (McClelland, Bowles, & Koopman, 2012). Remember that males have only one X chromosome. Thus, if there is an absent or altered, disease-relevant gene on the X chromosome, males have no "backup" copy to counter the harmful gene and therefore may develop an X-linked disease. However, females have a second X chromosome, which is likely to be unchanged. As a result, they are not likely to have the X-linked disease. Thus, most individuals who have X-linked diseases are males. Females who have one abnormal copy of the gene on the X chromosome are known as carriers, and they usually do not show any signs of the X-linked disease. Fragile X syndrome, which we will discuss later in the chapter, is an example of X-linked inheritance.

Calvin and Hobbes

by Bill Watterson

CALVIN & HOBBES, Copyright © 1991 Watterson. Reprinted with permission of Universal Uclick. All Rights Reserved.

Name	Description	Treatment	Incidence
Down syndrome	An extra chromosome causes mild to severe retardation and physical abnormalities.	Surgery, early intervention, infant stimulation, and special learning programs	1 in 1,900 births at age 20 1 in 300 births at age 35 1 in 30 births at age 45
Klinefelter syndrome (XXY)	An extra X chromosome causes physical abnormalities.	Hormone therapy can be effective	1 in 600 male births
Fragile X syndrome	An abnormality in the X chromosome can cause intellectual disability, learning disabilities, or short attention span.	Special education, speech and language therapy	More common in males than in females
Turner syndrome (XO)	A missing X chromosome in females can cause intellectual disability and sexual underdevelopment.	Hormone therapy in childhood and puberty	1 in 2,500 female births
XYY syndrome	An extra Y chromosome can cause above-average height.	No special treatment required	1 in 1,000 male births

Figure 2.4 Some Chromosome Abnormalities
The treatments for these abnormalities do not necessarily erase the problem but may improve the individual's adaptive behavior and quality of life.

Polygenic Inheritance

Genetic transmission is usually more complex than the simple examples we have examined thus far (Lewis, 2012). Few characteristics reflect the influence of only a single gene or pair of genes. Most are determined by the interaction of many different genes; they are said to be *polygenically* determined (Lu, Yu, & Deng, 2012). Even a simple characteristic such as height reflects the interaction of many genes as well as the influence of the environment. Most diseases, such as cancer and diabetes, develop as a consequence of complex gene interactions and environmental factors (Dastani & others, 2012).

The term *gene-gene interaction* is increasingly used to describe studies that focus on the interdependence of two or more genes in influencing characteristics, behavior, diseases, and development (Chen, Wang, & Chan, 2012). For example, recent studies have documented gene-gene interaction in children's immune system functioning (Reijmerink & others, 2011), asthma (Su & others, 2012), cancer (Bushel & others, 2012), cardiovascular disease (Xiao & others, 2012), and arthritis (Ronninger & others, 2012).

Chromosome- and Gene-Linked Abnormalities

In some (relatively rare) cases, genetic inheritance involves an abnormality. Some of these abnormalities come from whole chromosomes that do not separate properly during meiosis. Others are produced by defective genes.

Chromosome Abnormalities

Sometimes a gamete is formed in which the combined sperm and ovum do not have their normal set of 23 chromosomes. The most notable examples involve Down syndrome and abnormalities of the sex chromosomes. Figure 2.4 describes some chromosome abnormalities, along with their treatment and incidence.

Down Syndrome Down syndrome is one of the most common genetically linked causes of intellectual disability; it is also characterized by certain physical features. An individual with Down syndrome has a round face, a flattened skull, an extra fold of skin over the eyelids, a thickened tongue, short limbs, and retardation of motor and mental abilities (Peters & Petrill, 2011). The syndrome is caused by the presence of an extra copy of chromosome 21. It is not known why the extra chromosome is present, but the

Down syndrome A chromosomally transmitted form of intellectual disability, caused by the presence of an extra copy of chromosome 21.

health of the male sperm or female ovum may be involved.

Down syndrome appears approximately once in every 700 live births. Women between the ages of 16 and 34 are less likely to give birth to a child with Down syndrome than are younger or older women. African American children are rarely born with Down syndrome.

Sex-Linked Chromosome Abnormalities Recall that a newborn normally has either an X and a Y chromosome, or two X chromosomes. Human embryos must possess at least one X chromosome to be viable. The most common sex-linked chromosome abnormalities involve the presence of an extra chromosome (either an X or a Y) or the absence of one X chromosome in females.

These athletes, several of whom have Down syndrome, are participating in a Special Olympics competition. Notice the distinctive facial features of the individuals with Down syndrome, such as a round face and a flattened skull. *What causes Down syndrome?*

How Would You…?

As a social worker, how would you respond to a 33-year-old pregnant woman who is concerned about the risk of giving birth to a baby with Down syndrome?

Klinefelter syndrome is a chromosomal disorder in which males have an extra X chromosome, making them XXY instead of XY. Males with this disorder have undeveloped testes, and they usually have enlarged breasts and become tall (Ross & others, 2012). Klinefelter syndrome occurs approximately once in every 800 live male births.

Fragile X syndrome is a genetic disorder that results from an abnormality in the X chromosome, which becomes constricted and often breaks. A lower level of intelligence often is an outcome, and it may take the form of intellectual disability, a learning disability, or a short attention span. This disorder occurs more frequently in males than in females, possibly because the second X chromosome in females negates the effects of the other, abnormal X chromosome (Fung & others, 2012).

Turner syndrome is a chromosome disorder in females in which either an X chromosome is missing, making the person XO instead of XX, or part of one X chromosome is deleted. Females with Turner syndrome are short in stature and have a webbed neck (Kaur & Phadke, 2012). In some cases, they are infertile. They have difficulty in mathematics, but their verbal ability is often quite good. Turner syndrome occurs in approximately 1 of every 2,500 live female births (Pinsker, 2012).

The *XYY syndrome* is a chromosomal disorder in which the male has an extra Y chromosome (Stockholm & others, 2012). Early interest in this syndrome focused on the belief that the extra Y chromosome found in some males contributed to aggression and violence. However, researchers subsequently found that XYY males are no more likely to commit crimes than are XY males (Witkin & others, 1976).

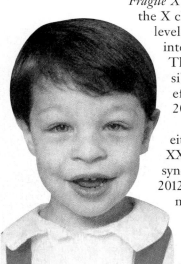

A boy with fragile X syndrome.

Gene-Linked Abnormalities

Abnormalities can be produced not only by an abnormal number of chromosomes, but also by defective genes. Figure 2.5 describes some gene-linked abnormalities, including their treatment and incidence.

Phenylketonuria (PKU) is a genetic disorder in which the individual cannot properly metabolize phenylalanine, an amino acid that naturally occurs in many food sources. It results from a recessive gene and occurs about once in every 10,000 to 20,000 live births. Today,

How Would You…?

As a health-care professional, how would you explain heredity-environment interaction to new parents who are upset when they discover that their child has a treatable genetic defect?

Name	Description	Treatment	Incidence
Cystic fibrosis	Glandular dysfunction that interferes with mucus production; breathing and digestion are hampered, resulting in a shortened life span.	Physical and oxygen therapy, synthetic enzymes, and antibiotics; most individuals live to middle age.	1 in 2,000 births
Diabetes	Body does not produce enough insulin, which causes abnormal metabolism of sugar.	Early onset can be fatal unless treated with insulin.	1 in 2,500 births
Hemophilia	Delayed blood clotting causes internal and external bleeding.	Blood transfusions/injections can reduce or prevent damage due to internal bleeding.	1 in 10,000 males
Huntington disease	Central nervous system deteriorates, producing problems in muscle coordination and mental deterioration.	Does not usually appear until age 35 or older; death likely 10 to 20 years after symptoms appear.	1 in 20,000 births
Phenylketonuria (PKU)	Metabolic disorder that, left untreated, causes mental retardation.	Special diet can result in average intelligence and normal life span.	1 in 10,000 to 1 in 20,000 births
Sickle-cell anemia	Blood disorder that limits the body's oxygen supply; it can cause joint swelling, as well as heart and kidney failure.	Penicillin, medication for pain, antibiotics, and blood transfusions.	1 in 400 African American children (lower among other groups)
Spina bifida	Neural tube disorder that causes brain and spine abnormalities.	Corrective surgery at birth, orthopedic devices, and physical/medical therapy.	2 in 1,000 births
Tay-Sachs disease	Deceleration of mental and physical development caused by an accumulation of lipids in the nervous system.	Medication and special diet are used, but death is likely by 5 years of age.	1 in 30 American Jews is a carrier.

Figure 2.5 Some Gene-Linked Abnormalities

phenylketonuria is easily detected in infancy, and it is treated by a diet that prevents an excess accumulation of phenylalanine (Di Ciommo, Forcella, & Cotugno, 2012; Giovannini & others, 2012). If phenylketonuria is left untreated, however, excess phenylalanine builds up in the child, producing intellectual disability and hyperactivity. Phenylketonuria accounts for approximately 1 percent of institutionalized individuals who are mentally retarded, and it occurs primarily in Whites.

Sickle-cell anemia, which occurs most often in African Americans, is a genetic disorder that impairs functioning of the body's red blood cells. Red blood cells, which carry oxygen to the body's other cells, are usually shaped like a disk. In sickle-cell anemia, a recessive gene causes the red blood cell to become a hook-shaped "sickle" that cannot carry oxygen properly and dies quickly. As a result, the body's cells do not receive adequate oxygen, causing anemia and early death (Mehari & others, 2012). About 1 in 400 African American babies is affected by sickle-cell anemia. One in 10 African Americans is a carrier, as is 1 in 20 Latin Americans.

Other diseases that result from genetic abnormalities include cystic fibrosis, some forms of diabetes, hemophilia, Huntington disease, spina bifida, and Tay-Sachs disease. Someday, scientists may be able to identify why these and other genetic abnormalities occur and discover how to cure them (Tabara, Kohara, & Miki, 2012; Wu & others, 2012).

During a physical examination for a college football tryout, Jerry Hubbard, 32, learned that he carried the gene for sickle-cell anemia. Daughter Sara is healthy but daughter Avery (in the print dress) has sickle-cell anemia. *If you were a genetic counselor, would you recommend that this family have more children? Explain.*

Holly Ishmael, Genetic Counselor

Holly Ishmael is a genetic counselor at Children's Mercy Hospital in Kansas City. She obtained an undergraduate degree in psychology and then a master's degree in genetic counseling from Sarah Lawrence College.

Genetic counselors work as members of a health-care team, providing information and support to families with birth defects or genetic disorders. They identify families at risk by analyzing inheritance patterns and explore options with the family. Some genetic counselors, like Holly, become specialists in prenatal and pediatric genetics; others might specialize in cancer genetics or psychiatric genetic disorders.

Holly says, "Genetic counseling is a perfect combination for people who want to do something science-oriented, but need human contact and don't want to spend all of their time in a lab or have their nose in a book" (Rizzo, 1999, p. 3).

Genetic counselors have specialized graduate degrees in the areas of medical genetics and counseling. They enter graduate school with undergraduate backgrounds from a

Holly Ishmael (*left*) in a genetic counseling session.

variety of disciplines, including biology, genetics, psychology, public health, and social work. There are approximately 30 graduate genetic counseling programs in the United States. If you are interested in this profession, you can obtain further information from the National Society of Genetic Counselors at www.nsgc.org.

Genetic counselors, usually physicians or biologists who are well-versed in the field of medical genetics, understand the kinds of diseases just described, the odds of encountering them, and helpful strategies for offsetting some of their effects (Kingsmore & others, 2012). To read about the career and work of a genetic counselor, see *Careers in Life-Span Development*.

The Interaction of Heredity and Environment: The Nature-Nurture Debate

Is it possible to untangle the influence of heredity from that of environment and discover the role of each in producing individual differences in development? When heredity and environment interact, how does heredity influence the environment, and vice versa?

Behavior Genetics

Behavior genetics is the field that seeks to discover the influence of heredity and environment on individual differences in human traits and development. Behavior geneticists often study either twins or adoption situations (Maxson, 2013).

In a **twin study,** the behavioral similarities between identical twins (who are genetically identical) is compared with the behavioral similarities between fraternal twins. Recall that although fraternal twins share the same womb, they are no more genetically alike than

behavior genetics The field that seeks to discover the influence of heredity and environment on individual differences in human traits and development.

twin study A study in which the behavioral similarity of identical twins is compared with the behavioral similarity of fraternal twins.

are non-twin siblings. By comparing groups of identical and fraternal twins, behavior geneticists capitalize on this basic knowledge that identical twins are more similar genetically than are fraternal twins: If they observe that a behavioral trait is more often shared by identical twins than by fraternal twins, they can infer that the trait has a genetic basis (Bell & Saffery, 2012). For example, one study revealed a higher incidence of conduct problems shared by identical twins than by fraternal twins; the researchers discerned an important role for heredity in conduct problems (Scourfield & others, 2004).

However, several issues complicate the interpretation of twin studies. For example, perhaps the environments of identical twins are more similar than those of fraternal twins. Parents and caregivers might stress the similarities of identical twins more than those of fraternal twins, and identical twins might perceive themselves as a "set" and play together more than fraternal twins do. If so, the observed similarities between identical twins might have a significant environmental basis.

In an **adoption study,** investigators seek to discover whether the behavior and psychological characteristics of adopted children are more like those of their adoptive parents, who have provided a home environment, or more like those of their biological parents, who have contributed their heredity (Kendler & others, 2012). Another form of the adoption study compares adoptees with their adoptive siblings and their biological siblings.

adoption study A study in which investigators seek to discover whether, in behavior and psychological characteristics, adopted children are more like their adoptive parents, who provided a home environment, or more like their biological parents, who contributed their heredity. Another form of the adoption study compares adoptive and biological siblings.

Heredity-Environment Correlations

The difficulties that researchers encounter in interpreting the results of twin and adoption studies reflect the complexities of heredity-environment interactions. Some of these interactions are heredity-environment correlations, which means that individuals' genes may influence the types of environments to which they are exposed. In a sense, individuals "inherit" environments that may be related or linked to genetic "propensities" (Loehlin, 2010; Plomin & others, 2009). Behavior geneticist Sandra Scarr (1993) described three ways in which heredity and environment are correlated:

- *Passive genotype-environment correlations* occur because biological parents, who are genetically related to the child, provide a rearing environment for the child. For example, the parents might have a genetic predisposition to be intelligent and read skillfully. Because they read well and enjoy reading, they provide their children with books to read. The likely outcome is that their children, given their own inherited predispositions from their parents and their book-filled environment, will become skilled readers.

- *Evocative genotype-environment correlations* occur because a child's characteristics elicit certain types of environments. For example, active, smiling children receive more social stimulation than passive, quiet children do. Cooperative, attentive children evoke more pleasant and instructional responses from the adults around them than uncooperative, distractible children do.

- *Active (niche-picking) genotype-environment correlations* occur when children seek out environments that they find compatible and stimulating. *Niche-picking* refers to finding a setting that is suited to one's abilities. Children select from their surrounding environment some aspect that they respond to, learn about, or ignore. Their active selections of environments are related to their particular genotype. For example, outgoing children tend to seek out social contexts in which to interact with people, whereas shy children don't. Children who are musically inclined are likely to select musical environments in which they can successfully perform their skills.

How might heredity-environment correlations be at work in a child learning to play the piano?

The Epigenetic View and Gene x Environment (G x E) Interaction

Notice that Scarr's view gives the preeminent role in development to heredity: her analysis describes how heredity may influence the types of environments that children experience. Critics argue that the concept of heredity-environment correlation gives heredity too great an influence in determining development because it does not consider the role of prior environmental influences in shaping the correlation itself (Gottlieb, 2007). In this section we look at some approaches that place greater emphasis on the role of the environment.

The Epigenetic View

In line with the concept of a collaborative gene, Gilbert Gottlieb (2007) proposed an **epigenetic view,** which states that development is the result of an ongoing, bidirectional interchange between heredity and the environment. Figure 2.6 compares the heredity-environment correlation and epigenetic views of development.

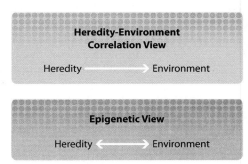

Let's look at an example that reflects the epigenetic view. A baby inherits genes from both parents at conception. During prenatal development, toxins, nutrition, and stress can influence some genes to stop functioning while others become stronger or weaker. During infancy, additional environmental experiences, such as exposure to toxins, nutrition, stress, learning, and encouragement, continue to modify genetic activity and the activity of the nervous system that directly underlies behavior.

Figure 2.6 Comparison of the Heredity-Environment Correlation and Epigenetic Views

Heredity and environment thus operate together—or collaborate—to produce a person's intelligence, temperament, health, ability to pitch a baseball, ability to read, and so on (Gottlieb, 2007; Moore, 2013; Wright & Christiani, 2010).

How Would You...?

As a human development and family studies professional, how would you apply the epigenetic view to explain why one identical twin can develop alcoholism, while the other twin does not?

Gene x Environment (G x E) Interaction

An increasing number of studies are exploring how the interaction between heredity and environment influences development, including interactions that involve specific DNA sequences (Bihagi & others, 2012; Slomko, Heo, & Einstein, 2012). The epigenetic mechanisms involve the actual molecular modification of the DNA strand as a result of environmental inputs in ways that alter gene functioning (Feil & Fraga, 2012; Meaney, 2010).

One study found that individuals who have a short version of a gene labeled 5-HTTLPR (a gene involving the neurotransmitter serotonin) have an elevated risk of developing depression only if they *also* lead stressful lives (Caspi & others, 2003). Thus, the specific gene did not directly cause the development of depression; rather the gene interacted with a stressful environment in a way that allowed the researchers to predict whether individuals would develop depression. Recent studies also have found support for the interaction between the 5-HTTLPR gene and stress levels in predicting depression in adolescents and older adults (Petersen & others, 2012; Zannas & others, 2012).

Other research involving interaction between genes and environmental experiences has focused on attachment, parenting, and supportive child rearing environments (Berry & others, 2012). In one study, adults who experienced parental loss as young children were more likely to have unresolved attachment issues as adults only when they had the short version of the 5-HTTLPR gene (Caspers & others, 2009). The long version of the serotonin transporter gene apparently provided some protection and ability to cope better with parental loss. Other recent research has found that variations in dopamine-related genes interact with supportive or unsupportive rearing environments to influence children's development (Bakermans-Kranenburg & van IJzendoorn, 2011). The type of research just described is referred to as studies of **gene x environment (g x e) interaction**—the interaction of a specific measured variation in DNA and a specific measured aspect of the environment (Alexander & others, 2012; Karg & Sen, 2012).

Conclusions About Heredity-Environment Interaction

If an attractive, popular, intelligent girl is elected president of her high school senior class, is her success due to heredity or to environment? Of course, the answer is "both."

The relative contributions of heredity and environment are not additive. That is, we can't say that such-and-such a percentage of nature and such-and-such a percentage of experience make us who we are. Nor is it accurate to say that full genetic expression happens once, at the time of conception or birth, after which we carry our genetic legacy into the world to see how far it takes us. Genes produce proteins throughout the life span, in many different environments. Or they don't produce these proteins, depending in part on how harsh or nourishing those environments are.

The emerging view is that complex behaviors are influenced by genes in a way that gives people a propensity for a particular developmental trajectory (Maxson, 2013; Plomin, 2012). However, the individual's actual development requires more: a particular environment. And that environment is complex, just like the mixture of genes we inherit (Grusec & others, 2013; Mistry, Conteras, & Dutta, 2013; Moore, 2013). Environmental influences range from the things we lump together under "nurture" (such as culture, parenting, family dynamics, schooling, and neighborhood quality) to biological encounters (such as viruses, birth complications, and even biological events in cells).

Imagine for a moment that there is a cluster of genes that are somehow associated with youth violence. (This example is hypothetical because we don't know of any such combination.) The adolescent who carries this genetic mixture might experience a world of loving parents, regular nutritious meals, lots of books, and a series of competent teachers. Or the adolescent's world might include parental neglect, a neighborhood in which gunshots and crime are everyday occurrences, and inadequate schooling. In which of these environments are the adolescent's genes likely to manufacture the biological underpinnings of criminality?

If heredity and environment interact to determine the course of development, is that all there is to answering the question of what causes development? Are humans completely at the mercy of their genes and their environment as they develop through the life span? Genetic heritage and environmental experiences are pervasive influences on development. But in thinking about what causes development, recall from Chapter 1 our discussion of development as the co-construction of biology, culture, *and* the individual. Not only are we the outcomes of our heredity and the environment we experience, but we also can author a unique developmental path by changing our environment. As one psychologist recently concluded:

> In reality, we are both the creatures and creators of our worlds. We are . . . the products of our genes and environments. Nevertheless, . . . the stream of causation that shapes the future runs through our present choices . . . Mind matters . . . Our hopes, goals, and expectations influence our future. (Myers, 2010, p. 168)

Prenatal Development

We turn now to a description of how the process of development unfolds from its earliest moment—the moment of conception—when two parental cells, with their unique genetic contributions, meet to create a new individual.

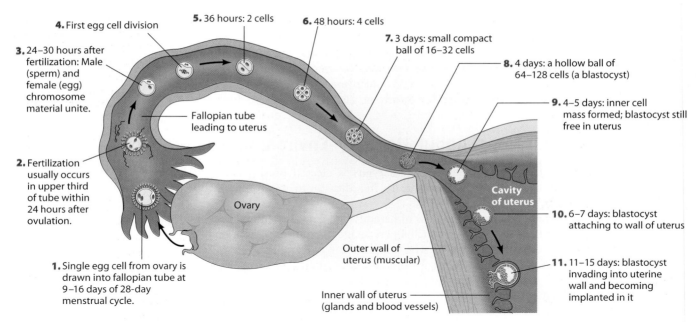

4. First egg cell division

5. 36 hours: 2 cells

6. 48 hours: 4 cells

7. 3 days: small compact ball of 16–32 cells

3. 24–30 hours after fertilization: Male (sperm) and female (egg) chromosome material unite.

8. 4 days: a hollow ball of 64–128 cells (a blastocyst)

Fallopian tube leading to uterus

9. 4–5 days: inner cell mass formed; blastocyst still free in uterus

2. Fertilization usually occurs in upper third of tube within 24 hours after ovulation.

Ovary

Cavity of uterus

10. 6–7 days: blastocyst attaching to wall of uterus

1. Single egg cell from ovary is drawn into fallopian tube at 9–16 days of 28-day menstrual cycle.

Outer wall of uterus (muscular)

11. 11–15 days: blastocyst invading into uterine wall and becoming implanted in it

Inner wall of uterus (glands and blood vessels)

Figure 2.7 **Major Developments in the Germinal Period**

Conception occurs when a single sperm cell from a male unites with an ovum (egg) in a female's fallopian tube in a process called fertilization. Over the next few months the genetic code discussed earlier directs a series of changes in the fertilized egg, but many events and hazards will influence how that egg develops and becomes a person.

The Course of Prenatal Development

Prenatal development lasts approximately 266 days, beginning with fertilization and ending with birth. Pregnancy can be divided into three periods: germinal, embryonic, and fetal.

The Germinal Period

The **germinal period** is the period of prenatal development that takes place in the first two weeks after conception. It includes the creation of the fertilized egg (the zygote), cell division, and the attachment of the multicellular organism to the uterine wall.

Rapid cell division by the zygote begins the germinal period. (Recall from earlier in the chapter that this cell division occurs through a process called mitosis.) Within one week after conception, the differentiation of these cells—their specialization for different tasks—has already begun. At this stage the organism, now called the blastocyst, consists of a hollow ball of cells that will eventually develop into the embryo, and the trophoblast, an outer layer of cells that later provides nutrition and support for the embryo. Implantation, the embedding of the blastocyst in the uterine wall, takes place during the second week after conception. Figure 2.7 summarizes these significant developments in the germinal period.

The Embryonic Period

The **embryonic period** is the period of prenatal development that occurs from two to eight weeks after conception. During the embryonic period, the rate of cell differentiation intensifies, support systems for cells form, and organs develop.

germinal period The period of prenatal development that takes place in the first two weeks after conception. It includes the creation of the zygote, continued cell division, and the attachment of the zygote to the uterine wall.

embryonic period The period of prenatal development that occurs two to eight weeks after conception. During the embryonic period, the rate of cell differentiation intensifies, support systems for the cells form, and organs appear.

The mass of cells is now called an *embryo*, and three layers of cells form. The embryo's *endoderm* is the inner layer of cells, which will develop into the digestive and respiratory systems. The *ectoderm* is the outermost layer, which will become the nervous system, sensory receptors (ears, nose, and eyes, for example), and skin parts (hair and nails, for example). The *mesoderm* is the middle layer, which will become the circulatory system, bones, muscles, excretory system, and reproductive system. Every body part eventually develops from these three layers. The endoderm primarily produces internal body parts, the mesoderm primarily produces parts that surround the internal areas, and the ectoderm primarily produces surface parts. **Organogenesis** is the name given to the process of organ formation during the first two months of prenatal development. While they are being formed, the organs are especially vulnerable to environmental influences.

How Would You...?

As a human development and family studies professional, how would you characterize the greatest risks at each period of prenatal development?

organogenesis Organ formation that takes place during the first two months of prenatal development.

fetal period The prenatal period of development that begins two months after conception and lasts for seven months, on the average.

As the embryo's three layers form, life-support systems for the embryo develop rapidly. These systems include the amnion, the umbilical cord (both of which develop from the fertilized egg, not the mother's body), and the placenta. The amnion is like a bag or an envelope; it contains a clear fluid in which the developing embryo floats. The amniotic fluid provides an environment that is temperature- and humidity-controlled, as well as shockproof. The *umbilical cord*, which typically contains two arteries and one vein, connects the baby to the placenta. The *placenta* consists of a disk-shaped group of tissues in which small blood vessels from the mother and the offspring intertwine but do not join.

Very small molecules—oxygen, water, salt, and nutrients from the mother's blood, as well as carbon dioxide and digestive wastes from the baby's blood—pass back and forth between the mother and the embryo or fetus (Woolett, 2011). Large molecules cannot pass through the placental wall; these include red blood cells and some harmful substances, such as most bacteria, maternal wastes, and hormones (Eshkoli & others, 2011). Virtually any drug or chemical substance a pregnant woman ingests can cross the placenta to some degree, unless it is metabolized or altered during passage, or is too large (Iqbal & others, 2012). A recent study revealed that cigarette smoke weakened and increased the oxidative stress of fetal membranes, from which the placenta develops (Menon & others, 2011). The mechanisms that govern the transfer of substances across the placental barrier are complex and still not entirely understood (Saunders, Liddelow, & Dziegielewska, 2012).

The Fetal Period

The **fetal period,** which lasts about seven months, is the prenatal period that extends from two months after conception until birth in typical pregnancies. Growth and development continue their dramatic course during this time.

Three months after conception, the fetus is about 3 inches long and weighs about 1 ounce. It has become active, moving its arms and legs, opening and closing its mouth, and moving its head. The face, forehead, eyelids, nose, and chin are distinguishable, as are the upper arms, lower arms, hands, and lower limbs. In most cases, the genitals can be identified as male or female. By the end of the fourth month of pregnancy, the fetus has grown to 6 inches in length and weighs 4 to 7 ounces. At this time, a growth spurt occurs in the body's lower parts. For the first time, the mother can feel arm and leg movements.

By the end of the fifth month, the fetus is about 12 inches long and weighs close to a pound. Structures of the skin have formed—including toenails and fingernails. The fetus is more active, showing a preference for a particular position in the womb. By the end of the sixth month, the fetus is about 14 inches long and has gained another 6 to 12 ounces. The eyes and eyelids are completely formed, and a fine layer of hair covers the head. A grasping reflex is present and irregular breathing movements occur.

First trimester (first 3 months)

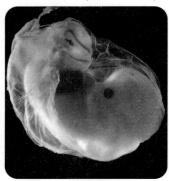

Conception to 4 weeks

- Is less than $1/10$ inch long
- Beginning development of spinal cord, nervous system, gastrointestinal system, heart, and lungs
- Amniotic sac envelops the preliminary tissues of entire body
- Is called a "zygote," then a "blastocyst"

8 weeks

- Is just over 1 inch long
- Face is forming with rudimentary eyes, ears, mouth, and tooth buds
- Arms and legs are moving
- Brain is forming
- Fetal heartbeat is detectable with ultrasound
- Is called an "embryo"

12 weeks

- Is about 3 inches long and weighs about 1 ounce
- Can move arms, legs, fingers, and toes
- Fingerprints are present
- Can smile, frown, suck, and swallow
- Sex is distinguishable
- Can urinate
- Is called a "fetus"

Second trimester (middle 3 months)

16 weeks

- Is about 6 inches long and weighs about 4 to 7 ounces
- Heartbeat is strong
- Skin is thin, transparent
- Downy hair (lanugo) covers body
- Fingernails and toenails are forming
- Has coordinated movements; is able to roll over in amniotic fluid

20 weeks

- Is about 12 inches long and weighs close to 1 pound
- Heartbeat is audible with ordinary stethoscope
- Sucks thumb
- Hiccups
- Hair, eyelashes, eyebrows are present

24 weeks

- Is about 14 inches long and weighs about 1 to $1 1/2$ pounds
- Skin is wrinkled and covered with protective coating (vernix caseosa)
- Eyes are open
- Waste matter is collected in bowel
- Has strong grip

Third trimester (last 3 months)

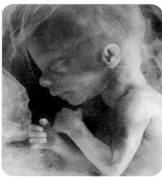

28 weeks

- Is about 16 inches long and weighs about 3 pounds
- Is adding body fat
- Is very active
- Rudimentary breathing movements are present

32 weeks

- Is $16 1/2$ to 18 inches long and weighs 4 to 5 pounds
- Has periods of sleep and wakefulness
- Responds to sounds
- May assume the birth position
- Bones of head are soft and flexible
- Iron is being stored in liver

36 to 38 weeks

- Is 19 to 20 inches long and weighs 6 to $7 1/2$ pounds
- Skin is less wrinkled
- Vernix caseosa is thick
- Lanugo is mostly gone
- Is less active
- Is gaining immunities from mother

Figure 2.8 Growth and Development in the Three Trimesters of Prenatal Development

As early as six months of pregnancy (about 24 to 25 weeks after conception), the fetus for the first time has a chance of surviving outside the womb—that is, it is *viable*. Infants that are born early, or between 24 and 37 weeks of pregnancy, usually need help breathing because their lungs are not yet fully mature. By the end of the seventh month, the fetus is about 16 inches long and weighs about 3 pounds.

During the last two months of prenatal development, fatty tissues develop and the functioning of various organ systems—heart and kidneys, for example—steps up. During the eighth and ninth months, the fetus grows longer and gains substantial weight—about 4 more pounds. At birth, the average American baby weighs 7½ pounds and is about 20 inches long. In addition to describing prenatal development in terms of germinal, embryonic, and fetal periods, prenatal development also can be divided into equal three-month periods, called *trimesters*. Figure 2.8 gives an overview of the main events during each trimester. Remember that the three trimesters are not the same as the three prenatal periods we have discussed. The germinal and embryonic periods occur in the first trimester. The fetal period begins toward the end of the first trimester and continues through the second and third trimesters.

Figure 2.9 Early Formation of the Nervous System
The photograph shows the primitive, tubular appearance of the nervous system at six weeks in the human embryo.

The Brain

One of the most remarkable aspects of the prenatal period is the development of the brain (Nelson, 2012, 2013). By the time babies are born, they have approximately 100 billion **neurons,** or nerve cells, which handle information processing at the cellular level in the brain. During prenatal development, neurons move to specific locations and start to become connected. The basic architecture of the human brain is assembled during the first two trimesters of prenatal development. In typical development, the third trimester of prenatal development and the first two years of postnatal life are characterized by connectivity and functioning of neurons (Nelson, 2013).

neurons Nerve cells that handle information processing at the cellular level in the brain.

As the human embryo develops inside its mother's womb, the nervous system begins forming as a long, hollow tube located on the embryo's back. This pear-shaped *neural tube,* which forms at about 18 to 24 days after conception, develops out of the ectoderm. The tube closes at the top and bottom ends at about 24 days after conception. Figure 2.9 shows that the nervous system still has a tubular appearance 6 weeks after conception.

Two birth defects related to a failure of the neural tube to close are anencephaly and spina bifida. When a fetus has anencephaly (that is, when the head end of the neural tube fails to close), the highest regions of the brain fail to develop and the baby dies in the womb, during childbirth, or shortly after birth (Stoll & others, 2011). Spina bifida, an incomplete development of the spinal cord, results in varying degrees of paralysis of the lower limbs. Individuals with spina bifida usually need assistive devices such as crutches, braces, or wheelchairs. Both maternal diabetes and obesity also place the fetus at risk for developing neural tube defects (Stern & others, 2011). A strategy that can help to prevent neural tube defects is for women to take adequate amounts of the B vitamin folic acid, a topic we will discuss later in the chapter (Collins & others, 2011).

In a normal pregnancy, once the neural tube has closed, a massive proliferation of new immature neurons begins to take place about the fifth prenatal week and continues throughout the remainder of the prenatal period. The production of new neurons is called *neurogenesis.* At the peak of neurogenesis, it is estimated that as many as 200,000 neurons are being generated every minute.

At approximately 6 to 24 weeks after conception, *neuronal migration* occurs (Nelson, 2012, 2013). Cells begin moving outward from their point of origin to their appropriate locations and creating the different levels, structures, and regions of the brain (Zeisel, 2011). Once a cell has migrated to its target destination, it must mature and develop a more complex structure.

At about the 23rd prenatal week, connections between neurons begin to form, a process that continues postnatally (Kostovic, Judas, & Sedmak, 2011). We will have much more to say about the structure of neurons, their connectivity, and the development of the infant brain in Chapter 3.

Prenatal Tests

Together with her doctor, a pregnant woman will decide the extent to which she should undergo prenatal testing. A number of tests can indicate whether a fetus is developing normally; these include ultrasound sonography, fetal MRI, chorionic villus sampling, amniocentesis, maternal blood screening, and noninvasive prenatal diagnosis. The decision to have a given test depends on several criteria, such as the mother's age, medical history, and genetic risk factors.

Ultrasound Sonography

An ultrasound test is generally performed 7 weeks into a pregnancy and at various times later in pregnancy. *Ultrasound sonography* is a noninvasive prenatal medical procedure in which high-frequency sound waves are directed into the pregnant woman's abdomen. The echo from the sounds is transformed into a visual representation of the fetus's inner structures. This technique can detect many structural abnormalities in the fetus, including microencephaly, a form of intellectual disability involving an abnormally small brain; it can also give clues to the baby's sex and indicate whether there is more than one fetus (Masselli & others, 2011). There is virtually no risk to the woman or fetus when this technique is used.

Chorionic Villus Sampling

At some point between the 10th and 12th weeks of pregnancy, chorionic villus sampling may be used to screen for genetic defects and chromosome abnormalities (Basaran, Basaran, & Topatan, 2011). *Chorionic villus sampling (CVS)* is a prenatal medical procedure in which a tiny tissue sample from the placenta is removed and analyzed (Bauland & others, 2012). The results are available in about 10 days.

Amniocentesis

Between the 15th and 18th weeks of pregnancy, *amniocentesis* may be performed. In this procedure, a sample of amniotic fluid is withdrawn by syringe and tested for chromosome or metabolic disorders (Athanasiadis & others, 2011). The later in the pregnancy amniocentesis is performed, the better its diagnostic potential. However, the earlier it is performed, the more useful it is in deciding how to handle a pregnancy when the fetus is found to have a disorder. It may take two weeks for enough cells to grow so that amniocentesis test results can be obtained. Amniocentesis brings a small risk of miscarriage: about 1 woman in every 200 to 300 miscarries after amniocentesis.

Maternal Blood Screening

During the 16th to 18th weeks of pregnancy, maternal blood screening may be performed. *Maternal blood screening* identifies pregnancies that have an elevated risk for birth defects such as spina bifida and Down syndrome (Ballard, 2011). The current blood test is called the *triple screen* because it measures three substances in the mother's blood. After an abnormal triple screen result, the next step is usually an ultrasound examination. If an ultrasound does not explain the abnormal triple screen results, amniocentesis typically is used.

Fetal MRI

The development of brain-imaging techniques has led to increasing use of *fetal MRI* to diagnose fetal malformations (To, 2012) (see Figure 2.10). MRI, which stands for magnetic resonance imaging, uses a powerful magnet and radio images to generate detailed images of the body's organs and structures. Currently, ultrasound is still the first choice in fetal screening, but fetal MRI can provide more detailed images than ultrasound. In many instances, ultrasound will indicate a possible abnormality and fetal MRI will then be used to obtain a clearer, more detailed image (Martin & others, 2012). Among the fetal malformations that fetal MRI may be able to detect better than ultrasound sonography are certain abnormalities of the central nervous system, chest, gastrointestinal tract, genital/urinary organs, and placenta (Panigraphy & others, 2012).

Noninvasive Prenatal Diagnosis (NIPD)

Noninvasive prenatal diagnosis (NIPD) is increasingly being explored as an alternative to procedures such as chorionic villus sampling and amniocentesis (Avent, 2012; Chiu & Lo, 2012). At this

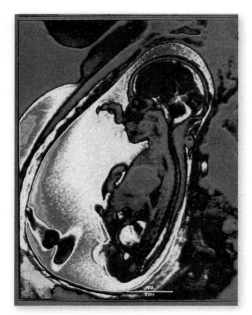

Figure 2.10 A Fetal MRI
Increasingly, MRI is being used to diagnose fetal malformations.

How Would You...?

As a psychologist, how would you advise a 25-year-old mother who is concerned about the possibility of birth defects but has no genetic history of these types of problems?

point, NIPD has mainly focused on brain imaging techniques and the isolation and examination of fetal cells circulating in the mother's blood and analysis of cell-free fetal DNA in maternal plasma (Geaghan, 2012; Zugazaga Cortazar, & Martin Martinez, 2012).

Researchers already have used NIPD to successfully test for genes inherited from a father that cause cystic fibrosis and Huntington disease. They also are exploring the potential for using NIPD very early in fetal development to diagnose a baby's sex and detect Down syndrome (Fernandez-Martinez & others, 2012; Miura & others, 2011).

Fetal Sex Determination

Chorionic villus sampling has often been used to determine the sex of the fetus at some point between 11 and 13 weeks of gestation. Recently, though, some noninvasive techniques have been able to detect the sex of the fetus at an earlier point (Kolialexi & others, 2012). A recent meta-analysis of studies confirmed that a baby's sex can be detected as early as 7 weeks into pregnancy (Devaney & others, 2011). Being able to detect an offspring's sex as well as the presence of various diseases and defects at such an early stage raises ethical concerns about couples' motivation to terminate a pregnancy (Lewis & others, 2012).

Infertility and Reproductive Technology

Recent advances in biological knowledge have also opened up many choices for infertile people (Beall & Decherney, 2012; Ming & others, 2012). Approximately 10 to 15 percent of couples in the United States experience infertility, which is defined as the inability to conceive a child after 12 months of regular intercourse without contraception. The cause of infertility can rest with either the woman or the man, or both (Reindollar & Goldman, 2012). The woman may not be ovulating (releasing eggs to be fertilized); she may be producing abnormal ova; her fallopian tubes (by which ova normally reach the womb) may be blocked; or she may have a condition that prevents implantation of the embryo into the uterus. The man may produce too few sperm; the sperm may lack motility (the ability to move adequately); or he may have a blocked passageway (Kini & others, 2010).

Surgery can correct some causes of infertility; for others, hormone-based drugs may be effective. Of the 2 million U.S. couples who seek help for infertility every year, about 40,000 try assisted reproduction technologies. *In vitro fertilization (IVF)*, the technique that produced the world's first "test tube baby" in 1978, involves eggs and sperm being combined in a laboratory dish. If any eggs are successfully fertilized, one or more of the resulting fertilized eggs is transferred into the woman's uterus.

The creation of families by means of assisted reproduction techniques raises important questions about the physical and psychological consequences for children. For example, one result of fertility treatments is an increase in multiple births (Steel & Sutcliffe, 2010). Twenty-five to 30 percent of pregnancies achieved by fertility treatments—including in vitro fertilization—result in multiple births. Any multiple birth increases the likelihood that the babies will have life-threatening and costly problems, such as extremely low birth weight (McDonald & others, 2010).

Hazards to Prenatal Development

For most babies, the course of prenatal development goes smoothly. Their mother's womb protects them as they develop. Despite this protection, however, the environment can affect the embryo or fetus in many well-documented ways.

General Principles

A **teratogen** is any agent that can potentially cause a birth defect or negatively alter cognitive and behavioral outcomes. The field of study that investigates the causes of birth defects is called *teratology* (Hyoun & others, 2012; Rasmussen, 2012). Teratogens include drugs, incompatible blood types, environmental pollutants, infectious diseases, nutritional deficiencies, maternal stress, advanced maternal and paternal age, and environmental pollutants.

The dose, genetic susceptibility, and time of exposure to a particular teratogen influence both the severity of the damage to an embryo or fetus and the type of defect: (1) *Dose*—The dose effect is rather obvious—the greater the dose of an agent, such as a drug, the greater the effect. (2) *Genetic susceptibility*—The type or severity of abnormalities caused by a teratogen is linked to the genotype of the pregnant woman and the genotype of the embryo or fetus (Charlet & others, 2012). (3) *Time of exposure*—Teratogens do more damage when they occur at some points in development than at others. The probability of a structural defect is greatest early in the embryonic period, when organs are being formed (Holmes, 2011). After organogenesis is complete, teratogens are less likely to cause anatomical defects. Instead, exposure during the fetal period is more likely to stunt growth or create problems in the way organs function. To examine some key teratogens and their effects, let's begin with drugs.

Prescription and Nonprescription Drugs

Prescription drugs that can function as teratogens include antibiotics, such as streptomycin and tetracycline; some antidepressants; certain hormones, such as progestin and synthetic estrogen; and Accutane (often prescribed for acne) (Crijns & others, 2012; Koren & Nordeng, 2012). Nonprescription drugs that can be harmful include diet pills and aspirin. However, recent research revealed that low doses of aspirin pose no harm to the fetus but that high doses can contribute to maternal and fetal bleeding (Bennett, Bagot, & Arya, 2012).

Psychoactive Drugs

Psychoactive drugs act on the nervous system to alter states of consciousness, modify perceptions, and change moods. Examples include caffeine, alcohol, and nicotine, as well as illegal drugs such as cocaine, methamphetamine, marijuana, and heroin.

Caffeine People often consume caffeine by drinking coffee, tea, or colas, or by eating chocolate. The U.S. Food and Drug Administration recommends that pregnant women either not consume caffeine or consume it only sparingly.

Alcohol Heavy drinking by pregnant women can be devastating to offspring (Brocardo, Gil-Mohapel, & Christie, 2011). **Fetal alcohol spectrum disorders (FASD)** are a cluster of abnormalities and problems that appear in the offspring of mothers who drink alcohol heavily during pregnancy. The abnormalities include facial deformities and defective limbs, face, and heart (Painter, Williams, & Burd, 2012a). Most children with FASD have learning problems, and many are below average in intelligence; some have an intellectual disability (Painter, Williams, & Burd, 2012b). A recent study revealed that children with FASD have deficiencies in the brain pathways involved in working memory (Diwadkar & others, 2012). Although mothers of FASD infants are heavy drinkers, many mothers who are heavy drinkers may not have children with FASD or may have one child with FASD and other children who do not have it.

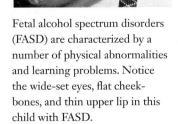

Fetal alcohol spectrum disorders (FASD) are characterized by a number of physical abnormalities and learning problems. Notice the wide-set eyes, flat cheekbones, and thin upper lip in this child with FASD.

fetal alcohol spectrum disorders (FASD) A cluster of abnormalities that appears in the offspring of mothers who drink alcohol heavily during pregnancy.

What are some guidelines for alcohol use during pregnancy? Even drinking just one or two servings of beer or wine or one serving of hard liquor a few days a week can have negative effects on the fetus, although it is generally agreed that this level of alcohol use will not cause fetal alcohol spectrum disorders (Cheng & others, 2011; Valenzeula & others, 2012). The U.S. Surgeon General recommends that no alcohol be consumed during pregnancy. And research suggests that it may not be wise to consume alcohol at the time of conception. One study revealed that intakes of alcohol by both men and women during the weeks of conception increased the risk of early pregnancy loss (Henriksen & others, 2004).

Nicotine Cigarette smoking by pregnant women can also adversely influence prenatal development, birth, and postnatal development. Preterm births and low birth weights, fetal and neonatal deaths, respiratory problems, sudden infant death syndrome (SIDS, also known as crib death), and cardiovascular problems are all more common among the offspring of mothers who smoked during pregnancy (Burstyn & others, 2012). Researchers also have found that maternal smoking during pregnancy is a risk factor for the development of attention deficit hyperactivity disorder in children (Abbott & Winzer-Serhan, 2012; Sagiv & others, 2012). Researchers also have documented that environmental tobacco smoke is linked to an increased risk of low birth weight in offspring (Leonardi-Bee & others, 2008) and to diminished ovarian functioning in female offspring (Kilic & others, 2012). And a recent study revealed that environmental tobacco smoke was associated with 114 deregulations in the development of fetal cells in offspring, especially those involving immune functioning (Votavova & others, 2012).

Cocaine Does cocaine use during pregnancy harm the developing embryo and fetus? A recent research study found that cocaine quickly crossed the placenta to reach the fetus (De Giovanni & Marchetti, 2012). The most consistent finding is that cocaine exposure during prenatal development is associated with reduced birth weight, length, and head circumference (Gouin & others, 2011). In other studies, prenatal cocaine exposure has been linked to lower arousal, less effective self-regulation, higher excitability, and lower quality of reflexes at 1 month of age (Ackerman, Riggins, & Black, 2010; Lester & others, 2002); impaired motor development at 2 years of age and a slower rate of growth through 10 years of age (Richardson, Goldschmidt, & Willford, 2008); impaired language development and information processing, including attention deficits (especially impulsivity) (Accornero & others, 2006; Richardson & others, 2011); increased behavioral problems, especially externalizing problems such as high rates of aggression and delinquency (Minnes & others, 2010; Richardson & others, 2011); and increased likelihood of being in a special education program that involves support services (Levine & others, 2008).

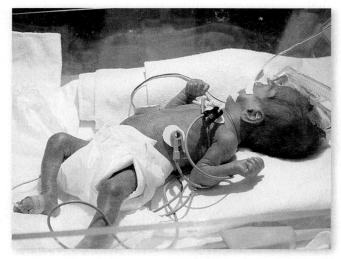

Some researchers argue that these findings should be interpreted cautiously (Accornero & others, 2006). Why? Because other factors in the lives of pregnant women who use cocaine (such as poverty, malnutrition, and other substance abuse) often cannot be ruled out as possible contributors to the problems found in their children (Hurt & others, 2005; Messiah & others, 2011). For example, cocaine users are more likely than nonusers to smoke cigarettes, use marijuana, drink alcohol, and take amphetamines.

This baby was exposed to cocaine prenatally. *What are some of the possible effects on development of being exposed to cocaine prenatally?*

Despite these cautions, the weight of research evidence indicates that children born to mothers who use cocaine are likely to have neurological, medical, and cognitive deficits (Field, 2007; Mayer & Zhang, 2009; Richardson & others, 2011). Cocaine use by pregnant women is never recommended.

Methamphetamine Methamphetamine, like cocaine, is a stimulant, speeding up an individual's nervous system. Babies born to mothers who use methamphetamine, or "meth," during pregnancy are at risk for a number of problems, including high infant mortality, low birth weight, memory deficits, and developmental and behavioral problems (Piper & others, 2011). A recent study found that prenatal exposure to meth was linked to less brain activation in a number of areas, especially the frontal lobes, in 7- to 15-year-olds (Roussotte & others, 2011). Another recent study revealed that prenatal meth exposure was associated with smaller head circumference, neonatal intensive care unit (NICU) admission, and referral to child protective services (Shah & others, 2012).

Marijuana An increasing number of studies find that marijuana use by pregnant women also has negative outcomes for offspring. For example, a recent study found that prenatal marijuana exposure was related to lower intelligence in children (Goldschmidt & others, 2008). Another study indicated that prenatal exposure to marijuana was linked to marijuana use at 14 years of age (Day, Goldschmidt, & Thomas, 2006). In sum, marijuana use is not recommended for pregnant women.

How Would You...?

As a social worker, how would you advise women in their childbearing years who frequently abuse drugs and other psychoactive substances?

Heroin It is well documented that infants whose mothers are addicted to heroin show several behavioral difficulties at birth (Ortigosa Gomez & others, 2011). The difficulties include withdrawal symptoms, such as tremors, irritability, abnormal crying, disturbed sleep, and impaired motor control. Many still show behavioral problems at their first birthday, and attention deficits may appear later in development. The most common treatment for heroin addiction, methadone, is associated with very severe withdrawal symptoms in newborns (Blandthorn, Forster, & Love, 2011).

Incompatible Blood Types

Incompatibility between the mother's and the father's blood types poses another risk to prenatal development (Matsuda & others, 2011). Blood types are created by differences in the surface structure of red blood cells. One such difference creates the familiar blood groups—A, B, O, and AB. A second difference creates what is called Rh-positive and Rh-negative blood. If a surface marker, called the *Rh factor*, is present in an individual's red blood cells, the person is said to be Rh-positive; if the Rh marker is not present, the person is said to be Rh-negative. If a pregnant woman is Rh-negative and her partner is Rh-positive, the fetus may be Rh-positive. If the fetus's blood is Rh-positive and the mother's is Rh-negative, the mother's immune system may produce antibodies that will attack the fetus. This can result in any number of problems, including miscarriage or stillbirth, anemia, jaundice, heart defects, brain damage, or death soon after birth (Li & others, 2010).

Generally, the first Rh-positive baby of an Rh-negative mother is not at risk, but with each subsequent pregnancy the risk increases. A serum (RhoGAM) may be given to the mother within three days of the child's birth to prevent her body from making antibodies that will attack future Rh-positive fetuses. Also, babies affected by Rh incompatibility can be given blood transfusions before or right after birth (Goodnough & others, 2011).

Environmental Hazards

Many aspects of our modern industrial world can endanger the embryo or fetus. Some specific hazards to the embryo or fetus include radiation, toxic wastes, and other environmental pollutants (Wiesel & others, 2011).

X-ray radiation can affect the developing embryo or fetus, especially in the first several weeks after conception, when women do not yet know they are pregnant. Women and their physicians should weigh the risk of an X-ray when the woman is or might be pregnant (Rajaraman & others, 2011). However, a routine diagnostic X-ray of a body area other than the abdomen, with the woman's abdomen protected by a lead apron, is generally considered safe (Brent, 2009, 2011).

Maternal Diseases

Maternal diseases and infections can produce defects in offspring by crossing the placental barrier, or they can cause damage during birth. Rubella (German measles) is one disease that can cause prenatal defects. Women who plan to have children should have a blood test before they become pregnant to determine if they are immune to the disease (Rasmussen, 2012; Reef & others, 2011).

Syphilis (a sexually transmitted infection) is more damaging later in prenatal development—four months or more after conception. Damage includes eye lesions, which can cause blindness, and skin lesions (Caddy & others, 2011).

Another infection that has received widespread attention is genital herpes. Newborns contract this virus when they are delivered through the birth canal of a mother with genital herpes (Nigro & others, 2011). About one-third of babies delivered through an infected birth canal die; another one-fourth suffer brain damage. If an active case of genital herpes is detected in a pregnant woman close to her delivery date, a cesarean section can be performed (in which the infant is delivered through an incision in the mother's abdomen) to keep the virus from infecting the newborn (Patel & others, 2011).

AIDS is a sexually transmitted infection that is caused by the human immunodeficiency virus (HIV), which destroys the body's immune system. A mother can infect her offspring with HIV/AIDS in three ways: (1) across the placenta during gestation, (2) through contact with maternal blood or fluids during delivery, and (3) through breast feeding. The transmission of AIDS through breast feeding is a particular problem in many developing countries (UNICEF, 2012). Babies born to HIV-infected mothers can be (1) infected and symptomatic (show HIV symptoms), (2) infected but asymptomatic (not show HIV symptoms), or (3) not infected at all. An infant who is infected and asymptomatic may still develop HIV symptoms up to 15 months of age.

The more widespread disease of diabetes, characterized by high levels of sugar in the blood, also affects offspring (Heude & others, 2012). A research review indicated that newborns with physical defects are more likely to have diabetic mothers than newborns without such defects (Eriksson, 2009). Moreover, women who have gestational diabetes (a condition in which women without previously diagnosed diabetes develop high blood glucose levels during pregnancy) may deliver very large infants (weighing 10 pounds or more), and the infants themselves are at risk for diabetes (Gluck & others, 2009).

Other Parental Factors

So far we have discussed a number of drugs, environmental hazards, maternal diseases, and incompatible blood types that can harm the embryo or fetus. Here we will explore other characteristics of the mother and father that can affect prenatal and child development, including nutrition, age, and emotional states and stress.

Maternal Diet and Nutrition A developing embryo or fetus depends completely on its mother for nutrition, which comes from the mother's blood (Lowdermilk & Perry, 2012). The nutritional status of the embryo or fetus is determined by the mother's total caloric intake, as well as her intake of proteins, vitamins, and minerals. Children born to malnourished mothers are more likely than other children to be malformed.

Being overweight before and during pregnancy can also put the embryo or fetus at risk, and an increasing number of pregnant women in the United States are overweight (Heude & others, 2012; Poston & others, 2011). Maternal obesity

Because the fetus depends entirely on its mother for nutrition, it is important for the pregnant woman to have good nutritional habits. In Kenya, this government clinic provides pregnant women with information about how their diet can influence the health of their fetus and offspring. *What might the information about diet be like?*

adversely affects pregnancy outcomes through elevated rates of hypertension, diabetes, respiratory complications, and infections in the mother (Nodine & Hastings-Tolsma, 2012). Management of obesity that includes weight loss and increased exercise prior to pregnancy is likely to benefit the mother and the baby (Vesco & others, 2012).

One aspect of maternal nutrition that is important for normal prenatal development is folic acid, a B-complex vitamin (Waddell, 2012). A study of more than 34,000 women found that taking folic acid either alone or as part of a multivitamin for at least one year prior to conceiving was linked with a 70 percent lower risk of delivering at 20 to 28 weeks and a 50 percent lower risk of delivering at 28 to 32 weeks (Bukowski & others, 2008). Another study revealed that toddlers of mothers who did not use folic acid supplements in the first trimester of pregnancy had more behavioral problems (Roza & others, 2010). Also, as indicated earlier in the chapter, lack of folic acid is related to neural tube defects in offspring (Collins & others, 2011). The U.S. Department of Health and Human Services (2012) recommends that pregnant women consume a minimum of 400 micrograms of folic acid per day (about twice the amount the average woman gets in one day). Orange juice and spinach are examples of foods that are rich in folic acid.

Fish is often recommended as part of a healthy diet, but pollution has made many kinds of fish a risky choice for pregnant women. Some fish contain high levels of mercury, which is released into the air both naturally and by industrial processes (Wells, 2011). Mercury that falls into the water can accumulate in large fish, such as shark, swordfish, king mackerel, and some species of large tuna (American Pregnancy Association, 2012; Mayo Clinic, 2012). Mercury is easily transferred across the placenta, and the embryo's developing brain and nervous system are highly sensitive to the metal. Researchers have found that prenatal mercury exposure is linked to adverse outcomes, including miscarriage, preterm birth, and lower intelligence (Xue & others, 2007).

Maternal Age When possible harmful effects on the fetus and infant are considered, two maternal ages are of special interest: adolescence and 35 years and older (Malizia, Hacker, & Penzias, 2009; Rudang & others, 2012). The mortality rate of infants born to adolescent mothers is double that of infants born to mothers in their twenties. Adequate prenatal care decreases the probability that a child born to an adolescent girl will have physical problems. However, adolescents are the least likely of women in all age groups to obtain prenatal assistance from clinics and health services.

Maternal age is also linked to the risk that a child will have Down syndrome (Ghosh & others, 2010). A baby with Down syndrome rarely is born to a mother 16 to 34 years of age. However, when the mother reaches 40 years of age, the probability is slightly higher than 1 in 100 that a baby born to her will have Down syndrome, and by age 50 it is almost 1 in 10. When mothers are 35 years and older, risks also increase for low birth weight, preterm delivery, and fetal death (Koo & others, 2012; Mbugua Gitau & others, 2009).

We still have much to learn about the role of the mother's age in pregnancy and childbirth. As women remain active, exercise regularly, and are careful about their nutrition, their reproductive systems may remain healthier at older ages than was thought possible in the past.

Emotional States and Stress When a pregnant woman experiences intense fears, anxieties, and other emotions or negative mood states, physiological changes occur that may affect her fetus (Howerton & Bale, 2012). A mother's stress may also influence the fetus indirectly by increasing the likelihood that the mother will engage in unhealthy behaviors such as taking drugs and receiving poor prenatal care.

How Would You...?

As a health-care professional, what advice would you give to an expectant mother who is experiencing extreme psychological stress?

High maternal anxiety and stress during pregnancy can have long-term consequences for the offspring (Dunkel Schetter, 2011). A research review indicated that pregnant women with high levels of stress are at increased risk for having a child with emotional or cognitive problems, attention deficit hyperactivity disorder (ADHD), and language delay (Taige & others, 2007).

Might maternal depression also have an adverse effect on birth outcomes? A recent research review concluded that maternal depression during pregnancy is linked to preterm birth (Dunkel Schetter, 2011).

Paternal Factors So far, we have discussed how characteristics of the mother—such as drug use, disease, diet and nutrition, age, and emotional states—can influence prenatal development and the development of the child. Might there also be some paternal risk factors? Indeed, there are several. Men's exposure to lead, radiation, certain pesticides, and petrochemicals may cause abnormalities in sperm that lead to miscarriage or diseases such as childhood cancer (Cordier, 2008). The father's smoking during the mother's pregnancy also can cause problems for the offspring. In one study, heavy paternal smoking was associated with an increased risk of early miscarriage (Venners & others, 2004). This negative outcome may be related to the mother's exposure to secondhand smoke. And in a recent study, paternal smoking around the time of the child's conception was linked to an increased risk of the child developing leukemia (Milne & others, 2012). Also, a recent research review concluded that there is an increased risk of spontaneous abortion, autism, and schizophrenic disorders when the father is 40 years of age or older (Reproductive Endocrinology and Infertility Committee & others, 2011).

In one study, in China, the longer fathers smoked, the higher the risk that their children would develop cancer (Ji & others, 1997). *What are some other paternal factors that can influence the development of the fetus and the child?*

Much of our discussion on prenatal development has focused on what can go wrong. Prospective parents should take steps to avoid the vulnerabilities to fetal development that we have described. But it is important to keep in mind that most of the time, prenatal development does not go awry and development occurs along a positive path.

Prenatal Care

Although prenatal care varies enormously from one woman to another, it usually involves a defined schedule of visits for medical care, which typically includes screening for manageable conditions and treatable diseases that can affect the baby or the mother. In addition to medical care, prenatal programs often include comprehensive educational, social, and nutritional services.

Information about pregnancy, labor, delivery, and caring for the newborn can be especially valuable for first-time mothers (Gabbe & others, 2012; Lowdermilk & Perry 2012). Prenatal care is also very important for women in poverty and immigrant women because it links them with other social services (Lyberg & others, 2012).

A CenteringPregnancy program. This increasingly widespread program alters routine prenatal care by bringing women out of exam rooms and into relationship-oriented groups.

An innovative program that is rapidly expanding in the United States is CenteringPregnancy (Ickovics & others, 2011; Steming, 2008). This program is relationship-centered and provides complete prenatal care in a group setting. It replaces traditional 15-minute physician visits with 90-minute peer group support sessions and self-examination led by a physician or certified nurse-midwife. Groups of up to 10 women (and often their partners) meet regularly beginning at 12 to 16 weeks of pregnancy. The sessions emphasize empowering women to play an active role in experiencing a positive pregnancy. In a recent study, high-stress women were randomly assigned to a CenteringPregnancy Plus group, group prenatal care, or standard individual care from 18 weeks gestation to birth (Ickovics & others, 2011). The most stressed women in the CenteringPregnancy Plus group showed increased self-esteem and decreased stress and social conflict in their third trimester of pregnancy; their social conflict and depression also were lower at one year postpartum.

Some prenatal programs for parents focus on home visitation (Issel & others, 2011). Research evaluations indicate that the Nurse-Family Partnership created by David Olds and his colleagues (2004, 2007) is successful. The Nurse-Family Partnership involves home visits by trained nurses beginning in the second or third trimester of prenatal development. The extensive program consists of approximately 50 home visits beginning during the prenatal period and extending through the child's first two years. Research has revealed that the Nurse-Family Partnership has numerous positive outcomes, including fewer pregnancies, better work circumstances, and stability in relationship partners for the mother, and improved academic success and social development for the child (Olds & others, 2004, 2007).

Exercise increasingly is recommended as part of a comprehensive prenatal care program. Exercise during pregnancy helps prevent constipation, conditions the body, reduces excessive weight gain, and is associated with a more positive mental state, including a reduced level of depression (Robledo-Colonia & others, 2012; Ruchat & others, 2012; Streuling & others, 2011). A recent study found that exercise during pregnancy improved mothers' perception of their health (Barakat & others, 2011). In another recent study, following 12 weeks of twice-weekly yoga or massage therapy, both therapy groups had a greater decrease in depression, anxiety, and back and leg pain than a control group (Field & others, 2012).

Birth and the Postpartum Period

The long wait for the moment of birth is over, and the infant is about to appear. What happens during childbirth, and what can be done to make the experience a positive one?

Nature writes the basic script for how birth occurs, but parents make important choices about the conditions surrounding birth. We look first at the sequence of physical steps through which a child is born.

The Birth Process

The birth process occurs in three stages. It may take place in different contexts and in most cases involves one or more attendants.

Stages of Birth

The first stage of the birth process is the longest. Uterine contractions are 15 to 20 minutes apart at the beginning and last up to a minute each. These contractions cause the woman's cervix to stretch and open. As the first stage progresses, the contractions come closer together, occurring every two to five minutes. Their intensity increases. By the end of the first stage, contractions dilate the cervix to an opening of about 10 centimeters (4 inches) so that the baby can move from the uterus to the birth canal. For a woman having her first child, the first stage lasts an average of 6 to 12 hours; for subsequent children, this stage typically is much shorter.

The second birth stage begins when the baby's head starts to move through the cervix and the birth canal. It terminates when the baby completely emerges from the mother's body. With each contraction, the mother bears down hard to push the baby out of her body. By the time the baby's head is out of the mother's body, the contractions come almost every minute and last for about a minute. This stage typically lasts approximately 45 minutes to an hour.

Afterbirth is the third stage, during which the placenta, umbilical cord, and other membranes are detached and expelled. This final stage is the shortest of the three birth stages, lasting only minutes.

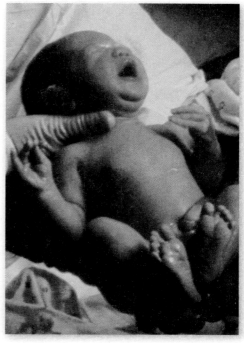

After the long journey of prenatal development, birth takes place. During birth the baby is on a threshold between two worlds. *What are the characteristics of the three stages of birth?*

Childbirth Setting and Attendants

A doula assisting a birth. *What types of support do doulas provide?*

In the United States, 99 percent of births take place in hospitals, a figure that has remained constant for several decades (Martin & others, 2005). Who helps a mother during birth varies across cultures. In U.S. hospitals, it has become the norm for fathers or birth coaches to be with the mother throughout labor and delivery. In the East African Nigoni culture, by contrast, men are completely excluded from the childbirth process. When a woman is ready to give birth, female relatives move into the woman's hut and the husband leaves, taking his belongings (clothes, tools, weapons, and so on) with him. He is not permitted to return until after the baby is born. In some cultures, childbirth is an open, community affair. For example, in the Pukapukan culture in the Pacific Islands, women give birth in a shelter that is open to villagers, who may observe the birth.

Midwives *Midwifery* is practiced in most countries throughout the world (Kitzinger, 2011). In Holland, more than 40 percent of babies are delivered by *midwives* rather than by doctors. However, in 2003, 91 percent of U.S. births were attended by physicians, and only 8 percent of women who delivered a baby were attended by a midwife (Martin & others, 2005). Nevertheless, the 8 percent figure for 2003 represents a substantial increase from less than 1 percent in 1975 (Martin & others, 2005). Ninety-five percent of the midwives who delivered babies in the United States in 2003 were certified nurse-midwives.

Doulas In some countries, a doula attends a childbearing woman. *Doula* is a Greek word that means "a woman who helps." A *doula* is a caregiver who provides continuous physical, emotional, and educational support for the mother before, during, and after childbirth (Hansard, 2012). Doulas remain with the parents throughout labor, assessing and responding to their needs. Researchers have found positive effects when a doula is present at the birth of a child (Akhavan & Lundgren, 2012).

In the United States, most doulas work as independent providers hired by the expectant parents. Doulas typically function as part of a "birthing team," serving as an adjunct to the midwife or the hospital's obstetric staff.

Methods of Childbirth

U.S. hospitals often allow the mother and her obstetrician a range of options regarding their method of delivery. Key choices involve the use of medication, whether to use any of a number of nonmedicated techniques to reduce pain, and when to have a cesarean delivery.

Medication Three basic kinds of drugs that are used for labor are analgesia, anesthesia, and oxytocin/Pitocin.

Analgesia is used to relieve pain. Analgesics include tranquilizers, barbiturates, and narcotics such as Demerol.

Anesthesia is used in late first-stage labor and during delivery to block sensation in an area of the body or to block consciousness. There is a trend toward not using general anesthesia, which blocks consciousness, in normal births because general anesthesia can be transmitted through the placenta to the fetus (Pennell & others, 2011). An *epidural block* is regional anesthesia that numbs the woman's body from the waist down.

Oxytocin is a synthetic hormone that is used to stimulate contractions; Pitocin is the most widely used oxytocin. The benefits and risks of oxytocin as a part of childbirth continue to be debated (Buchanan & others, 2012).

Predicting how a drug will affect an individual woman and her fetus is difficult (Davidson & others, 2012). A particular drug might have only a minimal effect on one fetus yet have a much stronger effect on another. The drug's dosage is also a factor. Stronger doses of tranquilizers and narcotics given to decrease the mother's pain potentially have a more negative effect on the fetus than do mild doses. It is important for the mother to assess her level of pain and have a voice in deciding whether she should receive medication.

Natural and Prepared Childbirth For a brief time not long ago, the idea of avoiding all medication during childbirth gained favor in the United States. Instead, many women chose to reduce the pain of childbirth through techniques known as natural childbirth and prepared childbirth. Today, at least some medication is used in the typical childbirth, but elements of natural childbirth and prepared childbirth remain popular (Oates & Abraham, 2010).

Natural childbirth is a childbirth method in which no drugs are given to relieve pain or assist in the birth process. The mother and her partner are taught to use breathing methods and relaxation techniques during delivery. French obstetrician Ferdinand Lamaze developed a method similar to natural childbirth that is known as **prepared childbirth,** or the Lamaze method. It includes a special breathing technique to control pushing in the final stages of labor, as well as more detailed education about anatomy and physiology. The Lamaze method has become very popular in the United States. The pregnant woman's partner usually serves as a coach; the partner attends childbirth classes with her and helps her with her breathing and relaxation during delivery. In sum, proponents of current prepared childbirth methods conclude that when information and support are provided, women *know* how to give birth.

Other Nonmedicated Techniques to Reduce Pain The effort to reduce stress and control pain during labor has recently led to an increase in

natural childbirth A childbirth method in which no drugs are given to relieve pain or assist in the birth process. The mother and her partner are taught to use breathing methods and relaxation techniques during delivery.

prepared childbirth Developed by French obstetrician Ferdinand Lamaze, this childbirth strategy is similar to natural childbirth but includes a special breathing technique to control pushing in the final stages of labor and more detailed anatomy and physiology instruction.

the use of some older and some newer nonmedicated techniques (Kalder & others, 2011; Simpkin & Bolding, 2004). These include waterbirth, massage, and acupuncture.

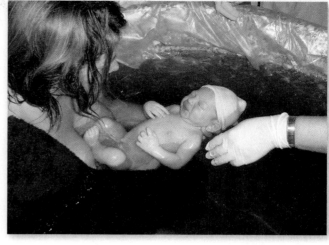

Waterbirth involves giving birth in a tub of warm water. Some women go through labor in the water and get out for delivery; others remain in the water for delivery. The rationale for waterbirth is that the baby has been in an amniotic sac for many months and that delivery in a similar environment is likely to be less stressful for the baby and the mother (Meyer, Weible, & Woeber, 2010). Reviews of research have indicated mixed results for waterbirths (Cluett & Burns, 2009), although a recent study did find that waterbirth was linked with a shorter second stage of labor (Cortes, Basra, & Kelleher, 2011). Waterbirth has been practiced more often in European countries such as Switzerland and Sweden in recent decades than in the United States, but is increasingly being included in U.S. birth plans.

What is the rationale for the waterbirth technique?

Massage is increasingly used during pregnancy, labor, and delivery. Two recent research reviews concluded that massage therapy reduced pain during labor (Jones & others, 2012; Smith & others, 2012). *Acupuncture*, the insertion of very fine needles into specific locations in the body, is used as a standard procedure to reduce the pain of childbirth in China, although it only recently has begun to be used for this purpose in the United States (Moleti, 2009). Recent research indicates that acupuncture can have positive effects on labor and delivery (Borup & others, 2009; Citkovitz, Schnyer, & Hoskins, 2011; Smith & others, 2011, 2012).

Cesarean Delivery

Normally, the baby's head comes through the vagina first. But if the baby is in a *breech position*, its buttocks are the first part to emerge from the vagina. In 1 of every 25 deliveries, the baby's head is still in the uterus when the rest of the body is out. Because breech births can cause respiratory problems, if the baby is in a breech position a surgical procedure known as a cesarean delivery is usually performed. In a *cesarean delivery* (or cesarean section), the baby is removed from the uterus through an incision made in the mother's abdomen. The benefits and risks of cesarean sections continue to be debated (Minguez-Milio & others, 2011). Some critics argue that far too many babies are delivered by cesarean section in the United States and around the world (Gibbons & others, 2012). In 2009, 34 percent of U.S. babies were cesarean deliveries (U.S. Center for Health Statistics, 2011).

How Would You...?

As a health-care provider, how would you advise a woman in her first trimester about the options available for her baby's birth and for her own comfort during the process?

The Transition from Fetus to Newborn

Much of our discussion of birth so far has focused on the mother. However, birth also involves considerable stress for the baby. If the delivery takes too long, the baby can develop anoxia, a condition in which the fetus or newborn has an insufficient supply of oxygen. Anoxia can cause brain damage (Aylott, 2006).

The baby has considerable capacity to withstand the stress of birth. Large quantities of adrenaline and noradrenaline, hormones that protect the fetus in the event of oxygen deficiency, are secreted in the newborn's body during the birth process (Van Beveren, 2012).

Careers in life-span development

Linda Pugh, Perinatal Nurse

Perinatal nurses work with childbearing women to support health and growth during the childbearing experience. Linda Pugh, Ph.D., R.N.C., is a perinatal nurse on the faculty at The Johns Hopkins University School of Nursing. She is certified as an inpatient obstetric nurse and specializes in the care of women during labor and delivery. She teaches undergraduate and graduate students, educates professional nurses, and conducts research. In addition, Pugh consults with hospitals and organizations about women's health issues and many of the topics we discuss in this chapter.

Her research interests include nursing interventions with low-income breast feeding women, discovering ways to prevent and ameliorate fatigue during childbearing, and using breathing exercises during labor.

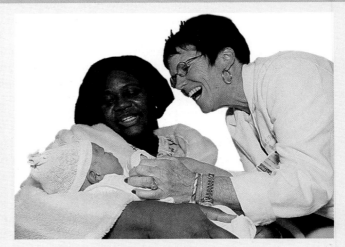

Linda Pugh (*right*) with a mother and her newborn.

Immediately after birth, the umbilical cord is cut and the baby is on its own. Before birth, oxygen came from the mother via the umbilical cord, but now the baby can breathe independently.

Almost immediately after birth, a newborn is taken to be weighed, cleaned up, and tested for signs of developmental problems that might require urgent attention (Therrell & others, 2010). The **Apgar Scale** is widely used to assess the health of newborns at one and five minutes after birth. The Apgar Scale evaluates infants' heart rate, respiratory effort, muscle tone, body color, and reflex irritability. An obstetrician or nurse does the evaluation and gives the newborn a score, or reading, of 0, 1, or 2 on each of these five health signs. A total score of 7 to 10 indicates that the newborn's condition is good. A score of 5 indicates that there may be developmental difficulties. A score of 3 or below signals an emergency and warns that the baby might not survive. The Apgar Scale is especially good at assessing the newborn's ability to respond to the stress of delivery and its new environment (Shehata & others, 2011). It also identifies high-risk infants who need resuscitation.

Nurses often play important roles in the birth of a baby. To read about the work of a nurse who specializes in the care of women during labor and delivery, see *Careers in Life-Span Development*.

Low Birth Weight and Preterm Infants

Three related conditions pose threats to many newborns: low birth weight, preterm birth, and being small for date. *Low birth weight* infants weigh less than 5 pounds at birth. *Very low birth weight* newborns weigh under 3 pounds, and *extremely low birth weight* newborns weigh under 2 pounds. Preterm infants are born three weeks or more before the pregnancy has reached its full term—in other words, 35 or fewer weeks after conception. Small for date infants (also called *small for gestational age infants*) have a birth weight that is below normal when the length of the pregnancy is considered. They weigh less than 90 percent of all babies of the same gestational age. Small for date infants may be preterm or full term. One study found that small for date infants have a 400 percent greater risk of death (Regev & others, 2003).

Apgar Scale A widely used assessment of the newborn's health at 1 and 5 minutes after birth.

In 2009, 12.2 percent of U.S. infants were born preterm—a 35 percent increase since the 1980s and a decrease of .6 percent since 2006 (National Center for Health Statistics, 2011). The increase in preterm birth is likely due to such factors as the increasing number of births to women 35 years and older, increasing rates of multiple births, increased management of maternal and fetal conditions (for example, inducing labor preterm if medical technology indicates it will increase the likelihood of survival), increased substance abuse (tobacco, alcohol), and increased stress (Goldenberg & Culhane, 2007). Ethnic variations characterize preterm birth (Lhila & Long, 2011). For example, in 2009, the likelihood of being born preterm was 12.2 percent for all U.S. infants and 10.9 percent for non-Latino White infants, but the rate was 17.5 percent for African American infants (National Center for Health Statistics, 2011).

Incidence and Causes of Low Birth Weight

Most, but not all, preterm babies are also low birth weight babies. The incidence of low birth weight varies considerably from one country to another. In some developing countries, such as Bangladesh, where poverty is rampant and the health and nutrition of mothers are poor, the percentage of low birth weight babies reaches as high as 50 percent. In the United States, there has been an increase in low birth weight infants in the last two decades, and the U.S. low birth weight rate of 8.1 percent in 2011 is considerably higher than that of many other developed countries (Centers for Disease Control and Prevention, 2012; Hoyert, 2012). For example, only 4 percent of the infants born in Sweden, Finland, the Netherlands, and Norway are low birth weight, and only 5 percent of those born in New Zealand, Australia, France, and Japan are low birth weight.

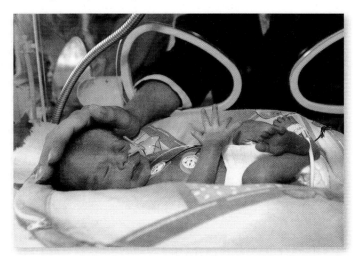

A "kilogram kid," weighing less than 2.3 pounds at birth. *What are some long-term outcomes of weighing so little at birth?*

Recently, there has been considerable interest in the role that progestin might play in reducing preterm births (Lucovnik & others, 2011). Recent research indicates that progestin is most effective when it is given to women with a history of previous spontaneous birth at less than 37 months (da Fonseca & others, 2009), to women who have a short cervical length of 15 mm or less (da Fonseca & others, 2009), and to women with a singleton rather than multiple offspring (Lucovnik & others, 2011).

Consequences of Low Birth Weight

Although most preterm and low birth weight infants are healthy, as a group they have more health and developmental problems than do normal birth weight infants (Minde & Zelkowitz, 2008). The number and severity of these problems increase when infants are born very early and as their birth weight decreases (Baron & others, 2011). Survival rates for infants who are born very early and very small have risen, but with this improved survival rate have come increased rates of severe brain damage (Faroogi & others, 2011).

For preterm birth, the terms *extremely preterm* and *very preterm* are increasingly used (Lowdermilk, Perry, & Cashion, 2011). *Extremely preterm infants* are those born less than 28 weeks preterm, and *very preterm infants* are those born at less than 33 weeks of gestational age.

Low birth weight children are more likely than their normal birth weight counterparts to develop a learning disability, attention deficit hyperactivity disorder, or breathing problems such as asthma (Anderson & others, 2011). And a recent study found that low birth weight was associated with childhood autism (Lampl

a substantial percentage of women reported loss of sleep during pregnancy and in the postpartum period (National Sleep Foundation, 2007). The loss of sleep can contribute to stress, marital conflict, and impaired decision making (Meerlo, Sgoifo, & Suchecki, 2008).

After delivery, the mother's body undergoes sudden and dramatic changes in hormone production. When the placenta is delivered, estrogen and progesterone levels drop steeply and remain low until the ovaries start producing hormones again.

Involution is the process by which the uterus returns to its prepregnant size five or six weeks after birth. Immediately following birth, the uterus weighs 2 to 3 pounds. By the end of five or six weeks, the uterus weighs 2 to 3½ ounces. Nursing the baby helps contract the uterus at a more rapid rate.

Emotional and Psychological Adjustments

Emotional fluctuations are common for mothers in the postpartum period. For some women, emotional fluctuations decrease within several weeks after the delivery, but other women experience more long-lasting emotional swings.

As shown in Figure 2.11, about 70 percent of new mothers in the United States have what are called the postpartum blues. About two to three days after birth, they begin to feel depressed, anxious, and upset. These feelings may come and go for several months after the birth, often peaking about three to five days after birth. Even without treatment, these feelings usually go away after one or two weeks.

However, some women develop postpartum depression, which involves a major depressive episode that typically occurs about four weeks after delivery. In other words, women with postpartum depression have such strong feelings of sadness, anxiety, or despair that for at least a two-week period they have trouble coping with their daily tasks. Without treatment, postpartum depression may become worse and last for many months (Nolen-Hoeksema, 2011). And many women with postpartum depression don't seek help. For example, one study found that 15 percent of the women reported postpartum depression symptoms but less than half sought help (McGarry & others, 2009). Estimates indicate that 10 to 14 percent of new mothers experience postpartum depression.

Several antidepressant drugs are effective in treating postpartum depression and appear to be safe for breast feeding women (Logsdon, Wisner, & Hanusa, 2009). Psychotherapy, especially cognitive therapy, also is an effective treatment of postpartum depression for many women (Beck, 2006). In addition, engaging in regular exercise may help to relieve postpartum depression (Daley, Macarthur, & Winter, 2007).

Can a mother's postpartum depression affect the way she interacts with her infant? A research review concluded that the interaction difficulties of depressed mothers and their infants occur across cultures and socioeconomic status groups, and encompass less sensitivity of the mothers and less responsiveness on the part of infants (Field, 2010a). Several caregiving activities also are compromised, including feeding, sleep routines, and safety practices.

Postpartum blues
Symptoms appear 2 to 3 days after delivery and usually subside within 1 to 2 weeks.

70%

10%

20%

Postpartum depression
Symptoms linger for weeks or months and interfere with daily functioning.

No symptoms

Figure 2.11 Postpartum Blues and Postpartum Depression Among U.S. Women
Some health professionals refer to the postpartum period as the "fourth trimester." Though the time span of the postpartum period does not necessarily cover three months, the term "fourth trimester" suggests continuity and emphasizes the importance of the first several months after birth for the mother.

The postpartum period is a time of considerable adjustment and adaptation for both the mother and the father. Fathers can provide an important support system for mothers, especially in helping mothers care for young infants. *What kinds of tasks might the father of a newborn do to support the mother?*

Fathers also undergo considerable adjustment in the postpartum period, even when they work away from home all day. Many fathers feel that the baby comes first and gets all of the mother's attention; some feel that they have been replaced by the baby.

The father's support and caring can play a role in whether the mother develops postpartum depression or not (Persson & others, 2011). One study revealed that higher support by fathers was related to lower incidence of postpartum depression in women (Smith & Howard, 2008).

Summary

The Evolutionary Perspective

- Darwin proposed that natural selection fuels evolution. In evolutionary theory, adaptive behavior is behavior that promotes the organism's survival in a natural habitat.

- Evolutionary psychology holds that adaptation, reproduction, and "survival of the fittest" are important in shaping behavior. Evolutionary developmental psychology emphasizes that humans need an extended "juvenile" period to develop a large brain and learn the complexity of social communities.

Genetic Foundations of Development

- Except in the sperm and egg, the nucleus of each human cell contains 46 chromosomes, which are composed of DNA. Short segments of DNA constitute genes, the units of hereditary information that direct cells to reproduce and manufacture proteins. Genes act collaboratively, not independently.

- Genes are passed on to new cells when chromosomes are duplicated during the processes of mitosis and meiosis.

- Genetic principles include those involving dominant-recessive genes, sex-linked genes, and polygenic inheritance.

- Chromosome abnormalities can produce Down syndrome and other problems; gene-linked disorders, such as PKU, involve defective genes.

The Interaction of Heredity and Environment: The Nature-Nurture Debate

- Behavior geneticists use twin studies and adoption studies to determine the strength of heredity's influence on development.

- In Scarr's heredity-environment correlation view, heredity directs the types of environments that children experience. Scarr identified three types of genotype-environment interactions: passive, evocative, and active (niche-picking).

- The epigenetic view emphasizes that development is the result of an ongoing, bidirectional interchange between heredity and environment. Recently, interest has developed in how gene interaction influences development.

- The interaction of heredity and environment is complex, but we can create a unique developmental path by changing our environment.

Prenatal Development

- Prenatal development can be divided into three periods: germinal, embryonic, and fetal. The growth of the brain during prenatal development is remarkable.

- A number of prenatal tests, including ultrasound sonography, chorionic villus sampling, amniocentesis, maternal blood screening, and fetal MRI, can reveal whether a fetus is developing normally. Noninvasive prenatal diagnosis is increasingly being used.

- Approximately 10 to 15 percent of U.S. couples have infertility problems. Assisted reproduction techniques, such as in vitro fertilization, are increasingly being used by infertile couples.

- Some prescription drugs and nonprescription drugs can harm the unborn child. In particular, the psychoactive drugs caffeine, alcohol, nicotine, cocaine, methamphetamine, marijuana, and heroin can endanger developing offspring. Other potential sources of harmful effects on the fetus include incompatibility of the mother's and the father's blood types, environmental hazards, maternal diseases, maternal diet and nutrition, age, emotional states and stress, and paternal factors.

- Prenatal care usually involves medical care services with a defined schedule of visits and often encompasses educational, social, and nutritional services as well. Inadequate prenatal care may increase the risk of infant mortality and result in low birth weight.

Birth and the Postpartum Period

- Childbirth occurs in three stages. Childbirth strategies involve the childbirth setting and attendants. In many countries, a midwife attends a childbearing woman. In some countries, a doula helps with the birth. Methods of delivery include medicated, natural and prepared, and cesarean.

- Being born involves considerable stress for the baby, but the baby is well prepared and adapted to handle the stress. Low birth weight, preterm, and small for date infants are at risk for developmental problems, although most of these infants are normal and healthy. Kangaroo care and massage therapy have been shown to produce benefits for preterm infants.

- Early bonding has not been found to be critical in the development of a competent infant, but close contact during the first few days after birth may reduce the mother's anxiety and lead to better interaction later.

- The postpartum period lasts for about six weeks after childbirth or until the body has returned to a nearly prepregnant state; postpartum depression is a serious condition that may become worse if not treated.

Key Terms

evolutionary psychology 35
chromosomes 37
DNA 37
genes 37
mitosis 38
meiosis 38

genotype 39
phenotype 39
Down syndrome 41
behavior genetics 44
twin study 44
adoption study 45
epigenetic view 46

gene x environment (g x e) interaction 47
germinal period 48
embryonic period 48
organogenesis 49
fetal period 49
neurons 51

teratogen 54
fetal alcohol spectrum disorders (FASD) 54
natural childbirth 62
prepared childbirth 62
Apgar Scale 64
postpartum period 67

Physical and Cognitive Development in Infancy

3

Stories of Life-Span Development: Newborn Babies in Ghana and Nigeria

Latonya is a newborn baby in Ghana. During her first days of life she has been kept apart from her mother and bottle fed. Manufacturers of infant formula provide the hospital where she was born with free or subsidized milk powder. Latonya's mother has been persuaded to bottle feed rather than breast feed her. When her mother bottle feeds Latonya, she overdilutes the milk formula with unclean water. Latonya's feeding bottles have not been sterilized. Latonya becomes very sick. She dies before her first birthday.

Ramona was born in Nigeria in a "baby-friendly" program. In this program, babies are not separated from their mothers when they are born, and the mothers are encouraged to breast feed them. The mothers are told of the perils that bottle feeding can cause because of unsafe water and unsterilized bottles. They also are informed about the advantages of breast milk, which include its nutritious and hygienic qualities, its ability to immunize babies against common illnesses, and its role in reducing the mother's risk of breast and ovarian cancer. Ramona's mother is breast feeding her. At 1 year of age, Ramona is very healthy.

For many years, maternity units in hospitals favored bottle feeding and did not give mothers adequate information about the benefits of breast feeding. In recent years, the World Health Organization and UNICEF have tried to reverse the trend toward bottle feeding of infants in many impoverished countries. They instituted the "baby-friendly" program in many countries. They also persuaded the International Association of Infant Formula Manufacturers to stop marketing their baby formulas to hospitals in countries where governments support the baby-friendly initiatives (Grant, 1993). For the hospitals themselves, costs actually were reduced as infant formula, feeding bottles, and separate nurseries became

71

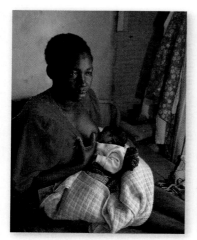

unnecessary. For example, baby-friendly Jose Fabella Memorial Hospital in the Philippines reported saving 8 percent of its annual budget. Still, there are many places in the world where the baby-friendly initiatives have not been implemented (UNICEF, 2004).

The advantages of breast feeding in impoverished countries are substantial (UNICEF, 2013). However,

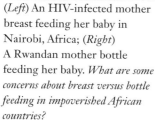

(*Left*) An HIV-infected mother breast feeding her baby in Nairobi, Africa; (*Right*) A Rwandan mother bottle feeding her baby. *What are some concerns about breast versus bottle feeding in impoverished African countries?*

these advantages must be balanced against the risk of passing HIV to the baby through breast milk if the mother has the virus; the majority of mothers with HIV don't know that they are infected. In some areas of Africa more than 30 percent of mothers have the virus.

In the first two years of life, an infant's body and brain undergo remarkable growth and development. In this chapter we explore how this takes place: through physical growth, motor development, sensory and perceptual development, cognitive development, and language development. ■

Physical Growth and Development in Infancy

At birth, an infant has few of the physical abilities we associate with being human. Its head, which is huge relative to the rest of the body, flops around uncontrollably. Apart from some basic reflexes and the ability to cry, the newborn is unable to perform many actions. Over the next 12 months, however, the infant becomes capable of sitting, standing, stooping, climbing, and usually walking. During the second year, while growth slows, rapid increases in such activities as running and climbing take place. Let's now examine in greater detail the sequence of physical development in infancy.

Patterns of Growth

During prenatal development and early infancy, the head occupies an extraordinary proportion of the total body (see Figure 3.1). The **cephalocaudal pattern** is the sequence in which the earliest growth always occurs at the top—the head—with physical growth and differentiation of features gradually working their way down from top to bottom (shoulders, middle trunk, and so on). This same pattern occurs in the head area, as the top parts of the head—the eyes and brain—grow faster than the lower parts, such as the jaw.

Sensory and motor development generally proceed according to the cephalocaudal pattern. For example, infants see objects before they can control their torso, and they can use their hands long before they can crawl or walk. However, development does not follow a rigid blueprint. One study found that infants reached for toys with their feet four weeks earlier, on average, than they reached for them with their hands (Galloway & Thelen, 2004).

Growth also follows the **proximodistal pattern,** a sequence in which growth starts at the center of the body and moves toward the

cephalocaudal pattern The sequence in which the earliest growth always occurs at the top—the head—with physical growth in size, weight, and feature differentiation gradually working from top to bottom.

proximodistal pattern The sequence in which growth starts at the center of the body and moves toward the extremities.

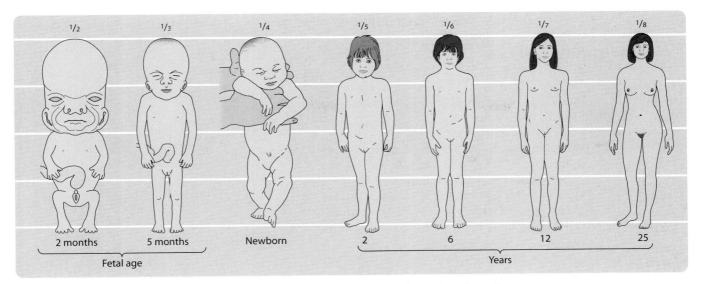

Figure 3.1 Changes in Proportions of the Human Body During Growth
As individuals develop from infancy through adulthood, one of the most noticeable physical changes is that the head becomes smaller in relation to the rest of the body. The fractions listed refer to head size as a proportion of total body length at different ages.

extremities. For example, infants control the muscles of their trunk and arms before they control their hands, and they use their whole hands before they can control several fingers.

Height and Weight

The average North American newborn is 20 inches long and weighs 7½ pounds. Ninety-five percent of full-term newborns are 18 to 22 inches long and weigh between 5½ and 10 pounds.

In the first several days of life, most newborns lose 5 to 7 percent of their body weight before they adjust to feeding by sucking, swallowing, and digesting. They then grow rapidly, gaining an average of 5 to 6 ounces per week during the first month. They double their birth weight by the age of 4 months and nearly triple it by their first birthday. Infants grow about 3/4 inch per month during the first year, increasing their birth length by about 40 percent by their first birthday.

Growth slows considerably in the second year of life (Burns & others, 2013). By 2 years of age, children weigh approximately 26 to 32 pounds, having gained a quarter to half a pound per month during the second year; now they have reached about one-fifth of their adult weight. At 2 years of age, the average child is 32 to 35 inches tall, nearly half of his or her eventual adult height.

The Brain

At birth, the infant that began as a single cell has a brain that contains tens of billions of nerve cells, or neurons. Extensive brain development continues after birth, through infancy, and later (Diamond, 2013; Nelson, 2012, 2013). Because the brain is still developing so rapidly in infancy, the infant's head should be protected from falls or other injuries and the baby should never be shaken. *Shaken baby syndrome*, which includes brain swelling and hemorrhaging, affects hundreds of babies in the United States each year (Swaiman & others, 2012). A recent analysis found that fathers were most often the perpetrators of shaken baby syndrome, followed by child care providers and a boyfriend of the victim's mother (National Center on Shaken Baby Syndrome, 2012).

lateralization Specialization of function in one hemisphere of the cerebral cortex or the other.

The Brain's Development

At birth, the brain weighs about 25 percent of its adult weight. By the second birthday, it is about 75 percent of its adult weight. However, the brain's areas do not mature uniformly.

Mapping the Brain Scientists analyze and categorize areas of the brain in numerous ways (Geng & others, 2012; South & Isaacs, 2013). Of greatest interest is the portion farthest from the spinal cord, known as the *forebrain*, which includes the cerebral cortex and several structures beneath it. The *cerebral cortex* covers the forebrain like a wrinkled cap. It has two halves, or hemispheres. Based on ridges and valleys in the cortex, scientists distinguish four main areas, called lobes, in each hemisphere: the *frontal lobes*, the *occipital lobes*, the *temporal lobes*, and the *parietal lobes* (see Figure 3.2).

Although these areas are found in the cerebral cortex of each hemisphere, the two hemispheres are not identical in anatomy or function. **Lateralization** is the specialization of function in one hemisphere or the other. Researchers continue to explore the degree to which each is involved in various aspects of thinking, feeling, and behavior (Griffiths & others, 2012). At birth, the hemispheres of the cerebral cortex have already started to specialize: Newborns show greater electrical brain activity in the left hemisphere than in the right hemisphere when listening to speech sounds (Hahn, 1987).

The most extensive research on brain lateralization has focused on language. Speech and grammar are localized in the left hemisphere in most people, but some aspects of language, such as appropriate language use in different contexts and the use of metaphor and humor, involve the right hemisphere (Marinkovic & others, 2011; McGettigan & others, 2012). Thus, language is not controlled exclusively by the brain's left hemisphere. Further, most neuroscientists agree that complex functions—such as reading, performing music, and creating art—are the outcome of communication between the two sides of the brain (Ibrahim & Eviatar, 2012).

How do the areas of the brain in the newborn and the infant differ from those of an adult, and why do the differences matter? Important differences have been documented at both the cellular and the structural levels.

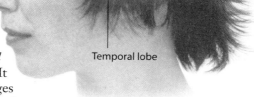

Figure 3.2 The Brain's Four Lobes

Shown here are the locations of the brain's four lobes: frontal, occipital, temporal, and parietal.

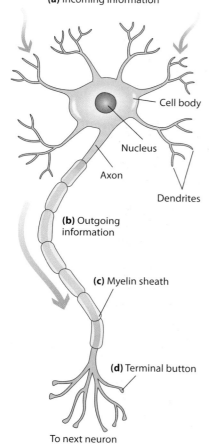

(a) Incoming information

Cell body

Nucleus

Axon

Dendrites

(b) Outgoing information

(c) Myelin sheath

(d) Terminal button

To next neuron

Figure 3.3 The Neuron

(*a*) The dendrites of the cell body receive information from other neurons, muscles, or glands through the axon. (*b*) Axons transmit information away from the cell body. (*c*) A myelin sheath covers most axons and speeds information transmission. (*d*) As the axon ends, it branches out into terminal buttons.

Changes in Neurons Within the brain, neurons send electrical and chemical signals, communicating with each other. As we indicated in Chapter 2, a *neuron* is a nerve cell that handles information processing (see Figure 3.3). Extending from the neuron's cell body are two types of fibers, known as *axons* and *dendrites*. Generally, the axon carries signals away from the cell body and dendrites carry signals toward it. A *myelin sheath*, which is a layer of fat cells, encases many axons (see Figure 3.3). The myelin sheath provides insulation and helps electrical signals travel faster down the axon.

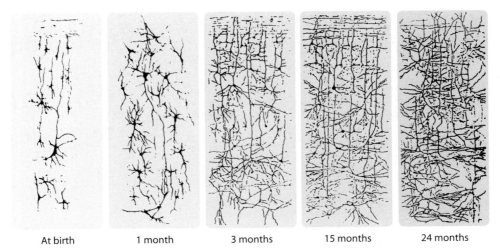

| At birth | 1 month | 3 months | 15 months | 24 months |

Figure 3.4 Dendritic Spreading
Note the increase in connectedness between neurons over the course of the first two years of
life. Reprinted by permission of the publisher from *The Postnatal Development of the Human Cerebral Cortex, Vols. I–VIII*
by J. LeRoy Conel, Cambridge, MA: Harvard University Press. Copyright © 1939, 1941, 1947, 1951, 1955, 1959, 1963,
1967 by the President and Fellows of Harvard College.

Myelination also is involved in providing energy to neurons and in facilitating communication (Fancy & others, 2012; Harris & Atwell, 2012). At the end of the axon are terminal buttons, which release chemicals called *neurotransmitters* into *synapses*, tiny gaps between neurons. Chemical interactions in synapses connect axons and dendrites, allowing information to pass from one neuron to another (Emes & Grant, 2013).

Neurons change in two very significant ways during the first years of life. First, *myelination*, the process of encasing axons with fat cells, begins prenatally and continues throughout childhood, even into adolescence (Lebel & others, 2012). Second, connectivity among neurons increases, creating new neural pathways, as Figure 3.4 illustrates. New dendrites grow, connections among dendrites increase, and synaptic connections between axons and dendrites proliferate. Whereas myelination speeds up neural transmissions, the expansion of dendritic connections facilitates the spreading of neural pathways in infant development.

Researchers have discovered an intriguing aspect of synaptic connections: Nearly twice as many of these connections are made as will ever be used (Huttenlocher & Dabholkar, 1997). The connections that are used become stronger and survive, while the unused ones are replaced by other pathways or disappear. In the language of neuroscience, these connections will be "pruned" (Campbell & others, 2012).

Changes in Regions of the Brain Figure 3.5 vividly illustrates the dramatic growth and later pruning of synapses in the visual, auditory, and prefrontal cortex (Huttenlocher & Dabholkar, 1997). Notice that "blooming and pruning" vary considerably by brain region. For example, the peak of synaptic overproduction in the visual cortex occurs at about the fourth postnatal month, followed by a gradual retraction until the middle to end of the preschool years (Huttenlocher & Dabholkar, 1997). In areas of the brain involved in hearing and language, a similar, though somewhat later, course is detected. However, in the *prefrontal cortex*, the area of the brain where higher-level thinking and self-regulation occur, the peak of overproduction takes place at about 1 year of age; it is not until middle to late adolescence that the adult density of synapses is achieved (Blakemore, 2012). Both heredity and environment are thought to influence the timing and course of synaptic overproduction and subsequent retraction.

Meanwhile, the pace of myelination also varies in different areas of the brain (Gogtay & Thompson, 2010). Myelination for visual pathways occurs rapidly after

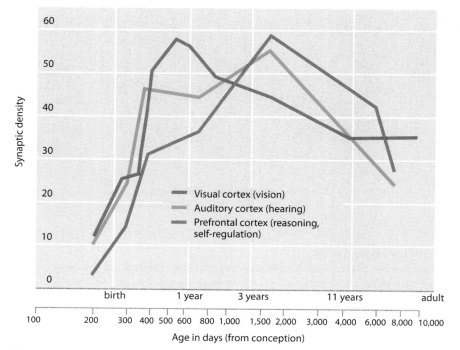

Figure 3.5 Synaptic Density in the Human Brain from Infancy to Adulthood
The graph shows the dramatic increase and then pruning in synaptic density for three regions of the brain: visual cortex, auditory cortex, and prefrontal cortex. Synaptic density is believed to be an important indication of the extent of connectivity between neurons.

birth and is completed in the first six months. Auditory myelination is not completed until 4 or 5 years of age.

Early Experience and the Brain

What determines how these changes in the brain occur? The infant's brain is literally waiting for experiences to determine how connections are made. Before birth, it appears that genes mainly direct how the brain establishes basic wiring patterns; after birth, environmental experiences guide the brain's development. The inflowing stream of sights, sounds, smells, touches, language, and eye contact help shape neural connections (Nelson, 2012, 2013). It may not surprise us, then, that depressed brain activity has been found in children who grow up in a deprived environment (Fox, Levitt, & Nelson, 2010; McLaughlin & others, 2011). Infants whose caregivers expose them to a variety of stimuli—talking, touching, playing—are most likely to develop to their full potential.

The profusion of neural connections described earlier provides the growing brain with flexibility and resilience. As an extreme example, consider 16-year-old Michael Rehbein. When Michael was 4½, he began to experience uncontrollable seizures—as many as 400 a day. Doctors said that the only solution was to remove the left hemisphere of his brain, where the seizures were occurring. Michael had his first major surgery at age 7 and another at age 10. Although recovery was slow, his right hemisphere began to reorganize and eventually took over functions, such as speech, that normally occur in the brain's left hemisphere (see Figure 3.6). Individuals like Michael are living proof of the growing brain's remarkable ability to adapt and recover from a loss of brain tissue.

The Neuroconstructivist View

Not long ago, scientists thought that our genes determined how our brains were "wired" and that the cells in the brain responsible for processing information just maturationally unfolded with little or no input from environmental

(a)

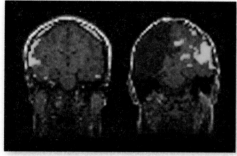

(b)

Figure 3.6 Plasticity in the Brain's Hemispheres
(*a*) Michael Rehbein at 14 years of age. (*b*) Brain scans of Michael Rehbein. Michael's right hemisphere has reorganized to take over the language functions normally carried out by corresponding areas in the left hemisphere of an intact brain. However, the right hemisphere is not as efficient as the left, and more areas of the brain are recruited to process speech.

experiences. Whatever brain your heredity dealt you, you were essentially stuck with. This view, however, turned out to be wrong. Instead, the brain has plasticity and its development depends on context (Diamond, 2013; Nelson, 2012, 2013; Westermann, Thomas, & Karmiloff-Smith, 2011; Peltzer-Karph, 2012).

The infant's brain depends on experiences to determine how connections are made (Johnson & de Haan, 2011). Before birth, it appears that genes mainly direct basic wiring patterns. Neurons grow and travel to distant places awaiting further instructions (Nelson, 2012, 2013). After birth, the inflowing stream of sights, sounds, smells, touches, language, and eye contact help shape the brain's neural connections.

In the increasingly popular **neuroconstructivist view,** (a) biological processes (genes, for example) and environmental experiences (enriched or impoverished, for example) influence the brain's development; (b) the brain has plasticity and is context dependent; and (c) development of the brain and the child's cognitive development are closely linked. These factors constrain or advance children's construction of their cognitive skills (Johnson & de Haan, 2011; Westermann, Thomas, & Karmiloff-Smith, 2011). The neuroconstructivist view emphasizes the importance of interactions between experiences and gene expression in the brain's development, much as the epigenetic view proposes (see Chapter 2, "Biological Beginnings").

neuroconstructivist view
Developmental perspective in which biological processes and environmental conditions influence the brain's development; the brain has plasticity and is context dependent; and cognitive development is closely linked with brain development.

Sleep

The typical newborn sleeps 16 to 17 hours a day, but there is considerable individual variation in how much infants sleep. For newborns, the range is from about 10 hours to about 21 hours per day. A recent research review concluded that infants 0 to 2 years of age slept an average of 12.8 hours out of the 24, within a range of 9.7 to 15.9 hours (Galland & others, 2012). A recent study also revealed that by 6 months of age the majority of infants slept through the night, awakening their mothers only once or twice a week (Weinraub & others, 2012).

The most common infant sleep-related problem reported by parents is nighttime waking (The Hospital for Sick Children & others, 2010). Surveys indicate that 20 to 30 percent of infants have difficulty going to sleep at night and have nighttime waking problems (Sadeh, 2008). A recent study found that nighttime wakings at 1 year of age predicted lower sleep efficiency at four years of age (Tikotzky & Shaashua, 2012). Infant nighttime waking problems have consistently been linked to excessive parental involvement in sleep-related interactions with their infant (Sadeh, 2008).

REM Sleep

A much greater amount of time is taken up by *REM (rapid eye movement)* sleep in infancy than at any other point in the life span. Unlike adults, who spend about one-fifth of their night in REM sleep, infants spend about half of their sleep time in REM sleep, and they often begin their sleep cycle with REM sleep

sudden infant death syndrome (SIDS) A condition that occurs when an infant stops breathing, usually during the night, and suddenly dies without an apparent cause.

rather than non-REM sleep. By the time infants reach 3 months of age, the percentage of time they spend in REM sleep decreases to about 40 percent, and REM sleep no longer begins their sleep cycle.

Why do infants spend so much time in REM sleep? Researchers are not certain. The large amount of REM sleep may provide infants with added self-stimulation, since they spend less time awake than do older children. REM sleep also might promote the brain's development in infancy (Graven, 2006).

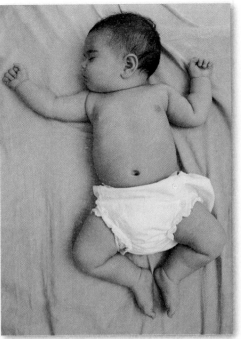

SIDS

Sudden infant death syndrome (SIDS) is a condition that occurs when an infant stops breathing, usually during the night, and dies suddenly without an apparent cause. SIDS remains the highest cause of infant death in the United States, with nearly 3,000 infant deaths annually attributed to SIDS (Montagna & Chokroverty, 2011). Risk of SIDS is highest at 2 to 4 months of age (NICHD, 2012). Since 1992, the American Academy of Pediatrics (AAP) has recommended that infants be placed to sleep on their backs to reduce the risk of SIDS, and since then far fewer infants have

Is this a good sleep position for infants? Why or why not?

How Would You...?

As a health-care provider, how would you advise parents about preventing SIDS?

been placed on their stomachs to sleep (AAP, 2000). Researchers have found that SIDS does indeed decrease when infants sleep on their backs rather than on their stomachs or sides (Yiallourou & others, 2011). Among the reasons given for the high risk of SIDS in infants lying face downward are that it impairs the infant's arousal from sleep and restricts the infant's ability to swallow effectively (Franco & others, 2011).

SIDS also occurs more often in infants with abnormal brain stem functioning involving the neurotransmitter serotonin (Broadbent & others, 2012). Also, heart arrhythmias are estimated to occur in as many as 10 to 15 percent of SIDS cases, and two recent studies revealed that gene mutations are linked to the occurrence of these arrhythmias in SIDS cases (Brion & others, 2012; Van Norstrand & others, 2012). A recent meta-analysis concluded that breast feeding is linked to a lower incidence of SIDS (Hauck & others, 2011). And SIDS is more likely to occur in low birth weight infants, African American and Eskimo infants, infants who are passively exposed to cigarette smoke, when infants and parents share the same bed, when infants don't use a pacifier when they go to sleep, and when they sleep in a bedroom without a fan (Coleman-Phox, Odouli, & Li, 2008; Kitsantas & Gaffney, 2010; Moon & others, 2012; Senter & others, 2010).

Nutrition

From birth to 1 year of age, human infants nearly triple their weight and increase their length by 40 percent. What kind of nourishment do they need to sustain this growth?

Breast Feeding Versus Bottle Feeding

For the first four to six months of life, human milk or an alternative formula is the baby's source of nutrients and energy. For years, debate has focused on whether breast feeding is better for the infant than bottle feeding. The growing consensus is that breast feeding is better for the baby's health (McKinney & Murray, 2013; Vasquez & Berg, 2012). Since the 1970s, breast feeding by U.S. mothers has become widespread. In 2008, more than 75 percent of U.S. mothers breast fed their newborns, and 44 percent breast fed their 6-month-olds (Centers for Disease Control and Prevention, 2012). A recent large-scale study that examined feeding practices in 28 developing countries found that the practices were far from optimal (Arbib & others, 2012). In this study, only 25 percent of infants 5 months of age and younger were breast fed.

What are some of the benefits of breast feeding? During the first two years of life and beyond, benefits include appropriate weight gain and lowered risk of childhood obesity (McKinney & Murray, 2013; Scott, Ng, & Cobiac, 2012); reduced risk of SIDS (Zotter & Pichler, 2012); fewer gastrointestinal infections (Garofalo, 2010); and fewer lower respiratory tract infections (Prameela, 2011). However, in a large-scale review, no evidence for the benefits of breast feeding was found for children's cognitive development and cardiovascular functioning (Agency for Healthcare Research and Quality, 2007). Benefits of breast feeding for the mother include a lower incidence of breast cancer (Akbari & others, 2011) and a reduction in ovarian cancer (Stuebe & Schwartz, 2010).

Human milk or an alternative formula is a baby's source of nutrients for the first four to six months. The growing consensus is that breast feeding is better for the baby's health, although controversy still swirls about the issue of breast feeding versus bottle feeding. *What do research studies indicate are the outcomes of breast feeding for children and mothers?*

Many health professionals have argued that breast feeding facilitates the development of an attachment bond between mother and infant (Wittig & Spatz, 2008). However, a recent research review found that the positive effect of breast feeding on the mother-infant relationship is not supported by research (Jansen, de Weerth, & Riksen-Walraven, 2008). The review concluded that recommending breast feeding should not be based on its role in improving the mother-infant relationship but rather on its positive effects on infant and maternal health.

The American Academy of Pediatrics Section on Breastfeeding (2012) recently reconfirmed its recommendation of exclusive breast feeding in the first six months followed by continued breast feeding as complementary foods are introduced, and further breastfeeding for one year or longer as mutually desired by the mother and infant. Are there circumstances when mothers should not breast feed? Yes. A mother should not breast feed if she (1) is infected with AIDS or any other infectious disease that can be transmitted through her milk, (2) has active tuberculosis, or (3) is taking any drug that may not be safe for the infant (Goga & others, 2012).

Some women cannot breast feed their infants because of physical difficulties; others feel guilty if they terminate breast feeding early. Mothers also may worry that they are depriving their infants of important emotional and psychological benefits if they bottle feed rather than breast feed. Some researchers have found, however, that there are no psychological differences between breast fed and bottle fed infants (Ferguson, Harwood, & Shannon, 1987; Young, 1990).

A further issue in interpreting the benefits of breast feeding was underscored in a large-scale research review (Agency for Healthcare Research and Quality, 2007). While highlighting a number of benefits of breast feeding for children and mothers, the report issued a caution about research on breast feeding: None of the findings imply causality. Breast feeding versus bottle feeding studies are correlational, not experimental, and women who breast feed tend to be wealthier, older, and better educated, and are likely to be more health-conscious than those who bottle feed, which could explain why breast fed children are healthier.

Nutritional Needs

Individual differences among infants in terms of their nutrient reserves, body composition, growth rates, and activity patterns make it difficult to define actual nutrient needs (Byrd-Bredbenner & others, 2013; Schiff, 2013). However,

T. Berry Brazelton, Pediatrician

T. Berry Brazelton is America's best-known pediatrician as a result of his numerous books, television appearances, and newspaper and magazine articles about parenting and children's health. He takes a family-centered approach to child development issues and communicates with parents in easy-to-understand ways.

Dr. Brazelton founded the Child Development Unit at Boston Children's Hospital and created the Brazelton Neonatal Behavioral Assessment Scale, a widely used measure of the newborn's health and well-being. He also has conducted a number of research studies on infants and children and has been president of the Society for Research in Child Development, a leading research organization.

T. Berry Brazelton with a young child.

because parents need guidelines, nutritionists recommend that infants consume approximately 50 calories per day for each pound they weigh—more than twice an adult's requirement per pound.

A national study of more than 3,000 randomly selected 4- to 24-month-olds documented that many U.S. parents are feeding their babies too few fruits and vegetables and too much junk food (Fox & others, 2004). Up to one-third of the babies ate no vegetables and fruit; almost half of the 7- to 8-month-old babies were fed desserts, sweets, or sweetened drinks. By 15 months, French fries were the most common vegetables the babies ate.

Caregivers play very important roles in infants' early development of eating patterns (Lumeng & others, 2012). Caregivers who are not sensitive to developmental changes in infants' nutritional needs, neglectful caregivers, and conditions of poverty can contribute to the development of eating problems in infants (Black & Lozoff, 2008). A recent study found that low maternal sensitivity when infants were 15 and 24 months of age was linked to a higher risk of obesity in adolescence (Anderson & others, 2012).

In sum, adequate early nutrition is an important aspect of healthy development (Golley & others, 2012). To be healthy, children need a nurturant, supportive environment. One individual who has stood out as an advocate of caring for children is T. Berry Brazelton, who is featured in the *Careers in Life-Span Development* profile.

Motor Development

Meeting infants' nutritional needs helps them to develop the strength and coordination required for motor development. How do infants develop their motor skills, and which skills do they develop when?

Dynamic Systems Theory

dynamic systems theory The perspective on motor development that seeks to explain how motor behaviors are assembled for perceiving and acting.

According to **dynamic systems theory**, infants assemble motor skills for perceiving and acting; perception and action are coupled (Thelen & Smith, 2006). In order to develop motor skills, infants must perceive something in the environment that motivates them to act, then use their perceptions to fine-tune their movements. Motor skills thus represent solutions to the infant's goals (Adolph & Berger, 2013).

How is a motor skill developed, according to this theory? When infants are motivated to do something, they might create a new motor behavior. The new behavior is the result of many converging factors: the development of the nervous system, the body's physical properties and its possibilities for movement, the goal the child is motivated to reach, and environmental support for the skill. For example, babies will learn to walk only when their nervous system has matured sufficiently to allow them to control certain leg muscles, their legs have grown enough to support their weight, and they have decided they want to walk.

Mastering a motor skill requires the infant's active efforts to coordinate several components of the skill. Infants explore and select possible solutions to the demands of a new task; they assemble adaptive patterns by modifying their current movement patterns. The first step, for example, occurs when the infant is motivated by a new challenge—such as the desire to cross a room—and initiates this task by taking a few stumbling steps. The infant then "tunes" these movements to make them smoother and more effective. The tuning is achieved through repeated cycles of action and perception of the consequences of that action. According to the dynamic systems view, even universal milestones such as crawling, reaching, and walking are learned through this process of adaptation: Infants modulate their movement patterns to fit a new task by exploring and selecting possible configurations (Adolph & Robinson, 2013).

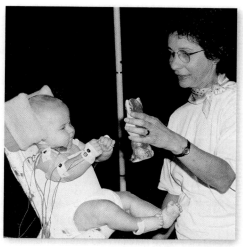

Esther Thelen is shown conducting an experiment to discover how infants learn to control their arms to reach and grasp for objects. A computer device is used to monitor the infant's arm movements and to track muscle patterns. Thelen's research is conducted from a dynamic systems perspective. *What is the nature of this perspective?*

Thus, according to dynamic systems theory, motor development is not a passive process in which genes dictate the unfolding of a sequence of skills. Rather, the infant actively puts together a skill in order to achieve a goal within the constraints set by the infant's body and environment. Nature and nurture, the infant and the environment, are all working together as part of an ever-changing system.

As we examine the course of motor development, we will describe how dynamic systems theory applies to some specific skills. First, though, let's examine how the story of motor development begins with reflexes.

Reflexes

The newborn is not completely helpless. Among other things, the newborn has some basic reflexes. Reflexes are built-in reactions to stimuli, and they govern the newborn's movements. Reflexes are genetically carried survival mechanisms that are automatic and involuntary. They allow infants to respond adaptively to their environment before they have had the opportunity to learn. For example, if immersed in water, the newborn automatically holds its breath and contracts its throat to keep water out.

Other important examples are the rooting and sucking reflexes. Both have survival value for newborn mammals, who must find a mother's breast to obtain nourishment. The *rooting reflex* occurs when the infant's cheek is stroked or the side of the mouth is touched. In response, the infant turns its head toward the side that was touched in an apparent effort to find something to suck. The *sucking reflex* occurs when newborns automatically suck an object placed in their mouth. This reflex enables newborns to get nourishment before they have associated a nipple with food.

Another example is the *Moro reflex*, which occurs in response to a sudden, intense noise or movement. When startled, the newborn arches its back, throws back its head, and flings out its arms and legs. Then the newborn rapidly closes its arms

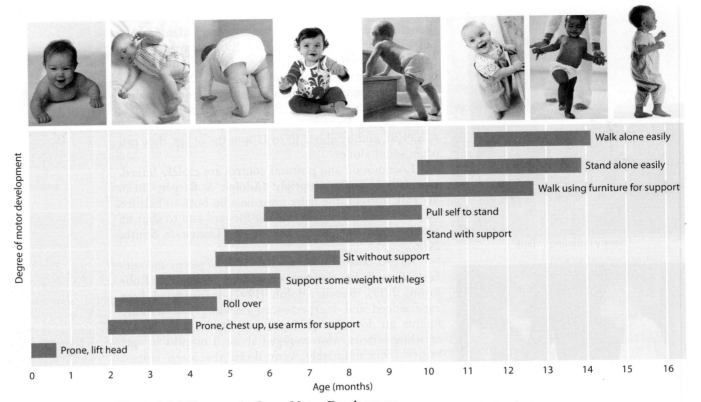

Figure 3.9 Milestones in Gross Motor Development
The horizontal red bars indicate the range in which most infants reach various milestones in gross motor development.

How Would You...?

As a human development and family studies professional, how would you advise parents who are concerned that their infant is one or two months behind the average gross motor milestones?

crawling (Davis & others, 1998). In the African Mali tribe, most infants do not crawl (Bril, 1999).

According to Karen Adolph and Sarah Berger (2005), "The old-fashioned view that growth and motor development reflect merely the age-related output of maturation is, at best, incomplete. Rather, infants acquire new skills with the help of their caregivers in a real-world environment of objects, surfaces, and planes" (p. 273).

Development in the Second Year

The motor accomplishments of the first year bring increasing independence, allowing infants to explore their environment more extensively and to initiate interaction with others more readily. In the second year of life, toddlers become more mobile as their motor skills are honed. Child development experts believe that motor activity during the second year is vital to the child's competent development and that few restrictions, except those having to do with safety, should be placed on their adventures (Fraiberg, 1959).

By 13 to 18 months, toddlers can pull a toy attached to a string and use their hands and legs to climb up steps. By 18 to 24 months, toddlers can walk quickly or run stiffly for a short distance, balance on their feet in a squatting position while playing with objects on the floor, walk backward without losing their balance, stand and kick a ball without falling, stand and throw a ball, and jump in place.

Practice is especially important in learning to walk (Adolph & Joh, 2009). Infants and toddlers accumulate an immense number of experiences with balance and locomotion. For example, the average toddler traverses almost 40 football fields a day and has 15 falls an hour (Adolph, 2010).

Fine Motor Skills

fine motor skills Motor skills that involve more finely tuned movements, such as finger dexterity.

Whereas gross motor skills involve large-muscle activity, **fine motor skills** involve finely tuned movements. Grasping a toy, using a spoon, buttoning a shirt, or anything that requires finger dexterity demonstrates fine motor skills. At birth, infants have very little control over fine motor skills, but they do have many components of what will become finely coordinated arm, hand, and finger movements (McCormack, Hoerl, & Butterfill, 2012).

The onset of reaching and grasping marks a significant achievement in infants' ability to interact with their surroundings (Greif & Needham, 2012; Ziemer, Plumert, & Pick, 2012). During the first two years of life, infants refine how they reach and grasp. Initially, they reach by moving the shoulder and elbow crudely, swinging toward an object. Later, when they reach for an object they move the wrist, rotate the hand, and coordinate the thumb and forefinger. An infant does not have to see his or her own hand in order to reach for an object (Clifton & others, 1993); rather, reaching is guided by cues from muscles, tendons, and joints.

Experience plays a role in reaching and grasping (Keen, 2011). In one study, 3-month-old infants participated in play sessions wearing "sticky mittens"— "mittens with palms that stuck to the edges of toys and allowed the infants to pick up the toys" (Needham, Barrett, & Peterman, 2002, p. 279) (see Figure 3.10). Infants who participated in sessions with the mittens grasped and manipulated objects earlier in their development than a control group of infants who did not receive the "mitten" experience. The experienced infants looked at the objects longer, swatted at them more during visual contact, and were more likely to mouth the objects. In a recent study, 5-month-old infants whose parents trained them to use the sticky mittens for 10 minutes a day over a two-week period showed advances in their reaching behavior at the end of the two weeks (Libertus & Needham, 2011).

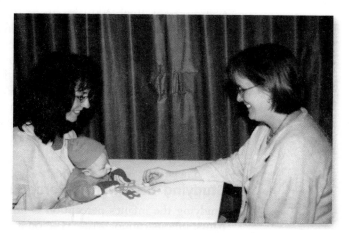

Figure 3.10 Infants' Use of "Sticky Mittens" to Explore Objects
Amy Needham and her colleagues (2002) found that "sticky mittens" enhanced young infants' object exploration skills.

Just as infants need to exercise their gross motor skills, they also need to exercise their fine motor skills (Loucks & Sommerville, 2012). Especially when they can manage a pincer grip, infants delight in picking up small objects. Many develop the pincer grip and begin to crawl at about the same time, and infants at this time pick up virtually everything in sight, especially on the floor, and put the objects in their mouth. Thus, parents need to be vigilant in monitoring objects within the infant's reach.

Sensory and Perceptual Development

Can a newborn see? If so, what can it perceive? How do sensations and perceptions develop? Can an infant put together information from two modalities, such as sight and sound? These are among the intriguing questions that we explore in this section.

Exploring Sensory and Perceptual Development

How does a newborn know that her mother's skin is soft rather than rough? How does a 5-year-old know what color his hair is? Infants and children "know" these things as a result of information that comes through the senses.

areas of infant perception in which eye-tracking equipment is being used are memory, joint attention, and face processing (Falck-Ytter & others, 2012; Wheeler & others, 2011). Further, eye-tracking equipment is improving our understanding of atypically developing infants, such as those with autism (Sasson & Elison, 2012), and infants at risk for atypical developmental outcomes, including preterm infants and infants at risk for developing autism (Bedford & others, 2012).

A recent eye-tracking study shed light on the effectiveness of TV programs and DVDs that claim to educate infants (Kirkorian, Anderson, & Keen, 2012). In this study, 1-year-olds, 4-year-olds, and adults watched *Sesame Street* while the eye-tracking equipment recorded precisely what they looked at on the screen. The 1-year-olds were far less likely than their older counterparts to consistently look at the same part of the screen, suggesting that the 1-year-olds showed little understanding of the *Sesame Street* video but instead were more likely to be attracted by what was salient than by what was relevant.

Visual Perception

Psychologist William James (1890/1950) called the newborn's perceptual world a "blooming, buzzing confusion." A century later, we can safely say that he was wrong (Johnson, 2012, 2013). Even the newborn perceives a world with some order.

Visual Acuity and Color

Just how well can infants see? The newborn's vision is estimated to be 20/600 on the well-known Snellen eye examination chart (Banks & Salapatek, 1983). This means that an object 20 feet away is only as clear to the newborn's eyes as it would be if it were viewed from a distance of 600 feet by an adult with normal vision (20/20). By 6 months of age, though, an average infant's vision is 20/40 (Aslin & Lathrop, 2008). Figure 3.13 shows a computer estimation of what a picture of a face looks like to an infant at different ages from a distance of about 6 inches.

The infant's color vision also improves. By 8 weeks, and possibly even by 4 weeks, infants can discriminate among some colors (Kelly, Borchert, & Teller, 1997).

Perceiving Occluded Objects

Look around the context in which you are right now. You likely see that some objects are partly occluded by other objects that are in front of them—possibly a desk behind a chair, some books behind a computer, or a car parked behind a

Figure 3.13 Visual Acuity During the First Months of Life
The four photographs represent a computer estimation of what a picture of a face looks like to a 1-month-old, 2-month-old, 3-month-old, and 1-year-old (which approximates the visual acuity of an adult).

tree. Do infants perceive an object as complete when it is occluded by an object in front of it?

In the first two months of postnatal development, infants do not perceive occluded objects as complete, instead only perceiving what is visible. Beginning at about 2 months of age, infants develop the ability to perceive that occluded objects are whole (Slater, Field, & Hernandez-Reif, 2007). How does perceptual completion develop? In Scott Johnson's (2004, 2010, 2011, 2012, 2013) research, learning, experience, and self-directed exploration via eye movements play key roles in the development of perceptual completion in young infants.

Many objects that are occluded appear and disappear behind closer objects, as when you are walking down the street and see cars appear and disappear behind buildings. Infants develop the ability to track briefly occluded moving objects at about 3 to 5 months (Bertenthal, 2008). One study explored the ability of 5- to 9-month-old infants to track moving objects that disappeared gradually behind an occluded partition, disappeared abruptly, or imploded (shrank quickly) (Bertenthal, Longo, & Kenny, 2007) (see Figure 3.14). In this study, the infants were more likely to accurately track the moving object when it disappeared gradually rather than vanishing abruptly or imploding.

Depth Perception

To investigate whether infants have depth perception, Eleanor Gibson and Richard Walk (1960) constructed a miniature cliff with a drop-off covered by glass. They placed 6- to 12-month-old infants on the edge of this visual cliff and had their mothers coax them to crawl onto the glass (see Figure 3.15). Most infants would not crawl out on the glass, choosing instead to remain on the shallow side, an indication that they could perceive depth, according to Gibson and Walk. Although researchers do not know exactly how early in life infants can perceive depth, they have found that infants develop the ability to use binocular (two-eyed) cues to depth by about 3 to 4 months of age.

Other Senses

Other sensory systems besides vision also develop during infancy. In this section, we explore development in hearing, touch and pain, smell, and taste.

Hearing

During the last two months of pregnancy, as the fetus nestles in its mother's womb, it can hear sounds such as the mother's voice (Kisilevsky & others, 2009). In one study, researchers had 16 women read *The Cat in the Hat* aloud to their fetuses during the last months of pregnancy (DeCasper & Spence, 1986). Then, shortly after their babies were born, the mothers read aloud either *The Cat in the Hat* or a story with a different rhyme and pace, *The King, the Mice and the Cheese* (which had not been read during prenatal development). The infants

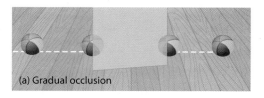

(a) Gradual occlusion

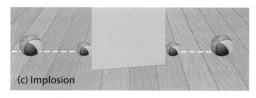
(b) Abrupt occlusion

(c) Implosion

Figure 3.14 Infants' Predictive Tracking of a Briefly Occluded Moving Ball
The top photograph shows the visual scene that infants experienced. At the beginning of each event, a multicolored ball bounced up and down with an accompanying bouncing sound, and then rolled across the floor until it disappeared behind the partition. The bottom drawing shows the three stimulus events that the 5- to 9-month-old infants experienced: (*a*) gradual occlusion—the ball gradually disappears behind the right side of the occluding partition located in the center of the display; (*b*) abrupt occlusion—the ball abruptly disappears when it reaches the location of the white circle and then abruptly reappears 2 seconds later at the location of the second white circle on the other side of the occluding partition; (*c*) implosion—the rolling ball quickly decreases in size as it approaches the occluding partition and rapidly increases in size as it reappears on the other side of the occluding partition.

Figure 3.15 Examining Infants' Depth Perception on the Visual Cliff
Eleanor Gibson and Richard Walk (1960) found that most infants would not crawl out on the glass, which, according to Gibson and Walk, indicated that they had depth perception. However, critics point out that the visual cliff is a better indication of the infant's social referencing and fear of heights than of the infant's perception of depth.

sucked on a nipple in a different way when the mothers read the two stories, suggesting that the infants recognized the pattern and tone of *The Cat in the Hat*. A recent fMRI study confirmed that the fetus can hear at 33 to 34 weeks into the prenatal period by assessing fetal brain response to auditory stimuli (Jardri & others, 2012). Newborns are especially sensitive to human speech sounds (Saffran, Werker, & Warner, 2006). Just a few days after birth, newborns will turn to the sound of a familiar caregiver's voice.

What changes in hearing take place during infancy? They involve perception of a sound's loudness, pitch, and localization. Immediately after birth, infants cannot hear soft sounds quite as well as adults can; a stimulus must be louder for the newborn to hear it (Trehub & others, 1991). Infants are also less sensitive to the pitch of a sound than adults are. *Pitch* is the frequency of a sound; a soprano voice sounds high-pitched, a bass voice low-pitched. Infants are less sensitive to low-pitched sounds and are more likely to hear high-pitched sounds (Aslin, Jusczyk, & Pisoni, 1998). By 2 years of age, infants have considerably improved their ability to distinguish sounds with different pitches.

Even newborns can determine the general location from which a sound is coming, but by 6 months they are more proficient at localizing sounds, detecting their origins. The ability to localize sounds continues to improve in the second year (Saffran, Werker, & Warner, 2006).

Touch and Pain

Newborns respond to touch. A touch to the cheek produces a turning of the head; a touch to the lips produces sucking movements. Newborns can also feel pain (Gunnar & Quevado, 2007). The issue of an infant's pain perception often becomes important to parents who give birth to a son and need to consider whether he should be circumcised (Gunnar & Quevado, 2007). An investigation by Megan Gunnar and her colleagues (1987) found that although newborn infant males cry intensely during circumcision, they also display amazing resiliency. Within several minutes after the surgery (which is often performed without general anesthesia), they can nurse and interact in a normal manner with their mothers. Many newly circumcised infants go into a deep sleep not long after the procedure, probably as a coping mechanism. Also, once researchers discovered that newborns feel pain, the practice of operating on newborns without anesthesia began to be reconsidered. Anesthesia is now used in some circumcisions (Morris & others, 2012).

Smell

Newborns can differentiate among odors (Doty & Shah, 2008). For example, the expressions on their faces indicate that they like the scents of vanilla and strawberry but do not like the scent of rotten eggs or fish (Steiner, 1979).

It may take time to develop other odor preferences, however. By the time they were 6 days old, breast fed infants in one study showed a clear preference for smelling their mother's breast pad rather than a clean breast pad (MacFarlane, 1975). When they were 2 days old they did not show this preference, indicating that they require several days of experience to recognize this scent.

Taste

Sensitivity to taste might be present even before birth (Doty & Shah, 2008). In one very early experiment, when saccharin was added to the amniotic fluid of a near-term fetus, swallowing increased (Windle, 1940). In another study, even at only 2 hours of age, babies made different facial expressions when they tasted sweet, sour, and bitter solutions (Rosenstein & Oster, 1988) (see Figure 3.16). At about 4 months, infants begin to prefer salty tastes, which as newborns they had found to be aversive (Harris, Thomas, & Booth, 1990).

intermodal perception The ability to relate and integrate information from two or more sensory modalities, such as vision and hearing.

Intermodal Perception

How do infants put all these stimuli together? Imagine yourself playing basketball or tennis. You are experiencing many visual inputs: the ball coming and going, other players moving around, and so on. However, you are experiencing many auditory inputs as well: the sound of the ball bouncing or being hit, the grunts and groans, and so on. There is good correspondence between much of the visual and auditory information: When you see the ball bounce, you hear a bouncing sound; when a player stretches to hit a ball, you hear a groan. When you look at and listen to what is going on, you do not experience just the sounds or just the sights; you put all these things together. You experience a unitary episode. This is **intermodal perception,** which involves integrating information from two or more sensory modalities, such as vision and hearing (Bremner & others, 2012). Most perception is intermodal (Bahrick, 2010).

Early, exploratory forms of intermodal perception exist even in newborns (Bahrick & Hollich, 2008). For example, newborns turn their eyes and their head toward the sound of a voice or rattle when the sound is maintained for several seconds (Clifton & others, 1981). Intermodal perception becomes sharper with experience in the first year of life (Kirkham & others, 2012). In the first six months, infants have difficulty connecting sensory input from different modes (such as vision and sound), but in the second half of the first year they show an increased ability to make this connection mentally.

Nature, Nurture, and Perceptual Development

Now that we have discussed many aspects of perceptual development, let's explore one of developmental psychology's key issues as it relates to perceptual development: the nature-nurture issue. There has been a longstanding interest in how strongly infants' perception is influenced by nature or nurture (Johnson, 2011, 2012, 2013; Slater & others, 2011). In the field of perceptual development, those

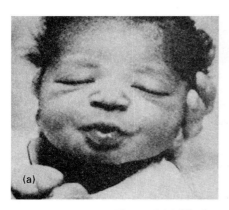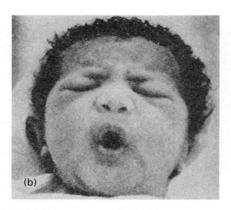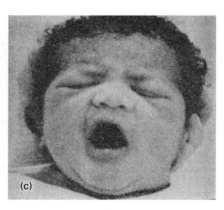

Figure 3.16 Newborns' Facial Responses to Basic Tastes
Facial expressions elicited by (*a*) a sweet solution, (*b*) a sour solution, and (*c*) a bitter solution.

who emphasize nature are referred to as *nativists* and those who emphasize learning and experience are called *empiricists*.

In the nativist view, the ability to perceive the world in a competent, organized way is inborn or innate. At the beginning of our discussion of perceptual development, we examined the Gibsons' ecological view because it has played such a pivotal role in guiding research in perceptual development. This approach leans toward a nativist explanation of perceptual development because it holds that perception is direct and evolved over time to allow the detection of size and shape constancy, a three-dimensional world, intermodal perception, and so on early in infancy. However, the Gibsons' view is not entirely nativist because they emphasized that perceptual development involves distinctive features that are detected at different ages (Slater & others, 2011).

The Gibsons' ecological view is quite different from Piaget's constructivist view, which reflects an empiricist approach to explaining perceptual development. According to Piaget, much of perceptual development in infancy must await the development of a sequence of cognitive stages in which infants become able to construct more complex perceptual tasks. Thus, in Piaget's view the ability to perceive size and shape constancy, a three-dimensional world, intermodal perception, and so on develops later in infancy than the Gibsons envision.

Today it is clear that an extreme empiricist position on perceptual development is unwarranted. Much of early perception develops from innate (nature) capabilities, and the basic foundation of many perceptual abilities can be detected in newborns, whereas others unfold through maturation (Bornstein, Arterberry, & Mash, 2011). However, as infants develop, environmental experiences (nurture) refine or calibrate many perceptual functions, and they may be the driving force behind some functions (Amos & Johnson, 2011; Johnson, 2012, 2013). The accumulation of experience with and knowledge about their perceptual world contributes to infants' ability to perceive coherent impressions of people and things (Slater & others, 2011). Thus, a full portrait of perceptual development includes the influence of nature, nurture, and a developing sensitivity to information (Arterberry, 2008).

Perceptual Motor Coupling

A central theme of the ecological approach is the interplay between perception and action. Action can guide perception, and perception can guide action. Only by moving one's eyes, head, hands, and arms and by moving from one location to another can an individual fully experience his or her environment and learn how to adapt to it. Thus, perception and action are coupled (Adolph & Robinson, 2013).

Babies, for example, continually coordinate their movements with perceptual information to learn how to maintain balance, reach for objects in space, and move across various surfaces and terrains (Adolph & Berger, 2013; Thelen & Smith, 2006). They are motivated to move by what they perceive. Consider the sight of an attractive toy across the room. In this situation, infants must perceive the current state of their bodies and learn how to use their limbs to reach the toy. Although their movements at first are awkward and uncoordinated, babies soon learn to select patterns that are appropriate for reaching their goals.

Equally important is the other part of the perception-action coupling. That is, action educates perception (Adolph & Robinson, 2013). For example, watching an object while exploring it manually helps infants discover its texture, size, and hardness. Moving around in their environment teaches babies about how objects and people look from different perspectives,

What roles do nature and nurture play in the infant's perceptual development? How are perceptual and motor development coupled?

or whether surfaces will support their weight. In short, infants perceive in order to move and move in order to perceive. Perceptual and motor development do not occur in isolation from each other but instead are coupled.

Cognitive Development

The competent infant not only develops motor and perceptual skills, but also develops cognitive skills. Our coverage of cognitive development in infancy focuses on Piaget's theory and sensorimotor stages as well as on how infants learn, remember, and conceptualize.

Piaget's Theory

Piaget's theory is a general, unifying story of how biology and experience sculpt cognitive development. The Swiss child psychologist Jean Piaget thought that, just as our physical bodies have structures that enable us to adapt to the world, we build mental structures that help us to adapt to the world. *Adaptation* involves adjusting to new environmental demands. Piaget stressed that children actively construct their own cognitive worlds; information is not just poured into their minds from the environment. He sought to discover how children at different points in their development think about the world and how systematic changes in their thinking occur.

Processes of Development

What processes do children use as they construct their knowledge of the world? Piaget developed several concepts to answer this question.

Schemes According to Piaget (1954), as the infant or child seeks to construct an understanding of the world, the developing brain creates **schemes.** These are actions or mental representations that organize knowledge. In Piaget's theory, infants create behavioral schemes (physical activities), whereas toddlers and older children create mental schemes (cognitive activities) (Lamb, Bornstein, & Teti, 2002). A baby's schemes are structured by simple actions that can be performed on objects such as sucking, looking, and grasping. Older children's schemes include strategies and plans for solving problems.

Assimilation and Accommodation To explain how children use and adapt their schemes, Piaget offered two concepts: assimilation and accommodation. **Assimilation** occurs when children use their existing schemes to deal with new information or experiences. **Accommodation** occurs when children adjust their schemes to account for new information and experiences.

Think about a toddler who has learned the word *car* to identify the family's automobile. The toddler might call all moving vehicles on roads "cars," including motorcycles and trucks; the child has assimilated these objects to his or her existing scheme. But the child soon learns that motorcycles and trucks are not cars and fine-tunes the category to exclude those vehicles. The child has accommodated the scheme.

Organization To make sense out of their world, said Piaget, children cognitively organize their experiences. **Organization,** in Piaget's theory, is the grouping of isolated behaviors and thoughts into a higher-order system. Continual refinement

schemes In Piaget's theory, actions or mental representations that organize knowledge.

assimilation Piagetian concept of using existing schemes to deal with new information or experiences.

accommodation Piagetian concept of adjusting schemes to fit new information and experiences.

organization Piaget's concept of grouping isolated behaviors and thoughts into a higher-order, more smoothly functioning cognitive system.

In Piaget's view, what is a scheme? What schemes might this young infant be displaying?

93

of this organization is an inherent part of development. A child who has only a vague idea about how to use a hammer may also have a vague idea about how to use other tools. After learning how to use each one, she relates these uses to one another, thereby organizing her knowledge.

Equilibration and Stages of Development Assimilation and accommodation always take the child to a higher level, according to Piaget. In trying to understand the world, the child inevitably experiences cognitive conflict, or *disequilibrium*. That is, the child is constantly faced with inconsistencies and counterexamples to his or her existing schemes. For example, if a child believes that pouring water from a short, wide container into a tall, narrow container changes the amount of water in the container, the child might wonder where the "extra" water came from and whether there is actually more water to drink. This puzzle creates disequilibrium; and in Piaget's view the resulting search for equilibrium creates motivation for change. The child assimilates and accommodates, adjusting old schemes, developing new schemes, and organizing and reorganizing the old and new schemes. Eventually, the organization is fundamentally different from the old organization; it becomes a new way of thinking.

Equilibration is the name Piaget gave to this mechanism by which children shift from one stage of thought to the next. Equilibration does not, however, happen all at once. There is considerable movement between states of cognitive equilibrium and disequilibrium as assimilation and accommodation work in concert to produce cognitive change.

A result of these processes, according to Piaget, is that individuals go through four stages of development. A different way of understanding the world makes one stage more advanced than another. Cognition is *qualitatively* different in one stage compared with another. In other words, the way children reason at one stage is different from the way they reason at another stage. Here our focus is on Piaget's stage of infant cognitive development. In Chapters 5, 7, and 9, we explore the last three Piagetian stages.

The Sensorimotor Stage

The **sensorimotor stage** lasts from birth to about age 2. In this stage, infants construct an understanding of the world by coordinating sensory experiences (such as seeing and hearing) with physical, motor actions—hence the term *sensorimotor*. At the beginning of this stage, newborns have little more than reflexes to work with. At the end of the sensorimotor stage, 2-year-olds can produce complex sensorimotor patterns and use primitive symbols. We first summarize Piaget's descriptions of how infants develop. Later we consider criticisms of his view.

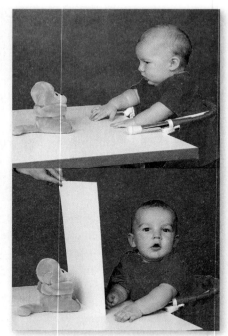

Figure 3.17 Object Permanence
Piaget argued that object permanence is one of infancy's landmark cognitive accomplishments. For this 5-month-old boy, "out of sight" is literally out of mind. The infant looks at the toy monkey, but when his view of the toy is blocked, he does not search for it. Several months later, he will search for the hidden toy monkey, an action reflecting the presence of object permanence.

Object Permanence **Object permanence** is the understanding that objects continue to exist even when they cannot be seen, heard, or touched. Acquiring the sense of object permanence is one of the infant's most important accomplishments, according to Piaget.

How could anyone know whether or not an infant had a sense of object permanence? The principal way in which object permanence is studied is by watching an infant's reaction when an interesting object disappears (see Figure 3.17). If infants search for the object, it is inferred that they know it continues to exist.

equilibration A mechanism that Piaget proposed to explain how children shift from one stage of thought to the next.

sensorimotor stage The first of Piaget's stages, which lasts from birth to about 2 years of age; during this stage, infants construct an understanding of the world by coordinating sensory experiences with motoric actions.

object permanence The Piagetian term for understanding that objects and events continue to exist, even when they cannot directly be seen, heard, or touched.

Evaluating Piaget's Sensorimotor Stage Piaget opened up a new way of looking at infants with his view that their main task is to coordinate their sensory impressions with their motor activity. However, the infant's cognitive world is not as neatly packaged as Piaget portrayed it, and some of Piaget's explanations for the cause of change are debated. In the past several decades, there have been many research studies on infant development using sophisticated experimental techniques. Much of the new research suggests that Piaget's view of sensorimotor development needs to be modified (Baillargeon & Carey, 2012; Diamond, 2013; Johnson, 2012, 2013).

A-not-B error is the term used to describe the tendency of infants to reach where an object was located earlier rather than where the object was last hidden. Older infants are less likely to make the A-not-B error because their concept of object permanence is more complete.

Researchers have found, however, that the A-not-B error does not show up consistently (Sophian, 1985). The evidence indicates that A-not-B errors are sensitive to the delay between hiding the object at B and the infant's attempt to find it (Diamond, 1985). Thus, the A-not-B error might be due to a failure in memory. Another explanation is that infants tend to repeat a previous motor behavior (Clearfield & others, 2006).

A number of theorists, such as Eleanor Gibson (1989) and Elizabeth Spelke (2004, 2011), have concluded that infants' perceptual abilities are highly developed very early in life. For example, intermodal perception—the ability to coordinate information from two or more sensory modalities, such as vision and hearing—develops much earlier than Piaget would have predicted (Spelke & Owsley, 1979).

Object permanence also develops earlier than Piaget thought. In his view, object permanence does not develop until approximately 8 to 9 months. However, research by Renée Baillargeon and her colleagues (2004; Baillargeon & others, 2012) documents that infants as young as 3 to 4 months expect objects to be *substantial* (in the sense that other objects cannot move through them) and *permanent* (in the sense that they continue to exist when they are hidden).

Today researchers believe that infants see objects as bounded, unitary, solid, and separate from their background, possibly at birth or shortly thereafter, but definitely by 3 to 4 months, much earlier than Piaget envisioned. Young infants still have much to learn about objects, but the world appears both stable and orderly to them.

In considering the big issue of whether nature or nature plays a more important role in infant development, Elizabeth Spelke (2011) comes down clearly on the side of nature. Spelke endorses a **core knowledge approach,** which states that infants are born with domain-specific innate knowledge systems. Among these knowledge systems are those involving space, number sense, object permanence, and language (which we will discuss later in this chapter). Strongly influenced by evolution, the core knowledge domains are theorized to be "prewired" to allow infants to make sense of their world. After all, Spelke concludes, how could infants possibly grasp the complex world in which they live if they did not come into the world equipped with core sets of knowledge? In this approach, the innate core knowledge domains form a foundation around which more mature cognitive functioning and learning develop. The core knowledge approach argues that Piaget greatly underestimated the cognitive abilities of infants, especially young infants.

A-not-B error This term is used to describe the tendency of infants to reach where an object was located earlier rather than where the object was last hidden.

core knowledge approach States that infants are born with domain-specific innate knowledge systems.

A 4-month-old in Elizabeth Spelke's infant perception laboratory is tested to determine whether she knows that an object in motion will not stop in midair. Spelke concluded that at 4 months babies don't expect objects like these balls to obey gravitational constraints, but that they do expect objects to be solid and continuous. Research by Spelke, Renée Baillargeon, and others suggests that infants develop an ability to understand how the world works earlier than Piaget envisioned. However, critics such as Andrew Meltzoff fault their research and conclude there is still controversy about how early some infant cognitive accomplishments occur.

In criticizing the core knowledge approach, British developmental psychologist Mark Johnson (2008) says that the infants Spelke assesses in her research have already accumulated hundreds, and in some cases even thousands, of hours of experience in grasping what the world is about, which gives considerable room for the environment's role in the development of infant cognition (Highfield, 2008). According to Johnson (2008), infants likely come into the world with "soft biases to perceive and attend to different aspects of the environment, and to learn about the world in particular ways."

In sum, many researchers conclude that Piaget wasn't specific enough about how infants learn about their world and that infants, especially young infants, are more competent than Piaget thought (Baillargeon & others, 2012; Diamond, 2013; Hyde & Spelke, 2012; Johnson, 2012, 2013). As researchers have examined the specific ways that infants learn, the field of infant cognition has become very specialized. There are many researchers working on different questions, with no general theory emerging that can connect all of the different findings. Their theories often are local theories, focused on specific research questions, rather than grand theories like Piaget's (Kuhn, 1998). Among the unifying themes in the study of infant cognition are seeking to understand more precisely how developmental changes in cognition take place, the big issue of nature and nurture, and the brain's role in cognitive development (Aslin, 2012). Recall from Chapter 1 that exploring connections between brain, cognition, and development involve the recently emerging field of *developmental cognitive neuroscience* (Bell, 2012; Cuevas & others, 2012; Diamond, 2013; Morasch & others, 2013).

Learning, Remembering, and Conceptualizing

In Chapter 1, we described the behavioral and social cognitive theories, as well as information-processing theory. These theories emphasize that cognitive development does not unfold in a stage-like process as Piaget proposed, but rather advances more gradually. In this section we explore what researchers using these approaches can tell us about how infants learn, remember, and conceptualize.

Conditioning

In Chapter 1, we discussed Skinner's theory of operant conditioning, in which the consequences of a behavior influence the probability of the behavior's occurrence. Infants can learn through operant conditioning: If an infant's behavior is followed by a rewarding stimulus, the behavior is likely to recur.

Operant conditioning has been especially helpful to researchers in their efforts to determine what infants perceive (Rovee-Collier & Barr, 2010). For example, infants will suck faster on a nipple when the sucking behavior is followed by a visual display, music, or a human voice (Rovee-Collier, 2007).

Carolyn Rovee-Collier (1987) has demonstrated that infants can retain information from the experience of being conditioned. In a characteristic experiment, Rovee-Collier places a 2½-month-old baby in a crib under an elaborate mobile (see Figure 3.18). She then ties one end of a ribbon to the baby's ankle and the other end to the mobile. Subsequently, she observes that the baby kicks and makes the mobile move. The movement of the mobile is the reinforcing stimulus (which increases the baby's kicking behavior) in this experiment. Weeks later, the baby is returned to the crib, but its foot is not tied to the mobile. The baby kicks, suggesting that it has retained the information that if it kicks a leg, the mobile will move.

Figure 3.18 The Technique Used in Rovee-Collier's Investigation of Infant Memory

In Rovee-Collier's experiment, operant conditioning was used to demonstrate that infants as young as 2½ months of age can retain information from the experience of being conditioned. *What did infants recall in Rovee-Collier's experiment?*

Attention

Attention, the focusing of mental resources on select information, improves cognitive processing on many tasks. Even newborns can detect a contour and fix their attention on it. Older infants scan patterns more thoroughly. By 4 months, infants can selectively attend to an object.

Closely linked with attention are the processes of habituation and dishabituation, which we discussed earlier in this chapter (Colombo, Brez, & Curtindale, 2013). Infants' attention is strongly governed by novelty and habituation. When an object becomes familiar, attention becomes shorter, making infants more vulnerable to distraction (Richards, 2010).

Another important aspect of infant development is **joint attention,** in which individuals focus on the same object or event. Joint attention requires (1) the ability to track each other's behavior, such as following someone's gaze; (2) one person directing another's attention; and (3) reciprocal interaction. Early in infancy, joint attention usually involves a caregiver pointing or using words to direct an infant's attention. Emerging forms of joint attention occur at about 7 to 8 months, but it is not until 10 to 11 months that joint attention skills are frequently observed (Meltzoff & Brooks, 2009). By their first birthday, infants have begun to direct adults' attention to objects that capture their interest (Heimann & others, 2006).

Joint attention plays important roles in many aspects of infant development and considerably increases infants' ability to learn from other people (Carpenter, 2011; Meltzoff, 2011). Nowhere is this more apparent than in observations of interchanges between caregivers and infants as infants are learning language (Tomasello, 2011). When caregivers and infants frequently engage in joint attention, infants say their first word earlier and develop a larger vocabulary (Flom & Pick, 2003). A recent study also revealed that the extent to which 9-month-old infants engaged in joint attention was linked to their long-term memory (a one-week delay), possibly because joint attention enhances the relevance of attended items (Kopp & Lindenberger, 2011). Joint attention skills in infancy also are associated with the development of self-regulation later in childhood. For example, a recent study revealed that responding to joint attention at 12 months of age was linked to self-regulation skills at 3 years of age that involved delaying gratification for an attractive object (Vaughan Van Hecke & others, 2012).

Imitation

Infant development researcher Andrew Meltzoff (2004, 2007, 2011) has conducted numerous studies of infants' imitative abilities. He sees infants' imitative abilities as biologically based, because infants can imitate a facial expression within the first few days after birth. He also emphasizes that the infant's imitative abilities do not resemble a hardwired response but rather involve flexibility and adaptability (Meltzoff & Williamson, 2013). In Meltzoff's observations of infants during the first 72 hours of life, the infants gradually displayed more complete imitation of an adult's facial expression, such as protruding the tongue or opening the mouth wide (see Figure 3.19).

Meltzoff (2007, 2011) concludes that infants don't blindly imitate everything they see and often make creative errors. He also argues that beginning at birth there is an interplay between learning by observing and learning by doing (Piaget emphasized learning by doing).

How Would You...?

As a human development and family studies professional, what strategies would likely help parents improve an infant's development of attention?

attention The focusing of mental resources on select information.

joint attention Process that occurs when (1) individuals focus on the same object and track each other's behavior, (2) one individual directs another's attention, and (3) reciprocal interaction takes place.

Figure 3.19 Infant Imitation Infant development researcher Andrew Meltzoff protrudes his tongue in an attempt to get the infant to imitate his behavior. *How do Meltzoff's findings about imitation compare with Piaget's descriptions of infants' abilities?*

the following (Slobin, 1972): identification—"See doggie"; location—"Book there"; repetition—"More milk"; negation—"Not wolf"; possession—"My candy"; attribution—"Big car"; and question—"Where ball?" These examples are from children whose first language is English, German, Russian, Finnish, Turkish, or Samoan.

Language milestones

Figure 3.23 Variation in Language Milestones *What are some possible explanations for variations in the timing of these milestones?*

for six years (Lane, 1976). When found, he made no effort to communicate, and he never did learn to communicate effectively.

Sadly, a modern-day wild child was discovered in Los Angeles in 1970. Despite intensive intervention, the child, named Genie by researchers, has never acquired more than a primitive form of language. Both of these cases—the Wild Boy of Aveyron and Genie— raise questions about the biological and environmental influences on language.

This interaction of biology and experience can be seen in variations in the acquisition of language. Children vary in their ability to acquire language, and this variation cannot be completely explained by differences in environmental input alone. However, virtually every child benefits enormously from opportunities to talk and be talked with. Children whose parents and teachers provide them with a rich verbal environment show many positive outcomes (Gunning, 2013; Tamis-LeMonda & Song, 2013). Parents and teachers who pay attention to what children are trying to say, expand their children's utterances, read to them, and label things in the environment, are providing valuable, if unintentional, benefits (Hirsh-Pasek & Golinkoff, 2013).

Summary

Physical Growth and Development in Infancy

- Most development follows cephalocaudal and proximodistal patterns.
- Physical growth is rapid in the first year but rate of growth slows in the second year.
- Dramatic changes characterize the brain's development in the first two years. The neuroconstructivist view is an increasingly popular view of the brain's development.
- Newborns usually sleep 16 to 17 hours a day, but by 4 months many American infants approach adult-like sleeping patterns. Sudden infant death syndrome (SIDS) is a condition that occurs when a sleeping infant suddenly stops breathing and dies without an apparent cause.
- Infants need to consume about 50 calories per day for each pound they weigh. The growing consensus is that breast feeding is more beneficial than bottle feeding.

Motor Development

- Dynamic systems theory seeks to explain how motor behaviors are assembled for perceiving and acting. This theory emphasizes that experience plays an important role in motor development, and that perception and action are coupled.
- Reflexes—automatic movements—govern the newborn's behavior.
- Key gross motor skills, which involve large-muscle activities, developed during infancy include control of posture and walking.
- Fine motor skills involve finely tuned movements. The onset of reaching and grasping marks a significant accomplishment, and this becomes more refined during the first two years of life.

Sensory and Perceptual Development

- Sensation occurs when information interacts with sensory receptors. Perception is the interpretation of sensation.
- Created by the Gibsons, the ecological view states that perception brings people into contact with the environment to interact with and adapt to it.
- The infant's visual acuity increases dramatically in the first year of life. By 3 months of age, infants show size and shape constancy. In Gibson and Walk's classic study, infants had depth perception as young as 6 months of age.
- The fetus can hear several weeks prior to birth. Just after being born, infants can hear but their sensory threshold is higher than that of adults. Newborns can respond to touch, feel pain, differentiate among odors, and may be sensitive to taste at birth.
- A basic form of intermodal perception is present in newborns and sharpens over the first year of life.
- In perception, nature advocates are referred to as nativists and nurture proponents are called empiricists. A strong empiricist approach is unwarranted. A full account of perceptual development includes the roles of nature, nurture, and the infant's developing sensitivity to information.

Cognitive Development

- In Piaget's theory, children construct their own cognitive worlds, building mental structures to adapt to their world. Schemes, assimilation and accommodation, organization, and equilibration are key processes in Piaget's theory. According to Piaget, there are four qualitatively different stages of thought. In sensorimotor thought, the first of Piaget's four stages, the infant organizes and coordinates sensations with physical movements. The stage lasts from birth to about 2 years of age. One key accomplishment of this stage is object permanence. In the past several decades, revisions of Piaget's view have been proposed based on research.

- An approach different from Piaget's focuses on infants' operant conditioning, attention, imitation, memory, and concept formation.

Language Development

- Rules describe the way language works. Language is characterized by infinite generativity.

- Infants reach a number of milestones in development, including first words and two-word utterances.
- Chomsky argues that children are born with the ability to detect basic features and rules of language. The behavioral view has not been supported by research. How much of language is biologically determined, and how much depends on interaction with others, is a subject of debate among linguists and psychologists. However, all agree that both biological capacity and relevant experience are necessary. Parents should talk extensively with an infant, especially about what the baby is attending to.

Key Terms

cephalocaudal pattern 72
proximodistal pattern 72
lateralization 74
neuroconstructivist
    view 77
sudden infant death
    syndrome (SIDS) 78
dynamic systems
    theory 80
gross motor skills 82
fine motor skills 85

sensation 86
perception 86
ecological view 86
visual preference
    method 86
habituation 86
dishabituation 86
intermodal
    perception 91
schemes 93
assimilation 93

accommodation 93
organization 93
equilibration 94
sensorimotor stage 94
object permanence 94
A-not-B error 95
core knowledge
    approach 95
attention 97
joint attention 97
deferred imitation 98

memory 98
implicit memory 98
explicit memory 98
concepts 99
language 100
infinite generativity 100
telegraphic speech 102
language acquisition
    device (LAD) 103
child-directed
    speech 104

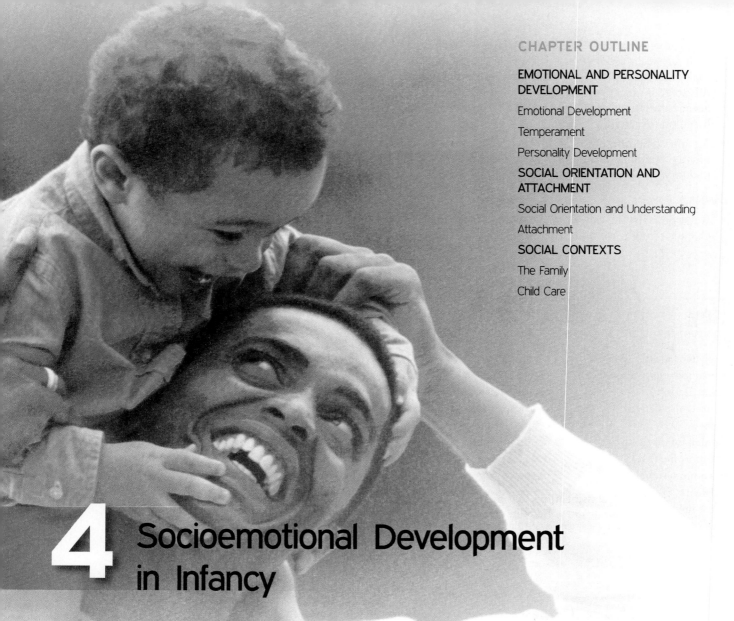

4 Socioemotional Development in Infancy

Stories of Life-Span Development: Darius and His Father

An increasing number of fathers are staying home to care for their children (Lamb, 2010). Consider 17-month-old Darius. On weekdays, Darius' father, a writer, cares for him during the day while his mother works full-time as a landscape architect. Darius' father is doing a great job of caring for him. He keeps Darius nearby while he is writing and spends lots of time talking to him and playing with him. From their interactions, it is clear that they genuinely enjoy each other's company.

Last month, Darius began spending one day a week at a child-care center.

His parents selected the center after observing a number of centers and interviewing teachers and center directors. His parents placed him in the center because they wanted him to get some experience with peers and his father to have some time out from caregiving.

Darius' father looks to the future and imagines the Little League games Darius will play in and the many other activities he can enjoy with his son. Remembering how little time his own father spent with him, he is dedicated to making sure that Darius has an involved, nurturing relationship with his father.

When Darius' mother comes home in the evening, she spends considerable time with him. Darius is securely attached to both his mother and his father.

In Chapter 3, you read about how infants perceive, learn, and remember. Infants also are socioemotional beings, capable of displaying emotions and initiating social interaction with people close to them. The main topics that we explore in this chapter are emotional and personality development, attachment, and the social contexts of the family and child care. ■

Emotional and Personality Development

Anyone who has been around infants for even a brief time can tell that they are emotional beings. Not only do infants express emotions, but they also vary in temperament. Some are shy and others are outgoing. Some are active and others much less so. Let's explore these and other aspects of emotional and personality development in infants.

Emotional Development

Imagine what your life would be like without emotion. Emotion is the color and music of life, as well as the tie that binds people together. How do psychologists define and classify emotions, and why are they important to development? How do emotions develop during the first two years of life?

What Are Emotions?

For our purposes, we will define **emotion** as feeling, or affect, that occurs when a person is in a state or an interaction that is important to him or her, especially to his or her well-being. Especially in infancy, emotions have important roles in (1) communication with others and (2) behavioral organization. Through emotions, infants communicate important aspects of their lives such as joy, sadness, interest, and fear (Witherington & others, 2010). In terms of behavioral organization, emotions influence infants' social responses and adaptive behavior as they interact with others in their world (Easterbrook & others, 2013; Thompson, 2013a).

Psychologists classify the broad range of emotions in many ways, but almost all classifications designate an emotion as either positive (pleasant) or negative (unpleasant). Positive emotions include happiness, joy, love, and enthusiasm. Negative emotions include anxiety, anger, guilt, and sadness.

Biological and Environmental Influences

Emotions are influenced both by biological foundations and by a person's experiences (Easterbrooks & others, 2013; Thompson, 2013a, b). For example, children who are blind from birth and have never observed the smile or frown on another person's face smile and frown in the same way that children with normal vision do. Moreover, facial expressions of basic emotions such as happiness, surprise, anger, and fear are the same across cultures.

These biological factors, however, are only part of the story of emotion. Biological evolution has endowed human beings to be emotional, but embeddedness in relationships and cultural contexts provides diversity in emotional experiences (Tamis-LeMonda & Song, 2013). Display rules—rules governing when, where, and how emotions should be expressed—are not universal. For example, researchers have found that East Asian infants display less frequent and less intense positive and negative emotions than do non-Latino White infants (Cole & Tan, 2007). Throughout childhood, East Asian parents encourage their children to show emotional reserve rather than to be emotionally expressive (Chen & others, 1998).

How do East Asian mothers handle their infants' and children's emotional development differently from non-Latina White mothers?

| Joy | Sadness | Fear | Surprise |

Figure 4.1 Expression of Different Emotions in Infants

Emotions serve important functions in our relationships (Slatcher & Trentacosta, 2012). As we discuss later in this section, emotions are the first language with which parents and infants communicate (Duncombe & others, 2012). Emotion-linked interchanges provide the foundation for the infant's developing attachment to the parent (Thompson, 2013a, b).

Early Emotions

Emotions that infants express in the first six months of life include surprise, interest, joy, anger, sadness, fear, and disgust (see Figure 4.1). Other emotions that appear in infancy include jealousy, empathy, embarrassment, pride, shame, and guilt; most of these occur for the first time at some point in the second half of the first year or during the second year. These later-developing emotions have been called self-conscious or other-conscious emotions because they involve the emotional reactions of others (Lewis, 2007, 2010).

Some experts on infant socioemotional development, such as Jerome Kagan (2010), conclude that the structural immaturity of the infant brain makes it unlikely that emotions that require thought—such as guilt, pride, despair, shame, empathy, and jealousy—can be experienced in the first year. Thus, both Kagan (2010) and Joseph Campos (2009) argue that so-called "self-conscious" emotions don't occur until after the first year, a view that increasingly reflects that of most developmental psychologists.

Emotional Expressions and Relationships

Emotional expressions are involved in infants' first relationships. The ability of infants to communicate emotions permits coordinated interactions with their caregivers and the beginning of an emotional bond between them (Easterbrooks & others, 2013; Thompson, 2013c). Not only do parents change their emotional expressions in response to those of their infants (and each other), but infants also modify their emotional expressions in response to those of their parents. In other words, these interactions are mutually regulated. Because of this coordination, the interactions between parents and infants are described as *reciprocal*, or *synchronous*, when all is going well. Sensitive, responsive parents help their infants grow emotionally, whether the infants respond in distressed or happy ways (Wilson, Havighurst, & Harley, 2012).

Crying Cries and smiles are two emotional expressions that infants display when interacting with parents. These are babies' first forms of emotional communication. Crying is the most important mechanism newborns have for communicating with their world. Cries may also provide information about the health of the newborn's central nervous system. Newborns even tend to respond with cries and negative facial expressions when they hear other newborns cry (Dondi, Simion, & Caltran, 1999). However, a recent study revealed that newborns of depressed

How Would You…?

As a human development and family studies professional, how would you respond to the parents of a 13-month-old baby who are concerned because their son has suddenly started crying every morning when they drop him off at child care despite the fact that he has been going to the same child care for over six months?

mothers showed less vocal distress when another infant cried, reflecting emotional and physiological dysregulation (Jones, 2012).

Babies have at least three types of cries:

- **Basic cry:** A rhythmic pattern that usually consists of a cry, followed by a briefer silence, then a shorter whistle that is somewhat higher in pitch than the main cry, then another brief rest before the next cry. Some experts believe that hunger is one of the conditions that incite the basic cry.

- **Anger cry:** A variation of the basic cry, with more excess air forced through the vocal cords.

- **Pain cry:** A sudden long, initial loud cry followed by the holding of the breath; no preliminary moaning is present. The pain cry may be stimulated by physical pain or by any high-intensity stimulus.

Most adults can determine whether an infant's cries signify anger or pain (Zeskind, Klein, & Marshall, 1992). Parents can distinguish among the cries of their own baby better than among those of another baby.

Should parents respond to an infant's cries? Many developmental psychologists recwommend that parents soothe a crying infant, especially in the first year. This reaction should help infants develop a sense of trust and secure attachment to the caregiver. A recent study revealed that mothers' emotional reactions (anger and anxiety) to crying increased the risk of subsequent attachment insecurity (Leerkes, Parade, & Gudmundson, 2011). And another recent study found that problems in infant soothability at 6 months of age were linked to insecure attachment at 12 months of age (Mills-Koonce, Propper, & Barnette, 2012).

What are some different types of cries?

basic cry A rhythmic pattern usually consisting of a cry, a briefer silence, a shorter inspiratory whistle that is higher pitched than the main cry, and then a brief rest before the next cry.

anger cry A cry similar to the basic cry, with more excess air forced through the vocal cords.

pain cry A sudden outburst of loud crying without preliminary moaning, followed by breath holding.

Smiling Smiling is a critical social skill and a key social signal (Witherington & others, 2010). Two types of smiling can be distinguished in infants:

- **Reflexive smile:** A smile that does not occur in response to external stimuli and appears during the first month after birth, usually during sleep.

- **Social smile:** A smile that occurs in response to an external stimulus, typically a face in the case of the young infant. Social smiling occurs as early as two months of age.

Fear One of a baby's earliest emotions is fear, which typically first appears at about 6 months and peaks at about 18 months. However, abused and neglected infants can show fear as early as 3 months (Witherington & others, 2010). The most frequent expression of an infant's fear involves **stranger anxiety,** in which an infant shows fear and wariness of strangers.

Stranger anxiety usually emerges gradually. It first appears at about 6 months in the form of wary reactions. By 9 months, fear of

reflexive smile A smile that does not occur in response to external stimuli. It appears during the first month after birth, usually during sleep.

social smile A smile in response to an external stimulus, which, early in development, typically is a face.

stranger anxiety An infant's fear and wariness of strangers that typically appears in the second half of the first year of life.

strangers is often more intense, and it continues to escalate through the infant's first birthday (Emde, Gaensbauer, & Harmon, 1976).

Not all infants show distress when they encounter a stranger. Besides individual variations, whether an infant shows stranger anxiety also depends on the social context and the characteristics of the stranger. Infants show less stranger anxiety when they are in familiar settings. For example, in one study, 10-month-olds showed little stranger anxiety when they met a stranger in their own home but much greater fear when they encountered a stranger in a research laboratory (Sroufe, Waters, & Matas, 1974). Also, infants show less stranger anxiety when they are sitting on their mothers' laps than when they are in an infant seat several feet away from their mothers (Bohlin & Hagekull, 1993). Thus, it appears that when infants feel secure they are less likely to show stranger anxiety.

Who the stranger is and how the stranger behaves also influence stranger anxiety in infants. Infants are less fearful of child strangers than of adult strangers. They also are less fearful of friendly, outgoing, smiling strangers than of passive, unsmiling strangers (Bretherton, Stolberg, & Kreye, 1981).

In addition to stranger anxiety, infants experience fear of being separated from their caregivers. The result is **separation protest**—crying when the caregiver leaves. Separation protest tends to peak at about 15 months among U.S. infants. A study of four different cultures found, similarly, that separation protest peaked at about 13 to 15 months (Kagan, Kearsley, & Zelazo, 1978). As indicated in Figure 4.2, the percentage of infants who engaged in separation protest varied across cultures, but the infants reached a peak of protest at about the same age—just before the middle of the second year.

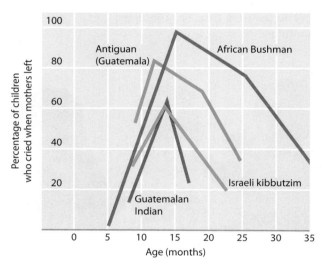

Figure 4.2 Separation Protest in Four Cultures

Note that separation protest peaked at about the same age in all four cultures in this study (13 to 15 months) (Kagan, Kearsley, & Zelazo, 1978). However, 100 percent of infants in an African Bushman culture engaged in separation protest compared with only about 60 percent of infants in Guatemalan Indian and Israeli kibbutzim cultures. *What might explain the fact that separation protest peaks at about the same time in different cultures?*

Reprinted by permission of the publisher from *Infancy: Its Place in Human Development* by Jerome Kagan, Richard B. Kearsley, and Philip R. Zelazo, p. 107, Cambridge, Mass.: Harvard University Press. Copyright © 1978 by the President and Fellows of Harvard College.

Social Referencing Infants not only express emotions like fear but also "read" the emotions of other people (Cornew & others, 2012). **Social referencing** involves "reading" emotional cues in others to help determine how to act in a particular situation. The development of social referencing helps infants interpret ambiguous situations more accurately, as when they encounter a stranger (Pelaez, Virues-Ortega, & Gewirtz, 2012). By the end of the first year, a parent's facial expression—either smiling or fearful—influences whether an infant will explore an unfamiliar environment.

Infants become better at social referencing in the second year of life. At this age, they tend to "check" with their mother before they act; they look at her to see if she is happy, angry, or fearful.

Emotional Regulation and Coping

During the first year, the infant gradually develops an ability to inhibit, or minimize, the intensity and duration of emotional reactions (Calkins, 2012; Morasch & Bell, 2012). From early in infancy, babies put their thumbs in their mouths to soothe themselves. In their second year, they may say things to help soothe themselves. When placed in his bed for the night, after a little crying and whimpering, a 20-month-old was overhead saying, "Go sleep, Alex. Okay." But at first, infants depend mainly on caregivers to help them soothe their emotions, as when a caregiver rocks an infant to sleep, sings lullabies, gently strokes the infant, and so on.

Caregivers' actions influence the infant's neurobiological regulation of emotions (Easterbrooks & others, 2013; Thompson, 2013a, b). By soothing the infant, caregivers help infants modulate their emotions and reduce the level of stress hormones (de Haan & Gunnar, 2009). Many developmental psychologists believe it is a good strategy for a caregiver to soothe an infant before the infant gets into an intense, agitated, uncontrolled state (Thompson, 2013a, b).

Later in infancy, when they become aroused, infants sometimes redirect their attention or distract themselves in order to reduce their arousal. By age 2, children can use language to define their feeling states and identify the context that is upsetting them (Calkins & Markovitch, 2010). A 2-year-old might say, "Doggy scary." This type of communication may cue caregivers to help the child regulate emotion.

Contexts can influence emotional regulation (Easterbrooks & others, 2013; Thompson, 2013a). Infants are often affected by fatigue, hunger, time of day, which people are around them, and where they are. Infants must learn to adapt to different contexts that require emotional regulation. Further, new demands appear as the infant becomes older and parents modify their expectations. For example, a parent may take it in stride if a 6-month-old infant screams in a restaurant but may react very differently if a 1½-year-old starts screaming.

temperament An individual's behavioral style and characteristic way of responding emotionally.

Temperament

Do you get upset easily? Does it take much to get you angry or to make you laugh? Even at birth, babies seem to have different emotional styles. One infant is cheerful and happy much of the time; another seems to cry constantly. These tendencies reflect **temperament,** or individual differences in behavioral styles, emotions, and characteristic ways of responding. With regard to its link to emotion, temperament refers to individual differences in how quickly the emotion is shown, how strong it is, how long it lasts, and how quickly it fades away (Campos, 2009).

Describing and Classifying Temperament

How would you describe your temperament or the temperament of a friend? Researchers have described and classified the temperaments of individuals in different ways. Here we examine three of those ways.

Chess and Thomas' Classification Psychiatrists Alexander Chess and Stella Thomas (Chess & Thomas, 1977; Thomas & Chess, 1991) identified three basic types, or clusters, of temperament:

- **Easy child:** This child is generally in a positive mood, quickly establishes regular routines in infancy, and adapts easily to new experiences.
- **Difficult child:** This child reacts negatively and cries frequently, engages in irregular daily routines, and is slow to accept change.
- **Slow-to-warm-up child:** This child has a low activity level, is somewhat negative, and displays a low intensity of mood.

easy child A child who is generally in a positive mood, who quickly establishes regular routines in infancy, and who adapts easily to new experiences.

difficult child A child who tends to react negatively and cry frequently, who engages in irregular daily routines, and who is slow to accept new experiences.

slow-to-warm-up child A child who has a low activity level, is somewhat negative, and displays a low intensity of mood.

In their longitudinal investigation, Chess and Thomas found that 40 percent of the children they studied could be classified as easy, 10 percent as difficult, and 15 percent as slow to warm up. Notice that 35 percent did not fit any of the three patterns. Researchers have found that these three basic clusters of temperament are moderately stable across the childhood years.

One study revealed that young children with a difficult temperament showed more problems when they experienced low-quality child care and fewer problems when they experienced high-quality child care than did young children with an easy temperament (Pluess & Belsky, 2009).

Kagan's Concept of Behavioral Inhibition Another way of classifying temperament focuses on the differences between a shy, subdued, timid child and a sociable, extraverted, bold child. Jerome Kagan (2002, 2010, 2013) regards shyness with strangers (peers or adults) as one feature of a broad temperament category called *inhibition to the unfamiliar:* Inhibited children react to many aspects of unfamiliarity with initial avoidance, distress, or subdued affect, beginning around 7 to 9 months. A recent study revealed that behavioral inhibition at 3 years of age was linked to shyness four years later (Volbrecht & Goldsmith, 2010). In another study, shyness/inhibition in infancy/childhood was linked to social anxiety at 21 years of age (Bohlin & Hagekull, 2009).

Effortful Control (Self-Regulation) Mary Rothbart and John Bates (2006) stress that effortful control (self-regulation) is an important dimension of temperament. Infants who are high in effortful control show an ability to keep their arousal from getting too intense and have strategies for soothing themselves. By contrast, children who are low in effortful control are often unable to control their arousal; they are easily agitated and become intensely emotional. A recent study found that infants of mothers who were more stressed had a lower level of effortful control while infants of extraverted mothers showed a higher level of effortful control (Gartstein & others, 2012).

An important point about temperament classifications such as Chess and Thomas' and Rothbart and Bates' is that children should not be pigeonholed as having only one temperament dimension, such as "difficult" or "negative affectivity." A good strategy when attempting to classify a child's temperament is to think of temperament as consisting of multiple dimensions (Bates, 2012a, b). For example, a child might be extraverted, show little emotional negativity, and have good self-regulation. Another child might be introverted, show little emotional negativity, and have a low level of self-regulation.

The development of temperament capabilities such as effortful control allows individual differences to emerge. For example, although maturation of the brain's prefrontal lobes must occur for any child's attention to improve and the child to achieve effortful control, some children develop effortful control while others do not. And it is these individual differences in children that are at the heart of what temperament is (Bates, 2012a, b).

Biological Foundations and Experience

How does a child acquire a certain temperament? Kagan (2010, 2013) argues that children inherit a physiology that predisposes them to have a particular type of temperament. However, through experience they may learn to modify their temperament to some

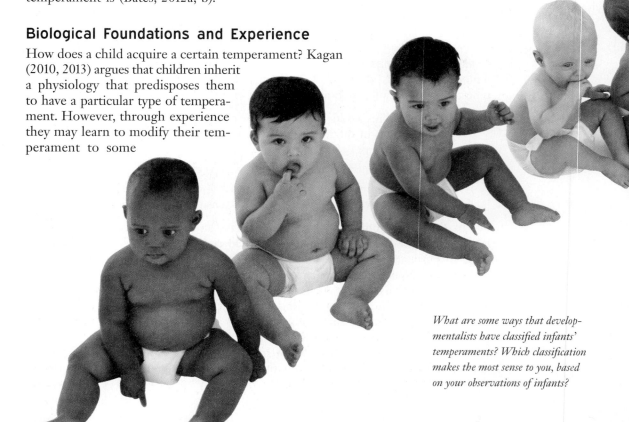

What are some ways that developmentalists have classified infants' temperaments? Which classification makes the most sense to you, based on your observations of infants?

degree. For example, children may inherit a physiology that predisposes them to be fearful and inhibited but then learn to reduce their fear and inhibition to some degree.

How might caregivers help a child become less fearful and inhibited? An important first step is to find out what frightens the child. Comforting and reassuring the child, and addressing their specific fears, are good strategies.

Biological Influences Physiological characteristics have been linked with different temperaments (Frodl & O'Keane, 2012; Kagan, 2013; Mize & Jones, 2012). In particular, an inhibited temperament is associated with a unique physiological pattern that includes a high and stable heart rate, high levels of the hormone cortisol, and high activity in the right frontal lobe of the brain (Kagan, 2010). This pattern may be tied to the excitability of the amygdala, a structure in the brain that plays an important role in fear and inhibition. Twin and adoption studies also suggest that heredity has a moderate influence on differences in temperament within a group of people (Plomin & others, 2009).

Too often the biological foundations of temperament are interpreted as meaning that temperament cannot develop or change. However, important self-regulatory dimensions of temperament such as adaptability, soothability, and persistence look very different in a 1-year-old and a 5-year-old (Easterbrooks &

others, 2013). These temperament dimensions develop and change with the growth of the neurobiological foundations of self-regulation (Calkins, 2012).

Gender, Culture, and Temperament Gender may be an important factor shaping the context that influences temperament. Parents might react differently to an infant's temperament based on whether the baby is a boy or a girl (Gaias & others, 2012). For example, in one study, mothers were more responsive to the crying of irritable girls than to that of irritable boys (Crockenberg, 1986).

Similarly, the reaction to an infant's temperament may depend in part on culture (Fung, 2011; Rothbart, 2011). For example, an active temperament might be valued in some cultures (such as the United States) but not in others (such as China) (Gartstein & others, 2009). Indeed, children's temperament can vary across cultures. For example, behavioral inhibition is valued more highly in China than in North America (Cole & Tan, 2007). Also, a recent study revealed that U.S infants showed more temperamental fearfulness while Finnish infants

goodness of fit Refers to the match between a child's temperament and the environmental demands with which the child must cope.

engaged in more positive affect, such as effortful control (Gaias & others, 2012).

In short, many aspects of a child's environment can encourage or discourage the persistence of temperament characteristics (Bates, 2012a, b; Easterbrooks & others, 2013). One useful way of thinking about these relationships applies the concept of goodness of fit, which we examine next.

Goodness of Fit and Parenting

Goodness of fit refers to the match between a child's temperament and the environmental demands the child must cope with. Suppose Jason is an active toddler who is made to sit still for long periods and Jack is a slow-to-warm-up toddler who is abruptly pushed into new situations on a regular basis. Both Jason and Jack face a lack of fit between their temperament and environmental demands. Lack of fit can produce adjustment problems (Rothbart, 2011). Researchers have found that decreases in infants' negative emotionality are linked to higher levels of parental sensitivity, involvement, and responsivity (Wachs & Bates, 2010).

What are some good strategies for parents to adopt when responding to their infant's temperament?

Many parents don't come to believe in the importance of temperament until the birth of their second child. They viewed their first child's behavior as stemming from how they treated the child. But then they find that some strategies that worked with their first child are not as effective with the second child. Some problems experienced with the first child (such as those associated with feeding, sleeping, and coping with strangers) may not arise with the second child, but new problems arise. Such experiences strongly suggest that children differ from each other very early in life, and that these differences have important implications for parent-child interaction (Rothbart, 2011).

What are the implications of temperamental variations for parenting? Decreases in infants' negative emotionality occur when parents are more involved, responsive, and sensitive when interacting with their children (Bates, 2012a, b; Penela & others, 2012). Temperament experts Ann Sanson and Mary Rothbart (1995) also recommend the following strategies for temperament-sensitive parenting:

- *Attention to and respect for individuality.* One implication is that it is difficult to generate general prescriptions for "good parenting." A goal might be accomplished in one way with one child and in another way with another child, depending on each child's temperament. Parents need to be flexible and sensitive to the infant's signals and needs.

- *Structuring the child's environment.* Crowded, noisy environments can pose greater problems for some children (such as a "difficult child") than for others (such as an "easy child"). We might also expect that a fearful, withdrawing child would benefit from slower entry into new contexts.

- *Avoid applying negative labels to the child.* Acknowledging that some children are harder to parent than others is often helpful, and advice on how to handle particular kinds of difficult circumstances can be helpful. However, labeling a child "difficult" runs the risk

How Would You...?

As a social worker, how would you apply information about an infant's temperament to maximize goodness of fit?

of becoming a self-fulfilling prophecy. That is, if a child is identified as "difficult," people may treat him or her in a way that elicits "difficult" behavior.

Personality Development

Emotions and temperament are key aspects of personality, the enduring personal characteristics of individuals (Shiner & DeYoung, 2013). Let's now examine characteristics that are often thought of as central to personality development during infancy: trust, the development of a sense of self, and progress toward independence.

Trust

According to Erik Erikson (1968), the first year of life is characterized by the trust-versus-mistrust stage of development. Upon emerging from a life of regularity, warmth, and protection in the mother's womb, the infant faces a world that is less secure. Erikson proposed that infants learn trust when they are cared for in a consistently nurturant manner. If the infant is not well fed and kept warm on a consistent basis, a sense of mistrust is likely to develop.

In Erikson's view, the issue of trust versus mistrust is not resolved once and for all in the first year of life. It arises again at each successive stage of development, and the outcomes can be positive or negative. For example, children who leave infancy with a sense of trust can still have their sense of mistrust activated at a later stage, perhaps if their parents become separated or divorced.

The Developing Sense of Self

It is difficult to study the self in infancy mainly because infants cannot tell us how they experience themselves. Infants cannot verbally express their views of the self. They also cannot understand complex instructions from researchers.

A rudimentary form of self-recognition—being attentive and positive toward one's image in a mirror—appears as early as 3 months (Mascolo & Fischer, 2007; Pipp, Fischer, & Jennings, 1987). However, a central, more complete index of self-recognition—the ability to recognize one's physical features—does not emerge until the second year (Thompson, 2006).

One ingenious strategy to test infants' visual self-recognition is the use of a mirror technique in which an infant's mother first puts a dot of rouge on the infant's nose. Then, an observer watches to see how often the infant touches its nose. Next, the infant is placed in front of a mirror and observers detect whether nose touching increases. Why does this matter? The idea is that increased nose touching indicates that the infant recognizes itself in the mirror and is trying to touch or rub off the rouge because the rouge violates the infant's view of itself; that is, the infant thinks something is not right, since it believes its real self does not have a dot of rouge on it.

Figure 4.3 displays the results of two investigations that used the mirror technique. The researchers found that before they were 1 year old, infants did not recognize themselves in the mirror (Amsterdam, 1968; Lewis & Brooks-Gunn, 1979). Signs of self-recognition began

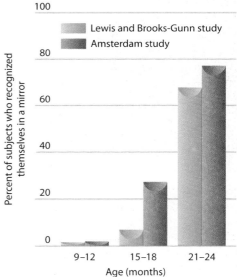

Figure 4.3 The Development of Self-Recognition in Infancy The graph shows the findings of two studies in which infants less than 1 year of age did not recognize themselves in the mirror. A slight increase in the percentage of infant self-recognition occurred around 15 to 18 months of age. By 2 years of age, a majority of children recognized themselves. *Why do researchers study whether infants recognize themselves in a mirror?*

to appear among some infants when they were 15 to 18 months old. By the time they were 2 years old, most children recognized themselves in the mirror. In sum, infants begin to develop a self-understanding, called self-recognition, at approximately 18 months of age (Hart & Karmel, 1996; Lewis, 2005).

In one study, biweekly assessments of infants from 15 to 23 months of age were conducted (Courage, Edison, & Howe, 2004). Self-recognition emerged gradually over this period, first appearing in the form of mirror recognition, followed by use of the personal pronoun and then by recognizing a photo of themselves. These aspects of self-recognition are often referred to as the first indications of toddlers' understanding of the mental state of "me," "that they are objects in their own mental representation of the world" (Lewis, 2005, p. 363).

Late in the second year and early in the third year, toddlers show other emerging forms of self-awareness that reflect a sense of "me" (Thompson & Virmani, 2010). For example, they refer to themselves by saying "Me big"; they label internal experiences such as emotions; they monitor themselves, as when a toddler says, "Do it myself"; and they say that things are theirs (Bullock & Lutkenhaus, 1990; Fasig, 2000). A recent study revealed that it is not until the second year that infants develop a conscious awareness of their own bodies. This developmental change in body awareness marks the beginning of children's representation of their own three-dimensional body shape and appearance, providing an early step in the development of their self-image and identity (Brownell & others, 2010).

Independence

Not only does the infant develop a sense of self in the second year of life, but independence also becomes a more central theme in the infant's life. Erikson (1968) stressed that independence is an important issue in the second year of life. Erikson's second stage of development is identified as autonomy versus shame and doubt. Autonomy builds as the infant's mental and motor abilities develop. At this point, not only can infants walk, but they can also climb, open and close, drop, push and pull, and hold and let go. Infants feel pride in these new accomplishments and want to do everything themselves, whether the activity is flushing a toilet, pulling the wrapping off a package, or deciding what to eat. It is important to recognize toddlers' motivation to do what they are capable of doing at their own pace. Then they can learn to control their muscles and their impulses themselves. Conversely, when caregivers are impatient and do for toddlers what they are capable of doing themselves, shame and doubt develop. To be sure, every parent has rushed a child from time to time, and one instance of rushing is unlikely to result in impaired development. It is only when parents consistently overprotect toddlers or criticize accidents (wetting, soiling, spilling, or breaking, for example) that children are likely to develop an excessive sense of shame and doubt about their ability to control themselves and their world.

How Would You...?

As a human development and family studies professional, how would you work with parents who showed signs of being overly protective or critical to the point of impairing their toddler's autonomy?

Erikson also argued that the stage of autonomy versus shame and doubt has important implications for the development of independence and identity during adolescence. The development of autonomy during the toddler years gives adolescents the courage to be independent individuals who can choose and guide their own future.

Social Orientation and Attachment

So far, we have discussed how emotions and emotional competence change as children develop. We have also examined the role of emotional style; in effect, we have seen how emotions set the tone of our experiences in life. But emotions also write the lyrics because they are at the core of our interest in the social world and our relationships with others.

Social Orientation and Understanding

As socioemotional beings, infants show a strong interest in their social world and are motivated to orient themselves toward it and to understand it. In earlier chapters we described many of the biological and cognitive foundations that contribute to the infant's development of social orientation and understanding. We will call attention to relevant biological and cognitive factors as we explore social orientation; locomotion; intention, goal-directed behavior and cooperation; and social referencing. Discussing biological, cognitive, and social processes together reminds us of an important aspect of development that was pointed out in Chapter 1—that these processes are intricately intertwined (Diamond, 2009).

Social Orientation

From early in their development, infants are captivated by the social world. Young infants stare intently at faces and are attuned to the sounds of human voices, especially their caregiver's (Gaither, Pauker, & Johnson, 2012; Lowe & others, 2012). Later, they become adept at interpreting the meaning of facial expressions. Face-to-face play often begins to characterize caregiver-infant interactions when the infant is about 2 to 3 months of age. Such play reflects many mothers' motivation to create a positive emotional state in their infants (Thompson, 2006, 2013a, b).

Infants also learn about the social world through contexts other than face-to-face play with a caregiver (Easterbrooks & others, 2013). Even though infants as young as 6 months show an interest in each other, their interaction with peers increases considerably in the latter half of the second year. Between 18 and 24 months, children markedly increase their imitative and reciprocal play—for example, imitating nonverbal actions like jumping and running (Eckerman & Whitehead, 1999). One study involved presenting 1- and 2-year-olds with a simple cooperative task that consisted of pulling a lever to get an attractive toy (Brownell, Ramani, & Zerwas, 2006) (see Figure 4.4). Any coordinated actions of the 1-year-olds appeared to be coincidental rather than cooperative, whereas the 2-year-olds' behavior was characterized as active cooperation to reach a goal.

Figure 4.4 The Cooperation Task
The cooperation task consisted of two handles on a box, atop which was an animated musical toy, surreptitiously activated by remote control when both handles were pulled. The handles were placed far enough apart that one child could not pull both handles. The experimenter demonstrated the task, saying, "Watch! If you pull the handles, the doggie will sing" (Brownell, Ramani, & Zerwas, 2006).

Locomotion

Recall from earlier in the chapter how important independence is for infants, especially in the second year of life. As infants develop the ability to crawl, walk, and run, they are able to explore and expand their social world. These newly developed self-produced locomotor skills allow the infant to independently initiate social interchanges on a more frequent basis.

Locomotion is also important for its motivational implications (Adolph & Berger, 2013; Adolph & Robinson, 2013). Once infants have the ability to move in goal-directed pursuits, the rewards gained from these pursuits lead to further efforts to explore and develop skills.

Intention, Goal-Directed Behavior, and Cooperation

The ability to perceive people as engaging in intentional and goal-directed behavior is an important social-cognitive accomplishment, and this initially occurs toward the end of the first year (Thompson, 2013a, b). Joint attention and gaze-following help the infant understand that other people have intentions (Bedford & others, 2012). By their first birthday, infants have begun to direct their caregiver's attention to objects that capture their interest (Heimann & others, 2006).

Infants' Social Sophistication and Insight

In sum, researchers are discovering that infants are more socially sophisticated and insightful at younger ages than was previously envisioned (Thompson, 2006, 2013a, b). This sophistication and insight is reflected in infants' perceptions of others' actions as intentionally motivated and goal-directed and their motivation to share and participate in that intentionality by their first birthday (Tomasello & Hamann, 2012). The more advanced social-cognitive skills of infants could be expected to influence their understanding and awareness of attachment to a caregiver.

Attachment

Attachment is a close emotional bond between two people. There is no shortage of theories about infant attachment. Three theorists discussed in Chapter 1—Freud, Erikson, and Bowlby—proposed influential views of attachment.

Freud theorized that infants become attached to the person or object that provides them with oral satisfaction. For most infants, this is the mother, since she is most likely to feed the infant. Is feeding as important as Freud thought? A classic study by Harry Harlow (1958) indicates that the answer is no (see Figure 4.5).

Harlow removed infant monkeys from their mothers at birth; for six months they were reared by two surrogate (substitute) "mothers." One surrogate mother was made of wire, the other of cloth. Half of the infant monkeys were fed by the wire mother, half by the cloth mother. Periodically, the amount of time the infant monkeys spent with either the wire or the cloth mother was computed. Regardless of which mother fed them, the infant monkeys spent far more time with the cloth mother. Even if the wire mother, but not the cloth mother, provided nourishment, the infant monkeys spent more time with the cloth mother. And when Harlow frightened the monkeys, those who were "raised" by the cloth mother ran to that mother and clung to it; those who were raised by the wire mother did not. Whether the mother provided comfort seemed to determine whether the monkeys associated that mother with security. This study clearly demonstrated that feeding is not the crucial element in the attachment process and that contact comfort is important.

Physical comfort also plays a role in Erik Erikson's (1968) view of the infant's development. Recall Erikson's proposal that during the first year of life infants are in the stage of trust versus mistrust. Physical comfort and sensitive care, according to Erikson (1968), are key to establishing a basic level of trust in infants. The infant's sense of

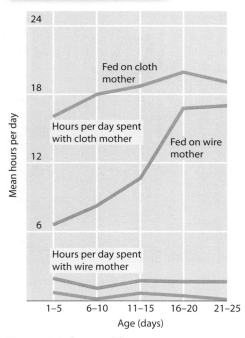

Figure 4.5 Contact Time with Wire and Cloth Surrogate Mothers
Regardless of whether the infant monkeys were fed by a wire or a cloth mother, they overwhelmingly preferred to spend contact time with the cloth mother. *How do these results compare with what Freud's theory and Erikson's theory would predict about human infants?*

trust, in turn, is the foundation for attachment and sets the stage for a lifelong expectation that the world will be a good and pleasant place.

The ethological perspective of British psychiatrist John Bowlby (1969, 1989) also stresses the importance of attachment in the first year of life and the responsiveness of the caregiver. Bowlby believed that both the infant and its primary caregivers are biologically predisposed to form attachments. He argued that the newborn is biologically equipped to elicit attachment behavior. The baby cries, clings, coos, and smiles. Later, the infant crawls, walks, and follows the mother. The immediate result is to keep the primary caregiver nearby; the long-term effect is to increase the infant's chances of survival (Thompson, 2006).

Attachment does not emerge suddenly but rather develops in a series of phases, moving from a baby's general preference for human figures to a partnership with primary caregivers. Following are four such phases based on Bowlby's conceptualization of attachment (Schaffer, 1996):

- *Phase 1: From birth to 2 months.* Infants instinctively direct their attachment to human figures. Strangers, siblings, and parents are equally likely to elicit smiling or crying from the infant.

- *Phase 2: From 2 to 7 months.* Attachment becomes focused on one figure, usually the primary caregiver, as the baby gradually learns to distinguish between familiar and unfamiliar people.

- *Phase 3: From 7 to 24 months.* Specific attachments develop. With increased locomotor skills, babies actively seek contact with regular caregivers, such as the mother or father.

- *Phase 4: From 24 months on.* Children become aware of other people's feelings, goals, and plans and begin to take these into account in directing their own actions.

Bowlby argued that infants develop an *internal working model* of attachment, a simple mental model of the caregiver, their relationship to him or her, and the self as deserving of nurturant care. The infant's internal working model of attachment with the caregiver influences the infant's, and later the child's, subsequent responses to other people (Roisman & Groh, 2011). The internal model of attachment also has played a pivotal role in the discovery of links between attachment and subsequent emotion, understanding, conscious development, and self-concept (Thompson, 2013d).

Individual Differences in Attachment

Although attachment to a caregiver intensifies midway through the first year, isn't it likely that the quality of a baby's attachment experiences varies? Mary Ainsworth (1979) thought so. Ainsworth created the **Strange Situation,** an observational measure of infant attachment in which the infant experiences a series of introductions, separations, and reunions with the caregiver and an adult stranger in a prescribed order. In using the Strange Situation, researchers hope that their observations will provide information about the infant's motivation to be near the caregiver and the degree to which the caregiver's presence provides the infant with security and confidence.

Based on how babies respond in the Strange Situation, they are described as being securely attached or insecurely attached (in one of three ways) to the caregiver:

- **Securely attached babies** use the caregiver as a secure base from which to explore the environment. When in the presence of their caregiver, securely attached infants explore the room and examine toys that have been placed in it. When the caregiver departs, securely attached infants might protest mildly; when the caregiver returns, these infants reestablish positive interaction with her, perhaps by smiling or climbing on her lap. Subsequently, they often resume playing with the toys in the room.

Strange Situation An observational measure of infant attachment that requires the infant to move through a series of introductions, separations, and reunions with the caregiver and an adult stranger in a prescribed order.

securely attached babies Babies that use the caregiver as a secure base from which to explore their environment.

insecure avoidant babies Babies that show insecurity by avoiding their mothers.

insecure resistant babies Babies that often cling to the caregiver, then resist her by fighting against the closeness, perhaps by kicking or pushing away.

insecure disorganized babies Babies that show insecurity by being disorganized and disoriented.

- **Insecure avoidant babies** show insecurity by avoiding the caregiver. In the Strange Situation, these babies engage in little interaction with the caregiver, are not distressed when she leaves the room, usually do not reestablish contact with her upon her return, and may even turn their back on her. If contact is established, the infant usually leans away or looks away.

- **Insecure resistant babies** often cling to the caregiver and then resist her by fighting against the closeness, perhaps by kicking or pushing away. In the Strange Situation, these babies often cling anxiously to the caregiver and don't explore the playroom. When the caregiver leaves, they often cry loudly and then push away if she tries to comfort them upon her return.

- **Insecure disorganized babies** are disorganized and disoriented. In the Strange Situation, these babies might appear dazed, confused, and fearful. To be classified as disorganized, babies must show strong patterns of avoidance and resistance or display certain specified behaviors, such as extreme fearfulness around the caregiver.

Do individual differences in attachment matter? Ainsworth proposed that secure attachment in the first year of life provides an important foundation for psychological development later in life. The securely attached infant moves freely away from the caregiver but keeps track of where she is through periodic glances. The securely attached infant responds positively to being picked up by others and, when put back down, freely moves away to play. An insecurely attached infant, by contrast, avoids the caregiver or is ambivalent toward her, fears strangers, and is upset by minor, everyday separations.

What is the nature of secure and insecure attachment?

How Would You…?

As a psychologist, how would you identify an insecurely attached toddler? How would you encourage a parent to strengthen the attachment bond?

If early attachment to a caregiver is important, it should relate to a child's social behavior later in development. For some children, early attachments seem to foreshadow later functioning (Bretherton, 2012; Brisch, 2012). In an extensive longitudinal study conducted by Alan Sroufe and his colleagues (2005), early secure attachment (assessed by the Strange Situation at 12 and 18 months) was linked with positive emotional health, high self-esteem, self-confidence, and socially competent interaction with peers, teachers, camp counselors, and romantic partners through adolescence. And a recent meta-analysis found that disorganized attachment was more strongly linked to externalizing problems (aggression and hostility, for example) than were avoidant attachment and resistant attachment (Fearon & others, 2010).

An important issue regarding attachment is whether infancy is a critical or sensitive period for development. The studies just described show continuity, with secure attachment in infancy predicting subsequent positive development in childhood and adolescence. For some children, though, there is little continuity. Not all research reveals the power of infant attachment to predict subsequent development (Roisman & Groh, 2011; Thompson, 2013d). In one longitudinal study, attachment classification in infancy did not predict attachment classification at 18 years of age (Lewis, Feiring, & Rosenthal, 2000). In this study, the best predictor of an insecure attachment classification at 18 was the occurrence of parental divorce in the intervening years. Consistently positive caregiving over a number of years is likely an important factor in connecting early attachment with the child's functioning later in development. Indeed, researchers have found that early secure attachment and subsequent experiences, especially maternal care and life stresses, are linked with children's later behavior and adjustment (Thompson, 2013d). For example, a longitudinal study revealed that changes in attachment security/insecurity from infancy to adulthood were linked to stresses and supports in socioemotional contexts (Van Ryzin, Carlson, & Sroufe, 2011). These results suggest that attachment continuity may reflect stable social contexts as much as early working models. The study just described (Van Ryzin, Carlson, & Sroufe, 2011) reflects an increasingly accepted view of the development of attachment and its influence on development. That is, it is important to recognize that attachment security in infancy does not always by itself produce long-term positive outcomes, but rather is linked to later outcomes through connections with the way children and adolescents subsequently experience various social contexts as they develop.

developmental cascade model
Involves connections across domains over time that influence developmental pathways and outcomes.

The Van Ryzin, Carlson, and Sroufe (2011) study reflects a **developmental cascade model,** which involves connections across domains over time that influence developmental pathways and outcomes (Cicchetti, 2013; Masten, 2013). Developmental cascades can include connections between a wide range of biological, cognitive, and socioemotional processes (attachment, for example), and also can involve social contexts such as families, peers, schools, and culture. Further, links can produce positive or negative outcomes at different points in development, such as infancy, early childhood, middle and late childhood, adolescence, and adulthood.

In addition to challenging the assumption that secure attachment in infancy serves as a critical or sensitive period, some developmentalists argue that the secure attachment concept does not adequately consider certain biological factors in development, such as genes and temperament. For example, Jerome Kagan (1987, 2002) points out that infants are highly resilient and adaptive; he argues that they are evolutionarily equipped to stay on a positive developmental course, even in the face of wide variations in parenting. Kagan and others stress that genetic characteristics and temperament play more important roles in a child's social competence than the attachment theorists, such as Bowlby and Ainsworth, are willing to acknowledge (Bakermans-Kranenburg & van IJzendoorn, 2011). For example, if some infants inherit a low tolerance for stress, this, rather than an insecure attachment bond, may be responsible for an inability to get along with peers. One study found links between disorganized attachment in infancy, a specific gene, and levels of maternal responsiveness (Spangler & others, 2009). In this study, infants with the short version of the gene—serotonin transporter gene 5-HTTLPR—developed a disorganized attachment style only when their mothers were slow in responding to them.

Another criticism of attachment theory is that it ignores the diversity of socializing agents and contexts that exists in an infant's world. A culture's value system can influence the nature of attachment (Mistry, Contreras, & Dutta, 2013). In northern Germany, for example, expectations for an infant's independence may be responsible for infants showing little distress upon a brief separation from the mother, whereas the Japanese mother's motivation for extreme close proximity to her infant may explain why Japanese infants become upset when they are separated from the mother. Also, in some cultures infants show attachments to many people. Among the Hausa (who live in Nigeria), both grandmothers and siblings provide a significant amount of care for infants (Harkness & Super, 1995). Infants in agricultural societies tend to form attachments to older siblings, who have major responsibility for their younger siblings' care. Researchers recognize the importance of competent, nurturant caregivers in an infant's development (Grusec & others, 2013).

In the Hausa culture, siblings and grandmothers provide a significant amount of care for infants. *How might these variations in care affect attachment?*

At issue, though, is whether or not secure attachment, especially to a single care-giver, is essential (Lamb, 2010; Thompson, 2013d).

Despite such criticisms, there is ample evidence that security of attachment is important to development (Sroufe, Coffino, & Carlson, 2010; Thompson, 2013d). Secure attachment in infancy is important because it reflects a positive parent-infant relationship and provides a foundation that supports healthy socio-emotional development in the years that follow.

Caregiving Styles and Attachment

Is the style of caregiving linked with the quality of the infant's attachment? Securely attached babies have caregivers who are sensitive to their signals and are consistently available to respond to the infant's needs (Cassidy & others, 2011; Jin & others, 2012). These caregivers often let their babies take an active part in determining the onset and pacing of interactions in the first year of life. A recent study revealed that sensitive maternal responding was linked to infant attachment security (Finger & others, 2009).

How do the caregivers of insecurely attached babies interact with them? Care-givers of avoidant babies tend to be unavailable or rejecting (Cassidy & others, 2011).

How Would You…?

As a health-care professional, how would you use an infant's at-tachment style and/or a parent's caregiving style to determine whether an infant may be at risk for neglect or abuse?

They often don't respond to their babies' signals and have little physical contact with them. When they do interact with their babies, they may behave in an angry and irri-table way. Caregivers of resistant babies tend to be incon-sistent; sometimes they respond to their babies' needs, and sometimes they don't. In gen-eral, they tend not to be very affectionate with their babies and show little synchrony when interacting with them. Caregiv-ers of disorganized babies often neglect or physically abuse them (Bernard & others, 2012; Cicchetti, 2013).

Social Contexts

Now that we have explored the infant's emotional and personality development and attachment, let's examine the social contexts in which these occur. We begin by studying a number of aspects of the family and then turn to a social context in which infants increasingly spend time: child care.

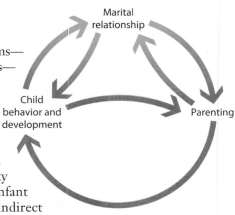

The Family

The family can be thought of as a constellation of subsystems—a complex whole made up of interrelated, interacting parts—defined in terms of generation, gender, and role. Each family member participates in several subsystems (Parke & Clarke-Stewart, 2011). The father and child represent one subsystem, the mother and father another; the mother, father, and child represent yet another; and so on.

These subsystems have reciprocal influences on each other, as Figure 4.6 highlights. For example, Jay Belsky (1981) stresses that marital relations, parenting, and infant behavior and development can have both direct and indirect effects on each other. An example of a direct effect is the influence of the parents' behavior on the child. An indirect effect is how the relationship between the spouses mediates the way a parent acts toward the child. For example, marital conflict might reduce the

Figure 4.6 Interaction Between Children and Their Parents: Direct and Indirect Effects

efficiency of parenting, in which case marital conflict would indirectly affect the child's behavior (Cummings, Braungart-Rieker, & Du Rocher-Schudlich, 2013). The simple fact that two people are becoming parents may have profound effects on their relationship.

The Transition to Parenthood

Whether people become parents through pregnancy, adoption, or stepparenting, they face disequilibrium and must adapt to it. Parents want to develop a strong attachment with their infant, but they still want to maintain strong attachments to their spouse and friends, and possibly to continue their careers. Parents ask themselves how this new being will change their lives. A baby places new restrictions on partners; no longer will they be able to rush out to a movie at a moment's notice, and money may not be readily available for vacations and other luxuries. Dual-career parents ask, "Will it harm the baby to place her in child care? Will we be able to find responsible baby-sitters?"

In a longitudinal investigation of couples from late pregnancy until three years after the baby was born, couples enjoyed more positive marital relations before the baby was born than afterward (Cowan & Cowan, 2000, 2009; Cowan & others, 2005). Still, almost one-third reported an increase in marital satisfaction. Some couples said that the baby had both brought them closer together and moved them farther apart; being parents enhanced their sense of themselves and gave them a new, more stable identity as a couple. Babies opened men up to greater concern with intimate relationships, and the demands of juggling work and family roles stimulated women to manage family tasks more efficiently and pay attention to their own personal growth.

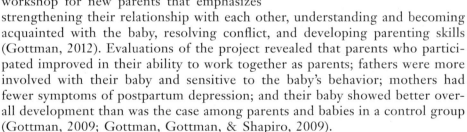

What kinds of adaptations do parents need to make?

The Bringing Home Baby project is a workshop for new parents that emphasizes strengthening their relationship with each other, understanding and becoming acquainted with the baby, resolving conflict, and developing parenting skills (Gottman, 2012). Evaluations of the project revealed that parents who participated improved in their ability to work together as parents; fathers were more involved with their baby and sensitive to the baby's behavior; mothers had fewer symptoms of postpartum depression; and their baby showed better overall development than was the case among parents and babies in a control group (Gottman, 2009; Gottman, Gottman, & Shapiro, 2009).

Other recent studies have explored the transition to parenthood (Brown, Feinberg, & Kan, 2012; Menendez & others, 2011). One study found similar negative change in relationship satisfaction for married and cohabiting women during the transition to parenthood (Mortensen & others, 2012). Another study revealed that mothers experienced unmet expectations in the transition to parenting, with fathers doing less than their partners had anticipated (Biehle & Mickelson, 2012).

Reciprocal Socialization

For many years, socialization was viewed as a one-way process: Children were considered to be the products of their parents' socialization techniques. According to more recent research, however, parent-child interaction is reciprocal (Gault-Sherman, 2011). **Reciprocal socialization** is socialization that is bidirectional. That is, children socialize their parents just as parents socialize their children (Grusec & others, 2013). These reciprocal

reciprocal socialization Socialization that is bidirectional, meaning that children socialize parents, just as parents socialize children.

scaffolding Process in which parents time interactions so that infants experience turn-taking with their parents.

interchanges and mutual influence processes are sometimes referred to as *transactional* (Sameroff, 2009, 2012).

An important form of reciprocal socialization is **scaffolding,** in which parents time interactions in such a way that the infant experiences turn-taking with the parents. Scaffolding can be used to support children's efforts at any age.

The game peek-a-boo, in which parents initially cover their babies, then remove the covering, and finally register "surprise" at the babies' reappearance, reflects the concept of scaffolding. As infants become more skilled at this game, they gradually do some of the covering and uncovering themselves. Parents try to time their actions in such a way that the infant takes turns with the parent.

Caregivers often play games with infants such as peek-a-boo and pat-a-cake. *How is scaffolding involved in these games?*

How Would You…?

As an educator, how would you explain the value of games and the role of scaffolding in the development of infants and toddlers?

Managing and Guiding Infants' Behavior

In addition to sensitive parenting involving warmth and caring that can result in infants being securely attached to their parents, other important aspects of parenting infants involve managing and guiding their behavior in an attempt to reduce or eliminate undesirable behaviors (Holden, Vittrup, & Rosen, 2011). This management process includes (1) being proactive and childproofing the environment so infants won't encounter potentially dangerous objects or situations, and (2) engaging in corrective methods when infants engage in undesirable behaviors, such as excessive fussing and crying, throwing objects, and so on.

One study assessed the discipline and corrective methods that parents had used by the time their infants were 12 and 24 months old (Vittrup, Holden, & Buck, 2006) (See Figure 4.7). Notice in Figure 4.7 that the main method parents used by the time infants were 12 months old was diverting the infants' attention, followed by reasoning, ignoring, and negotiating. Also note in Figure 4.7 that more than one-third of parents had yelled at their infant, about one-fifth had slapped the infant's hands or threatened the infant, and approximately one-sixth had spanked the infant by their first birthday.

Method	12 Months	24 Months
Spank with hand	14	45
Slap infant's hand	21	31
Yell in anger	36	81
Threaten	19	63
Withdraw privileges	18	52
Time-out	12	60
Reason	85	100
Divert attention	100	100
Negotiate	50	90
Ignore	64	90

Figure 4.7 Parents' Methods for Managing and Correcting Infants' Undesirable Behavior
Shown here are the percentages of parents who had used various corrective methods by the time the infants were 12 and 24 months old. *Source:* Based on data presented in Table 1 in Vittrup, Holden, G.W. & Buck, M. (2006). Attitudes predict the use of physical punishment: A prospective study of the emergence of disciplinary practices. Pediatrics, 117, 2055–2064.

As infants move into the second year of life and become more mobile and capable of exploring a wider range of environments, parental management of the toddler's behavior often triggers even more corrective feedback and discipline (Holden, Vittrup, & Rosen, 2011). As indicated in Figure 4.7, in the study just described, yelling increased from 36 percent at 1 year of age to 81 percent at 2 years of age, slapping the infant's hands increased from 21 percent at 1 year to 31 percent at age 2, and spanking increased from 14 percent at 1 to 45 percent at 2 (Vittrup, Holden, & Buck, 2006).

A special concern is that such corrective discipline tactics not become abusive. Too often what starts out as mild to moderately intense discipline on the part of parents can move into highly intense anger. In Chapter 6, you will read more extensively about the use of punishment with children and child maltreatment.

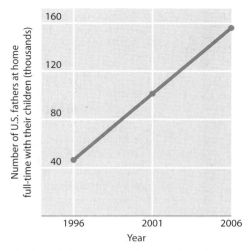

Figure 4.8 **Increase in the Number of U.S. Fathers Staying at Home Full-Time with Their Children**

Maternal and Paternal Caregiving

Much of our discussion of attachment has focused on mothers as caregivers. Do mothers and fathers differ in their caregiving roles? In general, mothers on average still spend considerably more time in caregiving with infants and children than do fathers (Blakemore, Berenbaum, & Liben, 2009). Mothers especially are more likely to engage in the managerial role with their children, coordinating their activities, making sure their health-care needs are met, and so on (Parke & Clarke-Stewart, 2011).

However, an increasing number of U.S. fathers stay home full-time with their children (Lamb, 2010). As indicated in Figure 4.8, there was a 300-plus percent increase in stay-at-home fathers in the United States from 1996 to 2006. A large portion of these full-time fathers have career-focused wives who are the primary providers of family income (O'Brien & Moss, 2010). One study revealed that the stay-at-home fathers were as satisfied with their marriage as traditional parents, although they indicated that they missed their daily life in the workplace (Rochlen & others, 2008). In this study, the stay-at-home fathers reported that they tended to be ostracized when they took their children to playgrounds and often were excluded from parent groups.

Observations of fathers and their infants suggest that fathers have the ability to act as sensitively and responsively with their infants as mothers do (Lamb, 2010; Rutherford & Przednowek, 2012). Consider the Aka pygmy culture in Africa, in which fathers spend as much time interacting with their infants as mothers do (Hewlett, 1991, 2000; Hewlett & MacFarlan, 2010). A recent study also found that marital intimacy and partner support during prenatal development were linked to father-infant attachment following childbirth (Yu & others, 2012). And another recent study revealed that fathers with a college-level education engaged in more stimulating physical activities with their infants and that fathers in a conflictual couple relationship participated in less caregiving and physical play with their infants (Cabrera, Hofferth, & Chae, 2011). Remember, however, that although fathers can be active, nurturant, involved caregivers, as in the case of Aka pygmies, in many cultures men have not chosen to follow this pattern (Lamb, 2005).

Do fathers interact with their infants differently from the way mothers do? Maternal interactions usually center on child-care activities—feeding, changing

An Aka pygmy father with his infant son. In the Aka culture, fathers were observed to be holding or near their infants 47 percent of the time (Hewlett, 1991).

diapers, and bathing. Paternal interactions are more likely to include play, especially rough-and-tumble play (Parke & Clarke-Stewart, 2011). They bounce infants, throw them up in the air, tickle them, and so on (Lamb, 1986, 2000). Mothers do play with their infants, but their play is less physical and arousing than that of fathers.

Do children benefit when fathers are positively involved in their caregiving? A study of more than 7,000 children who were assessed from infancy to adulthood revealed that those whose fathers were extensively involved in their lives (such as engaging in various activities with them and showing a strong interest in their education) were more successful in school (Flouri & Buchanan, 2004). However, if fathers have mental health problems, they may not interact as effectively with their infants. A recent study revealed that depressed fathers focused more on their own needs than on their infants' needs and directed more negative and critical speech toward infants (Sethna, Murray, & Ramchandani, 2012).

Child Care

Many U.S. children today experience multiple caregivers. Most do not have a parent staying home to care for them; instead, the children receive "child care"—that is, some type of care provided by others. Many parents worry that child care will have adverse effects such as reducing their infants' emotional attachment to them, retarding the infants' cognitive development, failing to teach them how to control anger, or allowing them to be unduly influenced by their peers. Are these concerns justified?

In the United States, approximately 15 percent of children age 5 and younger experience more than one child-care arrangement. A recent study of 2- and 3-year-old children revealed that an increase in the number of child-care arrangements the children experienced was linked to an increase in behavioral problems and a decrease in prosocial behavior (Morrissey, 2009).

Parental Leave

Today far more young children are in child care than at any other time in U.S. history. About 2 million children in the United States currently receive formal, licensed child care, and uncounted millions of children are cared for by unlicensed baby-sitters. In part, these numbers reflect the fact that U.S. adults cannot receive paid leave from their jobs to care for their young children.

Child-care policies around the world vary (Tolani & Brooks-Gunn, 2008). Europe has led the way in creating new standards of parental leave: In 1992, the European Union (EU) mandated a paid 14-week maternity leave. In most European countries today, working parents on leave receive 70 to 100 percent of the worker's prior wage, and paid leave averages about 16 weeks (Tolani & Brooks-Gunn, 2008). The United States currently allows up to 12 weeks of unpaid leave for parents who are caring for a newborn.

Most countries restrict eligible benefits to women who have been employed for a minimum length of time prior to childbirth. In Denmark, even unemployed mothers are eligible for extended parental leave related to childbirth. In Germany, child-rearing leave is available to almost all parents. The Nordic countries (Denmark, Norway, and Sweden) have extensive gender-equity family leave policies for childbirth that emphasize the contributions of both women and men (O'Brien & Moss, 2010). For example, in Sweden parents can take an 18-month, job-protected parental leave with benefits to be shared by parents and applied to full-time or part-time work.

How are child-care policies in many European countries, such as Sweden, different from those in the United States?

Variations in Child Care

Because the United States does not have a policy of paid leave for child care, child care in the United States has become a major national concern (Berlin, 2012; Lamb, 2012). Many factors influence the effects of child care, including the age of the child, the type of child care, and the quality of the program.

The type of child care varies extensively. Child care is provided in large centers with elaborate facilities and in private homes. Some child-care centers are commercial operations; others are nonprofit centers run by churches, civic groups, and employers. Some child-care providers are professionals; others are untrained adults who want to earn extra money. Figure 4.9 presents the primary care arrangement for U.S. children under age 5 with employed mothers (Clarke-Stewart & Miner, 2008).

Child-care quality makes a difference. What constitutes a high-quality child-care program for infants? In high-quality child care (Clarke-Stewart & Miner, 2008, p. 273):

> caregivers encourage the children to be actively engaged in a variety of activities, have frequent, positive interactions that include smiling, touching, holding, and speaking at the child's eye level, respond properly to the child's questions or requests, and encourage children to talk about their experiences, feelings, and ideas.

High-quality child care also involves providing children with a safe environment, access to age-appropriate toys and participation in age-appropriate activities, and a low caregiver-child ratio that allows caregivers to spend considerable time with children on an individual basis.

Children are more likely to experience poor-quality child care if they come from families with few resources (psychological, social, and economic) (Carta & others, 2012). Many researchers have examined the role of poverty in quality of child care (Lucas & others, 2008). One study found that extensive child care was harmful to low-income children only when the care was of low quality (Votruba-Drzal & others, 2004). Even if the child was in child care more than 45 hours a week, high-quality care was associated with fewer internalizing problems (anxiety, for example) and externalizing problems (aggressive and destructive behaviors, for example). A recent study revealed that children from low-income families benefited in terms of school readiness and language development when their parents selected higher-quality child care (McCartney & others, 2007).

To read about one individual who provides quality child care to individuals from impoverished backgrounds, see the *Careers in Life-Span Development* profile.

How Would You...?

As an educator, how would you design the ideal child-care program to promote optimal infant development?

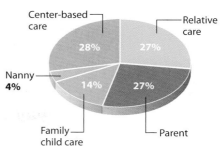

Figure 4.9
Primary Care Arrangements in the United States for Children Under 5 Years of Age with Employed Mothers

---

Careers in life-span development

Wanda Mitchell, Child-Care Director

Wanda Mitchell is the Center Director at the Hattie Daniels Day Care Center in Wilson, North Carolina. Her responsibilities include directing the operation of the center, which involves creating and maintaining an environment in which young children can learn effectively, and ensuring that the center meets state licensing requirements. Wanda obtained her undergraduate degree from North Carolina A & T University, majoring in Child Development. Prior to her current position, she had been an education coordinator for Head Start and an instructor at Wilson Technical Community College. Describing her chosen career, Wanda says, "I really enjoy working in my field. This is my passion. After graduating from college, my goal was to advance in my field."

Wanda Mitchell, child-care director, working with some of the children at her center.

The National Longitudinal Study of Child Care

In 1991, the National Institute of Child Health and Human Development (NICHD) began a comprehensive longitudinal study of child-care experiences. Data were collected from a diverse sample of almost 1,400 children and their families at 10 locations across the United States over a period of seven years. Researchers used multiple methods (trained observers, interviews, questionnaires, and testing) and measured many facets of children's development, including physical health, cognitive development, and socioemotional development. Following are some of the results of what is now referred to as the NICHD Study of Early Child Care and Youth Development or NICHD SECCYD (NICHD Early Child Care Research Network, 2001, 2002, 2003, 2004, 2005, 2006, 2009).

- *Quality of care.* Evaluations of quality of care were based on characteristics such as group size, child–adult ratio, physical environment, caregiver characteristics (such as formal education, specialized training, and child-care experience), and caregiver behavior (such as sensitivity to children). An alarming conclusion is that a majority of the child care in the first three years of life was of unacceptably low quality. Positive caregiving by nonparents in child-care settings was infrequent—only 12 percent of the children in the study experienced positive nonparental child care (such as positive talk and language stimulation). Further, infants from low-income families experienced lower-quality child care than did infants from higher-income families. When quality of caregivers' care was high, children performed better on cognitive and language tasks, were more cooperative with their mothers during play, showed more positive and skilled interaction with peers, and had fewer behavior problems. Caregiver training and favorable child–staff ratios were linked with higher cognitive and social competence when children were 54 months of age. In recent research involving the NICHD sample, links were found between nonrelative child care from birth to 4 years of age and adolescent development at 15 years of age (Vandell & others, 2010). In this analysis, better quality of early care was related to a higher level of academic achievement and a lower level of externalizing problems at age 15.

- *Amount of child care.* The quantity of child care predicted some outcomes (Vandell & others, 2010). When children spent extensive amounts of time in child care beginning in infancy, they experienced fewer sensitive interactions with their mothers, showed more behavior problems, and had higher rates of illness. In general, when children spent 30 hours or more per week in child care, their development was less than optimal.

- *Family and parenting influences.* The influence of families and parenting was not weakened by extensive child care. Parents played a significant role in helping children regulate their emotions. Especially important parenting influences were being sensitive to children's needs, being involved with children, and providing cognitive stimulation. Indeed, parental sensitivity has been the most consistent predictor of secure attachment (Friedman, Melhuish, & Hill, 2009). An important final point about the extensive NICHD SECCYD research is that findings have consistently shown that family factors are considerably stronger and more consistent predictors of a wide variety of child outcomes than are child-care experiences (quality, quantity, type). The worst outcomes for children occur when both home and child care settings are of poor quality. For example, a recent study involving the NICHD SECCYD data revealed that worse socioemotional

What are some important findings from the national longitudinal study of child care conducted by the National Institute of Child Health and Human Development?

outcomes (more problem behavior, lower levels of prosocial behavior) for children occurred when they experienced both home and child care environments that conferred risk (Watamura & others, 2011).

What are some strategies parents can follow in regard to child care? Child-care expert Kathleen McCartney (2003, p. 4) offers this advice:

- *Recognize that the quality of your parenting is a key factor in your child's development.*
- *Make decisions that will improve the likelihood that you will be good parents.* "For some this will mean working full-time"—for personal fulfillment, income, or both. "For others, this will mean working part-time or not working outside the home."
- *Monitor your child's development.* "Parents should observe for themselves whether their children seem to be having behavior problems." They should also talk with child-care providers and their pediatrician about their child's behavior.
- *Take some time to find the best child care.* Observe different child-care facilities and be certain that you like the one you choose. "Quality child care costs money, and not all parents can afford the child care they want."

How Would You...?

As a psychologist, based on the findings from the NICHD study, how would you advise parents about their role in their child's development versus the role of nonparental child care?

Summary

Emotional and Personality Development

- Emotion is feeling, or affect, that occurs when a person is in a state or an interaction that is important to them. Infants display a number of emotions early in their development, such as by crying, smiling, and showing fear. Two fears that infants develop are stranger anxiety and fear of separation from a caregiver. As infants develop, it is important for them to increase their ability to regulate their emotions.

- Temperament is an individual's behavioral style and characteristic way of responding emotionally. Chess and Thomas classified infants as (1) easy, (2) difficult, or (3) slow to warm up. Kagan proposed that inhibition to the unfamiliar is an important temperament category. Rothbart and Bates emphasized that effortful control (self-regulation) is an important temperament dimension. Goodness of fit can be an important aspect of a child's adjustment.

- Erikson argued that an infant's first year is characterized by the stage of trust versus mistrust. Independence becomes a central theme in the second year of life, which is characterized by the stage of autonomy versus shame and doubt.

Social Orientation and Attachment

- Infants show a strong interest in the social world and are motivated to understand it. Infants are more socially sophisticated and insightful at an earlier age than was previously thought.

- Attachment is a close emotional bond between two people. In infancy, contact comfort and trust are important in the development of attachment. Securely attached babies use the caregiver, usually the mother, as a secure base from which to explore their environment. Three types of insecure attachment are avoidant, resistant, and disorganized. Caregivers of secure babies are more sensitive to the babies' signals and are consistently available to meet their needs.

Social Contexts

- The transition to parenthood requires considerable adaptation and adjustment on the part of parents. Children socialize parents just as parents socialize children. Parents use a wide range of methods to manage and guide infants' behavior. In general, mothers spend more time in caregiving than fathers; fathers tend to engage in more physical, playful interaction with infants than mothers.

- The quality of child care is uneven, and child care remains a controversial topic. Quality child care can be achieved and seems to have few adverse effects on children.

Key Terms

Physical and Cognitive Development in Early Childhood

5

Stories of Life-Span Development: Reggio Emilia's Children

The Reggio Emilia approach is an educational program for young children that was developed in the northern Italian city of Reggio Emilia. Children of single parents and children with disabilities have priority in admission; other children are admitted according to a scale of needs. Parents pay on a sliding scale based on income.

The children are encouraged to learn by investigating and exploring topics that interest them. A wide range of stimulating media and materials are available for children to use as they learn music, movement, drawing, painting, sculpting, collage, puppetry, and photography, among other things (Stremmel, 2011).

In this program, children often explore topics in a group, which fosters a sense of community, respect for diversity, and a collaborative approach to problem solving (Jones & Reynolds, 2011). In this group setting, two co-teachers guide the children in their exploration. The Reggio Emilia teachers treat each project as an adventure. It can start from an adult's suggestion, from a child's idea, or from an unexpected event such as a snowfall. Every project is based on what the children say and do. The teachers allow children enough time to think of and craft a project.

At the core of the Reggio Emilia approach is an image of children who are competent and have rights, especially the right to outstanding care and education (Martin & Evaldsson, 2012). Parent participation is considered essential, and cooperation is a major theme in the schools. Many experts on early childhood education believe that the Reggio Emilia approach provides a supportive, stimulating context in which children are motivated to explore their world in a competent and confident manner.

A Reggio Emilia classroom in which young children explore topics that interest them.

Parents and educators who clearly understand how young children develop can play an active role in creating programs that foster their natural interest in learning, rather than stifling it (Squires & others, 2013). In this chapter, the first of two chapters on early childhood (ages 3 to 5), we explore the physical, cognitive, and language changes that typically occur as the toddler develops into the preschooler, and then we look at early childhood education. ■

Physical Changes

Remember from Chapter 3 that a child's growth in infancy is rapid and follows cephalocaudal and proximodistal patterns. Fortunately, the growth rate slows in early childhood; otherwise, we would be a species of giants.

Body Growth and Change

Despite the slowing of growth in height and weight that characterizes early childhood, this growth is still the most obvious physical change during this period of development. Yet unseen changes in the brain and nervous system are no less significant in preparing children for advances in cognition and language.

Height and Weight

The average child grows 2½ inches in height and gains between 5 and 7 pounds a year during early childhood. As the preschool child grows older, the percentage of increase in height and weight decreases with each additional year (Wilson & Hockenberry, 2012). Girls are only slightly smaller and lighter than boys during these years, a difference that continues until puberty. In addition, girls have more fatty tissue than boys, and boys have more muscle tissue than girls.

During the preschool years, both boys and girls slim down as the trunk of the body lengthens (Burns & others, 2013). Although the head is still somewhat large for the body, by the end of the preschool years most children have lost the top-heavy look they had as toddlers. Body fat also shows a slow, steady decline during the preschool years. The chubby baby often looks much leaner by the end of early childhood.

Growth patterns vary from one individual to another (Florin & Ludwig, 2011). Think back to your preschool years. That was probably the first time you noticed that some children were taller than you, some shorter; some were fatter, some thinner; some were stronger, some weaker. Much of the variation was due to heredity, but environmental experiences were also involved. A review of the height and weight of children around the world concluded that the two most important contributors to height differences are ethnic origin and nutrition (Meredith, 1978). Urban, middle-socioeconomic status, and firstborn children were taller than rural, lower-socioeconomic status, and later-born children. In the United States, African American children are also taller than White children.

The bodies of 5-year-olds and 2-year-olds are different. Notice that the 5-year-old not only is taller and weighs more, but also has a longer trunk and legs than the 2-year-old. *Can you think of some other physical differences between 2- and 5-year-olds?*

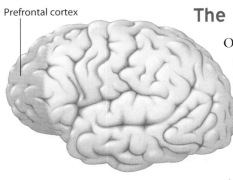

Prefrontal cortex

The Brain

myelination The process by which the axons are covered and insulated with a layer of fat cells, which increases the speed at which information travels through the nervous system.

One of the most important physical developments during early childhood is the continuing development of the brain and other parts of the nervous system (Diamond, 2013). The increasing maturation of the brain, combined with opportunities to experience a widening world, contribute to children's emerging cognitive abilities. In particular, changes in the brain during early childhood enable children to plan their actions, attend to stimuli more effectively, and make considerable strides in language development.

Figure 5.1
The Prefrontal Cortex
The brain pathways and circuitry involving the prefrontal cortex (shaded in purple) show significant advances in development during middle and late childhood. *What cognitive processes are linked with these changes in the prefrontal cortex?*

Although the brain does not grow as rapidly during early childhood as in infancy, it does undergo remarkable changes. By repeatedly obtaining brain scans of the same children for up to four years, researchers have found that children's brains experience rapid, distinct spurts of growth (Gogtay & Thompson, 2010). The overall size of the brain does not increase dramatically from ages 3 to 15; what does change dramatically are local patterns within the brain. The amount of brain material in some areas can nearly double in as little as a year, followed by a dramatic loss of tissue as unneeded cells are pruned and the brain continues to reorganize itself. From 3 to 6 years of age the most rapid growth in the brain takes place in the part of the frontal lobes known as the *prefrontal cortex* (see Figure 5.1), which plays a key role in planning and organizing new actions and maintaining attention to tasks (Gogtay & Thompson, 2010).

The continuation of two changes that began before birth contributes to the brain's growth during early childhood. First, the number and size of dendrites increase, and second, myelination continues. Recall from Chapter 3 that **myelination** is the process through which axons (nerve fibers that carry signals away from the cell body) are covered with a layer of fat cells, which increases the speed and efficiency of information traveling through the nervous system. Myelination is important in the development of a number of abilities (Lebel & others, 2012). For example, myelination in the areas of the brain related to hand-eye coordination is not complete until about age 4. Myelination in the areas of the brain related to focusing attention is not complete until the end of middle or late childhood.

Motor Development

Running as fast as you can, falling down, getting right back up and running just as fast as you can . . . building towers with blocks . . . scribbling, scribbling, and scribbling some more . . . cutting paper with scissors . . . During your preschool years, you probably developed the ability to perform all these activities. What physical changes made this possible?

Gross Motor Skills

The preschool child no longer has to make an effort simply to stay upright and move around. As children move their legs with more confidence and carry themselves more purposefully, moving around in the environment becomes more automatic (Burns & others, 2013).

Around age 3, children enjoy simple movements such as hopping, jumping, and running back and forth, just for the sheer delight of performing them. They delight in showing how they can run across a room and jump all of 6 inches. The run-and-jump will win no Olympic medals, but for the 3-year-old it brings considerable pride and a sense of accomplishment.

At age 4, children are still enjoying the same kinds of activities, but they have become more adventurous. They scramble over low jungle gyms as they display their athletic prowess. Although they have been able to climb stairs with one foot on each step for some time, they are just beginning to be able to come down the same way.

By age 5, children are even more adventuresome than when they were 4. It is not unusual for self-assured 5-year-olds to perform hair-raising stunts on practically any climbing object. Five-year-olds also run hard and enjoy races with each other and their parents.

Fine Motor Skills

By the time they turn 3, children have had the ability to pick up the tiniest objects between their thumb and forefinger for some time, but they are still somewhat clumsy at it. Three-year-olds can build surprisingly high block towers, each block placed with intense concentration but often not in a completely straight line. When 3-year-olds play with a simple jigsaw puzzle, they are rather rough in placing the pieces. Even when they recognize the hole a piece fits into, they are not very precise in positioning the piece. They often try to force the piece into the hole or pat it vigorously.

By age 4, children's fine motor coordination has improved substantially and is much more precise. Sometimes 4-year-olds have trouble building high towers with blocks because, in their desire to place each of the blocks perfectly, they may upset those already in the stack. Fine motor coordination continues to improve so that by age 5, hand, arm, and body all move together under better command of the eye. Mere towers no longer interest the 5-year-old, who now wants to build a house or a church, complete with steeple, though adults might still need to be told what each finished project is meant to be.

Nutrition and Exercise

Eating habits are important aspects of development during early childhood (Schiff, 2013; Wardlaw & Smith, 2012). What children eat affects their skeletal growth, body shape, and susceptibility to disease. Exercise and physical activity are also very important aspects of young children's lives (Lumpkin, 2011).

Overweight Young Children

Being overweight has become a serious health problem in early childhood (Thompson & Manore, 2013). A recent national study revealed that 45 percent of children's meals exceed recommendations for saturated and trans fat, which can raise cholesterol levels and increase the risk of heart disease (Center for Science in the Public Interest, 2008). This study also found that one-third of children's daily caloric intake comes from restaurants, twice the percentage consumed away from home in the 1980s. Further, 93 percent of almost 1,500 possible choices at 13 major fast-food chains exceeded 430 calories—one-third of what the National Institute of Medicine recommends that 4- to 8-year-old children consume in a day. Nearly all of the children's meal offerings at KFC, Taco Bell, Sonic, Jack in the Box, and Chick-fil-A were too high in calories. A recent study of U.S. 2- and 3-year-olds found that French fries and other fried potatoes were the vegetable they were most likely to consume (Fox & others, 2010).

Young children's eating behavior is strongly influenced by their caregivers' behavior (Black & Hurley, 2007; Farrow, 2012; Gibson & others, 2012). Children's eating behavior improves when caregivers eat with children on a predictable schedule, model eating healthy food, make mealtimes pleasant occasions, and engage in certain feeding styles. Distractions created by television, family arguments, and competing activities should be minimized so that children can focus on eating. Experts recommend a sensitive, responsive caregiver feeding style, in which the caregiver is nurturant, provides clear information about what is expected, and responds appropriately to children's cues (Black & Lozoff, 2008). Forceful and restrictive caregiver behaviors are not recommended, as they can lead to excessive weight gain (Riesch & others, 2012).

How Would You...?

As a health-care professional, how would you work with parents to increase the nutritional value of meals and snacks they provide to their young children?

The Centers for Disease Control and Prevention (2012) designates categories for obesity, overweight, and at risk for being overweight. These categories are determined by body mass index (BMI), which is computed using a formula that takes into account height and weight. Only children and adolescents at or above the 97th percentile are classified as obese; those at the 95th or 96th percentile as overweight; and those from the 85th to the 94th percentile as at risk of being overweight.

The percentages of young children who are overweight or at risk of being overweight in the United States have increased dramatically in recent decades, and these percentages are likely to climb further unless changes occur in children's lifestyles (Summerbell & others, 2012). In 2009–2010, 12.1 percent of U.S. 2- to 5-year-olds were classified as obese compared to 5 percent in 1976–1980 and 10.4 percent in 2007–2008 (Ogden & others, 2012). Being overweight in early childhood is a risk factor for later weight problems. For example, a recent study revealed that preschool children who were overweight were at significant risk for being overweight or obese in adolescence (Shankaran & others, 2011).

What are some trends in the eating habits and weight of young children?

A comparison of 34 countries revealed that the United States had the second highest rate of child obesity (Janssen & others, 2005). Childhood obesity contributes to a number of health problems in young children (Anspaugh & Ezell, 2013). For example, physicians are now seeing type 2 (adult-onset) diabetes (a condition directly linked with obesity and a low level of fitness) in children as young as age 5 (Riley & Bluhm, 2012). We will have much more to consider about children's eating behavior and weight status in Chapter 7.

Exercise

Young children should engage in physical activity every day (Wuest & Fisette, 2012). Guidelines recommend that preschool children engage in two hours of physical activity per day, comprising one hour of structured activity and one hour of unstructured free-play (National Association for Sport and Physical Education, 2002). The child's life should center on activities, not meals (Graber & Woods, 2012). Following are some recent research studies that examine young children's exercise and activities:

- Observations of 3- to 5-year-old children during outdoor play at preschools revealed that the preschool children were mainly sedentary even when participating in outdoor play (Brown & others, 2009). In this study, throughout the day the preschoolers were sedentary 89 percent of the time, engaged in light activity 8 percent of the time, and participated in moderate to vigorous physical activity only 3 percent of the time.

How much physical activity should preschool children engage in per day?

- Preschool children's physical activity was enhanced by family members engaging in sports together and by parents' perception that it was safe for their children to play outside (Beets & Foley, 2008).

- Incorporation of a "move and learn" physical activity curriculum increased the activity level of 3- to 5-year-old children in a half-day preschool program (Trost, Fees, & Dzewaltowski, 2008).

How Would You...?

As a health-care professional, how would you advise parents who want to get their talented 4-year-old child into a soccer league for preschool children?

Malnutrition

Poor nutrition affects many young children from low-income families. Many of these children do not obtain essential amounts of iron, vitamins, or protein. Poor nutrition is a particular concern in the lives of infants from low-income families (Imdad & others, 2011).

To address this problem in the United States, the WIC (Women, Infants, and Children) program provides federal grants to states for healthy supplemental foods, health care referrals, and nutrition education for women from low-income families beginning in pregnancy, and to infants and young children up to 5 years of age who are at nutritional risk (Hillier & others, 2012; WIC New York, 2011; Whaley & others, 2012). WIC serves approximately 7,500,000 participants in the United States.

Positive influences on infants' and young children's nutrition and health, as well as mothers' health, have been found for participants in WIC (Sekhobo & others, 2010). For example, a recent multiple-year literacy intervention with Spanish-speaking families in the WIC program in Los Angeles increased literacy resources and activities at home, which in turn led to a higher level of school readiness in children (Whaley & others, 2011).

Illness and Death

The vast majority of children in the United States go through the physical changes just described and reach adulthood without serious illness or death. However, some do not. In the United States accidents are the leading cause of death in young children, followed by cancer and cardiovascular disease (National Center for Health Statistics, 2012). In addition to motor vehicle accidents, other accidental deaths in children involve drowning, falls, and poisoning (Green, Muir, & Maher, 2011).

Children's safety is influenced not only by their own skills and safety-related behaviors but also by characteristics of their family and home, school and peers, and the community (Trasande & others, 2010). Figure 5.2 describes steps that can be taken in each of these contexts to enhance children's safety and prevent injury (Sleet & Mercy, 2003).

One major danger to children is parental smoking (Hwang & others, 2012). An estimated 22 percent of children and adolescents in the United States are exposed to tobacco smoke in the home. An increasing number of studies indicate that children are at risk for health problems when they live in homes in which a parent smokes (Chang, 2009). Children exposed to tobacco smoke in the home are more likely to develop wheezing and asthma than are children in homes where no one smokes (Yi & others, 2012). A recent study found that parental smoking was a risk factor for higher blood pressure in children (Simonetti & others, 2011). And another recent study revealed that exposure to second-hand smoke was related to young children's sleep problems, including sleep-disordered breathing (Yolton & others, 2010).

Although accidents and serious illnesses such as cancer are the leading causes of death among children in the United States, this is not the case elsewhere in the world, where many children die of preventable infectious diseases. Many of the deaths of young children around the world could be prevented by a reduction in poverty and improvements in nutrition, sanitation, education, and health services (UNICEF, 2012). High poverty rates have devastating effects on the health of a country's young children, as they often experience lives of hunger, malnutrition, illness, inadequate access to health care, unsafe water, and a lack of protection from harm (UNICEF, 2012). In the last decade, there has been a dramatic increase in the number of young children who have died because of HIV/AIDS transmitted to them by their parents. Deaths of young children due to HIV/AIDS especially occur in countries with high rates of poverty and low levels of education (UNICEF, 2012).

How Would You...?

As a health-care professional, how would you talk with parents about the impact of secondhand smoke on children's health to encourage parents to stop smoking?

Individual

- Development of social skills and ability to regulate emotions
- Impulse control (such as not darting out into a street to retrieve a ball)
- Frequent use of personal protection (such as bike helmets and safety seats)

Family/Home

- High awareness and knowledge of child management and parenting skills
- Frequent parent protective behaviors (such as use of child safety seats)
- Presence of home safety equipment (such as smoke alarms and cabinet locks)

School/Peers

- Promotion of home/school partnerships
- Absence of playground hazards
- Injury prevention and safety promotion policies and programs

Community

- Availability of positive activities for children and their parents
- Active surveillance of environmental hazards
- Effective prevention policies in place (such as pool fencing)

Figure 5.2
Characteristics That Enhance Young Children's Safety
In each context of a child's life, steps can be taken to create conditions that enhance the child's safety and reduce the likelihood of injury. How are the contexts listed in the figure related to Bronfenbrenner's theory (described in Chapter 1)?

Many children in impoverished countries die before reaching the age of 5 from dehydration and malnutrition brought about by diarrhea. *What are some of the other main causes of death in young children around the world?*

Cognitive Changes

The cognitive world of the preschool child is creative, free, and fanciful. Preschool children's imaginations work overtime, and their mental grasp of the world improves. Our coverage of cognitive development in early childhood focuses on three theories: Piaget's, Vygotsky's, and information processing.

Piaget's Preoperational Stage

Remember from Chapter 3 that during Piaget's first stage of development, the sensorimotor stage, the infant becomes increasingly able to organize and coordinate sensations and perceptions with physical

preoperational stage Piaget's second stage, lasting from about 2 to 7 years of age, during which children begin to represent the world with words, images, and drawings, and symbolic thought goes beyond simple connections of sensory information and physical action; stable concepts are formed, mental reasoning emerges, egocentrism is present, and magical beliefs are constructed.

operations In Piaget's theory, these are internalized, reversible sets of actions that allow children to do mentally what they formerly did physically.

symbolic function substage Piaget's first substage of preoperational thought, in which the child gains the ability to mentally represent an object that is not present (between about 2 and 4 years of age).

egocentrism The inability to distinguish between one's own perspective and someone else's (salient feature of the first substage of preoperational thought).

movements and actions. The **preoperational stage,** which lasts from approximately ages 2 to 7, is the second stage in Piaget's theory. In this stage, children begin to represent the world with words, images, and drawings. They form stable concepts and begin to reason. At the same time, the young child's cognitive world is dominated by egocentrism and magical beliefs.

Because Piaget called this stage "preoperational," it might sound like an unimportant waiting period. Not so. However, the label *pre-operational* emphasizes that the child does not yet perform **operations,** which are reversible mental actions that allow children to do mentally what before they could do only physically. Mentally adding and subtracting numbers are examples of operations. *Preoperational thought* is the beginning of the ability to reconstruct in thought what has been established in behavior. It can be divided into two substages: the symbolic function substage and the intuitive thought substage.

The Symbolic Function Substage

The **symbolic function substage** is the first substage of preoperational thought, occurring roughly between the ages of 2 and 4. In this substage, the young child gains the ability to mentally represent an object that is not present. This ability vastly expands the child's mental world (Mandler & DeLoache, 2012). In this substage, children use scribble designs to represent people, houses, cars, clouds, and so on; they begin to use language more effectively and engage in pretend play. However, although young children make distinct progress during this substage, their thought still has important limitations, two of which are egocentrism and animism.

Egocentrism is the inability to distinguish between one's own perspective and someone else's perspective. The following telephone conversation between 4-year-old Marie, who is at home, and her father, who is at work, typifies Marie's egocentric thought:

> **Father:** Marie, is Mommy there?
> Marie silently nods.
>
> **Father:** Marie, may I speak to Mommy?
> Marie nods again, silently.

Marie's response is egocentric in that she fails to consider her father's perspective before replying. A nonegocentric thinker would have responded verbally.

Piaget and Barbel Inhelder (1969) initially studied young children's egocentrism by devising the three mountains task (see Figure 5.3). The child walks around the

Model of Mountains

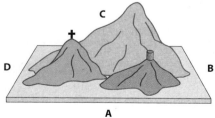
A
Child seated here

Photo 1
(View from A)

Photo 2
(View from B)

Photo 3
(View from C)

Photo 4
(View from D)

Figure 5.3 The Three Mountains Task
Photo 1 shows the child's perspective from where he or she is sitting (location A). Photos 2, 3, and 4 show what the mountains would look like to a person sitting at locations B, C, and D, respectively. When asked to choose the photograph that shows what the mountains look like from position B, the preoperational child selects a photograph taken from location A, the child's view at the time. A child who thinks in a preoperational way cannot take the perspective of a person sitting at another spot.

model of the mountains and becomes familiar with what the mountains look like from different perspectives, and she can see that there are different objects on the mountains. The child is then seated on one side of the table on which the mountains are placed. The experimenter moves a doll to different locations around the table, and at each location asks the child to select from a series of photos the one that most accurately reflects the view that the doll is seeing. Children in the preoperational stage often pick their own view rather than the doll's view. Preschool children frequently show the ability to take another's perspective on some tasks but not others.

Animism, another limitation of preoperational thought, is the belief that inanimate objects have lifelike qualities and are capable of action. A young child might show animism by saying, "That tree pushed the leaf off, and it fell down," or "The sidewalk made me mad; it made me fall down." A young child who shows animism fails to distinguish among appropriate and inappropriate occasions for using human perspectives.

animism The belief that inanimate objects have lifelike qualities and are capable of action.

intuitive thought substage Piaget's second substage of preoperational thought, in which children begin to use primitive reasoning and want to know the answers to all sorts of questions (between about 4 and 7 years of age).

The Intuitive Thought Substage

The **intuitive thought substage** is the second substage of preoperational thought, occurring between ages 4 and 7. In this substage, children begin to use primitive reasoning and want to know the answers to all sorts of questions. Consider 4-year-old Terrell, who is at the beginning of the intuitive thought substage. Although he is starting to develop his own ideas about the world he lives in, his ideas are still simple, and he is not very good at thinking things out. He has difficulty understanding events that he knows are taking place but that he cannot see. His fantasized thoughts bear little resemblance to reality. He cannot yet answer the question "What if?" in any reliable way. For example, he has only a vague idea of why he needs to avoid getting hit by a car. He also has difficulty negotiating traffic because he cannot do the mental calculations necessary to estimate whether an approaching car will hit him when he crosses the road.

"I still don't have all the answers, but I'm beginning to ask the right questions." © Lee Lorenz/The New Yorker Collection/www.cartoonbank.

By age 5 children have just about exhausted the adults around them with "why" questions. The child's questions signal the emergence of interest in reasoning and in figuring out why things are the way they are. Following are some samples of the questions children ask during the intuitive thought substage (Elkind, 1976): "What makes you grow up?" "Why does a woman have to be married to have a baby?" "Who was the mother when everybody was a baby?" "Why do leaves fall?" "Why does the sun shine?"

Piaget called this substage *intuitive* because young children seem so sure about their knowledge and understanding, yet are unaware of how they know what they know. That is, they know something but know it without the use of rational thinking and are sometimes wrong as a result.

Centration and the Limits of Preoperational Thought

Another limitation of preoperational thought is **centration**, a centering of attention on one characteristic to the exclusion of all others. Centration is most clearly evidenced in young children's lack of **conservation;** that is, they lack the awareness that altering an object or substance's appearance does not change its basic properties. For

centration The focusing of attention on one characteristic to the exclusion of all others.

conservation In Piaget's theory, awareness that altering an object's or a substance's appearance does not change its basic properties.

example, to adults it is obvious that a certain amount of liquid remains the same when it is poured from one container to another, regardless of the containers' shapes. But this is not at all obvious to young children.

The situation that Piaget devised to study conservation is his most famous task. In the conservation task, children are presented with two identical beakers, each filled to the same level with liquid (see Figure 5.4). They are asked if these beakers contain the same amount of liquid, and they usually say yes. Then the liquid from one beaker is poured into a third beaker, which is taller and thinner than the first two. The children are then asked if the amount of liquid in the tall, thin beaker is equal to that which remains in one of the original beakers. Children who are less than 7 or 8 years old usually say no and justify their answers in terms of the differing height or width of the two beakers. They are typically struck by the height of the liquid in a tall, narrow container and focus on that characteristic to the exclusion of others. Older children usually answer yes and justify their answers appropriately ("If you poured the water back, the amount would still be the same").

In Piaget's theory, failing the conservation of liquid task is a sign that children are at the preoperational stage of cognitive development. The failure demonstrates not only centration but also inability to mentally reverse actions. For example, in the conservation of matter example shown in Figure 5.5, preoperational children say that the longer shape contains more clay because they assume that "longer is more." Preoperational children cannot mentally reverse the clay-rolling process to see that the amount of clay is the same in both the shorter ball shape and the longer stick shape.

In addition to failing to conserve volume, preoperational children fail to conserve number, matter, length, and area. However, children often vary in their performance on different conservation tasks. Thus, a child might be able to conserve volume but not number. A recent fMRI brain imaging study of conservation of number revealed that advances in a network in the parietal and frontal lobes were linked to 9- and

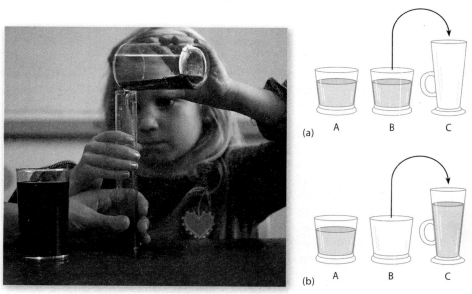

Figure 5.4 Piaget's Conservation Task
The beaker test is a well-known Piagetian test to determine whether a child can think operationally—that is, can mentally reverse actions and show conservation of the substance. (*a*) Two identical beakers, A and B, are presented to the child. Then the experimenter pours the liquid from B into C, which is taller and thinner than A or B. (*b*) The child is asked if these beakers (A and C) have the same amount of liquid. The preoperational child says "no." When asked to point to the beaker that has more liquid, the preoperational child points to the tall, thin beaker.

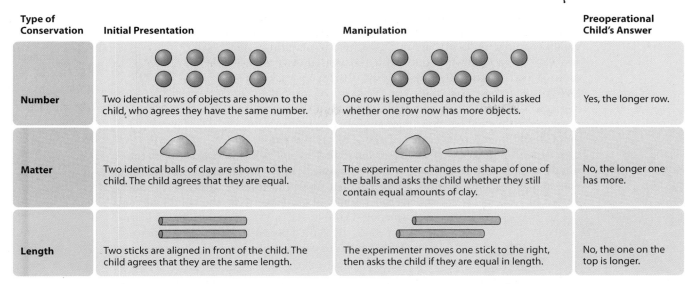

Type of Conservation	Initial Presentation	Manipulation	Preoperational Child's Answer
Number	Two identical rows of objects are shown to the child, who agrees they have the same number.	One row is lengthened and the child is asked whether one row now has more objects.	Yes, the longer row.
Matter	Two identical balls of clay are shown to the child. The child agrees that they are equal.	The experimenter changes the shape of one of the balls and asks the child whether they still contain equal amounts of clay.	No, the longer one has more.
Length	Two sticks are aligned in front of the child. The child agrees that they are the same length.	The experimenter moves one stick to the right, then asks the child if they are equal in length.	No, the one on the top is longer.

Figure 5.5 Some Dimensions of Conservation: Number, Matter, and Length
What characteristics of preoperational thought do children demonstrate when they fail these conservation tasks?

How Would You…?

As a human development and family studies professional, how would you explain the child's response in the following scenario: A parent gives a 3-year-old a cookie. The child says, "I want two cookies." The parent breaks the cookie in half and hands the two pieces to the child, who happily accepts them.

10-year-olds' conservation success in comparison with nonconserving 5- and 6-year-olds (Houde & others, 2011).

Some developmental psychologists do not believe that Piaget was entirely correct in his estimate of when children's conservation skills emerge. For example, Rochel Gelman (1969) showed that when children's attention to relevant aspects of the conservation task is improved, they are more likely to conserve. Gelman has also demonstrated that attentional training on one dimension, such as number, improves preschool children's performance on another dimension, such as mass. Thus, Gelman believes that conservation appears earlier than Piaget thought and that attention is especially important in explaining conservation.

Vygotsky's Theory

Like Piaget, Vygotsky was a constructivist, but Vygotsky's theory is a **social constructivist approach,** and it emphasizes the social contexts of learning and the construction of knowledge through social interaction (Gauvain, 2013). In Chapter 1, we described some basic elements of Vygotsky's theory. Here we expand on his theory, exploring his ideas about the zone of proximal development, scaffolding, and the young child's use of language.

The Zone of Proximal Development and Scaffolding

Vygotsky's belief in the importance of social influences, especially instruction, on children's cognitive development is reflected in his concept of the zone of proximal development (Daniels, 2011). **Zone of proximal development (ZPD)** is Vygotsky's term for the range of tasks that are too difficult for the child to master alone but can be learned with the guidance and assistance of adults or more-skilled children. Thus, the lower limit of the ZPD is the level of skill reached by the child working independently. The upper limit is the level of additional

social constructivist approach An approach that emphasizes the social contexts of learning and that knowledge is mutually built and constructed. Vygotsky's theory reflects this approach.

zone of proximal development (ZPD) Vygotsky's term for tasks that are too difficult for children to master alone but can be mastered with assistance.

responsibility the child can accept with the assistance of an able instructor (see Figure 5.6). The ZPD captures the child's cognitive skills that are in the process of maturing and can be accomplished only with the assistance of a more-skilled person (Petrick-Steward, 2012). Vygotsky (1962) called these the "buds" or "flowers" of development, to distinguish them from the "fruits" of development, which the child can already accomplish independently.

Closely linked to the idea of the ZPD is the concept of scaffolding, which was introduced in Chapter 4 in the context of parent-infant interaction. *Scaffolding* means changing the level of support. Over the course of a teaching session, a more-skilled person (a teacher or advanced peer) adjusts the amount of guidance to fit the child's current performance (Daniels, 2011). When the student is learning a new task, the skilled person may use direct instruction. As the student's competence increases, less guidance is given.

How Would You...?

As an educator, how would you apply Vygotsky's ZPD theory and the concept of scaffolding to help a young child complete a puzzle?

Upper limit

Level of additional responsibility child can accept with assistance of an able instructor

Zone of proximal development (ZPD)

Lower limit

Level of problem solving reached on these tasks by child working alone

Figure 5.6 Vygotsky's Zone of Proximal Development
Vygotsky's zone of proximal development has a lower limit and an upper limit. Tasks in the ZPD are too difficult for the child to perform alone. They require assistance from an adult or a more-skilled child. As children experience the verbal instruction or demonstration, they organize the information in their existing mental structures so they can eventually perform the skill or task alone.

Language and Thought

According to Vygotsky, children use speech not only for social communication but also to help them solve tasks. Vygotsky (1962) further believed that young children use language to plan, guide, and monitor their behavior. This use of language for self-regulation is called *private speech*. For Piaget, private speech is egocentric and immature, but for Vygotsky it is an important tool of thought during the early-childhood years (Wertsch, 2007).

Vygotsky saw that language and thought initially develop independently of each other and then merge. He emphasized that all mental functions have external, or social, origins. Children must use language to communicate with others before they can focus inward on their own thoughts. Children also must communicate externally and use language for a long time before they can make the transition from external to internal speech. This transition period occurs between ages 3 and 7 and involves talking to oneself. After a while, self-talk becomes second nature to children, and they can act without verbalizing. When this occurs, children have internalized their egocentric speech in the form of *inner speech*, which becomes their thoughts.

Vygotsky saw children who use a lot of private speech as more socially competent than those who don't. He argued that private speech represents an early transition toward becoming more socially communicative. For Vygotsky, when young children talk to themselves they are using language to govern their behavior and guide themselves. For example, a child working on a puzzle might say to herself, "Which pieces should I put together first? I'll try those green ones first. Now I need some blue ones. No, that blue one doesn't fit there. I'll try it over here." Researchers have found support for Vygotsky's view that private speech plays a positive role in children's development (Winsler, Carlton, & Barry, 2000). Children use private speech more often when tasks are difficult, when they have made errors, and when they are not sure how to proceed (Berk, 1994). Researchers have also found that children who use private speech are more attentive and improve their performance more than do children who do not use private speech (Berk & Spuhl, 1995).

Teaching Strategies Based on Vygotsky's Theory

Vygotsky's theory has been embraced by many teachers and has been successfully applied to education (Daniels, 2011; Gauvain, 2013; Goncu & Gauvain, 2011). Here are some ways in which educators can apply Vygotsky's theory:

1. *Assess the child's ZPD.* Like Piaget, Vygotsky did not believe that formal, standardized tests are the best way to assess children's learning. Rather, Vygotsky argued that assessment should focus on determining the child's zone of proximal development. The skilled helper presents the child with tasks of varying difficulty to determine the best level at which to begin instruction.

2. *Use the child's zone of proximal development in teaching.* Teaching should begin near the zone's upper limit, so that the child can reach the goal with help and move to a higher level of skill and knowledge. Offer just enough assistance. You might ask, "What can I do to help you?" Or simply observe the child's intentions and attempts, providing support only when it is needed.

3. *Use more-skilled peers as teachers.* Remember that it is not just adults who are important in helping children learn. Children also benefit from the support and guidance of more-skilled children.

4. *Monitor and encourage children's use of private speech.* Be aware of the developmental change from talking to oneself externally when solving a problem during the preschool years to talking to oneself privately in the early elementary school years. In the elementary school years, encourage children to internalize and self-regulate their talk to themselves.

How can Vygotsky's ideas be applied to educating children?

5. *Place instruction in a meaningful context.* Educators today are moving away from abstract presentations of material, instead providing students with opportunities to experience learning in real-world settings. For example, instead of just memorizing math formulas, students work on math problems with real-world implications.

Tools of the Mind is an early-childhood education curriculum that emphasizes children's development of self-regulation and the cognitive foundations of literacy. The curriculum was created by Elena Bodrova and Deborah Leong (2007) and has been implemented in more than 200 classrooms. Most of the children in the Tools of the Mind programs are considered at risk of academic failure because of their living circumstances, which in many instances are characterized by poverty and other difficult conditions such as being homeless and having parents with drug problems.

With these applications of Vygotsky's theory in mind, let's examine an early childhood program that reflects these applications. Tools of the Mind is grounded in Vygotsky's (1962) theory, with special attention to cultural tools and the development of self-regulation, the zone of proximal development, scaffolding, private speech, shared activity, and play as important activity. In a Tools of the Mind classroom, dramatic play has a central role. Teachers guide children in creating themes that are based on the children's interests, such as treasure hunt, store, hospital, and restaurant. Teachers also incorporate field trips, visitor presentations, videos, and books in the development of children's play. They help children develop a play plan, which increases the maturity of their play. Play plans describe what the children expect to do in the play period, including the imaginary context, roles, and props to be used. The play plans increase the quality of their play and self-regulation.

Scaffolding children's writing is another important theme in the Tools of the Mind classroom. Teachers guide children in planning their own message by drawing a line to stand for each word the child says. Children then repeat the message, pointing to each line as they say the word. Then the child writes on the lines, trying to represent each word with some letters or symbols.

Research assessments of children's writing in Tools of the Mind classrooms revealed that they have more advanced writing skills than do children in other early childhood programs (Bodrova & Leong, 2007). For example, they write more complex messages, use more words, spell more accurately, show better letter recognition, and have a better understanding of the concept of a sentence. Also, one study assessed the effects of the Tools of the Mind curriculum on at-risk preschool children (Diamond & others, 2007). The results indicated that the Tools of the Mind curriculum improved the self-regulatory and cognitive control skills (such as resisting distractions and temptations) of such children. Other research on the Tools of the Mind curriculum has found that it improves young children's cognitive skills (Barnett & others, 2006; Saifer, 2007).

Evaluating Vygotsky's Theory

How does Vygotsky's theory compare with Piaget's? We already have mentioned several comparisons, such as Vygotsky's emphasis on the importance of inner speech in cognitive development and Piaget's view that such speech is immature. Figure 5.7 compares the two theories. The implication of Piaget's theory for teaching is that children need support to explore their world and discover knowledge. The main implication of Vygotsky's theory is that students need many opportunities to learn with a teacher and more-skilled peers. In both theories, teachers serve as facilitators and guides rather than as directors and molders.

Even though their theories were proposed at about the same time, most of the world learned about Vygotsky's theory later than they did about Piaget's, so Vygotsky's theory has not yet been evaluated as thoroughly. Vygotsky's view of the importance of sociocultural influences on children's development fits with the current belief that it is important to evaluate contextual factors in learning (Gauvain, 2013; Gredler, 2012; Mahn & John-Steiner, 2013).

	Vygotsky	Piaget
Sociocultural Context	Strong emphasis	Little emphasis
Constructivism	Social constructivist	Cognitive constructivist
Stages	No general stages of development proposed	Strong emphasis on stages (sensorimotor, preoperational, concrete operational, and formal operational)
Key Processes	Zone of proximal development, language, dialogue, tools of the culture	Schema, assimilation, accommodation, operations, conservation, classification
Role of Language	A major role; language plays a powerful role in shaping thought	Language has a minimal role; cognition primarily directs language
View on Education	Education plays a central role, helping children learn the tools of the culture	Education merely refines the child's cognitive skills that have already emerged
Teaching Implications	Teacher is a facilitator and guide, not a director; establish many opportunities for children to learn with the teacher and more-skilled peers	Also views teacher as a facilitator and guide, not a director; provide support for children to explore their world and discover knowledge

Figure 5.7 **Comparison of Vygotsky's and Piaget's Theories**

Some critics say that Vygotsky was not specific enough about age-related changes (Goncu & Gauvain, 2011). Another criticism is that he overemphasized the role of language in thinking. His emphasis on collaboration and guidance also has potential pitfalls. Might facilitators be too helpful in some cases, as when a parent becomes overbearing and controlling? Further, some children might become lazy and expect help when they could have done something on their own.

executive attention Involves action planning, allocating attention to goals, error detection and compensation, monitoring progress on tasks, and dealing with novel or difficult circumstances.

sustained attention Focused and extended engagement with an object, task, event, or other aspect of the environment.

Information Processing

Piaget's and Vygotsky's theories provided important ideas about how young children think and how their thinking changes. More recently, the information-processing approach has generated research that illuminates how children process information during the preschool years (Bjorklund, 2013; Cohen, 2012; Siegler, 2013). What are the limitations and advances in young children's ability to pay attention to the environment, to remember, to develop strategies and solve problems, and to understand their own mental processes and those of others?

Attention

Recall that in Chapter 3 we defined *attention* as the focusing of mental resources on select information. Children's ability to pay attention improves significantly during the preschool years (Bell & Cuevas, 2013; Rothbart, 2011). Toddlers wander around, shift attention from one activity to another, and seem to spend little time focused on any one object or event. By comparison, a preschool child might be observed watching television for half an hour. However, a recent research study revealed that television watching and video game playing were both linked to attention problems in children (Swing & others, 2010).

Young children especially make advances in two aspects of attention: executive attention and sustained attention (Bell & Cuevas, 2013; Rothbart, 2011). **Executive attention** involves planning actions, allocating attention to goals, detecting and compensating for errors, monitoring progress on tasks, and dealing with novel or difficult circumstances. **Sustained attention** is focused and extended engagement with an object, task, event, or other aspect of the environment.

In at least two ways, however, the preschool child's control of attention is still deficient:

1. *Salient versus relevant dimensions.* Preschool children are likely to pay attention to stimuli that stand out, or are *salient*, even when those stimuli are not relevant to solving a problem or performing a task. For example, if a flashy, attractive clown presents the directions for solving a problem, preschool children are likely to pay more attention to the clown than to the directions. After age 6 or 7, children attend more efficiently to the dimensions of the task that are relevant, such as the directions for solving a problem. This change reflects a shift to cognitive control of attention, so that children act less impulsively and reflect more.

2. *Planfulness.* When experimenters ask children to judge whether two complex pictures are the same, preschool children tend to use a haphazard comparison strategy, not examining all the details before making a judgment. By comparison, elementary school age children are more likely to systematically compare the details across the pictures, one detail at a time (Vurpillot, 1968).

In Central European countries such as Hungary, kindergarten children participate in exercises designed to improve their attention (Posner & Rothbart, 2007). For example, in one eye-contact exercise, the teacher sits in the center of a circle of children and each child is required to catch the teacher's eye before being permitted to leave the group. In other exercises created to improve attention, teachers have children participate in stop-go activities during which they have to listen

What are some advances in children's attention in early childhood?

for a specific signal, such as a drumbeat or an exact number of rhythmic beats, before stopping the activity.

Computer exercises recently have been developed to improve children's attention (Jaeggi, Berman, & Jonides, 2009; Steiner & others, 2011; Tang & Posner, 2009). For example, one study revealed that five days of computer exercises that involved learning how to use a joystick, relying on working memory, and resolving conflict improved the attention of 4- to 6-year-old children (Rueda & others, 2005). Although not commercially available, further information about computer exercises for improving children's attention is available at www.teach-the-brain.org/learn/attention/index.

The ability of preschool children to control and sustain their attention is related to school readiness (Posner & Rothbart, 2007). For example, a study of more than 1,000 children revealed that their ability to sustain their attention at 54 months of age was linked to their school readiness (which included achievement and language skills) (NICHD Early Child Care Research Network, 2005). A later study showed that children whose parents and teachers rated them higher on a scale of having attention problems at 54 months of age had a lower level of social skills in peer relations in the first and third grades than their counterparts who were rated lower on the attention problems scale (NICHD Early Child Care Research Network, 2009).

Memory

Memory—the retention of information over time—is a central process in children's cognitive development. In Chapter 3, we saw that most of an infant's memories are fragile and, for the most part, short-lived—except for the memory of perceptual-motor actions, which can be substantial (Bauer, 2013; Bauer & Fivush, 2013). Thus, we saw that to understand the infant's capacity to remember, we need to distinguish *implicit memory* from *explicit memory*. Explicit memory itself, however, comes in many forms. One distinction is between relatively permanent or *long-term memory* and short-term memory.

Short-Term Memory In **short-term memory,** individuals retain information for up to 30 seconds if there is no rehearsal of the information. Using *rehearsal* (repeating information after it has been presented), we can keep information in short-term memory for a much longer period. One method of assessing short-term memory is the memory-span task. You hear a short list of stimuli—usually digits—presented at a rapid pace (one per second, for example). Then you are asked to repeat the digits.

Research with the memory-span task suggests that short-term memory increases during early childhood. For example, in one investigation memory span increased from about 2 digits in 2- to 3-year-old children to about 5 digits in 7-year-old children, yet between ages 7 and 13 memory span increased by only 1½ digits (Dempster, 1981) (see Figure 5.8). Keep in mind, though, that memory span varies from one individual to another.

Why does memory span change with age? Rehearsal of information is important; older children rehearse the digits more than younger children do. Also important are efficiency of processing and speed, especially the speed with which memory items can be identified (Schneider, 2011).

short-term memory The memory component in which individuals retain information for up to 30 seconds, assuming there is no rehearsal of the information.

The speed-of-processing explanation highlights a key point in the information-processing perspective: The speed with which a child processes information is an important aspect of the child's cognitive abilities, and there is abundant evidence that the speed with which many cognitive tasks are completed improves dramatically during the childhood years (Kail, 2007).

How Accurate Are Young Children's Long-Term Memories? While toddlers' short-term memory span increases during the early childhood years, their memory also becomes more accurate. Young children can remember a great deal of information if they are given appropriate cues and prompts (Bauer, 2013; Ghetti & Bauer, 2012; Riggins, 2012). Increasingly, young children are even being allowed to testify in court, especially if they are the only witnesses to abuse or a crime (Bruck & Ceci, 2012). Several factors can influence the accuracy of a young child's memory, however (Bruck & Ceci, 1999):

- *There are age differences in children's susceptibility to suggestion.* Preschoolers are the most suggestible age group (Lehman & others, 2010). For example, preschool children are more susceptible to believing misleading or incorrect information given after an event (Ghetti & Alexander, 2004). Despite these age differences, there is still concern about the reaction of older children when they are subjected to suggestive interviews (Bruck & Ceci, 2012).

- *There are individual differences in susceptibility.* Some preschoolers are highly resistant to interviewers' suggestions, whereas others immediately succumb to the slightest suggestion.

- *Interviewing techniques can produce substantial distortions in children's reports about highly salient events.* Children are suggestible not just about peripheral details but also about the central aspects of an event (Bruck & Ceci, 2012; Malloy & others, 2012). In some cases, children's false reports can be tinged with sexual connotations. In laboratory studies, young children have made false claims about "silly events" that involved body contact (such as "Did the nurse lick your knee?" or "Did she blow in your ear?"). A significant number of preschool children have falsely reported that someone touched their private parts, kissed them, or hugged them, when these events clearly did not happen. Nevertheless, young children are capable of recalling much that is relevant about an event (Fivush, 1993). When young children do recall information accurately, the interviewer often has a neutral tone and avoids asking misleading questions, and there is no reason for the child to make a false report (Bruck & Ceci, 2012).

In sum, whether a young child's eyewitness testimony is accurate or not may depend on a number of factors, such as the type, number,

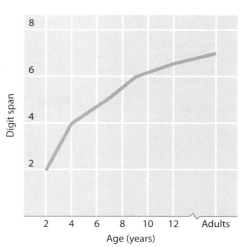

Figure 5.8 Developmental Changes in Memory Span In one study, from 2 years of age to 7 years of age children's memory span increased from 2 digits to about 5 digits (Dempster, 1981). Between 7 and 13 years of age, memory span had increased on average only another 1½ digits, to about 7 digits. *What factors might contribute to the increase in memory span during childhood?*

Four-year-old Jennifer Royal was the only eyewitness to one of her playmates' being shot to death. She was allowed to testify in open court, and the clarity of her statements helped to convict the gunman. *What are some issues involved in deciding whether young children should be allowed to testify in court?*

executive functioning An umbrella-like concept that consists of a number of higher level cognitive processes linked to the development of the brain's prefrontal cortex. Executive functioning involves managing one's thoughts to engage in goal-directed behavior and exercise self-control.

and intensity of the suggestive techniques the child has experienced (Lamb & Malloy, 2013; Orbach & others, 2012). It appears that the reliability of young children's reports has as much to do with the skills and motivation of the interviewer as with any natural limitations on young children's memory (Bruck & Ceci, 2012).

Executive Functioning

Recently, interest has increased in the development of children's **executive functioning,** an umbrella-like concept that encompasses a number of higher-level cognitive processes linked to the development of the brain's prefrontal cortex. Executive functioning involves managing one's thoughts to engage in goal-directed behavior and exercise self control (Carlson, Zelazo, & Faja, 2013; Liew, 2012; Zhou, Chen, & Main, 2012). Earlier in this chapter, we described the recent interest in *executive attention*, which comes under the umbrella of executive functioning.

In early childhood, executive functioning especially involves developmental advances in cognitive inhibition (such as inhibiting a strong tendency that is incorrect), cognitive flexibility (such as shifting attention to another item or topic), goal-setting (such as sharing a toy or mastering a skill like catching a ball), and delay of gratification (the ability to forego an immediate pleasure or reward for a more desirable one later) (Beck & others, 2011; Bell & Cuevas, 2013; Carlson, Zelazo, & Faja, 2013; Zelazo & Muller, 2011). During early childhood, the relatively stimulus-driven toddler is transformed into a child capable of flexible, goal-directed problem solving that characterizes executive functioning (Zelazo & Muller, 2011). Figure 5.9 describes a research study on young children's executive functioning (Carlson & White, 2011).

Researchers have found that advances in executive functioning in the preschool years are linked with school readiness (Ursache, Blair, & Raver, 2012). Parents and teachers play important roles in the development of executive functioning. Ann Masten and her colleagues (Herbers & others, 2011; Masten, 2013; Masten & others, 2008) have found that executive functioning and parenting skills are linked to homeless children's success in school. Masten believes that executive functioning and good parenting skills are related. In her words, "When we see kids with good executive function, we often see adults around them that are good self-regulators . . . Parents model, they support, and they scaffold these skills." (Masten, 2012, p. 11).

Significant advances in the development of executive functioning occur in middle and late childhood (Diamond, 2013). Adult-level executive functioning emerges in early adolescence on many tasks, but on some tasks executive functioning continues to improve during adulthood (Zelazo & Muller, 2011).

Some developmental psychologists use their training in areas such as cognitive development to pursue careers in applied areas. To read about the work of Helen Hadani, an individual who followed this path, see the *Careers in Life-Span Development* profile.

Figure 5.9 Studying Executive Functioning in Young Children

Researcher Stephanie Carlson has conducted a number of research studies on young children's executive functioning. In one study, young children were read either *Planet Opposite*—a fantasy book in which everything is turned upside down—or *Fun Town*—a reality-oriented fiction book (Carlson & White, 2011). After being read one of the books, the young children completed the Less Is More Task, in which they were shown two trays of candy—one with five pieces, the other with two— and told that the tray they picked would be given to the stuffed animal seated at the table. Sixty percent of the 3-year-olds who heard the *Planet Opposite* story gave away the five pieces of candy, compared with only 20 percent of their counterparts who heard the more straightforward story. The results indicated that learning about a topsy-turvy imaginary world likely helped the young children become more flexible in their thinking.

Helen Hadani, Developmental Psychologist, Toy Designer, and LANGO Regional Director

Helen Hadani obtained a Ph.D. from Stanford University in developmental psychology. As a graduate student at Stanford, she worked part-time for Hasbro toys testing its children's software on preschoolers. Her first job after graduate school was with Zowie Entertainment, which was subsequently bought by LEGO. In her work as a toy designer there, Helen conducted experiments and focus groups at different stages of a toy's development and also studied the age-effectiveness of the toy. In Helen's words, "Even in a toy's most primitive stage of development . . . you see children's creativity in responding to challenges, their satisfaction when a problem is solved or simply their delight in having fun" (Schlegel, 2000, p. 50).

More recently, she began working for LANGO, a company established on the premise that every American child should learn a foreign language. LANGO uses music, games, and art to help children learn a second language. Helen is currently a regional director for LANGO.

Helen Hadani, a developmental psychologist, with some of the toys and materials for guiding children in learning a second language.

The Child's Theory of Mind

Even young children are curious about the nature of the human mind (Apperly, 2012; Astington & Hughes, 2013; Wellman, 2011). They have a **theory of mind,** a term that refers to awareness of one's own mental processes and those of others. Studies of theory of mind view the child as "a thinker who is trying to explain, predict, and understand people's thoughts, feelings, and utterances" (Harris, 2006). Children's theory of mind changes as they develop through childhood (Gelman, 2013; Wellman, 2011). Although whether infants have a theory of mind continues to be questioned by some (Rakoczy, 2012), the consensus is that some changes occur quite early in development, as we see next. The main changes occur at ages 2 to 3, 4 to 5, and beyond age 5.

Ages 2 to 3 In this time frame, children begin to understand the following three mental states: (1) *Perceptions*—the child realizes that other people see what is in front of their eyes and not necessarily what is in front of the child's eyes. (2) *Emotions*— the child can distinguish between positive and negative emotions. A child might say, "Vic feels bad." (3) *Desires*—the child understands that if someone wants something, he or she will try to get it. A child might say, "I want my mommy."

Children refer to desires earlier and more frequently than they refer to cognitive states such as thinking and knowing (Harris, 2006). Two- to 3-year-olds understand the way desires are related to actions and to simple emotions (Harris, 2006). For example, they understand that people will search for what they want and that if they obtain it, they are likely to feel happy, but if they don't, they will keep searching for it and are likely to feel sad or angry (Hadwin & Perner, 1991).

Ages 4 to 5 Children come to understand that the mind can represent objects and events accurately or inaccurately (Low & Simpson,

theory of mind Refers to the awareness of one's own mental processes and the mental processes of others.

2012). The realization that people can have *false beliefs*—beliefs that are not true—develops in a majority of children by the time they are 5 years old (Wellman, Cross, & Watson, 2001) (see Figure 5.10).

In a classic false-belief task, children are told a story about Sally and Anne. In the story, Sally places a toy in a basket and then leaves the room. In her absence, Anne takes the toy from the basket and places it in a box. Children are asked where Sally will look for the toy when she returns. The major finding is that 3-year-olds tend to fail false-belief tasks, saying that Sally will look in the box (even though Sally could not know that the toy has been moved to this new location). Four-year-olds and older children tend to pass the task, correctly saying that Sally will have a "false belief"—she will think the object is in the basket, even though that belief is now false. The conclusion from these studies is that children younger than age 4 do not understand that it is possible to have a false belief.

Young children's understanding of thinking has some limitations (Gelman & Frazier, 2012; Wellman, 2011). They often underestimate when mental activity is likely occurring. For example, they fail to attribute mental activity to someone who is sitting quietly, reading, or talking (Flavell, Green, & Flavell, 1995). Their understanding of their own thinking is also limited.

Beyond Age 5 It is only beyond the preschool years that children have a deepening appreciation of the mind itself rather than just an understanding of mental states (Wellman, 2011). Not until middle and late childhood do children see the mind as an active constructor of knowledge or a processing center (Flavell, Green, & Flavell, 2000). It is only then that they move from understanding that beliefs can be false to realizing that the same event can be open to multiple interpretations (Carpendale & Chandler, 1996).

Individual Differences As in other developmental research, there are individual differences in the ages when children reach certain milestones in their theory of mind (Astington & Hughes, 2013; Pellicano, 2010; Wellman, 2011). For example, children who talk with their parents about feelings frequently as 2-year-olds perform better on theory of mind tasks (Ruffman, Slade, & Crowe, 2002), as do children who frequently engage in pretend play (Harris, 2000).

Executive functioning, which involves goal-directed behavior and self-control (as discussed earlier in the chapter), is linked to the development of a theory of mind (Carroll & others, 2012; Muller & others, 2012). For example, in one executive function task, children are asked to say the word "night" when they see a picture of a sun and the word "day" when they see a picture of a moon and stars. Children who perform better at executive function tasks seem also to have a better understanding of theory of mind (Sabbagh & others, 2006).

Another individual difference in understanding the mind involves autism (Doherty, 2008). Children with autism show a number of behaviors that differ from those of most children their age, including deficits in social interaction and communication as well as repetitive behaviors or interests. Researchers have found that autistic children have difficulty developing a theory of mind, especially when it comes to understanding other people's beliefs and emotions (Boucher, 2012a). However, children with autism might have difficulty in understanding others' beliefs and

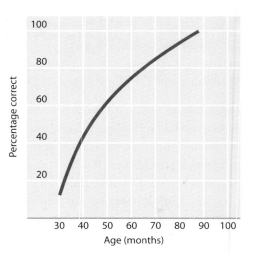

Figure 5.10 Development Changes in False-Belief Performance
False-belief performance—the child's understanding that a person has a false belief that contradicts reality—dramatically increases from 2½ years of age through the middle of the elementary school years. In a summary of the results of many studies, 2½-year-olds gave incorrect responses about 80 percent of the time (Wellman, Cross, & Watson, 2001). At 3 years, 8 months, they were correct about 50 percent of the time, and after that, gave increasingly correct responses.

emotions not solely due to theory of mind deficits but to other aspects of cognition such as problems involving attention, eye gaze, face recognition, memory, language impairment, or some general intellectual impairment (Boucher, 2012b; Boucher, Mayes, & Bigham, 2012).

phonology The sound system of a language, including the sounds used and how they may be combined.

morphology Units of meaning involved in word formation.

Language Development

Toddlers move rather quickly from producing two-word utterances to creating three-, four-, and five-word combinations. Between ages 2 and 3, they begin the transition from saying simple sentences that express a single proposition to saying complex sentences.

As young children learn the special features of their own language, there are extensive regularities in how they acquire that particular language (Berko Gleason, 2009; Wagner & Hoff, 2013). For example, all children learn the prepositions *on* and *in* before other prepositions. Children learning other languages, such as Russian or Chinese, also acquire the particular features of those languages in a consistent order.

Understanding Phonology and Morphology

Phonology refers to the sound system of a language, including the sounds used and how they may be combined. During the preschool years, most children gradually become more sensitive to the sounds of spoken words and increasingly capable of producing all the sounds of their language. By their third birthday they can produce all the vowel sounds and most of the consonant sounds (Menn & Stoel-Gammon, 2009).

By the time children move beyond two-word utterances, they demonstrate a knowledge of morphology rules (Park & others, 2012). **Morphology** refers to the units of meaning involved in word formation. Children begin using the plural and possessive forms of nouns (such as *dogs* and *dog's*). They put appropriate endings on verbs (such as *-s* when the subject is third-person singular and *-ed* for the past tense). They use prepositions (such as *in* and *on*), articles (such as *a* and *the*), and various forms of the verb *to be* (such as "I *was* going to the store"). Some of the best evidence for changes in children's use of morphological rules occurs in their overgeneralization of the rules, as when a preschool child says "foots" instead of "feet," or "goed" instead of "went."

In a classic experiment that was designed to study children's knowledge of morphological rules, such as how to make a plural, Jean Berko (1958) presented preschool and first-grade children with cards such as the one shown in Figure 5.11. The children were asked to look at the card while the experimenter read aloud the words on the card. Then the children were asked to supply the missing word. This might sound easy, but Berko was interested in the children's ability to apply the appropriate morphological rule—in this case, to say "wugs" with the *z* sound that indicates the plural.

Although the children's answers were not perfect, they were much better than chance. What makes Berko's study impressive is that most of the words were made up for the experiment. Thus, the children could not base their responses on remembering past instances of hearing the words. That they could make the plurals or past tenses of words they had never heard before was proof that they knew the morphological rules.

This is a wug.

Now there is another one.
There are two of them.
There are two _____.

Figure 5.11 Stimuli in Berko's Study of Young Children's Understanding of Morphological Rules In Jean Berko's (1958) study, young children were presented with cards such as this one with a "wug" on it. Then the children were asked to supply the missing word; in supplying the missing word, they also had to say it correctly. "Wugs" is the correct response here.

syntax The ways words are combined to form acceptable phrases and sentences.

semantics The meaning of words and sentences.

Changes in Syntax and Semantics

Preschool children also learn and apply rules of **syntax,** which involves the way words are combined to form acceptable phrases and sentences (Gertner & Fisher, 2012). They show a growing mastery of complex rules for how words should be ordered (deVilliers & deVilliers, 2013). Consider *wh-* questions, such as "Where is Daddy going?" or "What is that boy doing?" To ask these questions properly, the child must know two important differences between *wh-* questions and affirmative statements (for instance, "Daddy is going to work" and "That boy is waiting for the school bus"). First, a *wh-* word must be added at the beginning of the sentence. Second, the auxiliary verb must be inverted—that is, exchanged with the subject of the sentence. Young children learn quite early where to put the *wh-* word, but they take much longer to learn the auxiliary-inversion rule. Thus, preschool children might ask, "Where Daddy is going?" and "What that boy is doing?"

Gains in **semantics,** the aspect of language that refers to the meaning of words and sentences, also characterize early childhood. Vocabulary development is dramatic (Crain & Zhou, 2012). Some experts have concluded that between 18 months and 6 years, young children learn an average of about one new word every waking hour (Gelman & Kalish, 2006)! By the time they enter first grade, it is estimated that children know about 14,000 words (Clark, 1993).

What are some important aspects of how word learning optimally occurs? Kathy Hirsh-Pasek and Roberta Golinkoff (Harris, Golinkoff, & Hirsh-Pasek, 2011; Hirsh-Pasek & Golinkoff, 2013) emphasize six key principles in young children's vocabulary development:

1. *Children learn the words they hear most often.* They learn the words that they encounter when interacting with parents, teachers, siblings, peers, as well as words from books. They especially benefit from encountering words that they do not know.

2. *Children learn words for things and events that interest them.* Parents and teachers can direct young children to experience words in contexts that interest the children; playful peer interactions are especially helpful in this regard.

3. *Children learn words best in responsive and interactive contexts rather than passive contexts.* Children who experience turn-taking opportunities, joint focusing experiences, and positive, sensitive socializing contexts with adults encounter the scaffolding necessary for optimal word learning. They learn words less effectively when they are passive learners.

4. *Children learn words best in contexts that are meaningful.* Young children learn new words more effectively when new words are encountered in integrated contexts rather than as isolated facts.

5. *Children learn words best when they access clear information about word meaning.* Children whose parents and teachers are sensitive to words the children might not understand and provide support and elaboration with hints about word meaning learn words better than children whose parents and teachers quickly state a new word and don't monitor whether children understand its meaning.

6. *Children learn words best when grammar and vocabulary are considered.* Children who experience a large number of words and diversity in verbal stimulation develop a richer vocabulary and better understanding of grammar. In many cases, vocabulary and grammar development are connected.

Advances in Pragmatics

Changes in **pragmatics,** the appropriate use of language in different contexts, also characterize young children's language development (Bryant, 2009, 2012). A 6-year-old is simply a much better conversationalist than a 2-year-old. What are some of the improvements in pragmatics during the preschool years?

pragmatics The appropriate use of language in different contexts.

Young children begin to engage in extended discourse (Akhtar & Herold, 2008). For example, they learn culturally specific rules of conversation and politeness, and they become sensitive to the need to adapt their speech to different settings. Their developing linguistic skills and increasing ability to take the perspective of others contribute to their generation of more competent narratives.

As children grow older, they become increasingly able to talk about things that are not here (Grandma's house, for example) and not now (what happened to them yesterday or might happen tomorrow, for example). A preschool child can tell you what she wants for lunch tomorrow, something that would not have been possible at the two-word stage of language development.

Around age 4 or 5, children learn to change their speech style to suit the situation. For example, even 4-year-old children speak to a 2-year-old differently from the way they talk to a same-aged peer; they use shorter sentences with the 2-year-old. They also speak to an adult differently from a same-aged peer, using more polite and formal language with the adult (Shatz & Gelman, 1973).

Young Children's Literacy

Concern about U.S. children's ability to read and write has led to a careful examination of preschool and kindergarten children's experiences, with the hope that a positive orientation toward reading and writing can be developed early in life (Giorgis, 2012; Giorkas & Glazer, 2013). Parents and teachers need to provide young children with a supportive environment for the development of literacy skills (Tamis-LeMonda & Song, 2013). Children should be active participants in a wide range of interesting listening, talking, writing, and reading experiences (Gunning, 2013).

Instruction should be built on what children already know about oral language, reading, and writing. Further, early precursors of literacy and academic success include language skills, phonological and syntactic knowledge, letter identification, and enjoyment of books (McGee & Richgels, 2012).

What are some strategies for using books effectively with preschool children? Ellen Galinsky (2010) recently emphasized these strategies:

- *Use books to initiate conversation with young children.* Ask them to put themselves in the book characters' places and imagine what they might be thinking or feeling.

- *Use what and why questions.* Ask young children what they think is going to happen next in a story and then to see if it occurs.

- *Encourage children to ask questions about stories.*

- *Choose some books that play with language.* Creative books on the alphabet, including those with rhymes, often interest young children.

Anna Mudd began writing stories when she was 4 years old. Above is her story, "The devl and the babe goste," which she wrote as a 6-year-old. The story includes poetic images, sophisticated syntax, and vocabulary that reflects advances in language development. *What are some guidelines parents and teachers can follow in helping young children develop literacy skills?*

child-centered kindergarten
Education that involves the whole child by considering both the child's physical, cognitive, and socioemotional development and the child's needs, interests, and learning styles.

Montessori approach An educational philosophy in which children are given considerable freedom and spontaneity in choosing activities and are allowed to move from one activity to another as they desire.

Early Childhood Education

How do early education programs treat children, and how do the children fare? Our exploration of early childhood education focuses on variations in programs, education for children who are disadvantaged, and some controversies in early childhood education.

Variations in Early Childhood Education

There are many variations in the way young children are educated (Feeney, Moravcik, & Nolte, 2013; Henninger, 2013). The foundation of early childhood education is the child-centered kindergarten.

The Child-Centered Kindergarten

Nurturing is a key aspect of the **child-centered kindergarten,** which emphasizes educating the whole child and promoting his or her physical, cognitive, and socioemotional development (Morrison, 2012). Instruction is organized around the child's needs, interests, and learning styles. Emphasis is on the process of learning, rather than what is learned. The child-centered kindergarten honors three principles: (1) each child follows a unique developmental pattern; (2) young children learn best through firsthand experiences with people and materials; and (3) play is extremely important in the child's total development. *Experimenting, exploring, discovering, trying out, restructuring, speaking,* and *listening* are frequent activities in excellent kindergarten programs. Such programs are closely attuned to the developmental status of 4- and 5-year-old children.

Larry Page and Sergey Brin, founders of the highly successful Internet search engine, Google, recently said that their early years at Montessori schools were a major factor in their success (International Montessori Council, 2006). During an interview with Barbara Walters, they said they learned how to be self-directed and self-starters at Montessori (ABC News, 2005). They commented that their Montessori experiences encouraged them to think for themselves and allowed them the freedom to develop their own interests.

The Montessori Approach

Montessori schools are patterned on the educational philosophy of Maria Montessori (1870–1952), an Italian physician-turned-educator who at the beginning of the twentieth century crafted a revolutionary approach to young children's education. The **Montessori approach** is a philosophy of education in which children are given considerable freedom and spontaneity in choosing activities. They are allowed to move from one activity to another as they desire, and the teacher acts as a facilitator rather than a director. The teacher shows the child how to perform intellectual activities, demonstrates interesting ways to explore curriculum materials, and offers help when the child requests it (Isaacs, 2012). "By encouraging children to make decisions from an early age, Montessori programs seek to develop self-regulated problem solvers who can make choices and manage their time effectively" (Hyson, Copple, & Jones, 2006, p. 14). The number of Montessori schools in the United States has expanded dramatically in recent years, from one school in 1959 to 355 schools in 1970 to more than 4,000 today.

Some developmental psychologists favor the Montessori approach, but others believe that it neglects children's socioemotional development. For example, although the Montessori approach fosters independence and the development of cognitive skills, it deemphasizes verbal interaction between the teacher and child and between peers. Montessori's critics also argue that it restricts imaginative play and that its heavy reliance on self-corrective materials may not adequately allow for creativity and for a variety of learning styles.

Developmentally Appropriate Education

Many educators and psychologists conclude that preschool and young elementary school children learn best through active, hands-on teaching methods such as games and dramatic play. They believe that schools need to accommodate individual differences in children's development. They also argue that schools should focus on improving children's socioemotional development as well as their cognitive development. Educators refer to this type of schooling as **developmentally appropriate practice (DAP),** which is based on knowledge of the typical development of children within a particular age span (age-appropriateness), as well as on the uniqueness of the individual child (individual-appropriateness). DAP emphasizes the importance of creating settings that encourage children to be active learners and reflect children's interests and capabilities (Bredekamp, 2011; Squires & others, 2013). Desired outcomes for DAP include thinking critically, working cooperatively, solving problems, developing self-regulatory skills, and enjoying learning. The emphasis in DAP is on the process of learning rather than on its content (Bredekamp, 2011).

> **developmentally appropriate practice (DAP)** Education that focuses on the typical developmental patterns of children (age appropriateness) and the uniqueness of each child (individual appropriateness).

How Would You...?
As an educator, how would you design a developmentally appropriate lesson to teach kindergartners the concept of gravity?

Do developmentally appropriate educational practices improve young children's development? Some researchers have found that young children in developmentally appropriate classrooms are likely to feel less stress, be more motivated, be more socially skilled, have better work habits, be more creative, have better language skills, and demonstrate better math skills than children in developmentally inappropriate classrooms (Hart & others, 2003). However, not all studies find DAP to have significant positive effects (Hyson, Copple, & Jones, 2006). Among the reasons that it is difficult to generalize about research on developmentally appropriate education is that individual programs often vary, and developmentally appropriate education is an evolving concept. Recent changes in the concept have given more attention to sociocultural factors and the teacher's active involvement and implementation of systematic intentions, as well as how strongly academic skills should be emphasized and how they should be taught.

Education for Young Children Who Are Disadvantaged

For many years, U.S. children from low-income families did not receive any education before they entered the first grade. Often when they began first grade they were already several steps behind their classmates in readiness to learn. In the summer of 1965, the federal government began striving to break the cycle of poverty and poor education for young children through **Project Head Start.** Head Start is a compensatory program designed to give children from low-income families the opportunity to acquire skills and experiences that are important for success in school (Hustedt, Friedman, & Barnett, 2012; Zigler & Styfco, 2010). After almost half a century, Head Start continues to be the largest federally funded program for U.S. children, with almost 1 million children enrolled in it annually (Hagen & Lamb-Parker, 2008). In 2007, 3 percent of Head Start children were 5 years old, 51 percent were 4 years old, 36 percent were 3 years old, and 10 percent were under age 3 (Administration for Children & Families, 2008).

Early Head Start was established in 1995 to serve children from birth to 3 years of age. In 2007, half of all new funds appropriated

How Would You...?
As a health-care professional, how would you explain the importance of including health services as part of an effective Head Start program?

> **Project Head Start** A government-funded program that is designed to provide children from low-income families the opportunity to acquire the skills and experiences important for school success.

EARLY CHILDHOOD EDUCATION

157

Yolanda Garcia, Director of Children's Services, Head Start

Yolanda Garcia has been the director of the Children's Services Department of the Santa Clara, California, County Office of Education since 1980. As director, she is responsible for managing child development programs for 2,500 children 3 to 5 years old in 127 classrooms. Her training includes two master's degrees: one in public policy and child welfare from the University of Chicago and another in education administration from San Jose State University.

Yolanda Garcia, Director of Children's Services/Head Start, working with a Head Start child in Santa Clara, California.

Garcia has served on many national advisory committees that have produced improvements in the staffing of Head Start programs. Most notably, she served on the Head Start Quality Committee that recommended the development of Early Head Start and revised performance standards for Head Start programs. Garcia currently is a member of the American Academy of Science Committee on the Integration of Science and Early Childhood Education.

for Head Start programs were used for the expansion of Early Head Start. Researchers have found positive effects for Early Head Start (Hoffman & Ewen, 2007). A recent study revealed that Early Head Start had a protective effect on risks young children might experience in parenting stress, language development, and self-control (Ayoub, Vallotton, & Mastergeorge, 2011).

Head Start programs are not all created equal. One estimate is that 40 percent of the 1,400 Head Start programs are of questionable quality (Zigler & Styfco, 1994). More attention needs to be given to developing consistently high-quality Head Start programs (Hillemeier & others, 2012). One person who is strongly motivated to make Head Start a valuable learning experience for young children from disadvantaged backgrounds is Yolanda Garcia. To read about her work, see the *Careers in Life-Span Development* profile.

Evaluations support the positive influence of quality early childhood programs on both the cognitive and social worlds of disadvantaged young children (Lamy, 2012). A recent national evaluation of Head Start revealed that the program had a positive influence on the language and cognitive development of 3- and 4-year-olds (Puma & others, 2010). However, by the end of the first grade, there were few lasting outcomes. One exception was a larger vocabulary for those who went to Head Start as 4-year-olds and better oral comprehension for those who went to Head Start as 3-year-olds. Another recent study found that when young children initially began Head Start, they were well below their more academically advantaged peers in literacy and math (Hindman & others, 2010). However, by the end of the first grade, the Head Start children were on par with national averages in literacy and math.

One high-quality early childhood education program (although not a Head Start program) is the Perry Preschool program in Ypsilanti, Michigan, a two-year preschool program that includes weekly home visits from program personnel. In analyses of the long-term effects of the program, adults who had been in the Perry Preschool program were compared with a control group of adults from the same background who had not received the enriched early childhood education (Schweinhart & others, 2005; Weikert, 1993). Those who had been in the Perry Preschool program had fewer teen pregnancies and better high school graduation rates, and at age 40 more were in the workforce, owned their own homes, had a savings account, and had fewer arrests.

Controversies in Early Childhood Education

Two current controversies in early childhood education involve (1) what the curriculum for early childhood education should be (Hauser-Cram & Mitchell, 2012), and (2) whether preschool education should be universal in the United States (Zigler, Gilliam, & Barnett, 2011).

Controversy Over Curriculum

A current controversy in early childhood education involves what the curriculum for early childhood education should be (Bredekamp, 2011). On one side are those who advocate a child-centered, constructivist approach much like that emphasized by the National Association for the Education of Young Children (NAEYC), along the lines of developmentally appropriate practice. On the other side are those who advocate an academic, direct-instruction approach.

How Would You…?

As a psychologist, how would you advise preschool teachers to balance the development of young children's skills for academic achievement with opportunities for healthy social interaction?

In practice, many high-quality early-childhood education programs include both academic and constructivist approaches. Many education experts, such as Lilian Katz (1999), though, worry about academic approaches that place too much pressure on young children to achieve and don't provide opportunities to actively construct knowledge. Competent early childhood programs also should focus on both cognitive development *and* socioemotional development, not exclusively on cognitive development (Bredekamp, 2011; NAEYC, 2009).

Universal Preschool Education

Another controversy in early childhood education focuses on whether preschool education should be instituted for all U.S. 4-year-old children. Edward Zigler and his colleagues (2006, 2011) argue that the United States should have universal preschool education. They emphasize that quality preschools prepare children for later academic success. Zigler and his colleagues (2006) cite research showing that quality preschool programs decrease the likelihood that children will be retained in a grade or drop out before graduating from high school. They also point to analyses indicating that universal preschool would bring cost savings on the order of billions of dollars because of a diminished need for remedial and justice services (Karoly & Bigelow, 2005).

What is the curriculum controversy in early childhood education?

Critics of universal preschool education argue that the gains attributed to preschool and kindergarten education are often overstated. They especially stress that research has not proven that nondisadvantaged children improve as a result of attending a preschool. Thus, the critics say it is more important to improve preschool education for young children who are disadvantaged than to fund preschool education for all 4-year-old children. Some critics, especially home-schooling advocates, emphasize that young children should be educated by their parents, not by schools. Thus, universal preschool education remains a subject of controversy.

Summary

Physical Changes

- The average child grows 2½ inches in height and gains between 5 and 7 pounds a year during early childhood, although growth patterns vary from one child to another. Some of the brain's growth in early childhood is due to increases in the number and size of dendrites, some to myelination. From ages 3 to 6, the most rapid growth in the brain occurs in the frontal lobes.

- Gross and fine motor skills improve dramatically during early childhood.

- Too many young children in the United States are being raised on diets that are too high in fat. The child's life should be centered on activities, not meals. Other nutritional concerns include malnutrition in early childhood and the inadequate diets of many children living in poverty.

- Accidents are the leading cause of death in young children. A special concern is the poor health status of many young children in low-income families. There has been a dramatic increase in HIV/AIDS in young children in developing countries in recent decades.

Cognitive Changes

- According to Piaget, in the preoperational stage children cannot yet perform operations, but they begin to present the world with symbols, to form stable concepts, and to reason. Preoperational thought is characterized by two substages: symbolic function (2 to 4 years) and intuitive thought (4 to 7 years). Centration and a lack of conservation also characterize the preoperational stage.

- Vygotsky's theory represents a social constructivist approach to development. Vygotsky argues that it is important to discover the child's zone of proximal development to improve the child's learning.

- Young children make substantial strides in executive and sustained attention. Significant improvement in short-term memory occurs during early childhood.

Advances in executive functioning, an umbrella-like concept that consists of a number of higher-level cognitive processes linked to the development of the prefrontal cortex, occur in early childhood. Theory of mind is the awareness of one's own mental processes and the mental processes of others. Children begin to understand mental states involving perceptions, emotions, and desires at 2 to 3 years of age and at 4 to 5 years of age realize that people can have false beliefs.

Language Development

- Young children increase their grasp of language's rule systems. In terms of phonology, children become more sensitive to the sounds of spoken language. Berko's classic study demonstrated that young children understand morphological rules.

- Preschool children learn and apply rules of syntax, which involves how words should be ordered. In terms of semantics, vocabulary development increases dramatically in early childhood.

- Young children's conversational skills improve in early childhood.

- Early precursors of literacy and academic success develop in early childhood.

Early Childhood Education

- The child-centered kindergarten emphasizes the education of the whole child. The Montessori approach has become increasingly popular. Developmentally appropriate practice focuses on the typical patterns of children (age appropriateness) and the uniqueness of each child (individual appropriateness).

- The U.S. government has tried to break the poverty cycle with programs such as Head Start. Model programs have had positive effects on young children's education.

- Controversy over early childhood education involves what the curriculum should be and whether universal preschool education should be implemented.

Key Terms

myelination 135
preoperational stage 140
operations 140
symbolic function
    substage 140
egocentrism 140
animism 141
intuitive thought
    substage 141

centration 141
conservation 141
social constructivist
    approach 143
zone of proximal
    development
    (ZPD) 143
executive
    attention 147

sustained attention 147
short-term memory 148
executive functioning 150
theory of mind 151
phonology 153
morphology 153
syntax 154
semantics 154
pragmatics 154

child-centered
    kindergarten 156
Montessori approach 156
developmentally
    appropriate practice
    (DAP) 157
Project Head Start 157

6 Socioemotional Development in Early Childhood

Stories of Life-Span Development: Craig Lesley's Complicated Early Emotional and Social Life

In his memoir *Burning Fence: A Western Memoir of Fatherhood*, award-winning novelist Craig Lesley describes one memory from his early childhood:

Lifting me high above his head, my father placed me in the crotch of the Bing cherry tree growing beside my mother's parents' house in The Dalles. A little frightened at the dizzying height, I pressed my palms into the tree's rough, peeling bark. My father stood close, reassuring. I could see his olive skin, dazzling smile, and sharp-creased army uniform.

"Rudell, don't let him fall." My mother watched, her arms held out halfway, as if to catch me. . . .

The cherries were ripe and robins flittered through the green leaves, pecking at the Bings. Tipping my head back I could see blue sky beyond the extended branches.

"That's enough. Bring him down now." My mother's arms reached out farther.

Laughing, my father grabbed me under the arms, twirled me around, and plunked me into the grass. I wobbled a little. Imprinted on my palms was the pattern of the tree bark, and I brushed off the little bark pieces on my dungarees.

In a moment, my grandmother gave me a small glass of lemonade. . . .

This first childhood memory of my father remains etched in my mind. . . .

When I grew older, I realized that my father had never lifted me into the cherry tree. After Rudell left, I never saw him until I was fifteen. My grandfather had put me in the tree. Still, the memory of my father lifting me into the tree persists. Even today, I remain half-convinced by the details, the press of bark against my palms, the taste of lemonade, the texture of my father's serge uniform. Apparently, my mind has cross-wired the photographs of my handsome father in his army uniform with the logical reality that my grandfather set me in the crotch of the tree.

162

Why can I remember the event so vividly? I guess because I wanted so much for my father to be there. I have no easy answers. (Lesley, 2005, pp. 8–10)

Like millions of children, Lesley experienced a family torn by divorce; he would also experience abuse by a stepfather. When his father left, Lesley was an infant, but even as a preschooler he felt his father's absence. Once he planned to win a gift for his father so that his grandmother "could take it to him and then he'd come to see me" (Lesley, 2005, p. 16). In just a few years, the infant had become a child with a complicated emotional and social life.

In early childhood, young children's emotional lives and personalities develop in significant ways, and their small worlds widen. In addition to the continuing influence of family relationships, peers assume a more significant role in children's development, play fills the days of many young children's lives—and, for many, more time is spent watching television. ■

Emotional and Personality Development

Many changes characterize young children's socioemotional development in early childhood. Children's developing minds and social experiences produce remarkable advances in the development of the self, emotional maturity, moral understanding, and gender awareness.

The Self

You learned in Chapter 4 that during the second year of life children make considerable progress in self-recognition. In the early childhood years, young children develop in many ways that enable them to enhance their self-understanding.

Initiative Versus Guilt

In Chapter 1, you read about Erik Erikson's (1968) eight developmental stages, which are encountered during certain time periods in the human life span. As you learned in Chapter 4, Erikson's first stage, trust versus mistrust, describes what he considers to be the main developmental task of infancy. According to Erikson, the psychosocial stage associated with early childhood is *initiative versus guilt*. At this point in development, children have become convinced that they are persons of their own; during early childhood, they begin to discover what kind of person they will become. They identify intensely with their parents, who most of the time appear to them to be powerful and beautiful, though often unreasonable, disagreeable, and sometimes even dangerous. During early childhood, children use their perceptual, motor, cognitive, and language skills to make things happen. They have a surplus of energy that permits them to forget failures quickly and to approach new areas that seem desirable—even if dangerous—with undiminished zest and some increased sense of direction. On their own initiative, then, children at this stage exuberantly move out into a wider social world.

The great governor of initiative is conscience. Children's initiative and enthusiasm may bring them not only rewards but also guilt, which lowers self-esteem.

Self-Understanding and Understanding Others

Recent research studies have revealed that young children are more psychologically aware—of themselves and others—than was formerly thought (Easterbrooks & others, 2013; Thompson, 2013b, c). This increased awareness reflects young children's expanding psychological sophistication.

In Erikson's portrait of early childhood, the young child clearly has begun to develop **self-understanding**, which is the representation of self, the substance and content of self-conceptions (Harter, 2012). Though not the whole of personal identity, self-understanding provides its rational underpinnings. Mainly through interviews,

self-understanding The child's cognitive representation of self, the substance and content of the child's self-conceptions.

researchers have probed children's conceptions of many aspects of self-understanding (Harter, 2006, 2012).

As we saw in Chapter 4, early self-understanding involves self-recognition. In early childhood, young children think the self can be described by material characteristics such as size, shape, and color. They distinguish themselves from others through physical and material attributes. Says 4-year-old Sandra, "I'm different from Jennifer because I have brown hair and she has blond hair." Says 4-year-old Ralph, "I am different from Hank because I am taller and I am different from my sister because I have a bicycle." Physical activities are also a central component of the self in early childhood (Keller, Ford, & Meacham, 1978). For example, preschool children often describe themselves in terms of activities such as play. In sum, in early childhood, children often provide self-descriptions that involve body attributes, material possessions, and physical activities.

Although young children mainly describe themselves in terms of concrete, observable features and activities, at age 4 to 5, as they hear others use psychological trait and emotion terms, they begin to include these in their self-descriptions (Marsh, Ellis, & Craven, 2002). Thus, in a self-description a 4-year-old might say, "I'm not scared. I'm always happy."

What characterizes young children's self-understanding?

Young children's self-descriptions are typically unrealistically positive, as reflected in the comment of the 4-year-old who says he is always happy, which he is not (Harter, 2012). They express this optimism because they don't yet distinguish between their desired competence and their actual competence, tend to confuse ability and effort (thinking that differences in ability can be changed as easily as can differences in effort), don't engage in spontaneous social comparison of their abilities with those of others, and tend to compare their present abilities with what they could do at an earlier age (which usually makes them look quite good).

Understanding Others

Children also make advances in their understanding of others (Harter, 2012; Mills & others, 2012). Young children's theory of mind includes understanding that other people have emotions and desires. And at age 4 to 5 children not only start describing themselves in terms of psychological traits but also begin to perceive others in terms of psychological traits. Thus, a 4-year-old might say, "My teacher is nice."

It is important for children to develop an understanding that people don't always give accurate reports of their beliefs (Mills & Landrum, 2012) Researchers have found

Young children are more psychologically aware of themselves and others than used to be thought. Some children are better than others at understanding people's feelings and desires—and, to some degree, these individual differences are influenced by conversations caregivers have with young children about feelings and desires.

that even 4-year-olds understand that people may make statements that aren't true in order to obtain what they want or to avoid trouble (Lee & others, 2002). For example, one study revealed that 4- and 5-year-olds were increasingly skeptical of another child's claim to be sick when the children were informed that the child was motivated to avoid having to go to camp (Gee & Heyman, 2007). This and other research on young children's social understanding provides clear evidence that young children are not as egocentric as Piaget believed them to be.

Another important aspect of understanding others involves understanding joint commitments. As children approach their third birthday, their collaborative interactions with others increasingly involve obligations to the partner (Tomasello & Hamann, 2012). One study revealed that 3-year-olds, but not 2-year-olds, recognized when an adult is committed and when they themselves are committed to joint activity that involves obligation to a partner (Grafenhain & others, 2009).

Both the extensive theory of mind research and the recent research on young children's social understanding underscore that young children are not as egocentric as Piaget envisioned (Sokol, Snjezana, & Muller 2010; Thompson, 2012). Piaget's concept of egocentrism has become so ingrained in people's thinking about young children that too often the current research on social awareness in infancy and early childhood has been overlooked. Research increasingly shows that young children are more socially sensitive and perceptive than was previously envisioned, suggesting that parents and teachers can help them to better understand and interact in the social world by how they interact with them (Thompson 2013a, b). If young children are seeking to better understand various mental and emotional states (intentions, goals, feelings, desires) that they know underlie people's actions, then talking with them about these internal states can improve young children's understanding of them (Thompson, 2011, 2013c, d).

However, debate continues to surround the question of whether young children are socially sensitive or basically egocentric. Ross Thompson (2012, 2013c, d) comes down on the side of viewing young children as socially sensitive, while Susan Harter (2012) argues that there is still evidence to support the conclusion that young children are essentially egocentric.

Emotional Development

The young child's growing awareness of self is linked to the ability to feel an expanding range of emotions. Young children, like adults, experience many emotions during the course of a day. Their emotional development allows them to try to make sense of other people's emotional reactions and to begin to control their own emotions (Cummings, Braungart-Rieker, & Sherman, 2013; Thompson, 2013d).

Expressing Emotions

Recall from Chapter 4 that even young infants experience emotions such as joy and fear, but to experience *self-conscious emotions* children must be able to refer to themselves and be aware of themselves as distinct from others (Lewis, 2010). Pride, shame, embarrassment, and guilt are examples of self-conscious emotions. These emotions do not appear to develop until self-awareness appears around 18 months of age.

During the early childhood years, emotions such as pride and guilt become more common. They are especially influenced by parents' responses to children's behavior. For example, a young child may experience shame when a parent says, "You should feel bad about biting your sister."

Understanding Emotions

Among the most important changes in emotional development in early childhood is an increased understanding of emotions (Bassett & others, 2012; Denham & others, 2012). Young children increasingly understand that certain situations are likely to evoke particular emotions, facial expressions indicate specific emotions, and emotions affect behavior and can be used to influence others. A recent study also found that young children's understanding of emotions was linked to an increase in prosocial behavior (Ensor, Spencer, & Hughes, 2011).

Between ages 2 and 4, children considerably increase the number of terms they use to describe emotions. During this time, they are also learning about the causes and consequences of feelings (Denham & others, 2012).

When they are 4 to 5 years old, children show an increased ability to reflect on emotions. They also begin to understand that the same event can elicit different feelings in different people. Moreover, they show growing awareness that they need to manage their emotions to meet social standards. And by age 5 most children can accurately determine emotions that are produced by challenging circumstances and describe strategies they might call on to cope with everyday stress (Cole & others, 2009).

Regulating Emotions

As you read in Chapter 4, emotion regulation is an important aspect of development. In particular, it plays a key role in children's ability to manage the demands and conflicts they face in interacting with others (Thompson, 2013c, d).

Many researchers consider the growth of emotion regulation in children as fundamental to their development of social competence (Cole & Hall, 2012; Nelson & others, 2012; Perry & others, 2012; Thompson, 2013a, b). Emotion regulation can be conceptualized as an important component of self-regulation or of executive functioning. Recall from Chapter 5 that executive functioning is increasingly thought to be a key concept in describing the young child's higher level cognitive functioning (Carlson & White, 2013). Cybelle Raver and her colleagues (Blair & Raver, 2012; McCoy & Raver, 2012; Raver & others, 2011, 2012; Zhai, Raver, & Jones, 2012) are using interventions such as increasing caregiver emotional expressiveness to improve young children's emotion regulation and reduce behavior problems in Head Start families.

Emotion-Coaching and Emotion-Dismissing Parents Parents can play an important role in helping young children regulate their emotions. Depending on how they talk with their children about emotion, parents can be described as taking an *emotion-coaching* or an *emotion-dismissing* approach (Gottman, 2012). The distinction between these approaches is most evident in the way the parent deals with the child's negative emotions (anger, frustration, sadness, and so on). *Emotion-coaching parents* monitor their children's emotions, view their children's negative emotions as opportunities for teaching, assist them in labeling emotions, and coach them in how to deal effectively with emotions. In contrast, *emotion-dismissing parents* view their role as to deny, ignore, or change negative emotions. Emotion-coaching parents interact with their children in a less rejecting manner, use more scaffolding and praise, and are more nurturant than are emotion-dismissing parents. Moreover, children of emotion-coaching parents are better at soothing themselves when they get upset, are more effective in regulating their negative affect, focus their attention better, and have fewer behavior problems than do children of emotion-dismissing parents. Recent studies have found that fathers' emotion coaching was related to children's social competence (Baker, Fenning, & Crnic, 2011) and that mothers' emotion coaching was linked to less oppositional behavior (Dunsmore, Booker, & Ollendick, 2012).

Parents' knowledge of their children's emotional world can help them to guide their children's emotional development and teach them how to cope effectively with problems. A recent study found that mothers' knowledge about what distresses and comforts their children predicts the children's coping, empathy, and prosocial behavior (Vinik, Almas, & Grusec, 2011).

An emotion-coaching parent. *What are some differences in emotion-coaching and emotion-dismissing parents?*

Regulation of Emotion and Peer Relations Emotions play a strong role in determining the success of a child's peer relationships (Denham & others, 2011). Specifically, the ability to modulate one's emotions is an important skill that benefits children in their relationships with peers. Moody and emotionally negative children are more likely to experience rejection by peers, whereas emotionally positive children are more popular. A recent study revealed that 4-year-olds recognized and generated strategies for controlling their anger more than did 3-year-olds (Cole & others, 2009).

moral development Development that involves thoughts, feelings, and actions regarding rules and conventions about what people should do in their interactions with other people.

Moral Development

Unlike a crying infant, a screaming 5-year-old is likely to be considered responsible for making a fuss. The parents may worry about whether the 5-year-old is a "bad" child. Although there are some who view children as innately good, many developmental psychologists believe that just as parents help their children become good readers, musicians, or athletes, parents must nurture goodness and help their children develop morally. **Moral development** involves the development of thoughts, feelings, and behaviors regarding rules and conventions about what people should do in their interactions with other people. Major developmental theories have focused on different aspects of moral development.

Moral Feelings

Feelings of anxiety and guilt are central to the account of moral development provided by Freud's psychoanalytic theory (introduced in Chapter 1). According to Freud, to reduce anxiety, avoid punishment, and maintain parental affection, children identify with their parents, internalizing their standards of right and wrong, and in this way develop the *superego*, the moral element of the personality.

Freud's ideas are not backed by research, but guilt certainly can motivate moral behavior. Other emotions, however, also contribute to moral development, including positive feelings. One important example is *empathy*, or responding to another person's feelings with an emotion that echoes those feelings (Denham & others, 2012).

Infants have the capacity for some purely empathic responses, but empathy often requires the ability to discern another person's emotional states, or what is called *perspective taking*. Learning how to identify a wide range of emotional states in others, and to anticipate what kinds of action will improve another person's emotional state, helps to advance children's moral development (Thompson, 2012).

Moral Reasoning

Interest in how children think about moral issues was stimulated by Piaget (1932), who extensively observed and interviewed children from ages 4 through 12. Piaget watched children play marbles to learn how they used and thought about the game's rules. He also asked children about ethical issues—theft, lies, punishment, and justice, for example. He concluded that children go through two distinct stages in how they think about morality:

heteronomous morality The first stage of moral development in Piaget's theory, occurring from approximately 4 to 7 years of age. Justice and rules are conceived of as unchangeable properties of the world, removed from the control of people.

- From ages 4 to 7, children display **heteronomous morality,** the first stage of moral development in Piaget's theory. Children think of justice and rules as unchangeable properties, removed from the control of people.

- From ages 7 to 10, children are in a period of transition, showing some features of the first stage of moral reasoning and some of the second stage, autonomous morality.

autonomous morality The second stage of moral development in Piaget's theory, displayed by older children (about 10 years of age and older). The child becomes aware that rules and laws are created by people and, in judging an action, one should consider the actor's intentions as well as the consequences.

- From about age 10 and older, children show **autonomous morality.** They become aware that rules and laws are created by people, and in judging an action they consider the actor's intentions as well as the action's consequences.

immanent justice The concept that, if a rule is broken, punishment will be meted out immediately.

Piaget extensively observed and interviewed 4- to 12-year-old children as they played games to learn how they used and thought about the games' rules.

Because young children are heteronomous moralists, they judge the rightness or goodness of behavior by considering its consequences, not the intentions of the actor. For example, to the heteronomous moralist, breaking twelve cups accidentally is worse than breaking one cup intentionally. As children develop into moral autonomists, intentions become more important than consequences.

The heteronomous thinker also believes that rules are unchangeable and are handed down by all-powerful authorities. When Piaget suggested to young children that they use new rules in a game of marbles, they resisted. By contrast, older children—moral autonomists—accept change and recognize that rules are merely conventions, subject to change.

The heteronomous thinker also believes in **immanent justice,** the concept that if a rule is broken, punishment will be meted out immediately. The young child believes that a violation is connected automatically to its punishment. Thus, young children often look around worriedly after doing something wrong, expecting the inevitable punishment. Immanent justice also implies that if something unfortunate happens to someone, that person must have transgressed earlier. Older children, who are moral autonomists, recognize that punishment occurs only if someone witnesses the wrongdoing and that, even then, punishment is not inevitable.

How do these changes in moral reasoning occur? Piaget argued that as children develop, they become more sophisticated in their thinking about social matters, especially about the possibilities and conditions of cooperation. Piaget stressed that this social understanding comes about through the mutual give-and-take of peer relations. In the peer group, where others have power and status similar to the child's, plans are negotiated and coordinated, and disagreements are reasoned about and eventually settled. Parent-child relations, in which parents have the power and children do not, are less likely to advance moral reasoning, because rules are often handed down in an authoritarian manner.

How Would You...?

As a health-care professional, how would you expect a child in the heteronomous stage of moral development to judge the behaviors of a doctor who unintentionally caused pain to a child during a medical procedure?

Earlier in this chapter you read about Ross Thompson's view that young children are not as egocentric as Piaget envisioned. Thompson (2012) recently further elaborated on this view, arguing that recent research indicates that young children often show a non-egocentric awareness of others' goals, feelings, and desires and how such internal states are influenced by the actions of others. These ties between advances in moral understanding and theory of mind indicate that young children possess cognitive resources that allow them to be aware of others' intentions and know when someone violates a moral prohibition. One study of 3-year-olds found that they were less likely to offer assistance to an adult they had previously observed being harmful to another person (Vaish, Carpenter, & Tomasello, 2010). However, because of limitations in their self-control skills, social understanding, and cognitive flexibility, young children's moral advancements often are inconsistent and vary across situations. They still have a long way to go before they have the capacity for developing a consistent moral character and making ethical judgments.

Moral Behavior

The behavioral and social cognitive approach, initially described in Chapter 1, focuses on moral behavior rather than moral reasoning. It holds that the processes of reinforcement, punishment, and imitation explain the development of moral behavior. When children are rewarded for behavior that is consistent with laws and social conventions, they are likely to repeat that behavior. When models who behave morally are provided, children are likely to adopt their actions. And when children are punished for immoral behavior, those behaviors are likely to be reduced or eliminated. However, because punishment may have adverse side effects, as discussed later in this chapter, it needs to be used judiciously and cautiously.

If a mother has rewarded a 4-year-old boy for telling the truth when he broke a glass at home, does this mean that he is likely to tell the truth to his preschool teacher when he knocks over a vase and breaks it? Not necessarily; the situation influences behavior. More than half a century ago, a comprehensive study of thousands of children in many situations—at home, at school, and at church, for example—found that a totally honest child is virtually nonexistent; so is a child who cheats in all situations (Hartshorne & May, 1928–1938). Behavioral and social cognitive researchers emphasize that what children do in one situation is often only weakly related to what they do in other situations. A child might cheat in class but not in a game; a child might steal a piece of candy when alone but not when others are present.

Social cognitive theorists also emphasize that the ability to resist temptation is closely tied to the development of self-control (Mischel, 2004), which involves learning to delay gratification. According to social cognitive theorists, cognitive factors are important in the child's development of self-control (Bandura, 2010a).

Gender

Recall from Chapter 1 that gender refers to the social and psychological dimensions of being male or female, and even preschool children display many of these dimensions. **Gender identity** is the sense of being male or female, which most children acquire by the time they are 3 years old. **Gender roles** are sets of expectations that prescribe how females or males should think, act, and feel. During the preschool years, most children increasingly act in ways that match their culture's gender roles.

How do these and other gender differences come about? Biology clearly plays a role, as we saw in Chapter 2. Among the possible biological influences are chromosomes, hormones, and evolution (Arnold, 2012; Buss, 2012). However, our focus in this chapter is on the social aspects of gender.

Social Influences

Many social scientists do not locate the cause of psychological gender differences in biological dispositions. Rather, they argue that these differences are due to social experiences (Eagly, 2012; Matlin, 2012). Their explanations include both social and cognitive theories.

Social Theories of Gender Three main social theories of gender have been proposed: social role theory, psychoanalytic theory, and social cognitive theory. Alice Eagly (2001, 2010, 2012) proposed **social role theory,** which states that gender differences result from the contrasting roles of women and men. In most cultures around the world, women have less power and status than men do, and they control fewer resources (UNICEF, 2012). Compared with men, women perform more domestic work, spend fewer hours in paid employment, receive lower pay, and are more thinly represented in the highest levels of organizations. In Eagly's (2010, 2012) view, as women adapted to roles with less power and less status in society, they showed more cooperative, less dominant profiles than men did. Thus, the social hierarchy and division of labor are important causes of gender differences in power, assertiveness, and nurture (Carli & Eagly, 2012).

The **psychoanalytic theory of gender** stems from Freud's view that the preschool child develops a sexual attraction to the opposite-sex parent. This is the process known as the Oedipus (for boys) or

gender identity The sense of being male or female, which most children acquire by the time they are 3 years old.

gender roles Sets of expectations that prescribe how females or males should think, act, and feel.

social role theory A theory that gender differences result from the contrasting roles of men and women.

psychoanalytic theory of gender A theory deriving from Freud's view that the preschool child develops a sexual attraction to the opposite-sex parent, by approximately 5 or 6 years of age renounces this attraction because of anxious feelings, and subsequently identifies with the same-sex parent, unconsciously adopting the same-sex parent's characteristics.

social cognitive theory of gender
A theory emphasizing that children's gender development occurs through the observation and imitation of gender behavior and through the rewards and punishments children experience for gender-appropriate and gender-inappropriate behavior.

Electra (for girls) complex. At age 5 or 6, the child renounces this attraction because of anxious feelings. Subsequently, the child identifies with the same-sex parent, unconsciously adopting that parent's characteristics. However, developmental psychologists have observed that gender development does not proceed in the manner that Freud proposed (Callan, 2001). Children become gender-typed much earlier than age 5 or 6, and they become masculine or feminine even when the same-sex parent is not present in the family.

The social cognitive approach discussed in Chapter 2 provides an alternative explanation. According to the **social cognitive theory of gender,** children's gender development occurs through observation and imitation of what other people say and do, and through being rewarded and punished for gender-appropriate and gender-inappropriate behavior (Bussey & Bandura, 1999). From birth onward, males and females are treated differently. When infants and toddlers show gender differences, adults tend to reward them. Parents often use rewards and punishments to teach their daughters to be feminine ("Karen, you are being a good girl when you play gently with your doll") and their sons to be masculine ("Keith, a boy as big as you are is not supposed to cry"). Parents, however, are only one of many sources from which children learn gender roles (Leaper, 2013). Culture, schools, peers, the media, and other family members also provide gender role models (Hyde & Else-Quest, 2013). For example, children learn about gender by observing other adults in the neighborhood and on television. As children grow older, peers become increasingly important. Let's look more closely at the influence of parents and peers.

First imagine that this is a photograph of a baby girl. What expectations would you have of her? Then imagine that this is a photograph of a baby boy. What expectations would you have of him?

Parental Influences

Parents influence their children's gender development by action and by example. (Hilliard & Liben, 2012). Both mothers and fathers are psychologically important to their children's gender development (Matlin, 2012). Cultures around the world, however, can vary in the roles assigned to mothers and fathers (Mistry, Contreras, & Dutta, 2013). A research review provided these conclusions (Bronstein, 2006):

- *Mothers' socialization strategies.* In many cultures, mothers socialize their daughters to be more obedient and responsible than their sons. They also place more restrictions on their daughters' autonomy.

- *Fathers' socialization strategies.* Fathers show more attention to their sons than to their daughters, engage in more activities with their sons, and put forth more effort to promote their sons' intellectual development.

Thus, according to Bronstein (2006, pp. 269–270), "Despite an increased awareness in the United States and other Western cultures of the detrimental effects of gender stereotyping, many parents continue to foster behaviors and perceptions that are consonant with traditional gender role norms."

How Would You...?

As a human development and family studies professional, how would you describe the ways in which parents influence their children's notions of gender roles?

Peer Influences

Parents provide the earliest discrimination of gender roles, but before long, peers join the process of responding to and modeling masculine and feminine behavior (Bukowski & Juang, 2012). In fact, peers become so important to gender development that the playground has been described as "gender school" (Luria & Herzog, 1985).

Peers extensively reward and punish gender behavior (Leaper, 2013; Leaper & Bigler, 2011). For example, when children play in ways that the culture considers sex-appropriate, their peers tend to reward them. But peers often reject children who act in a manner that is considered more characteristic of the other gender

(Handrinos & others, 2012). A little girl who brings a doll to the park may find herself surrounded by new friends; a little boy might be jeered. However, there is greater pressure for boys to conform to a traditional male role than for girls to conform to a traditional female role (Fagot, Rodgers, & Leinbach, 2000). For example, a preschool girl who wants to wear boys' clothing receives considerably more approval than a boy who wants to wear a dress. The very term "tomboy" implies broad social acceptance of girls' adopting traditional male behaviors.

Gender molds important aspects of peer relations (Field & others, 2012; Zozuls & others, 2012). It influences the composition of children's groups, the size of groups, and interactions within a group (Maccoby, 1998, 2002).

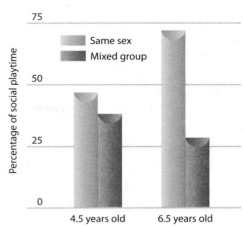

Figure 6.1
Developmental Changes in Percentage of Time Spent in Same-Sex and Mixed-Group Settings
Observations of children show that they are more likely to play in same-sex than mixed-sex groups. This tendency increases between 4 and 6 years of age.

- *Gender composition of children's groups.* Around age 3, children already show a preference for spending time with same-sex playmates. This preference increases until around age 12, and during the elementary school years children spend a large majority of their free time with children of their own sex (see Figure 6.1). Observations of children show that they are more likely to play in same-sex than mixed-sex groups. This tendency increases between 4 and 6 years of age.

- *Group size.* From about age 5, boys are more likely to associate together in larger clusters than girls are. Boys are also more likely to participate in organized group games than girls are. In one study, same-sex groups of six children were permitted to use play materials in any way they wished (Benenson, Apostolaris, & Parnass, 1997). Girls were more likely than boys to play in dyads or triads, while boys were more likely to interact in larger groups and seek to attain a group goal.

- *Interaction in same-sex groups.* Boys are more likely than girls to engage in rough-and-tumble play, competition, conflict, ego displays, risk taking, and seeking dominance. By contrast, girls are more likely to engage in "collaborative discourse," in which they talk and act in a more reciprocal manner.

Cognitive Influences

Observation, imitation, rewards and punishment—these are the mechanisms by which gender develops, according to social cognitive theory. Interactions between the child and the social environment are the main keys to gender development.

How Would You...?

As an educator, how would you create a classroom climate that promotes healthy gender development for both boys and girls?

Some critics argue that this explanation pays too little attention to the child's own mind and understanding, and portrays the child as passively acquiring gender roles (Martin & Ruble, 2010).

One influential cognitive theory is **gender schema theory,** which states that gender typing emerges as children gradually develop gender schemas of what is gender-appropriate and gender-inappropriate in their culture (Martin & Ruble, 2010). A schema is a cognitive structure, a network of associations that guide an individual's perceptions. A gender schema organizes the world in terms of female and male. Children are internally motivated to perceive the world and to act in accordance with their developing schemas. Bit by bit, children pick up what is gender-appropriate and gender-inappropriate in their culture, developing gender schemas that shape how they perceive the world and what they remember (Conry-Murray, Kim, & Turiel, 2012). Children are motivated to act in ways that conform with these gender schemas. Thus, gender schemas fuel gender typing.

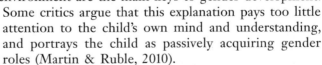

gender schema theory The theory that gender typing emerges as children gradually develop gender schemas of what is gender-appropriate and gender-inappropriate in their culture.

Families

Attachment to a caregiver is a key social relationship during infancy, but we saw in Chapter 4 that some experts maintain that secure attachment and the infant's early experiences have been overdramatized as determinants of life-span development. Social and emotional development is also shaped by other relationships and by temperament, contexts, and social experiences in the early childhood years and later (Grusec & others, 2013). In this section, we discuss aspects of social relationships in early childhood that go beyond attachment.

Parenting

Good parenting takes time and effort (Grusec & others, 2013). You can't do it in a minute here and a minute there. You can't do it with CDs or DVDs. Of course, it's not just the quantity of time parents spend with children that is important for children's development—the quality of the parenting is clearly important (Huberman & Mendelsohn, 2012; Iruka, Laforett, & Odom, 2012).

Baumrind's Parenting Styles

Baumrind (1971, 2012) stresses that parents should be neither punitive nor aloof. Rather, they should develop rules for their children and be affectionate with them. She has described four parenting styles:

- **Authoritarian parenting** is a restrictive, punitive style in which parents exhort the child to follow their directions and respect their work and effort. The authoritarian parent places firm limits and controls on the child and allows little verbal exchange. For example, an authoritarian parent might say, "You do it my way or else." Authoritarian parents also might spank the child frequently, enforce rules rigidly but not explain them, and show anger toward the child. Children of authoritarian parents are often unhappy, fearful, and anxious about comparing themselves with others; they also fail to initiate activity and have weak communication skills.

- **Authoritative parenting** encourages children to be independent but still places limits and controls on their actions. Extensive verbal give-and-take is allowed, and parents are warm and nurturant toward the child. An authoritative parent might put his arm around the child in a comforting way and say, "You know you shouldn't have done that. Let's talk about how you could handle the situation better next time." Authoritative parents show pleasure and support in response to their children's constructive behavior. They also expect independent, age-appropriate behavior. Children whose parents are authoritative are often cheerful, self-controlled and self-reliant, and achievement-oriented; they tend to maintain friendly relations with peers, cooperate with adults, and cope well with stress.

- **Neglectful parenting** is a style in which the parent is uninvolved in the child's life. Children whose parents are neglectful develop the sense that other aspects of the parents' lives are more important than they are. These children tend to be socially incompetent. Many have poor self-control and don't handle independence well. They frequently have low self-esteem, are immature, and may be alienated from the family. In adolescence, they may show patterns of truancy and delinquency.

- **Indulgent parenting** is a style in which parents are highly involved with their children but place few demands or controls on them. Such parents let their children do what they want. Some parents deliberately rear their children in this way because they believe the combination of warm involvement and few restraints will produce

authoritarian parenting A restrictive punitive style in which parents exhort the child to follow their directions and to respect work and effort. The authoritarian parent places firm limits and controls on the child and allows little verbal exchange. Authoritarian parenting is associated with children's social incompetence.

authoritative parenting A parenting style in which parents encourage their children to be independent but still place limits and controls on their actions. Extensive verbal give-and-take is allowed, and parents are warm and nurturant toward the child. Authoritative parenting is associated with children's social competence.

neglectful parenting A style of parenting in which the parent is very uninvolved in the child's life; it is associated with children's social incompetence, especially a lack of self-control.

indulgent parenting A style of parenting in which parents are highly involved with their children but place few demands or controls on them. Indulgent parenting is associated with children's social incompetence, especially a lack of self-control.

a creative, confident child. However, children whose parents are indulgent rarely learn respect for others and have difficulty controlling their behavior. They might be domineering, egocentric, and noncompliant, and have unsatisfactory peer relations.

These four classifications of parenting involve combinations of acceptance and responsiveness on the one hand and demand and control on the other (Maccoby & Martin, 1983). How these dimensions combine to produce authoritarian, authoritative, neglectful, and indulgent parenting is shown in Figure 6.2.

Keep in mind that research on parenting styles and children's development is correlational, not causal, in nature. Thus, if a study reveals that authoritarian parenting is linked to higher levels of aggression in children, it may be just as likely that aggressive children elicited authoritarian parenting as it is that authoritarian parenting produced aggressive children. Also recall from Chapter 1 that a third factor may influence the correlation between two factors. Thus, in the example of the correlation between authoritarian parenting and aggressive children, possibly authoritarian parents (first factor) and aggressive children (second factor) share genes (third factor) that predispose them to behave in ways that produced the correlation.

How Would You...?

As a psychologist, how would you use the research on parenting styles to design a parent education class that teaches effective skills for interacting with young children?

How Would You...?

As a human development and family studies professional, how would you characterize the parenting style that prevails within your own family?

	Accepting, responsive	Rejecting, unresponsive
Demanding, controlling	Authoritative	Authoritarian
Undemanding, uncontrolling	Indulgent	Neglectful

Figure 6.2 Classification of Parenting Styles
The four types of parenting styles (authoritative, authoritarian, indulgent, and neglectful) involve the dimensions of acceptance and responsiveness, on the one hand, and demand and control on the other. For example, authoritative parenting involves being both accepting/responsive and demanding/controlling.

Parenting Styles in Context

Among Baumrind's four parenting styles, authoritative parenting clearly conveys the most benefits to the child and to the family as a whole. Do the benefits of authoritative parenting transcend the boundaries of ethnicity, socioeconomic status, and household composition? Although some exceptions have been found, evidence linking authoritative parenting with competence on the part of the child occurs in research across a wide range of ethnic groups, social strata, cultures, and family structures (Steinberg & Silk, 2002).

Nevertheless, researchers have found that in some ethnic groups, aspects of the authoritarian style may be associated with more positive outcomes than Baumrind predicts. In the Arab world, many families are very authoritarian, dominated by the father's rule, and children are taught strict codes of conduct and family loyalty (Booth, 2002). As another example, Asian American parents often continue aspects of traditional Asian child-rearing practices that have sometimes been described as authoritarian. The parents exert considerable control over their children's lives. However, Ruth Chao (2001, 2005, 2007; Chao & Otsuki-Clutter, 2011; Chao & Tseng, 2002) argues that the style of parenting used by many Asian American

According to Ruth Chao, which type of parenting style do many Asian American parents use?

parents is distinct from the domineering control that is characteristic of the authoritarian style. Instead, Chao argues that it reflects concern and involvement in children's lives and is best conceptualized as a type of training. The high academic achievement of Asian American children may be a consequence of their parents' "training" (Stevenson & Zusho, 2002). In recent research involving Chinese American adolescents and their parents, parental control was endorsed as were the Confucian goals of perseverance, working hard in school, obedience, and being sensitive to parents' wishes (Russell, Crockett, & Chao, 2010).

Punishment

Use of corporal punishment is legal in every state in the United States. A national survey of U.S. parents with 3- and 4-year-old children found that 26 percent of parents reported spanking their children frequently, and 67 percent reported yelling at their children frequently (Regalado & others, 2004). A cross-cultural comparison found that individuals in the United States and Canada were among those with the most favorable attitudes toward corporal punishment and were most likely to remember it being used by their parents (see Figure 6.3) (Curran & others, 2001).

A research review concluded that corporal punishment by parents is associated with higher levels of immediate compliance and aggression by the children (Gershoff, 2002). The review also found that corporal punishment is linked to lower levels of moral internalization and mental health (Gershoff, 2002). A study in six countries revealed that mothers' use of physical punishment was linked to the highest rates of aggression in their children (Gershoff & others, 2010). And several recent longitudinal studies have found that physical punishment of children is associated with higher levels of aggression later in childhood and adolescence (Gershoff & others, 2012; Taylor & others, 2010).

What are some reasons for avoiding spanking or similar punishments? They include the following:

- When adults punish a child by yelling, screaming, or spanking, they are presenting children with out-of-control models for handling stressful situations. Children may imitate this behavior.

- Punishment can instill fear, rage, or avoidance. For example, spanking the child may cause the child to avoid being near the parent and to fear the parent.

- Punishment tells children what not to do rather than what to do. Children should be given feedback, such as "Why don't you try this?"

- Parents might unintentionally become so aroused when they are punishing the child that they become abusive (Knox, 2010).

Most child psychologists recommend handling misbehavior by reasoning with the child, especially explaining the consequences of the child's actions for others. *Time out*, in which the child is removed from a setting that offers positive reinforcement, can also be effective.

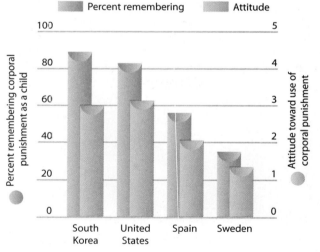

Figure 6.3 Corporal Punishment in Different Countries

A 5-point scale was used to assess attitudes toward corporal punishment, with scores closer to 1 indicating an attitude against its use and scores closer to 5 suggesting an attitude favoring its use. *Why are studies of corporal punishment correlational studies, and how does that affect their usefulness?*

For example, when the child has misbehaved, a parent might forbid TV viewing for a specified time.

Debate about the effects of punishment on children's development continues (Gershoff & others, 2012; Grusec, 2011; Grusec & others, 2013; Lansford & Deater-Deckard, 2012). A research review of 26 studies concluded that only severe or predominant use of spanking, not mild spanking, compared unfavorably with alternative discipline practices (Larzelere & Kuhn, 2005).

In addition to considering whether physical punishment is mild or out of control, another factor in evaluating its effects on children's development involves cultural contexts. Recently research has indicated that in countries such as Kenya where physical punishment is considered normal and necessary for handling children's transgressions, the effects of physical punishment are less harmful than in countries such as Thailand where physical punishment is perceived as detrimental to children's development (Lansford & others, 2005, 2012).

In the view of some experts, it is still difficult to determine whether the effects of physical punishment are always harmful to children's development, although such a view might be distasteful to some individuals (Grusec, 2011). It is nonetheless clear that when physical punishment involves abuse, it can be very harmful to children's development, as discussed later in this chapter (Cicchetti, 2013).

Coparenting

The relationship between marital conflict and the use of punishment highlights the importance of *coparenting*, the support that parents give each other in raising a child. Poor coordination between parents, undermining by one parent of the other, lack of cooperation and warmth, and aloofness by one parent are conditions that place children at risk (McHale & Sullivan, 2008; Solmeyer & others, 2011). In addition, one study revealed that coparenting is more beneficial than either maternal or paternal parenting in terms of children's development of self-control (Karreman & others, 2008). And a recent study found that greater father involvement in young children's play was linked to an increase in supportive coparenting (Jia & Schoppe-Sullivan, 2011).

Parents who do not spend enough time with their children or have problems in child rearing can benefit from counseling and therapy. To read about the work of marriage and family counselor Darla Botkin, see *Careers in Life-Span Development*.

FAMILIES

175

Child Maltreatment

Unfortunately, punishment sometimes leads to the abuse of infants and children (Cicchetti, 2011, 2013). In 2009, approximately 702,000 U.S. children were found to be victims of child abuse at least once during that year (U.S. Department of Health and Human Services, 2010).

Types of Child Maltreatment

The four main types of child maltreatment are physical abuse, child neglect, sexual abuse, and emotional abuse (National Clearinghouse on Child Abuse and Neglect, 2004):

- *Physical abuse* is characterized by the infliction of physical injury as a result of punching, beating, kicking, biting, burning, shaking, or otherwise harming a child. The parent or other person may not intend to hurt the child; the injury may result from excessive physical punishment (Hornor, 2012).

- *Child neglect* is characterized by failure to provide for the child's basic needs. Neglect can be physical (abandonment, for example), educational (allowing chronic truancy, for example), or emotional (marked inattention to the child's needs, for example) (Newton & Vandeven, 2010). Child neglect is by far the most common form of child maltreatment. In every country where relevant data have been collected, neglect occurs up to three times as often as abuse (Benoit, Coolbear, & Crawford, 2008).

Eight-year-old Donnique Hein lovingly holds her younger sister, 6-month-old Maria Paschel, after a meal at Laura's Home, a crisis shelter in Westpark run by the City Mission, in March 2010.

- *Sexual abuse* includes fondling of genitals, intercourse, incest, rape, sodomy, exhibitionism, and commercial exploitation through prostitution or production of pornographic materials (Bahali & others, 2010).

- *Emotional abuse (psychological/verbal abuse/mental injury)* includes acts or omissions by parents or other caregivers that have caused, or could cause, serious behavioral, cognitive, or emotional problems (van Harmelen & others, 2010).

How Would You...?

As a health-care professional, how would you work with parents during infant and toddler checkups to prevent child maltreatment?

Although any of these forms of child maltreatment may be found separately, they often occur in combination. Emotional abuse is almost always present when other forms are identified.

The Context of Abuse

No single factor causes child maltreatment (Cicchetti, 2013; Cicchetti & Rogosch, 2012; Cicchetti & others, 2013). A combination of factors, including the culture, characteristics of the family, and developmental characteristics of the child, likely contribute to child maltreatment.

The extensive violence that characterizes American culture, including TV violence, is reflected in the occurrence of violence in the family (Durrant, 2008). The family itself is obviously a key part of the context of abuse (Cichetti, 2013). Among the family and family-associated characteristics that may contribute to child maltreatment are parenting stress, substance abuse, social isolation, single parenting, and socioeconomic difficulties (especially poverty) (Cicchetti, 2013; Laslett & others, 2012; Turner & others, 2012). The interactions among all family members need to be considered, regardless of who performs violent acts against the child. For example, even though the father may be the one who physically abuses the child, the behavior of the mother, the child, and siblings should also be evaluated.

About one-third of parents who were abused themselves when they were young go on to abuse their own children (Cicchetti, Toth, & Rogosch, 2005). Thus, some, but not a majority, of parents are involved in an intergenerational transmission of abuse.

Developmental Consequences of Abuse

Among the consequences of maltreatment in childhood and adolescence are poor emotion regulation, attachment problems, problems in peer relations, difficulty in adapting to school, and other psychological problems, such as depression and delinquency (Cicchetti & Rogosch, 2012). Compared with their peers, adolescents who experienced abuse or neglect as children are more likely to engage in violent romantic relationships, delinquency, sexual risk taking, and substance abuse (Trickett, Negriff, & Perkins, 2011). And a recent study revealed that a significant increase in suicide attempts before age 18 occurred with repeated child maltreatment (Jonson-Reid, Kohl, & Drake, 2012).

Later, during the adult years, individuals who were maltreated as children are more likely to experience physical and mental health issues as well as sexual problems (Lacelle & others, 2012). A 30-year longitudinal study found that middle-aged adults who had experienced child maltreatment had increased risk for diabetes, lung disease, malnutrition, and vision problems (Widom & others, 2012). Another study revealed that child maltreatment was linked to depression in adulthood and to unfavorable outcomes for treatment of depression (Nanni, Uher, & Danese, 2012). Further, adults who were maltreated as children often have difficulty in establishing and maintaining healthy intimate relationships (Dozier, Stovall-McClough, & Albus, 2009). As adults, maltreated children are also at higher risk for violent behavior toward other adults—especially dating partners and marital partners—as well as for substance abuse, anxiety, and depression (Miller-Perrin, Perrin, & Kocur, 2009). One study also revealed that adults who had experienced child maltreatment were at increased risk for financial and employment-related difficulties (Zielinski, 2009).

How Would You...?

As an educator, how would you explain the potential impact of maltreatment at home on a child's performance in school?

An important research agenda is to discover how to prevent child maltreatment or intervene in children's lives when they have been maltreated (Cicchetti & others, 2013; Preer, Sorrentino, & Newton, 2012). In one study of maltreating mothers and their 1-year-olds, two treatments were effective in reducing child maltreatment: (1) home visitation that emphasized improved parenting, coping with stress, and increasing support for the mother; and (2) parent-infant psychotherapy that focused on improving maternal-infant attachment (Cicchetti, Toth, & Rogosch, 2005).

Sibling Relationships and Birth Order

How do developmental psychologists characterize sibling relationships? And how does birth order influence behavior, if at all?

Sibling Relationships

Approximately 80 percent of American children have one or more siblings—that is, sisters and brothers (Dunn, 2007). If you grew up with siblings, you probably have rich memories of your relationships with them. Two- to 4-year-old siblings in each other's presence have a conflict once every 10 minutes, on average; the rate of conflict declines somewhat from ages 5 to 7 (Kramer, 2006). What do parents do when they encounter siblings having a verbal or physical confrontation? One study revealed that they do one of three things: (1) intervene and try to help them resolve the conflict, (2) admonish or threaten them, or (3) do nothing at all (Kramer & Perozynski, 1999). Of interest is that in families with two siblings ages 2 to 5 the most frequent parental reaction is to do nothing at all.

Laurie Kramer (2006), who has conducted a number of research studies on siblings, says that not intervening and letting sibling conflict escalate are not good strategies. She developed a program titled "More Fun with Sisters and Brothers" that teaches 4- to 8-year-old siblings social skills for developing positive interactions (Kramer & Radey, 1997). Among the skills taught in the program are how to appropriately initiate play, how to accept and refuse invitations to play, perspective taking, how to deal with angry feelings, and how to manage conflict.

However, conflict is only one of the many dimensions of sibling relations (Howe, Ross, & Recchia, 2011). Sibling relations include helping, sharing, teaching, fighting, compromising, and playing, and siblings can act as emotional supports, rivals, and communication partners. A recent review concluded that sibling relationships in adolescence are not as close, are less intense, and are more egalitarian than in childhood (East, 2009).

Judy Dunn (2007), a leading expert on sibling relationships, described three important characteristics of sibling relationships:

1. *The emotional quality of the relationship.* Siblings often express both intense positive and negative emotions toward each other. Many children and adolescents have mixed feelings toward their siblings.

2. *The familiarity and intimacy of the relationship.* Siblings typically know each other very well, and this intimacy suggests that they can either provide support or tease and undermine each other, depending on the situation.

What characterizes children's sibling relationships?

3. *The variation in sibling relationships.* Some siblings describe their relationships more positively than others do. Thus, there is considerable variation in sibling relationships. We just noted that many siblings have mixed feelings about each other, but some children and adolescents describe their siblings mainly in warm, affectionate ways, whereas others primarily talk about how irritating and mean a sibling is.

Birth Order

Whether a child has older or younger siblings has been linked to the development of certain personality characteristics. For example, a recent review concluded that "firstborns are the most intelligent, achieving, and conscientious, while later-borns are the most rebellious, liberal, and agreeable" (Paulhus, 2008, p. 210). Compared with later-born children, firstborn children have also been described as more adult-oriented, helpful, conforming, and self-controlled. However, when such birth-order differences are reported, they often are small.

The one-child family is becoming much more common in China because of the strong motivation to limit the population growth in the People's Republic of China. The policy is still relatively new, and its effects on children have not been fully examined. *In general, though, what have researchers found the only child to be like?*

What accounts for such differences related to birth order? Proposed explanations usually point to variations in interactions associated with a particular position in the family. In one study, mothers became more negative, coercive, and restraining and played less with the firstborn following the birth of a second child (Dunn & Kendrick, 1982).

What about children who don't have siblings? The popular conception is that an only child is a "spoiled brat" with undesirable characteristics such as dependency, lack of self-control, and self-centered

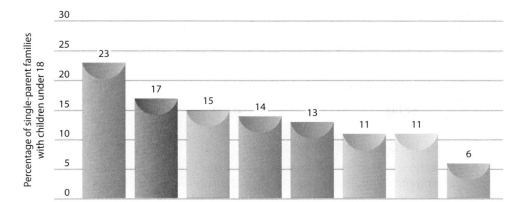

Figure 6.4 **Single-Parent Families in Different Countries**

behavior. But researchers present a more positive portrayal, in which only children are often achievement-oriented and display desirable personality characteristics, especially in comparison with later-borns and children from large families (Falbo & Poston, 1993; Jiao, Ji, & Jing, 1996).

So far, our discussion suggests that birth order might be a strong predictor of behavior. However, an increasing number of family researchers stress that, when all the factors that influence behavior are considered, birth order itself has limited ability to predict behavior. Think about some of the other important factors in children's lives that influence their behavior. They include heredity, models of competency or incompetency that parents present to children on a daily basis, peer and school influences, socioeconomic and sociohistorical factors, and cultural variations. When someone says that firstborns are always like this but last-borns are always like that, he or she is making overly simplistic statements that do not adequately take into account the complexity of influences on a child's development.

The Changing Family in a Changing Society

Beyond variations in number of siblings, the families that children experience differ in many important ways. As shown in Figure 6.4, the United States has one of the highest percentages of single-parent families in the world. Among two-parent families, there are those in which both parents work, those in which parents have found new spouses after divorce, and those in which the parents are gay or lesbian. Differences in culture and socioeconomic status (SES) also influence families. How do these variations in families affect children?

Working Parents

More than one of every two U.S. mothers with a child under age 5 is in the labor force; more than two of every three with a child ages 6 to 17 is. Maternal employment is a part of modern life, but its effects are still being debated.

Parental employment can have positive and negative effects on parenting (Han, 2009). Recent research indicates that what matters for children's development is the nature of the parents' work rather than whether or not both parents work outside the home (Goldberg & Lucas-Thompson, 2008; Parke & Clarke-Stewart, 2011). Ann Crouter (2006) described how parents bring their experiences at work into their homes. She concluded that parents who experience poor working conditions, such

How does work affect parenting?

as long hours, overtime work, stressful working conditions, and lack of autonomy at work, are likely to be more irritable at home and engage in less effective parenting than their counterparts who experience better working conditions. A consistent finding is that children (especially girls) whose mothers are employed engage in less gender stereotyping and have more egalitarian views of gender than do children whose mothers do not work outside the home (Goldberg & Lucas-Thompson, 2008).

Children in Divorced Families

Divorce rates changed rather dramatically in the United States and many countries around the world in the late twentieth century (Amato & Dorius, 2010). The U.S. divorce rate increased dramatically in the 1960s and 1970s but has declined since the 1980s. However, the divorce rate in the United States is still much higher than in most other countries.

It is estimated that 40 percent of children born to married parents in the United States will experience their parents' divorce (Hetherington & Stanley-Hagan, 2002). Let's examine some important questions about children in divorced families:

- *Are children better adjusted in intact, never-divorced families than in divorced families?* Most researchers agree that children from divorced families show poorer adjustment than their counterparts in never-divorced families (Amato & Dorius, 2010; Hetherington, 2006; Lansford, 2012; Robbers & others, 2012) (see Figure 6.5). Those who have experienced multiple divorces are at greater risk. Children in divorced families are more likely than those in never-divorced families to have academic problems, to exhibit externalized problems (such as acting out and delinquency) and experience internalized problems (such as anxiety and depression), to be less socially responsible, to have less competent intimate relationships, to drop out of school, to become sexually active at an earlier age, to take drugs, to associate with antisocial peers, to have low self-esteem, and to be less securely attached as young adults (Lansford, 2009). One study found that experiencing parental divorce in childhood was associated with insecure attachment in early adulthood (Brockmeyer, Treboux, & Crowell, 2005). Another study revealed that when individuals experienced the divorce of their parents in childhood and adolescence, they were more likely to have unstable romantic and marital relationships and low levels of education in adulthood (Amato, 2006). Keep in mind, however, that a majority of children (75 percent) in divorced families do not have significant adjustment problems.

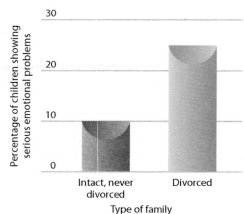

Figure 6.5 **Divorce and Children's Emotional Problems**
In Hetherington's research, 25 percent of children from divorced families showed serious emotional problems, compared with only 10 percent of children from intact, never-divorced families. However, keep in mind that a substantial majority (75 percent) of the children from divorced families did not show serious emotional problems.

- *Should parents stay together for the sake of the children?* Whether parents should stay in an unhappy or conflictual marriage for the sake of their children is one of the most commonly asked questions about divorce (Hetherington, 2006). If the stresses and disruptions in family relationships associated with an unhappy marriage that erode the well-being of children are reduced by the move to a divorced, single-parent family, divorce can be advantageous. However, if the diminished resources and increased risks associated with divorce are accompanied by inept parenting and sustained or increased conflict, not only between the divorced couple but also among the parents, children, and siblings, the best choice for the children would be for an unhappy marriage to be continued (Hetherington & Stanley-Hagan, 2002). It is difficult to determine how these "ifs" will play out when parents either remain together in an acrimonious marriage or become divorced.

Many of the problems experienced by children of divorced parents begin during the predivorce period, a time when parents often are in active conflict. Thus, when children of divorced parents show problems, the problems may be due not only to the divorce itself but also to the marital conflict that led to it. E. Mark Cummings and his colleagues (Cummings & Davies, 2010; Cummings & Merrilees, 2009; Koss & others, 2011) have proposed emotion security theory, which has its roots in attachment theory and states that children appraise marital conflict in terms of their sense of security and safety in the family. These researchers make a distinction between marital conflict that is negative for children (such as hostile emotional displays and destructive conflict tactics) and marital conflict that can be positive for children (such as marital disagreement that involves calmly discussing each person's perspective and then working together to reach a solution).

- *How much do family processes matter after a divorce?* They matter a great deal (Lansford, 2012; Sutherland, Altenhofen, & Biringen, 2012). When divorced parents' relationship with each other is harmonious and when they use authoritative parenting, children's adjustment improves (Hetherington, 2006). A number of researchers have shown that a disequilibrium, which includes diminished parenting skills, occurs in the year following the divorce—but by two years after the divorce, restabilization has occurred and parenting skills have improved (Hetherington, 1989). When the divorced parents can agree on childrearing strategies and can maintain a cordial relationship with each other, frequent visits by the noncustodial parent usually benefit the child (Fabricius & others, 2010). Following a divorce, father involvement with children drops off more than mother involvement, especially for fathers of girls. Also, a recent study in divorced families revealed that an intervention focused on improving the mother-child relationship was linked to improvements in relationship quality that increased children's coping skills over the short term (six months) and long term (six years) (Velez & others, 2011).

What concerns are involved in whether parents should stay together for the sake of the children or become divorced?

- *What factors influence an individual child's vulnerability to suffering negative consequences as a result of divorce?* Among the factors involved are the child's adjustment prior to the divorce, as well as the child's personality and temperament, gender, and custody situation (Hetherington, 2006). Children whose parents later divorce show poorer adjustment before the breakup (Lansford, 2009). Children who are socially mature and responsible, who show few behavioral problems, and who have an easy temperament are better able to cope with their parents' divorce. Children with a difficult temperament often have problems coping with their parents' divorce (Hetherington, 2006). Joint custody works best for children when the parents can get along with each other (Parke & Clarke-Stewart, 2011).

- *What role does socioeconomic status play in the lives of children whose parents have divorced?* Mothers who have custody of their children experience the loss of about one-fourth to one-half of their predivorce income, compared with a loss of only one-tenth by fathers who have custody. This income loss for divorced mothers is accompanied by increased workloads, high rates of job instability, and residential moves to less desirable neighborhoods with inferior schools (Lansford, 2009).

Gay and Lesbian Parents

Increasingly, gay and lesbian couples are creating families that include children (Patterson & D'Augelli, 2013; Patterson & Farr, 2012). Approximately 20 percent

What are the research findings regarding the development and psychological well-being of children raised by gay and lesbian couples?

of lesbians and 10 percent of gay men are parents. There may be more than 1 million gay and lesbian parents in the United States today.

Like heterosexual couples, gay and lesbian parents vary greatly. They may be single, or they may have same-gender partners. Many lesbian mothers and gay fathers are noncustodial parents because they lost custody of their children to heterosexual spouses after a divorce.

Parenthood among lesbians and gay men is controversial. Opponents claim that being raised by gay or lesbian parents harms the child's development. But researchers have found few differences between children growing up with lesbian mothers or gay fathers on the one hand, and children growing up with heterosexual parents on the other (Golombok, 2011a, b; Golombok & Tasker, 2010). For example, children raised by gay or lesbian parents are just as popular with their peers, and no differences are found in the adjustment and mental health of children living in these families when they are compared with children raised by heterosexual parents (Hyde & Else-Quest, 2013; Patterson, 2013). Contrary to the once-popular expectation that being raised by a gay or lesbian parent would result in the child's growing up to be gay or lesbian, in reality the overwhelming majority of children from gay or lesbian families have a heterosexual orientation (Golombok, 2011a, b).

Cultural, Ethnic, and Socioeconomic Variations

Parenting can be influenced by culture, ethnicity, and socioeconomic status (Parra Cardona & others, 2012; Wright & others, 2012). Recall from Bronfenbrenner's ecological theory (see Chapter 1) that a number of social contexts influence the child's development. In Bronfenbrenner's theory, culture, ethnicity, and socioeconomic status are classified as part of the macrosystem because they represent broader societal contexts.

Cross-Cultural Studies Different cultures often give different answers to such basic questions as what the father's role in the family should be, what support systems are available to families, and how children should be disciplined (Bekman & Aksu-Koc, 2012). There are important cross-cultural variations in parenting (Trommsdorff, 2012). In some cultures, such as rural areas of many countries, authoritarian parenting is widespread.

Cultural change, brought about by factors such as increasingly frequent international travel, the Internet and electronic communications, and economic globalization, is affecting families in many countries around the world. There are trends toward greater family mobility, migration to urban areas, and separation as some family members work in cities or countries far from their homes. Other trends include smaller families, fewer extended-family households, and increases in maternal employment (Brown & Larson, 2002). These trends can change the nature of the resources available to children. For example, when several generations no longer live in close proximity, children may lose the support and guidance of grandparents, aunts, and uncles. On the positive side, smaller families may produce more openness and communication between parents and children.

Ethnicity Families within various ethnic groups in the United States differ in their typical size, structure, composition, reliance on kinship networks, and levels of income and education (Conger & others, 2012; Gonzales & others, 2012). Large and extended families are more common among minority groups than among the White majority. For example, 19 percent of Latino families have three or more children, compared with 14 percent of African American and 10 percent of White families. African American and Latino children interact more with grandparents, aunts, uncles, cousins, and more distant relatives than do White children.

Single-parent families are more common among African Americans and Latinos than among non-Latino White Americans (Zeiders, Roosa, & Tein, 2011). In comparison with two-parent households, single parents often have more limited resources in terms of time, money, and energy (Wright & others, 2012). Ethnic minority parents also tend to be less educated and are more likely to live in low-income circumstances than their non-Latino White counterparts. Still, many impoverished ethnic minority families manage to find ways to raise competent children (Hattery & Smith, 2007).

Of course, individual families vary, and how ethnic minority families deal with stress depends on many factors (Nieto & Bode, 2012). Whether the parents are native-born or immigrants, how long the family has been in this country, its socioeconomic status, and its national origin all make a difference (Gonzales & others, 2012). The characteristics of the family's social context also influence its adaptation. What are the attitudes toward the family's ethnic group within its neighborhood or city? Can the family's children attend good schools? Are there community groups that welcome people from the family's ethnic group? Do members of the family's ethnic group form community groups of their own?

Recently immigrated families may face special problems. Many individuals in immigrant families are dealing with the problem of being undocumented. Living in an undocumented family can affect children's developmental outcomes through parents being unwilling to sign up for services for which they may be eligible, through parental stress and other conditions linked to low-wage work and lack of benefits, and through a lack of cognitive stimulation in the home (Yoshikawa, 2012).

What are some characteristics of families within different ethnic groups?

Recent research indicates that many members of families that have recently immigrated to the United States adopt a bicultural orientation, selecting characteristics of the U.S. culture that help them to survive and advance, while still retaining aspects of their culture of origin (Mok & Morris, 2012). In adopting characteristics of the U.S. culture, Latino families are increasingly embracing the importance of education (Cooper, 2011). Although their school dropout rates have remained higher than the rates for other ethnic groups, toward the end of the first decade of the twenty-first century they declined considerably (National Center for Education Statistics, 2010).

However, although many ethnic/immigrant families adopt aspects of the majority culture, parenting in many ethnic minority families also focuses on issues associated with promoting children's ethnic pride, knowledge of their ethnic group, and awareness of discrimination (Ho & others, 2012; Rogers & others, 2012; Simpkins & others, 2012).

Socioeconomic Status Low-income families have less access to resources than do higher-income families (Conger & others, 2012; Duncan, 2012; Evans & others, 2012). The resources in question include nutrition, health care, protection from danger, and enriching educational and socialization opportunities, such as tutoring and lessons in various activities. These differences are compounded in low-income families characterized by long-term poverty (Maholmes & King, 2012; Widom & Nikulina, 2012). A recent study found that persistent economic hardship as well as very early poverty was linked to lower cognitive functioning in children at 5 years of age (Schoon & others, 2012).

In the United States and most Western cultures, researchers have identified differences in child-rearing practices among groups of different socioeconomic-status (SES) (Hoff, Laursen, & Tardif, 2002, p. 246):

- "Lower-SES parents (1) are more concerned that their children conform to society's expectations, (2) create a home atmosphere in which it is clear that parents have authority over children," (3) are more likely to use physical punishment in disciplining their children, and (4) are more directive and less conversational with their children.

- "Higher-SES parents (1) are more concerned with developing children's initiative" and delay of gratification, (2) "create a home atmosphere in which children are more nearly equal participants and in which rules are discussed as opposed to being laid down" in an authoritarian manner, (3) are less likely to use physical punishment, and (4) "are less directive and more conversational" with their children.

Peer Relations, Play, and Media/Screen Time

The family is an important social context for children's development. However, children's development also is strongly influenced by what goes on in other social contexts, such as in peer groups and when children are playing or using various media (DeWall, Anderson, & Bushman, 2013; Hirsh-Pasek & Golinkoff, 2013).

Peer Relations

As children grow older, they spend an increasing amount of time with their peers—children of about the same age or maturity level.

What are the functions of a child's peer group? One of its most important functions is to provide a source of information and comparison about the world outside the family. Children receive feedback about their abilities from their peer group. They evaluate what they can do in terms of whether it is better than, as good as, or worse than what other children can do. It is hard to make these judgments at home because siblings are usually older or younger.

Good peer relations can be necessary for normal socioemotional development (Ladd & others, 2012). Special concerns in peer relations focus on children who are withdrawn and aggressive (Rubin & others, 2013; Underwood, 2011). Withdrawn children who are rejected by peers or are victimized and feel lonely are at risk for depression. Children who are aggressive with their peers are at risk for developing a number of problems, including delinquency and dropping out of school (Wentzel, 2013).

Recall from our discussion of gender that by about age 3, children already prefer to spend time with same-sex rather than opposite-sex playmates, and this preference increases in early childhood. During these same years, the frequency of peer interactions, both positive and negative, picks up considerably (Cillessen & Bellmore, 2011). Although aggressive interactions and rough-and-tumble play increase, the proportion of aggressive exchanges, compared with friendly exchanges, decreases. Many preschool children spend considerable

What are some characteristics of young children's peer relations?

time in peer interaction just conversing with playmates about such matters as "negotiating roles and rules in play, arguing, and agreeing" (Rubin, Bukowski, & Parker, 2006). We discuss peer relations further in Chapter 8.

Play

An extensive amount of peer interaction during childhood involves play, but social play is only one type of play (Pellegrini, 2013). Play is a pleasurable activity that is engaged in for its own sake, and its functions and forms vary.

Functions of Play

Play makes important contributions to young children's cognitive and socioemotional development (Hirsh-Pasek & Golinkoff, 2013). Theorists have focused on different aspects of play and have highlighted a long list of functions of play.

According to Freud and Erikson, play helps the child master anxieties and conflicts. Because pent-up tensions are released through play, the child can cope better with life's problems. Therapists use *play therapy* both to allow the child to work off frustrations and to analyze the child's conflicts and ways of coping with them (Sanders, 2008). Children may feel less threatened and be more likely to express their true feelings in the context of play.

Play is also an important context for cognitive development (Power, 2011). Both Piaget and Vygotsky concluded that play is the child's work. Piaget (1962) maintained that play advances children's cognitive development. At the same time, he said that children's cognitive development *constrains* the way they play. Play permits children to practice their competencies and acquired skills in a relaxed, pleasurable way. Piaget thought that cognitive structures need to be exercised, and play provides the perfect setting for this exercise.

Vygotsky (1962) also considered play to be an excellent setting for cognitive development. He was especially interested in the symbolic and make-believe aspects of play, as when a child substitutes a stick for a horse and rides the stick as if it were a horse. For young children, the imaginary situation is real. Parents should encourage such imaginary play because it advances the child's cognitive development, especially creative thought.

Daniel Berlyne (1960) described play as exciting and pleasurable in itself because it satisfies our exploratory drive. This drive involves curiosity and a desire for information about something new or unusual. Play encourages exploratory behavior by offering children the possibilities of novelty, complexity, uncertainty, surprise, and incongruity.

More recently, play has been described as an important context for the development of language and communication skills (Hirsh-Pasek & Golinkoff, 2013). Language and communication skills may be enhanced through discussions and negotiations regarding roles and rules in play as young children practice various words and phrases. These types of social interactions during play can benefit young children's literacy skills (Hirsh-Pasek & Golinkoff, 2013). And, as we saw in Chapter 5, play is a central focus of the child-centered kindergarten and is thought to be an essential aspect of early childhood education (Henninger, 2013).

Types of Play

The contemporary perspective on play emphasizes both the cognitive and the social aspects of it (Fung & Cheng, 2012; Pellegrini, 2013; Vong, 2012). Among the most widely studied types of children's play are sensorimotor and practice play, pretense/symbolic play, social play, constructive play, and games (Bergen, 1988).

Sensorimotor and Practice Play **Sensorimotor play** is behavior that allows infants to derive pleasure from exercising their sensorimotor schemes. The development of sensorimotor play follows Piaget's description of sensorimotor thought, which we discussed in

sensorimotor play Behavior engaged in by infants to derive pleasure from exercising their existing sensorimotor schemes.

practice play Play that involves repetition of behavior when new skills are being learned or when physical or mental mastery and coordination of skills are required for games or sports.

pretense/symbolic play Play in which the child transforms the physical environment into a symbol.

Chapter 4. Infants begin to engage in exploratory and playful visual and motor transactions during the second quarter of the first year of life. By the age of 9 months, many infants can select novel objects for exploration and play, especially responsive objects such as toys that make noise or bounce.

Practice play involves the repetition of behavior when new skills are being learned or when physical or mental mastery and coordination of skills are required for games or sports. Sensorimotor play, which often involves practice play, is primarily confined to infancy, whereas practice play can continue to occur throughout life. During the preschool years, children often engage in practice play.

Pretense/Symbolic Play **Pretense/symbolic play** occurs when the child transforms the physical environment into a symbol. Between 9 and 30 months, children increasingly use objects in symbolic play. They learn to transform objects—substituting them for other objects and acting toward them as if they were these other objects. For example, a preschool child may treat a table as if it were a car and say, "I'm fixing the car," as he grabs a leg of the table.

A preschool "superhero" at play.

Many experts on play consider the preschool years the "golden age" of pretense/symbolic play that is dramatic or sociodramatic in nature. This type of make-believe play often appears at about 18 months and reaches a peak at ages 4 to 5, then gradually declines.

Some child psychologists believe that pretend play is an important aspect of young children's development and often reflects advances in their cognitive development, especially as an indication of symbolic understanding. For example, Catherine Garvey (2000) and Angeline Lillard (2006) emphasize that hidden in young children's pretend-play narratives are remarkable capacities for role-taking, balancing of social roles, metacognition (thinking about thinking), testing of the distinction between reality and pretense, and numerous nonegocentric capacities that reveal young children's remarkable cognitive skills.

Social Play **Social play** is play that involves interaction with peers. It increases dramatically during the preschool years. For many children, social play is the main context for their social interactions with peers (Coplan & Arbeau, 2009). Social play includes varied interchanges such as turn taking, conversations about numerous topics, social games and routines, and physical play. It often provides a high degree of pleasure to the participants.

Constructive Play **Constructive play** combines sensorimotor/practice play with symbolic representation. It occurs when children engage in the self-regulated creation of a product or solution. Constructive play increases in the preschool years as symbolic play increases and sensorimotor play decreases. Constructive play is also a frequent form of play in the elementary school years, both in and out of the classroom.

social play Play that involves social interactions with peers.

constructive play Play that combines sensorimotor and repetitive activity with symbolic representation of ideas. Constructive play occurs when children engage in self-regulated creation or construction of a product or a problem solution.

How Would You…?

As an educator, how would you integrate play into the learning process?

Trends in Play

Kathy Hirsh-Pasek, Roberta Golinkoff, and Dorothy Singer (Hirsh-Pasek & others, 2009; Singer, Golinkoff, & Hirsh-Pasek, 2006) are concerned about the decline in the amount of time young children have for free play, reporting that it has declined considerably in recent decades. They are especially worried about young children's playtime being restricted at home and school so they can spend more time on academic subjects. They also point out that many schools have eliminated recess. And it is not just the decline in free play time that bothers them. They underscore that learning in playful contexts captivates children's minds in ways that enhance their cognitive and socioemotional development—Singer, Golinkoff, and Hirsh-Pasek's (2006) first book on play was titled: *Play = Learning*. Among the cognitive benefits of play, they identified the development of creativity; abstract thinking; imagination; attention, concentration, and persistence; problem-solving; social cognition, empathy, and perspective taking; language skills; and mastery of new concepts. Among the socioemotional experiences and development they believe play promotes are enjoyment, relaxation, and self-expression; cooperation, sharing, and turn-taking; anxiety reduction; and self-confidence. With so many positive cognitive and socioemotional outcomes of play, clearly it is important that we find more time for play in young children's lives.

games Activities engaged in for pleasure that include rules and often involve competition between two or more individuals.

Games Games are activities that are engaged in for pleasure and have rules. Often they involve competition. Preschool children may begin to participate in social games that involve simple rules of reciprocity and turn taking. However, games take on a much stronger role in the lives of elementary school children. In one study, the highest incidence of game playing occurred between ages 10 and 12 (Eiferman, 1971). After age 12, games decline in popularity (Bergen, 1988).

Kathy Hirsh-Pasek in a play setting with a young child. *What are some concerns of Hirsh-Pasek and her colleagues about trends in children's play?*

Media and Screen Time

Few developments in society in the second half of the twentieth century had a greater impact on children than television (Zimmerman & others, 2012). Television continues to have a strong influence on children's development, but children's use of other media and information/communication devices has led to the use of the term *screen time*, which includes how much time individuals spend watching television programs and DVDs, using computers, playing video games, and using mobile media such as iPhones (De Decker & others, 2012; Schmidt & others, 2012). Television is still the elephant in young children's media life, with 2- to 4-year-old children watching TV approximately 2 to 4 hours per day (Roberts & Foehr, 2008). However, a recent study revealed that 12 percent of 2- to 4-year-old U.S. children use computers every day and 22 percent of 5- to 8-year-olds use computers daily (Common Sense Media, 2011). A recent recommendation stated that for children 2 to 4 years of age screen time should be limited to no more than 1 hour per day (Tremblay & others, 2012). Many children spend more time with various screen media than they do interacting with their parents and peers.

Screen time can have a negative influence on children by making them passive learners, distracting them from doing homework, teaching them stereotypes, providing them with violent models of aggression, and presenting them with unrealistic views of the world.

Among other concerns about young children having so much screen time are decreased time spent in play, less time interacting with peers, reductions in physical activity, increased rates of being overweight or obese, poor sleep habits, and higher rates of aggression. Consider the following recent research: a research review concluded that a higher level of screen time at 4 to 6 years of age was linked to increased obesity and lower physical activity from preschool through adolescence (te Velde & others, 2012).

What are some concerns about young children's media and screen time?

The extent to which children are exposed to violence and aggression on television raises special concerns (Matos, Ferreira, & Haase, 2012). Children who watch higher levels of aggression and violence in TV shows are more likely to engage in aggressive behavior (DeWall, Anderson, & Bushman, 2013). In addition to television violence, there is increased concern about violent video games, especially those that are highly realistic (Escobar-Chaves & Anderson, 2008). Recent research reviews concluded that playing violent video games is linked to aggression in both males and females (DeWall, Anderson, & Bushman, 2013; Gentile, 2011).

How Would You...?

As a human development and family studies professional, how would you talk with parents about strategies for improving television viewing by their children?

Summary

Emotional and Personality Development

- In Erikson's theory, early childhood is a period when development involves resolving the conflict of initiative versus guilt. Young children improve their self-understanding and understanding of others.

- Young children's range of emotions expands during early childhood as they increasingly experience self-conscious emotions such as pride, shame, and guilt. Children benefit from having emotion-coaching parents.

- Moral development involves thoughts, feelings, and actions regarding rules and regulations about what people should do in their interactions with others. Piaget proposed cognitive changes in children's moral reasoning. Behavioral and social cognitive theorists argue that there is considerable situational variability in moral behavior.

- Gender refers to the social and psychological dimensions of being male or female. Both psychoanalytic theory and social cognitive theory emphasize the adoption of parents' gender characteristics. Peers are especially adept at rewarding gender-appropriate behavior. Gender schema theory emphasizes the role of cognition in gender development.

Families

- Authoritarian, authoritative, neglectful, and indulgent parenting styles produce different results. Authoritative parenting is the style most often associated with children's social competence. Ethnic variations characterize parenting styles. Physical punishment is widely used by U.S. parents, but there are a number of reasons why it is not a good choice. Coparenting has positive effects on children's development.

- Child maltreatment may take the form of physical abuse, child neglect, sexual abuse, and emotional abuse.

- Siblings interact with each other in positive and negative ways. Birth order is related in certain ways to child characteristics, but by itself it is not a good predictor of behavior.

- In general, having both parents employed full-time outside the home has not been shown to have negative effects on children. If divorced parents develop a harmonious relationship and practice authoritative parenting, children's adjustment improves. Researchers have found few differences between children growing up in gay or lesbian families and children growing up in heterosexual families. Culture, ethnicity, and socioeconomic status are linked to a number of aspects of families and children's development.

Peer Relations, Play, and Media/Screen Time

- Peers are powerful socialization agents. Peers provide a source of information and comparison about the world outside the family.

- Play's functions include affiliation with peers, tension release, advances in cognitive development, exploration, and provision of a safe haven. The contemporary perspective on play emphasizes both the cognitive and the social aspects of play. Among the most widely studied types of children's play are sensorimotor play, practice play, pretense/symbolic play, social play, constructive play, and games.

Media and Screen Time

- There are serious concerns about the extensive amount of time young children are spending with various media and electronic devices. Both watching TV violence and playing violent video games have been linked to children's aggressive behavior.

Key Terms

7 Physical and Cognitive Development in Middle and Late Childhood

Stories of Life-Span Development: Angie and Her Weight

The following comments are by Angie, an elementary-school-age girl:

> When I was eight years old, I weighed 125 pounds. My clothes were the size that large teenage girls wear. I hated my body, and my classmates teased me all the time. I was so overweight and out of shape that when I took a P.E. class my face would get red and I had trouble breathing. I was jealous of the kids who played sports and weren't overweight like I was.
>
> I'm nine years old now and I've lost 30 pounds. I'm much happier and proud of myself. How did I lose the weight? My mom said she had finally

decided enough was enough. She took me to a pediatrician who specializes in helping children lose weight and keep it off. The pediatrician counseled my mom about my eating and exercise habits, then had us join a group that he had created for overweight children and their parents. My mom and I go to the group once a week, and we've now been participating in the program for six months. I no longer eat fast-food meals, and my mom is cooking more healthy meals. Now that I've lost weight, exercise is not as hard for me, and I don't get teased by the kids at school. My mom's pretty happy, too, because she's lost 15 pounds herself

since we've been in the counseling program.

Not all overweight children are as successful as Angie at reducing their weight. Indeed, being overweight in childhood has become a major national health concern in the United States. Later in the chapter, we further explore being overweight in childhood.

During the middle and late childhood years, which last from approximately 6 years of age to 10 or 11 years of age, children grow taller, heavier, and stronger, and become more adept at using their physical skills. During these years, disabilities may emerge that call for special attention and intervention. It is also in this age period that children's cognitive abilities increase dramatically. Their command of grammar becomes proficient, they learn to read, and they may acquire a second language. ■

Physical Changes and Health

Continued growth and change in proportions characterize children's bodies during middle and late childhood. During this time period, some important changes in the brain also take place and motor skills improve. Developing a healthy lifestyle that involves regular exercise and good nutrition is a key aspect of making sure these years are a time of healthy growth and development.

Body Growth and Change

The period of middle and late childhood involves slow, consistent growth. This is a period of calm before the rapid growth spurt of adolescence. During the elementary school years, children grow an average of 2 to 3 inches a year until, at the age of 11, the average girl is 4 feet, 10¼ inches tall, and the average boy is 4 feet, 9 inches tall. During the middle and late childhood years, children gain about 5 to 7 pounds a year. The weight increase is due mainly to increases in the size of the skeletal and muscular systems, as well as the size of some body organs.

Proportional changes are among the most pronounced physical changes in middle and late childhood (Burns & others, 2013). Head and waist circumference decrease in relation to body height. A less noticeable physical change is that bones continue to ossify during middle and late childhood, although they still yield to pressure and pull more than do mature bones.

Muscle mass and strength gradually increase during these years as "baby fat" decreases. The loose movements and knock-knees of early childhood give way to improved muscle tone. Thanks both to heredity and to exercise, children double their strength capabilities during these years. Because of their greater number of muscle cells, boys are usually stronger than girls.

What characterizes physical growth during middle and late childhood?

The Brain

Total brain volume stabilizes by the end of middle and late childhood, but significant changes in various structures and regions of the brain continue to occur (Thomason & Thompson, 2011). As children develop, activation in some brain areas increases while it decreases in other areas (Diamond, 2013). One shift in activation that occurs is from diffuse, larger areas to more focal, smaller areas

(Turkeltaub & others, 2003). This shift is characterized by synaptic pruning, in which areas of the brain not being used lose synaptic connections and those areas being used show an increase in connections. In one study, researchers found less diffusion and more focal activation in the prefrontal cortex from 7 to 30 years of age (Durston & others, 2006). This shift in activation was accompanied by increased efficiency in cognitive performance, especially *cognitive control*, which involves effective control and flexibility in a number of areas (Diamond, 2013).

Leading researchers in developmental cognitive neuroscience have recently proposed that the prefrontal cortex likely orchestrates the functions of many other brain regions during development (Johnson, Grossmann, & Cohen-Kadosh, 2009). As part of this organizational role, the prefrontal cortex may provide an advantage to neural networks and connections that include the prefrontal cortex. In this view, the prefrontal cortex coordinates which neural connections are the most effective for solving a problem at hand.

Motor Development

During middle and late childhood, children's motor skills become much smoother and more coordinated than they were in early childhood. For example, only one child in a thousand can hit a tennis ball over the net at the age of 3, yet by the age of 10 or 11 most children can learn to play the sport. Running, climbing, skipping rope, swimming, bicycle riding, and skating are just a few of the many physical skills elementary school children can master. In gross motor skills that involve large muscle activity, boys usually outperform girls.

Increased myelination of the central nervous system is reflected in the improvement of fine motor skills during middle and late childhood. Children can more adroitly use their hands as tools. Six-year-olds can hammer, paste, tie shoes, and fasten clothes. By 7 years of age, children's hands have become steadier. At this age, children prefer a pencil to a crayon for printing, and they reverse letters less often. Printing becomes smaller. At 8 to 10 years of age, they can use their hands independently with more ease and precision. Fine motor coordination develops to the point at which children can write rather than print words. Cursive letter size becomes smaller and more even. At 10 to 12 years of age, children begin to show manipulative skills similar to the abilities of adults. They can master the complex, intricate, and rapid movements needed to produce fine-quality crafts or to play a difficult piece on a musical instrument. Girls usually outperform boys in their use of fine motor skills.

What are some good strategies for increasing children's exercise?

Exercise

American children and adolescents are not getting enough exercise (Gao, 2012; Graber & Woods, 2013). Increasing children's exercise levels has positive outcomes (Graham, Holt/Hale, & Parker, 2013). One study found that 45 minutes of moderate physical activity and 15 minutes of vigorous physical activity daily were related to decreased odds of children being overweight (Wittmeier, Mollard, & Kriellaars, 2008). And a recent study of 9-year-olds revealed that a higher level of physical activity was linked to a lower level of metabolic disease risk based on measures such as cholesterol, waist circumference, and insulin levels (Parrett & others, 2011).

Parents and schools play important roles in determining children's exercise levels (Wuest & Fisette, 2012). Growing up with parents who exercise regularly provides positive models of exercise for children (Crawford & others, 2010; Loprinzi & Trost, 2010). A recent study revealed that mothers were more likely than fathers to limit sedentary behavior in boys and girls (Edwardson & Gorely, 2010). In this study, fathers did have an influence on their sons' physical activity, but primarily through explicit modeling of physical activity, such as showing their sons how to shoot a basketball. Another recent study found that a school-based physical activity was successful in improving children's fitness and lowering their fat content (Kriemler & others, 2010).

How Would You...?
As an educator, how would you structure the curriculum to ensure that elementary school students are getting adequate physical activity throughout the day?

As you read in Chapter 6, screen time is linked with low activity levels and obesity in children (Goldfield, 2012; te Velde & others, 2012). Researchers have found that the total time that children and adolescents spend in front of a television or computer screen places them at risk for reduced activity and being overweight (Rey-Lopez & others, 2008).

Health, Illness, and Disease

For the most part, middle and late childhood is a time of excellent health. Disease and death are less prevalent at this time than during other periods in childhood and in adolescence. However, many children in middle and late childhood face health problems that threaten their development (Barakat, Hocking, & Kazak, 2013).

How Would You...?
As a social worker, how would you use your knowledge of overweight risk factors to design a workshop for parents and children about healthy lifestyle choices?

Overweight Children

Being overweight is an increasingly prevalent health problem in children (Schiff, 2013; Summerbell & others, 2012). Over the last three decades, the percentage of U.S. children who are at risk for being overweight has doubled from 15 percent in the 1970s to almost 30 percent today, and the percentage of children who are overweight has tripled during this time frame (Orsi, Hale, & Lynch, 2011). We indicated that 12.1 percent of 2- to 5-year-old U.S. children are obese. That figure is 50 percent higher for 6- to 11-year-old U.S. children—in 2009–2010, 18 percent of U.S. 6- to 11-year-olds were classified as obese (Ogden & others, 2012).

What are some concerns about overweight children?

Causes of Children Being Overweight Heredity and environmental contexts are related to being overweight in childhood. Recent genetic analysis indicates that heredity is an important factor in children becoming overweight (Freitag, Asherson, & Hebebrand, 2012). Overweight parents tend to have overweight children (Pufal & others, 2012). Environmental factors that influence whether children become overweight include availability of food (especially food high in fat content), energy-saving devices, declining physical activity, parents' eating habits and monitoring of children's eating habits, the context in which a child eats, and heavy screen time (Faith & others, 2012; Riesch & others, 2012). One study found that having two overweight/obese parents significantly increased the likelihood that children would be overweight/obese (Xu & others, 2011). A recent behavior modification study of overweight and obese children made watching TV contingent on their engagement in exercise (Goldfield, 2012). The intervention markedly increased their exercise and reduced their TV viewing time.

Consequences of Children Being Overweight The increase in overweight children in recent decades is cause for great concern because being overweight raises the risk for many medical and psychological problems (Schiff, 2013). Diabetes, hypertension (high blood pressure), and elevated blood cholesterol levels are common in children who are overweight (Lytle, 2012; Trasande & Elbel, 2012). A recent research review concluded that obesity was linked with low self-esteem in children (Gomes & others, 2011). And in a recent study, overweight children reported being teased more by their peers and family members than did normal-weight children (McCormack & others, 2011).

Intervention Programs A combination of diet, exercise, and behavior modification is often recommended to help children lose weight (Cronk & others, 2011). Intervention programs that emphasize getting parents to engage in healthier life styles themselves, as well as feeding their children healthier food and getting them to exercise more, can produce weight reduction in overweight and obese children (Brotman & others, 2012). For example, a recent study found that a combination of a child-centered activity program and a parent-centered dietary modification program were successful in helping overweight children lose pounds over a two-year period (Collins & others, 2011).

Cancer

Cancer is the second leading cause of death in U.S. children 5 to 14 years of age. One in every 330 children in the United States develops cancer before the age of 19. The incidence of cancer in children has increased slightly in recent years (National Cancer Institute, 2012).

Child cancers mainly attack the white blood cells (leukemia), brain, bone, lymph system, muscles, kidneys, and nervous system. All are characterized by an uncontrolled proliferation of abnormal cells (Fabbri & others, 2012). As indicated in Figure 7.1, the most common cancer in children is leukemia, a cancer in which bone marrow manufactures an abundance of abnormal white blood cells that crowd out normal cells, making the child susceptible to bruising and infection (Lund & others, 2011).

Because of advancements in cancer treatment, children with cancer are surviving longer than in the past (National Cancer Institute, 2012). For example, approximately 80 percent of children with acute lymphoblastic leukemia are cured with current chemotherapy treatment (Wayne, 2011).

Child life specialists are among the health professionals who work to make the lives of children with diseases less stressful. To read about the work of child life specialist Sharon McLeod, see *Careers in Life-Span Development*.

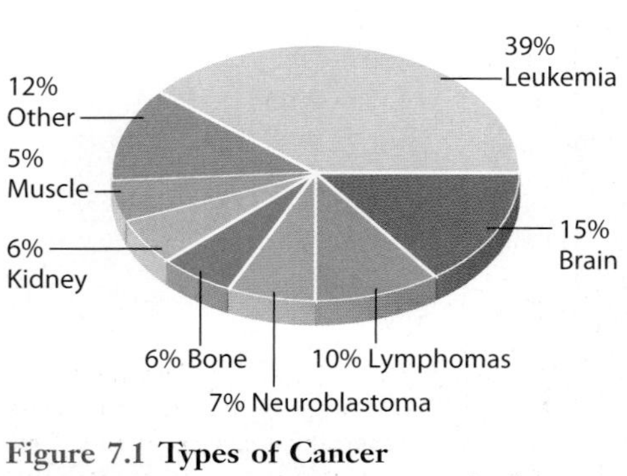

12% Other
5% Muscle
6% Kidney
6% Bone
7% Neuroblastoma
10% Lymphomas
39% Leukemia
15% Brain

Figure 7.1 Types of Cancer in Children

Cancers in children have a different profile from adult cancers, which attack mainly the lungs, colon, breast, prostate, and pancreas.

Children with Disabilities

The elementary school years are a time when disabilities become prominent for some children. What are some of the disabilities that children have? What characterizes the educational issues facing children with disabilities?

The Scope of Disabilities

Of all children from 3 to 21 years of age in the United States, 14 percent received special education or related services in 2008-2009 (Aud & others, 2011). Figure 7.2 shows the four largest groups of students with a disability who were served by federal programs in the 2008–2009 school year (Condition of Education, 2012). As indicated in Figure 7.2, students with a learning disability were by far the largest group of students with a disability to be given special education, followed by children with speech or language impairments, intellectual disability, and emotional disturbance.

Learning Disabilities

The U.S. government uses the following definition to determine whether a child should be classified as having a learning disability: A child with a **learning disability** has difficulty in learning that involves understanding or using spoken or written language, and the difficulty can appear in listening, thinking, reading, writing, and spelling. A learning disability also may involve difficulty in doing mathematics (Jitendra & Montague, 2013). To be classified as a learning disability, the learning problem is not primarily the result

Disability	Percentage of All Children in Public Schools
Learning disabilities	4.9
Speech or hearing impairments	2.9
Intellectual disability	0.9
Emotional disturbance	0.8

Figure 7.2 U.S. Children with a Disability Who Receive Special Education Services
Figures are for the 2009–2010 school year and represent the four categories with the highest numbers and percentages of children. Both learning disability and attention deficit hyperactivity disorder are combined in the learning disabilities category (Condition of Education, 2012).

learning disability Describes a child who has difficulty understanding or using spoken or written language or doing mathematics. To be classified as a learning disability, the problem is not primarily the result of visual, hearing, or motor disabilities; intellectual disability; emotional disorders; or due to environmental, cultural, or economic disadvantage.

attention deficit hyperactivity disorder (ADHD) A disability in which children consistently show one or more of the following characteristics: (1) inattention, (2) hyperactivity, and (3) impulsivity.

of visual, hearing, or motor disabilities; intellectual disability; emotional disorders; or due to environmental, cultural, or economic disadvantage.

About three times as many boys as girls are classified as having a learning disability. Among the explanations for this gender difference are a greater biological vulnerability among boys and *referral bias*. That is, boys are more likely than girls to be referred by teachers for treatment because of troublesome behavior.

Approximately 80 percent of children with a learning disability have a reading problem (Shaywitz, Gruen, & Shaywitz, 2007). Three types of learning disabilities are dyslexia, dysgraphia, and dyscalculia:

- *Dyslexia* is a category reserved for individuals who have a severe impairment in their ability to read and spell (Allor & Al Otaiba, 2013).

- *Dysgraphia* is a learning disability that involves difficulty in handwriting (Mason, Harris, & Graham, 2013). Children with dysgraphia may write very slowly, their writing products may be virtually illegible, and they may make numerous spelling errors because of their inability to match up sounds and letters (Hayes & Berninger, 2013).

- *Dyscalculia*, also known as developmental arithmetic disorder, is a learning disability that involves difficulty in math computation (Bryant & others, 2013).

The precise causes of learning disabilities have not yet been determined (Hallahan, Kaufmann, & Pullen, 2012). To reveal any regions of the brain that might be involved in learning disabilities, researchers use brain-imaging techniques, such as magnetic resonance imaging (Shaywitz, Lyon, & Shaywitz, 2006) (see Figure 7.3). This research indicates that it is unlikely learning disabilities reside in a single, specific brain location. More likely, learning disabilities are due to problems in integrating information from multiple brain regions or subtle difficulties in brain structures and functions.

Many children with ADHAD show impulsive behavior, such as this boy reaching to pull a girl's hair. *How would you handle this situation if you were a teacher in this context?*

Interventions with children who have a learning disability often focus on improving reading ability (Carlisle, Kenney, & Vereb, 2013; Lerner & Johns, 2012). Intensive instruction over a period of time by a competent teacher can help many children (Berninger & Dunn, 2013).

Attention Deficit Hyperactivity Disorder (ADHD)

Attention deficit hyperactivity disorder (ADHD) is a disability in which children consistently show one or more of these characteristics over a period of time: (1) inattention, (2) hyperactivity, and (3) impulsivity. Children who are inattentive have such difficulty focusing on any one thing that they may get bored with a task after only a few minutes—or even seconds. Children who are hyperactive show high levels of physical activity, seeming to be almost constantly in motion. Children who are impulsive have difficulty curbing their reactions; they do not do a good job of thinking before they act.

How Would You...?

As an educator, how would you explain the nature of learning disabilities to a parent whose child has recently been diagnosed with a learning disability?

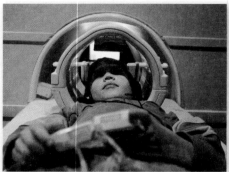

Figure 7.3 Brain Scans and Learning Disabilities
An increasing number of studies are using MRI brain scans to examine the brain pathways involved in learning disabilities. Shown here is 9-year-old Patrick Price, who has dyslexia. Patrick is going through an MRI scanner disguised by drapes to look like a child-friendly castle. Inside the scanner, children must lie virtually motionless as words and symbols flash on a screen, and they are asked to identify them by clicking different buttons.

Depending on the characteristics that children with ADHD display, they can be diagnosed as (1) ADHD with predominantly inattention, (2) ADHD with predominantly hyperactivity/impulsivity, or (3) ADHD with both inattention and hyperactivity/impulsivity.

The number of children diagnosed and treated for ADHD has increased substantially in recent decades. The disorder is diagnosed four to nine times more often in boys than in girls. There is controversy, however, about the increased diagnosis of ADHD (Friend, 2011). Some experts attribute the increase mainly to heightened awareness of the disorder; others are concerned that many children are being incorrectly diagnosed (Parens & Johnston, 2009).

A recent study examined the possible misdiagnosis of ADHD (Bruchmiller, Margraf, & Schneider, 2012). In this study, child psychologists, psychiatrists, and social workers were given vignettes of children with ADHD (some vignettes matched the diagnostic criteria for the disorder, while others did not). Whether each child was male or female varied. The researchers assessed whether the mental health professionals gave a diagnosis of ADHD to the child described in the vignette. The professionals overdiagnosed ADHD almost 20 percent of the time, and regardless of the symptoms described, boys were twice as likely as girls to be given a diagnosis of ADHD.

How Would You...?

As a health-care professional, how would you respond to these statements by a parent? "I do not believe that ADHD is a real disorder. Children are supposed to be active."

Adjustment and optimal development are difficult for children who have ADHD, so it is important that the diagnosis be accurate. Children diagnosed with ADHD have an increased risk of school dropout, adolescent pregnancy, substance use problems, and antisocial behavior (Chang, Lichtenstein, & Larsson, 2012; Von Polier, Vioet, & Herpertz-Dahlmann, 2012).

Definitive causes of ADHD have not been found. However, a number of causes have been proposed (Purper-Ouakil & others, 2011). Some children likely inherit a tendency to develop ADHD from their parents (Williams & others, 2012). Other children likely develop ADHD because of damage to their brain during prenatal or postnatal development (Lindblad & Hjern, 2010). Among early possible contributors to ADHD are cigarette and alcohol exposure during prenatal development and low birth weight (Choudhry & others, 2012; Knopik, 2009). For example, a recent study revealed cigarette smoking during pregnancy was linked to ADHD in 6- to 7-year-old children (Sciberras, Ukoumunne, & Efron, 2011).

As with learning disabilities, the development of brain-imaging techniques is leading to a better understanding of ADHD (Cubillo & others, 2012; Sonuga-Barke, 2013). One study revealed that peak thickness of the cerebral cortex occurred three years later (10.5 years) in children with ADHD than in children without ADHD (peak at 7.5 years) (Shaw & others, 2007). The delay was more prominent in the prefrontal regions of the brain that are especially important in attention and planning (see Figure 7.4). Another study also found delayed development in the brain's frontal lobes among children with ADHD, which likely was due to delayed or decreased myelination (Nagel & others, 2011). Researchers also are exploring the roles that various neurotransmitters, such as serotonin and dopamine, might play in ADHD (Dalley & Roiser, 2012; Shen, Liao, & Tseng, 2012).

The delays in brain development just described are in areas linked to executive functioning. An increasing focus of study regarding children with ADHD is their difficulty on executive functioning tasks, such as inhibiting behavior when necessary, using working memory, and effective planning (Jacobson & others, 2011). Researchers also have found deficits in theory of mind in children with ADHD (Buhler & others, 2011).

Prefrontal cortex   Prefrontal cortex

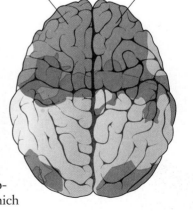

Greater than 2 years delay

0 to 2 years delay

Figure 7.4 Regions of the Brain in Which Children with ADHD Had a Delayed Peak in the Thickness of the Cerebral Cortex

Note: The greatest delays occurred in the prefrontal cortex.

autism spectrum disorders (ASD) Also called pervasive developmental disorders, they range from the severe disorder labeled autistic disorder to the milder disorder called Asperger syndrome. These disorders are characterized by problems in social interaction, verbal and nonverbal communication, and repetitive behaviors.

Stimulant medication such as Ritalin or Adderall (which has fewer side effects than Ritalin) is effective in improving the attention of many children with ADHD, but it usually does not improve their attention to the same level as in children who do not have ADHD (Sclar & others, 2012). A meta-analysis (statistical analysis that combines the results of many different studies) concluded that behavior management treatments are effective in reducing the effects of ADHD (Fabiano & others, 2009). Researchers have often found that a combination of medication (such as Ritalin) and behavior management improves the behavior of children with ADHD better than medication alone or behavior management alone, although this treatment does not work in all cases (Parens & Johnston, 2009).

How Would You...?

As a human development and family studies professional, how would you advise parents who are hesitant about medicating their child who was recently diagnosed with a mild form of ADHD?

Autism Spectrum Disorders

Autism spectrum disorders (ASD), also called pervasive developmental disorders, range from the more severe disorder called *autistic disorder* to the milder disorder called *Asperger syndrome.* Autism spectrum disorders are characterized by problems in social interaction, problems in verbal and nonverbal communication, and repetitive behaviors (Hall, 2013). Children with these disorders may also show atypical responses to sensory experiences (National Institute of Mental Health, 2011). Autism spectrum disorders can often be detected in children as young as 1 to 3 years of age.

Recent estimates of autism spectrum disorders indicate that they are dramatically increasing in occurrence or are increasingly being detected. Once thought to affect only 1 in 2,500 children decades ago, they were estimated to be present in about 1 in 150 children in 2002 (Centers for Disease Control and Prevention, 2007). However, the most recent estimate is that 1 in 88 children had an autism spectrum disorder in 2008 (Centers for Disease Control & Prevention, 2012). In the most recent survey, autism spectrum disorders were identified five times more often in boys than in girls.

What characterizes autism spectrum disorders?

Autistic disorder is a severe developmental autism spectrum disorder that has its onset in the first three years of life and includes deficiencies in social relationships; abnormalities in communication; and restricted, repetitive, and stereotyped patterns of behavior.

Asperger syndrome is a relatively mild autism spectrum disorder in which the child has relatively good verbal language skills, milder nonverbal language problems, and a restricted range of interests and relationships (Soares & Patel, 2012). Children with Asperger syndrome often engage in obsessive, repetitive routines and preoccupations with a particular subject. For example, a child may be obsessed with baseball scores or railroad timetables.

What causes autism spectrum disorders? The current consensus is that autism is a brain dysfunction characterized by abnormalities in brain structure and neurotransmitters (Mendez & others, 2012; Toma & others, 2012). Recent interest has focused on a lack of connectivity between brain regions as a key factor in autism (Just & others, 2012; Philip & others, 2012). Genetic factors also likely play a role in the development of autism spectrum disorders (Yates, 2012). There is no evidence that family socialization causes autism. Intellectual disability is present in some children with autism, while others show average or above-average intelligence (Memari & others, 2012).

Children with autism benefit from a well-structured classroom, individualized instruction, and small-group instruction. Behavior modification techniques are sometimes effective in helping autistic children learn (Iovannone, 2013).

Educational Issues

Until the 1970s most U.S. public schools either refused enrollment to children with disabilities or inadequately served them. This changed in 1975, when *Public Law 94-142*, the Education for All Handicapped Children Act, required that all students with disabilities be given a free, appropriate public education. In 1990, Public Law 94-142 was recast as the *Individuals with Disabilities Education Act* (IDEA). IDEA was amended in 1997 and then reauthorized in 2004 and renamed the Individuals with Disabilities Education Improvement Act.

IDEA spells out broad mandates for services to children with disabilities of all kinds (Turnbull & others, 2013). These services include evaluation and eligibility determination, appropriate education and an individualized education plan (IEP), and education in the least restrictive environment (LRE) (Yudof & others, 2012).

An **individualized education plan (IEP)** is a written statement that spells out a program that is specifically tailored for a student with a disability. The **least restrictive environment (LRE)** is a setting that is as similar as possible to the one in which children who do not have a disability are educated. This provision of the IDEA has given a legal basis to efforts to educate children with a disability in the regular classroom. The term **inclusion** describes educating a child with special education needs full-time in the regular classroom (McLeskey, Rosenberg, & Westling, 2013).

Many legal changes regarding children with disabilities have been extremely positive (Smith & others, 2012). Compared with several decades ago, far more children today are receiving competent, specialized services. For many children, inclusion in the regular classroom, with modifications or supplemental services, is appropriate. However, some leading experts on special education argue that some children with disabilities may not benefit from inclusion in the regular classroom. James Kauffman and his colleagues, for example, advocate a more individualized approach that does not necessarily involve full inclusion but allows options such as special education outside the regular classroom with trained professionals and adapted curricula (Kauffman, McGee, & Brigham, 2004). They go on to say, "We sell students with disabilities short when we pretend that they are not different from typical students. We make the same error when we pretend that they must *not* be expected to put forth extra effort if they are to learn to do some things—or learn to do something in a different way" (p. 620). Like general education, special education should challenge students with disabilities "to become all they can be."

individualized education plan (IEP) A written statement that spells out a program tailored to a child with a disability.

least restrictive environment (LRE) The concept that a child with a disability should be educated in a setting that is as similar as possible to the one in which children who do not have a disability are educated.

inclusion Educating a child who requires special education full-time in the regular classroom.

IDEA mandates free, appropriate education for all children. *What services does IDEA mandate for children with disabilities?*

Cognitive Changes

It is the wisdom of the human life span that at no time are children more ready to learn than during the period of expansive imagination at the end of early childhood. Do children enter a new stage of cognitive development in middle and late childhood?

Piaget's Cognitive Developmental Theory

According to Piaget (1952), the preschool child's thought is preoperational. Preschool children can form stable concepts, and they have begun to reason, but their thinking is flawed by egocentrism and magical belief systems. As we discussed in

Chapter 5, however, Piaget may have underestimated the cognitive skills of preschool children. Some researchers argue that under the right conditions, young children may display abilities that are characteristic of Piaget's next stage of cognitive development, the stage of concrete operational thought (Gelman, 1969). Here we will cover the characteristics of concrete operational thought and evaluate Piaget's portrait of this stage.

The Concrete Operational Stage

Piaget proposed that the *concrete operational stage* lasts from approximately 7 to 11 years of age. In this stage, children can perform concrete operations, and they can reason logically as long as reasoning can be applied to specific or concrete examples. Remember that *operations* are mental actions that are reversible, and *concrete operations* are operations that are applied to real, concrete objects.

The conservation tasks described in Chapter 5 indicate whether children are capable of concrete operations. For example, recall that in one task involving conservation of matter, the child is presented with two identical balls of clay. The experimenter rolls one ball into a long, thin shape; the other remains in its original ball shape. The child is then asked if there is more clay in the ball or in the long, thin piece of clay. By the time children reach the age of 7 or 8, most answer that the amount of clay is the same. To answer this problem correctly, children have to imagine the clay rolling back into a ball. This type of imagination involves a reversible mental action applied to a real, concrete object. Concrete operations allow the child to consider several characteristics rather than focus on a single property of an object. In the clay example, the preoperational child is likely to focus on height *or* width. The concrete operational child coordinates information about both dimensions.

What other abilities are characteristic of children who have reached the concrete operational stage? One important skill is the ability to classify or divide things into different sets or subsets and to consider their interrelationships. Consider the family tree of four generations that is shown in Figure 7.5 (Furth & Wachs, 1975). This family tree suggests that the grandfather (A) has three children (B, C, and D), each of whom has two children (E through J), and that one of these children (J) has three children (K, L, and M). A child who comprehends the classification system can move up and down a level, across a level, and up and down and across within the system. The concrete operational child understands that person J can at the same time be father, brother, and grandson, for example.

Children who have reached the concrete operational stage are also capable of **seriation,** which is the ability to order stimuli along a quantitative dimension (such as length). To see if students can serialize, a teacher might haphazardly place eight sticks of different lengths on a table. The teacher then asks the students to order the sticks by length. Many young children end up with two or three small groups of "big" sticks or "little" sticks, rather than a correct ordering of all eight sticks. Another ineffective strategy they use is to line up the tops of the sticks evenly but ignore the bottoms. The concrete operational thinker simultaneously understands that each stick must be longer than the one that precedes it and shorter than the one that follows it.

Another aspect of reasoning about the relations between classifications is **transitivity,** which is the ability to logically combine relations to understand certain conclusions. In this case, consider three sticks (A, B, and C) of differing lengths. A is the longest, B is intermediate in length, and C is the shortest. Does the child understand

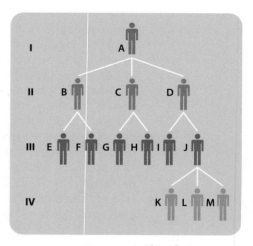

Figure 7.5 Classification: An Important Ability in Concrete Operational Thought
A family tree of four generations (I to IV): The preoperational child has trouble classifying the members of the four generations; the concrete operational child can classify the members vertically, horizontally, and obliquely (up and down and across). For example, the concrete operational child understands that a family member can be a son, a brother, and a father, all at the same time.

seriation The concrete operation that involves ordering stimuli along a quantitative dimension (such as length).

transitivity The ability to logically combine relations to understand certain conclusions.

that if A is longer than B and B is longer than C, then A is longer than C? In Piaget's theory, concrete operational thinkers do; preoperational thinkers do not.

Evaluating Piaget's Concrete Operational Stage

Has Piaget's portrait of the concrete operational child stood the test of research? According to Piaget, various aspects of a stage should emerge at the same time. In fact, however, some concrete operational abilities do not appear in synchrony. For example, children do not learn to conserve at the same time they learn to cross-classify.

> **How Would You...?**
>
> As a psychologist, how would you characterize the contribution Piaget made to our current understanding of cognitive development in childhood?

Furthermore, education and culture exert stronger influences on children's development than Piaget reasoned (Gauvain, 2013; Goncu & Gauvain, 2012; Mistry, Contreras, & Dutta, 2013). Some preoperational children can be trained to reason at a concrete operational stage. And the age at which children acquire conservation skills is related to how much practice their culture provides in these skills.

Thus, although Piaget was a giant in the field of developmental psychology, his conclusions about the concrete operational stage have been challenged. In Chapter 9, after examining the final stage in his theory of cognitive development, we will further evaluate Piaget's contributions and the criticisms of his theory.

Neo-Piagetians argue that Piaget got some things right but that his theory needs considerable revision. They give more emphasis to how children use attention, memory, and strategies to process information (Case & Mueller, 2001). They especially believe that a more accurate portrayal of children's thinking requires attention to children's strategies, the speed at which children process information, the particular task involved, and the division of problems into smaller, more precise steps (Morra & others, 2008). These are issues addressed by the information-processing approach, and we discuss some of them later in this chapter.

Information Processing

If we examine how children handle information during middle and late childhood instead of analyzing the type of thinking they display, what do we find? During these years, most children dramatically improve their ability to sustain and control attention (Columbo, Brez, & Curtindale, 2013). Other changes in information processing during middle and late childhood involve memory, thinking, and metacognition.

An outstanding teacher, and education in the logic of science and mathematics, are important cultural experiences that promote the development of operational thought. *Might Piaget have underestimated the roles of culture and schooling in children's cognitive development?*

Memory

In Chapter 5 you learned that short-term memory increases considerably during early childhood but after the age of 7 does not show as much increase. **Long-term memory,** a relatively permanent and unlimited type of memory, increases with age during middle and late childhood. In part, improvements in memory reflect children's increased knowledge and their increased use of strategies. Keep in mind that it is important not to view memory in terms of how children add something to it but rather to underscore how children actively construct their memory (Baddeley, 2012; Cohen, 2012).

Knowledge and Expertise Much of the research on the role of knowledge in memory has compared experts and novices. *Experts* have acquired extensive knowledge about a particular content area; this knowledge influences what they notice and how they organize, represent, and interpret information. This in turn affects their ability to remember, reason, and solve problems. When individuals have expertise about a particular subject, their memory also tends to be good regarding material related to that subject (Staszewski, 2013).

For example, one study found that 10- and 11-year-olds who were experienced chess players ("experts") were able to remember more information about chess pieces than college students who were not chess players ("novices") (Chi, 1978). In contrast, when the college students were presented with other stimuli, they were able to remember them better than the children were. Thus, the children's expertise in chess gave them superior memories, but only regarding chess.

There are developmental changes in expertise (Blair & Somerville, 2009). Older children usually have more expertise about a subject than younger children do, which can contribute to their better memory for the subject.

Strategies Long-term memory depends on the learning activities individuals engage in when learning and remembering information. **Strategies** consist of deliberate mental activities to improve the processing of information. They do not occur automatically but require effort and work (MacArthur, 2012). Following are some effective strategies for adults to use in helping children improve their memory skills:

- *Guide children to elaborate about the information they are to remember.* **Elaboration** involves more extensive processing of the information, such as thinking of examples or relating the information to one's own life. Elaboration makes the information more meaningful (Schneider, 2011).

- *Encourage children to engage in mental imagery.* Mental imagery can help even young school children to remember visuals. However, for remembering verbal information, mental imagery works better for older children than for younger children (Schneider, 2011).

- *Motivate children to remember material by understanding it rather than by memorizing it.* Children will remember information better over the long term if they understand the information rather than just rehearse and memorize it. Rehearsal works well for encoding information into short-term memory, but when children need to retrieve the information from long-term memory, it is much less efficient. For most information, encourage children to understand it, give it meaning, elaborate on it, and personalize it.

- *Repeat and vary instructional information, and link it to other information early and often.* These recommendations improve children's consolidation and reconsolidation of the information they are learning (Bauer, 2009a, b). Varying the themes of a lesson increases the number of associations in memory storage, and linking the information expands the network of associations in memory storage; both strategies expand the routes for retrieving information from storage in the brain.

- *Embed memory-relevant language when instructing children.* Teachers who use mnemonic devices and metacognitive questions that encourage children to think about their thinking can improve student performance. In recent research that involved extensive

strategies Consist of deliberate mental activities to improve the processing of information.

elaboration An important strategy that involves engaging in more extensive processing of information.

observations of a number of first-grade teachers in the classroom, Peter Ornstein and his colleagues (2007, 2010) found that for the time segments observed, the teachers rarely used strategy suggestions or metacognitive (thinking about thinking) questions. However, lower-achieving students increased their performance when they were placed in classrooms with teachers who frequently embedded memory-relevant information in their teaching (Ornstein, Coffman, & Grammer, 2007).

Fuzzy Trace Theory Might something other than knowledge and strategies be responsible for the improvement in memory during the elementary school years? Charles Brainerd and Valerie Reyna (2004) argue that fuzzy traces account for much of this improvement. Their **fuzzy trace theory** states that memory is best understood by considering two types of memory representations: (1) verbatim memory trace and (2) gist. The *verbatim memory trace* consists of the precise details of the information, whereas *gist* refers to the central idea of the information. When gist is used, fuzzy traces are built up. Although individuals of all ages extract gist, young children tend to store and retrieve verbatim traces. At some point during the early elementary school years, children begin to use gist more, and according to the theory, this contributes to the improved memory and reasoning of older children because fuzzy traces are more enduring and less likely to be forgotten than verbatim traces.

Thinking

Thinking involves manipulating and transforming information in memory. Two important aspects of thinking are being able to think critically and creatively.

Critical Thinking Currently there is considerable interest among psychologists and educators in critical thinking (Barnett & Francis, 2012; Choy & Oo, 2012). **Critical thinking** involves thinking reflectively and productively, and evaluating evidence. In this book, the "How Would You . . . ?" questions in the margins of each chapter challenge you to think critically about a topic or an issue related to the discussion.

Jacqueline and Martin Brooks (2001) lament that few schools really teach students to think critically and develop a deep understanding of concepts. Deep understanding occurs when students are stimulated to rethink previously held ideas. In Brooks and Brooks' view, schools spend too much time getting students to give a single correct answer in an imitative way, rather than encouraging them to expand their thinking by coming up with new ideas and rethinking earlier conclusions. They observe that too often teachers ask students to recite, define, describe, state, and list, rather than to analyze, infer, connect, synthesize, criticize, create, evaluate, think, and rethink. Many successful students complete their assignments, do well on tests and get good grades, yet they don't ever learn to think critically and deeply. They think superficially, staying on the surface of problems rather than stretching their minds and becoming deeply engaged in meaningful thinking.

Creative Thinking Cognitively competent children not only think critically, but also creatively (Kaufman & Sternberg, 2012, 2013). **Creative thinking** is the ability to think in novel and unusual ways and to come up with unique solutions to problems. Thus, intelligence and creativity are not the same thing. This difference was recognized by J. P. Guilford (1967), who distinguished between **convergent thinking,** which produces one correct answer and characterizes the kind

S. GROSS

"For God's sake, think! Why is he being so nice to you?" © Sam Gross/ The New Yorker Collection/www. cartoonbank.com

fuzzy trace theory States that memory is best understood by considering two types of memory representations: (1) verbatim memory trace and (2) gist. In this theory, older children's better memory is attributed to the fuzzy traces created by extracting the gist of information.

thinking Manipulating and transforming information in memory.

critical thinking Thinking reflectively and productively, as well as evaluating the evidence.

creative thinking The ability to think in novel and unusual ways and to come up with unique solutions to problems.

convergent thinking The type of thinking that produces one correct answer and is typically assessed by standardized intelligence tests.

divergent thinking Thinking that produces many answers to the same question and is characteristic of creativity.

metacognition Cognition about cognition, or knowing about knowing.

of thinking that is required on conventional tests of intelligence, and **divergent thinking,** which produces many different answers to the same question and characterizes creativity. For example, a typical item on a conventional intelligence test is "How many quarters will you get in return for 60 dimes?" In contrast, the following question has many possible answers: "What images come to mind when you hear the phrase 'sitting alone in a dark room' or 'some unique uses for a paper clip'?"

It is important to recognize that children will show more creativity in some domains than others (Kaufman & Sternberg, 2012, 2013). A child who shows creative thinking skills in mathematics may not exhibit these skills in art, for example. An important goal is to help children learn to think creatively.

A special concern today is that the creative thinking of children in the United States appears to be declining. A study of approximately 300,000 U.S. children and adults found that creativity scores rose until 1990, but since then have been steadily declining (Kim, 2010). Among the likely causes of this decline are the amount of time U.S. children spend watching TV and playing video games instead of engaging in creative activities, as well as the lack of emphasis on creative thinking skills in schools (Baer & Kaufman, 2013; Gregerson, Kaufman, & Snyder, 2013). In some countries, though, there has been increasing emphasis on creative thinking in schools. For example, historically, creative thinking has typically been discouraged in Chinese schools. However, Chinese educators are now encouraging teachers to spend more classroom time on creative activities (Plucker, 2010).

How Would You...?

As a psychologist, how would you talk with teachers and parents about ways to improve children's creative thinking?

Metacognition

Metacognition is cognition about cognition, or knowing about knowing (Flavell, 2004). Many studies classified as "metacognitive" have focused on *metamemory*, or knowledge about memory. This includes general knowledge about memory, such as knowing that recognition tests are easier than recall tests. It also encompasses knowledge about one's own memory, such as a student's ability to monitor whether she has studied enough for a test that is coming up next week (Dimmitt & McCormick, 2012).

Young children do have some general knowledge about memory (Schneider, 2011). By 5 or 6 years of age, children usually already know that familiar items are easier to learn than unfamiliar ones, that short lists are easier than long ones, that recognition is easier than recall, and that forgetting is more likely to occur over time (Lyon & Flavell, 1993). However, in other ways young children's metamemory is limited. They don't understand that related items are easier to remember than unrelated ones and that remembering the gist of a story is easier than remembering information verbatim (Kreutzer, Leonard, & Flavell, 1975). By the fifth grade, children do understand that gist recall is easier than verbatim recall.

Cognitive developmentalist John Flavell is a pioneer in providing insights about children's thinking. Among his many contributions are establishing the field of metacognition and conducting numerous studies in this area, including metamemory and theory of mind studies.

Young children also have only limited knowledge about their own memory. They have an inflated opinion of their memory abilities. For example, in one study a majority of young children predicted that they would be able to recall all 10 items on a list of 10 items. When tested for this, however, none of the young children managed this feat (Flavell, Friedrichs,

How Would You...?

As an educator, how would you advise teachers and parents about ways to improve children's metacognitive skills?

& Hoyt, 1970). As they move through the elementary school years, children can give more realistic evaluations of their memory skills.

In addition to metamemory, metacognition includes knowledge about memory strategies (McCormick, Dimmitt, & Sullivan, 2013; Sperling, 2012). In the view of Michael Pressley (2007), the key to education is helping students learn a rich repertoire of strategies that produce solutions to problems. Good thinkers routinely use strategies and effective planning to solve problems. Good thinkers also know when and where to use strategies. Understanding when and where to use strategies often results from monitoring the learning situation (Dimmitt & McCormick, 2012).

Executive Functioning

In Chapter 7, you read about executive functioning and its characteristics in early childhood (Carlson & White, 2013; Carlson, Zelazo, & Faja, 2013). Some of the cognitive topics we already have discussed in this chapter—working memory, critical thinking, creative thinking, and metacognition—can be considered under the umbrella of executive functioning and linked to the development of the brain's prefrontal cortex (Dimmitt & McCormick, 2012). Also, earlier in the chapter in the coverage of brain development in middle and late childhood, you read about the increase in cognitive control, which involves flexible and effective control in a number of areas such as focusing attention, reducing interfering thoughts, inhibiting motor actions, and exercising flexibility in deciding between competing choices.

Adele Diamond and Kathleen Lee (2011) recently highlighted the following dimensions of executive functioning that they conclude are the most important for 4- to 11-year-old children's cognitive development and school success:

- *Self-control/inhibition.* Children need to develop self-control that will allow them to concentrate and persist on learning tasks, to inhibit their tendencies to repeat incorrect responses, and to resist the impulse to do something that they later would regret.

- *Working memory.* Children need an effective working memory to mentally work with the masses of information they will encounter as they go through school and beyond.

- *Flexibility.* Children need to be flexible in their thinking so as to consider different strategies and perspectives.

Researchers have found that executive functioning is a better predictor of school readiness than general IQ (Blair & Razza, 2007). A number of diverse activities have been found to increase children's executive functioning, such as computerized training that uses games to improve working memory (CogMed, 2013), aerobic exercise (Chang & others, 2012), mindfulness (the Tools of the Mind program discussed in Chapter 5, for example) (Bodrova, Leong, & Akhutina, 2011), and some types of school curricula (the Montessori curriculum, for example) (Diamond, 2013; Diamond & Lee, 2011).

Intelligence

How can intelligence be defined? **Intelligence** is the ability to solve problems and to adapt and learn from experiences. Interest in intelligence has often focused on individual differences and assessment. *Individual differences* are the stable, consistent ways in which people differ from each other. We can talk about individual differences in personality or any other domain, but it is in the domain of intelligence that the most attention has been directed at individual differences. For example, an intelligence test purports to inform us about whether a student can reason better than others who have taken the test. Let's go back in history and see what the first intelligence test was like.

intelligence Problem-solving skills and the ability to learn from, and adapt to, the experiences of everyday life.

mental age (MA) Binet's measure of an individual's level of mental development, compared with that of others.

intelligence quotient (IQ) A person's mental age divided by chronological age and multiplied by 100.

normal distribution A symmetrical distribution with most scores falling in the middle of the possible range of scores and few scores appearing toward the extremes of the range.

The Binet Tests

In 1904, the French Ministry of Education asked psychologist Alfred Binet to devise a method of identifying children who were unable to learn in school. School officials wanted to reduce crowding by placing students who did not benefit from regular classroom teaching in special schools. Binet and his student Theophile Simon developed an intelligence test to meet this request. The test is called the *1905 Scale*. It consists of 30 questions on topics ranging from the ability to touch one's ear to the ability to draw designs from memory and define abstract concepts.

Binet developed the concept of **mental age (MA),** an individual's level of mental development relative to others. A few years later, in 1912, William Stern created the concept of **intelligence quotient (IQ),** a person's mental age divided by chronological age (CA) and multiplied by 100. That is: IQ = MA/CA × 100. If mental age is the same as chronological age, then the person's IQ is 100. If mental age is above chronological age, then IQ is more than 100. If mental age is below chronological age, then IQ is less than 100.

The Binet test has been revised many times to incorporate advances in the understanding of intelligence and intelligence tests. These revisions are called the *Stanford-Binet tests* (Stanford University is where the revisions have been done). In 2004, the test—now called the *Stanford-Binet 5*—was revised to analyze an individual's response in five content areas: fluid reasoning, knowledge, quantitative reasoning, visual-spatial reasoning, and working memory. A general composite score also is still obtained.

By administering the test to large numbers of people of different ages (from preschool through late adulthood) from different backgrounds, researchers have found that scores on the Stanford-Binet approximate a normal distribution (see Figure 7.6). A **normal distribution** is symmetrical, with a majority of the scores falling in the middle of the possible range of scores and few scores appearing toward the extremes of the range.

The Wechsler Scales

Another set of tests widely used to assess students' intelligence is called the *Wechsler scales,* developed by psychologist David Wechsler. They include the *Wechsler Preschool and Primary Scale of Intelligence—Third Edition (WPPSI-III)* to test children

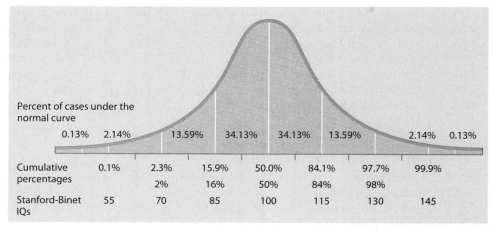

Figure 7.6 The Normal Curve and Stanford-Binet IQ Scores
The distribution of IQ scores approximates a normal curve. Most of the population falls in the middle range of scores. Notice that extremely high and extremely low scores are very rare. Slightly more than two-thirds of the scores fall between 85 and 115. Only about 1 in 50 individuals has an IQ of more than 130, and only about 1 in 50 individuals has an IQ of less than 70.

from the ages of 2 years 6 months to 7 years 3 months; the *Wechsler Intelligence Scale for Children—Fourth Edition (WISC-IV)* for children and adolescents 6 to 16 years of age; and the *Wechsler Adult Intelligence Scale—Fourth Edition (WAIS-IV).*

The Wechsler subscales not only provide an overall IQ score but also yield several composite indexes, such as the Verbal Comprehension Index, the Working Memory Index, and the Processing Speed Index. These types of indexes allow the examiner to quickly identify the areas in which the child is strong or weak. Three of the Wechsler subscales are shown in Figure 7.7.

Types of Intelligence

Is it more appropriate to think of a child's intelligence as a general ability or as a number of specific abilities? Robert Sternberg and Howard Gardner have proposed influential theories that reflect this second viewpoint.

Sternberg's Triarchic Theory Robert J. Sternberg (1986, 2004, 2010, 2011, 2012a, 2013a, b) developed the **triarchic theory of intelligence,** which states that intelligence comes in three forms: (1) *analytical intelligence*, which refers to the ability to analyze, judge, evaluate, compare, and contrast; (2) *creative intelligence*, which consists of the ability to create, design, invent, originate, and imagine; and (3) *practical intelligence*, which involves the ability to use, apply, implement, and put ideas into practice.

Sternberg says that children with different triarchic patterns "look different" in school. Students with high analytic ability tend to be favored in conventional schooling. They often do well under direct instruction, in which the teacher lectures and gives students objective tests. They often are considered to be "smart" students who get good grades, show up in high-level tracks, do well on traditional tests of intelligence and the SAT, and later get admitted to competitive colleges.

In contrast, children who are high in creative intelligence often are not on the top rung of their class. Many teachers have specific expectations about how assignments should be done, and creatively intelligent students may not conform to those expectations. Instead of giving conformist answers, they give unique answers, for which they might get reprimanded or marked down. No teacher wants to discourage creativity, but Sternberg stresses that too often a teacher's desire to improve students' knowledge suppresses creative thinking.

Like children high in creative intelligence, children who are practically intelligent often do not relate well to the demands of school. However, many of these children do well outside of the classroom's walls. They may have excellent social skills and good common

"You're wise, but you lack tree smarts." © Donald Reilly/The New Yorker Collection/www.cartoonbank.com

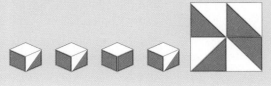

Verbal Subscales

Similarities

A child must think logically and abstractly to answer a number of questions about how things might be similar.

Example: "In what way are a lion and a tiger alike?"

Comprehension

This subscale is designed to measure an individual's judgment and common sense.

Example: "What is the advantage of keeping money in a bank?"

Nonverbal Subscales

Block Design

A child must assemble a set of multicolored blocks to match designs that the examiner shows.
Visual-motor coordination, perceptual organization, and the ability to visualize spatially are assessed.

Example: "Use the four blocks on the left to make the pattern on the right."

Figure 7.7 Sample Subscales of the Wechsler Intelligence Scale for Children—Fourth Edition (WISC-IV)
The Wechsler includes 11 subscales, 6 verbal and 5 nonverbal. Three of the subscales are shown here. Simulated items similar to those found in the Wechsler Intelligence Scale for Children—Fourth Edition. Copyright © 2004 by NCS Pearson, Inc. Reproduced by permission. All rights reserved. "Wechsler Intelligence Scale for Children" and "WISC" are trademarks of Harcourt Assessment, Inc. registered in the United States of America and/or other jurisdictions.

triarchic theory of intelligence Sternberg's theory that intelligence consists of analytical intelligence, creative intelligence, and practical intelligence.

sense. As adults, some become successful managers, entrepreneurs, or politicians in spite of having undistinguished school records.

Gardner's Eight Frames of Mind Howard Gardner (1983, 1993, 2002) suggests there are eight types of intelligence, or "frames of mind." These are described here, with examples of the types of vocations in which they are reflected as strengths (Campbell, Campbell, & Dickinson, 2004):

Verbal: The ability to think in words and use language to express meaning. Occupations: Authors, journalists, speakers.

Mathematical: The ability to carry out mathematical operations. Occupations: Scientists, engineers, accountants.

Spatial: The ability to think three-dimensionally. Occupations: Architects, artists, sailors.

Bodily-kinesthetic: The ability to manipulate objects and be physically adept. Occupations: Surgeons, craftspeople, dancers, athletes.

Musical: A sensitivity to pitch, melody, rhythm, and tone. Occupations: Composers, musicians, and sensitive listeners.

Interpersonal: The ability to understand and interact effectively with others. Occupations: Successful teachers, mental health professionals.

Intrapersonal: The ability to understand oneself. Occupations: Theologians, psychologists.

Naturalist: The ability to observe patterns in nature and understand natural and human-made systems. Occupations: Farmers, botanists, ecologists, landscapers.

Howard Gardner, shown here working with a young child, developed the concept that intelligence comprises eight kinds of skills: verbal, mathematical, spatial, bodily-kinesthetic, musical, intrapersonal, interpersonal, and naturalist.

How Would You...?

As a psychologist, how would you use Gardner's theory of multiple intelligences to respond to children who are distressed by their below-average score on a traditional intelligence test?

According to Gardner, everyone has all of these intelligences to varying degrees. As a result, we prefer to learn and process information in specific ways. People learn best when they can do so in a way that uses their stronger intelligences.

Evaluating the Multiple-Intelligences Approaches Sternberg's and Gardner's approaches have much to offer. They have stimulated teachers to think more broadly about what makes up children's competencies. And they have motivated educators to develop programs that instruct students in multiple domains. These approaches have also contributed to interest in assessing intelligence and classroom learning in innovative ways, such as by evaluating student portfolios (Moran & Gardner, 2007).

Still, doubts about multiple-intelligences approaches persist. A number of psychologists think that the multiple-intelligences views have taken the concept of specific intelligences too far (Reeve & Charles, 2008). Some argue that a research base to support the three intelligences of Sternberg or the eight intelligences of Gardner has not yet emerged. One expert on intelligence, Nathan Brody (2007), observes that people who excel at one type of intellectual task are likely to excel in others. Thus, individuals who do well at memorizing lists of digits are also likely to be good at solving verbal problems and spatial layout problems. If musical skill reflects a distinct type of intelligence, ask other critics, why not label the skills of outstanding chess players, prizefighters, painters, and poets as types of intelligence?

The argument between those who support the concept of general intelligence and those who advocate the multiple-intelligences view is ongoing (Brody, 2007; Sternberg, 2012a, 2013a, b). Sternberg (2012a, 2013a, b) actually accepts that there is a general intelligence for the kinds of analytical tasks that traditional IQ tests assess but thinks that the range of tasks those tests measure is far too narrow.

Culture and Intelligence

Differing conceptions of intelligence occur not only among psychologists but also among cultures (Zhang & Sternberg, 2012). What is viewed as intelligent in one culture may not be thought of as intelligent in another. For example, people in Western cultures tend to view intelligence in terms of reasoning and thinking skills, whereas people in Eastern cultures see intelligence as a way for members of a community to engage successfully in social roles (Nisbett, 2003).

Interpreting Differences in IQ Scores

The IQ scores that result from tests such as the Stanford-Binet and Wechsler scales provide information about children's mental abilities. However, interpretation of scores on intelligence tests is a controversial topic.

The Influence of Genetics How strong is the effect of genetics on intelligence? This question is difficult to answer because, as we discussed in Chapter 2, teasing apart the influences of heredity and environment is virtually impossible. Also, most research on heredity and environment does not include environments that differ radically. Thus, it is not surprising that many genetic studies show environment to be a fairly weak influence on intelligence.

Have scientists been able to pinpoint specific genes that are linked to intelligence? A recent research review concluded that there may be more than 1,000 genes that affect intelligence, each possibly having a small influence on an individual's intelligence (Davies & others, 2011). However, researchers have not been able to identify the specific genes that contribute to intelligence (Deary, 2012).

One strategy for examining the role of heredity in intelligence is to compare the IQs of identical and fraternal twins, as we initially discussed in Chapter 2. Recall that identical twins have exactly the same genetic makeup but fraternal twins do not. If intelligence is genetically determined, say some investigators, identical twins' IQs should be more similar than the intelligence of fraternal twins. A research review of many studies found that the difference in the average correlation of intelligence between identical and fraternal twins was 0.15, a relatively low correlation (Grigorenko, 2000) (see Figure 7.8).

Today, most researchers agree that genetics and environment interact to influence intelligence (Cooper, 2012). For most people, this means that modifications in environment can change their IQ scores considerably. Although genetic endowment may always influence a person's intellectual ability, the environmental influences and opportunities we provide children and adults do make a difference (Sternberg, 2012a, 2013a, b).

Environmental Influences The environment's role in intelligence is reflected in the 12- to 18-point increase in IQ when children are adopted from lower-SES to middle-SES homes (Nisbett & others, 2012). Environmental influences on intelligence also involve schooling (Gustafsson, 2007). The biggest effects have been found when large groups of children have been deprived of formal education for

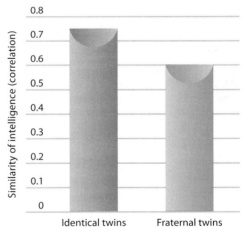

Figure 7.8 Correlation Between Intelligence Test Scores and Twin Status The graph represents a summary of research findings that have compared the intelligence test scores of identical and fraternal twins. An approximate .15 difference has been found, with a higher correlation for identical twins (.75) and a lower correlation for fraternal twins (.60).

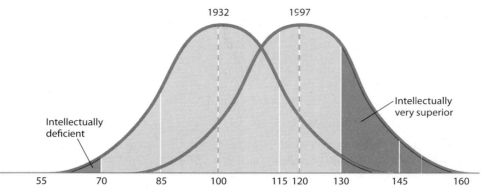

Figure 7.9 **The Increase in IQ Scores from 1932 to 1997**
As measured by the Stanford-Binet intelligence test, American children seem to be getting smarter. Scores of a group tested in 1932 fell along a bell-shaped curve with half below 100 and half above. Studies show that if children took that same test today, half would score above 120 on the 1932 scale. Very few of them would score in the "intellectually deficient" end, on the left side, and about one-fourth would rank in the "very superior" range.

Students in an elementary school in South Africa. *How might schooling influence the development of children's intelligence?*

an extended period, resulting in lower intelligence (Ceci & Gilstrap, 2000). Another possible effect of education can be seen in rapidly increasing IQ test scores around the world (Flynn, 1999, 2007, 2011, 2012; Flynn & Blair, 2013). IQ scores have been increasing so fast that a high percentage of people regarded as having average intelligence at the turn of the century would be considered below average in intelligence today (see Figure 7.9). If a representative sample of people today took the Stanford-Binet test version used in 1932, about 25 per-cent would be defined as having very superior intelligence, a label usually accorded to fewer than 3 percent of the population. Because the increase has taken place in a relatively short time, it can't be due to heredity, but rather may be due to increasing levels of education attained by a much greater percentage of the world's population, or to other environmental factors such as the explosion of information to which people are exposed (Flynn & Blair, 2013). The worldwide increase in intelligence test scores that has occurred over a short time frame has been called the *Flynn effect* after the researcher who discovered it, James Flynn.

Researchers are increasingly concerned about improving the early environ-ment of children who are at risk for impoverished intelligence (Bagnato & Macy, 2012; Huberman & Mendelsohn, 2012). For various reasons, many low-income parents have difficulty providing an intellectually stimulating environment for their children. Programs that educate parents to be more sensitive caregivers and better teachers, as well as support services such as quality child-care programs, can make a difference in a child's intellectual development (Johnson & Brooks-Gunn, 2012; Squires & others, 2013). Thus the efforts to counteract a deprived early environment's effect on intelligence emphasize prevention rather than remediation.

A review of the research on early interventions concluded that (1) high-quality child-care center–based interventions are associated with increases in chil-dren's intelligence and school achievement; (2) the interventions are most successful with poor children and children whose parents have little education; (3) the positive benefits continue through adolescence but are not as strong as in

CHAPTER 7 PHYSICAL AND COGNITIVE DEVELOPMENT IN MIDDLE AND LATE CHILDHOOD early childhood or the beginning of elementary school; and (4) the programs that continue into middle and late childhood have the best long-term results (Brooks-Gunn, 2003).

In sum, there is a consensus among psychologists that both heredity and environment influence intelligence (Grigorenko & Takanishi, 2012). This consensus reflects the nature-nurture issue that was highlighted in Chapter 1. Recall that this issue focuses on the extent to which development is influenced by nature (heredity) and nurture (environment). Although psychologists agree that intelligence is the product of both nature and nurture, there is still disagreement about how strongly each influences intelligence.

Group Differences On average, African American schoolchildren in the United States score 10 to 15 points lower on standardized intelligence tests than non-Latino White American schoolchildren do (Brody, 2000). Children from Latino families also score lower than non-Latino White children. These are *average scores*, however; there is significant overlap in the distribution of scores. About 15 to 25 percent of African American schoolchildren score higher than half of White schoolchildren do, and many White schoolchildren score lower than most African American schoolchildren. As African Americans have gained social, economic, and educational opportunities, the gap between African Americans and Whites on standardized intelligence tests has begun to narrow. This gap especially narrows in college, where African American and White students often experience more similar environments than in the elementary and high school years (Myerson & others, 1998).

Creating Culture-Fair Tests **Culture-fair tests** are tests of intelligence that are intended to be free of cultural bias. Two types of culture-fair tests have been devised. The first includes items that are familiar to children from all socioeconomic and ethnic backgrounds, or items that at least are familiar to the children taking the test. For example, a child might be asked how a bird and a dog are different, on the assumption that all children have been exposed to birds and dogs. The second type of culture-fair test has no verbal questions.

Why is it so hard to create culture-fair tests? Most tests tend to reflect what the dominant culture thinks is important (Zhang & Sternberg, 2012). If tests have time limits, that will bias the test against groups not concerned with time. If languages differ, the same words might have different meanings for different language groups. Even pictures can produce bias because some cultures have less experience with drawings and photographs. Because of such difficulties in creating culture-fair tests, Robert Sternberg (2012b) concludes that there are no culture-fair tests, only *culture-reduced tests*.

Extremes of Intelligence

Intelligence tests have been used to discover indications of intellectual disability or giftedness, the extremes of intelligence. At times, they have been misused for this purpose. Keeping in mind the theme that an intelligence test should not be used as the sole indicator of intellectual disability or giftedness, we will explore the nature of these intellectual extremes.

Intellectual Disability **Intellectual disability** is a condition of limited mental ability in which an individual has a low IQ, usually below 70 on a traditional intelligence test, and has difficulty adapting to everyday life. About 5 million Americans fit this definition of intellectual disability.

culture-fair tests Tests of intelligence that are designed to be free of cultural bias.

intellectual disability A condition of limited mental ability in which an individual has a low IQ, usually below 70 on a traditional test of intelligence, and has difficulty adapting to everyday life.

A child with Down syndrome. *What causes a child to develop Down syndrome? In which major classification of intellectual disability does the condition fall?*

organic intellectual disability
Intellectual disability that involves some physical damage and is caused by a genetic disorder or brain damage.

cultural-familial intellectual disability Intellectual disability that is characterized by no evidence of organic brain damage, but the individual's IQ generally is between 50 and 70.

gifted Having above-average intelligence (an IQ of 130 or higher) and/or superior talent for something.

There are several classifications of intellectual disability (Hallahan, Kaufmann, & Pullen, 2012). About 89 percent of the individuals with an intellectual disability fall into the mild category, with IQs of 55 to 70; most of them are able to live independently as adults and work at a variety of jobs. About 6 percent are classified as having a moderate intellectual disability, with IQs of 40 to 54; these people can attain a second-grade level of skills and may be able to support themselves as adults through some types of labor. About 3.5 percent are in the severe category, with IQs of 25 to 39; these individuals learn to talk and accomplish very simple tasks but require extensive supervision. Less than 1 percent have IQs below 25; they fall into the profound classification and need constant supervision.

Intellectual disability can have an organic cause, or it can be social and cultural in origin:

- **Organic intellectual disability** is intellectual disability that is caused by a genetic disorder or by brain damage; the word *organic* refers to the tissues or organs of the body, indicating physical damage. Most people who suffer from organic intellectual disability have IQs that range between 0 and 50. However, children with Down syndrome have an average IQ of approximately 50. As discussed in Chapter 2, Down syndrome is caused by an extra copy of chromosome 21.

- **Cultural-familial intellectual disability** is a mental deficit in which no evidence of organic brain damage can be found; individuals' IQs generally range from 50 to 70. Psychologists suspect that such mental deficits result from the normal variation that distributes people along the range of intelligence scores combined with growing up in a below-average intellectual environment.

Giftedness There have always been people whose abilities and accomplishments outshine others'—the whiz kid in class, the star athlete, the natural musician. People who are **gifted** have above-average intelligence (an IQ of 130 or higher) or superior talent for something or both. When it comes to programs for the gifted, most school systems select children who have intellectual superiority and academic aptitude, whereas children who are talented in the visual and performing arts (arts, drama, dance, music), athletics, or other special aptitudes tend to be overlooked (Grigorenko & others, 2012; Winner, 2009).

What are the characteristics of children who are gifted? Despite speculation that giftedness is linked with having a mental disorder, no relation between giftedness and mental disorder has been found. Similarly, the idea that gifted children are maladjusted is a myth, as Lewis Terman (1925) found when he conducted an extensive study of 1,500 children whose Stanford-Binet IQs averaged 150. The children in Terman's study were socially well adjusted, and many went on to become successful doctors, lawyers, professors, and scientists. Studies support the conclusion that gifted people tend to be more mature than others, have fewer emotional problems than others, and grow up in a positive family climate (Feldman, 2001).

Ellen Winner (1996) described three criteria that characterize gifted children, whether in art, music, or academic domains:

1. *Precocity.* Gifted children are precocious. They begin to master an area earlier than their peers. Learning in their domain is more effortless for them than for ordinary children. In most instances, these gifted children are precocious because they have an inborn high ability in a particular domain or domains.

2. *Marching to a different drummer.* Gifted children learn in a qualitatively different way than ordinary children. One way that they

At 2 years of age, art prodigy Alexandra Nechita colored in coloring books for hours and also took up pen and ink. She had no interest in dolls or friends. By age 5 she was using watercolors. Once she started school, she would start painting as soon as she got home. At the age of 8, in 1994, she saw the first public exhibition of her work. In succeeding years, working quickly and impulsively on canvases as large as 5 feet by 9 feet, she has completed hundreds of paintings, some of which sell for close to $100,000 apiece. As a teenager, she continues to paint—relentlessly and passionately. It is, she says, what she loves to do. *What are some characteristics of children who are gifted?*

march to a different drummer is that they need minimal help, or scaffolding, from adults to learn. In many instances, they resist any kind of explicit instruction. They often make discoveries on their own and solve problems in unique ways.

3. *A passion to master.* Gifted children are driven to understand the domain in which they have high ability. They display an intense, obsessive interest and an ability to focus. They motivate themselves, says Winner, and do not need to be "pushed" by their parents.

Is giftedness a product of heredity or environment? The answer is, likely both (Sternberg, Jarvin, & Grigorenko, 2011). Individuals who are gifted recall that they had signs of high ability in a particular area at a very young age, prior to or at the beginning of formal training (Howe & others, 1995). This suggests the importance of innate ability in giftedness. However, researchers have also found that individuals with world-class status in the arts, mathematics, science, and sports all report strong family support and years of training and practice (Bloom, 1985). Deliberate practice is an important characteristic of individuals who become experts in a particular domain. For example, in one study, the best musicians engaged in twice as much deliberate practice over their lives as did the least successful ones (Ericsson, Krampe, & Tesch-Romer, 1993).

Individuals who are highly gifted are typically not gifted in many domains, and research on giftedness is increasingly focused on domain-specific developmental paths (Sternberg, Jarvin, & Grigorenko, 2011). During the childhood years, the domain(s) in which individuals are gifted usually emerges. Thus, at some point in the childhood years, the child who will become a gifted artist or the child who will become a gifted mathematician begins to show expertise in that domain. Regarding domain-specific giftedness, software genius Bill Gates (1998), the founder of Microsoft and one of the world's richest people, commented that when you are good at something, you may have to resist the urge to think that you will be good at everything. Because he has been so successful at software development, he has found that people also expect him to be brilliant in other domains in which he is far from gifted.

An increasing number of experts argue that the education of children who are gifted in the United States requires a significant overhaul (Ambrose, Sternberg, & Sriraman, 2012; Olszewski-Kubilius & Thomson, 2013). Ellen Winner (1996, 2009) argues that too often children who are gifted are socially isolated and underchallenged in the classroom. It is not unusual for other students to label them "nerds" or "geeks." Many eminent adults report that school was a negative experience for them, that they were bored and sometimes knew more than their teachers (Bloom, 1985). Winner argues that American students will benefit more from their education when standards are raised for all children. She recommends that some underchallenged students be allowed to attend advanced classes in their domain of exceptional ability, such as allowing some precocious middle school students to take college classes in their area of expertise. For example, at age 13, Bill Gates took college math classes and hacked a computer security system; Yo-Yo Ma, famous cellist, graduated from high school at 15 and attended Juilliard School of Music in New York City.

A young Bill Gates, founder of Microsoft and now one of the world's richest people. Like many highly gifted students, Gates was not especially fond of school. He hacked a computer security system when he was 13 and as a high school student, he was allowed to take some college math classes. He dropped out of Harvard University and began developing a plan for what was to become Microsoft Corporation. *What are some ways that schools can enrich the education of highly talented students like Gates to make it a more challenging, interesting, and meaningful experience?*

How Would You...?

As an educator, how would you structure educational programs for children who are gifted that would challenge and expand their unique cognitive abilities?

Language Development

Children gain new skills as they enter school that make it possible for them to learn to read and write. These include increased use of language to talk about things that are not physically present, learning what a word is, and learning how to recognize and talk about sounds (Berko Gleason, 2003). They also learn the *alphabetic principle*—that the letters of the alphabet represent sounds of the language.

Vocabulary, Grammar, and Metalinguistic Awareness

During middle and late childhood, changes occur in the way children's mental vocabulary is organized. When asked to say the first word that comes to mind when they hear a word, preschool children typically provide a word that often follows the word in a sentence. For example, when asked to respond to "dog" the young child may say "barks," or to the word "eat" respond with "lunch." At about 7 years of age, children begin to respond with a word that is the same part of speech as the stimulus word. For example, a child may now respond to the word "dog" with "cat" or "horse." To "eat," they now might say "drink." This is evidence that children of this age have begun to categorize their vocabulary by parts of speech (Berko Gleason, 2003).

The process of categorizing becomes easier as children increase their vocabulary (Clark, 2012). Children's vocabulary increases from an average of about 14,000 words at age 6 to an average of about 40,000 words by age 11.

Children make similar advances in grammar (Behrens, 2012). During the elementary school years, children's improvement in logical reasoning and analytical skills helps them understand such constructions as the appropriate use of comparatives (*shorter, deeper*) and subjectives ("If you were president . . . "). During the elementary school years, children become increasingly able to understand and use complex grammar, such as the following sentence: *The boy who kissed his mother wore a hat*. They also learn to use language in a more connected way, producing connected discourse. They become able to relate sentences to one another to produce descriptions, definitions, and narratives that make sense. Children must be able to do these things orally before they can be expected to deal with them in written assignments.

These advances in vocabulary and grammar during the elementary school years are accompanied by the development of **metalinguistic awareness,** which is knowledge about language, such as knowing what a preposition is or being able to discuss the sounds of a language. Metalinguistic awareness allows children "to think about their language, understand what words are, and even define them" (Berko Gleason, 2009, p. 4). It improves considerably during the elementary school years (Pan & Uccelli, 2009). Defining words becomes a regular part of classroom discourse, and children increase their knowledge of syntax as they study and talk about the components of sentences, such as subjects and verbs (Crain, 2012).

Children also make progress in understanding how to use language in culturally appropriate ways—a process called pragmatics (Bryant, 2012). By the time they enter adolescence, most children know the rules for the use of language in everyday contexts—that is, what is appropriate and inappropriate to say.

Reading

Before learning to read, children learn to use language to talk about things that are not present; they learn what a word is; and they learn how to recognize sounds and talk about them. Children who begin elementary school with a robust vocabulary have an advantage when it comes to learning to read (Vacca & others, 2012).

metalinguistic awareness Refers to knowledge about language, such as knowing what a preposition is or being able to discuss the sounds of a language.

How should children be taught to read? Currently, debate focuses on the whole-language approach versus the phonics approach (Reutzel & Cooter, 2012, 2013; Vacca & others, 2012).

The **whole-language approach** stresses that reading instruction should parallel children's natural language learning. In some whole-language classes, beginning readers are taught to recognize whole words or even entire sentences, and to use the context of what they are reading to guess at the meaning of words. Reading materials that support the whole-language approach are whole and meaningful—that is, children are given material in its complete form, such as stories and poems, so that they learn to understand language's communicative function. Reading is connected with listening and writing skills. Although there are variations in whole-language programs, most share the premise that reading should be integrated with other skills and subjects, such as science and social studies, and that it should focus on real-world material. Thus, a class might read newspapers, magazines, or books, and then write about and discuss them.

In contrast, the **phonics approach** emphasizes that reading instruction should teach basic rules for translating written symbols into sounds. Early phonics-centered reading instruction should involve simplified materials. Only after children have learned correspondence rules that relate spoken phonemes to the alphabet letters that are used to represent them should they be given complex reading materials, such as books and poems (Fox, 2012).

Which approach is better? Research suggests that children can benefit from both approaches, but instruction in phonics needs to be emphasized (Fox, 2012; Tompkins, 2013). An increasing number of experts in the field of reading now conclude that direct instruction in phonics is a key aspect of learning to read (Cunningham, 2013; Dow & Baer, 2013; Fox, 2012).

Beyond the phonics/whole language issue in learning to read, becoming a good reader includes learning to read fluently (Gunning, 2013). Many beginning or poor readers do not recognize words automatically. Their processing capacity is consumed by the demands of word recognition, so they have less capacity to devote to comprehension of groupings of words as phrases or sentences. As their processing of words and passages becomes more automatic, it is said that their reading becomes more *fluent* (Fox, 2012). Metacognitive strategies, such as learning to monitor one's reading progress, getting the gist of what is being read, and summarizing also are important in becoming a good reader (McCormick, Dimmitt, & Sullivan, 2013).

whole-language approach An approach to reading instruction based on the idea that instruction should parallel children's natural language learning. Reading materials should be whole and meaningful.

phonics approach The idea that reading instruction should teach the basic rules for translating written symbols into sounds.

This teacher is helping a student sound out words. Researchers have found that phonics instruction is a key aspect of teaching students to read, especially beginning readers and students with weak reading skills.

Bilingualism and Second-Language Learning

Are there sensitive periods in learning a second language? That is, if individuals want to learn a second language, how important is the age at which they begin to learn it? What is the best way in the United States to teach children who come from homes in which English is not the primary language?

Second-Language Learning

For many years, it was claimed that if individuals did not learn a second language prior to puberty they would never reach native-language learners' proficiency in the second language (Johnson & Newport, 1991). However, recent research indicates a more complex conclusion: There are sensitive periods for learning a second language. Additionally, these sensitive periods likely vary across different areas of language systems (Thomas & Johnson, 2008). For example, late language learners, such as adolescents and adults, may learn new vocabulary more easily than new sounds or new grammar (Neville, 2006). Also, children's ability to pronounce words with a native-like accent in a second language typically decreases with age, with an especially sharp drop occurring after the age of about 10 to 12. Adults tend to learn a second language faster than children, but their level of second-language mastery is not as high as children's. And the way children and adults learn a second language differs somewhat. Compared with adults, children are less sensitive to feedback, less likely to use explicit strategies, and more likely to learn a second language from large amounts of input (Thomas & Johnson, 2008).

Students in the United States are far behind their counterparts in many developed countries in learning a second language. For example, in Russia, schools have 10 grades, called *forms*, which roughly correspond to the 12 grades in American schools. Russian children begin school at age 7 and begin learning English in the third form. Because of this emphasis on teaching English, most Russian citizens under the age of 40 today are able to speak at least some English. The United States is the only technologically advanced Western nation that does not have a national foreign language requirement at the high school level, even for students in rigorous academic programs.

U.S. students who do not learn a second language may be missing more than the chance to acquire a skill. *Bilingualism*—the ability to speak two languages—has a positive effect on children's cognitive development. Children who are fluent in two languages perform better than their single-language counterparts on tests of control of attention, concept formation, analytical reasoning, cognitive flexibility, and cognitive complexity (Bialystok, 2001, 2007; Bialystok & Craik, 2010). They also are more conscious of the structure of spoken and written language and better at noticing errors of grammar and meaning, skills that benefit their reading ability (Bialystok, 1997; Kuo & Anderson, 2012). However, recent research indicates that bilingual children have a smaller vocabulary in each language than monolingual children do (Bialystok, 2011).

How Would You...?

As a human development and family studies professional, how would you describe the advantages of promoting bilingualism in the home for school-age children in the United States who come from families whose first language is not English?

In the United States, many immigrant children go from being monolingual in their home language to bilingual in that language and in English, only to end up monolingual speakers of English. This is called *subtractive bilingualism*, and it can have negative effects on children, who often become ashamed of their home language.

Bilingual Education

A current controversy related to bilingualism involves the millions of U.S. children who come from homes in which English is not the primary language (Echevarria, Vogt, & Short, 2013; Lessow-Hurley, 2013). What is the best way to teach these English language learners (ELLs)?

For the last two decades, the preferred strategy has been *bilingual education*, which is to teach academic subjects to immigrant children in their native language while slowly teaching them English (Diaz-Rico, 2012; Horowitz, 2013). Advocates of bilingual education programs argue that if children who do not know English are taught only in English, they will fall behind in academic subjects. How, they ask, can 7-year-olds learn arithmetic or history taught only in English when they do not speak the language?

Some critics of bilingual programs argue that too often it is thought that immigrant children need only one year of bilingual education. However, most immigrant children take approximately three to five years to develop speaking proficiency and seven years to develop reading proficiency in English (Hakuta, Butler, & Witt, 2001). Also, immigrant children vary in their ability to learn English (Herrera & Murry, 2011). Children who come from lower socioeconomic backgrounds have more difficulty than those from higher socioeconomic backgrounds (Hakuta, 2001). Thus, especially for immigrant children from low socioeconomic backgrounds, more years of bilingual education may be needed than they currently are receiving.

A first- and second-grade bilingual English-Cantonese teacher instructing students in Chinese in Oakland, California. *What have researchers found about the effectiveness of bilingual education?*

Critics who oppose bilingual education argue that as a result of these programs, the children of immigrants are not learning English, which puts them at a permanent disadvantage in U.S. society. What have researchers found regarding outcomes of bilingual education programs? Drawing conclusions about the effectiveness of bilingual education programs is difficult because of variations across programs in the number of years they are in effect, type of instruction, qualities of schooling other than bilingual education, teachers, children, and other factors. Further, no effectively conducted experiments that compare bilingual education with English-only education in the United States have been conducted (Snow & Yang, 2006).

Research supports bilingual education in that (1) children have difficulty learning a subject when it is taught in a language they do not understand, and (2) when both languages are integrated in the classroom, children learn the second language more readily and participate more actively (Hakuta, 2005).

Summary

Physical Changes and Health

- The period of middle and late childhood involves slow, consistent growth.

- Changes in the brain in middle and late childhood include advances in functioning in the prefrontal cortex, which is associated with an increase in cognitive control.

- Motor development becomes much smoother and more coordinated. Boys usually are better at gross motor skills, girls at fine motor skills.

- Most U.S. children do not get nearly enough exercise.

- For the most part, middle and late childhood is a time of excellent health. However, being overweight in childhood poses serious health risks. Cancer is the second leading cause of death in children (after accidents).

Children with Disabilities

- Approximately 13 percent of U.S. children from 3 to 21 years of age receive special education or related services. Approximately 80 percent of children with a learning disability have a reading problem. The number of children diagnosed with ADHD has been increasing. Autism spectrum disorders recently have been estimated to characterize 1 in 150 U.S. children.

- U.S. legislation requires that all children with disabilities be given a free, appropriate public education. Increasingly, this education has involved full inclusion.

Cognitive Changes

- Piaget theorized that the stage of concrete operational thought characterizes children from about 7 to 11 years of age. During this stage children are capable of concrete operations, conservation, classification, seriation, and transitivity. Criticisms of Piaget's theory have been proposed.

- Changes in these aspects of information occur in middle and late childhood: attention, memory, critical thinking, creative thinking, and metacognition.

- Widely used intelligence tests today include the Stanford-Binet test and Wechsler scales. Sternberg proposed that intelligence comes in three main forms, whereas Gardner said there are eight types of intelligence. Intelligence is influenced by heredity and environment. Extremes of intelligence include intellectual disability and giftedness.

Language Development

- In the elementary school years, improvements in children's language development include vocabulary, grammar, and metalinguistic awareness.

- Both the phonics and whole-language approach can benefit children, but experts increasingly view phonics instruction as critical in learning to read.

- Recent research indicates a complex conclusion about whether there are sensitive periods in learning a second language. Bilingual education in the United States aims to teach academic subjects to immigrant children in their native languages while gradually adding English instruction.

Key Terms

learning disability 195
attention deficit
   hyperactivity disorder
   (ADHD) 196
autism spectrum disorders
   (ASD) 198
individualized education
   plan (IEP) 199
least restrictive
   environment
   (LRE) 199

inclusion 199
seriation 200
transitivity 200
neo-Piagetians 201
long-term memory 201
strategies 202
elaboration 202
fuzzy trace theory 203
thinking 203
critical thinking 203
creative thinking 203

convergent thinking 203
divergent thinking 204
metacognition 204
intelligence 205
mental age (MA) 206
intelligence quotient
   (IQ) 206
normal distribution 206
triarchic theory of
   intelligence 207
culture-fair tests 211

intellectual disability 211
organic retardation 212
cultural-familial
   retardation 212
gifted 212
metalinguistic
   awareness 214
whole-language
   approach 215
phonics approach 215

Socioemotional Development in Middle and Late Childhood

8

Stories of Life-Span Development: Learning in Troubled Schools

In *The Shame of the Nation*, Jonathan Kozol (2005) described his visits to 60 U.S. schools in urban low-income areas in 11 states. He saw many schools in which the minority population was 80 to 90 percent. Kozol observed numerous inequities—unkempt classrooms, hallways, and restrooms; inadequate textbooks and supplies; and lack of resources. He also saw teachers mainly instructing students to memorize material by rote, especially as preparation for mandated tests, rather than stimulating them to engage in

higher-level thinking. Kozol also frequently observed teachers using threatening disciplinary tactics to control the classroom.

However, some teachers Kozol observed were effective in educating children in these undesirable conditions. At P.S. 30 in the South Bronx, Mr. Bedrock teaches fifth grade. One student in his class, Serafina, recently lost her mother to AIDS. When Kozol visited the class, he was told that two other children had taken the role of "allies in the child's struggle for emotional survival" (Kozol,

2005, p. 291). Textbooks are in short supply for the class, and the social studies text is so out of date it claims that Ronald Reagan is the country's president. But Mr. Bedrock told Kozol that it's a "wonderful" class this year. About their teacher, 56-year-old Mr. Bedrock, one student said, "He's getting old . . . but we love him anyway" (p. 292). Kozol found the students orderly, interested, and engaged.

The years of middle and late childhood bring many changes to children's social and emotional lives. The

development of their self-conceptions, moral reasoning, and gendered behavior is significant. Transformations in their relationships with parents and peers occur, and schooling takes on a more academic flavor. ∎

Emotional and Personality Development

In this section, we explore how the self continues to develop during middle and late childhood and the emotional changes that take place during these years. We also discuss children's moral development and many aspects of the role that gender plays in their development in middle and late childhood.

What are some of the challenges faced by children growing up in the South Bronx?

The Self

What is the nature of the child's self-understanding, understanding of others, and self-esteem during the elementary school years? What roles do self-efficacy and self-regulation play in children's achievement?

The Development of Self-Understanding

In middle and late childhood, especially from 8 to 11 years of age, children increasingly describe themselves with psychological characteristics and traits rather than the more concrete self-descriptions of younger children. Older children are more likely to describe themselves as *"popular, nice, helpful, mean, smart,* and *dumb"* (Harter, 2006, p. 526).

In addition, during the elementary school years, children become more likely to recognize social aspects of the self (Harter, 2012). They include references to social groups in their self-descriptions, such as referring to themselves as Girl Scouts, as Catholics, or as someone who has two close friends (Livesly & Bromley, 1973).

Children's self-understanding in the elementary school years also includes increasing reference to social comparison (Harter, 2012). At this point in development, children are more likely to distinguish themselves from others in comparative rather than in absolute terms. That is, elementary-school-age children are no longer as likely to think about what they do or do not do, but are more likely to think about what they can do in comparison with others.

Consider a series of studies in which Diane Ruble (1983) investigated children's use of social comparison in their self-evaluations. Children were given a difficult task and then offered feedback on their performance as well as information about the performances of other children their age. The children were then asked for self-evaluations. Children younger than 7 made virtually no reference to the information about other children's performances. However, many children older than 7 included socially comparative information in their self-descriptions.

How Would You...?

As a psychologist, how would you explain the role of social comparison for the development of a child's sense of self?

Understanding Others

In Chapter 6 we described the advances and limitations of young children's social understanding. In middle and late childhood, **perspective taking,** the social cognitive process involved in assuming the perspective of others and understanding their thoughts and feelings, improves. Executive functioning, discussed in Chapter 5, "Physical and Cognitive Development in Early Childhood,"

What are some changes in children's understanding of others in middle and late childhood?

is at work in perspective taking (Galinsky, 2010). Among the executive functions called on when children engage in perspective taking are cognitive inhibition (controlling one's own thoughts to consider the perspective of others) and cognitive flexibility (seeing situations in different ways).

perspective taking The social cognitive process involved in assuming the perspective of others and understanding their thoughts and feelings.

self-esteem The global evaluative dimension of the self. Self-esteem is also referred to as self-worth or self-image.

self-concept Domain-specific evaluations of the self.

Self-Esteem and Self-Concept

High self-esteem and a positive self-concept are important characteristics of children's well-being (Marsh, Martin, & Xu, 2012). Investigators sometimes use the terms *self-esteem* and *self-concept* interchangeably or do not precisely define them, but there is a meaningful difference between them. **Self-esteem** refers to global evaluations of the self; it is also called *self-worth* or *self-image*. For example, a child may perceive that she is not merely a person but a *good* person. **Self-concept** refers to domain-specific evaluations of the self. Children can make self-evaluations in many domains of their lives—academic, athletic, appearance, and so on. In sum, *self-esteem* refers to global self-evaluations, *self-concept* to domain-specific evaluations.

The foundations of self-esteem and self-concept emerge from the quality of parent-child interaction in infancy and early childhood. Thus, if children have low self-esteem in middle and late childhood, they may have experienced neglect or abuse in relationships with their parents earlier in development. Children with high self-esteem are more likely to be securely attached to parents and have parents who engage in sensitive caregiving (Thompson, 2011, 2013a, b, c, d).

Self-esteem reflects perceptions that do not always match reality (Baumeister, 2013; Baumeister & others, 2003; Pauletti & others, 2012). A child's self-esteem might reflect a belief about whether he or she is intelligent and attractive, for example, but that belief is not necessarily accurate. Thus, high self-esteem may refer to accurate, justified perceptions of one's worth as a person and one's successes and accomplishments, but it can also refer to an arrogant, grandiose, unwarranted sense of superiority over others (Krueger, Vohs, & Baumeister, 2008). In the same manner, low self-esteem may reflect either an accurate perception of one's shortcomings or a distorted, even pathological insecurity and inferiority.

Variations in self-esteem have been linked with many aspects of children's development. However, much of the research is *correlational* rather than *experimental*. Recall from Chapter 1 that correlation does not equal causation. Thus, if a correlational study finds an association between children's low self-esteem and low academic achievement, low academic achievement could cause the low self-esteem as much as low self-esteem could cause low academic achievement.

Researchers have found only moderate correlations between school performance and self-esteem, and these correlations do not suggest that high self-esteem produces better school performance (Baumeister, 2013; Baumeister & others, 2003). In fact, efforts to increase students' self-esteem have not always led to improved school performance (Davies & Brember, 1999).

Children with high self-esteem have greater initiative, but this can produce positive or negative outcomes (Baumeister & others, 2003). High-self-esteem children are prone to both prosocial and antisocial actions (Krueger, Vohs, & Baumeister, 2008).

In addition, a current concern is that too many of today's children grow up receiving praise for mediocre or even poor performance and as a consequence have inflated self-esteem (Stipek, 2005). They may have difficulty handling competition and criticism. This theme

How Would You...?

As an educator, how would you work with children to improve their self-esteem in relation to their academic ability?

is vividly captured by the title of a book, *Dumbing Down Our Kids: Why American Children Feel Good About Themselves But Can't Read, Write, or Add* (Sykes, 1995).

Increasing Children's Self-Esteem

Teachers, social workers, health-care professionals and others are often concerned about low self-esteem in the children they serve. Researchers have suggested several strategies to improve self-esteem in at-risk children (Bednar, Wells, & Peterson, 1995; Harter, 2006, 2012).

- *Identify the causes of low self-esteem.* Intervention should target the causes of low self-esteem. Children have the highest self-esteem when they perform competently in domains that are important to them. Therefore, it is helpful to encourage children to identify and value their areas of competence, such as academic skills, athletic skills, physical attractiveness, and social acceptance.

- *Provide emotional support and social approval.* Some children with low self-esteem come from conflictual families or conditions of abuse or neglect—situations in which emotional support is unavailable. In some cases, alternative sources of support can be arranged either informally through the encouragement of a teacher, a coach, or another significant adult, or more formally through programs such as Big Brothers and Big Sisters.

- *Help children achieve.* Achievement also can improve children's self-esteem. For example, the straightforward teaching of real skills to children often results in increased achievement and thus in enhanced self-esteem. Children develop higher self-esteem when they know which tasks will achieve their goals and when they have successfully performed them or similar tasks.

- *Help children cope.* Self-esteem can be built when a child faces a problem and tries to cope with it, rather than avoiding it. If coping rather than avoidance prevails, children often face problems realistically, honestly, and nondefensively. This produces favorable self-evaluative thoughts, which lead to the self-generated approval that raises self-esteem.

How can parents help children develop higher self-esteem?

Self-Efficacy

Self-efficacy is the belief that one can master a situation and produce favorable outcomes. Albert Bandura (2001, 2006, 2010a, 2012), whose social cognitive theory was described in Chapter 1, states that self-efficacy is a critical factor in whether or not students achieve. Self-efficacy is the belief that "I can"; helplessness is the belief that "I cannot." Students with high self-efficacy endorse such statements as "I know that I will be able to learn the material in this class" and "I expect to be able to do well at this activity."

Dale Schunk (2008, 2012) has applied the concept of self-efficacy to many aspects of students' achievement. In his view, self-efficacy influences a student's choice of activities. Students with low self-efficacy for learning may avoid many learning tasks, especially those that are challenging. By contrast, their high-self-efficacy counterparts eagerly work at learning tasks (Schunk, 2012). Students with high self-efficacy are more likely to expend effort and persist longer at a learning task than students with low self-efficacy.

How Would You...?

As an educator, how would you encourage enhanced self-efficacy in a student who says, "I can't do this work"?

Self-Regulation

One of the most important aspects of the self in middle and late childhood is the increased capacity for self-regulation. This increased

self-efficacy The belief that one can master a situation and produce favorable outcomes.

capacity is characterized by deliberate efforts to manage one's behavior, emotions, and thoughts that lead to increased social competence and achievement (Schunk & Zimmerman, 2013; Thompson, 2013c, d). A recent study found that self-control increased from 4 to 10 years of age and that high self-control was linked to lower levels of deviant behavior (Vazsonyi & Huang, 2010).

The increased capacity for self-regulation is linked to developmental advances in the brain's prefrontal cortex, which was discussed in Chapter 7 (Diamond, 2013). In that discussion, increased focal activation in the prefrontal cortex was linked to improved cognitive control. Such cognitive control includes self-regulation.

Industry Versus Inferiority

In Chapter 1, we described Erik Erikson's (1968) eight stages of human development. His fourth stage, industry versus inferiority, appears during middle and late childhood. The term *industry* expresses a dominant theme of this period: Children become interested in how things are made and how they work. When children are encouraged in their efforts to make, build, and work—whether building a model airplane, constructing a tree house, fixing a bicycle, solving an addition problem, or cooking—their sense of industry increases. Conversely, parents who see their children's efforts at making things as "mischief" or "making a mess" will tend to foster a sense of inferiority in their children.

Emotional Development

In Chapter 6, we saw that preschoolers become more adept at talking about their own and others' emotions. They also show a growing awareness of the need to control and manage their emotions to meet social standards. In middle and late childhood, children further develop their understanding and self-regulation of emotion (McRae & others, 2012; Thompson, 2013c, d).

Developmental Changes

Developmental changes in emotions during the middle and late childhood years include the following (Denham & others, 2011; Kuebli, 1994; Thompson, 2013c, d):

- *Improved emotional understanding.* Children in elementary school, for example, develop an increased ability to understand such complex emotions as pride and shame. These emotions become less tied to the reactions of other people; they become more self-generated and integrated with a sense of personal responsibility.

- *Increased understanding that more than one emotion can be experienced in a particular situation.* A third-grader, for example, may realize that achieving something might involve both anxiety and joy.

- *Increased tendency to be aware of the events leading to emotional reactions.* A fourth-grader may become aware that her sadness today is influenced by her friend moving to another town last week.

- *Ability to suppress or conceal negative emotional reactions.* A fifth-grader has learned to tone down his anger better than he used to when one of his classmates irritates him.

What are some changes in emotion during the middle and late childhood years?

- *The use of self-initiated strategies for redirecting feelings.* In the elementary school years, children become more reflective about their emotional lives and increasingly use strategies to control their emotions. They become more effective at cognitively managing their emotions, such as soothing themselves after an upset.

- *A capacity for genuine empathy.* A fourth-grader, for example, feels sympathy for a distressed person and experiences vicariously the sadness the distressed person is feeling.

Coping with Stress

An important aspect of children's emotional lives is learning how to cope with stress. As children get older, they more accurately appraise a stressful situation and determine how much control they have over it (Masten, 2013). Older children generate more coping alternatives to stressful conditions and use more cognitive coping strategies (Saarni & others, 2006). They are better than younger children at intentionally shifting their thoughts to something that is less stressful; and at reframing, or changing their perception of a stressful situation. For example, a younger child may be very disappointed that a teacher did not say hello when the child arrived in the classroom. An older child may reframe the situation and think, "My teacher may have been busy with other things and just forgot to say hello."

By 10 years of age, most children are able to use these cognitive strategies to cope with stress (Saarni, 1999). However, in families that have not been supportive and are characterized by turmoil or trauma, children may be so overwhelmed by stress that they do not use such strategies (Klingman, 2006).

Disasters, such as the bombing of the World Trade Center in New York City in September 2001 or Hurricane Katrina in New Orleans in 2005, can especially harm children's development and produce adjustment problems (McDermott & Cobham, 2012). Among the outcomes for children who experience disasters are acute stress reactions, depression, panic disorder, and post-traumatic stress disorder (Salloum & Overstreet, 2012). The likelihood that a child will face these problems following a disaster depends on factors such as the nature and severity of the disaster and the type of support available to the child.

In research on disasters/trauma, the term *dose-response effects* is often used. A widely supported finding in this research area is that the more severe the disaster/trauma (dose), the worse the adaptation and adjustment (response) following the disaster/trauma (Masten, 2013; Masten & Narayan, 2012).

Researchers have offered some recommendations for parents, teachers, and other adults caring for children after a disaster (Gurwitch & others, 2001):

- Reassure children (numerous times, if necessary) of their safety and security.

- Allow children to retell events and be patient in listening to them.

A 7-year-old girl places a stuffed animal at a memorial near Sandy Hook Elementary School in Newtown, Connecticut, following the shooting there that left 26 people dead, 20 of them young children. What are some effective strategies to help children cope with traumatic events such as the terrorist attacks on the United States on 9/11/2001 and the Sandy Hook tragedy?

- Encourage children to talk about any disturbing or confusing feelings, reassuring them that such feelings are normal after a stressful event.

- Protect children from re-exposure to frightening situations and reminders of the trauma—for example, by limiting discussion of the event in front of the children.

- Help children make sense of what happened, keeping in mind that children may misunderstand what took place. For example, young children "may blame themselves, believe things happened that did not happen, believe that terrorists are in the school, etc. Gently help children develop a realistic understanding of the event" (p. 10).

How Would You...?
As a social worker, how would you counsel a child who has been exposed to a traumatic event?

Moral Development

Remember from Chapter 6 our description of Piaget's view of moral development. Piaget proposed that younger children are characterized by heteronomous morality but that by 10 years of age they have moved into a higher stage called autonomous morality. According to Piaget, older children consider the intentions of the individual, believe that rules are subject to change, and are aware that punishment does not always follow wrongdoing.

A second major perspective on moral development was proposed by Lawrence Kohlberg (1958, 1986). Piaget's cognitive stages of development serve as the underpinnings for Kohlberg's theory, but Kohlberg proposed six stages of moral development, which he believed are universal. Development from one stage to another, said Kohlberg, is fostered by opportunities to take the perspective of others and to experience conflict between one's current stage of moral thinking and the reasoning of someone at a higher stage.

The Kohlberg Stages

Kohlberg's stages fall into three levels of moral thinking, each of which is characterized by two stages (see Figure 8.1).

LEVEL 1	LEVEL 2	LEVEL 3
Preconventional Level	**Conventional Level**	**Postconventional Level**
Stage 1 Heteronomous Morality *Children obey because adults tell them to obey. People base their moral decisions on fear of punishment.*	**Stage 3** Mutual Interpersonal Expectations, Relationships, and Interpersonal Conformity *Individuals value trust, caring, and loyalty to others as a basis for moral judgments.*	**Stage 5** Social Contract or Utility and Individual Rights *Individuals reason that values, rights, and principles undergird or transcend the law.*
Stage 2 Individualism, Instrumental purpose, and Exchange *Individuals pursue their own interests but let others do the same. What is right involves equal exchange.*	**Stage 4** Social System Morality *Moral judgments are based on understanding of the social order, law, justice, and duty.*	**Stage 6** Universal Ethical Principles *The person has developed moral judgments that are based on universal human rights. When faced with a dilemma between law and conscience, a personal, individualized conscience is followed.*

Figure 8.1 Kohlberg's Three Levels and Six Stages of Moral Development
Kohlberg argued that people everywhere develop their moral reasoning by passing through these age-based stages. *Where does Kohlberg's theory stand on the nature-nurture and continuity-discontinuity issues discussed in Chapter 1?*

preconventional reasoning The lowest level in Kohlberg's theory of moral development. The individual's moral reasoning is controlled primarily by external rewards and punishment.

heteronomous morality Kohlberg's first stage in preconventional reasoning, in which moral thinking is tied to punishment.

individualism, instrumental purpose, and exchange The second Kohlberg stage of moral development. At this stage, individuals pursue their own interests but also let others do the same.

conventional reasoning The second, or intermediate, level in Kohlberg's theory of moral development. At this level, individuals abide by certain standards, but they are the standards of others, such as parents or the laws of society.

mutual interpersonal expectations, relationships, and interpersonal conformity Kohlberg's third stage of moral development. At this stage, individuals value trust, caring, and loyalty to others as a basis of moral judgments.

social systems morality The fourth stage in Kohlberg's theory of moral development. Moral judgments are based on understanding the social order, law, justice, and duty.

postconventional reasoning The highest level in Kohlberg's theory of moral development. At this level, the individual recognizes alternative moral courses, explores the options, and then decides on a personal moral code.

social contract or utility and individual rights The fifth Kohlberg stage. At this stage, individuals reason that values, rights, and principles undergird or transcend the law.

universal ethical principles The sixth and highest stage in Kohlberg's theory of moral development. Individuals develop a moral standard based on universal human rights.

Preconventional reasoning is Kohlberg's lowest level of moral reasoning. At this level, children interpret good and bad in terms of external rewards and punishments.

- *Stage 1.* **Heteronomous morality** is the first stage in preconventional reasoning. At this stage, moral thinking is tied to punishment. For example, children think that they must obey because they fear punishment for disobedience.

- *Stage 2.* **Individualism, instrumental purpose, and exchange** is the second stage of preconventional reasoning. At this stage, children reason that pursuing their own interests is the right thing to do, but they let others do the same. Thus, they think that what is right involves an equal exchange. They reason that if they are nice to others, others will be nice to them in return.

Conventional reasoning is the second, or intermediate, level in Kohlberg's theory of moral development. At this level, individuals apply certain standards, but they are the standards set by others, such as parents or the government.

- *Stage 3.* **Mutual interpersonal expectations, relationships, and interpersonal conformity** is Kohlberg's third stage of moral development. At this stage, individuals value trust, caring, and loyalty to others as a basis of moral judgments. Children and adolescents often adopt their parents' moral standards at this stage, seeking parental approval as a "good girl" or a "good boy."

- *Stage 4.* **Social systems morality** is the fourth stage in Kohlberg's theory of moral development. At this stage, moral judgments are based on understanding the social order, law, justice, and duty. For example, adolescents may reason that in order for a community to work effectively, it needs to be protected by laws that community members obey.

Postconventional reasoning is the highest level in Kohlberg's theory of moral development. At this level, the individual recognizes alternative moral courses, explores the options, and then decides on a personal moral code.

- *Stage 5.* **Social contract or utility and individual rights** is the fifth Kohlberg stage. At this stage, individuals reason that values, rights, and principles undergird or transcend the law. A person evaluates the validity of actual laws and may examine social systems in terms of the degree to which they preserve and protect fundamental human rights and values.

- *Stage 6.* **Universal ethical principles** is the sixth and highest stage in Kohlberg's theory of moral development. At this stage, the person has developed a moral standard based on universal human rights. When faced with a conflict between law and conscience, the person reasons that conscience should be followed, even though the decision might bring risk.

Kohlberg believed that these levels and stages occur in a sequence and are age related: Before age 9, most children use level 1, preconventional reasoning based on external rewards and punishments. By early adolescence, moral reasoning is increasingly based on level 2, the application of standards set by others. Most adolescents reason at the higher part of level 2 (stage 3), with some signs of stages 2 and 4. Not everyone progresses beyond level 2, even in adulthood, but by early adulthood a small number of individuals reason in postconventional ways (level 3).

What evidence supports this description of development? A 20-year longitudinal investigation found that use of stages 1 and 2 decreased with age (Colby & others, 1983) (see Figure 8.2). Stage 4, which did not appear at all in the moral reasoning of 10-year-olds, was reflected in the moral thinking of 62 percent of the 36-year-olds. Stage 5 did not appear in any individuals until age 20 to 22, and even later in adulthood it never characterized more than 10 percent of the individuals. Thus, this research found that the moral stages appeared somewhat later than Kohlberg initially envisioned, and reasoning at the higher stages, especially stage 6, was rare.

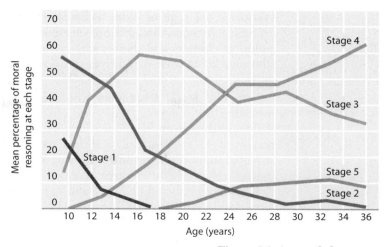

Figure 8.2 Age and the Percentage of Individuals at Each Kohlberg Stage
In one longitudinal study of males from 10 to 36 years of age, at age 10 most moral reasoning was at stage 2 (Colby & others, 1983). At 16 to 18 years of age, stage 3 became the most frequent type of moral reasoning, and it was not until the mid-twenties that stage 4 became the most frequent. Stage 5 did not appear until 20 to 22 years of age, and it never characterized more than 10 percent of the individuals. In this study, the moral stages appeared somewhat later than Kohlberg envisioned and stage 6 was absent. *Do you think it matters that all of the participants in this study were males? Why or why not?*

Influences on the Kohlberg Stages

What factors influence movement through Kohlberg's stages? Although moral reasoning at each stage presupposes a certain level of cognitive development, Kohlberg argued that advances in children's cognitive development did not ensure development of moral reasoning. Instead, moral reasoning also reflects children's experiences in dealing with moral questions and moral conflict.

Several investigators have tried to advance individuals' levels of moral development by having a model present arguments that reflect moral thinking one stage above the individuals' established levels. This approach applies Vygotsky's principle of scaffolding; it also applies the concepts of equilibrium and conflict that Piaget used to explain cognitive development. By presenting arguments slightly beyond the children's level of moral reasoning, the researchers created a disequilibrium that motivated the children to restructure their moral thought. The upshot of studies using this approach is that virtually any discussion about the adolescent's current stage seems to promote more advanced moral reasoning (Walker, 1982).

Kohlberg believed that peer interaction is a critical part of the social stimulation that challenges children to change their moral reasoning. Whereas adults characteristically impose rules and regulations on children, the give-and-take among peers gives children an opportunity to take the perspective of another person and to generate rules democratically. Kohlberg stressed that encounters with any peers can produce perspective-taking opportunities that may advance a child's moral reasoning.

Kohlberg's Critics

Kohlberg's theory has provoked debate, research, and criticism (Berkowitz, 2012; Lapsley & Yeager, 2013; Narvaez & others, 2012; Smetana, 2013). Key criticisms involve the link between moral thought and moral behavior, the roles of culture and the family in moral development, and the significance of concern for others.

Moral Thought and Moral Behavior Kohlberg's theory has been criticized for placing too much emphasis on moral thought and not enough emphasis on moral behavior (Walker, 2004). Moral reasons can sometimes be used as a shelter for immoral behavior. Corrupt CEOs and politicians have usually endorsed the loftiest of moral virtues in public before their own immoral behavior is exposed.

Whatever the type of public scandal, you will probably find that the culprits expressed virtuous thoughts but engaged in immoral behavior. No one wants a nation of cheaters and thieves who can reason at the postconventional level and who may know what is right yet still do what is wrong.

Culture and Moral Reasoning Kohlberg emphasized that his stages of moral reasoning are universal, but some critics claim his theory is culturally biased (Gibbs, 2010). Both Kohlberg and his critics may be partially correct. One review of 45 studies in 27 cultures around the world, mostly non-European, provided support for the universality of Kohlberg's first four stages (Snarey, 1987). Individuals in diverse cultures developed through these four stages in sequence as Kohlberg predicted. Stages 5 and 6, however, have not been found in all cultures (Gibbs & others, 2007; Snarey, 1987). Furthermore, Kohlberg's scoring system does not recognize the higher-level moral reasoning of certain cultures and thus does not acknowledge that moral reasoning is more culture-specific than Kohlberg envisioned (Snarey, 1987). In sum, although Kohlberg's approach does capture much of the moral reasoning used in various cultures around the world, his approach misses or misconstrues some important moral concepts in particular cultures (Gibbs, 2010).

A recent study explored links between culture, mindset, and moral judgment (Narváez & Hill, 2010). In this study, a higher level of multicultural experience was linked to open mindedness (being cognitively flexible), a growth mindset (perceiving that one's qualities can change and improve through effort), and higher moral judgment.

Families and Moral Development Kohlberg argued that family processes are essentially unimportant in children's moral development. As noted earlier, he argued that parent-child relationships usually provide children with little opportunity for give-and-take or perspective taking. Rather, Kohlberg said that such opportunities are more likely to be provided by children's peer relations.

Did Kohlberg underestimate the contribution of family relationships to moral development? Most experts on children's moral development conclude that parents' moral values and actions influence children's development of moral thoughts (Laible & Thompson, 2007; Walker & Frimer, 2011). Nonetheless, most developmentalists agree with Kohlberg, and Piaget, that peers play an important role in the development of moral reasoning.

Gender and the Care Perspective The most publicized criticism of Kohlberg's theory has come from Carol Gilligan (1982, 1996), who argues that Kohlberg's theory reflects a gender bias. According to Gilligan, Kohlberg's theory is based on a male norm that puts abstract principles above relationships and concern for others and sees the individual as standing alone and independently making moral decisions. It puts justice at the heart of morality. In contrast with Kohlberg's **justice perspective**, Gilligan argues for a **care perspective**, which is a moral perspective that views people in terms of their connectedness with others and emphasizes interpersonal communication, relationships with others, and concern for others. According to Gilligan, Kohlberg greatly underplayed the care perspective, perhaps because he was a male, because most of his research was with males rather than females, and because he used male responses as a model for his theory.

However, questions have been raised about Gilligan's gender conclusions (Walker & Frimer, 2011). For example, a meta-analysis casts doubt on Gilligan's claim of substantial gender differences in moral judgment (Jaffee & Hyde, 2000). And a recent review concluded that girls' moral orientations are "somewhat more likely to focus on care for others than on abstract principles of justice, but they can use both moral orientations when needed (as can boys . . .)" (Blakemore, Berenbaum, & Liben, 2009, p. 132).

justice perspective A moral perspective that focuses on the rights of the individual; individuals independently make moral decisions.

care perspective The moral perspective of Carol Gilligan, which views people in terms of their connectedness with others and emphasizes interpersonal communication, relationships with others, and concern for others.

Domain Theory: Moral, Social Conventional, Personal Reasoning

The **domain theory of moral development** states that there are different domains of social knowledge and reasoning, including moral, social conventional, and personal domains. In domain theory, children's and adolescents' moral, social conventional, and personal knowledge and reasoning emerge from their attempts to understand and deal with different forms of social experience (Helwig & Turiel, 2011; Smetana, 2011a, b, 2013).

Social conventional reasoning focuses on conventional rules that have been established by social consensus in order to control behavior and maintain the social system. The rules themselves are arbitrary, such as raising your hand in class before speaking, using one staircase at school to go up and the other to go down, not cutting in front of someone standing in line to buy movie tickets, and stopping at a stop sign when driving. There are sanctions if we violate these conventions, although the rules can be changed by consensus.

In contrast, moral reasoning focuses on ethical issues and rules of morality. Unlike conventional rules, moral rules are not arbitrary. They are obligatory, widely accepted, and somewhat impersonal (Helwig & Turiel, 2011). Rules pertaining to lying, cheating, stealing, and physically harming another person are moral rules because violation of these rules affronts ethical standards that exist apart from social consensus and convention. Moral judgments involve concepts of justice, whereas social conventional judgments are concepts of social organization. Violating moral rules is usually more serious than violating conventional rules.

The social conventional approach is a serious challenge to Kohlberg's approach because Kohlberg argued that social conventions are a stop-over on the road to higher moral sophistication. For social conventional reasoning advocates, social conventional reasoning is not lower than postconventional reasoning but rather something that needs to be disentangled from the moral thread (Helwig & Turiel, 2011; Smetana, 2011a, b, 2013).

Recently, a distinction also has been made between moral and conventional issues, which are viewed as legitimately subject to adult social regulation, and personal issues, which are more likely subject to the child's or adolescent's independent decision making and personal discretion (Helwig & Turiel, 2011; Smetana, 2011a, b, 2013). Personal issues include control over one's body, privacy, and choice of friends and activities. Thus, some actions belong to a *personal* domain not governed by moral strictures or social norms.

Prosocial Behavior

Whereas Kohlberg's and Gilligan's theories have focused primarily on the development of moral reasoning, the study of prosocial moral behavior has placed more emphasis on the behavioral aspects of moral development (Eisenberg, Spinrad, & Morris, 2013; Poorthuis & others, 2012). Children engage in both immoral antisocial acts, such as lying and cheating, and prosocial moral behavior, such as showing empathy or helping others altruistically. Even during the preschool years, children may care for others or comfort someone in distress, but prosocial behavior is more prevalent in adolescence than in childhood (Eisenberg & others, 2009).

Sharing is one aspect of prosocial behavior that researchers have studied. Children's sharing comes to reflect a more complex sense of what is just and right during middle and late childhood. By the start of the elementary school years,

domain theory of moral development Theory that identifies different domains of social knowledge and reasoning, including moral, social conventional, and personal domains. These domains arise from children's and adolescents' attempts to understand and deal with different forms of social experience.

social conventional reasoning Thoughts about social consensus and convention, in contrast with moral reasoning, which stresses ethical issues.

How does children's sharing change from the preschool to the elementary school years?

children begin to express objective ideas about fairness (Eisenberg, Fabes, & Spinrad, 2006). It is common to hear 6-year-old children use the word *fair* as synonymous with *equal* or *same*. By the middle to late elementary school years, children come to believe that equity can also mean that people with special merit or special needs deserve special treatment.

Gender

Gilligan's claim that Kohlberg's theory of moral development reflects gender bias reminds us of the pervasive influence of gender on development. Long before elementary school, boys and girls show preferences for different toys and activities. As we discussed in Chapter 6, preschool children display a gender identity and gender-typed behavior that reflects biological, cognitive, and social influences. Here we examine gender stereotypes, gender similarities and differences, and gender-role classification.

Gender Stereotypes

In the past, a well-adjusted boy was supposed to be independent, aggressive, and powerful. A well-adjusted girl was supposed to be dependent, nurturing, and uninterested in power. These notions reflect **gender stereotypes,** which are broad categories that reflect general impressions and beliefs about females and males.

Recent research has found that gender stereotypes are, to a great extent, still present in today's world, in the lives of both children and adults (Halpern, 2012; Leaper, 2013; Matlin, 2012). Gender stereotyping continues to change during middle and late childhood and adolescence (Blakemore, Berenbaum, & Liben, 2009). During the elementary school years, children have considerable knowledge about which activities are linked with being male or female. However, a recent study of 6- to 10-year-olds revealed gender stereotyping in math—both boys and girls indicated math is for boys (Cvencek, Meltzoff, & Greenwald, 2011). Researchers also have found that boys' gender stereotypes are more rigid than girls' (Blakemore, Berenbaum, & Liben, 2009).

Gender Similarities and Differences

What is the reality behind gender stereotypes? Let's examine some of the similarities and differences between boys and girls, keeping in mind that (1) the differences are averages—not characteristics of all boys versus all girls; (2) even when differences are reported, there is considerable gender overlap; and (3) the differences may be due primarily to biological factors, sociocultural factors, or both. First, we examine physical similarities and differences, and then we turn to cognitive and socioemotional similarities and differences.

Physical Development Women have about twice the body fat of men, with most of it concentrated around breasts and hips. In males, fat is more likely to go to the abdomen. On the average, males grow to be 10 percent taller than females. Other physical differences are less obvious. From conception onward, females have a longer life expectancy than males, and females are less likely than males to develop physical or mental disorders. Males have twice the risk of coronary disease that females do.

Does gender matter when it comes to brain structure and function? Human brains are much alike, whether the brain belongs to a male or a female (Halpern & others, 2007). However, researchers have found some differences in the brains of males and females (Hofer & others, 2007). For example, female brains are smaller than male brains, but female brains have more folds; the larger number of folds (called convolutions) allows more surface brain tissue within the skulls of females than males (Luders & others, 2004). An area of the parietal lobe that functions in visuospatial skills is larger in males than females (Frederikse & others,

2000). And the areas of the brain involved in emotional expression show more metabolic activity in females than males (Gur & others, 1995).

Although some differences in brain structure and function have been found, either many of these differences are small or research is inconsistent regarding the differences. Also, when sex differences in the brain have been revealed, in many cases they have not been directly linked to psychological differences (Blakemore, Berenbaum, & Liben, 2009). Although research on sex differences in the brain is still in its infancy, it is likely that there are far more similarities than differences in the brains of females and males. A further point is worth noting: Anatomical sex differences in the brain may be due to the biological origins of these differences, behavioral experiences (which underscores the brain's continuing plasticity), or a combination of these factors.

Cognitive Development No gender differences in general intelligence have been revealed, but some gender differences have been found in some cognitive areas (Blakemore, Berenbaum, & Liben, 2009). Research has shown that in general girls and women have slightly better verbal skills than boys and men, although in some verbal skill areas the differences are substantial (Blakemore, Berenbaum, & Liben, 2009). For example, in recent national assessments, girls were significantly better than boys in reading and writing (National Assessment of Educational Progress, 2005, 2007).

Are there gender differences in math? A very large-scale study of more than 7 million U.S. students in grades 2 through 11 revealed no differences in math scores for boys and girls (Hyde & others, 2008). And a recent meta-analysis found no gender differences in math for adolescents (Lindberg & others, 2010). A recent research review concluded that girls have more negative math attitudes and that parents' and teachers' expectancies for children's math competence are often gender-biased in favor of boys (Gunderson & others, 2012).

"So according to the stereotype, you can put two and two together, but I can read the handwriting on the wall." © Joel Pett. All rights reserved.

One area of math that has been examined for possible gender differences is visuospatial skills, which include being able to rotate objects mentally and determine what they would look like when rotated (Halpern, 2012). These types of skills are important in courses such as plane and solid geometry and geography. A research review revealed that boys have better visuospatial skills than girls (Halpern & others, 2007). For example, despite equal participation in the National Geography Bee, in most years all 10 finalists are boys (Liben, 1995). However, some experts argue that the gender difference in visuospatial skills is small (Hyde & Else-Quest, 2013).

Socioemotional Development Three areas of socioemotional development in which gender similarities and differences have been studied extensively are aggression, emotion, and prosocial behavior.

One of the most consistent gender differences is that boys are more physically aggressive than girls are (Coyne, Nelson, & Underwood, 2011). The difference occurs in all cultures and appears very early in children's development (White, 2001). The physical aggression difference is especially pronounced when children are provoked. Both biological and environmental factors have been proposed to account for gender differences in aggression. Biological factors include heredity and hormones. Environmental factors include cultural expectations, adult and peer models, and social agents that reward aggression in boys and punish aggression in girls.

Although boys are consistently more physically aggressive than girls, might girls show as much or more verbal aggression, such as yelling, than boys? When verbal aggression is examined, gender differences often disappear; sometimes, though, verbal aggression is more pronounced in girls (Eagly & Steffen, 1986).

Recently, increased interest has been shown in *relational aggression*, which involves harming someone by manipulating a relationship (Underwood, 2011).

Relational aggression includes such behaviors as trying to make others dislike a certain individual by spreading malicious rumors about the person (Kawabata & others, 2012). Relational aggression increases in middle and late childhood (Dishion & Piehler, 2009). Mixed findings have characterized research on whether girls show more relational aggression than boys, but one consistency in findings is that relational aggression comprises a greater percentage of girls' overall aggression than it does for boys (Putallaz & others, 2007). One research review revealed that girls engage in more relational aggression than boys in adolescence but not in childhood (Smith, Rose, & Schwartz-Mette, 2010).

Gender differences occur in some aspects of emotion (Hertenstein & Keltner, 2011; Nolen-Hoeksema, 2012). Females express emotion more than males do, are better than males at decoding emotion, smile more, cry more, and are happier. Males report experiencing and expressing more anger than females do (Kring, 2000). Males usually show less self-regulation of emotion than females do, and this low self-control can translate into behavioral problems (Eisenberg, Spinrad, & Smith, 2004).

Are there gender differences in prosocial behavior? Across childhood and adolescence, females engage in more prosocial behavior than males do. Females also view themselves as more prosocial and empathic than males do (Eisenberg & others, 2009). There is a small difference between boys and girls in the extent to which they share, with girls sharing slightly more than boys. However, the greatest gender difference in prosocial behavior occurs with kind and considerate behavior, which females perform more often than males.

How Would You...?

As a psychologist, how would you discuss gender similarities and differences with a parent or teacher who is concerned about a child's academic progress and social skills?

Gender-Role Classification

Not long ago, it was accepted that boys should grow up to be masculine and girls to be feminine. In the 1970s, however, as both females and males became dissatisfied with the burdens imposed by their stereotypic roles, alternatives to femininity and masculinity were proposed. Instead of describing masculinity and femininity as a continuum in which more of one means less of the other, it was proposed that individuals could have both masculine and feminine traits.

This thinking led to the development of the concept of **androgyny,** the presence of positive masculine and feminine characteristics in the same person (Bem, 1977; Spence & Helmreich, 1978). The androgynous boy might be assertive (masculine) and nurturing (feminine). The androgynous girl might be powerful (masculine) and sensitive to others' feelings (feminine). Measures have been developed to assess androgyny (see Figure 8.3).

Gender experts such as Sandra Bem argue that androgynous individuals are more flexible, competent, and mentally healthy than their masculine or feminine counterparts. To some degree, though, which gender-role classification is best depends on the context involved. For example, in close relationships, feminine and androgynous orientations might be more desirable. One study found that girls and individuals high in femininity showed a stronger interest in caring than did boys and individuals high in masculinity (Karniol, Grosz, & Schorr, 2003). However, masculine and androgynous orientations might be more desirable in traditional academic and work settings because of the achievement demands in these contexts.

androgyny The presence of positive masculine and feminine characteristics in the same individual.

Examples of masculine items

Defends own beliefs
Forceful
Willing to take risks
Dominant
Aggressive

Examples of feminine items

Does not use harsh language
Affectionate
Loves children
Understanding
Gentle

Figure 8.3 The Bem Sex-Role Inventory

These items are from the Bem Sex-Role Inventory (BSRI). When taking the BSRI, an individual is asked to indicate on a 7-point scale how well each of the 60 characteristics describes herself or himself. The scale ranges from 1 (never or almost never true) to 7 (always or almost always true). The items are scored on independent dimensions of masculinity and femininity. Individuals who score high on the masculine items and low on the feminine items are categorized as masculine; those who score high on the feminine items and low on the masculine items are categorized as feminine; and those who score high on both the masculine and feminine items are categorized as androgynous.

Despite talk about the "sensitive male," William Pollack (1999) argues that little has been done to change traditional ways of raising boys. He says that the "boy code" tells boys that they should show little if any emotion and should act tough. Boys learn the boy code in many contexts—sandboxes, playgrounds, schoolrooms, camps, hangouts. The result, according to Pollack, is a "national crisis of boyhood." Pollack and others suggest that boys would benefit from being socialized to express their anxieties and concerns and to better regulate their aggression.

Gender in Context

Both the concept of androgyny and gender stereotypes describe people in terms of personality traits such as "aggressive" or "caring." However, which traits people display may vary with the situation (Leaper, 2013; Leaper & Bigler, 2011). Thus, the nature and extent of gender differences may depend on the context (Blakemore, Berenbaum, & Liben, 2009).

Consider helping behavior. The stereotype is that females are better than males at helping. But it depends on the situation. Females are more likely than males to volunteer their time to help children with personal problems and to engage in caregiving behavior. However, in situations where males feel a sense of competence and those that involve danger, males are more likely than females to help (Eagly & Crowley, 1986). For example, a male is more likely than a female to stop and help a person stranded by the roadside with a flat tire. Indeed, one study documented that males are more likely to help when the context is masculine in nature (MacGeorge, 2003).

The importance of considering gender in context is nowhere more apparent than when examining what is culturally prescribed behavior for females and males in different countries around the world (Matlin, 2012). Although there has been greater acceptance of androgyny and similarities in male and female behavior in the United States, in many countries gender roles have remained gender-specific. For example, in many Middle Eastern and some Asian countries, the division of labor between males and females is dramatic. Males are socialized and schooled to work in the public sphere, females in the private world of home and child rearing. In Iran, the dominant view is that the man's duty is to provide for his family and the woman's is to care for her family and household. China also has been a male-dominant culture. Although women have made some strides in China, especially in urban areas, the male role is still dominant. Most males in China do not accept androgynous behavior and gender equity.

In China, females and males are usually socialized to behave, feel, and think differently. The old patriarchal traditions of male supremacy have not been completely uprooted. Chinese women still make considerably less money than Chinese men do, and in rural China (such as here in the Guangxi Province) male supremacy still governs many women's lives.

Families

Our discussion of parenting and families in this section focuses on how parent-child interactions typically change in middle and late childhood, how parents act as managers, the role of attachment, and how children are affected by living with stepparents.

Developmental Changes in Parent–Child Relationships

As children move into the middle and late childhood years, parents spend considerably less time with them (Grusec & others, 2013). In one study, parents spent less than half as much time with their children aged 5 to 12 in caregiving, instruction, reading, talking, and playing as when the children were younger (Hill & Stafford, 1980). Although parents spend less time with their children in middle and late childhood than in early childhood, parents continue to be extremely important in their children's lives. In an analysis of the contributions of parents in middle and late childhood, the following conclusion was reached: "Parents serve as gatekeepers and provide scaffolding as children assume more responsibility for themselves and . . . regulate their own lives" (Huston & Ripke, 2006, p. 422).

Parents especially play an important role in supporting and stimulating children's academic achievement in middle and late childhood (Pomerantz, Cheung, & Qin, 2013). The value parents place on education can make a difference in whether children do well in school. Parents not only influence children's in-school achievement, but they also make decisions about children's out-of-school activities. Whether children participate in sports, music, and other activities is heavily influenced by the extent to which parents sign up children for such activities and encourage their participation (Simpkins & others, 2006).

Elementary school children tend to receive less physical discipline than they did as preschoolers. Instead of spanking or coercive holding, their parents are more likely to use deprivation of privileges, appeals to the child's self-esteem, comments designed to increase the child's sense of guilt, and statements that the child is responsible for his or her actions.

What are some changes in the focus of parent-child relationships in middle and late childhood?

During middle and late childhood, some control is transferred from parent to child. The process is gradual, and it produces *coregulation* rather than control by either the child or the parent alone (Maccoby, 1984). Parents continue to exercise general supervision and control, while children are allowed to engage in moment-to-moment self-regulation. The major shift to autonomy does not occur until about the age of 12 or later. A key developmental task as children move toward autonomy is learning to relate to adults outside the family on a regular basis—adults such as teachers who interact with the child much differently from the way parents do.

Parents as Managers

Parents can play important roles as managers of children's opportunities, as monitors of their behavior, and as social initiators and arrangers (Grusec & others, 2013; Parke & Clarke-Stewart, 2011). Mothers are more likely than fathers to engage in a managerial role in parenting.

Researchers have found that family management practices are positively related to students' grades and self-responsibility, and negatively to school-related problems (Eccles, 2007). Among the most important family management practices in this regard are maintaining a structured and organized family environment, such as establishing routines for homework, chores, bedtime, and so on, and effectively monitoring the child's behavior. A research review of family functioning in African American students' academic achievement found that when African American parents monitored their son's academic achievement by ensuring that homework was completed, restricted time spent on nonproductive distractions (such as video games and TV), and participated in a consistent, positive dialogue with teachers and school officials, their son's academic achievement benefited (Mandara, 2006).

Attachment

In Chapter 4, you read about the importance of secure attachment in infancy and the role of sensitive parenting in attachment (Berlin, 2012; Bretherton, 2012;

Thompson, 2013a). The attachment process continues to be an important aspect of children's development during the childhood years. During middle and late childhood, attachment becomes more sophisticated. As children's social worlds expand to include peers, teachers, and others, they typically spend less time with parents.

Kathryn Kerns and her colleagues (Brumariu, Kerns, & Siebert, 2012; Kerns & Siebert, 2012; Kerns, Siener, & Brumariu, 2011; Siener & Kerns, 2012) have studied links between attachment to parents and various child outcomes in the middle and late childhood years. They have found that during this period of development, secure attachment is associated with a lower level of internalized symptoms, anxiety, and depression in children (Brumariu & Kerns, 2010). For example, a recent study revealed that children who were less securely attached to their mother reported having more anxiety (Brumariu, Kerns, & Seibert, 2012). Also in this study, secure attachment was linked to a higher level of children's emotion regulation and less difficulty in identifying emotions.

Stepfamilies

Not only has divorce become commonplace in the United States, so has getting remarried (Higginbotham & others, 2012). It takes time for parents to marry, have children, get divorced, and then remarry. Consequently, there are far more elementary and secondary school children than infants or preschool children living in stepfamilies.

The number of remarriages involving children has grown steadily in recent years. Also, divorces occur at a 10 percent higher rate in remarriages than in first marriages (Cherlin & Furstenberg, 1994). About half of all children whose parents divorce will have a stepparent within four years of the separation.

Remarried parents face some unique tasks. The couple must define and strengthen their marriage and at the same time renegotiate the biological parent-child relationships and establish stepparent-stepchild and stepsibling relationships (Ganong, Coleman, & Hans, 2006). The complex histories and multiple relationships make adjustment difficult in a stepfamily. Only one-third of stepfamily couples stay remarried.

In some cases, the stepfamily may have been preceded by the death of a spouse. However, by far the largest number of stepfamilies is preceded by divorce rather than death (Pasley & Moorefield, 2004). Three common types of stepfamily structure are (1) stepfather, (2) stepmother, and (3) blended or complex. In stepfather families, the mother typically had custody of the children and remarried, introducing a stepfather into her children's lives. In stepmother families, the father usually had custody and remarried, introducing a stepmother into his children's lives. In a blended or complex stepfamily, both parents bring children from previous marriages to live in the newly formed stepfamily.

How does living in a stepfamily influence a child's development?

In Hetherington's (2006) most recent longitudinal analyses, children and adolescents who had been in a simple stepfamily (stepfather or stepmother) for a number of years were adjusting better than in the early years of the remarried family and were functioning well in comparison with children and adolescents in conflictual families that have not gone through a divorce, and children and adolescents in complex (blended) stepfamilies. More than 75 percent of the adolescents in long-established simple stepfamilies described their relationships with their stepparents as "close" or "very close." Hetherington (2006) concluded that in long-established simple stepfamilies adolescents seem to eventually benefit from the presence of a stepparent and the resources provided by the stepparent.

Children often have better relationships with their custodial parents (mothers in stepfather families, fathers in stepmother families) than with stepparents (Santrock, Sitterle, & Warshak, 1988). Also, children in simple families (stepmother, stepfather) often show better adjustment than their counterparts in complex (blended) families (Hetherington, 2006).

As in divorced families, children in stepfamilies show more adjustment problems than children in never-divorced families (Hetherington, 2006). The adjustment problems are similar to those found among children of divorced parents—academic problems and lower self-esteem, for example (Anderson & others, 1999). However, it is important to recognize that a majority of children in stepfamilies do not have problems. In one analysis, 25 percent of children from stepfamilies showed adjustment problems, compared with 10 percent in intact, never-divorced families (Hetherington & Kelly, 2002).

How Would You...?

As a human development and family studies professional, how would you advise divorced parents on strategies to ease their children's adjustment to remarriage?

Peers

Having positive relationships with peers is especially important in middle and late childhood (Rodkin & Ryan, 2012; Wentzel, 2013). Engaging in positive interactions with peers, resolving conflicts with peers in nonaggressive ways, and having quality friendships in middle and late childhood not only bring positive outcomes at this time in children's lives, but also are linked to more positive relationship outcomes in adolescence and adulthood (Huston & Ripke, 2006). For example, in one longitudinal study, being popular with peers and engaging in low levels of aggression at 8 years of age were related to higher levels of occupational status at 48 years of age (Huesmann & others, 2006). Another study found that peer competence (a composite measure that included social contact with peers, popularity with peers, friendship, and social skills) in middle and late childhood was linked to having better relationships with coworkers in early adulthood (Collins & van Dulmen, 2006).

Developmental Changes

What are some key aspects of peer relationships in middle and late childhood?

As children enter the elementary school years, reciprocity becomes especially important in peer interchanges. Researchers estimate that the percentage of time spent in social interaction with peers increases from approximately 10 percent at 2 years of age to more than 30 percent in middle and late childhood (Rubin, Bukowski, & Parker, 2006). In an early classic study, a typical day in elementary school included approximately 300 episodes with peers (Barker & Wright, 1951). As children move through middle and late childhood, the size of their peer group increases, and peer interaction is less closely supervised by adults (Rubin, Bukowski, & Parker, 2006; Rubin & others, 2013). Until about 12 years of age, children's preference for same-sex peer groups increases.

Peer Status

Which children are likely to be popular with their peers and which ones tend to be disliked? Developmentalists address this and similar questions by examining *sociometric status*, a term that describes the extent to which children are liked or disliked by their peer group (Cillessen & van den Berg, 2012). Sociometric status is typically assessed by asking children to rate how much they like or dislike each of their classmates. Status may also be assessed by asking children to nominate the children they like the most and those they like the least.

Developmentalists have distinguished five peer statuses (Wentzel & Asher, 1995):

- **Popular children** are frequently nominated as a best friend and are rarely disliked by their peers.

- **Average children** receive an average number of both positive and negative nominations from their peers.

- **Neglected children** are infrequently nominated as a best friend but are not disliked by their peers.

- **Rejected children** are infrequently nominated as someone's best friend and are actively disliked by their peers.

- **Controversial children** are frequently nominated both as someone's best friend and as being disliked.

popular children Children who are frequently nominated as a best friend and are rarely disliked by their peers.

average children Children who receive an average number of both positive and negative nominations from their peers.

neglected children Children who are infrequently nominated as a best friend but are not disliked by their peers.

rejected children Children who are infrequently nominated as a best friend and are actively disliked by their peers.

controversial children Children who are frequently nominated both as someone's best friend and as being disliked.

Popular children have a number of social skills that contribute to their being well liked. They give out reinforcements, listen carefully, maintain open lines of communication with peers, are happy, control their negative emotions, act like themselves, show enthusiasm and concern for others, and are self-confident without being conceited (Hartup, 1983; Rubin, Bukowski, & Parker, 1998).

Rejected children often have significant adjustment problems (White & Kistner, 2011). What characterizes the social skills of peer-rejected boys who are aggressive? John Coie (2004, pp. 252–253) provided three reasons why aggressive, peer-rejected boys have problems in social relationships:

- "First, the rejected, aggressive boys are more impulsive and have problems sustaining attention. As a result, they are more likely to be disruptive of ongoing activities in the classroom and in focused group play.

- Second, rejected, aggressive boys are more emotionally reactive. They are aroused to anger more easily and probably have more difficulty calming down once aroused. Because of this they are more prone to become angry at peers and attack them verbally and physically. . . .

- Third, rejected children have fewer social skills in making friends and maintaining positive relationships with peers."

How Would You...?

As a social worker, how would you help a rejected child develop more positive relationships with peers?

Social Cognition

Social cognition involves thoughts about social matters, such as an aggressive boy's interpretation of an encounter as hostile and his classmates' perception of his behavior as inappropriate (Dodge, 2011a, b). Children's social cognition about their peers becomes increasingly important for understanding peer relationships in middle and late childhood. Of special interest are the ways in which children process information about peer relations and their social knowledge (Dodge, 2011b).

Kenneth Dodge (1983) argues that children go through six steps in processing information about their social world. They selectively attend to social cues, attribute intent, generate goals, access behavioral scripts from memory, make decisions, and enact behavior. Dodge has found that aggressive boys are more likely to perceive another child's actions as hostile when the child's intention is ambiguous. And, when aggressive boys search for cues to determine a peer's intention,

How Would You...?

As a psychologist, how would you characterize differences in the social cognition of aggressive children compared with children who behave in less hostile ways?

they respond more rapidly, less efficiently, and less reflectively than do nonaggressive children. These are among the social cognitive factors believed to be involved in children's conflicts.

Social knowledge also is involved in children's ability to get along with peers. They need to know what goals to pursue in poorly defined or ambiguous situations, how to initiate and maintain a social bond, and what scripts to follow to get other children to be their friends. For example, as part of the script for getting friends, it helps to know that saying nice things, regardless of what the peer does or says, will make the peer like the child more.

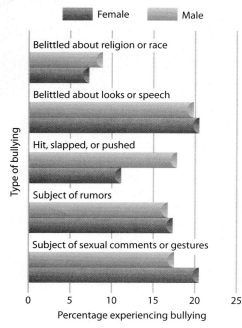

Figure 8.4 Bullying Behaviors Among U.S. Youth
This graph shows the type of bullying most often experienced by U.S. youth. The percentages reflect the extent to which bullied students said that they had experienced a particular type of bullying. In terms of gender, note that when they were bullied, boys were more likely to be hit, slapped, or pushed than girls were.

Bullying

Significant numbers of students are victimized by bullies (Lemstra & others, 2012). In a national survey of more than 15,000 students in grades 6 through 10, nearly one of every three students said that they had experienced occasional or frequent involvement as a victim or perpetrator in bullying (Nansel & others, 2001). In this study, bullying was defined as verbal or physical behavior intended to disturb someone less powerful (see Figure 8.4). Boys are more likely to be bullies than girls, but gender differences regarding victims of boys are less clear (Peets, Hodges, & Salmivalli, 2011).

Who is likely to be bullied? In the study just described, boys and younger middle school students were most likely to be affected (Nansel & others, 2001). Children who said they were bullied reported more loneliness and difficulty in making friends, while those who did the bullying were more likely to have low grades and to smoke and drink alcohol.

Researchers have found that anxious, socially withdrawn, and aggressive children are often the victims of bullying. Anxious and socially withdrawn children may be victimized because they are nonthreatening and unlikely to retaliate if bullied, whereas aggressive children may be the targets of bullying because their behavior is irritating to bullies (Rubin & others, 2011). A recent study revealed that having supportive friends was linked to a lower level of bullying and victimization (Kendrick, Jutengren, & Stattin, 2012).

How Would You...?

As a health-care professional, how would you characterize the health risks that bullying poses to the victims of bullying?

Social contexts also influence bullying (Schwartz & others, 2010). Recent research indicates that 70 to 80 percent of victims and their bullies are in the same school classroom (Salmivalli, Peets, & Hodges, 2011). Classmates are often aware of bullying incidents and in many cases witness bullying. The larger social context of the peer group plays an important role in bullying. In many cases, bullies torment victims to gain higher status in the peer group, and bullies need others to witness their power displays. Many bullies are not rejected by the peer group.

What are the outcomes of bullying? Researchers have found that children who are bullied are more likely to experience depression and to engage in suicide ideation and attempt suicide than their counterparts who have not been the victims of bullying (Fisher & others, 2012; Lemstra & others, 2012). A recent longitudinal study of more than 6,000 children found that children who were the victims of peer bullying from 4 to 10 years of age were more likely to engage in suicide ideation at 11½ years of age (Winsper & others, 2012). A recent study also revealed that 11 year olds who had were victims of peer bullying were more likely to have a heightened risk of developing borderline personality disorder symptoms (a pervasive pattern of unstable interpersonal relationships, low self-image, and emotional difficulties) (Wolke & others, 2012).

An increasing concern is peer bullying and harassment on the Internet (called *cyber-bullying*) (Donnerstein, 2012; Kowalksy, Limber, & Agatston, 2012). A recent study involving third- to sixth-graders revealed that engaging in cyber aggression was related to loneliness, lower self-esteem, fewer mutual friendships, and lower peer popularity (Schoffstall & Cohen, 2012). Information about preventing cyberbullying can be found at www. stopcyberbullying.org/.

Extensive interest is developing in preventing and treating bullying and victimization (Salmivalli, Garandeau, & Veenstra, 2012; Waasdorp, Bradshaw, & Leaf, 2012). A research review revealed mixed results for school-based intervention (Vreeman & Carroll, 2007). School-based interventions vary greatly, ranging from involving the whole school in an antibullying campaign to providing individualized social skills training (Alsaker & Valanover, 2012; Roland & Midthassel, 2012). One of the most promising bullying intervention programs has been created by Dan Olweus. This program focuses on 6- to 15-year-olds with the goal of decreasing opportunities and rewards for bullying. School staff is instructed in ways to improve peer relations and make schools safer. When properly implemented, the program reduces bullying by 30 to 70 percent (Olweus, 2003).

What characterizes bullying? What are some strategies to reduce bullying?

How Would You...?

As an educator, how would you design and implement a bullying reduction program at your school?

Friends

Friendship is an important aspect of children's lives in middle and late childhood (MacEvoy & Asher, 2012; Nurmsoo, Einav, & Hood, 2012). Like adult friendships, children's friendships are typically characterized by similarity (Brechwald & Prinstein, 2011). Throughout childhood, friends are more similar than dissimilar in terms of age, sex, race, and many other factors. Friends often have similar attitudes toward school, similar educational aspirations, and closely aligned achievement orientations.

Why are children's friendships important? Willard Hartup (1983, 1996, 2009) has studied peer relations and friendship for more than three decades. He recently concluded that friends can be cognitive and emotional resources from childhood through old age. Friends can foster self-esteem and a sense of well-being. More specifically, children's friendships can serve six functions (Gottman & Parker, 1987):

- *Companionship.* Friendship provides children with a familiar partner and playmate, someone who is willing to spend time with them and join in collaborative activities.

- *Stimulation.* Friendship provides children with interesting information, excitement, and amusement.

- *Physical support.* Friendship provides time, resources, and assistance.

- *Ego support.* Friendship provides the expectation of support, encouragement, and feedback, which helps children maintain an impression of themselves as competent, attractive, and worthwhile individuals.

performances are examples of contexts in which students participate cooperatively to reach a common goal; however, the jigsaw technique also lends itself to group science projects, history reports, and other learning experiences involving a variety of subject matter.

need for success in life (Pressley, 2007). Also, some individuals are concerned that in the era of No Child Left Behind policy there is a neglect of students who are gifted in the effort to raise the achievement level of students who are not doing well (Clark, 2008).

Consider also the following...

Adolescence is a transitional period in the human life span, entered at approximately 10 to 12 years of age and exited at about 18 to 22 years of age. We begin this chapter by examining some general characteristics of adolescence followed by coverage of major physical changes and health issues of adolescence. Then we describe the significant cognitive changes that take place during adolescence. Last, we consider various aspects of schools for adolescents. ▪

The Nature of Adolescence

There is a long history of worrying about how adolescents will "turn out." In 1904, G. Stanley Hall proposed the "storm-and-stress" view that adolescence is a turbulent time charged with conflict and mood swings. However, when Daniel Offer and his colleagues (1988) studied the self-images of adolescents in a number of countries, at least 73 percent of the adolescents displayed a healthy self-image rather than attitudes of storm-and-stress.

In matters of taste and manners, the young people of every generation have seemed unnervingly radical and different from adults—different in how they look, in how they behave, in the music they enjoy, in their hairstyles, and in the clothing they choose. It is an enormous error, though, to confuse adolescents' enthusiasm for trying on new identities and enjoying moderate amounts of outrageous behavior with hostility toward parental and societal standards. Acting out and boundary testing are time-honored ways in which adolescents move toward accepting, rather than rejecting, parental values.

Katie (*front*) and some of her volunteers.

Growing up has never been easy. However, adolescence is not best viewed as a time of rebellion, crisis, pathology, and deviance. A far more accurate vision of adolescence describes it as a time of evaluation, of decision making, of commitment, and of carving out a place in the world. Most of the problems of today's youth are not with the youth themselves. What adolescents need is access to a range of legitimate opportunities and to long-term support from adults who care deeply about them. *What might be some examples of such support and caring?*

Most adolescents negotiate the lengthy path to adult maturity successfully, but too large a group does not. Ethnic, cultural, gender, socioeconomic, age, and lifestyle differences influence the actual life trajectory of every adolescent (Astell-Burt & others, 2012; Chen & Brooks-Gunn, 2012). Different portrayals of adolescence emerge, depending on the particular group of adolescents being described. Today's adolescents are exposed to a complex menu of lifestyle options through the media, and many face the temptations of drug use and sexual activity at increasingly young ages. Too many adolescents are not provided with adequate opportunities and support to become competent adults (Eccles & Roeser, 2013; Lerner & others, 2013).

Peter Benson and his colleagues (Benson, 2010; Benson, Roehlkepartain, & Scales, 2012; Benson & Scales, 2009, 2011) argue that the United States has a fragmented social policy for youth that too often has focused only on the negative developmental deficits of adolescents, especially health-compromising behaviors such as drug use and delinquency, and not enough on positive strength-based approaches. According to Benson and his colleagues (2004, p. 783), a strength-based approach to social policy for youth

> adopts more of a wellness perspective, places particular emphasis on the existence of healthy conditions, and expands the concept of health to include the skills and competencies needed to succeed in employment, education, and life. It moves beyond the eradication of risk and deliberately argues for the promotion of well-being.

Physical Changes

One father remarked that the problem with his teenage son was not that he grew, but that he did not know when to stop growing. In addition to pubertal changes, other physical changes we will explore involve sexuality and the brain.

Puberty

Puberty is not the same as adolescence. For most of us, puberty ends long before adolescence does, although puberty is the most important marker of the beginning of adolescence. **Puberty** is a period of rapid physical maturation involving hormonal and bodily changes that occur primarily during early adolescence. Puberty is not a single, sudden event. We know whether a young boy or girl is going through puberty, but pinpointing puberty's beginning and end is difficult (Susman & Dorn, 2013). Among the most noticeable changes are signs of sexual maturation and increases in height and weight.

ZITS By Jerry Scott and Jim Borgman

© ZITS Partnership. Reprinted with permission of King Features Syndicate.

puberty A period of rapid physical and sexual maturation that occurs mainly during early adolescence.

menarche A girl's first menstruation.

hormones Powerful chemical substances secreted by the endocrine glands and carried through the body by the bloodstream.

hypothalamus A structure in the higher portion of the brain that monitors eating and sex.

pituitary gland An important endocrine gland that controls growth and regulates other glands, including the gonads.

gonads The sex glands—the testes in males and the ovaries in females.

Sexual Maturation, Height, and Weight

Think back to the onset of your puberty. Of the striking changes that were taking place in your body, what was the first to occur? Researchers have found that male pubertal characteristics typically develop in this order: increase in penis and testicle size, appearance of straight pubic hair, minor voice change, first ejaculation (which usually occurs through masturbation or a wet dream), appearance of kinky pubic hair, onset of maximum growth in height and weight, growth of hair in armpits, more detectable voice changes, and, finally, growth of facial hair.

What is the order of appearance of physical changes in females? First, either the breasts enlarge or pubic hair appears. Later, hair appears in the armpits. As these changes occur, the female grows in height and her hips become wider than her shoulders. **Menarche**—a girl's first menstruation—comes rather late in the pubertal cycle.

Marked weight gains coincide with the onset of puberty. During early adolescence, girls tend to outweigh boys, but by about age 14 boys begin to surpass girls. Similarly, at the beginning of the adolescent period, girls tend to be as tall as or taller than boys of their age, but by the end of the middle school years most boys have caught up, or, in many cases, surpassed girls in height.

As indicated in Figure 9.1, the growth spurt occurs approximately two years earlier for girls than for boys. The mean age at the beginning of the growth spurt in girls is 9; for boys, it is 11. The peak rate of pubertal change occurs at 11½ years for girls and 13½ years for boys. During their growth spurt, girls increase in height about 3½ inches per year, boys about 4 inches. Boys and girls who are shorter or taller than their peers before adolescence are likely to remain so during adolescence.

Hormonal Changes

Behind the first whisker in boys and the widening of hips in girls is a flood of **hormones,** powerful chemical substances secreted by the endocrine glands and carried through the body by the bloodstream. The endocrine system's role in puberty involves the interaction of the hypothalamus, the pituitary gland, and the gonads. The **hypothalamus** is a structure in the brain that monitors eating and sex. The **pituitary gland** is an important endocrine gland that controls growth and regulates other glands; among these, the **gonads**—the testes in males, the ovaries in females—are particularly important in giving rise to pubertal changes in the body.

The concentrations of certain hormones increase dramatically during adolescence (Nguyen & others, 2012). *Testosterone* is a hormone associated in boys with the development of genitals, an increase in height, and a change in voice. *Estradiol* is a type of estrogen; in girls it is associated with breast, uterine, and skeletal development. In one study, testosterone levels increased eighteenfold in boys but only twofold in girls during puberty; estradiol increased eightfold in girls but only twofold in boys (Nottelmann & others, 1987). Thus, both testosterone and estradiol are present in the hormonal makeup of both boys and girls, but testosterone dominates in male pubertal development, estradiol in female pubertal development.

The same influx of hormones that grows hair on a male's chest and increases the fatty tissue in a female's breasts may also contribute to psychological development in adolescence. However, hormonal effects by themselves do not account for adolescent development (Susman & Dorn, 2013). For example, in one study, social factors accounted for two to four times as much variance as did

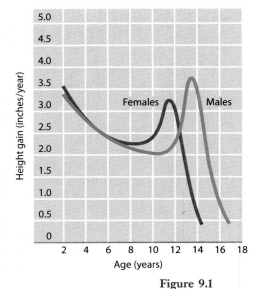

Figure 9.1
Pubertal Growth Spurt
On average, the peak of the growth spurt during puberty occurs two years earlier for girls (11½) than for boys (13½). *How are hormones related to the growth spurt and to the difference between the average height of adolescent boys and that of girls?*

How Would You...?
As a psychologist, how would you explain the influence of biological and physical changes on adolescent mood swings?

hormonal factors in young adolescent girls' depression and anger (Brooks-Gunn & Warren, 1989). Behavior and moods also can affect hormones. Stress, eating patterns, exercise, sexual activity, tension, and depression can activate or suppress various aspects of the hormonal system. In sum, the hormone-behavior link is complex (Susman & Dorn, 2013).

Timing and Variations in Puberty

In the United States—where children mature up to a year earlier than children in European countries—the average age of menarche has declined significantly since the mid-nineteenth century. Fortunately, however, we are unlikely to see pubescent toddlers, since what has happened in the past century is likely the result of improved nutrition and health (Hermann-Giddens, 2007).

What are some of the differences in the ways girls and boys experience pubertal growth?

Why do the changes of puberty occur when they do, and how can variations in their timing be explained? The basic genetic program for puberty is wired into the species (Dvornyk & Wagar-ul-Hag, 2012), but nutrition, health, family stress, and other environmental factors also affect puberty's timing and makeup (James & others, 2012). A recent cross-cultural study in 29 countries found that childhood obesity was linked to early puberty in girls (Currie & others, 2012). For most boys, the pubertal sequence may begin as early as age 10 or as late as 13½ and may end as early as age 13 or as late as 17. Thus, the normal range is wide enough that, given two boys of the same chronological age, one might complete the pubertal sequence before the other one has begun it. For girls, menarche is considered within the normal range if it appears between the ages of 9 and 15.

Body Image

One psychological aspect of physical change in puberty is certain: Adolescents are preoccupied with their bodies and develop images of what their bodies are like. One study revealed that adolescents with the most positive body images engaged in health-enhancing behaviors, especially regular exercise (Friesen & Holmqvist, 2010).

How Would You...?

As a human development and family studies professional, how would you counsel parents about communicating with their adolescent daughter about changes in her behavior that likely reflect a downward turn in her body image?

Gender differences characterize adolescents' perceptions of their bodies. In general, girls are less happy with their bodies and have more negative body images than boys throughout puberty (Bearman & others, 2006). Girls' more negative body images may be due to media portrayals of the attractiveness of being thin and the increase in body fat in girls during puberty (Benowitz-Fredericks & others, 2012). A recent study found that both boys' and girls' body images became more positive as they moved from the beginning to the end of adolescence (Holsen, Carlson Jones, & Skogbrott Birkeland, 2012).

Early and Late Maturation

You may have entered puberty earlier or later than average, or perhaps you were right on time. Adolescents who mature earlier or later than their peers perceive themselves differently (Susman & Dorn, 2013). In the Berkeley Longitudinal Study some years ago, early-maturing boys perceived themselves more positively and had more successful peer relations than did their late-maturing counterparts (Jones, 1965). When the late-maturing boys were in their thirties, however, they had developed a stronger sense of identity than the early-maturing boys had (Peskin, 1967). This may have occurred because the late-maturing

The Timing of Adolescent Sexual Behaviors

What is the current profile of sexual activity of adolescents? In a U.S. national survey conducted in 2011, 63 percent of twelfth-graders reported that they had experienced sexual intercourse, compared with 33 percent of ninth-graders (Eaton & others, 2010). By age 20, 77 percent of U.S. youth have engaged in sexual intercourse (Dworkin & Santelli, 2007). Nationally, 47.5 percent of twelfth-graders, 39 percent of eleventh-graders, 30 percent of tenth-graders, and 21 percent of ninth-graders recently reported being sexually active (Eaton & others, 2012).

What trends in adolescent sexual activity have occurred in the last two decades? From 1991 to 2011, fewer adolescents reported ever having had sexual intercourse, currently being sexually active, having had sexual intercourse before the age of 13, and having had sexual intercourse with four or more persons during their lifetime (Eaton & others, 2012).

How Would You…?

As a psychologist, how would you describe the gender differences in the timing of an adolescent's first sexual experience?

Until very recently, at all grade levels, adolescent males have been more likely than adolescent females to say that they have had sexual intercourse and are sexually active (MMWR, 2006). However, in the 2009 national survey, a higher percentage of twelfth-grade females (65 percent) reported having experienced sexual intercourse than did twelfth-grade males (60 percent); a higher percentage of ninth-grade males (34 percent) than ninth-grade females (29 percent) still reported having experienced sexual intercourse (Eaton & others, 2010). The gender reversals in the 12th grade continued in 2011.

Many adolescents are not emotionally prepared to handle sexual experiences, especially in early adolescence. Early sexual activity is linked with risky behaviors such as drug use, delinquency, and school-related problems (Sales & others, 2012). A study also revealed that alcohol use, early menarche, and poor parent-child communication were linked to early sexually intimate behavior in girls (Hipwell & others, 2010). A research review also found that earlier onset of sexual intercourse was linked to a lower level of parental monitoring (Zimmer-Gembeck & Helfand, 2008). Further, research has indicated that associating with more deviant peers in early adolescence was related to having more sexual partners at age 16 (Lansford & others, 2010). A study of middle school students revealed that better academic achievement was a protective factor in keeping boys and girls from engaging in early initiation of sexual intercourse (Laflin, Wang, & Barry, 2008). And one study also revealed that neighborhood poverty concentrations predicted 15- to 17-year-old girls' and boys' sexual initiation (Cubbin & others, 2010).

What are some risks for early initiation of sexual intercourse?

Contraceptive Use

Sexual activity brings considerable risks if appropriate safeguards are not taken. Youth encounter two kinds of risks: unintended, unwanted pregnancy and sexually transmitted infections. Both of these risks can be reduced significantly if contraception is used.

Are adolescents increasingly using condoms? A national study revealed a substantial increase in the use of a contraceptive (61 percent in 2009 compared with 46 percent in 1991) by U.S. high school students during the last time they had sexual intercourse (Eaton & others, 2010). However, in this study, condom use by U.S. adolescents did not significantly change from 2003 through 2009. A recent study also found that 50 percent of U.S. 15- to 19-year-old girls with unintended pregnancies ending in live births were not using any birth control method when they got pregnant, and 34 percent believed they could not get pregnant at the time (Centers for Disease Control and Prevention, 2012a).

Sexually Transmitted Infections

Some forms of contraception, such as birth control pills or implants, do not protect against sexually transmitted infections, or STIs. **Sexually transmitted infections (STIs)** are contracted primarily through sexual contact, including oral-genital and anal-genital contact. Every year more than 3 million American adolescents (about one-fourth of those who are sexually experienced) acquire an STI (Centers for Disease Control and Prevention, 2012b). In a single act of unprotected sex with an infected partner, a teenage girl has a 1 percent risk of getting HIV, a 30 percent risk of acquiring genital herpes, and a 50 percent chance of contracting gonorrhea (Glei, 1999). Other very widespread STIs are chlamydia and human papillomavirus (HPV). In Chapter 11, we will consider these and other sexually transmitted infections.

sexually transmitted infections (STIs) Infections contracted primarily through sexual contact, including oral-genital and anal-genital contact.

Adolescent Pregnancy

In cross-cultural comparisons, the United States continues to have one of the highest adolescent pregnancy and childbearing rates in the industrialized world, despite a considerable decline in the 1990s (Cooksey, 2009). The U.S. adolescent pregnancy rate is eight times as high as in the Netherlands. This dramatic difference exists in spite of the fact that U.S. adolescents are no more sexually active than their counterparts in the Netherlands.

Despite the negative comparisons of the United States with many other developed countries, there have been some encouraging trends in U.S. adolescent pregnancy rates. In 2009, births to adolescent girls fell to a record low (Ventura & Hamilton, 2011). The U.S. adolescent birth rate decreased 8 percent from 2007 to 2009 (Ventura & Hamilton, 2011). Fear of sexually transmitted infections, especially AIDS; school/community health classes; and a greater hope for the future are the likely reasons for the decrease in U.S. adolescent pregnancy rates in recent decades.

Ethnic variations characterize adolescent pregnancy (Casares & others, 2010) (see Figure 9.3). Latina adolescents are more likely than African American and non-Latina White adolescents to become pregnant (Ventura & Hamilton, 2011). Latina and African American adolescent girls who have a child are also more likely to have a second child than are non-Latina White adolescent girls (Rosengard, 2009). And daughters of teenage mothers are at risk for teenage childbearing, thus perpetuating an intergenerational cycle (Meade, Kershaw, & Ickovics, 2008).

Outcomes Adolescent pregnancy creates risks for both the mother and the baby. Adolescent mothers often drop out of school. Although many adolescent mothers resume their education later in life, they generally never catch up economically with women who postpone childbearing until their twenties. Infants born to adolescent mothers are more likely to have low birth weights—a prominent factor in infant mortality—as well as neurological problems and childhood illness (Khashan, Baker, & Kenny, 2010).

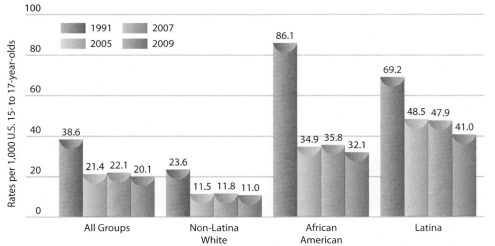

Figure 9.3

U.S. Adolescent Birth Rate by Ethnicity, 1991 to 2009
Birth rates for U.S. 15- to 17-year-olds from 1991 to 2009.

Though the consequences of America's high adolescent pregnancy rate are cause for great concern, it often is not pregnancy alone that leads to negative consequences for an adolescent mother and her offspring. Adolescent mothers are more likely to come from low-SES backgrounds (Molina & others, 2010). Many adolescent mothers also were not good students before they became pregnant (Malamitsi-Puchner & Boutsikou, 2006). However, not every adolescent female who bears a child lives a life of poverty and low achievement. Thus, although adolescent pregnancy is a high-risk circumstance and adolescents who do not become pregnant generally fare better than those who do, some adolescent mothers do well in school and have positive outcomes (Schaffer & others, 2012).

What are some consequences of adolescent pregnancy?

Serious, extensive efforts are needed to help pregnant adolescents and young mothers enhance their educational and occupational opportunities (Gruber, 2012). Adolescent mothers also need help in obtaining competent child care and in planning for the future.

Adolescents can benefit from age-appropriate family life education. Family and consumer science educators teach life skills, such as effective decision making, to adolescents. *Careers in Life-Span Development* describes the work of one family and consumer science educator.

Careers in life-span development

Lynn Blankenship, Family and Consumer Science Educator

Lynn Blankenship is a family and consumer science educator. She has an undergraduate degree in this area from the University of Arizona and has taught for more than 20 years, the last 14 at Tucson High Magnet School.

Lynn was awarded the Tucson Federation of Teachers Educator of the Year Award for 1999–2000 and was honored as the Arizona Teacher of the Year in 1999.

Lynn especially enjoys teaching life skills to adolescents. One of her favorite activities is having students care for an automated baby that imitates the needs of real babies. She says that this program has a profound impact on students because the baby must be cared for around the clock for the duration of the assignment. Lynn also coordinates real-world work experiences and training for students in several child-care facilities in the Tucson area.

Family and consumer science educators like Lynn Blankenship may specialize in early childhood education or instruct middle and high school students about such matters as nutrition, interpersonal relationships, human sexuality, parenting,

Lynn Blankenship (*center*) teaching life skills to students.

and human development. Hundreds of colleges and universities throughout the United States offer two- and four-year degree programs in family and consumer science. These programs usually require an internship. Additional education courses may be needed to obtain a teaching certificate. Some family and consumer science educators go on to graduate school for further training, which provides a background for possible jobs in college teaching or research.

Reducing Adolescent Pregnancy Girls Inc. has four programs that are intended to increase adolescent girls' motivation to avoid pregnancy until they are mature enough to make responsible decisions about motherhood (Roth & others, 1998). Growing Together, a series of five two-hour workshops for adolescent girls and their mothers, and Will Power/Won't Power, a series of six two-hour sessions that focus on assertiveness training, are designed for 12- to 14-year-old girls. For older adolescent girls, Taking Care of Business provides nine sessions that emphasize career planning as well as information about sexuality, reproduction, and contraception. The program Health Bridge coordinates health and education services—girls can participate in this program as one of their Girls Inc. club activities. Girls who participated in these programs were less likely to get pregnant than girls who did not participate (Girls Inc., 1991).

Currently, a major controversy in sex education is whether schools should have an abstinence-only program or a program that emphasizes contraceptive knowledge. A number of leading experts on adolescent sexuality now conclude that sex education programs that emphasize contraceptive knowledge do not increase the incidence of sexual intercourse and are more likely to reduce the risk of adolescent pregnancy and sexually transmitted infections than abstinence-only programs (Carroll, 2013; Hyde & DeLamater, 2011).

Some sex education programs are starting to include abstinence-plus sexuality by promoting abstinence as well as providing instructions for contraceptive use (Nixon & others, 2011; Realini & others, 2010).

How Would You...?

As an educator, how would you incorporate sex education throughout the curriculum to encourage adolescents' healthy, responsible sexual development?

Adolescent Health

Adolescence is a critical juncture in the adoption of behaviors that are relevant to health (Catalano & others, 2012). Many of the behaviors that are linked to poor health habits and early death in adults begin during adolescence. Conversely, the early formation of healthy behavior patterns, such as regular exercise and a preference for foods low in fat and cholesterol, not only has immediate health benefits but helps in adulthood to delay or prevent disability and mortality from heart disease, stroke, diabetes, and cancer (Insel & Roth, 2012; Schiff, 2013).

Nutrition and Exercise

Concerns are growing about adolescents' nutrition and exercise habits (Alberga & others, 2012; Dowdy & others, 2012). National data indicated that the percentage of overweight U.S. 12- to 19-year-olds increased from 11 to 17 percent from the early 1990s to 2009–2010 (Ogden & others, 2012). During this time frame, the prevalence of obesity in adolescent boys increased from 14 to 19 percent, but there was no significant change in obesity in adolescent girls.

Being obese in adolescence predicts obesity in emerging adulthood. For example, a longitudinal study of more than 8,000 adolescents found that obese adolescents were more likely to develop severe obesity in emerging adulthood than were overweight or normal-weight adolescents (The & others, 2010). In another longitudinal study, the

What are some characteristics of adolescents' exercise patterns?

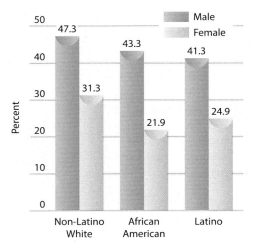

Figure 9.4 Exercise Rates of U.S. High School Students: Gender and Ethnicity
Note: Data are for high school students who were doing any kind of physical activity that increased their heart rate and made them breathe hard some of the time for a total of at least 60 minutes per day on five or more of the seven days preceding the survey.

percentage of overweight individuals increased from 20 percent at 14 years of age to 33 percent at 24 years of age (Patton & others, 2011).

Researchers have found that individuals become less active as they reach and progress through adolescence (Alberga & others, 2012; Kwan & others, 2012). A national study revealed that only 31 percent of U.S. 15-year-olds met the federal government's moderate to vigorous exercise recommendations (a minimum of 60 minutes a day) on weekdays and only 17 percent met the recommendations on weekends (Nader & others, 2008). This study also found that adolescent boys were more likely to engage in moderate to vigorous exercise than were girls. Another national study of U.S. adolescents revealed that physical activity increased until 13 years of age in boys and girls but then declined through 18 years of age (Kahn & others, 2008).

Ethnic differences in exercise participation rates of U.S. adolescents also occur, and these rates vary by gender. As indicated in Figure 9.4, in the National Youth Risk Survey, non-Latino White boys exercised the most, African American girls the least (Eaton & others, 2008).

Exercise is linked to a number of positive physical outcomes in adolescence (Alberga & others, 2012). Regular exercise has a positive effect on adolescents' weight status. Other positive outcomes of exercise in adolescence are reduced triglyceride levels, lower blood pressure, and a lower incidence of type II diabetes (Shi, de Groh, & Morrison, 2012). A recent study also found that eighth-, tenth-, and twelfth-grade students who engaged in higher levels of exercise had lower levels of alcohol, cigarette, and marijuana use (Terry-McElrath, O'Malley, & Johnston, 2011).

Screen-based activity (watching television, using computers, talking on the phone, texting, and instant messaging for long hours) may be involved in lower levels of physical fitness in adolescence (Leatherdale, 2010; Wang & others, 2012). A recent study revealed that children and adolescents who engaged in the highest amount of daily screen-based activity (TV/video/video game in this study) were less likely to exercise daily (Sisson & others, 2010). In this study, children and adolescents who engaged in low levels of physical activity and high levels of screen-based activity were almost twice as likely to be overweight as their more active, less sedentary counterparts (Sisson & others, 2010).

How Would You...?

As a health-care professional, how would you explain the benefits of physical fitness in adolescence to adolescents, parents, and teachers?

Sleep Patterns

Like nutrition and exercise, sleep is an important influence on well-being. Might changing sleep patterns in adolescence contribute to adolescents' health-compromising behaviors? Recently there has been a surge of interest in adolescent sleep patterns (Beebe, 2011; Bei & others, 2012; Hagenauer & Lee, 2012).

In a national survey of youth, only 31 percent of U.S. adolescents got eight or more hours of sleep on an average school night (Eaton & others, 2010). In this study, the percentage of adolescents getting this much sleep on an average school night decreased as they got older.

The National Sleep Foundation (2006) conducted a U.S. survey of 1,602 caregivers and their 11- to 17-year-olds. Forty-five percent of the adolescents got inadequate sleep on school nights (less than eight hours). Older adolescents (ninth- to twelfth-graders) got markedly less sleep on school nights than younger adolescents (sixth- to eighth-graders)—62 percent of the older adolescents got inadequate sleep compared with 21 percent of the younger adolescents. Adolescents who got inadequate sleep (less than eight hours) on school nights were more likely to feel tired, cranky, and irritable; to fall asleep in school; to be in a depressed mood; and to drink caffeinated beverages than their counterparts who got optimal sleep (nine or more hours).

In Mary Carskadon's sleep laboratory at Brown University, an adolescent girl's brain activity is being monitored. Carskadon (2006) says that in the morning, sleep-deprived adolescents' "brains are telling them it's night time . . . and the rest of the world is saying it's time to go to school" (p. 19).

Mary Carskadon and her colleagues (2006, 2011a, b; Jenni & Carskadon, 2007; Tarokh & Carskadon, 2010) have conducted a number of research studies on adolescent sleep patterns. They found that when given the opportunity, adolescents will sleep an average of 9 hours and 25 minutes a night. Most get considerably less than nine hours of sleep, however, especially during the week. This shortfall creates a sleep deficit, which adolescents often attempt to make up on the weekend. The researchers also found that older adolescents tend to be sleepier during the day than younger adolescents are. They theorized that this sleepiness was not due to academic work or social pressures. Rather, their research suggests that adolescents' biological clocks undergo a shift as they get older, delaying their period of wakefulness by about one hour. A delay in the nightly release of the sleep-inducing hormone melatonin, which is produced in the brain's pineal gland, seems to underlie this shift. Melatonin is secreted at about 9:30 p.m. in younger adolescents and approximately an hour later in older adolescents.

Carskadon concludes that early school starting times may cause grogginess, inattention in class, and poor performance on tests. Based on her research, school officials in Edina, Minnesota, decided to start classes at 8:30 a.m. rather than the usual 7:25 a.m. Since then, there have been fewer referrals for discipline problems, and the number of students who report being ill or depressed has decreased. The school system reports that test scores have improved for high school students but not for middle school students. This finding supports Carskadon's suspicion that early start times are likely to be more stressful for older than for younger adolescents.

How Would You...?

As an educator, how would you use developmental research to convince your school board to change the starting time of high school?

Do sleep patterns change in emerging adulthood? Research indicates that they do (Galambos, Howard, & Maggs, 2011). A recent study revealed that more than 60 percent of college students were categorized as poor-quality sleepers (Lund & others, 2010). In this study, the weekday bedtimes and rise times of first-year college students were approximately 1 hour and 15 minutes later than those of seniors in high school (Lund & others, 2010). However, the first-year college students had later bedtimes and rise times than third- and fourth-year college students, indicating that at about 20 to 22 years of age, a reverse shift in the timing of bedtimes and rise times occurs.

Leading Causes of Death in Adolescence

The three leading causes of death in adolescence are unintentional injuries, homicide, and suicide (Eaton & others, 2010). Almost half of all deaths occurring from 15 to 24 years of age are due to unintentional injuries, the majority of them involving motor vehicle accidents.

Risky driving habits, such as speeding, tailgating, and driving under the influence of alcohol or other drugs, may be more important contributors to these accidents than lack of driving experience (Marcotte & others, 2012). In about 50 percent of motor vehicle fatalities involving adolescents, the driver has a blood alcohol level of 0.10 percent—twice the level needed to be designated as "under the influence" in some states. A high rate of intoxication is also found in adolescents who die as pedestrians or while using recreational vehicles.

Homicide is the second leading cause of death in adolescence (National Vital Statistics Reports, 2008), especially among African American male adolescents. The rate of the third cause, adolescent suicide, has tripled since the 1950s. Suicide accounts for 6 percent of the deaths in the 10 to 14 age group and 12 percent of deaths in the 15 to 19 age group. We will discuss suicide further in Chapter 10.

Substance Use and Abuse

Each year since 1975, Lloyd Johnston and his colleagues at the Institute of Social Research at the University of Michigan have monitored the drug use of America's high school seniors in a wide range of public and private high schools. Since 1991, they also have surveyed drug use by eighth- and tenth-graders. In 2011, the study surveyed 47,000 secondary school students (Johnston & others, 2012).

According to this study, the proportions of eighth-, tenth-, and twelfth-grade U.S. students who used any illicit drug declined in the late 1990s and the first decade of the twenty-first century (Johnston & others, 2012) (see Figure 9.5). Marijuana is the illicit drug most widely used in the United States, and its use by adolescents increased from 2008 to 2011 (Johnston & others, 2012). As shown in Figure 9.5, in which marijuana is included, an increase in illicit drug use by U.S. adolescents occurred from 2008 to 2011. However, when marijuana use is subtracted from the illicit drug index, no increase in illicit drug use by adolescents occurred in this time frame (Johnston & others, 2012). The United States still has one of the highest rates of adolescent drug use of any industrialized nation.

A special concern involves adolescents who begin to use drugs early in adolescence or even in childhood (Kenney, 2012). A longitudinal study of individuals from 8 to 42 years of age also found that early onset of drinking was linked to increased risk of heavy drinking in middle age (Pitkänen, Lyrra, & Pulkkinen, 2005). And a recent study revealed that the onset of alcohol use before age 11 was linked to a higher risk for alcohol dependence in early adulthood (Guttmannova & others, 2012).

Parents play an important role in preventing adolescent drug abuse (Feinstein, Richter, & Foster, 2012). Researchers have found that parental monitoring is linked

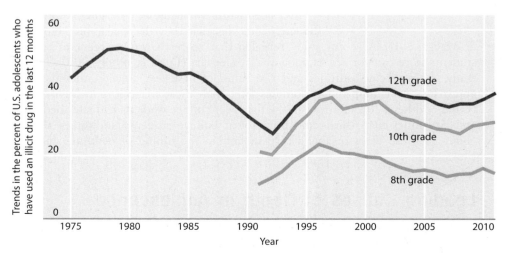

Figure 9.5 Trends in Drug Use by U.S. Eighth-, Tenth-, and Twelfth-Grade Students
This graph shows the percentage of U.S. eighth-, tenth, and twelfth-grade students who reported having taken an illicit drug in the last 12 months from 1991 to 2011 (for eighth- and tenth-graders), and from 1975 to 2011 (for twelfth-graders) (Johnston & others, 2012).

with a lower incidence of problem behavior by adolescents, including substance abuse (Tobler & Komro, 2010). A recent research review found that when adolescents ate dinner more often with their families they were less likely to have problems such as substance abuse (Sen, 2010). And recent research revealed that authoritative parenting was linked to lower adolescent alcohol consumption (Piko & Balazs, 2012) while parent-adolescent conflict was related to a higher level of adolescent alcohol use (Chaplin & others, 2012).

Along with parents, peers play a very important role in adolescent substance use (Tucker & others, 2012). A recent large-scale study of eighth- and tenth-graders found that of various risk factors the strongest predictors of substance use involved peer relations (Patrick & Schulenberg, 2010). In this study, spending more evenings out with peers, having friends who get drunk, feeling pressure to drink, and perceived availability of alcohol were linked to heavy episodic drinking.

Educational success is also a strong buffer for the emergence of drug problems in adolescence (Balsa, Giuliano, & French, 2011). An analysis by Jerald Bachman and his colleagues (2008) revealed that early educational achievement considerably reduced the likelihood that adolescents would develop drug problems, including alcohol abuse, smoking, and abuse of various illicit drugs.

How Would You...?

As a human development and family studies professional, how would you explain to parents the importance of parental monitoring in preventing adolescent substance abuse?

Eating Disorders

Earlier in the chapter under the topic of nutrition and exercise, we described the increasing numbers of adolescents who are overweight. Let's now examine two different eating problems—anorexia nervosa and bulimia nervosa—that are far more common in adolescent girls than boys.

Anorexia Nervosa

Although most U.S. girls have been on a diet at some point, slightly less than 1 percent ever develop anorexia nervosa. **Anorexia nervosa** is an eating disorder that involves the relentless pursuit of thinness through starvation. It is a serious disorder that can lead to death. Four main characteristics apply to people suffering from anorexia nervosa: (1) weight less than 85 percent of what is considered normal for their age and height; (2) an intense fear of gaining weight that does not decrease with weight loss; (3) a distorted image of their body shape (Stewart & others, 2012), and (4) *amenorrhea (lack of menstruation)* in girls who have reached puberty. Obsessive thinking about weight and compulsive exercise also are linked to anorexia nervosa (Hildebrant & others, 2012). Even when they are extremely thin, they see themselves as too fat. They never think they are thin enough, especially in the abdomen, buttocks, and thighs. They usually weigh themselves frequently, often take their body measurements, and gaze critically at themselves in mirrors.

Anorexia nervosa typically begins in the early to middle adolescent years, often following an episode of dieting and some type of life stress (Fitzpatrick, 2012). It is about 10 times more likely to occur in females than males. When anorexia nervosa does occur in males, the symptoms and other characteristics (such as a distorted body image and family conflict) are usually similar to those reported by females who have the disorder (Ariceli & others, 2005).

Most individuals with anorexia are non-Latina White adolescent or young adult females from well-educated, middle- and upper-income families and are competitive and high achieving (Darcy, 2012; Dodge, 2012). They set high standards, become stressed about not being able to reach the standards, and are intensely concerned about how others perceive them (Liechty, 2010; Woelders & others, 2011). Unable to meet these

Anorexia nervosa has become an increasing problem for adolescent girls and young adult women. *What are some possible causes of anorexia nervosa?*

anorexia nervosa An eating disorder that involves the relentless pursuit of thinness through starvation.

high expectations, they turn to something they can control—their weight. Offspring of mothers with anorexia nervosa are at risk for becoming anorexic themselves (Striegel-Moore & Bulik, 2007). Problems in family functioning are increasingly being found to be linked to the appearance of anorexia nervosa in adolescent girls (Stiles-Shields & others, 2012), and a recent research review indicated that family therapy is often the most effective treatment of adolescent girls with anorexia nervosa (Bulik & others, 2007).

Biology and culture are involved in anorexia nervosa. Genes play an important role in anorexia nervosa (Lock, 2012a). Also, the physical effects of dieting may change neural networks and thus sustain the disordered pattern (Lock, 2012b). The fashion image in U.S. culture likely contributes to the incidence of anorexia nervosa (Benowitz-Fredericks & others, 2012; Carr & Peebles, 2012). The media portray thin as beautiful in their choice of fashion models, whom many adolescent girls strive to emulate (Carr & Peebles, 2012). And many adolescent girls who strive to be thin hang out together.

Bulimia Nervosa

Whereas people with anorexia control their eating by restricting it, most individuals with bulimia cannot. **Bulimia nervosa** is an eating disorder in which the individual consistently follows a binge-and-purge pattern. They go on an eating binge and then purge by self-inducing vomiting or using a laxative. Although many people binge and purge occasionally and some experiment with it, a person is considered to have a serious bulimic disorder only if the episodes occur at least twice a week for three months (Uher & Rutter, 2012).

As with those who have anorexia, most people with bulimia are preoccupied with food, have a strong fear of becoming overweight, are depressed or anxious, and have a distorted body image. A study revealed that they overvalued their body weight and shape, and this overvaluation was linked to higher depression and lower self-esteem (Hrabosky & others, 2007). Unlike people who have anorexia, people who binge and purge typically fall within a normal weight range, which makes bulimia more difficult to detect.

How Would You...?

As a health-care professional, how would you educate parents to identify the signs and symptoms that may signal an eating disorder?

Approximately 1 to 2 percent of U.S. women are estimated to develop bulimia nervosa, and about 90 percent of people with bulimia are women. Bulimia nervosa typically begins in late adolescence or early adulthood. Many women who develop bulimia nervosa were somewhat overweight before the onset of the disorder, and the binge eating often began during an episode of dieting. As with anorexia nervosa, about 70 percent of individuals who develop bulimia nervosa eventually recover from the disorder (Agras & others, 2004). Like adolescents who are anorexic, bulimics are highly perfectionistic (Lampard & others, 2012). Unlike anorexics, individuals who binge and purge typically fall within a normal weight range, which makes bulimia more difficult to detect. Drug therapy and psychotherapy have been effective in treating bulimia nervosa (Hagman & Frank, 2012).

Adolescent Cognition

Adolescents' developing power of thought opens up new cognitive and social horizons. Let's examine what their developing power of thought is like, beginning with the perspective provided by Piaget's theory (1952).

Piaget's Theory

As we discussed in Chapter 7, Piaget proposed that around 7 years of age children enter the concrete operational stage of cognitive development. They can reason logically about concrete events and objects, and they make gains in their ability to classify objects and to reason about the relationships between classes of objects. Around age 11, according to Piaget, the fourth and final stage of cognitive development—the formal operational stage—begins.

hypothetical-deductive reasoning Piaget's formal operational concept that adolescents have the cognitive ability to develop hypotheses, or best guesses, about ways to solve problems.

The Formal Operational Stage

What are the characteristics of the formal operational stage? Formal operational thought is more abstract than concrete operational thought. Adolescents are no longer limited to actual, concrete experiences as anchors for thought. They can conjure up make-believe situations, abstract propositions, and events that are purely hypothetical, and can try to reason logically about them.

The abstract quality of thinking during the formal operational stage is evident in the adolescent's verbal problem-solving ability. The concrete operational thinker needs to see the concrete elements A, B, and C to be able to make the logical inference that if A = B and B = C, then A = C, whereas the formal operational thinker can solve this problem merely through verbal presentation.

Another indication of the abstract quality of adolescents' thought is their increased tendency to think about thought itself. One adolescent commented, "I began thinking about why I was thinking what I was. Then I began thinking about why I was thinking about what I was thinking about what I was." If this sounds abstract, it is, and it characterizes the adolescent's enhanced focus on thought and its abstract qualities.

Accompanying the abstract nature of formal operational thought is thought full of idealism and possibilities, especially during the beginning of the formal operational stage, when assimilation dominates. Adolescents engage in extended speculation about ideal characteristics—qualities they desire in themselves and in others. Such thoughts often lead adolescents to compare themselves with others in regard to such ideal standards. And their thoughts are often fantasy flights into future possibilities.

At the same time that adolescents think more abstractly and idealistically, they also think more logically. Children are likely to solve problems through trial and error; adolescents begin to think more as a scientist thinks, devising plans to solve problems and systematically testing solutions. This type of problem solving requires **hypothetical-deductive reasoning,** which involves creating a hypothesis and deducing its implications, which provides ways to test the hypothesis. Thus, formal operational thinkers develop hypotheses about ways to solve problems and then systematically deduce the best path to follow to solve the problem.

Evaluating Piaget's Theory

Researchers have challenged some of Piaget's ideas on the formal operational stage (Brynes, 2012; Diamond, 2013; Kuhn, 2009, 2011). Among their findings is that there is much more individual variation than Piaget envisioned: Only about one in three young adolescents is a formal operational thinker, and many

Might adolescents' ability to reason hypothetically and to evaluate what is ideal versus what is real lead them to engage in demonstrations, such as this one promoting better education? What other causes might be attractive to adolescents' newfound cognitive abilities of hypothetical-deductive reasoning and idealistic thinking?

American adults never become formal operational thinkers; neither do many adults in other cultures.

Furthermore, education in the logic of science and mathematics promotes the development of formal operational thinking. This point recalls a criticism of Piaget's theory that we discussed in Chapter 7: Culture and education exert stronger influences on cognitive development than Piaget argued (Goncu & Gauvain, 2012; Daniels, 2011).

Piaget's theory of cognitive development has been challenged on other points as well (Hyde & Spelke, 2012). As we noted in Chapter 7, Piaget conceived of stages as unitary structures of thought, with various aspects of a stage emerging at the same time. However, most contemporary developmentalists agree that cognitive development is not as stage-like as Piaget thought (Siegler, 2012). Furthermore, children can be trained to reason at a higher cognitive stage, and some cognitive abilities emerge earlier than Piaget thought (Baillargeon & Carey, 2012; Johnson, 2012, 2013). Some understanding of the conservation of number has been demonstrated as early as age 3, although Piaget did not think it emerged until 7. Other cognitive abilities can emerge later than Piaget thought (Brynes, 2012). As we just noted, many adolescents still think in concrete operational ways or are just beginning to master formal operations, and even many adults are not formal operational thinkers.

Despite these challenges to Piaget's ideas, we owe him a tremendous debt (Miller, 2011). Piaget was the founder of the present field of cognitive development, and he developed a long list of masterful concepts of enduring power and fascination: assimilation, accommodation, object permanence, egocentrism, conservation, and others. Psychologists also owe him the current vision of children as active, constructive thinkers. And they have a debt to him for creating a theory that generated a huge volume of research on children's cognitive development.

Piaget also was a genius when it came to observing children. His careful observations demonstrated inventive ways to discover how children act on, and adapt to, their world. He also showed us how children need to make their experiences fit their schemes yet simultaneously adapt their schemes to experience. Piaget also revealed how cognitive change is likely to occur if the context is structured to allow gradual movement to the next higher level. Concepts do not emerge suddenly, full-blown, but instead develop through a series of partial accomplishments that lead to increasingly comprehensive understanding (Mandler & DeLoache, 2012).

Adolescent Egocentrism

Adolescent egocentrism is the heightened self-consciousness of adolescents. David Elkind (1976) maintains that adolescent egocentrism has two key components—the imaginary audience and personal fable. The **imaginary audience** is adolescents' belief that others are as interested in them as they themselves are, as well as attention-getting behavior—attempts to be noticed, visible, and "on stage." For example, an eighth-grade boy might walk into the classroom thinking that all eyes are riveted on his spotty complexion. Adolescents sense that they are "on stage" in early adolescence, believing they are the main actors and all others are the audience.

According to Elkind, the **personal fable** is the part of adolescent egocentrism involving a sense of uniqueness and invincibility (or invulnerability). For example, 13-year-old Adrienne says this about herself: "No one understands me, particularly my parents. They have no idea of what I am feeling." Adolescents' sense of personal uniqueness makes them feel that no one can understand how they really feel. As part of their effort to retain a sense of personal uniqueness, adolescents might craft a story about the self that is filled with fantasy, immersing themselves in a world that is far removed from reality. Personal fables frequently show up in adolescent diaries.

Adolescents also often show a sense of invincibility or invulnerability. For example, during a conversation with a girl her own age, 14-year-old Margaret says, "Are you kidding? I won't get pregnant."

adolescent egocentrism The heightened self-consciousness of adolescents.

imaginary audience Involves adolescents' belief that others are as interested in them as they themselves are; attention-getting behavior motivated by a desire to be noticed, visible, and "on stage."

personal fable The part of adolescent egocentrism that involves an adolescent's sense of uniqueness and invincibility (or invulnerability).

This sense of invincibility may also lead adolescents to believe that they themselves are invulnerable to dangers and catastrophes (such as deadly car wrecks) that happen to other people. As a result, some adolescents engage in risky behaviors such as drag racing, drug use, suicide, and having sexual intercourse without using contraceptives or barriers against STIs (Alberts, Elkind, & Ginsberg, 2007). However, some research studies suggest that rather than perceiving themselves to be invulnerable, adolescents tend to portray themselves as vulnerable to experiencing a premature death (Bruine de Bruin, Parker, & Fischhoff, 2007; Fischhoff & others, 2010; Reyna & Rivers, 2008).

Many adolescent girls spend long hours in front of the mirror, depleting cans of hairspray, tubes of lipstick, and jars of cosmetics. *How might this behavior be related to changes in adolescent cognitive and physical development?*

Information Processing

Deanna Kuhn (2009) discussed some important characteristics of adolescents' information processing and thinking. In her view, in the later years of childhood and continuing in adolescence, individuals approach cognitive levels that may or may not be achieved, in contrast with the largely universal cognitive levels that young children attain. By adolescence, considerable variation in cognitive functioning is present across individuals. This variability supports the argument that adolescents are producers of their own development to a greater extent than are children. That is, adolescents are more likely than children to initiate changes in thinking rather than depend on others, such as parents and teachers, to direct their thinking.

Executive Functioning

Kuhn (2009) further argues that the most important cognitive change in adolescence is improvement in *executive functioning*, which we discussed earlier in Chapters 5 and 7. Recall from Chapters 5 and 7 the description of *executive functioning* as an umbrella-like concept that consists of a number of higher-level cognitive processes linked to the development of the prefrontal cortex. Executive functioning involves managing one's thoughts to engage in goal-directed behavior and to exercise self-control. Our further coverage of executive functioning in adolescence focuses on cognitive control and decision making.

Cognitive Control In Chapter 7, you read about the increase in cognitive control that occurs in middle and late childhood. Recall that cognitive control involves effective control in a number of areas, including controlling attention, reducing interfering thoughts, and being cognitively flexible (Diamond, 2013). Cognitive control continues to increase in adolescence and emerging adulthood (Casey, Jones, & Somerville, 2011).

Think about all the times adolescents need to engage in cognitive control, such as the following situations (Galinsky, 2010):

- making a real effort to stick with a task, avoiding interfering thoughts or environmental events, and instead doing what is most effective;
- stopping and thinking before acting to avoid blurting out something that a minute or two later they wished they hadn't said;
- continuing to work on something that is important but boring when there is something a lot more fun to do, inhibiting their behavior and doing the boring but important task, saying to themselves, "I have to show the self-discipline to finish this."

Controlling attention is a key aspect of learning and thinking in adolescence and emerging adulthood (Bjorklund, 2012). Distractions that can interfere with attention in adolescence and emerging adulthood come from the external environment (other students talking while the student is trying to listen to a lecture, or the student turning on a laptop or tablet PC during a lecture and looking at a new friend request on Facebook, for example) or intrusive distractions from competing thoughts in the individual's mind. Self-oriented thoughts, such as worrying, self-doubt, and intense emotionally laden thoughts may especially interfere with focusing attention on thinking tasks (Gillig & Sanders, 2011; Walsh, 2011).

Decision Making Adolescence is a time of increased decision making—which friends to choose; which person to date; whether to have sex, buy a car, go to college, and so on (Stanovich, West, & Toplak, 2012; Steinberg, 2012, 2013). How competent are adolescents at making decisions? Older adolescents are described as more competent than younger adolescents, who in turn are more competent than children (Keating, 1990). Compared with children, young adolescents are more likely to generate different options, examine a situation from a variety of perspectives, anticipate the consequences of decisions, and consider the credibility of sources.

Most people make better decisions when they are calm than when they are emotionally aroused. That may especially be true for adolescents, who have a tendency to be emotionally intense. The same adolescent who makes a wise decision when calm may make an unwise decision when emotionally aroused (Steinberg, 2012, 2013). In the heat of the moment, emotions may overwhelm decision-making ability.

How Would You...?

As an educator, how would you incorporate decision-making exercises into the school curriculum for adolescents?

The social context plays a key role in adolescent decision making. For example, adolescents' willingness to make risky decisions is more likely to occur in contexts where substances and other temptations are readily available (Reyna & Rivers, 2008). Recent research reveals that the presence of peers in risk-taking situations increases the likelihood that adolescents will make risky decisions (Albert & Steinberg, 2011a, b).

Adolescents need more opportunities to practice and discuss realistic decision making. Many real-world decisions on matters such as sex, drugs, and daredevil driving occur in an atmosphere of stress that includes time constraints and emotional involvement. One strategy for improving adolescent decision making is to provide more opportunities for them to engage in role playing and peer-group problem solving.

Schools

Our discussion of adolescents' schooling will focus on the transition from elementary to middle or junior high school, the characteristics of effective schools for adolescents, and how adolescents can benefit from service learning.

The Transition to Middle or Junior High School

The first year of middle school or junior high school can be difficult for many students (Anderman, 2012). For example, in one study of the transition from sixth grade in an elementary school to seventh grade in a junior high school, adolescents' perceptions of the quality of their school life plunged in the seventh grade

The transition from elementary to middle or junior high school occurs at the same time as a number of other developmental changes. *What are some of these other developmental changes?*

(Hirsch & Rapkin, 1987). Compared with their earlier feelings as sixth-graders, the seventh-graders were less satisfied with school, were less committed to school, and liked their teachers less. The drop in school satisfaction occurred regardless of how academically successful the students were.

top-dog phenomenon The circumstance of moving from the top position in elementary school to the lowest position in middle or junior high school.

The transition to middle or junior high school takes place at a time when many changes—in the individual, in the family, and in school—are occurring simultaneously (Eccles & Roeser, 2013). These changes include puberty and related concerns about body image; the emergence of at least some aspects of formal operational thought, including accompanying changes in social cognition; increased responsibility and decreased dependency on parents; change to a larger, more impersonal school structure; change from one teacher to many teachers and from a small, homogeneous set of peers to a larger, more heterogeneous set of peers; and an increased focus on achievement and performance. Moreover, when students make the transition to middle or junior high school, they experience the **top-dog phenomenon**, moving from being the oldest, biggest, and most powerful students in the elementary school to being the youngest, smallest, and least powerful students in the middle or junior high school.

How Would You...?

As an educator, how would you design school programs to enhance students' smooth transition into middle school?

There can also be positive aspects to the transition to middle or junior high school. Students are more likely to feel grown up, have more subjects from which to select, have more opportunities to spend time with peers and locate compatible friends, and enjoy increased independence from direct parental monitoring. They also may be more challenged intellectually by academic work.

Effective Schools for Young Adolescents

Educators and psychologists worry that junior high and middle schools have become watered-down versions of high schools, mimicking their curricular and extracurricular schedules. Critics argue that these schools should offer activities that reflect a wide range of individual differences in biological and psychological development among young adolescents. The Carnegie Foundation (1989) issued an extremely negative evaluation of our nation's middle schools. It concluded that most young adolescents attended massive, impersonal schools; were taught from irrelevant curricula; trusted few adults in school; and lacked access to health care and counseling. It recommended that the nation develop smaller "communities" or "houses" to lessen the impersonal nature of large middle schools, maintain lower student-to-counselor ratios (10 to 1 instead of several hundred to 1), involve parents and community leaders in schools, develop new curricula, have teachers team teach in more flexibly designed curriculum blocks that integrate several disciplines, boost students' health and fitness with more in-school programs, and help students who need public health care to get it. Twenty-five years later, experts are still finding that middle schools throughout the nation need a major redesign if they are to be effective in educating adolescents (Anderman, 2012; Eccles & Roeser, 2013).

High School

Just as there are concerns about U.S. middle school education, so are there concerns about U.S. high school education (Smith, 2009). Critics stress that many high schools have low expectations for success and inadequate standards for learning. Critics also argue that too often high schools foster passivity instead of creating a variety of pathways for students to achieve an identity. Many students graduate from high school with inadequate reading, writing, and mathematical skills—including many who go on to college and have to enroll in remediation classes there. Other students drop out of high school and do not have skills that will allow them to obtain decent jobs, much less to be informed citizens.

Robert Crosnoe's (2011) recent book, *Fitting in, Standing Out*, highlighted another major problem with U.S. high schools: How the negative social aspects of adolescents' lives undermine their academic achievement. In his view, adolescents become immersed in complex peer group cultures that demand conformity. High school is supposed to be about getting an education, but the reality for many youth is that it is as much about navigating the social worlds of peer relations that may or may not value education and academic achievement. The adolescents who fail to fit in, especially those who are obese or gay, become stigmatized. Crosnoe recommends increased school counseling services, expanded extracurricular activities, and improved parental monitoring to reduce such problems.

In the last half of the twentieth century and the first several years of the twenty-first century, U.S. high school dropout rates declined (National Center for Education Statistics, 2010). In the 1940s, more than half of U.S. 16- to 24-year-olds had dropped out of school; by 2008, this figure had decreased to 8 percent. The dropout rate of Latino adolescents remains high, although it has been decreasing in the twenty-first century (from 28 percent in 2000 to 18 percent in 2008). The lowest dropout rate in 2008 occurred for Asian American adolescents (3.2 percent), followed by non-Latino White adolescents (6.2 percent), African American adolescents (10.4 percent), then Latino adolescents (19 percent). Native American adolescents likely have the highest dropout rate. Although government statistics for this ethnic group have not been adequately assessed, some estimates indicate that their dropout rate is above 50 percent.

Gender differences characterize U.S. dropout rates, with males more likely to drop out than females (10.4 versus 7.9 percent, based on data from 2008) (National Center for Education Statistics, 2010). The gender gap in dropout rates is especially large for Latino adolescents (21.9 versus 15 percent). Figure 9.6 shows the dropout rates of 16- to 24-year-olds by ethnicity and gender in 2008.

The average U.S. high school dropout rates just described mask some very high dropout rates in low-income areas of inner cities. For example, in cities such as Detroit, Cleveland, and Chicago, dropout rates are above 50 percent. Also, the percentages cited in Figure 9.6 are for 16- to 24-year-olds. When dropout rates are calculated in terms of students who graduate from high school in four years, the percentage of students is also much higher than in Figure 9.6. Thus, in considering high school dropout rates, it is important to examine age, the number of

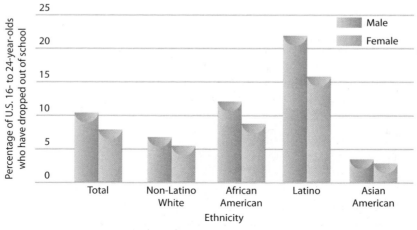

Figure 9.6 Trends in High School Dropout Rates
Source: National Center for Education Statistics (2010). *The condition education 2010.* Washington, D.C.: U.S. Department of Education.

years it takes to complete high school, and various contexts including ethnicity, gender, and school location.

service learning A form of education that promotes social responsibility and service to the community.

Students drop out of school for many reasons (Schoeneberger, 2012). In one study, almost 50 percent of the dropouts cited school-related reasons for leaving school, such as not liking school or being expelled or suspended (Rumberger, 1983). Twenty percent of the dropouts (but 40 percent of the Latino students) cited economic reasons for leaving school. One-third of the female students dropped out for personal reasons such as pregnancy or marriage.

According to a research review, the most effective programs to discourage dropping out of high school provide early reading programs, tutoring, counseling, and mentoring (Lehr & others, 2003). Clearly, then, early detection of children's school-related difficulties and getting children engaged with school in positive ways are important strategies for reducing the dropout rate (Fall & Roberts, 2012).

Service Learning

Service learning is a form of education that promotes social responsibility and service to the community. In service learning, adolescents engage in activities such as tutoring, helping older adults, working in a hospital, assisting at a child-care center, or cleaning up a vacant lot to make it into a play area. An important goal of service learning is to encourage adolescents to become less self-centered and more strongly motivated to help others (Zaff & others, 2010). Service learning is often more effective when two conditions are met (Nucci, 2006): (1) giving students some degree of choice in the service activities in which they participate, and (2) providing students opportunities to reflect about their participation.

Service learning takes education out into the community (Zaff & others, 2010). One eleventh-grade student worked as a reading tutor for students from low-income backgrounds with reading skills well below their grade levels. She commented that until she did the tutoring, she did not realize how many students had not experienced the same opportunities that she had when she was growing up. An especially rewarding moment was when one young girl told her, "I want to learn to read like you so I can go to college when I grow up." Thus, a key feature of service learning is that it benefits not only adolescents but also the recipients of their help.

What are some of the positive effects of service learning?

How Would You...?

As an educator, how would you devise a program to increase adolescents' motivation to participate in service learning?

Researchers have found that service learning also benefits adolescents in other ways (Gonsalves, 2011; Kielsmeier, 2011). Improvements in adolescent development related to service learning include higher grades in school, increased goal setting, higher self-esteem, an improved sense of being able to make a difference for others, and an increased likelihood that the adolescents will serve as volunteers in the future (Hart, Matsuba, & Atkins, 2008). One study found that adolescent girls participated in service learning more than did adolescent boys (Webster & Worrell, 2008).

Summary

The Nature of Adolescence

- Many stereotypes of adolescents are too negative. Most adolescents today successfully negotiate the path from childhood to adulthood. However, too many of today's adolescents are not provided with adequate opportunities and support to become competent adults. It is important to view adolescents as a heterogeneous group because different portraits of adolescents emerge, depending on the particular set of adolescents being described.

Physical Changes

- Puberty's determinants include nutrition, health, and heredity. Hormonal changes occurring in puberty are substantial. Puberty occurs approximately two years earlier for girls than for boys. Individual variation in pubertal changes is substantial. Adolescents show considerable interest in their body image, with girls having more negative body images than boys. Early-maturing girls are vulnerable to a number of risks.

- Changes in the brain during adolescence include an earlier maturation for the amygdala than the prefrontal cortex, as well as a thickening of the corpus callosum.

- Adolescence is a time of sexual exploration and sexual experimentation. About one in four sexually experienced adolescents acquires a sexually transmitted infection (STI). America's adolescent pregnancy rate is still too high.

Adolescent Health

- Adolescence is a critical juncture in health. Poor nutrition and lack of exercise are special concerns.

- Many adolescents stay up later than when they were children and are getting less sleep than they need.

- Accidents are the leading cause of death in adolescence.

- Although drug use in adolescence has declined in recent years, it still is a major concern.

- Eating disorders have increased in adolescence, with a substantial increase in the percentage of adolescents who are overweight. Two eating disorders that may emerge in adolescence are anorexia nervosa and bulimia nervosa.

Adolescent Cognition

- In Piaget's formal operational stage, thought is more abstract, idealistic, and logical than during the concrete operational stage. However, many adolescents are not formal operational thinkers.

- Adolescent egocentrism, which involves a heightened self-consciousness, reflects another cognitive change in adolescence.

- Changes in information processing in adolescence are mainly reflected in improved executive functioning, which includes advances in cognitive control and decision making.

Schools

- The transition to middle or junior high school is often stressful. One source of stress is the move from the top-dog to the lowest position in school.

- Some critics argue that a major redesign of U.S. middle schools is needed.

- The overall high school dropout rate declined considerably in the last half of the twentieth century, but the dropout rates for Native American and Latino adolescents remain very high.

- Service learning is linked to a number of positive benefits for adolescents.

Key Terms

10 Socioemotional Development in Adolescence

Stories of Life-Span Development: Jewel Cash, Teen Dynamo

The mayor of the city says she is "every-where." She recently persuaded the city's school committee to consider ending the practice of locking tardy students out of their classrooms. She also swayed a neighborhood group to support her proposal for a winter jobs program. According to one city councilman, "People are just impressed with the power of her arguments and the sophistication of the argument" (Silva, 2005, pp. B1, B4). She is Jewel E. Cash, and she is only 16 years old.

A junior at Boston Latin Academy, Jewel was raised in one of Boston's housing projects by her mother, a single parent. Today she is a member of the Boston Student Advisory Council, mentors children, volunteers at a women's shelter, manages and dances in two troupes, and is a member of a neighborhood watch group—among other activities. Jewel is far from typical, but her activities illustrate that cognitive and socioemotional development allows even adolescents to be capable, effective individuals.

Significant changes characterize socio-emotional development in adolescence. These changes include searching for identity. Changes also take place in the social contexts of adolescents' lives, with transformations occurring in relationships with families and peers in cultural contexts. Adolescents also may develop socioemotional problems such as delinquency and depression. ▪

Identity

Jewel Cash told an interviewer from the *Boston Globe*, "I see a problem and I say, 'How can I make a difference?'. . . I can't take on the world, even though I can try. . . . I'm moving forward but I want to make sure I'm bringing people with me" (Silva, 2005, pp. B1, B4). Jewel's confidence and positive identity sound at least as impressive as her activities. This section examines how adolescents develop characteristics like these. How well did you understand yourself during adolescence, and how did you acquire the stamp of your identity? Is your identity still developing?

Jewel Cash, seated next to her mother, participating in a crime watch meeting at a community center.

What Is Identity?

Questions about identity surface as common, virtually universal, concerns during adolescence. Some decisions made during adolescence might seem trivial: whom to date, whether or not to break up, which major to study, whether to study or play, whether or not to be politically active, and so on. Over the years of adolescence, however, such decisions begin to form the core of what the individual is all about as a human being—what is called his or her identity.

Identity is a self-portrait composed of many pieces, including these:

- The career and work path the person wants to follow (vocational/career identity)
- Whether the person is conservative, liberal, or middle-of-the-road (political identity)
- The person's spiritual beliefs (religious identity)
- Whether the person is single, married, divorced, and so on (relationship identity)
- The extent to which the person is motivated to achieve and is intellectually oriented (achievement, intellectual identity)
- Whether the person is heterosexual, homosexual, or bisexual (sexual identity)
- Which part of the world or country a person is from and how intensely the person identifies with his or her cultural heritage (cultural/ethnic identity)
- The kind of things a person likes to do, which can include sports, music, hobbies, and so on (interests)
- The individual's personality characteristics, such as being introverted or extraverted, anxious or calm, friendly or hostile, and so on (personality)
- The individual's body image (physical identity)

Synthesizing the identity components can be a lengthy process with many negations and affirmations of various roles and faces (Kroger, 2012). Identity development takes place in bits and pieces. Decisions are not made once

What are some important dimensions of identity?

and for all, but have to be made again and again. Identity development does not happen neatly, and it does not happen cataclysmically (Duriez & others, 2012; Schwartz & others, 2011, 2013).

Erikson's View

It was Erik Erikson (1950, 1968) who first understood that questions about identity are central to understanding adolescent development. Today, as a result of Erikson's masterful thinking and analysis, identity is considered a key aspect of adolescent development.

Erikson's theory was introduced in Chapter 1. Recall that his fifth developmental stage, which individuals experience during adolescence, is *identity versus identity confusion*. During this time, said Erikson, adolescents are faced with deciding who they are, what they are all about, and where they are going in life.

The search for an identity during adolescence is aided by a *psychosocial moratorium*, which is Erikson's term for the gap between childhood security and adult autonomy. During this period, society leaves adolescents relatively free of responsibilities and able to try out different identities. Adolescents in effect search their culture's identity files, experimenting with different roles and personalities. They may want to pursue one career one month (lawyer, for example) and another career the next month (doctor, actor, teacher, social worker, or astronaut, for example). They may dress neatly one day, sloppily the next. This experimentation is a deliberate effort on the part of adolescents to find out where they fit into the world. Most adolescents eventually discard undesirable roles.

Developmental Changes

Although questions about identity may be especially important during adolescence, identity formation neither begins nor ends during these years (McAdams & Cox, 2011). It begins with the appearance of attachment, the development of the sense of self, and the emergence of independence in infancy; the process reaches its final phase with a life review and integration in old age. What is important about identity development in adolescence, especially late adolescence, is that for the first time, physical development, cognitive development, and socioemotional development advance to the point at which the individual can begin to sort through and synthesize childhood identities and identifications to construct a viable path toward adult maturity.

How do individual adolescents go about the process of forming an identity? Eriksonian researcher James Marcia (1980, 1994) believes that Erikson's theory of identity development encompasses four *statuses* of identity, or ways of resolving the identity crisis: identity diffusion, identity foreclosure, identity moratorium, and identity achievement. What determines an individual's identity status? Marcia classifies individuals based on the existence or extent of their crisis or commitment (see Figure 10.1). **Crisis** is defined as a period of identity development during which the individual is exploring alternatives. Most researchers use the term *exploration* rather than crisis. **Commitment** is personal investment in identity.

The four statuses of identity are described as follows:

- **Identity diffusion** is the status of individuals who have not yet experienced a crisis or made any commitments. Not only are they undecided about occupational and ideological choices, they are also likely to show little interest in such matters.

- **Identity foreclosure** is the status of individuals who have made a commitment but have not experienced a crisis. This occurs most often when parents hand down commitments to their adolescents, usually in an authoritarian way, before adolescents have had a chance to explore different approaches, ideologies, and vocations on their own.

crisis Marcia's term for a period of identity development during which the adolescent is exploring alternatives.

commitment Marcia's term for the part of identity development in which adolescents show a personal investment in forming an identity.

identity diffusion Marcia's term for adolescents who have not yet experienced a crisis (explored meaningful alternatives) or made any commitments.

identity foreclosure Marcia's term for adolescents who have made a commitment but have not experienced a crisis.

| | Identity Status | | | |
Position on Occupation and Ideology	Identity Diffusion	Identity Foreclosure	Identity Moratorium	Identity Achievement
Crisis	Absent	Absent	Present	Present
Commitment	Absent	Present	Absent	Present

Figure 10.1 Marcia's Four Statuses of Identity
According to Marcia, an individual's status in developing an identity can be described as identity diffusion, identity foreclosure, identity moratorium, or identity achievement. The status depends on the presence or absence of (1) a crisis or exploration of alternatives and (2) a commitment to an identity. *What is the identity status of most young adolescents?*

- **Identity moratorium** is the status of individuals who are in the midst of a crisis but whose commitments are either absent or are only vaguely defined.
- **Identity achievement** is the status of individuals who have undergone a crisis and have made a commitment.

Researchers are developing a consensus that the key changes in identity are more likely to take place in emerging adulthood, the period from about 18 to 25 years of age (Moshman, 2011; Schwartz & others, 2013; Syed, 2013). For example, Alan Waterman (1985, 1992) has found that from the years preceding high school through the last few years of college, the number of individuals who are identity achieved increases, whereas the number of individuals who are identity diffused decreases. Many young adolescents are identity diffused. College upperclassmen are more likely than high school students or college freshmen to be identity achieved.

How Would You...?
As a psychologist, how would you apply Marcia's theory of identity formation to describe your current identity status or that of adolescents you know?

Why might college produce some key changes in identity? Increased complexity in the reasoning skills of college students combined with a wide range of new experiences that highlight contrasts between home and college and between themselves and others stimulate them to reach a higher level of integrating various dimensions of their identity (Phinney, 2008).

A recent meta-analysis of 124 studies revealed that during adolescence and emerging adulthood, identity moratorium status rose steadily to age 19 and then declined; identity achievement rose across late adolescence and emerging adulthood; and foreclosure and diffusion statuses declined across the high school years but fluctuated in the late teens and emerging adulthood (Kroger, Martinussen, & Marcia, 2010). The studies also found that a large portion of individuals were not identity achieved by the time they reached their twenties.

Resolution of the identity issue during adolescence and emerging adulthood does not mean that identity will be stable through the remainder of life (McAdams & Cox, 2011). Many individuals who develop positive identities follow what are called "MAMA" cycles; that is, their identity status changes from *m*oratorium to *a*chievement to *m*oratorium to *a*chievement (Marcia, 1994). These cycles may be repeated throughout life (Francis, Fraser, & Marcia, 1989). Marcia (2002) points out that the first identity is just that—it is not, and should not be regarded as, the final product.

Ethnic Identity

Throughout the world, ethnic minority groups have struggled to maintain their ethnic identities while blending in with the dominant

identity moratorium Marcia's term for adolescents who are in the midst of a crisis, but their commitments are either absent or vaguely defined.

identity achievement Marcia's term for adolescents who have undergone a crisis and have made a commitment.

culture (Erikson, 1968). **Ethnic identity** is an enduring aspect of the self that includes a sense of membership in an ethnic group, along with the attitudes and feelings related to that membership (Hudley & Irving, 2012). Most adolescents from ethnic minorities develop a *bicultural identity.* That is, they identify in some ways with their ethnic group and in other ways with the majority culture (Phinney, 2008).

For ethnic minority individuals, adolescence and emerging adulthood are often special junctures in their development (Syed, 2010, 2013). Although children are aware of some ethnic and cultural differences, individuals consciously confront their ethnicity for the first time in adolescence or emerging adulthood. Unlike children, adolescents and emerging adults have the ability to interpret ethnic and cultural information, to reflect on the past, and to speculate about the future. With their advancing cognitive skills of abstract thinking and self-reflection, adolescents (especially older adolescents) increasingly consider the meaning of their ethnicity and also have more ethnic-related experiences (O'Hara & others, 2012; Seaton & others, 2011). Because adolescents are more mobile and independent from their parents, they are more likely to experience ethnic stereotyping and discrimination as they interact with diverse individuals in school contexts and other public settings (Brody, Kogan, & Chen, 2012; Potochnick, Perreira, & Fuligni, 2012). Researchers have found that many ethnic minority groups experience stereotyping and discrimination, including African American, Latino, and Asian American adolescents (Roberts & others, 2012; Umana Taylor & others, 2012).

The indicators of identity change often differ for each succeeding generation (Phinney & Ong, 2007). First-generation immigrants are likely to be secure in their identities and unlikely to change much; they may or may not develop a new identity. The degree to which they begin to feel "American" appears to be related to whether or not they learn English, develop social networks beyond their ethnic group, and become culturally competent in their new country. Second-generation immigrants are more likely to

How Would You...?

As a human development and family studies professional, how would you design a community program that assists ethnic minority adolescents to develop a healthy bicultural identity?

think of themselves as "American," possibly because citizenship is granted at birth. Their ethnic identity is likely to be linked to retention of their ethnic language and social networks. In the third and later generations, the issues become more complex. Historical, contextual, and political factors that are unrelated to acculturation may affect the extent to which members of this generation retain their ethnic identities. For non-European ethnic groups, racism and discrimination influence whether ethnic identity is retained.

Families

Adolescence typically alters the relationship between parents and their children. Among the most important aspects of family relationships in adolescence are those that involve parental management and monitoring, autonomy and attachment, and parent-adolescent conflict.

Parental Management and Monitoring

A key aspect of the managerial role of parenting is effective monitoring, which is especially important as children move into the adolescent years (Smetana, 2010, 2011a, b). Monitoring includes supervising adolescents' choice of social settings, activities, and friends, as well as their academic efforts. Later in this chapter, we will describe lack of adequate parental monitoring as the parental factor most likely to be linked to juvenile delinquency.

A current interest involving parental monitoring focuses on adolescents' management of their parents' access to information, especially disclosing or concealing strategies regarding their activities (Amsel & Smetana, 2011; Rote & others, 2012). When parents engage in positive parenting practices, adolescents are more likely to disclose information (Rote & others, 2012). For example, disclosure increases when parents ask adolescents questions and when adolescents' relationship with parents is characterized by a high level of trust, acceptance, and quality (Keijsers & Laird, 2010). Researchers have found that adolescents' disclosure to parents about their whereabouts, activities, and friends is linked to positive adolescent adjustment (Laird & Marrero, 2010; Rote & others, 2012; Smetana, 2011a, b).

Autonomy and Attachment

With most adolescents, parents are likely to find themselves engaged in a delicate balancing act, weighing competing needs for autonomy and control, for independence and connection.

How Would You...?

As a social worker, how would you counsel a mother who is experiencing stress about anticipated family conflicts as her child enters adolescence?

The Push for Autonomy

The typical adolescent's push for autonomy and responsibility puzzles and angers many parents. As parents see their teenager slipping from their grasp, they may have an urge to take stronger control. Heated emotional exchanges may ensue, with either side calling names, making threats, and doing whatever seems necessary to gain control. Parents may feel frustrated because they *expect* their teenager to heed their advice, to want to spend time with the family, and to grow up to do what is right. Most parents anticipate that their teenager will have some difficulty adjusting to the changes that adolescence brings, but few parents imagine and predict just how strong an adolescent's desires will be to spend time with peers or how intensely adolescents will want to show that it is they—not their parents—who are responsible for their successes and failures.

Adolescents' ability to attain autonomy and gain control over their behavior is facilitated by appropriate adult reactions to their desire for control (McElhaney & Allen, 2012; Steinberg & Collins, 2011). At the onset of adolescence, the average individual does not have the knowledge to make appropriate or mature decisions in all areas of life. As the adolescent pushes for autonomy, the wise adult relinquishes control in those areas where the adolescent can make reasonable decisions, but continues to guide the adolescent to make reasonable decisions in areas in which the adolescent's knowledge is more limited. Gradually, adolescents acquire the ability to make mature decisions on their own.

Gender differences characterize autonomy-granting in adolescence. Boys are given more independence than girls. In one study, this was especially true in U.S. families with a traditional gender-role orientation (Bumpus, Crouter, & McHale, 2001). Also, Latino parents protect and monitor their daughters more closely than is the case for non-Latino parents (Updegraff & others, 2010).

What kinds of strategies can parents use to guide adolescents in effectively handling their increased motivation for autonomy?

Stacey Christensen, age 16: "I am lucky enough to have open communication with my parents. Whenever I am in need or just need to talk, my parents are there for me. My advice to parents is to let your teens grow at their own pace, be open with them so that you can be there for them. We need guidance; our parents need to help but not be too overwhelming."

The Role of Attachment

Recall from Chapter 4 that one of the most widely discussed aspects of socioemotional development in infancy is secure attachment to caregivers (Brisch, 2012; Easterbrooks & others, 2013). In the past decade, researchers have found that securely attached adolescents are less likely than those who are insecurely attached to have emotional difficulties and to engage in problem behaviors such as drug abuse and juvenile delinquency (Gorrese & Ruggieri, 2012; Schwarz, Stutz, & Ledermann, 2012). For example, Joseph Allen and his colleagues (2009) found that adolescents who were securely attached at age 14 were more likely to report that they were in an exclusive relationship, comfortable with intimacy in relationships, and increasing their financial independence at age 21. In a recent analysis, it was concluded that the most consistent outcomes of secure attachment in adolescence involve positive peer relations and development of the adolescent's emotion regulation capacities (Allen & Miga, 2010).

Parent-Adolescent Conflict

Although parent-adolescent conflict increases in early adolescence, it does not reach the tumultuous proportions G. Stanley Hall envisioned at the beginning of the twentieth century (Bornstein, Jager, & Steinberg, 2013). Rather, much of the conflict involves the everyday events of family life, such as keeping a bedroom clean, dressing neatly, getting home by a certain time, and not talking endlessly on the phone. The conflicts rarely involve major dilemmas such as drugs or delinquency.

Conflict with parents often escalates during early adolescence, remains somewhat stable during the high school years, and then lessens as the adolescent reaches 17 to 20 years of age. Parent-adolescent relationships become more positive if adolescents go away to college than if they attend college while living at home (Sullivan & Sullivan, 1980).

The everyday conflicts that characterize parent-adolescent relationships may actually serve a positive developmental function. These minor disputes and negotiations facilitate the adolescent's transition from being dependent on parents to becoming an autonomous individual. Recognizing that conflict and negotiation can serve a positive developmental function can tone down parental hostility.

The old model of parent-adolescent relationships suggested that as adolescents mature they detach themselves from parents and move into a world of autonomy apart from parents. The old model also suggested that parent-adolescent conflict is intense and stressful throughout adolescence. The new model emphasizes that parents serve as important attachment figures and support systems while adolescents explore a wider, more complex social world. The new model also emphasizes that in most families, parent-adolescent conflict is moderate rather than severe and that the everyday negotiations and minor disputes not only are normal but also can serve the positive developmental function of helping the adolescent make the transition from childhood dependency to adult independence (see Figure 10.2).

Old Model

Autonomy, detachment from parents; parent and peer worlds are isolated

Intense, stressful conflict throughout adolescence; parent-adolescent relationships are filled with storm and stress on virtually a daily basis

New Model

Attachment and autonomy; parents are important support systems and attachment figures; adolescent-parent and adolescent-peer worlds have some important connections

Moderate parent-adolescent conflict is common and can serve a positive developmental function; conflict greater in early adolescence

Figure 10.2 Old and New Models of Parent-Adolescent Relationships

Still, a high degree of conflict characterizes some parent-adolescent relationships (Schwarz, Stutz, & Ledermann, 2012). And this prolonged, intense conflict is associated with various adolescent problems: movement out of the home, juvenile delinquency, school dropout, pregnancy and early marriage, membership in religious cults, and drug abuse (Brook & others, 1990).

Peers

Peers play powerful roles in the lives of adolescents (Wentzel, 2013). When you think back to your own adolescent years, you probably recall many of your most enjoyable moments as experiences shared with peers. Peer relations undergo important changes in adolescence, including changes in friendships, peer groups, and the beginning of romantic relationships.

Friendships

For most children, being popular with their peers is a strong motivator. Beginning in early adolescence, however, teenagers typically prefer to have a smaller number of friendships that are more intense and intimate than those of young children.

Harry Stack Sullivan (1953) was the most influential theorist to discuss the importance of adolescent friendships. In contrast with other psychoanalytic theorists who focused almost exclusively on parent-child relationships, Sullivan argued that friends are also important in shaping the development of children and adolescents. Everyone, said Sullivan, has basic social needs, such as the need for tenderness (secure attachment), playful companionship, social acceptance, intimacy, and sexual relations. Whether or not these needs are fulfilled largely determines our emotional well-being. For example, if the need for playful companionship goes unmet, then we become bored and depressed; if the need for social acceptance is not met, we suffer a diminished sense of self-worth.

During adolescence, said Sullivan, friends become increasingly important in meeting social needs. In particular, Sullivan argued that the need for intimacy intensifies during early adolescence, motivating teenagers to seek out close friends. If adolescents fail to forge such close friendships, they experience loneliness and a reduced sense of self-worth. The nature of relationships with friends during adolescence can foreshadow the quality of romantic relationships in emerging adulthood. For example, a longitudinal study revealed that having more secure relationships with close friends at age 16 was linked with more positive romantic relationships at age 20 to 23 (Simpson & others, 2007).

Many of Sullivan's ideas have withstood the test of time. For example, adolescents report disclosing intimate and personal information to their friends more often than do younger children (Buhrmester, 1998) (see Figure 10.3). Adolescents also say they depend more on friends than on parents to satisfy

What changes take place in friendship during the adolescent years?

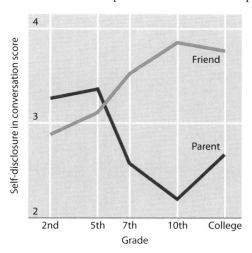

Figure 10.3 Developmental Changes in Self-Disclosing Conversations
Self-disclosing conversations with friends increased dramatically in adolescence while declining in an equally dramatic fashion with parents. However, self-disclosing conversations with parents began to pick up somewhat during the college years. The measure of self-disclosure involved a 5-point rating scale completed by the children and youth, with a higher score representing greater self-disclosure. The data shown represent the means for each age group.

clique A small group that ranges from 2 to about 12 individuals, averaging about 5 or 6 individuals, and often consists of adolescents who engage in similar activities.

their needs for companionship, reassurance of worth, and intimacy. The ups and downs of experiences with friends shape adolescents' well-being (Cook, Buehler, & Blair, 2012). Adolescent girls are more likely to disclose information about problems to a friend than are adolescent boys (Rose & others, 2012).

Developmental advantages occur when adolescents have friends who are socially skilled, supportive, and oriented toward academic achievement (Rodkin & Ryan, 2012). Positive friendship relationships in adolescence are associated with a host of positive outcomes, including lower rates of delinquency, substance abuse, risky sexual behavior, bullying, and victimization, and higher levels of academic achievement (Tucker & others, 2012; Way & Silverman, 2012; Wentzel, 2013).

Although most adolescents develop friendships with individuals who are close to their own age, some adolescents become best friends with younger or older individuals. Adolescents who interact with older youth engage in deviant behavior more frequently, but it is not known whether the older youth guide younger adolescents toward deviant behavior or whether the younger adolescents were already prone to deviant behavior before they developed friendships with older youth.

Peer Groups

How extensive is peer pressure in adolescence? What roles do cliques and crowds play in adolescents' lives? As we see next, researchers have found that the standards of peer groups and the influence of crowds and cliques become increasingly important during adolescence.

Peer Pressure

Young adolescents conform more to peer standards than children do. Around the eighth and ninth grades, conformity to peers—especially to their antisocial standards—peaks (Brown & Larson, 2009). At this point, adolescents are most likely to go along with a peer to steal hubcaps off a car, paint graffiti on a wall, or steal cosmetics from a store counter. One study found that U.S. adolescents are more likely than Japanese adolescents to put pressure on their peers to resist parental influence (Rothbaum & others, 2000). Adolescents are more likely to conform to their peers when they are uncertain about their social identity and when they are in the presence of someone they perceive to have higher status than they do (Prinstein & Dodge, 2010; Prinstein & others, 2009).

What characterizes adolescent cliques? How are they different from crowds?

Cliques and Crowds

Cliques and crowds assume more important roles during adolescence than during childhood (Brown, 2011; Brown & Larson, 2009). **Cliques** are small groups that range from 2 to about 12 individuals and average about 5 or 6 individuals. The clique members are usually of the same sex and about the same age.

Cliques can form because adolescents engage in similar activities, such as being in a club or on a sports team. Some cliques also form because of friendship. Several adolescents may form a clique because they have spent time with each other, share mutual interests, and enjoy each other's company. Not necessarily friends to start with, they often develop a friendship if they stay in the clique. What do adolescents do in cliques? They share ideas and hang out together. Often they develop an in-group identity in which they believe that their clique is better than other cliques.

Crowds are larger than cliques and less personal. Adolescents are usually members of a crowd based on reputation, and they may or may not spend much time together. Many crowds are defined by the activities adolescents engage in (such as "jocks" who are good at sports or "druggies" who take drugs).

crowd A larger group structure than a clique, a crowd is usually formed based on reputation, and members may or may not spend much time together.

Dating and Romantic Relationships

Adolescents spend considerable time either dating or thinking about dating (Shulman, Davila, & Shachar-Shapira, 2011). Dating can be a form of recreation, a source of status, a setting for learning about close relationships, and a way to find a mate.

Developmental Changes in Dating and Romantic Relationships

Three stages characterize the development of romantic relationships in adolescence (Connolly & McIsaac, 2009):

1. *Entering into romantic attractions and affiliations at about age 11 to 13.* This initial stage is triggered by puberty. From age 11 to 13, adolescents become intensely interested in romance and it dominates many conversations with same-sex friends. Developing a crush on someone is common, and the crush often is shared with a same-sex friend. Young adolescents may or may not interact with the individual who is the object of their infatuation. When dating occurs, it usually takes place in a group setting.

2. *Exploring romantic relationships at approximately age 14 to 16.* At this point in adolescence, two types of romantic involvement occur: (a) *Casual dating* emerges between individuals who are mutually attracted. These dating experiences are often short-lived, last a few months at best, and usually endure no longer than a few weeks. (b) *Dating in groups* is common and reflects the importance of peers in adolescents' lives. A friend often acts as a third-party facilitator of a potential dating relationship by communicating their friend's romantic interest and confirming whether the other person feels a similar attraction.

3. *Consolidating dyadic romantic bonds at about age 17 to 19.* At the end of the high school years, more serious romantic relationships develop. This is characterized by strong emotional bonds more closely resembling those in adult romantic relationships. These bonds often are more stable and enduring than earlier bonds, typically lasting one year or more.

What are some developmental changes in dating and romantic relationships in adolescence?

Two variations on these stages in the development of romantic relationships in adolescence involve early and late bloomers (Connolly & McIsaac, 2009). *Early bloomers* include 15 to 20 percent of 11- to 13-year-olds who say that they currently are in a romantic relationship and 35 percent who indicate that they have

had some prior experience in romantic relationships. *Late bloomers* comprise approximately 10 percent of 17- to 19-year-olds who say that they have had no experience with romantic relationships and another 15 percent who report that they have not engaged in any romantic relationships that lasted more than four months.

Dating in Gay and Lesbian Youth

Recently, researchers have begun to study romantic relationships among gay and lesbian youth (Diamond & Savin-Williams, 2011, 2013; Savin-Williams, 2013). Many sexual minority youth date other-sex peers, which can help them to clarify their sexual orientation or disguise it from others (Cohen & Savin-Williams, 2013). Most gay and lesbian youth have had some same-sex sexual experience, often with peers who are "experimenting," and then go on to a primarily heterosexual orientation (Diamond & Savin-Williams, 2011, 2013; Vrangalova & Savin-Williams, 2013).

What are some ethnic variations in dating during adolescence?

Sociocultural Contexts and Dating

The sociocultural context exerts a powerful influence on adolescents' dating patterns (Cheng & others, 2012; Holloway & others, 2012). This influence may be seen in differences in dating patterns among ethnic groups within the United States. Values, religious beliefs, and traditions often dictate the age at which dating begins, how much freedom in dating is allowed, whether dates must be chaperoned by adults or parents, and the roles of males and females in dating. For example, Latino and Asian American cultures have more conservative standards regarding adolescent dating than does the Anglo-American culture. Dating may become a source of conflict within a family if the parents have immigrated from cultures in which dating begins at a late age, little freedom in dating is allowed, dates are chaperoned, and dating is especially restricted for adolescent girls. When immigrant adolescents choose to adopt the ways of the dominant U.S. culture (such as unchaperoned dating), they often clash with parents and extended-family members who have more traditional values.

Dating and Adjustment

Researchers have linked dating and romantic relationships with various measures of how well adjusted adolescents are (Connolly & McIsaac, 2009). For example, one study of 200 tenth-graders revealed that the more romantic experiences they had

How Would You...?

As a psychologist, how would you explain the risks of dating and romantic relationships during early adolescence?

had, the more likely they were to report high levels of social acceptance, friendship competence, and romantic competence; however, having more romantic experience also was linked to a higher level of substance use, delinquency, and sexual behavior (Furman, Low, & Ho, 2009). Another study of adolescent girls found that those who engaged in *co-rumination* (excessive discussion of problems with friends) were more likely to be involved in a romantic relationship, and together co-rumination and romantic involvement predicted an increase in depressive symptoms (Starr & Davila, 2009). And in a study conducted among adolescent girls but not adolescent males, having an older romantic partner was linked to an increase in depressive symptoms, largely influenced by an increase in substance use (Haydon & Halpern, 2010).

Dating and romantic relationships at an early age can be especially problematic (Connolly & McIsaac, 2009). A recent study found that romantic activity was linked to depression in early adolescent girls (Starr & others, 2012). Researchers also have found that early dating and "going with" someone are linked with adolescent pregnancy and problems at home and school (Florsheim, Moore, & Edgington, 2003).

Culture and Adolescent Development

We live in an increasingly diverse world, one that includes more extensive contact between adolescents from different cultures and ethnic groups. In this section, we explore these differences as they relate to adolescents. We explore how adolescents in various cultures spend their time, and some of the rites of passage they undergo. We also examine how ethnicity and the media affect U.S. adolescents and influence their development.

Asian Indian adolescents in a marriage ceremony.

Cross-Cultural Comparisons

What traditions remain for adolescents around the globe? What circumstances are changing adolescents' lives?

Traditions and Changes in Adolescence Around the Globe

Depending on the culture being observed, adolescence may involve many different experiences (Arnett, 2012).

Health Adolescent health and well-being have improved in some respects but not in others. Overall, fewer adolescents around the world die from infectious diseases and malnutrition now than in the past (UNICEF, 2012). However, a number of adolescent health-compromising behaviors (especially illicit drug use and unprotected sex) are increasing in frequency. Extensive increases in the rates of HIV in adolescents have occurred in many sub-Saharan countries (UNICEF, 2012).

Muslim school in Middle East with boys only.

How Would You...?
As a health-care professional, how would you explain to policy makers and insurance providers the importance of cultural context when creating guidelines for adolescent health coverage?

Gender Around the world, the experiences of male and female adolescents continue to be quite different (Larson, Wilson, & Rickman, 2009). Except in a few regions such as Japan, the Philippines, and Western countries, males have far greater access to educational opportunities than females do (UNICEF, 2012). In many countries, adolescent females have less freedom than males to pursue a variety of careers and engage in various leisure activities. Gender differences in sexual expression are widespread, especially in India, Southeast Asia, Latin America, and Arab countries where there are far more restrictions on the sexual activity of adolescent females than on that of males. These gender differences do appear to be narrowing over time, however. In some countries,

Street youth in Rio de Janeiro.

rite of passage A ceremony or ritual that marks an individual's transition from one status to another. Most rites of passage focus on the transition to adult status.

educational and career opportunities for women are expanding, and control over adolescent girls' romantic and sexual relationships is weakening.

Family In some countries, adolescents grow up in closely knit families with extensive extended-kin networks that retain a traditional way of life. For example, in Arab countries, "adolescents are taught strict codes of conduct and loyalty" (Brown & Larson, 2002, p. 6). However, in Western countries such as the United States, parenting is less authoritarian than in the past, and much larger numbers of adolescents are growing up in divorced families and stepfamilies.

In many countries around the world, current trends "include greater family mobility, migration to urban areas, family members working in distant cities or countries, smaller families, fewer extended-family households, and increases in mothers' employment" (Brown & Larson, 2002, p. 7). Unfortunately, many of these changes may reduce the ability of families to spend time with their adolescents.

Peers Some cultures give peers a stronger role in adolescence than other cultures do (Brown & Larson, 2002). In most Western nations, peers figure prominently in adolescents' lives, in some cases taking on roles that are otherwise assumed by parents. Among street youth in South America, the peer network serves as a surrogate family that supports survival in dangerous and stressful settings. In other regions of the world, such as in Arab countries, peer relations are restricted, especially for girls (Booth, 2002).

Adolescents' lives, then, are shaped by a combination of change and tradition. Researchers have found both similarities and differences in the experiences of adolescents in different countries (Larson & Angus, 2011; Larson & Dawes, 2013).

Rites of Passage

Another variation in the experiences of adolescents in different cultures is whether the adolescents go through a rite of passage. Some societies have elaborate ceremonies that signal the adolescent's move to maturity and achievement of adult status (Kottak, 2009). A **rite of passage** is a ceremony or ritual that marks an individual's transition from one status to another. Most rites of passage focus on the transition to adult status. In many primitive cultures, rites of passage are the avenue through which adolescents gain access to sacred adult practices, to knowledge, and to sexuality. These rites often involve dramatic practices intended to facilitate the adolescent's separation from the immediate family, especially the mother. The transformation is usually characterized by some form of ritual death and rebirth, or by means of contact with the spiritual world. Bonds are forged between the adolescent and the adult instructors through shared rituals, hazards, and secrets to allow the adolescent to enter the adult world. This kind of ritual provides a forceful and discontinuous entry into the adult world at a time when the adolescent is perceived to be ready for the change.

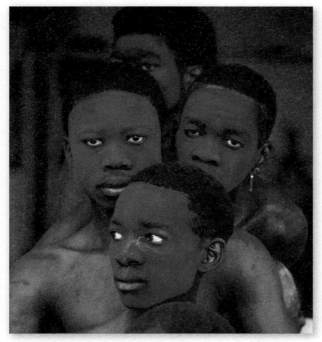

These Congolese Kota boys painted their faces as part of a rite of passage to adulthood. *What rites of passage do American adolescents have?*

An especially rich tradition of rites of passage for adolescents has prevailed in African cultures, especially sub-Saharan

Africa. Under the influence of Western industrialized culture, many of these rites are disappearing today, although they are still prevalent in locations where formal education is not readily available.

Do we have such rites of passage for American adolescents? We certainly do not have universal formal ceremonies that mark the passage from adolescence to adulthood. Certain religious and social groups do, however, have initiation ceremonies that indicate that an advance in maturity has been reached: the Jewish bar and bat mitzvah, the Catholic confirmation, and social debuts, for example. School graduation ceremonies come the closest to being culture-wide rites of passage in the United States. The high school graduation ceremony has become nearly universal for middle-class adolescents and increasing numbers of adolescents from low-income backgrounds.

How Would You...?

As an educator, how would you modify high school graduation to make it a more meaningful rite of passage for adolescents in the United States?

Ethnicity

Earlier in this chapter we explored the identity development of ethnic minority adolescents. Here, we further examine immigration and the relationship between ethnicity and socioeconomic status.

Immigration

Relatively high rates of immigration are contributing to the growth of ethnic minorities in the United States. Immigrants often experience stressors uncommon to or less prominent among longtime residents such as language barriers, dislocations and separations from support networks, changes in socioeconomic status (SES), and the dual struggle to preserve identity and to acculturate (Urdan, 2012).

Recent research indicates that many members of families that have recently immigrated to the United States adopt a bicultural orientation, selecting characteristics of the U.S. culture that help them to survive and advance, while still retaining aspects of their culture of origin. Immigration also involves cultural brokering, which has increasingly occurred in the United States as children and adolescents serve as mediators (cultural and linguistic) for their immigrant parents (Villanueva & Buriel, 2010).

In adopting characteristics of the U.S. culture, Latino families are increasingly embracing the importance of education. Although their school dropout rates have remained higher than for other ethnic groups, toward the end of the first decade of the twenty-first century they declined considerably (National Center for Education Statistics, 2010). In retaining positive aspects of their culture of origin, as research by Ross Parke and his colleagues (2011) indicates, Latino families maintain a strong commitment to family when they immigrate to the United States, even in the face of dealing with low-paying jobs and challenges in advancing economically. For example, divorce rates for Latino families are lower than for non-Latino White families of similar socioeconomic status.

What are some cultural adaptations these Mexican American girls likely have made as immigrants to the United States?

Ethnicity and Socioeconomic Status

Much of the research on ethnic minority adolescents has failed to tease apart the influences of ethnicity and socioeconomic status (SES). These factors can interact in ways that exaggerate the influence of ethnicity because ethnic minority individuals are overrepresented in the lower socioeconomic levels of American society (Chen & Brooks-Gunn, 2012;

Wright & others, 2012). Consequently, researchers too often have given ethnic explanations for aspects of adolescent development that were largely attributable to SES.

Not all ethnic minority families are poor. However, poverty contributes to the stressful life experiences of many ethnic minority adolescents (Way & Silverman, 2012). Thus, many ethnic minority adolescents experience a double disadvantage: (1) prejudice, discrimination, and bias because of their ethnic minority status; and (2) the stressful effects of poverty (Seaton & others, 2011).

Although some ethnic minority youth come from middle-income backgrounds, economic advantage does not entirely enable them to escape the prejudice, discrimination, and bias associated with being a member of an ethnic minority group (Duncan, 2012; Duncan & others, 2013). Even Japanese Americans, who are often characterized as a "model minority" because of their strong achievement orientation and family cohesiveness, still experience stress associated with ethnic minority status.

The Media

The culture adolescents experience involves not only cultural values, SES, and ethnicity, but also media influences (Hogan, 2012; Jackson & others, 2012). To better understand various aspects of U.S. adolescents' media use, the Kaiser Family Foundation funded national surveys in 1999, 2004, and 2009. The 2009 survey documented that adolescent media use had increased dramatically in the past decade (Rideout, Foehr, & Roberts, 2010). Today's youth live in a world in which they are encapsulated by media. In this 2009 survey, 8- to 11-year-olds used media 5 hours and 29 minutes a day, but 11- to 14-year-olds used media an average of 8 hours and 40 minutes a day, and 15- to 18-year-olds an average of 7 hours and 58 minutes a day. Thus, media use jumps more than 3 hours in early adolescence! Adding up the daily media use figures to obtain weekly media use leads to the staggering levels of more than 60 hours a week of media use by 11- to 14-year-olds and almost 56 hours a week by 15- to 18-year-olds!

A major trend in the use of technology is the dramatic increase in media multitasking (Pea & others, 2012). In the 2009 survey, when the amount of time spent multitasking was included in computing media use, 11- to 14-year-olds spent nearly 12 hours a day (compared with almost 9 hours a day when multitasking was not included) exposed to media (Rideout, Foehr, & Roberts, 2010)! A recent study of 8- to 12-year-old girls also found that a higher level of media multitasking was linked to negative social well-being while a higher level of face-to-face communication was associated with positive social well-being indicators, such as greater social success, feeling more normal, and having fewer friends whom parents thought were a bad influence (Pea & others, 2012).

Mobile media, such as cell phones and iPods, are mainly driving the increased media use by adolescents. For example, in the 2004 survey, only 18 percent of youth owned an iPod or MP3 player but in 2009, 76 percent owned them; in 2004, 39 percent owned a cell phone, a figure that jumped to 66 percent in 2009 (Rideout, Foehr, & Roberts, 2010).

The digitally mediated social environment of adolescents and emerging adults includes e-mail, instant messaging, social networking sites such as Facebook, chat rooms, videosharing and photosharing, multiplayer online computer games, and virtual worlds (Gross, 2013; Levinson, 2013). The remarkable increase in the popularity of Facebook was reflected in its replacement of Google in 2010 as the most frequently visited Internet site. Most of these digitally mediated social interactions began on computers but more recently have also shifted to cell phones, especially smartphones (Underwood & others, 2012; Valkenburg & Peter, 2011).

What are some trends in adolescents' media use?

A national survey revealed dramatic increases in adolescents' use of social media and text messaging (Lenhart & others, 2010). In 2009, nearly three-fourths of U.S. 12- to 17-year-olds reported using social networking sites. Eighty-one percent of 18- to 24-year-olds had created a profile on a social networking site and 31 percent of them visited a social networking site several times a day. More emerging adult women visit a social networking site several times a day (33 percent) than do their male counterparts (24 percent).

Text messaging has become the main way that adolescents connect with their friends, surpassing face-to-face contact, e-mail, instant messaging, and voice calling (Lenhart & others, 2010). However, voice mailing is the primary way that most adolescents prefer to connect with parents.

These recent studies explored the role of parents in guiding adolescents' use of the Internet and media:

- Both maternal and paternal authoritative parenting predicted proactive monitoring of adolescent media use, including restriction of certain media from adolescent use and parent-adolescent discussion of exposure to questionable media content (Padilla-Walker & Coyne, 2011).

- Problematic mother-adolescent (age 13) relationships that involved undermining attachment and autonomy predicted emerging adults' preference for online communication and greater probability of forming a poor-quality relationship with someone met online (Szwedo, Mikami, & Allen, 2011).

Adolescent Problems

In Chapter 9, we described several adolescent problems: substance abuse, sexually transmitted infections, and eating disorders. In this chapter, we examine the problems of juvenile delinquency, depression, and suicide. We also explore interrelationships among adolescent problems and how such problems can be prevented or remedied.

Juvenile Delinquency

The label **juvenile delinquent** is applied to an adolescent who breaks the law or engages in behavior that is considered illegal. Like other categories of disorders, juvenile delinquency is a broad concept; legal infractions range from littering to murder. Because the adolescent technically becomes a juvenile delinquent only after being judged guilty of a crime by a court of law, official records do not accurately reflect the number of illegal acts juvenile delinquents commit.

Males are more likely to engage in delinquency than females are. However, delinquency caseloads involving females increased from 19 percent in 1985 to 27 percent in 2005 (Puzzanchera & Sickmund, 2008).

Delinquency rates among minority groups and lower-socioeconomic-status youth are especially high in proportion to the overall population of these groups. However, such groups have less influence over the judicial decision-making process in the United States and therefore may be judged delinquent more readily than their White, middle-socioeconomic-status counterparts.

Causes of Delinquency

What causes delinquency? Many causes have been proposed, including heredity, identity problems, community influences, and family experiences. Erik Erikson (1968), for example, argues that adolescents whose development has restricted them from acceptable social roles, or made them feel that they cannot measure up to the demands placed on them, may choose a negative identity. Adolescents with a negative identity may find support for their delinquent image among peers, reinforcing the negative identity. For Erikson, delinquency is an attempt to establish an identity, even if it is a negative one.

juvenile delinquent An adolescent who breaks the law or engages in behavior that is considered illegal.

Although delinquency is less exclusively a phenomenon of lower socioeconomic status (SES) than it was in the past, some characteristics of lower-SES culture might promote delinquency (Ghazarian & Roche, 2010). The norms of many lower-SES peer groups and gangs are antisocial, or counterproductive to the goals and norms of society at large. Getting into or staying out of trouble are prominent features of life for some adolescents in low-income neighborhoods (Thio, 2010). A recent study found that youth whose families had experienced repeated poverty were more than twice as likely to be delinquent at 14 and 21 years of age (Najman & others, 2010).

Certain characteristics of family support systems are also associated with delinquency (Tolou-Shams & others, 2012; Van Ryzin & Dishion, 2012). Parental monitoring of adolescents is especially important in determining whether an adolescent becomes a delinquent (Fosco & others, 2012). A recent study found that early parental monitoring in adolescence and ongoing parental support were linked to a lower incidence of criminal behavior in emerging adulthood (Johnson & others, 2011). Further, recent research indicates that family therapy is often effective in reducing delinquency (Baldwin & others, 2012; Henggeler & Sheidow, 2012). A recent meta-analysis found that of five program types (case management, individual treatment, youth court, restorative justice, and family treatment), family treatment was the only one that was linked to a reduction in recidivism for juvenile offenders (Schwalbe & others, 2012).

An increasing number of studies have found that siblings can influence whether an adolescent becomes a delinquent (Bank, Burraston, & Snyder, 2004). And having delinquent friends and hanging out with delinquent peers greatly increases the risk of becoming delinquent (Fosco, Frank, & Dishion, 2012).

Rodney Hammond is an individual whose goal is to help at-risk adolescents, such as juvenile delinquents, cope more effectively with their lives. Read about his work in *Careers in Life-Span Development*.

How Would You...?

As a social worker, how would you apply your knowledge of juvenile delinquency and adolescent development to improve the juvenile justice system?

Careers in life-span development

Rodney Hammond, Health Psychologist

In describing his college experiences, Rodney Hammond said:

> When I started as an undergraduate at the University of Illinois, Champaign-Urbana, I hadn't decided on my major. But to help finance my education, I took a part-time job in a child development research program sponsored by the psychology department. There, I observed inner-city children in settings designed to enhance their learning. I saw firsthand the contribution psychology can make, and I knew I wanted to be a psychologist. (American Psychological Association, 2003, p. 26)

Rodney Hammond, counseling an adolescent girl about the risks of adolescence and how to effectively cope with them.

Depression and Suicide

What is the nature of depression in adolescence? What causes an adolescent to commit suicide?

Depression

How extensive is depression in adolescence? Rates of ever experiencing major depressive disorder range from 15 to 20 percent for adolescents (Graber & Sontag, 2009). By about age 15, adolescent females have a rate of depression that is twice that of adolescent males. Among the reasons for this gender difference are that females tend to ruminate in their depressed mood and amplify it; females' self-images, especially their body images, are more negative than males'; females face more discrimination than males do; and puberty occurs earlier for girls than for boys (Nolen-Hoeksema, 2011, 2012).

Do gender differences in adolescent depression hold for other cultures? In many cultures the gender difference of females experiencing more depression does hold, but a recent study of more than 17,000 Chinese 11- to 22-year-olds revealed that the male adolescents and emerging adults experienced more depression than their female counterparts (Sun & others, 2010). Explanation of the greater depression by males in China focused on stressful life events and a less positive coping style.

Genes are linked to adolescent depression (Hansell & others, 2012). A recent study found that certain dopamine-related genes were associated with depressive symptoms in adolescents (Adkins & others, 2012). And another recent study revealed that the link between adolescent girls' perceived stress and depression occurred only when the girls had the short version of the serotonin-related gene—5HTTLPR (Beaver & others, 2012).

Certain family factors place adolescents at risk for developing depression (Kitts & Goldman, 2012). These include having a depressed parent, emotionally unavailable parents, parents who have high marital conflict, and parents with financial problems. A recent study also revealed that mother-adolescent co-rumination, especially when focused on their mother's problems, were linked to adolescents' depression (Waller & Rose, 2010).

Poor peer relationships also are associated with adolescent depression (Vanhalst & others, 2012). Not having a close relationship with a best friend, having less contact with friends, having friends who are depressed, and experiencing peer

Rodney Hammond went on to obtain a doctorate in school and community psychology with a focus on children's development. For a number of years, he trained clinical psychologists at Wright State University in Ohio and directed a program to reduce violence in ethnic minority youth. There, he and his associates taught at-risk youth how to use social skills to effectively manage conflict and to recognize situations that could lead to violence. Today, Rodney is Director of Violence Prevention at the Centers for Disease Control and Prevention in Atlanta, Georgia. Rodney says that if you are interested in people and problem solving, psychology is a wonderful way to put these subjects together.

School psychology was one of Rodney Hammond's doctoral concentrations. School psychologists focus on improving the psychological and intellectual well-being of elementary, middle/junior, and high school students. They give psychological tests, interview students and their parents, consult with teachers, and may provide counseling to students and their families. They may work in a centralized office in a school district or in one or more schools. School psychologists usually have a master's or doctoral degree in school psychology. In graduate school, they take courses in counseling, assessment, learning, and other areas of education and psychology.

rejection all increase depressive tendencies in adolescents (Brendgen & others, 2010). Another recent study found that relational aggression was linked to depression for girls (Spieker & others, 2012). And as indicated earlier in this chapter, problems in adolescent romantic relationships can also trigger depression (Starr & others, 2012).

What type of treatment is most likely to reduce depression in adolescence? A recent research review concluded that drug therapy using serotonin reuptake inhibitors, cognitive behavior therapy, and interpersonal therapy are effective in treating adolescent depression (Maalouf & Brent, 2012). However, in this review, the most effective treatment was a combination of drug therapy and cognitive behavior therapy.

Suicide

What are some characteristics of adolescents who become depressed? What are some factors that are linked with suicide attempts by adolescents?

Suicide behavior is rare in childhood but escalates in adolescence and then increases further in emerging adulthood (Park & others, 2006). Suicide is the third-leading cause of death in 10- to 19-year-olds today in the United States (National Center for Health Statistics, 2012). Approximately 4,400 adolescents commit suicide each year (Eaton & others, 2010).

Although a suicide threat should always be taken seriously, far more adolescents contemplate or attempt it unsuccessfully than actually commit it. In the last two decades there has been a considerable decline in the percentage of adolescents who think about committing suicide, although from 2009 to 2011 this percentage increased from 14 to 16 percent (Youth Risk Behavior Survey, 2011). This national study found that in 2011, 8 percent of adolescents attempted suicide and 2 percent engaged in suicide attempts that required medical attention.

Females are more likely to attempt suicide than males, but males are more likely to succeed in committing suicide. Males use more lethal means, such as guns, in their suicide attempts, whereas adolescent females are more likely to cut their wrists or take an overdose of sleeping pills—methods less likely to result in death.

What is the psychological profile of the suicidal adolescent? Suicidal adolescents often have depressive symptoms. Although not all depressed adolescents are suicidal, depression is the most frequently cited factor

How Would You…?

As a psychologist, how would you talk with an adolescent who has just threatened suicide?

associated with adolescent suicide (Thapar & others, 2012). Further, a study indicated that adolescents who used alcohol while they were sad or depressed were at risk for attempting suicide (Schilling & others, 2009). A recent study also found that the strongest link between self-reported adolescent suicide attempts and drug use was any lifetime use of tranquilizers or sedatives (Kokkevi & others, 2012). Another recent study revealed that family support, peer support, and community connectedness was linked to a lower risk of suicidal tendencies in African American adolescents (Matlin, Molock, & Tebes, 2011). And in yet another study, sexual victimization was linked to a risk for suicide attempts in adolescence (Plener, Singer, & Goldbeck, 2011). Further, as discussed in Chapter 8, being victimized by bullying is associated with suicide-related thoughts and behaviour (McMahon & others, 2012).

The Interrelation of Problems and Successful Prevention/Intervention Programs

We have described some of the major adolescent problems in this chapter and in Chapter 9, including substance abuse; juvenile delinquency; school-related problems such as dropping out of school; adolescent pregnancy and sexually transmitted infections; eating disorders; depression; and suicide. The four problems that affect the most adolescents are (1) drug abuse, (2) juvenile delinquency, (3) sexual problems, and (4) school-related problems (Dryfoos, 1990; Dryfoos & Barkin, 2006). The adolescents most at risk have more than one of these problems.

Researchers are increasingly finding that problem behaviors in adolescence are interrelated (Milburn & others, 2012; Passini, 2012). For example, heavy substance abuse is related to early sexual activity, lower grades, dropping out of school, and delinquency (Marti, Stice, & Springer, 2010; Tull & others, 2012). Early initiation of sexual activity is associated with the use of cigarettes and alcohol, the use of marijuana and other illicit drugs, lower grades, dropping out of school, and delinquency (Harden & Mendle, 2011). Delinquency is related to early sexual activity, early pregnancy, substance abuse, and dropping out of school (Pedersen & Mastekaasa, 2011). As many as 10 percent of adolescents in the United States have been estimated to engage in all four of these problem behaviors (for example, adolescents who have dropped out of school are behind in their grade level, are users of heavy drugs, regularly use cigarettes and marijuana, and are sexually active but do not use contraception). In 1990, it was estimated that another 15 percent of high-risk youth engage in two or three of the four main problem behaviors (Dryfoos, 1990). Recently, this figure was increased to 20 percent of all U.S. adolescents (Dryfoos & Barkin, 2006).

What are some strategies for preventing and intervening in adolescent problems?

A review of the programs that have been successful in preventing or reducing adolescent problems found these common components (Dryfoos, 1990; Dryfoos & Barkin, 2006):

1. *Intensive individualized attention.* In successful programs, high-risk adolescents are attached to a responsible adult who gives the adolescent attention and deals with the adolescent's specific needs. This theme occurs in a number of programs. In a successful substance-abuse program, a student assistance counselor is available full-time for individual counseling and referral for treatment.

2. *Community-wide multiagency collaborative approaches.* The basic philosophy of community-wide programs is that a number of different programs and services have to be in place. In one successful substance-abuse program, a community-wide health promotion campaign has been implemented that uses local media and community education in concert with a substance-abuse curriculum in the schools.

3. *Early identification and intervention.* Reaching younger children and their families before children develop problems, or at the onset of their problems, is a successful strategy (Miller & others, 2010). One preschool program serves as an excellent model for the prevention of delinquency, pregnancy, substance abuse, and dropping out of school. Operated by the High/Scope Foundation in Ypsilanti, Michigan, the Perry Preschool has had a long-term positive impact on its students. This enrichment program, directed by David Weikart, serves disadvantaged African American children. They attend a high-quality, two-year preschool program and receive weekly home visits from program personnel. Based on official police records, by age 19, individuals who had attended the Perry Preschool program were less likely to

have been arrested and reported fewer adult offenses than a control group did. The Perry Preschool students also were less likely to drop out of school, and teachers rated their social behavior as more competent than that of a control group who had not received the enriched preschool experience (High/Scope Resource, 2005).

Summary

Identity

- Identity is a self-portrait composed of many pieces.
- Identity versus identity confusion is Erikson's fifth stage of the human life span, which individuals experience during adolescence.
- James Marcia proposed four identity statuses—identity diffusion, foreclosure, moratorium, and achievement—that are based on crisis (exploration) and commitment. Increasingly, experts argue that the main changes in identity occur in emerging adulthood rather than adolescence.
- Ethnicity is an important influence on identity.

Families

- A key aspect of the managerial role of parenting in adolescence is effectively monitoring the adolescent's development. Adolescents' disclosure to parents about their whereabouts is linked to positive adolescent adjustment.
- The adolescent's push for autonomy is one of the hallmarks of adolescence. Attachment to parents increases the probability that an adolescent will be socially competent.
- Parent-adolescent conflict increases in adolescence. The conflict is usually moderate rather than severe.

Peers

- Harry Stack Sullivan argued that there is a dramatic increase in the psychological importance and intimacy of close friends in early adolescence. Peer conformity and cliques and crowds assume more importance in adolescence.

- Three stages characterize adolescent dating and romantic relationships. Many gay and lesbian youth date other-sex peers. Culture can exert a powerful influence on adolescent dating. Some aspects of dating and romantic relationships are linked to adjustment difficulties.

Culture and Adolescent Development

- Adolescent development varies across cultures, and rites of passage still characterize adolescents in some cultures.
- Immigration is an important aspect of many ethnic adolescents' lives. Although not all ethnic minority families are poor, poverty contributes to the stress experienced by many ethnic minority adolescents.
- There has been a dramatic increase in adolescents' media multitasking and use of the Internet for social connections.

Adolescent Problems

- Juvenile delinquency is a major problem in adolescence. Numerous causes have been proposed to explain delinquency.
- Adolescents have a higher rate of depression than children, and females have a much higher rate of depression than males. Adolescent suicide is the third leading cause of death in U.S. adolescents, and numerous factors are linked to suicide.
- Researchers are increasingly finding that problem behaviors in adolescence are interrelated, and common components characterize successful programs designed to prevent or reduce adolescent problems.

Key Terms

crisis 276
commitment 276
identity diffusion 276

identity foreclosure 276
identity moratorium 277
identity achievement 277

ethnic identity 278
clique 282
crowd 283

rite of passage 286
juvenile delinquent 289

Physical and Cognitive Development in Early Adulthood

11

Stories of Life-Span Development: Dave Eggers, Pursuing a Career in the Face of Stress

He was a senior in college when both of his parents died of cancer within five weeks of each other. What would he do? He and his 8-year-old brother left Chicago to live in California, where his older sister was entering law school. Dave would take care of his younger brother, but he needed a job. That first summer, he took a class in furniture painting; then he worked for a geologi-

cal surveying company, re-creating maps on a computer. Soon, though, he did something very different: With friends from high school, Dave Eggers started *Might*, a satirical magazine for twenty-somethings. It was an edgy, highly acclaimed publication, but not a money-maker. After a few years, Eggers had to shut down the magazine, and he abandoned California for New York.

This does not sound like a promising start for a career. But within a decade after his parents' death, Eggers had not only raised his young brother but had also founded a quarterly journal and Web site, *McSweeney's*, and had written a best-seller, *A Heartbreaking Work of Staggering Genius*, which received the National Book Critics Circle Award and was nominated for a Pulitzer Prize. It is a slightly

fictionalized account of Eggers' life as he helped care for his dying mother, raised his brother, and searched for his own place in the world. Despite the pain of his loss and the responsibility for his brother, Eggers quickly built a record of achievement as a young adult. ▪

The Transition from Adolescence to Adulthood

When does an adolescent become an adult? In Chapter 9, we saw that it is not easy to tell when a girl or a boy enters adolescence. The task of determining when an individual becomes an adult is more difficult.

Dave Eggers, talented and insightful author.

Becoming an Adult

For most individuals, becoming an adult involves a lengthy transition period. The transition from adolescence to adulthood has been referred to as **emerging adulthood,** which occurs from approximately 18 to 25 years of age (Arnett, 2006, 2010, 2012). Experimentation and exploration characterize the emerging adult. At this point in their development, many individuals are still exploring which career path they want to follow, what they want their identity to be, and which lifestyle they want to adopt (for example, being single, cohabiting, or getting married).

Key Features of Emerging Adulthood

Jeffrey Arnett (2006) has concluded that five key features characterize emerging adulthood:

- *Identity exploration, especially in love and work.* Emerging adulthood is the time during which key changes in identity take place for many individuals (Kroger, 2012; Schwarz & others, 2013).
- *Instability.* Residential changes peak during early adulthood, a time during which there also is often instability in love, work, and education.
- *Self-focused.* According to Arnett (2006, p. 10), emerging adults "are self-focused in the sense that they have little in the way of social obligations, little in the way of duties and commitments to others, which leaves them with a great deal of autonomy in running their own lives."
- *Feeling in-between.* Many emerging adults don't consider themselves adolescents or full-fledged adults.
- *The age of possibilities, a time when individuals have an opportunity to transform their lives.* Arnett (2006) describes two ways in which emerging adulthood is the age of possibilities: (1) many emerging adults are optimistic about their future; and (2) for emerging adults who have experienced difficult times while growing up, emerging adulthood presents an opportunity to reorient their lives in a more positive direction.

Recent research indicates that these five aspects characterize not only individuals in the United States as they make the transition from adolescence to early adulthood, but also their counterparts in European countries and Australia (Arnett, 2012; Buhl & Lanz, 2007; Sirsch & others, 2009). Although emerging adulthood does not characterize development in all cultures, it does appear to occur in those where assuming adult roles and responsibilities is postponed (Kins & Beyers, 2010). Criticism of the concept of emerging adulthood is that it applies mainly to privileged adolescents and is not always a self-determined choice

emerging adulthood The transition from adolescence to adulthood (approximately 18 to 25 years of age), which involves experimentation and exploration.

for many young people, especially those in limiting socioeconomic conditions (Cote & Bynner, 2008).

An important aspect of emerging adulthood is the resilience that some individuals have and their ability to change their life in a positive direction following a troubled adolescence (Burt & Paysnick, 2012; Masten, 2013; Masten & Tellegen, 2012). In a longitudinal study, Ann Masten and her colleagues (2006) found that emerging adults who became competent after experiencing difficulties while growing up were more intelligent, experienced higher parenting quality, and were less likely to grow up in poverty or low-income circumstances than their counterparts who did not become competent as emerging adults. A further analysis focused on individuals who were still showing maladaptive patterns in emerging adulthood but had gotten their lives together by the time they were in the late twenties and early thirties. The three characteristics shared by these "late bloomers" were support by adults, being planful, and showing positive aspects of autonomy. In some cases, ". . . military service, marriage and romantic relationships, higher education, religious affiliations, and work opportunities may provide turning-point opportunities for changing the life course during emerging adulthood" (Masten, Obradovic, & Burt, 2006, p. 179).

Markers of Becoming an Adult

In the United States, the most widely recognized marker of entry into adulthood is holding a more or less permanent, full-time job, which usually happens when an individual finishes school—high school for some, college for others, graduate or professional school for still others. However, other criteria are far from clear. Economic independence is one marker of adult status, but achieving it is often a long process. College graduates are increasingly returning to live with their parents as they attempt to establish themselves economically. A longitudinal study found that at age 25 only slightly more than half of the participants were fully financially independent of their family of origin (Cohen & others, 2003). The most dramatic findings in this study, though, involved the extensive variability in the individual trajectories of adult roles across ten years from 17 to 27 years of age; many of the participants moved back and forth between increasing and decreasing economic dependency. A recent study revealed that continued co-residence with parents during emerging adulthood slowed down the process of becoming a self-sufficient and independent adult (Kins & Beyers, 2010).

Other studies show that taking responsibility for oneself is likely an important marker of adult status for many individuals. In one study, both parents and college students agreed that taking responsibility for one's actions and developing emotional control are important aspects of becoming an adult (Nelson & others, 2007).

What we have discussed about the markers of adult status mainly characterizes individuals in industrialized societies, especially Americans. In developing countries, marriage is more often a significant marker for entry into adulthood, and this usually occurs much earlier than the adulthood markers in the United States (Arnett, 2004).

Chris Barnard, 24-year-old emerging adult, in the apartment he shares with two roommates. Chris is a single 24-year-old. Two years ago he moved back in with his parents, worked as a temp, and thought about his next step in life. One of the temp jobs became permanent. He now works with a trade association in Washington, D.C. With the exception of technology, he says that his life is similar to what his parents' lives must have been like as they made the transition to adulthood. Chris's living arrangements reflect the "instability" characteristic of emerging adulthood. While in college, he changed dorms each year, then as a senior moved to an off-campus apartment. Following college, he moved back home, then moved to another apartment, and now is in yet another apartment. In Chris' words, "This is going to be the longest stay I've had since I went to college . . . I've sort of settled in" (Jayson, 2006, p. 2D).

How Would You...?

As a social worker, how would you apply your knowledge of contemporary society to counsel a client making the transition into adulthood?

How Would You...?

As a psychologist, how would you offer guidance to emerging adults who are concerned because they have not yet settled into a career and a long-term relationship?

In a recent study, the majority of 18- to 26-year-olds in India felt that they had achieved adulthood (Seiter & Nelson, 2010).

The Transition from High School to College

For many individuals in developed countries, going from high school to college is an important aspect of the transition to adulthood (Bowman, 2010). Just as the transition from elementary school to middle or junior high school involves change and possible stress, so does the transition from high school to college. The two transitions have many parallels. Going from being a senior in high school to being a freshman in college replays the top-dog phenomenon of transferring from the oldest and most powerful group of students to the youngest and least powerful group of students that occurred earlier as adolescence began. For many students, the transition from high school to college involves movement to a larger, more impersonal school structure; interaction with peers from more diverse geographical and sometimes more diverse ethnic backgrounds; and increased focus on achievement and its assessment. And like the transition from elementary to middle or junior high school, the transition from high school to college can involve positive features. Students are more likely to feel grown up, have more subjects from which to select, have more time to spend with peers, have more opportunities to explore different lifestyles and values, enjoy greater independence from parental monitoring, and be challenged intellectually by academic work (Halonen & Santrock, 2013).

The transition from high school to college often involves positive as well as negative features. In college, students are likely to feel grown up, be able to spend more time with peers, have more opportunities to explore different lifestyles and values, and enjoy greater freedom from parental monitoring. However, college involves a larger, more impersonal school structure and an increased focus on achievement and its assessment. *What was your transition to college like?*

How Would You...?

As an educator, how would you prepare high school students to ease the transition to college?

College counselors can provide good information about coping with stress and academic matters. To read about the work of college counselor Grace Leaf, see *Careers in Life-Span Development*.

Careers in life-span development

Grace Leaf, College/Career Counselor

Grace Leaf is a counselor at Spokane Community College in Washington. She has a master's degree in educational leadership and is working toward a doctoral degree in educational leadership at Gonzaga University in Washington. Her job involves teaching orientation for international students, conducting individual and group advising, and doing individual and group career planning. Grace tries to connect students with goals and values and helps them design an educational program that fits their needs and visions.

College counselors help students to cope with adjustment problems, identify their abilities and interests, develop academic plans, and explore career options. Some have an undergraduate degree, others a master's degree like Grace Leaf. Some college

Grace Leaf, counseling college students at Spokane Community College about careers.

counselors have a graduate degree in counseling; others may have an undergraduate degree in psychology or another discipline.

Physical Development

As emerging and young adults learn more about healthy lifestyles and how they contribute to a longer life span, they are increasingly interested in learning about their physical performance, health, nutrition, exercise, and substance use.

Physical Performance and Development

Most of us reach our peak physical performance before the age of 30, often between the ages of 19 and 26. This peak of physical performance occurs not only for the average young adult, but for outstanding athletes as well. Even though athletes as a group keep getting better than their predecessors—running faster, jumping higher, and lifting more weight—the age at which they reach their peak performance has remained virtually the same.

Different types of athletes, however, reach their peak performances at different ages. Most swimmers and gymnasts peak in their late teens. Golfers and marathon runners tend to peak in their late twenties. In other areas of athletics, peak performance often occurs in the early to mid-twenties.

Not only do we reach our peak in physical performance during early adulthood, it is also during this age period that we begin to decline in physical performance. Muscle tone and strength usually begin to show signs of decline around the age of 30. Sagging chins and protruding abdomens also may begin to appear for the first time. The lessening of physical abilities is a common complaint among the just-turned thirties. Sensory systems show little change in early adulthood, but the lens of the eye loses some of its elasticity and becomes less able to change shape and focus on near objects. Hearing peaks in adolescence, remains constant in the first part of early adulthood, and then begins to decline in the last part of early adulthood. And in the middle to late twenties, the body's fatty tissue increases.

Health

Emerging adults have more than twice the mortality rate of adolescents (Park & others, 2006) (see Figure 11.1). As indicated in Figure 11.1, males are mainly responsible for the higher mortality rate of emerging adults.

Although emerging adults have a higher death rate than adolescents, emerging adults have few chronic health problems, and they have fewer colds and respiratory problems than when they were children (Rimsza & Kirk, 2005). Although most college students know what it takes to prevent illness and promote health, they don't fare very well when it comes to applying this information to themselves (Murphy-Hoefer, Alder, & Higbee, 2004). In many cases, emerging adults are not as healthy as they seem (Fatusi & Hindin, 2010).

A longitudinal study revealed that most bad health habits that were engaged in during adolescence increased in emerging adulthood (Harris & others, 2006). Inactivity, diet, obesity, substance use, reproductive health care, and health-care access worsened in emerging adulthood. For example, when they were 12 to 18 years of age, only 5 percent reported no weekly exercise, but when they became 19 to 26 years of age, 46 percent said they did not exercise during a week. A recent

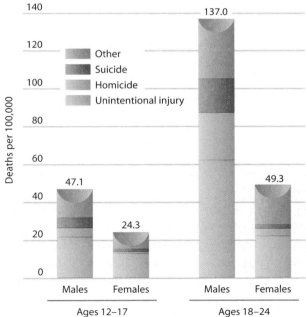

Figure 11.1
Mortality Rates of U.S. Adolescents and Emerging Adults

Why might it be easy to develop bad health habits in emerging and early adulthood?

study also found that college students from low-SES backgrounds engaged in lower levels of physical activity, ate more fast food and less fruits/vegetables, and showed more unhealthy weight control than their higher-SES counterparts (VanKim & Laska, 2012).

In emerging and early adulthood, few individuals stop to think about how their personal lifestyles will affect their health later in their adult lives. As emerging adults, many of us develop a pattern of not eating breakfast, not eating regular meals, and relying on snacks as our main food source during the day, eating excessively to the point where we exceed the normal weight for our age, smoking moderately or excessively, drinking moderately or excessively, failing to exercise, and getting by with only a few hours of sleep at night (Cousineau, Goldstein, & Franco, 2005; Waldron & Dieser, 2010). These lifestyles are associated with poor health, which in turn reduces life satisfaction. In the Berkeley Longitudinal Study—in which individuals were evaluated over a period of 40 years—physical health at age 30 predicted life satisfaction at age 70, more so for men than for women (Mussen, Honzik, & Eichorn, 2002).

Another study explored links between health behavior and life satisfaction of more than 17,000 individuals who were 17 to 30 years old in 21 countries (Grant, Wardle, & Steptoe, 2009). The young adults' life satisfaction was positively related to not smoking, exercising regularly, using sun protection, eating fruit, and limiting fat intake, but it was not related to alcohol consumption and fiber intake.

Eating and Weight

In Chapters 5 and 7, we discussed aspects of overweight children's lives, and in Chapter 9 we examined the eating disorders of anorexia nervosa and bulimia nervosa in adolescence. Now, we turn our attention to obesity and the extensive preoccupation that many young adults have with dieting.

Obesity Obesity is a serious and pervasive health problem for many individuals (Corsica & Perri, 2013; Schiff, 2013). A recent national survey found that 27 percent of U.S. 20- to 39-year-olds were obese (National Center for Health Statistics, 2011a). A recent analysis predicted that by 2030, 42 percent of U.S. adults will be obese (Finkelstein & others, 2012).

A recent international comparison of 33 developed countries revealed that the United States had the highest percentage of obese adults (OECD, 2010). Figure 11.2 shows the developed countries with the highest and lowest percentages of obese adults.

How Would You...?

As a health-care professional, how would you counsel young women of normal weight to accept their body image and set point for weight management?

Obesity is linked to increased risk of hypertension, diabetes, and cardiovascular disease (Insel & Roth, 2012; O'Callahan & others, 2013). For individuals who are 30 percent overweight, the probability of dying in middle adulthood increases by about 40 percent. Overweight and obesity also are associated with mental health problems. For example, a recent meta-analysis revealed that overweight women were more likely to be depressed than women who were not overweight, but no significant difference was found for men (de Wit & others, 2010).

Dieting Ironically, although obesity is on the rise, dieting has become an obsession with many Americans (Schiff, 2013; Willett, 2012). Although many Americans regularly embark on a diet, few are successful in keeping weight off over the long term (Dulloo, Jacquet, & Montani, 2012; Pietilainen & others, 2012). A research

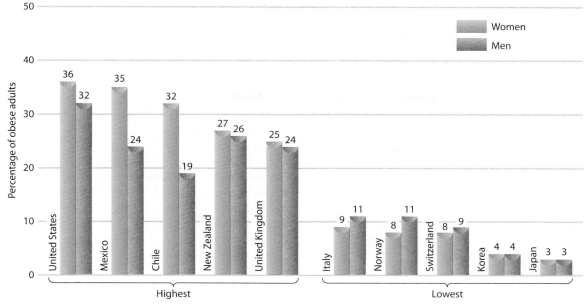

Figure 11.2 Countries with the Highest and Lowest Percentages of Obese Adults Among 33 Developed Countries

Source: OECD (2010). *Obesity and the Economics of Prevention—Fit Not Fat.* Paris, FR: OECD.

review of the long-term outcomes of calorie-restricting diets revealed that one-third to two-thirds of dieters eventually regain more weight than they lost on their diets (Mann & others, 2007). However, some individuals do lose weight and maintain the loss (Chambers & Swanson, 2012; Cooper & others, 2012). How often this occurs and whether some diet programs work better than others are still open questions.

What we do know about losing weight is that the most effective programs include exercise (Snel & others, 2012; Thompson & Manore, 2013). A research review concluded that adults who engaged in diet-plus-exercise programs lost more weight than those who followed diet-only programs (Wu & others, 2009). A study of approximately 2,000 U.S. adults found that exercising 30 minutes a day, planning meals, and weighing themselves daily were the strategies used more often by successful dieters than by unsuccessful dieters (Kruger, Blanck, & Gillespie, 2006) (see Figure 11.3).

The National Weight Control Registry is an ongoing examination of individuals who have lost 30 pounds and kept it off for at least one year. Research on these successful dieters provides important information about losing weight and maintaining the weight loss (Ogden & others, 2012). One of the most consistent findings regarding these successful dieters is that they engage in a high level of physical activity (Catenacci & others, 2008).

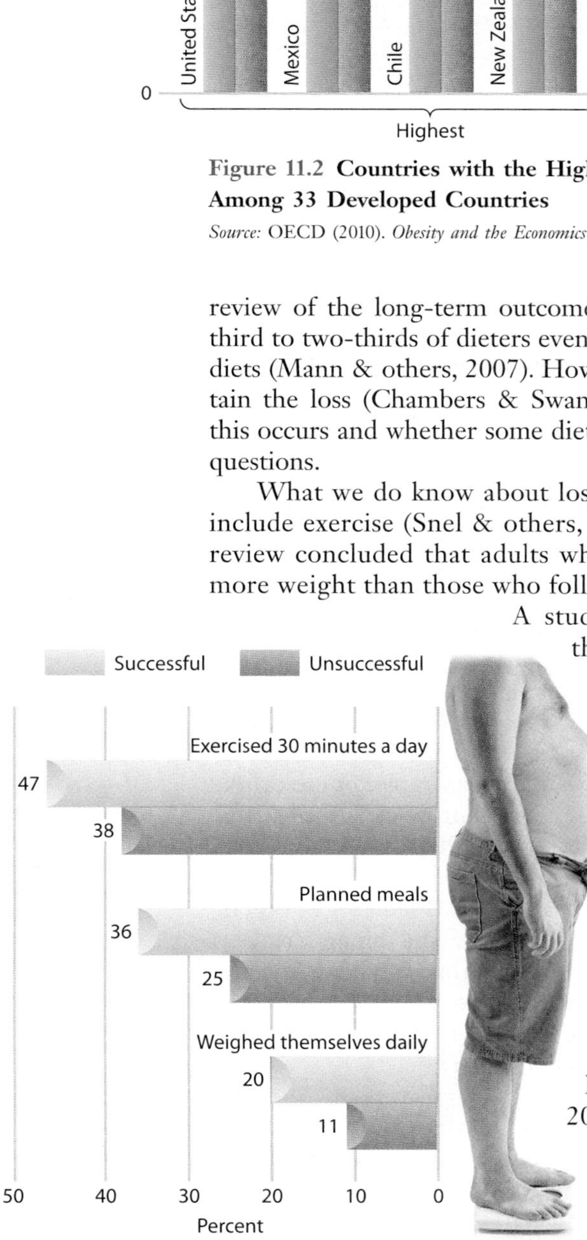

Regular Exercise

One of the main reasons that health experts want people to exercise is that it helps to prevent diseases, such as heart disease and diabetes (Fahey, Insel, & Roth, 2013). Many health experts recommend that young adults engage in 30 minutes or more of aerobic exercise daily.

Figure 11.3 Comparison of Strategies Used by Successful and Unsuccessful Dieters

Aerobic exercise is sustained exercise—jogging, swimming, or cycling, for example—that stimulates heart and lung activity. Most health experts recommend that you raise your heart rate to at least 60 percent of your maximum heart rate. Only about one-fifth of adults, however, meet these recommended levels of physical activity.

Researchers have found that exercise benefits not only physical health, but mental health as well (Donatelle, 2013; Kocer & others, 2011). In particular, exercise improves self-concept and reduces anxiety and depression (Jazaieri & others, 2012; Sturm & others, 2012). Meta-analyses have shown that exercise can be as effective in reducing depression as psychotherapy (Richardson & others, 2005). A recent study of college students revealed that males' motivation to exercise involved strength, challenge, and competition, whereas females' motivation focused more on weight management and appearance (Egli & others, 2011).

How Would You...?

As a health-care professional, how would you design a community education program to emphasize the importance of regular exercise for young adults?

Substance Abuse

In Chapter 9, we explored substance abuse in adolescence. Fortunately, by the time individuals reach their mid-twenties, many have reduced their use of alcohol and drugs (Bachman & others, 2002). As in adolescence, male college students and young adults are more likely to take drugs than their female counterparts (Johnston & others, 2008). One study revealed that only 20 percent of college students reported abstaining from drinking alcohol (Huang & others, 2009).

In 2010, 37 percent of U.S. college students reported having had five or more drinks in a row at least once in the last two weeks (Johnston & others, 2011). In the most recent survey, the Institute of Social Research introduced the term *extreme binge drinking* to describe individuals who had 10 or more drinks in a row. In 2010, approximately 13 percent of college students reported drinking this heavily (Johnston & others, 2011). While still at very high rates, college student drinking, including binge drinking, has declined in recent years. For example, binge drinking declined 4 percent from 2007 to 2010 (Johnston & others, 2011).

In a national survey of drinking patterns on 140 campuses (Wechsler & others, 1994), almost half of the binge drinkers

What kinds of problems are associated with binge drinking in college?

reported problems that included missing classes, sustaining physical injuries, experiencing troubles with police, and having unprotected sex. For example, binge-drinking college students were 11 times more likely to fall behind in school, 10 times more likely to drive after drinking, and twice as likely to have unprotected sex in comparison with college students who did not binge drink. Also, one study found that after an evening of binge drinking, memory retrieval was significantly impaired during the alcohol hangover the next morning (Verster & others, 2002).

How Would You...?

As a social worker, how would you apply your understanding of binge drinking to develop a program to encourage responsible alcohol use on college campuses?

Drinking alcohol before going out—called *pregaming*—has become common among college students (Bachrach & others, 2012; LaBrie & others, 2011). A

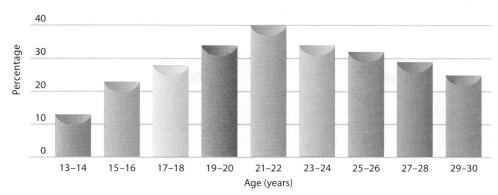

Figure 11.4 Binge Drinking in the Adolescence–Early Adulthood Transition
Note that the percentage of individuals engaging in binge drinking peaked at 21 or 22 years of age and then gradually declined through the remainder of the twenties. Binge drinking was defined as having five or more alcoholic drinks in a row in the previous two weeks.

recent study revealed that almost two-thirds of students on one campus had pregamed at least once in a two-week period (DeJong, DeRicco, & Schneider, 2010). Another recent study found that two-thirds of 18- to 24-year-old women at one college pregamed (Read, Merrill, & Bytschkow, 2010). Drinking games, in which the goal is to become intoxicated, also have become common on college campuses (Cameron & others, 2010). Higher levels of alcohol use have been consistently linked to higher rates of sexual risk taking, such as engaging in casual sex, sex without contraceptives, and sexual assaults (Gilmore, Granato, & Lewis, 2012; Khan & others, 2012; Olmstead, Pasley, & Fincham, 2012).

A special concern is the increase in binge drinking by females during emerging adulthood (Davis & others, 2010). In a national longitudinal study, binge drinking by 19- to 22-year-old women increased from 28 percent in 1995 to 34 percent in 2007 (Johnston & others, 2008).

When does binge drinking peak during development? A longitudinal study revealed that binge drinking peaks at about 21 to 22 years of age and then declines through the remainder of the twenties (Bachman & others, 2002) (see Figure 11.4).

Sexuality

In Chapter 9, we explored how adolescents develop a sexual identity and become sexually active. What happens to their sexuality in adulthood?

Sexual Activity in Emerging Adulthood

At the beginning of emerging adulthood (age 18), surveys indicate that slightly more than 60 percent of individuals have experienced sexual intercourse, but by the end of emerging adulthood (age 25), most individuals have had sexual intercourse (Lefkowitz & Gillen, 2006). Also, the average age of marriage in the United States is currently 28 for males and 26 for females (Copen & others, 2012). Thus, emerging adulthood is a time during which most individuals are "both sexually active and unmarried" (Lefkowitz & Gillen, 2006, p. 235).

Patterns of heterosexual behavior for males and females in emerging adulthood include the following (Lefkowitz & Gillen, 2006): (1) Males have more casual sexual partners, and females report being more selective about their choice of a sexual partner. (2) Casual sex is more common in emerging adulthood than

SEXUALITY

in young adulthood. A recent trend has involved "hooking up" to have nonrelationship sex (from kissing to intercourse) (Holman & Sillars, 2011; Lewis & others, 2012).

Sexual Orientation and Behavior

A recent national study of sexual behavior in the United States among adults 25 to 44 years of age found that 98 percent of the women and 97 percent of the men said that they had ever engaged in vaginal intercourse (Chandra & others, 2011). Also in this study, 89 percent of the women and 90 percent of the men reported that they had ever had oral sex with an opposite-sex partner, and 36 percent of the women and 44 percent of the men stated that they had ever had anal sex with an opposite-sex partner.

Detailed information about various aspects of sexual activity in adults of different ages comes from the 1994 Sex in America survey. In this study Robert Michael and his colleagues (1994) interviewed more than 3,000 people from 18 to 59 years of age who were randomly selected, in sharp contrast with earlier samples that were based on unrepresentative groups of volunteers.

Heterosexual Attitudes and Behavior

Here are some of the key findings from the 1994 Sex in America survey:

- Americans tend to fall into three categories: One-third have sex twice a week or more, one-third a few times a month, and one-third a few times a year or not at all.
- Married (and cohabiting) couples have sex more often than noncohabiting couples (see Figure 11.5).
- Most Americans do not engage in kinky sexual acts. When asked about their favorite sexual acts, the vast majority (96 percent) said that vaginal sex was "very" or "somewhat" appealing. Oral sex was in third place, after an activity that many have not labeled a sexual act—watching a partner undress.

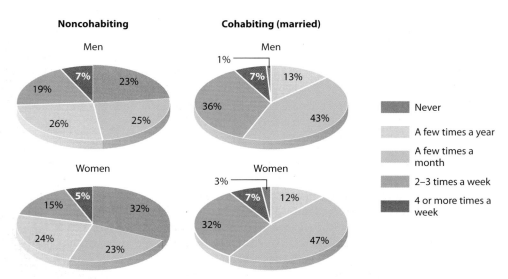

Figure 11.5 The Sex in America Survey
The percentages show noncohabiting and cohabiting (married) males' and females' responses to the question "How often have you had sex in the past year?" in a 1994 survey (Michael & others, 1994). *What was one feature of the Sex in America survey that made it superior to most surveys of sexual behavior?*

- Adultery is clearly the exception rather than the rule. Nearly 75 percent of the married men and 85 percent of the married women in the survey indicated that they had never been unfaithful.

- Men think about sex far more than women do—54 percent of the men said they thought about it every day or several times a day, whereas 67 percent of the women said they thought about it only a few times a week or a few times a month.

In sum, one of the most powerful messages in the 1994 survey was that Americans' sexual lives are more conservative than was previously believed. Although 17 percent of the men and 3 percent of the women said they had had sex with at least 21 partners, the overall impression from the survey was that sexual behavior is ruled by marriage and monogamy for most Americans.

How extensive are gender differences in sexuality? A recent meta-analysis revealed that men reported having slightly more sexual experiences and more permissive attitudes than women for most aspects of sexuality (Peterson & Hyde, 2010). For the following factors, stronger differences were found: Men said that they engaged more in masturbation, pornography use, and casual sex, and had more permissive attitudes about casual sex than their female counterparts did.

How Would You...?

As a human development and family studies professional, what information would you include in a program designed to educate young adults about healthy sexuality and sexual relationships?

Given all the media and public attention focusing on the negative aspects of sexuality—such as adolescent pregnancy, sexually transmitted infections, rape, and so on—it is important to underscore that research strongly supports the role of sexuality in well-being (Brody, 2010). For example, in a recent Swedish study frequency of sexual intercourse was strongly linked to life satisfaction for both women and men (Brody & Costa, 2009).

Sources of Sexual Orientation

Until the end of the nineteenth century, it was generally believed that people were either heterosexual or homosexual. Today, the more accepted view of sexual orientation depicts it not as an either/or proposition but as a continuum from exclusive male-female relations to exclusive same-sex relations (King, 2013). Some individuals are also bisexual, being sexually attracted to people of both sexes.

In the Sex in America survey, 2.7 percent of the men and 1.3 percent of the women reported that they had had same-sex relations in the past year (Michael & others, 1994). Why are some individuals lesbian, gay, or bisexual (LGB) and others heterosexual? Speculation surrounding this question has been extensive (Diamond & Savin-Williams, 2013).

All people, regardless of their sexual orientation, have similar physiological responses during sexual arousal and seem to be aroused by the same types of tactile stimulation. Investigators typically find no differences between LGBs and heterosexuals in a wide range of attitudes, behaviors, and adjustments (Fingerhut & Peplau, 2013).

What likely determines an individual's sexual preference?

Recently, researchers have explored the possible biological basis of same-sex relations. The results of hormone studies have been inconsistent. If gay males are given male sex hormones (androgens), their sexual orientation doesn't change. Their sexual desire merely increases. A very early prenatal critical period might influence sexual orientation (Berenbaum & Beltz, 2011). If this critical-period hypothesis turns out to be correct, it would explain why clinicians have found that sexual orientation is difficult, if not impossible, to modify.

Researchers have also examined genetic influences on sexual orientation by studying twins. A recent Swedish study of almost 4,000 twins found that only about 35 percent of the variation in homosexual behavior in men and 19 percent in women were explained by genetic differences (Langstrom & others, 2010). This result suggests that although genes likely play a role in sexual orientation, they are not the only factor involved (King, 2013).

An individual's sexual orientation—same-sex, heterosexual, or bisexual—is most likely determined by a combination of genetic, hormonal, cognitive, and environmental factors (King, 2013; Yarber, Sayad, & Strong, 2013). Most experts on same-sex relations believe that no one factor alone causes sexual orientation and that the relative weight of each factor can vary from one individual to the next.

Attitudes and Behavior of Lesbians and Gay Males

Many gender differences that appear in heterosexual relationships occur in same-sex relationships (Diamond & Savin-Williams, 2013; Savin-Williams, 2013). For example, like heterosexual women, lesbians have fewer sexual partners than gays, and lesbians have less permissive attitudes about casual sex outside a primary relationship than gays do (Fingerhut & Peplau, 2013).

According to psychologist Laura Brown (1989), lesbians and gays experience life as a minority in a dominant, majority culture. For lesbians and gays, developing a bicultural identity creates new ways of defining themselves. Brown believes that lesbians and gays adapt best when they don't define themselves in polarities, such as trying to live in an encapsulated lesbian or gay world completely divorced from the majority culture or completely accepting the dictates and biases of the majority culture.

Sexually Transmitted Infections

Sexually transmitted infections (STIs) are diseases that are primarily contracted through sex—intercourse as well as oral-genital and anal-genital sex. STIs affect about one of every six U.S. adults (National Center for Health Statistics, 2011b). Among the most prevalent STIs are bacterial infections—such as gonorrhea, syphilis, and chlamydia—and STIs caused by viruses—such as AIDS (acquired immune deficiency syndrome), genital herpes, and genital warts. Figure 11.6 describes these sexually transmitted infections.

No single disease has had a greater impact on sexual behavior, or created more public fear in the last several decades, than infection with the human immunodeficiency virus (HIV) (Crooks & Baur, 2011). HIV is a virus that destroys the body's immune system. Once a person is infected with HIV, the virus breaks down and overpowers the immune system, which leads to AIDS. An individual sick with AIDS has such a weakened immune system that a common cold can be life-threatening.

In 2010, more than 1 million people in the U.S. were living with an HIV infection (National Center for Health Statistics, 2012). In 2010, male-male sexual contact continued to be the most frequent AIDS transmission category. Because of education and the development of more effective drug treatments, deaths due to HIV/AIDS have begun to decline in the United States (National Center for Health Statistics, 2012).

sexually transmitted infections (STIs) Diseases that are contracted primarily through sex.

STI	Description/cause	Incidence	Treatment
Gonorrhea	Commonly called the "drip" or "clap." Caused by the bacterium *Neisseria gonorrhoeae*. Spread by contact between infected moist membranes (genital, oral-genital, or anal-genital) of two individuals. Characterized by discharge from penis or vagina and painful urination. Can lead to infertility.	500,000 cases annually in U.S.	Penicillin, other antibiotics
Syphilis	Caused by the bacterium *Treponema pallidum*. Characterized by the appearance of a sore where syphilis entered the body. The sore can be on the external genitals, vagina, or anus. Later, a skin rash breaks out on palms of hands and bottom of feet. If not treated, can eventually lead to paralysis or even death.	100,000 cases annually in U.S.	Penicillin
Chlamydia	A common STI named for the bacterium *Chlamydia trachomatis*, an organism that spreads by sexual contact and infects the genital organs of both sexes. A special concern is that females with chlamydia may become infertile. It is recommended that adolescent and young adult females have an annual screening for this STI.	About 3 million people in U.S. annually	Antibiotics
Genital herpes	Caused by a family of viruses with different strains. Involves an eruption of sores and blisters. Spread by sexual contact.	One of five U.S. adults	No known cure but antiviral medications can shorten outbreaks
AIDS	Caused by a virus, the human immunodeficiency virus (HIV), which destroys the body's immune system. Semen and blood are the main vehicles of transmission. Common symptoms include fevers, night sweats, weight loss, chronic fatigue, and swollen lymph nodes.	More than 300,000 cumulative cases of HIV virus in U.S. 25–34-year-olds; epidemic incidence in sub-Saharan countries	New treatments have slowed the progression from HIV to AIDS; no cure
Genital warts	Caused by the human papillomavirus, which does not always produce symptoms. Usually appear as small, hard painless bumps in the vaginal area, or around the anus. Very contagious. Certain high-risk types of this virus cause cervical cancer and other genital cancers. May recur despite treatment. A new HPV preventive vaccine, Gardasil, has been approved for girls and women 9–26 years of age.	About 5.5 million new cases annually; considered the most common STI in the U.S.	A topical drug, freezing, or surgery

Figure 11.6 **Sexually Transmitted Infections**

Globally, the total number of individuals living with HIV was 34 million at the end of 2010, with 22 million of these individuals with HIV living in sub-Saharan Africa. Approximately half of all new HIV infections around the world occur in the 15- to 24-year-old age category. The good news is that global rates of HIV infection fell nearly 25 percent from 2001 to 2009 with substantial decreases in India and South Africa (UNAIDS, 2011). In a recent study, only 49 percent of 15- to 24-year-old females in low- and middle-income countries knew that using a condom helps to prevent HIV infection, compared with 74 percent of young males (UNAIDS, 2011).

How Would You...?
As a health-care professional, what advice would you give to a patient who is sexually active, does not use condoms, and does not want to be tested for any sexually transmitted infections?

What are some good strategies for protecting against HIV and other sexually transmitted infections? They include:

- *Knowing your own and your partner's risk status.* Anyone who has had previous sexual activity with another person might have contracted an STI without being aware of it. Spend time getting to know a prospective partner before you have sex. Use this time to inform the other person of your STI status and inquire about your partner's. Remember that many people lie about their STI status.

- *Obtaining medical examinations.* Many experts recommend that couples who want to begin a sexual relationship should have a medical checkup to rule out STIs before they engage in sex. If cost is an issue, contact your campus health service or a public health clinic.

- *Having protected, not unprotected, sex.* When correctly used, latex condoms help to prevent many STIs from being transmitted. Condoms are most effective in preventing gonorrhea, syphilis, chlamydia, and HIV. They are less effective against the spread of herpes.

- *Not having sex with multiple partners.* One of the best predictors of getting an STI is having sex with multiple partners. Having more than one sex partner elevates the likelihood that you will encounter an infected partner.

Forcible Sexual Behavior and Sexual Harassment

Too often, sex involves the exercise of power. Here we briefly look at three of the problems that may result: two types of rape and sexual harassment.

What are some characteristics of acquaintance rape in colleges and universities?

Rape

Rape is forcible sexual intercourse with a person who does not give consent. Legal definitions of rape differ from state to state. For example, in some states, husbands are not prohibited from forcing their wives to have intercourse, although this has been challenged in several of those states.

Because victims may be reluctant to suffer the consequences of reporting rape, the actual number of incidents is not easily determined (Spohn & Tellis, 2012). Rape occurs most often in large cities, where it has been reported that 8 of every 10,000 women 12 years and older are raped each year. Nearly 200,000 rapes are reported each year in the United States. Although most victims of rape are women, rape of men does occur (McLean, Balding, & White, 2005). A recent study of college women who had been raped revealed that only 11.5 percent of them reported the rape to authorities and of those in which the rape involved drugs and/or alcohol, only 2.7 percent of the rapes were reported (Wolitzky-Taylor & others, 2011). Men in prisons are especially vulnerable to rape, usually by heterosexual males who use rape as a means of establishing their dominance and power (Barth, 2012).

Why does rape of women occur so often in the United States? Among the causes given are that males are socialized to be sexually aggressive, to regard women as inferior beings, and to view their own pleasure as the most important objective in sexual relations (Beech, Ward, & Fisher, 2006; Davies, Gilston, & Rogers, 2012). Researchers have found that male rapists share the following characteristics: aggression enhances their sense of power or masculinity; they are angry at women in general; and they want to hurt and humiliate their victims (Yarber, Sayad, & Strong, 2013). A recent study revealed that a higher level of men's sexual narcissism (assessed by these factors: sexual exploitation, sexual entitlement, low sexual empathy, and sexual skill) was linked to a greater likelihood that they would engage in sexual aggression (Widman & McNulty, 2010).

Rape is a traumatic experience for the victims and those close to them (Jozkowski & Sanders, 2012). As victims strive to get their lives back to normal, they may experience depression, fear, anxiety, and increased substance use for months or years (Amstadter & others, 2011). Recovery depends on the victim's coping abilities, psychological adjustments prior to the assault, and social support. Parents, a partner, and others close to the victim can provide important support for recovery, as can mental health professionals (Ahrens & Aldana, 2012; Resick & others, 2012).

An increasing concern is **date or acquaintance rape,** which is coercive sexual activity directed at someone with whom the perpetrator is at least casually acquainted (Albright, Stevens, & Beussman, 2012). By some estimates, one in three adolescent girls

rape Forcible sexual intercourse with a person who does not consent to it.

date or acquaintance rape Coercive sexual activity directed at someone with whom the perpetrator is at least casually acquainted.

will be involved in a controlling, abusive relationship before graduating from high school, and two-thirds of female college freshmen report having been date raped or having experienced an attempted date rape at least once (Watts & Zimmerman, 2002). About two-thirds of college men admit that they fondle women against their will, and half admit to forcing sexual activity.

A number of colleges and universities describe the *red zone* as a period of time early in the first year of college when women are at especially high risk for unwanted sexual experiences. A recent study revealed that first-year college women were more at risk for unwanted sexual experiences, especially early in the fall term, than second-year women (Kimble & others, 2008).

Sexual Harassment

Sexual harassment is a manifestation of power of one person over another. It takes many forms—from inappropriate sexual remarks and physical contact (patting, brushing against one's body) to blatant propositions and sexual assaults. Millions of women experience sexual harassment each year in work and educational settings (Snyder, Scherer, & Fisher, 2012). Sexual harassment of men by women also occurs but to a far lesser extent than sexual harassment of women by men (Bullock & Beckson, 2011).

In a survey of 2,000 college women, 62 percent reported that they had experienced sexual harassment while attending college (American Association of University Women, 2006). Most of the college women said that the sexual harassment involved noncontact forms such as crude jokes, remarks, and gestures. However, almost one-third said that the sexual harassment was physical in nature.

Sexual harassment can result in serious psychological consequences for the victim (Willoughby & others, 2012). A study of almost 1,500 college women revealed that when they had been sexually harassed they reported an increase in psychological distress, greater physical illness, and an increase in disordered eating (Huerta & others, 2006).

The elimination of such exploitation requires the improvement of work and academic environments. These types of improvements help to provide equal opportunities for people to be able to develop a career and obtain an education in a climate free of sexual harassment (Nielsen & Einarsen, 2012).

How Would You...?
As an educator, how would you develop a sensitivity workshop in sexual harassment?

Cognitive Development

Are there changes in cognitive performance during these years? To explore the nature of cognition in early adulthood, we focus on issues related to cognitive stages and creative thinking.

Cognitive Stages

Are young adults more advanced in their thinking than adolescents are? Let's examine how Piaget and others have answered this intriguing question.

Piaget's View

Piaget concluded that an adolescent and an adult think qualitatively in the same way. That is, Piaget argued that at approximately 11 to 15 years of age, adolescents enter the formal operational stage, which is characterized by more logical, abstract, and idealistic thinking than the concrete operational thinking of 7- to 11-year-olds. Piaget did believe that young adults are more quantitatively advanced in their thinking in the sense that they have more knowledge than adolescents possess. He also believed, as do information-processing psychologists, that adults especially increase their knowledge in a specific area, such as a physicist's understanding of physics or a financial analyst's knowledge about finance. According to Piaget, however, formal operational thought is the final stage in cognitive development, and it characterizes adults as well as adolescents.

Some developmentalists theorize it is not until adulthood that many individuals consolidate their formal operational thinking. That is, they may begin to plan and hypothesize about intellectual problems in adolescence, but they become more systematic and sophisticated at this as young adults. Nonetheless, even many adults do not think in formal operational ways at all (Kuhn, 2009).

Postformal Thought

It has been proposed that the idealism of Piaget's formal operational stage declines in young adults and is replaced by more realistic, pragmatic thinking. It also has been proposed that young adults move into a new qualitative stage of cognitive development, postformal thought (Sinnott, 2003). **Postformal thought** is:

- *Reflective, relativistic, and contextual.* As young adults engage in solving problems, they might think deeply about many aspects of work, politics, relationships, and other areas of life (Labouvie-Vief, 1986). They find that what might be the best solution to a problem at work (with a boss or co-worker) might not be the best solution at home (with a romantic partner). Thus, postformal thought holds that the correct answer to a problem requires reflective thinking and may vary from one situation to another. Some psychologists argue that reflective thinking continues to increase and becomes more internal and less contextual in middle age (Mascalo & Fischer, 2010; Labouvie-Vief, Gruhn, & Studer, 2010).

- *Provisional.* Many young adults also become more skeptical about the truth and seem unwilling to accept an answer as final. Thus, they come to see the search for truth as an ongoing and perhaps never-ending process.

What are some ways that young adults might think differently from adolescents?

- *Realistic.* Young adults understand that thinking can't always be abstract. In many instances, it must be realistic and pragmatic.

- *Recognized as being influenced by emotion.* Emerging and young adults are more likely than adolescents to understand that their thinking is influenced by emotions (Labouvie-Vief, 2009; Labouvie-Vief, Gruhn, & Studer, 2010). However, too often negative emotions produce thinking that is distorted and self-serving at this point in development.

How Would You…?

As an educator, how would you characterize the differences in the cognitive development of adolescents and adults? How would this distinction change the way you teach to these different populations?

Creativity

Early adulthood is a time of great creativity for some people. At the age of 30, Thomas Edison invented the phonograph, Hans Christian Andersen wrote his first volume of fairy tales, and Mozart composed *The Marriage of Figaro*. One early study of creativity found that individuals' most creative products were generated in their thirties, and that 80 percent of the most important creative contributions were completed by age 50 (Lehman, 1960). Even though a decline in creative contributions is often found in the fifties and later, the decline is not as great as was commonly thought.

How Would You…?

As an educator, how would you use your understanding of creativity to become a more effective teacher?

Any consideration of decline in creativity with age must take into account the field of creativity involved. In fields such as philosophy and history, older adults often show as much creativity as they did when they were in their thirties and forties. By contrast, in fields such as lyric poetry, abstract math, and theoretical physics, the peak of creativity is often reached in the twenties or thirties.

Can you make yourself more creative? Mihaly Csikszentmihalyi (1995) interviewed 90 leading figures in art, business, government, education, and science to learn how creativity works. He discovered that creative people regularly experience a state he calls *flow*, a heightened state of pleasure experienced when we are engaged in mental and physical challenges that absorb us. Csikszentmihalyi (2000) believes everyone is capable of achieving flow. Based on his interviews with some of the most creative people in the world, the first step toward a more creative life is cultivating your curiosity and interest. How can you do this?

- *Try to be surprised by something every day.* Maybe it is something you see, hear, or read about. Become absorbed in a lecture or a book. Be open to what the world is telling you. Life is a stream of experiences. Swim widely and deeply in it, and your life will be richer.

- *Try to surprise at least one person every day.* In a lot of things you do, you have to be predictable and patterned. Do something different for a change. Ask a question you normally would not ask. Invite someone to go to a show you haven't seen or a museum you never have visited.

- Write down each day what surprised you and how you surprised others. Most creative people keep a diary, notes, or lab records to ensure that their experience is not fleeting or forgotten. Start with a specific task. Each evening, record the most surprising event that occurred that day and your most surprising action. After a few days, reread your notes and reflect on your past experiences. After a few weeks, you might see a pattern of interest emerging in your notes, one that might suggest an area you can explore in greater depth.

- When something sparks your interest, follow it. Usually when something captures your attention, it is short-lived—an idea, a song, a flower. Too often we are too busy to explore the idea, song, or flower further. Or we think these areas are none of our business because we are not experts about them. Yet the world is our business. We can't know which part of it is best suited to our interests until we make a serious effort to learn as much about as many aspects of it as possible.

- Wake up in the morning with a specific goal to look forward to. Creative people wake up eager to start the day. Why? Not necessarily because they are cheerful, enthusiastic types but because they know that there is something meaningful to accomplish each day, and they can't wait to get started.

- Spend time in settings that stimulate your creativity. In Csikszentmihalyi's (1995) research, he gave people an electronic pager and beeped them randomly at different times of the day. When he asked them how they felt, they reported the highest levels of creativity when walking,

Mihaly Csikszentmihalyi, in the setting where he gets his most creative ideas. *When and where do you get your most creative thoughts?*

driving, or swimming. I (your author) do my most creative thinking when I'm jogging. These activities are semiautomatic in that they take a certain amount of attention while leaving some time free to make connections among ideas. Another setting in which highly creative people report coming up with novel ideas is the sort of half-asleep, half-awake state we are in when we are deeply relaxed or barely awake.

Careers and Work

Earning a living, choosing an occupation, establishing a career, and developing in a career—these are important themes of early adulthood. Let's consider some of the factors that go into choosing a career and a job, and examine how work typically affects the lives of young adults.

Careers

What are some developmental changes young adults experience as they choose a career? How effectively are individuals finding a path to purpose today?

"Did you think the ladder of success would be straight up?"
© Joseph Farris/The New Yorker Collection/www.cartoonbank.com

Developmental Changes

Many children have idealistic fantasies about what they want to be when they grow up. For example, many young children want to be superheroes, sports stars, or movie stars. In the high school years, they often have begun to think about careers on a somewhat less idealistic basis. In their late teens and early twenties, their career decision making has usually turned more serious as they explore different career possibilities and zero in on the career they want to enter. In college, this often means choosing a major or specialization that is designed to lead to work in a particular field. By their early and mid-twenties, many individuals have completed their education or training and started to enter a full-time occupation. From the mid-twenties through the remainder of early adulthood, individuals often seek to establish their emerging career in a particular field. They may work hard to move up the career ladder and improve their financial standing.

Phyllis Moen (2009a) described the career mystique, which includes ingrained cultural beliefs that engaging in hard work for long hours through adulthood will produce a path to status, security, and happiness. That is, many individuals have an idealized concept of a career path toward achieving the American dream of upward mobility through occupational ladders. However, the lockstep career mystique has never been a reality for many individuals, especially ethnic minority individuals, women, and poorly educated adults. Further, the career mystique has increasingly become a myth for many individuals in middle-income occupations as global outsourcing of jobs and the 2007–2009 recession have meant reduced job security for millions of Americans.

Finding a Path to Purpose

In his book *The Path to Purpose: Helping Our Children Find Their Calling in Life*, William Damon (2008) explored how purpose is a missing ingredient in many adolescents' and emerging adults' achievement and career development. Too many youth drift aimlessly through their high school and college years, Damon says, engaging in behavior that places them at risk for not fulfilling their potential and not finding a life pursuit that energizes them.

In interviews with 12- to 22-year-olds, Damon found that only about 20 percent had a clear vision of where they wanted to go in life, what they wanted to achieve, and why. The largest percentage—about 60 percent—had engaged in some potentially purposeful activities, such as service learning or fruitful discussions with a career counselor—but they still did not have a real commitment or any reasonable plans for reaching their goals. And slightly more than 20 percent expressed no aspirations and in some instances said they didn't see any reason to have aspirations.

Damon concludes that most teachers and parents communicate the importance of such goals as studying hard and getting good grades, but rarely discuss the purpose of these goals and where they might lead young adults. Damon emphasizes that too often students focus only on short-term goals and don't explore the big, long-term picture of what they want to do with their life. These interview questions that Damon (2008, p. 135) has used in his research are good springboards for getting individuals to reflect on their purpose:

Hari Prabhakar (*in rear*) at a screening camp in India that he created as part of his Tribal India Health Foundation. Hari reflects William Damon's concept of finding a path to purpose. His ambition is to become an international health expert. Hari graduated from Johns Hopkins University in 2006 with a double major in public health and writing. A top student (3.9 GPA), he took the initiative to pursue a number of activities outside the classroom, in the health field. As he made the transition from high school to college, Hari created the Tribal India Health Foundation (www.tihf.org), which provides assistance in bringing low-cost health care to rural areas in India. Juggling his roles as a student and as the foundation's director, Hari spent about 15 hours a week leading Tribal India Health throughout his four undergraduate years. In describing his work, Hari said (Johns Hopkins University, 2006): "I have found it very challenging to coordinate the international operation. . . . It takes a lot of work, and there's not a lot of free time. But it's worth it when I visit our patients and see how they and the community are getting better." *Sources:* Johns Hopkins University (2006); Prabhakar (2007).

- What's most important to you in your life?
- Why do you care about those things?
- Do you have any long-term goals?
- Why are these goals important to you?
- What does it mean to have a good life?
- What does it mean to be a good person?
- If you were looking back on your life now, how would you like to be remembered?

A recent study found that discussing such questions involving their values and life goals improved college students' goal direction (Bundick, 2011).

Work

Let's explore these aspects of work: Its impact on people's lives, the role of work in college, the occupational outlook, unemployment, dual-earner couples, and diversity in the workplace.

The Impact of Work

Work defines people in fundamental ways (Highhouse & Schmitt, 2013; Motowidlo & Kell, 2013). It is an important influence on their financial standing, housing, the way they spend their time, where they live, their friendships, and their health

(Allen, 2013). Some people define their identity through their work. Work also creates a structure and rhythm to life that is often missed when individuals do not work for an extended period. When they are unable to work, many individuals experience emotional distress and low self-esteem.

Most individuals spend about one-third of their lives at work. In one survey, 35 percent of Americans worked 40 hours a week, but 18 percent worked 51 hours or more per week (Center for Survey Research at the University of Connecticut, 2000). Only 10 percent worked less than 30 hours a week.

A trend in the U.S. workforce is the disappearing long-term career for an increasing number of adults, especially men in private-sector jobs (Hollister, 2011). Among the reasons for the disappearance of many long-term jobs is the dramatic increase in technology and cheaper labor in other countries. Many young and older adults are working at a series of jobs, and many work in short-term jobs (Greenhaus, 2013).

An important consideration regarding work is how stressful it is (Fernandez & others, 2010). A national survey of U.S. adults revealed that 55 percent indicated they were less productive because of stress (American Psychological Association, 2007). In this study, 52 percent reported that they considered or made a career decision, such as looking for a new job, declining a promotion, or quitting a job, because of stress in the workplace. In this survey, main sources of stress included low salaries (44 percent), lack of advancement opportunities (42 percent), uncertain job expectations (40 percent), and long hours (39 percent).

Many adults have changing expectations about work, yet employers often aren't meeting their expectations (Lavoie-Tremblay & others, 2010). For example, current policies and practices were designed for a single breadwinner (male) workforce and an industrial economy, making these policies and practices out of step with a workforce of women and men, and of single parents and dual earners. Many workers today want flexibility and greater control over the time and timing of their work, and yet most employers offer little flexibility, even though policies like flextime may be "on the books."

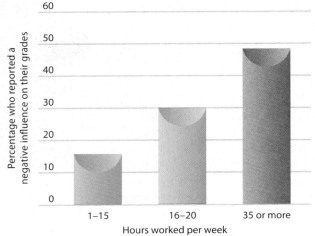

Work During College

The percentage of full-time U.S. college students who were employed increased from 34 percent in 1970 to 47 percent in 2008 (down from a peak of 52 percent in 2000) (National Center for Education Statistics, 2010). In this recent survey, 81 percent of part-time U.S. college students were employed.

Working can pay for schooling or help offset some of its costs, but working also can restrict students' opportunities to learn. For those who identified themselves primarily as students, one national study found that as the number of hours worked per week increased, their grades suffered (National Center for Education Statistics, 2002) (see Figure 11.7). Thus, college students need to carefully examine whether the number of hours they work is having a negative impact on their college success.

Of course, jobs also can contribute to your education. More than 1,000 colleges in the United States offer cooperative (co-op) programs, which are paid apprenticeships in a field that you are interested in pursuing. (You may not be permitted to participate in a co-op program

Figure 11.7 The Relation of Hours Worked Per Week in College to Grades
Among college students working to pay for school expenses, 16 percent of those working 1 to 15 hours per week reported that working negatively influenced their grades (National Center for Education Statistics, 2002). Thirty percent of college students who worked 16 to 20 hours a week said the same, as did 48 percent who worked 35 hours or more per week.

How Would You...?
As an educator, how would you advise a student who works a full-time job while taking college classes?

until your junior year.) Other useful opportunities for working while going to college include internships and part-time or summer jobs relevant to your field of study. Participating in these work experiences can be a key factor in landing the job you want when you graduate.

Monitoring the Occupational Outlook

As you explore the type of work you are likely to enjoy and in which you can succeed, it is important to be knowledgeable about different fields and companies. Occupations may have many job openings one year but few in another year as economic conditions change. Thus, it is critical to keep up with the occupational outlook in various fields. An excellent resource for doing this is the U.S. government's *Occupational Outlook Handbook, 2012–2013* (2012), which is revised every two years.

According to the 2012–2013 handbook, service industries, especially health services, professional and business services, and education are projected to account for the greatest numbers of new jobs in the next decade. Projected job growth varies widely by education requirements. Jobs that require a college degree are expected to grow the fastest. Most of the highest-paying occupations require a college degree.

Unemployment

Unemployment produces stress regardless of whether the job loss is temporary, cyclical, or permanent (Lundin, Backhans, & Hemmingsson, 2012). Banking problems and the recession toward the end of the first decade of the twenty-first century have produced very high unemployment rates, especially in the United States. Researchers have linked unemployment to physical problems (such as heart attack and stroke), mental problems (such as depression and anxiety), marital difficulties, and homicide (Backhans & Hemmingsson, 2012; Freyer-Adams & others, 2011). A 15-year longitudinal study of more than 24,000 adults found that their life satisfaction dropped considerably following unemployment and increased after they were reemployed but did not completely return to the same level

The economic recession that hit in 2007 resulted in millions of Americans losing their jobs, such as the individuals in line here waiting to apply for unemployment benefits in June 2009 in Chicago. *What are some of the potential negative outcomes of the stress caused by job loss?*

of life satisfaction previous to being unemployed (Lucas & others, 2004). Another study also revealed that immune system functioning declined with unemployment and increased with new employment (Cohen & others, 2007). A recent research review concluded that unemployment was associated with an increased mortality risk for individuals in the early and middle stages of their careers, but the link was weaker for those in the later years of their career (Roelfs & others, 2011).

Stress comes not only from a loss of income and the resulting financial hardships but also from decreased self-esteem (Howe & others, 2012). Individuals who cope best with unemployment have financial resources to rely on, often savings or the earnings of other family members. The support of understanding, adaptable family members also helps individuals to cope with unemployment. Job counseling and self-help groups can provide practical advice on job searching, résumé writing, and interviewing skills, and also can lend emotional support.

12 Socioemotional Development in Early Adulthood

Stories of Life-Span Development: Gwenna's Pursuit and Greg's Lack of Commitment

Commitment is an important issue in a romantic relationship for most individuals. Consider Gwenna, who decides that it is time to have a talk with Greg about his commitment to their relationship (Lerner, 1989, pp. 44–45):

> She shared her perspective on both the strengths and weaknesses of their relationship and what her hopes were for the future. She asked Greg to do the same. Unlike earlier conversations, this one was conducted without her pursuing him, pressuring him, or diagnosing his problems with women. At the same time, she asked Greg some clear questions, which exposed his vagueness.

> "How will you know when you are ready to make a commitment? What specifically would you need to change or be different than it is today?"

> "I don't know," was Greg's response. When questioned further, the best he could come up with was that he'd just feel it.

> "How much more time do you need to make a decision one way or another?"

> "I'm not sure," Greg replied. "Maybe a couple of years, but I really can't answer a question like that. I can't predict my feelings."

> And so it went.

> Gwenna really loved this man, but two years (and maybe longer) was longer than she could comfortably wait. So, after much thought, she told Greg that she would wait till fall (about ten months), but that she would move on if he couldn't commit himself to marriage by then. She was open about her wish to marry and have a family with him, but she was equally clear that her first priority was a mutually committed relationship. If Greg was not at that point by fall, then she would end the relationship—painful though it would be.

> During the waiting period, Gwenna was able to not pursue him and not get distant or otherwise reactive to his expressions of ambivalence and doubt. In this way she gave Greg emotional space

to struggle with his dilemma, and the relationship had its best chance of succeeding. Her bottom-line position ("a decision by fall") was not a threat or an attempt to rope Greg in, but rather a clear statement of what was acceptable to her.

When fall arrived, Greg told Gwenna he needed another six months to make up his mind. Gwenna deliberated a while and decided she could live with that. But when the six months were up, Greg was uncertain and asked for more time. It was then that Gwenna took the painful but ultimately empowering step of ending their relationship.

Love is of central importance in each of our lives, as it is in Gwenna's and Greg's lives. Shortly, we discuss the many faces of love, as well as the diversity of adult lifestyles, marriage and the family, and the role of gender in relationships. To begin, though, we will return to an issue we initially raised in Chapter 1: stability and change. ▪

Stability and Change from Childhood to Adulthood

For adults, socioemotional development revolves around adaptively integrating our emotional experiences into enjoyable relationships with others on a daily basis (Duck, 2011). Young adults like Gwenna and Greg face choices and challenges in adopting lifestyles that will be emotionally satisfying, predictable, and manageable for them. They do not come to these tasks as blank slates, but do their decisions and actions simply reflect the persons they had already become when they were 5 years old or 10 years old or 20 years old?

Current research shows that the first 20 years of life are not meaningless in predicting an adult's socioemotional life (Easterbrooks & others, 2013). And there is also every reason to believe that experiences in the early adult years are important in determining what the individual is like later in adulthood. A common finding is that the smaller the time intervals over which we measure socioemotional characteristics, the more similar an individual will look from one measurement to the next. Thus, if we measure an individual's self-concept at the age of 20, and then again at the age of 30, we will probably find more stability than if we measured the individual's self-concept at the age of 10 and then again at the age of 30.

In trying to understand the young adult's socioemotional development, it would be misleading to look at an adult's life only in the present tense, ignoring the unfolding of social relationships and emotions. So, too, it would be a mistake to search only through a 30-year-old's first five to ten years of life in trying to understand why he or she is having difficulty in a close relationship. To further explore stability and change, let's examine attachment.

Attachment appears during infancy and plays an important part in socioemotional development (Easterbrooks & others, 2013; Sroufe, Coffino, & Carlson, 2010). We discussed its role in infancy and adolescence (see Chapters 4 and 10). How do these earlier patterns of attachment and adults' attachment styles influence the lives of adults?

Although relationships with romantic partners differ from those with parents, romantic partners fulfill some of the same needs for adults as parents do for their children (Shaver & Mikulincer, 2013). Recall from Chapter 4 that *securely attached* infants are defined as those who use the caregiver as a secure base from which to explore the environment. Similarly, adults may count on their romantic partners to be a secure base to which they can return and obtain comfort and security in stressful times.

Do adult attachment patterns with partners reflect childhood attachment patterns with parents? In a retrospective study, Cindy Hazan & Phillip Shaver (1987) revealed that young adults who were securely attached in their romantic relationships were more likely to describe their early relationship with their parents as securely attached. In a longitudinal study, infants who were securely attached at

secure attachment style An attachment style that describes adults who have positive views of relationships, find it easy to get close to others, and are not overly concerned or stressed out about their romantic relationships.

avoidant attachment style An attachment style that describes adults who are hesitant about getting involved in romantic relationships and once they are in a relationship tend to distance themselves from their partner.

anxious attachment style An attachment style that describes adults who demand closeness, are less trusting, and are more emotional, jealous, and possessive.

age 1 were securely attached 20 years later in their adult romantic relationships (Steele & others, 1998). Also, a longitudinal study revealed that securely attached infants were in more stable romantic relationships in adulthood than their insecurely attached counterparts (Salvatore & others, 2011). However, in another longitudinal study, links between early attachment styles and later attachment styles were lessened by stressful and disruptive experiences such as the death of a parent or instability of caregiving (Lewis, Feiring, & Rosenthal, 2000).

Adults' attachment is categorized as secure, avoidant, or anxious:

How Would You...?

As a human development and family studies professional, how would you help individuals understand how early relationship experiences might influence their close relationships in adulthood?

- **Secure attachment style.** Securely attached adults have positive views of relationships, find it easy to get close to others, and are not overly concerned with or stressed out about their romantic relationships. These adults tend to enjoy sexuality in the context of a committed relationship and are less likely than others to have one-night stands.

- **Avoidant attachment style.** Avoidant individuals are hesitant about getting involved in romantic relationships, and once they are in a relationship, they tend to distance themselves from their partner.

- **Anxious attachment style.** These individuals demand closeness, are less trusting, and are more emotional, jealous, and possessive.

What are some key dimensions of attachment in adulthood, and how are they related to relationship patterns and well-being?

The majority of adults (about 60 to 80 percent) describe themselves as securely attached, and not surprisingly adults prefer having a securely attached partner (Zeifman & Hazan, 2008).

The following recent studies confirmed the importance of adult attachment in people's lives:

- Attachment security predicted more positive romantic relationships (Holland & Roisman, 2010).

- Adults with avoidant and anxious attachment patterns had a lower level of sexual satisfaction than their counterparts with a secure attachment pattern (Brassard & others, 2012).

- Anxiously attached adults were more ambivalent about relationship commitment than their securely attached counterparts (Joel, MacDonald, & Shimotomai, 2011).

- Individuals with an avoidant attachment style were less resistant to the temptations of infidelity, which was linked to their lower level of relationship commitment (Dewall & others, 2011).

- Attachment-anxious and attachment-avoidant adults had higher levels of depressive and anxious symptoms than attachment-secure adults (Jinyao & others, 2012).

- A national survey indicated that insecure attachment in adults was associated with the development of disease and chronic illness, especially cardiovascular system problems such as high blood pressure, heart attack, and stroke (McWilliams & Bailey, 2010).

If you have an insecure attachment style, are you stuck with it and does it doom you to have problematic relationships? Attachment categories are somewhat stable in adulthood, but adults do have the capacity to change their attachment thinking and behavior. Although attachment insecurities are linked to relationship problems, attachment style is only one factor that contributes to relationship functioning; other factors also contribute to relationship satisfaction and success. Later in the chapter, we will discuss some of these factors in our coverage of marital relationships.

Love and Close Relationships

Love refers to a vast and complex territory of human behavior, spanning a range of relationships that includes friendship, romantic love, affectionate love, and consummate love (Berscheid, 2010; Sternberg & Sternberg, 2012). In most of these types of love, one recurring theme is intimacy.

Intimacy

Self-disclosure and the sharing of private thoughts are hallmarks of intimacy (Miller, 2012). As we discussed in Chapter 10, adolescents have an increased need for intimacy. At the same time, they are engaged in the essential tasks of developing an identity and establishing their independence from their parents. Juggling the competing demands of intimacy, identity, and independence also becomes a central task of adulthood.

Erikson's Stage: Intimacy Versus Isolation

Recall from Chapter 10 that Erik Erikson (1968) argues that identity versus identity confusion—pursuing who we are, what we are all about, and where we are going in life—is the most important issue to be negotiated in adolescence. In early adulthood, according to Erikson, after individuals are well on their way to establishing stable and successful identities, they enter the sixth developmental stage, which is intimacy versus isolation. Erikson describes intimacy as finding oneself while losing oneself in another person, and it requires a commitment to another person.

Why is intimacy an important aspect of early adulthood?

A recent study confirmed Erikson's theory that identity development in adolescence is a precursor to intimacy in romantic relationships during emerging adulthood (Beyers & Seiffge-Krenke, 2010). And a meta-analysis revealed a positive link between identity development and intimacy, with the connection being stronger for men than women (Arseth & others, 2009).

An inability to develop meaningful relationships with others can harm an individual's personality. It may lead individuals to repudiate, ignore, or attack those who frustrate them. Such circumstances account for the shallow, almost pathetic attempts of youth to merge themselves with a leader. Many youth want to be apprentices or disciples of leaders and adults who will shelter them from the harm of the "out-group" world. If this fails, and Erikson believes that it must, sooner or later the individuals recoil into a self-search to discover where they went wrong. This introspection sometimes leads to painful depression and isolation. It also may contribute to a mistrust of others.

Intimacy and Independence

Development in early adulthood often involves balancing intimacy and commitment on the one hand, and independence and freedom on the other. At the same time that individuals are trying to establish an identity, they face the challenges of increasing their independence from their parents, developing an intimate relationship with another individual, and continuing their friendship commitments. They also face the task of making decisions for themselves without always relying on what others say or do.

The extent to which young adults develop autonomy has important implications for them. For example, young adults who have not sufficiently moved away from parental ties may have difficulty in both interpersonal relationships and a career.

The balance between intimacy and commitment—and independence and freedom—is delicate (Guerrero, Andersen, & Afifi, 2011). Some individuals are able to experience a healthy independence and freedom along with an intimate relationship. Keep in mind that intimacy and commitment, and independence and freedom, are not just concerns of early adulthood. They are important themes of development that recur throughout the adult years.

Friendship

Increasingly, researchers are finding that friendship plays an important role in development throughout the human life span (Blieszner & Roberto, 2012). Most U.S. men and women have a best friend. Ninety-two percent of women and 88 percent of men have a best friend of the same sex (Blieszner, 2009). Many friendships are long-lasting, as 65 percent of U.S. adults have known their best friend for at least 10 years and only 15 percent have known their best friend for less than 5 years. Adulthood brings opportunities for new friendships; when individuals move to new locations, they may establish new friendships in their neighborhood or at work (Blieszner, 2009).

As in the childhood years, there are gender differences in adult friendship (Bliezner & Roberto, 2012). Compared with men, women have more close friends and their friendships involve more self-disclosure and exchange of mutual support (Wood, 2012). Women are more likely to listen at length to what a friend has to say and be sympathetic, and women have been labeled "talking companions" because talk is so central to their relationships (Gouldner & Strong, 1987). Women's friendships tend to be characterized not only by depth but also by breadth: Women share many aspects of their experiences, thoughts, and feelings (Helgeson, 2012). A recent study revealed that in their early twenties, women showed more emotional intimacy with their closest friend than did men (Boden, Fischer, & Niehuis, 2010).

How is adult friendship different among female friends, male friends, and cross-gender friends?

Romantic and Affectionate Love

Although friendship is included in some conceptualizations of love, when we think about what love is, other types of love typically come to mind. In this section we explore two widely recognized types of love: romantic love and affectionate love.

Romantic Love

Some friendships evolve into **romantic love,** which is also called passionate love, or eros. Romantic love has strong components of sexuality and infatuation, and as well-known love researcher Ellen Berscheid (2010) has found, it often predominates in the early part

romantic love Also called passionate love, or eros; romantic love has strong sexual and infatuation components and often predominates in the early period of a love relationship.

How Would You...?

As a health-care professional, how would you advise individuals who are concerned about their sexual functioning because their romantic relationship seems to be losing its spark?

of a love relationship. A recent meta-analysis found that males show higher avoidance and lower anxiety about romantic love than females (Del Giudice, 2011).

A complex intermingling of different emotions goes into romantic love—including passion, fear, anger, sexual desire, joy, and jealousy. Sexual desire is the most important ingredient of romantic love (Berscheid, 2010). Obviously, some of these emotions are a source of anguish, which can lead to other issues such as depression. One study found that a relationship between romantic lovers was more likely than a relationship between friends to be a cause of depression (Berscheid & Fei, 1977).

affectionate love In this type of love, also called companionate love, an individual desires to have the other person near and has a deep, caring affection for the other person.

Affectionate Love

Love is more than just passion. **Affectionate love,** also called companionate love, is the type of love that occurs when someone desires to have the other person near and has a deep, caring affection for the person.

The early stages of love have more romantic love ingredients—but as love matures, passion tends to give way to affection (Berscheid, 2010). Phillip Shaver (1986) proposed a developmental model of love in which the initial phase of romantic love is fueled by a mixture of sexual attraction and gratification, a reduced sense of loneliness, uncertainty about the security of developing another attachment, and excitement from exploring the novelty of another human being. With time, he says, sexual attraction wanes, attachment anxieties either lessen or produce conflict and withdrawal, novelty is replaced with familiarity, and lovers find themselves either securely attached in a deeply caring relationship or distressed—feeling bored, disappointed, lonely, or hostile, for example. In the latter case, one or both partners may eventually end the relationship and then move on to another relationship.

Consummate Love

So far we have discussed two forms of love: romantic (or passionate) and affectionate (or companionate). According to Robert J. Sternberg (1988; Sternberg & Sternberg, 2012), these are not the only forms of love. Sternberg proposed a triarchic theory of love in which love can be thought of as a triangle with three main dimensions—passion, intimacy, and commitment. Passion involves physical and sexual attraction to another. Intimacy relates to the emotional feelings of warmth, closeness, and sharing in a relationship. Commitment is the cognitive appraisal of the relationship and the intent to maintain the relationship even in the face of problems.

In Sternberg's theory, the strongest, fullest form of love is *consummate love,* which involves all three dimensions (see Figure 12.1). If passion is the only ingredient in a relationship (with intimacy and commitment low or absent), we are merely *infatuated.* An affair or a fling in which there is little intimacy and even less commitment is an example. A relationship marked by intimacy and commitment but low or lacking in passion is called *affectionate love,* a pattern often found among couples who have been married for many years. If passion and commitment are present but intimacy is not, Sternberg calls the relationship *fatuous love,* as when one person worships another from a distance. But if

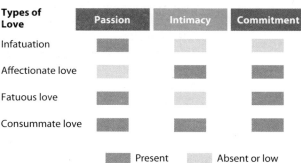

Figure 12.1 Sternberg's Triangle of Love
Sternberg identified three dimensions of love: passion, intimacy, and commitment. Various combinations of these dimensions result in infatuation, affectionate love, fatuous love, and consummate love.

couples share all three dimensions—passion, intimacy, and commitment—they experience consummate love (Sternberg & Sternberg, 2012).

Adult Lifestyles

A striking social change in recent decades has been the decreased stigma attached to individuals who do not maintain what were long considered conventional families. Adults today choose many lifestyles and form many types of families (Benokraitis, 2012; Klinenberg, 2012). They live alone, cohabit, marry, divorce, or live with someone of the same sex.

In a recent book, *The Marriage-Go-Round*, sociologist Andrew Cherlin (2009) concluded that the United States has more marriages and remarriages, more divorces, and more short-term cohabiting (living together) relationships than most countries. Combined, these lifestyles create more turnover and movement in and out of relationships in the United States than in virtually any other country. Let's explore these varying relationship lifestyles.

Single Adults

Recent decades have seen a dramatic rise in the percentage of single adults. Data from 2009 indicate that for the first time in history the proportion of individuals 25 to 34 years of age who have never been married (46 percent) exceeded those who were married (45 percent) (U.S. Census Bureau, 2010). The increasing number of single adults is the result of rising rates of cohabitation and a trend toward postponing marriage.

Even when singles enjoy their lifestyles and are highly competent individuals, they often are stereotyped (Schwartz & Scott, 2012). Stereotypes associated with being single range from the "swinging single" to the "desperately lonely, suicidal" single. Of course, most single adults are somewhere between these extremes.

Common challenges faced by single adults may include forming intimate relationships with other adults, confronting loneliness, and finding a niche in a society that is marriage-oriented. Bella DePaulo (2006, 2011) argues that society has a widespread bias against unmarried adults that is seen in everything from missed perks in jobs to deep social and financial prejudices.

Advantages of being single include having time to make decisions about one's life course, time to develop personal resources to meet goals, freedom to make autonomous decisions and pursue one's own schedule and interests, opportunities to explore new places and try out new experiences, and privacy.

A recent nationally representative U.S. survey of more than 5,000 single adults 21 years and older not in a committed relationship revealed that men are more interested in love, marriage, and children than their counterparts were in earlier generations (Match.com, 2011). In this study, today's women desire more independence in their relationships than their mothers did. Across every age group, more women than men reported wanting to pursue their own interests, have personal space, have their own bank account, have regular nights out with girlfriends, and take vacations on their own. In a second nationally representative survey, many single adults reported that they were looking for love but not marriage (Match.com, 2012). In this survey, almost 40 percent of the single adults were uncertain about whether they wanted to get married, 34 percent said they did want to marry, and 27 percent said they didn't want to get married.

Cohabiting Adults

Cohabitation refers to living together in a sexual relationship without being married. Cohabitation has undergone considerable changes in recent years (Benokraitis,

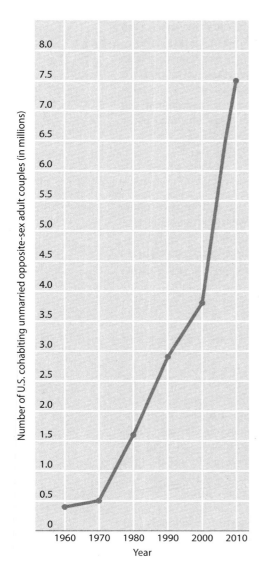

Figure 12.2
The Increase in Cohabitation in the United States
Since 1970, there has been a dramatic increase in the number of unmarried adults living together in the United States.

2012; Musick & Bumpass, 2012). As indicated in Figure 12.2, there has been a dramatic increase in the number of cohabiting U.S. couples since 1970, with more than 60 percent cohabiting prior to getting married (The National Marriage Project, 2011). And the trend shows no sign of letting up—from 3.8 million cohabiting couples in 2000 to 7.5 million cohabiting couples in 2010 (U.S. Census Bureau, 2010). Cohabitation rates are even higher in some countries—in Sweden, for example, cohabitation before marriage is virtually universal (Stokes & Raley, 2009).

A number of couples view their cohabitation not as a precursor to marriage but as an ongoing lifestyle (Klinenberg, 2012; Schwartz & Scott, 2012). These couples do not want the official aspects of marriage. In the United States, cohabiting arrangements tend to be short-lived, with one-third lasting less than a year (Hyde & DeLamater, 2011). Fewer than 1 out of 10 lasts five years. Of course, it is easier to dissolve a cohabitation relationship than a marriage.

A recent study revealed that young adults' main reasons for cohabiting are to spend time together, share expenses, and evaluate compatibility (Huang & others, 2011). In this study, gender differences emerged regarding drawbacks in cohabiting: men were more concerned about their loss of freedom while women were more concerned about delays in getting married.

Couples who cohabit face certain problems (Rhoades, Stanley, & Markman, 2009). Disapproval by parents and other family members can place emotional strain on the cohabiting couple. Some cohabiting couples have difficulty owning property jointly. Legal rights on the dissolution of the relationship are less certain than in a divorce. A recent study also found that cohabiting relationships were characterized by more commitment, lower satisfaction, more negative communication, and more physical aggression than dating (noncohabiting) relationships (Rhoades, Stanley, & Markman, 2012).

If a couple live together before they marry, does cohabiting help or harm their chances of later having a stable and happy marriage? The majority of studies have found lower rates of marital satisfaction and higher rates of divorce in couples who lived together before getting married (Copen & others, 2012; Whitehead & Popenoe, 2003). However, recent research indicates that the link between marital cohabitation and marital instability in first marriages has weakened in recent cohorts (Manning & Cohen, 2012; Reinhold, 2010).

What might explain the finding that cohabiting is linked with divorce more than not cohabiting? The most frequently given explanation is that the less traditional lifestyle of cohabitation may attract less conventional individuals who are not great believers in marriage in the first place (Whitehead & Popenoe, 2003). An alternative explanation is that the experience of cohabiting changes people's attitudes and habits in ways that increase their likelihood of divorce.

What are some potential advantages and disadvantages of cohabitation?

How Would You...?

As a psychologist, how would you counsel a couple deciding whether to cohabit before marriage?

Recent research has provided clarification of cohabitation outcomes. One meta-analysis found the negative link between cohabitation and marital instability did not hold up when only cohabitation with the eventual marital partner was examined, indicating that these cohabitors may attach more long-term positive meaning to living together (Jose, O'Leary, & Moyer, 2010). Also, a recent analysis indicated that cohabiting does not have a negative effect on marriage if the couple did not have any previous live-in lovers and did not have children prior to the marriage (Cherlin, 2009).

Married Adults

Until about 1930, stable marriage was widely accepted as the endpoint of adult development. In the last 80 years, however, personal fulfillment both inside and outside marriage has emerged as a goal that competes with marital stability. The changing norm of male-female equality in marriage has produced marital relationships that are more fragile and intense than they were in earlier generations (Lavner & Bradbury, 2012).

Marital Trends

In recent years, marriage rates in the United States have declined. From 2007 to 2010, the marriage rate continued to drop. In 2010, 51 percent of Americans were married, down from 72 percent in 1960 (Pew Research Center, 2010).

More adults are remaining single longer, with 27 percent of U.S. adults currently having never married (Pew Research Center, 2010). In 2011, the U.S. average age for a first marriage climbed to 28.7 years for men and 26.5 years for women, higher than at any other point in history (Pew Research Center, 2011). In 1980, the average age for a first marriage in the United States was 24 years for men and 21 years for women. In addition, the increase in cohabitation and a slight decline in the percentage of divorced individuals who remarry contribute to the decline in marriage rates in the United States (Copen & others, 2012).

Despite the decline in marriage rates, the United States is still a marrying society (Popenoe, 2009). In 2010, by 40 years of age, 77 percent of individuals had ever been married, although this figure is substantially below the figure of 93 percent in the 1960s (Pew Research Center, 2011). In a recent national poll, more than 40 percent of Americans under 30 believed that marriage was headed for extinction, yet only 5 percent of those young adults said they didn't want to get married (Pew Research Center, 2010). These findings may reflect marriage's role as a way to show friends and family that you have a successful social life (Cherlin, 2009).

Is there a best age to get married? Marriages in adolescence are more likely to end in divorce than marriages in adulthood (Copen & others, 2012). However, researchers have not been able to pin down a specific age range for getting married that is most likely to result in a successful marriage (Furstenberg, 2007).

How happy are people who do marry? The average duration of a marriage in the United States is currently just over nine years. As indicated in Figure 12.3, the percentage of married individuals in the United States who said their marriages were "very happy" declined from the 1970s through the early 1990s but recently the decline has begun to flatten out (Popenoe, 2009). Notice in Figure 12.3 that men consistently report being happier in their marriages than women do.

The Benefits of a Good Marriage

Are there any benefits to having a good marriage? There are several (Seccombe, 2012). Individuals who are happily married live longer, healthier lives than either divorced individuals or those who are unhappily married (Lee & others, 2011; Shor & others, 2012). A survey of U.S. adults 50 years and older also revealed that a lower portion of adult life spent in marriage was linked to an increased likelihood of dying at an earlier age (Henretta, 2010). And a recent large-scale

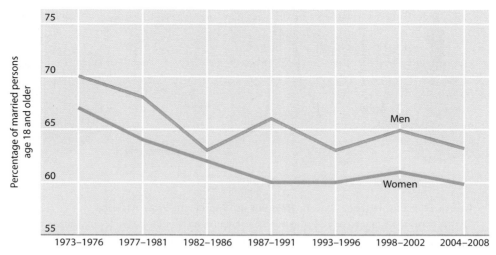

Figure 12.3 **Percentage of Married Persons Age 18 and Older With "Very Happy" Marriages**

analysis of data from a number of studies indicated a positive effect of marriage on life span, with being married benefitting the longevity of men more than women (Rendall & others, 2011). Further, an unhappy marriage can shorten a person's life by an average of four years (Gove, Style, & Hughes, 1990).

What are the reasons for these benefits of a happy marriage? People in happy marriages are likely to feel less physically and emotionally stressed, which puts less wear and tear on a person's body. Such wear and tear can lead to numerous physical ailments, such as high blood pressure and heart disease, as well as psychological problems such as anxiety, depression, and substance abuse.

Divorced Adults

Divorce has become an epidemic in the United States (Welch, 2012). The number of divorced adults rose from 1.8 percent of the adult population in 1960 to 4.8 percent in 1980 and to 8.6 percent in 2007, but it declined from 2007 to 2009 (National Center for Vital Statistics, 2010; Popenoe, 2009).

Individuals in some groups have higher rates of divorce (Amato, 2010; Repetti, Flook, & Sperling, 2011). Youthful marriage, low educational level, low income, not having a religious affiliation, having parents who are divorced, and having a baby before marriage are factors that are associated with increases in divorce (Hoelter, 2009). And certain characteristics of one's partner increase the likelihood of divorce: alcoholism, psychological problems, domestic violence, infidelity, and inadequate division of household labor (Hoelter, 2009).

Earlier, we indicated that researchers have not been able to pin down a specific age that is the best time to marry so that the marriage is unlikely to end in a divorce. However, if a divorce is going to occur, it usually takes place early in a marriage; most occur in the fifth to tenth years of marriage (National Center for Health Statistics, 2000) (see Figure 12.4). This timing may reflect an effort by partners in troubled marriages to stay in the marriage and try to work things out. If after several years these efforts have not improved the relationship, they may then seek a divorce.

Remarried Adults

Adults who remarry usually do so rather quickly, with approximately 50 percent remarrying within three years after they initially divorce (Sweeney, 2009, 2010). Men remarry sooner than women. Men with higher incomes are more likely to remarry than their counterparts with lower incomes. Remarriage occurs sooner for partners who initiate a divorce (especially in the first several years after divorce

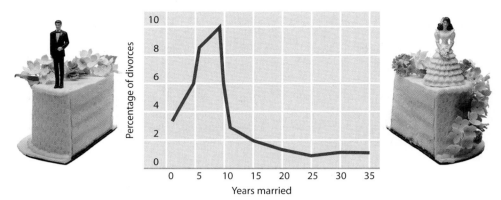

Figure 12.4 The Divorce Rate in Relation to Number of Years Married
Shown here is the percentage of divorces as a function of how long couples have been married. Notice that most divorces occur in the early years of marriage, peaking in the fifth to tenth years of marriage.

and for older women) than for those who do not initiate it (Sweeney, 2009, 2010). And some remarried individuals are more adult-focused, responding more to the concerns of their partner, while others are more child-focused, responding more to the concerns of the children (Anderson & Greene, 2011).

Evidence on the benefits of remarriage for adults is mixed (Seccombe, 2012). Remarried families are more likely to be unstable and divorce is more likely to occur, especially in the first several years of the remarriage, compared with first-marriage families (Waite, 2009). Adults who get remarried have a lower level of mental health (higher rates of depression, for example) than adults in first marriages, but remarriage often improves the financial status of remarried adults, especially women (Waite, 2009). Researchers have found that the relationship in remarriages is more egalitarian and more likely to be characterized by shared decision making than the relationship in first marriages (Waite, 2009). Remarried wives also report that they have more influence on financial matters in their new family than do wives in first marriages (Waite, 2009).

Gay and Lesbian Adults

The legal and social context of marriage creates barriers to breaking up that do not usually exist for same-sex partners (Rostosky & others, 2010). But in other ways, researchers have found that gay and lesbian relationships are similar—in their satisfactions, loves, joys, and conflicts—to heterosexual relationships (Fingerhut & Peplau, 2013). For example, like heterosexual couples, gay and lesbian couples need to find the balance of romantic love, affection, autonomy, and equality that is acceptable to both partners (Hope, 2009). An increasing number of gay and lesbian couples are creating families that include children.

There are a number of misconceptions about gay and lesbian couples. Contrary to stereotypes, one partner is masculine and the other feminine in only a small percentage of gay and lesbian couples. Only a small segment of the gay population has a large number of sexual partners, and this is uncommon among lesbians. Furthermore, researchers have found that gay and lesbian couples prefer long-term, committed relationships (Fingerhut & Peplau, 2013). About half of committed gay couples do have an open relationship that allows the possibility of sex (but not affectionate love) outside of the relationship. Lesbian couples usually do not have an open relationship.

A special concern is the stigma, prejudice, and discrimination that lesbian, gay, and bisexual individuals experience because of widespread social devaluation of same-sex relationships (Balsam & Hughes, 2013). However, a recent study indicated that many individuals in these relationships saw stigma as bringing them closer together and strengthening their relationship (Frost, 2011).

Challenges in Marriage, Parenting, and Divorce

No matter what lifestyles young adults choose, they will bring certain challenges. Because many choose the lifestyle of marriage, we'll consider some of the challenges in marriage and how to make it work. We also examine some challenges in parenting and trends in childbearing. Given the statistics about divorce rates in the previous section, we'll then consider how to deal with divorce.

Making Marriage Work

John Gottman (1994, 2006, 2011; Gottman & Gottman, 2009; Gottman & Silver, 2000) uses many methods to analyze what makes marriages work. He interviews couples about the history of their marriage, their philosophy about marriage, and how they view their parents' marriages. He videotapes them talking to each other about how their day went and evaluates what they say about the good and bad times of their marriages. Gottman also uses physiological measures to chart their heart rate, blood flow, blood pressure, and immune functioning moment by moment. In addition, he checks back with the couples every year to see how their marriage is faring. Gottman's research represents the most extensive assessment of marital relationships available. Currently, he and his colleagues are following 700 couples in seven studies.

Among the principles Gottman has found that determine whether a marriage will work are the following:

What makes marriages work? What are the benefits of having a good marriage?

- *Establishing love maps.* Individuals in successful marriages have personal insights and detailed maps of each other's life and world. They aren't psychological strangers. In good marriages, partners are willing to share their feelings with each other. They use these "love maps" to express not only their understanding of each other but also their fondness and admiration.

- *Nurturing fondness and admiration.* In successful marriages, partners sing each other's praises. More than 90 percent of the time, when couples put a positive spin on their marriage's history, the marriage is likely to have a positive future.

- *Turning toward each other instead of away.* In good marriages, spouses are adept at turning toward each other regularly. They see each other as friends. This friendship doesn't keep arguments from occurring, but it can prevent differences from overwhelming the relationship. In these good marriages, spouses respect each other and appreciate each other's point of view despite disagreements.

- *Letting your partner influence you.* Bad marriages often involve one spouse who is unwilling to share power with the other. Although power-mongering is more common in husbands, some wives also show this trait. A willingness to share power and to respect the other person's view is a prerequisite to compromising.

- *Creating shared meaning.* The more partners can speak candidly and respectfully with each other,

How Would You...?

As a human development and family studies professional, how would you counsel a newly married couple seeking advice on how to make their marriage work?

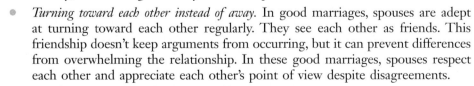

the more likely they will create shared meaning in their marriage. This also includes sharing goals with one's spouse and working together to achieve each other's goals.

In a provocative book, *Marriage, a History: How Love Conquered Marriage*, Stephanie Coontz (2005) concluded that marriages in America today are fragile not because Americans have become self-centered and career-minded, but because expectations for marriage have become unrealistically high compared with previous generations. To make a marriage work, she emphasizes like Gottman that partners need to develop a deep friendship, show respect for each other, and embrace commitment.

Becoming a Parent

For many young adults, parental roles are well planned, coordinated with other roles in life, and developed with the individual's economic situation in mind. For others, the discovery that they are about to become parents is a startling surprise. In either event, the prospective parents may have mixed emotions and romantic illusions about having a child (Carl, 2012).

Parenting requires a number of interpersonal skills and imposes emotional demands, yet there is little in the way of formal education for this task. Most parents learn parenting practices from their own parents—some they accept, some they discard. Unfortunately, when parenting practices are passed on from one generation to the next, both desirable and undesirable practices are perpetuated. Adding to the challenges of the task of parenting, husbands and wives may bring different parenting practices to the marriage (Huston & Holmes, 2004). The parents, then, may struggle with each other about which is a better way to interact with a child.

Parent educators seek to help individuals become better parents. To read about the work of one parent educator, see *Careers in Life-Span Development*.

Careers in life-span development

Janis Keyser, Parent Educator

Janis Keyser is a parent educator who teaches in the Department of Early Childhood Education at Cabrillo College in California. In addition to teaching college classes and conducting parenting workshops, she has co-authored a book with Laura Davis (1997), *Becoming the Parent You Want to Be: A Sourcebook of Strategies for the First Five Years*.

Janis writes as an expert on the iVillage Web site (www. parentsplace.com). She also co-authors a nationally syndicated parenting column, "Growing Up, Growing Together." She is the mother of three, stepmother of five, grandmother of twelve, and great-grandmother of six.

Parent educators may have different educational backgrounds and occupational profiles. Janis Keyser has a background in early childhood education and, as just indicated, teaches at a college. Many parent educators have majored in areas such as child development as an undergraduate and/or taken a specialization of parenting and family courses in a master's or doctoral degree program in human development

Janis Keyser (*right*), conducting a parenting workshop.

and family studies, clinical psychology, counseling psychology, or social work. As part of, or in addition to, their work in colleges and clinical settings, they may conduct parent education groups and workshops.

Like marriage, the age at which individuals have children has been increasing (Lauer & Lauer, 2012). In 2008, the average age at which women gave birth for the first time was 25, up from 21 years of age in 2001 (U.S. Census Bureau, 2011).

As birth control has become common practice, many individuals consciously choose when they will have children and how many children they will rear. The number of one-child families is increasing, for example, and U.S. women overall are having fewer children. These childbearing results are creating several trends:

- By giving birth to fewer children, and reducing the demands of child care, women free up a significant portion of their life spans for other endeavors.

- As working women increase in number, they invest less actual time in the child's development.

- Men are apt to invest a greater amount of time in fathering.

- Parental care is often supplemented by institutional care (child care, for example).

How Would You...?

As a human development and family studies professional, how would you advise a young woman who is inquiring about the best age to have children?

As more women show an increased interest in developing a career, they are not only marrying later, but also having fewer children and having them later in life. What are some of the advantages of having children early or late? Some of the advantages of having children early (in the twenties) are that the parents are likely to have more physical energy (for example, they can cope better with such matters as getting up in the middle of the night with infants and waiting up until adolescents come home at night); the mother is likely to have fewer medical problems with pregnancy and childbirth; and the parents may be less likely to build up expectations for their children, as do many couples who have waited many years to have children.

There are also advantages to having children later (in the thirties). The parents will have had more time to consider and achieve some of their goals in life, such as what they want from their family and career roles; the parents will be more mature and will be able to benefit from their life experiences to engage in more competent parenting; and the parents will be better established in their careers and have more income for child-rearing expenses.

Dealing with Divorce

If a marriage doesn't work, what happens after divorce? Psychologically, one of the most common characteristics of divorced adults is difficulty trusting someone else in a romantic relationship. Following a divorce, though, people's lives can take diverse turns (Ben-Zur, 2012; Smith & others, 2012). For example, in one research study 20 percent of the divorced group became more competent and better adjusted following their divorce (Hetherington & Kelly, 2002).

Strategies for divorced adults include the following (Hetherington & Kelly, 2002):

- Thinking of divorce as a chance to grow personally and to develop more positive relationships.

What are some strategies for coping with divorce?

rapport talk The language of
conversation; it is a way of establishing connections and negotiating
relationships.

report talk Talk that is designed
to give information and includes
public speaking.

- Making decisions carefully. The consequences of your decisions regarding work, lovers, and children may last a lifetime.

- Focusing more on the future than the past. Think about what is most important for you going forward in your life, set some challenging goals, and plan how to reach them.

- Using your strengths and resources to cope with difficulties.

- Not expecting to be successful and happy in everything you do. The path to a more enjoyable life will likely have a number of twists and turns, and moving forward will require considerable effort and resilience.

Gender, Communication, and Relationships

When Deborah Tannen (1990) analyzed the talk of women and men, she found that many wives complain about their husbands: "He doesn't listen to me anymore" and "He doesn't talk to me anymore." Lack of communication, though high on women's lists of reasons for divorce, is mentioned much less often by men.

Communication problems between men and women may come in part from differences in their preferred ways of communicating (Guerrero, Andersen, & Afifi, 2011; Wood, 2012). Tannen distinguishes two ways of communicating: rapport talk and report talk. **Rapport talk** is the language of conversation; it is a way of establishing connections and negotiating relationships. **Report talk** is talk that is designed to give information, which includes public speaking. According to Tannen, women enjoy rapport talk more than report talk, and men's lack of interest in rapport talk bothers many women. In contrast, men prefer to engage in report talk. Men hold center stage through such verbal performances as telling stories and jokes. They learn to use talk as a way of getting and keeping attention.

How extensive are the gender differences in communication? Research has yielded somewhat mixed results. Several studies do reveal some gender differences (Guerrero, Andersen, & Afifi, 2011). One study of a sampling of students' e-mails found that people could guess the writer's gender two-thirds of the time (Thompson & Murachver, 2001). Another study revealed that women make 63 percent of phone calls and, when talking to another woman, stay on the phone longer (7.2 minutes) than men do when talking with other men (4.6 minutes) (Smoreda & Licoppe, 2000). However, meta-analyses suggest that overall gender differences in communication are small for both children and adults (Hyde, 2005, 2007; Leaper & Smith, 2004). Further, one analysis revealed no gender differences in the average number of total words spoken by seven different samples of college men and women over 17 waking hours (Mehl & others, 2007).

A thorough study documented some gender differences in specific aspects of communication (Newman & others, 2008). In this study, women used words more for discussing people and what they were doing, as well as for communicating internal processes to others, including expression of doubts. By contrast, men used words more for external events, objects, and processes, including occupation, money, sports, and swearing. Contrary to popular stereotypes, men and women could not be distinguished in their references to sexuality and anger.

"You have no idea how nice it is to have someone to talk to."
Copyright © 1994 by Dan Orehek.

How Would You...?

As a social worker, how would you educate a marital therapy group about the role of gender in communication and relationships?

Summary

Stability and Change from Childhood to Adulthood

- The first 20 years are important in predicting an adult's personality, but so are ongoing experiences in the adult years. Attachment styles, for example, reflect childhood patterns and continue to influence relationships in adulthood. Adult attachments are categorized as secure, avoidant, or anxious. A secure attachment style is linked with positive aspects of relationships.

Love and Close Relationships

- Erikson theorized that intimacy versus isolation is the key developmental issue in early adulthood.

- Friendship plays an important role in adult development, especially in terms of emotional support.

- Romantic love, also called passionate love, includes passion, sexuality, and a mixture of emotions, not all of which are positive. Affectionate love, also called companionate love, usually becomes more important as relationships mature.

- Sternberg proposed a triarchic model of love: passion, intimacy, and commitment. If all three qualities are present, the result is consummate love.

Adult Lifestyles

- Being single has become an increasingly prominent lifestyle. Autonomy is one of its advantages. Challenges faced by single adults include achieving intimacy, coping with loneliness, and finding a positive identity in a marriage-oriented society.

- Cohabitation, an increasingly popular lifestyle, does not lead to greater marital happiness but is linked to possible negative consequences if a cohabiting couple marries.

- The age at which individuals marry in the United States is increasing. Though marriage rates have declined, a large percentage of Americans still marry. The benefits of marriage include better physical and mental health and a longer life.

- The U.S. divorce rate increased dramatically in the middle of the twentieth century but began to decline in the 1980s.

- Divorce is a complex and emotional experience.

- Stepfamilies are complex, and adjustment is difficult. Evidence on the benefits of remarriage after divorce is mixed.

- One of the most striking research findings about gay and lesbian couples is how similar their relationships are to heterosexual couples' relationships.

Challenges in Marriage, Parenting, and Divorce

- Gottman's research indicates that in marriages that work, couples establish love maps, nurture fondness and admiration, turn toward each other, accept the influence of the partner, and create shared meaning.

- Families are becoming smaller, and many women are delaying childbirth until they have become well established in a career.

- Divorced adults often have difficulty trusting someone else in a romantic relationship. Certain strategies are effective in dealing with divorce.

Gender, Communication, and Relationships

- Tannen distinguishes between rapport talk, which many women prefer, and report talk, which many men prefer, but the extent to which gender differences in communication exist continues to be debated.

Key Terms

secure attachment style 320

avoidant attachment style 320

anxious attachment style 320

romantic love 322

affectionate love 323

rapport talk 332

report talk 332

13 Physical and Cognitive Development in Middle Adulthood

Stories of Life-Span Development: Jim Croce, Time in a Bottle

Our perception of time depends on where we are in the life span. We are more concerned about time at some points in life than others (Charles & Carstensen, 2010; MacDonald, DeCarlo, & Dixon, 2011). Jim Croce's song "Time in a Bottle" reflects a time perspective that develops in the adult years:

If I could save time in a bottle
The first thing that I'd like to do
Is to save every day
Til Eternity passes away
Just to spend them with you . . .
But there never seems to be enough time

To do the things you want to do
Once you find them
I've looked around enough to know
That you're the one I want to go
Through time with

Jim Croce's song connects time with love and the hope of going through time with someone we love. Love and intimacy are important themes of adult development. So is time. In middle adulthood, individuals increasingly think about time-left-to-live instead of time-since-birth (Kotter-Gruhn & Smith, 2011; Setterson, 2009).

Middle-aged adults begin to look back to where they have been, reflecting on what they have done with the time they have had. They look toward the future in terms of how much time remains to accomplish what they hope to do with their lives.

In this first chapter on middle adulthood, we discuss physical changes; cognitive changes; changes in careers, work, and leisure. We also discuss the importance of religion and meaning in life. To begin, though, we explore how middle age is changing. ∎

The Nature of Middle Adulthood

Is midlife experienced the same way today as it was 100 years ago? How can middle adulthood be defined, and what are some of its main characteristics?

Changing Midlife

Many of today's 50-year-olds are in better shape, more alert, and more productive than their 40-year-old counterparts from a generation or two earlier. As more people lead healthier lifestyles and medical discoveries help to stave off the aging process, the boundaries of middle age are being pushed upward. It looks like middle age is starting later and lasting longer for increasing numbers of active, healthy, and productive people. A current saying is "60 is the new 40," implying that many 60-year-olds today are living a life that is as active, productive, and healthy as earlier generations did in their forties.

Questions such as, "To which age group do you belong?" and "How old do you feel?" reflect the concept of *age identity*. A consistent finding is that as adults become older their age identity is younger than their chronological age (Setterson & Trauten, 2009; Westerhof, 2009). One study found that almost half of the individuals 65 to 69 years of age considered themselves middle-aged (National Council on Aging, 2000), and another study found a similar pattern: Half of the 60- to 75-year-olds viewed themselves as being middle-aged (Lachman, Maier, & Budner, 2000). Also, some individuals consider the upper boundary of midlife to be the age at which they make the transition from work to retirement.

When Carl Jung studied midlife transitions early in the twentieth century, he referred to midlife as "the afternoon of life" (Jung, 1933). Midlife serves as an important preparation for late adulthood, "the evening of life" (Lachman, 2004, p. 306). But "midlife" came much earlier in Jung's time. In 1900 the average life expectancy was only 47 years of age; only 3 percent of the population lived past 65. Today, the average life expectancy is 78, and 12 percent of the U.S. population is older than 65. As a much greater percentage of the population lives to older ages, the midpoint of life and what constitutes middle age or middle adulthood

How is midlife changing?

are getting harder to pin down (Cohen, 2012). Statistically, the middle of life today is about 39 years of age, but most 39-year-olds don't want to be called "middle-aged." What we think of as middle age comes later—anywhere from 40 or 45 to about 60 or 65 years of age. And as more people live longer, the upper boundary of middle age will likely be nudged higher still.

In a recent book, *In Our Prime: the Invention of Middle Age*, Patricia Cohen (2012) notes that middle age wasn't thought of as a separate developmental period until the mid-1800s and the term *midlife* wasn't included in a dictionary until 1895. In Cohen's analysis, advances in health care and more people living to older ages especially fueled the emergence of thinking about middle age. People today take longer to grow up and longer to die than in past centuries.

In comparison with previous decades and centuries, an increasing percentage of today's population is made up of middle-aged and older adults. In the past, the age structure of the population could be represented by a pyramid, with the largest percentage of the population in the childhood years. Today, the percentages of people at different ages in the life span are more similar, creating what is called

middle adulthood The developmental period beginning at approximately 40 years of age and extending to about 60 to 65 years of age.

the "rectangularization" of the age distribution (a vertical rectangle) (Himes, 2009).

Although middle adulthood has been a relatively neglected period of the human life span (except for pop psychology portrayals of the midlife crisis), life-span developmentalists are beginning to give more attention to this age period (Schaie, 2011a; Willis & Martin, 2005). One reason for the increased attention is that the largest cohort in U.S. history is currently moving through the middle-age years. From 1990 to 2015, the middle-aged U.S. population is projected to increase from 47 million to 80 million, a 72 percent increase. Because of the size of the baby-boom cohort (recall from Chapter 1 that a *cohort* is a group of people born in a particular year or time period), the median age of the U.S. population will increase from 33 years in 1990 to 42 years in 2050. The baby boomers, born from 1946 to 1964, are of interest to developmentalists not only because of their large numbers but also because they are the best-educated and most affluent cohort in history to pass through middle age (Willis & Martin, 2005).

The portrait of midlife described so far here suggests that for too long the negative aspects of this developmental period have been overemphasized. However, as will be seen in the following sections, it is important not to go too far in describing midlife positively. Many physical aspects decline in middle adulthood and the increase in health problems such as obesity should be considered in taking a balanced approach to this age period.

Defining Middle Adulthood

Although the age boundaries are not set in stone, we will consider **middle adulthood** to be the developmental period that begins at approximately 40 years of age and extends to about 60 to 65 years of age. For many people, middle adulthood is a time of declining physical skills and expanding responsibility; a period in which people become more conscious of the young-old polarity and the shrinking amount of time left in life; a point when individuals seek to transmit something meaningful to the next generation; and a time when people reach and maintain satisfaction in their careers. In sum, middle adulthood involves "balancing work and relationship responsibilities in the midst of the physical and psychological changes associated with aging" (Lachman, 2004, p. 305).

In midlife, as in other age periods, individuals make choices, selecting what to do, deciding how to invest time and resources, and evaluating what aspects of their lives they need to change. In midlife, "a serious accident, loss, or illness" may be a "wake-up call" that produces "a major restructuring of time and a reassessment" of life's priorities (Lachman, 2004, p. 310).

What are the main characteristics of middle adulthood? What differentiates early and late midlife?

As we mentioned earlier, for many increasingly healthy adults, middle age is lasting longer. Indeed, a growing number of experts on middle adulthood describe the age period of 55 to 65 as *late midlife* (Deeg, 2005). Compared with earlier midlife, late midlife is more likely to be characterized by the death of a parent, the last child leaving the parental home, becoming a grandparent, preparing for retirement, and in most cases actual retirement. Many people in this age range experience their first confrontation with health problems. Overall, then, although gains and losses may balance each other in early midlife, losses may begin to outweigh gains for many individuals in late midlife (Baltes, Lindenberger, & Staudinger, 2006).

Keep in mind, though, that midlife is characterized by individual variations (Ailshire & Burgard, 2012; Wallin & others, 2012). As life-span expert Gilbert Brim (1992) commented, middle adulthood is full of changes, twists, and turns; the path is not fixed. People move in and out of states of success and failure.

Physical Development

What physical changes accompany the change to middle adulthood? How healthy are middle-aged adults? How sexually active are they?

Physical Changes

Although everyone experiences some physical changes due to aging in the middle adulthood years, the rates of this aging vary considerably from one individual to another. Genetic makeup and lifestyle factors play important roles in whether chronic disease will appear and when (Kaplan, Gurven, & Winking, 2009). Middle age is a window through which we can glimpse later life while there is still time to engage in prevention and to influence some of the course of aging (Bertrand, Graham, & Lachman, 2012; Lachman, 2004).

Visible Signs

One of the most visible signs of physical changes in middle adulthood is physical appearance. The first outwardly noticeable signs of aging usually are apparent by the forties or fifties. The skin begins to wrinkle and sag because of a loss of fat and collagen in underlying tissues (Stone & others, 2011). Small, localized areas of pigmentation in the skin produce age spots, especially in areas that are exposed to sunlight, such as the hands and face. For most people, their hair becomes thinner and grayer. Fingernails and toenails develop ridges and become thicker and more brittle.

How Would You...?

As a human development and family studies professional, how would you characterize the impact of the media in shaping middle-aged adults' expectations about their changing physical appearance?

Since a youthful appearance is valued in our culture, many individuals whose hair is graying, whose skin is wrinkling, whose bodies are sagging, and whose teeth are yellowing strive to make themselves look younger. Undergoing cosmetic surgery, dyeing hair, wearing wigs, enrolling in weight-reduction programs, participating in exercise regimens, and taking heavy doses of vitamins are common in middle age. Many baby boomers have shown a strong interest in plastic surgery and Botox, which may reflect their desire to take control of the aging process (Brun & Brock-Utne, 2012).

Height and Weight

Individuals lose height in middle age, and many gain weight (Onwudiwe & others, 2011). On average, from 30 to 50 years of age, men lose about half an inch in height; they may lose another 3/4 inch from 50 to 70 years of age (Hoyer & Roodin, 2009). The height loss for women can be as much as 2 inches over a 50-year span from 25 to 75 years of age. Note that there are large variations in the extent to which individuals become shorter with aging. The decrease in height is due to bone loss in the vertebrae.

Famous actor Sean Connery as a young adult in his twenties (*top*) and as a middle-aged adult in his fifties (*bottom*). *What are some of the most outwardly noticeable signs of aging in middle adulthood?*

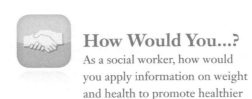

How Would You...?

As a social worker, how would you apply information on weight and health to promote healthier lifestyles for middle-aged adults?

Although people in middle age may lose height, many gain weight. On average, body fat accounts for about 10 percent of body weight in adolescence; it makes up 20 percent or more in middle age. Obesity increases from early to middle adulthood. In a national survey, 38 percent of U.S. adults 40 to 59 years of age were classified as obese (National Center for Health Statistics, 2011). In Chapter 11, we saw that 27 percent of U.S. adults age 20 to 39 were classified as obese. Being overweight is a critical health problem in middle adulthood and increases the risk that individuals will develop a number of other health problems such as hypertension and diabetes (Cheong & others, 2012; Nezu & others, 2013).

Strength, Joints, and Bones

As we saw in Chapter 11, maximum physical strength often is attained in the twenties. The term *sarcopenia* refers to age-related loss of muscle mass and strength (Doria & others, 2012). Muscle loss with age occurs at a rate of approximately 1 to 2 percent per year past the age of 50 (Marcell, 2003). A loss of strength especially occurs in the back and legs. Obesity is a risk factor for sarcopenia (Li & Heber, 2012). A recent research review concluded that weight management and resistance training were the best strategies to slow down the decline of muscle mass and muscle strength (Rolland & others, 2011).

Peak functioning of the body's joints also usually occurs in the twenties. The cartilage that cushions the movement of bones and other connective tissues, such as tendons and ligaments, become less efficient in the middle-adult years, a time when many individuals experience joint stiffness and greater difficulty in movement.

Maximum bone density occurs by the mid- to late thirties, from which point there is a progressive loss of bone. The rate of this bone loss begins slowly but accelerates during the fifties (Baron, 2012). Women lose bone mass about twice as quickly as men. By the end of midlife, bones break more easily and heal more slowly (Rachner, Khosia, & Hofbauer, 2011).

Vision and Hearing

Accommodation of the eye—the ability to focus and maintain an image on the retina—declines sharply between 40 and 59 years of age. In particular, middle-aged individuals begin to have difficulty viewing close objects, which means that many individuals have to wear glasses with bifocal lenses—lenses with two sections that enable the wearer to see items at different distances (Schieber, 2006). Also, there is some evidence that the retina becomes less sensitive to low levels of illumination. Laser surgery and implantation of intraocular lenses have become routine procedures for correcting vision in middle-aged adults (Ang, Evans, & Mehta, 2012).

Hearing also can start to decline by the age of 40 (Roring, Hines, & Charness, 2007). Sensitivity to high pitches usually declines first. The ability to hear low-pitched sounds does not seem to decline much in middle adulthood, though. Men usually lose their sensitivity to high-pitched sounds sooner than women do. However, this gender difference might be due to men's greater exposure to noise in occupations such as mining, automobile work, and so on (Scialfa & Kline, 2007). Also, recent advances in the effectiveness of hearing aids are dramatically improving the hearing of many aging adults (Banerjee, 2011).

Cardiovascular System

Midlife is the time when high blood pressure and high cholesterol take many individuals by surprise (Lachman, 2004). Cardiovascular disease increases considerably in middle age (Emery, Anderson, & Goodwin, 2013).

Members of the Masai tribe in Kenya, Africa, can stay on a treadmill for a long time because of their active lives. Incidence of heart disease is extremely low in the Masai tribe, which also can be attributed to their energetic lifestyle.

The level of cholesterol in the blood increases through the adult years and in midlife begins to accumulate on the artery walls, increasing the risk of cardiovascular disease (Sakuma, 2012). High blood pressure (hypertension), too, often occurs in the forties and fifties (Roberie & Elliot, 2012). At menopause, a woman's blood pressure often rises sharply and usually remains above that of a man through life's later years.

metabolic syndrome A condition characterized by hypertension, obesity, and insulin resistance. Metabolic syndrome often leads to the development of diabetes and cardiovascular disease.

Exercise, weight control, and a diet rich in fruits, vegetables, and whole grains can often help to stave off many cardiovascular problems in middle age (Currie, McKelvie, & MacDonald, 2012). For example, although heredity influences cholesterol levels, LDL (the bad cholesterol) can be reduced and HDL (the good cholesterol) increased by eating food that is very low in saturated fat and cholesterol and by exercising regularly (Logan, 2011). The health benefits of cholesterol-lowering and hypertension-lowering drugs are a major factor in improving the health of many middle-aged adults and increasing their life expectancy (de la Sierra & Barrios, 2012; Gadi & others, 2012).

An increasing problem in middle and late adulthood is **metabolic syndrome**, a condition characterized by hypertension, obesity, and insulin resistance. A recent research review concluded that chronic stress exposure is linked to metabolic syndrome (Tamashiro & others, 2011). Metabolic syndrome often leads to the development of diabetes and cardiovascular disease (Capoulade & others, 2012). A recent study found that individuals with metabolic syndrome who were physically active reduced their risk of developing cardiovascular disease (Broekhuizen & others, 2011). Another study revealed that a high body mass index (BMI) in adolescence was related to metabolic syndrome in middle-aged men and women (Gustafsson, Persson, & Hammarstrom, 2011).

Lungs

There is little change in lung capacity through most of middle adulthood. However, at about the age of 55, the proteins in lung tissue become less elastic. This change, combined with a gradual stiffening of connective tissues in the chest wall, decreases the lungs' capacity to shuttle oxygen from the air people breathe to the blood in their veins. The lung capacity of individuals who are smokers drops precipitously in middle age, but if the individuals quit smoking their lung capacity improves, although not to the level of individuals who have never smoked. Recent research also has found that low cognitive ability in early adulthood is linked to reduced lung functioning in middle age (Carroll & others, 2011).

Sleep

Some aspects of sleep become more problematic in middle age (Green & others, 2012). The total number of hours slept usually remains the same as in early adulthood, but beginning in the forties, wakeful periods are more frequent and there is less of the deepest type of sleep (stage 4). The amount of time spent lying awake in bed at night begins to increase in middle age, and this can produce a feeling of being less rested in the morning (Abbott, 2003). Sleep-disordered breathing and restless legs syndrome become more prevalent in middle age

(Polo-Kantola, 2011). A recent study found that middle-aged adults who sleep less than six hours a night on average had an increased risk of developing stroke symptoms (Ruiter & others, 2012). Another study found that change in sleep duration across five years in middle age was linked to cognitive functioning (Ferrie & others, 2011). In this study, a decrease from 6, 7, or 8 hours of sleep and an increase from 7 or 8 hours were related to lower scores on most assessments of cognitive functioning. Sleep problems in middle-aged adults are more common among those who use a higher number of prescription and nonprescription drugs, are obese, have cardiovascular disease, or are depressed (Loponen & others, 2010).

Health and Disease

In middle adulthood, the frequency of accidents declines, and individuals are less susceptible to colds and allergies than in childhood, adolescence, or early adulthood. Indeed, many individuals live through middle adulthood without having a disease or persistent health problem. For others, however, disease and persistent health problems become more common in middle adulthood than in earlier life stages (Hoyt & Stanton, 2012).

Stress is increasingly being found to be a factor in disease (Dougall & Baum, 2012). The cumulative effect of stress often takes a toll on the health of individuals by the time they reach middle age. David Almeida and his colleagues (2011) recently described how chronic stress or prolonged exposure to stressors can have damaging effects on an individuals' physical functioning, including an unhealthy overproduction of corticosteroids, such as cortisol. Chronic stress can interfere with immune system functioning, and this stress is linked to disease not only through the immune system but also through cardiovascular factors (Emery & others, 2013; Stowell, Robles, & Kane, 2013). A recent study indicated that aerobic fitness was related to the presence of a lower level of senescent T cells (prematurely aging cells that result from persistent immune activation) (Spielmann & others, 2011).

Stress and negative emotions can affect the development and course of cardiovascular disease by altering underlying physiological processes (Dougall & Baum, 2012). Sometimes, though, the link between stress and cardiovascular disease is indirect. For example, people who live in a chronically stressed condition, such as persistent poverty, are more likely to take up smoking, start overeating, and avoid exercising (Wilcox & others, 2011). All of these stress-related behaviors are linked with the development of cardiovascular disease (Emery, Anderson, & Goodwin, 2013).

Mortality Rates

Infectious disease was the main cause of death until the middle of the twentieth century. As infectious disease rates declined and more individuals lived through middle age, chronic disorders increased. These are characterized by a slow onset and a long duration (Kelley-Moore, 2009).

In middle age, many deaths are caused by a single, readily identifiable condition, whereas in old age, death is more likely to result from the combined effects of several chronic conditions. For many years heart disease was the leading cause of death in middle adulthood, followed by cancer; however, since 2005 more individuals 45 to 64 years of age in the United States died of cancer, followed by cardiovascular disease (Kochanek & others, 2011). The gap between cancer and the second highest cause of death widens as individuals age from 45 to 54 and from 55 to 64 years of age (National Center for Health Statistics, 2008). Men have higher mortality rates than women for all of the leading causes of death (Kochanek & others, 2011).

Sexuality

What kinds of changes characterize the sexuality of women and men as they go through middle age? **Climacteric** is a term used to describe the midlife transition in which fertility declines. Let's explore the substantial differences in the climacteric of women and men during middle adulthood.

Menopause

Menopause is the time in middle age, usually in the late forties or early fifties, when a woman's menstrual periods cease completely. The average age at which women have their last period is 51 (Wise, 2006). However, there is large variation in the age at which menopause occurs—from 39 to 59 years of age. Later menopause is linked with increased risk of breast cancer (Mishra & others, 2009).

In menopause, production of estrogen by the ovaries declines dramatically, and this decline produces uncomfortable symptoms in some women—"hot flashes," nausea, fatigue, and rapid heartbeat, for example. A recent study revealed that increased estradiol and improved sleep, but not hot flashes, predicted enhanced mood in women during their menopausal transition (Joffe & others, 2011).

Cross-cultural studies reveal wide variations in the menopause experience (Lerner-Geva & others, 2010; Sievert & Obermeyer, 2012). For example, hot flashes are uncommon in Mayan women (Beyene, 1986). Asian women report fewer hot flashes than women in Western societies (Payer, 1991). It is difficult to determine the extent to which these cross-cultural variations are due to genetic, dietary, reproductive, or cultural factors.

Menopause overall is not the negative experience for most women that it was once thought to be (Henderson, 2011). Most women do not have severe physical or psychological problems related to menopause. For example, a recent research review concluded that there is no clear evidence that depressive disorders occur more often during menopause than at other times in a woman's reproductive life (Judd, Hickey, & Bryant, 2011).

Hormone replacement therapy (HRT) augments the declining levels of reproductive hormone production by the ovaries (Yang & Reckelhoff, 2011). HRT can consist of various forms of estrogen, usually in combination with a progestin. A study of HRT's effects was halted as evidence emerged that participants who were receiving HRT faced an increased risk of stroke (National Institutes of Health, 2004). In the years since the finding linking HRT and increased risk of stroke was reported, there has been a 50 percent or more reduction in the use of HRT (Pines, Sturdee, & Maclennan, 2012). However, recent research has found a reduction of cardiovascular disease and minimal risks with HRT when it is initiated before 60 years of age and/or within 10 years of menopause and continued for six years or more (Hodis & others, 2012). Recent research studies on HRT have revealed that coinciding with the decreased use of HRT, evidence is mixed regarding changes in the incidence of breast cancer (Baber, 2011; Gompel & Santen, 2012; Howell & Evans, 2011).

The National Institutes of Health recommend that women with a uterus who are currently taking hormones should consult with their doctor to determine whether to continue their treatment. If they are taking HRT for

Researchers have found that almost 50 percent of Canadian and American women have occasional hot flashes, but only one in seven Japanese women do (Lock, 1998). *What factors might account for these variations?*

How Would You...?

As a human development and family studies professional, how would you counsel middle-aged women who voice the belief that hormone replacement therapy is necessary to "stay young"?

short-term relief of symptoms, the benefits may outweigh the risks. Many middle-aged women are seeking alternatives to HRT such as regular exercise, dietary supplements, herbal remedies, relaxation therapy, acupuncture, and nonsteroidal medications (Holloway, 2010).

The National Institutes of Health recommends that women with a uterus who are currently taking hormones consult with their doctor to determine whether they should continue the treatment. If they are taking HRT for short-term relief of symptoms, the benefits may outweigh the risks. However, the evidence of risks associated with HRT suggests that long-term hormone therapy should be seriously reevaluated (Warren, 2007). Consequently, many middle-aged women are choosing alternatives to HRT such as regular exercise, dietary supplements, herbal remedies, relaxation therapy, acupuncture, and nonsteroidal medications (Holloway, 2010).

Hormonal Changes in Middle-Aged Men

Do men go through anything like the menopause that women experience? In other words, is there a male menopause? During middle adulthood, most men do not lose their capacity to father children, although there usually is a modest decline in their sexual hormone level and activity (Yassin & others, 2011). They experience hormonal changes in their fifties and sixties, but nothing like the dramatic drop in estrogen that women experience. Testosterone production begins to decline about 1 percent a year during middle adulthood, and sperm count usually shows a slow decline, but men do not lose their fertility in middle age. What has been referred to as "male menopause," then, probably has less to do with hormonal change than with the psychological adjustment men must make when they are faced with declining physical energy and with family and work pressures. Testosterone therapy has not been found to relieve such symptoms, suggesting that they are not induced by hormonal change.

The gradual decline in men's testosterone levels in middle age can reduce their sexual drive (O'Connor & others, 2011). Their erections are less full and less frequent, and men require more stimulation to achieve them. Researchers once attributed these changes to psychological factors, but increasingly they find that as many as 75 percent of the erectile dysfunctions in middle-aged men stem from physiological problems. Smoking, diabetes, hypertension, elevated cholesterol levels, and obesity are at fault in many erectile problems in middle-aged men (Javaroni & Neves, 2012; Kolotkin, Zunker, & Ostbye, 2012).

Erectile dysfunction (ED), difficulty in attaining or maintaining an erection is present in approximately 50 percent of men 40 to 70 years of age (Berookhim & Bar-Charma, 2011). Treatment for men with erectile dysfunction has focused on the drug Viagra and on similar drugs, such as Levitra and Cialis (Lowe & Costabile, 2012; Rubio-Aurioles & others, 2012). Viagra works by allowing increased blood flow into the penis, which produces an erection. Its success rate is in the 60 to 85 percent range (Claes & others, 2010).

Sexual Attitudes and Behavior

Although the ability of men and women to function sexually shows little biological decline in middle adulthood, sexual activity usually occurs less frequently than in early adulthood (Burgess, 2004). Career interests, family matters, diminishing energy levels, and routine may contribute to this decline (Avis & others, 2009).

In the Sex in America survey (described initially in Chapter 11), the frequency of sexual activity was greatest for individuals 25 to 29 years old (47 percent had sex twice a week or more) and dropped off for individuals in their fifties (23 percent of 50- to

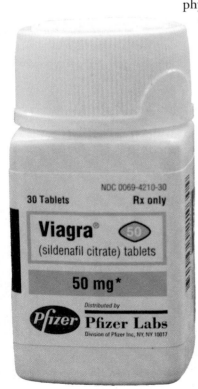

59-year-old males said they had sex twice a week or more, while only 14 percent of the females in this age group reported this frequency) (Michael & others, 1994). Note, though, that the Sex in America survey may underestimate the frequency of sexual activity of middle-aged adults because the data were collected prior to the widespread use of erectile dysfunction drugs such as Viagra.

Living with a spouse or partner makes all the difference in whether people engage in sexual activity, especially for women over 40 years of age. In one study conducted as part of the Midlife in the United States Study (MIDUS), 95 percent of women in their forties with partners said that they had been sexually active in the last six months, compared with only 53 percent of those without partners (Brim, 1999). By their fifties, 88 percent of women living with a partner have been sexually active in the last six months, but only 37 percent of those who are neither married nor living with someone say they have had sex in the last six months.

A large-scale study of U.S. adults 40 to 80 years of age found that early ejaculation (26 percent) and erectile difficulties (22 percent) were the most common sexual problems of older men (Laumann & others, 2009). In this study, the most common sexual problems of women were lack of sexual interest (33 percent) and lubrication difficulties (21 percent).

A person's health in middle age is a key factor in sexual activity in middle age. A recent study found that how often individuals have sexual intercourse, the quality of their sexual life, and their interest in sex were linked to how healthy they were (Lindau & Gavrilova, 2010).

How Would You...?

As a psychologist, how would you counsel a couple about the ways that the transition to middle adulthood might affect their sexual relationship?

How does the pattern of sexual activity change when individuals become middle-aged?

Cognitive Development

We have seen that middle-aged adults may not see as well, run as fast, or be as healthy as they were in their twenties and thirties. We've also seen a decline in their sexual activity. What about their cognitive skills? Do these skills decline as we enter and move through middle adulthood? To answer this question, we will explore the possibility of age-related changes in intelligence and information processing.

Intelligence

Our exploration of possible changes in intelligence in middle adulthood focuses on the concepts of fluid and crystallized intelligence, cohort effects, and the Seattle Longitudinal Study.

How Would You...?

As an educator, how would you explain how changes in fluid and crystallized intelligence might influence the way middle-aged adults learn?

Fluid and Crystallized Intelligence

John Horn argues that some abilities begin to decline in middle age, whereas others increase (Horn & Donaldson, 1980). He argues that **crystallized intelligence,** an individual's accumulated information and verbal skills, continues to increase in middle adulthood,

crystallized intelligence Accumulated information and verbal skills, which increase in middle age, according to Horn.

fluid intelligence The ability to reason abstractly, which steadily declines from middle adulthood on, according to Horn.

whereas **fluid intelligence**, one's ability to reason abstractly, begins to decline during middle adulthood (see Figure 13.1).

Horn's data were collected in a cross-sectional manner. Remember from Chapter 1 that a cross-sectional study assesses individuals of different ages at the same point in time. For example, a cross-sectional study might assess the intelligence of different groups of 40-, 50-, and 60-year-olds in a single evaluation, such as in 1980. The 40-year-olds in the study would have been born in 1940 and the 60-year-olds in 1920—different eras that offered different economic and educational opportunities. The 60-year-olds likely had fewer educational opportunities as they grew up. Thus, if we find differences between 40- and 60-year-olds on intelligence tests when they are assessed cross-sectionally, these differences might be due to cohort effects related to educational differences rather than to age.

By contrast, remember from Chapter 1 that in a longitudinal study, the same individuals are studied over a period of time. Thus, a longitudinal study of intelligence in middle adulthood might consist of giving the same intelligence test to the same individuals when they are 40, then 50, and then 60 years of age. As we see next, whether data on intelligence are collected cross-sectionally or longitudinally can make a difference in what is found about changes in crystallized and fluid intelligence and about intellectual decline.

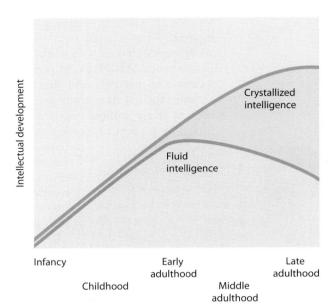

Figure 13.1 Fluid and Crystallized Intelligence Across the Life Span According to Horn, crystallized intelligence (based on cumulative learning experiences) increases throughout the life span, but fluid intelligence (the ability to perceive and manipulate information) steadily declines from middle adulthood onward.

The Seattle Longitudinal Study

K. Warner Schaie (1996, 2005, 2010, 2011a, 2012) is conducting an extensive study of intellectual abilities in adulthood. Five hundred individuals initially were tested in 1956. New waves of participants are added periodically. The main focus in the Seattle Longitudinal Study has been on individual change and stability in intelligence. The main mental abilities tested are *verbal comprehension* (ability to understand ideas expressed in words); *verbal memory* (ability to encode and recall meaningful language units, such as a list of words); *numeric ability* (ability to perform simple mathematical computations such as addition, subtraction, and multiplication); *spatial orientation* (ability to visualize and mentally rotate stimuli in two- and three-dimensional space); *inductive reasoning* (ability to recognize and understand patterns and relationships in a problem and use this understanding to solve other instances of the problem); and *perceptual speed* (ability to quickly and accurately make simple discriminations in visual stimuli).

The highest level of functioning for four of the six intellectual abilities occurred in the middle adulthood years (Schaie, 2012) (see Figure 13.2). For both women and men, peak performance on verbal ability, verbal memory, inductive reasoning, and spatial orientation was attained in middle age. Only two of the six abilities—numeric ability and perceptual speed—showed a decline in middle age. Perceptual speed showed the earliest decline, actually beginning in early adulthood. Interestingly, in terms of John Horn's ideas that were discussed earlier, for the participants in the Seattle Longitudinal Study, middle age was a time of peak performance for some aspects of both crystallized intelligence (verbal ability) and fluid intelligence (spatial orientation and inductive reasoning).

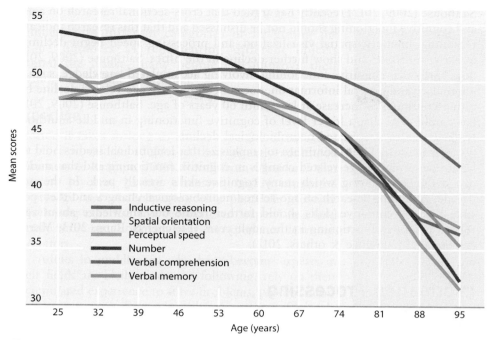

Figure 13.2 Longitudinal Changes in Six Intellectual Abilities from Age 25 to Age 95
Source: Adapted from Schaie, K.W. (2012). Developmental Influences on Adult Intelligence: The Seattle Longitudinal Study (2nd ed.), Fig. 5.8. New York: Oxford University Press.

Notice in Figure 13.2 that declines in functioning for most cognitive abilities began in the sixties, although verbal ability did not drop until the mid-seventies. From the mid-seventies through the mid-nineties, all cognitive abilities showed considerable decline.

When Schaie (1994) assessed intellectual abilities both cross-sectionally and longitudinally, he found declines more often in the cross-sectional than in the longitudinal assessments. For example, as shown in Figure 13.3, when assessed cross-sectionally, inductive reasoning showed a consistent decline in the middle adulthood years. In contrast, when assessed longitudinally, inductive reasoning increased until toward the end of middle adulthood, when it began to show a slight decline. In Schaie's (2009, 2010, 2011a, 2012) view, it is during middle adulthood, not early adulthood, that people reach a peak in their cognitive functioning for many intellectual skills.

Such differences across generations involve *cohort effects*. In a recent analysis, Schaie (2012b) concluded that the advances in cognitive functioning in middle age that have occurred in recent decades are likely due to a combination of factors: educational attainment, occupational structures (increasing numbers of workers in professional occupations with greater work complexity), changes in healthcare and lifestyles, immigration, and social interventions in poverty. The impressive gains in cognitive functioning in recent cohorts have been documented more clearly for fluid intelligence than for crystallized intelligence (Schaie, 2012).

Some researchers disagree with Schaie that middle adulthood is the time when the level of functioning in a number of cognitive domains is maintained or even increases (Finch, 2009). For example, Timothy

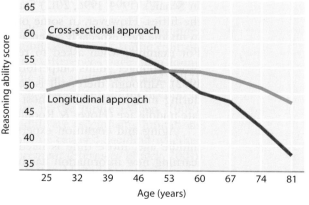

Figure 13.3 Cross-Sectional and Longitudinal Comparisons of Intellectual Change in Middle Adulthood
Why do you think reasoning ability peaks during middle adulthood?

HAGAR © 1987 King Features Syndicate.

developments in information technologies, downsizing of organizations, pressure to choose early retirement, and concerns about pensions and health care.

Globalization has replaced what was once a primarily non-Latino White male workforce in the United States with employees of different ethnic and national backgrounds who have immigrated from different parts of the world. To improve profits, many companies are restructuring, downsizing, and outsourcing jobs. One of the outcomes of this change has been for companies to offer incentives to middle-aged employees to retire early—in their fifties, or in some cases even forties, rather than their sixties.

The decline in defined-benefit pensions and increased uncertainty about the fate of health insurance are decreasing the sense of personal control for middle-aged workers. As a consequence, many are delaying retirement plans.

Some midlife career changes are self-motivated, while others are the consequence of losing one's job (Moen, 2009). Some individuals in middle age decide that they don't want to continue doing the same work for the rest of their working lives (Hoyer & Roodin, 2009). One aspect of middle adulthood involves adjusting idealistic hopes to realistic possibilities in light of how much time individuals have before they retire and how fast they are reaching their occupational goals (Levinson, 1978). Individuals could become motivated to change jobs if they perceive that they are behind schedule, if their goals are unrealistic, if they don't like the work they are doing, or if their job has become too stressful.

A final point to make about career development in middle adulthood is that cognitive factors earlier in development are linked to occupational attainment in middle age. In one study, task persistence at 13 years of age was related to occupational success in middle age (Andersson & Bergman, 2011).

How Would You...?

Sigmund Freud once commented that the two things adults need to do well to adapt to society's demands are to work and to love. To his list we add "to play." In our fast-paced society, it is all too easy to get caught up in the frenzied, hectic pace of our achievement-oriented work world and ignore leisure and play. Imagine your life as a middle-aged adult. *What would be the ideal mix of work and leisure? What leisure activities do you want to enjoy as a middle-aged adult?*

Leisure

As adults, not only must we learn how to work well, but we also need to learn how to relax and enjoy leisure (Hutchinson & Nimrod, 2012; Lin & others, 2012). **Leisure** refers to the pleasant times after work when individuals are free to pursue activities and interests of their own

leisure The pleasant times after work when individuals are free to pursue activities and interests of their own choosing.

choosing—hobbies, sports, or reading, for example. In one analysis of research on what U.S. adults regret the most, not engaging in more leisure-time pursuits was one of the top six regrets (Roese & Summerville, 2005).

Leisure can be an especially important aspect of middle adulthood (Parkes, 2006). By middle adulthood, more money may be available to many individuals, and there may be more free time and paid vacations. In short, midlife changes may produce expanded opportunities for leisure. For many individuals, middle adulthood is the first time in their lives when they have the opportunity to explore their leisure-time interests.

Adults in midlife need to begin preparing psychologically for retirement. Developing constructive and fulfilling leisure activities in middle adulthood is an important part of this preparation (Gibson, 2009). If an adult develops leisure activities that can be continued into retirement, the transition from work to retirement can be less stressful.

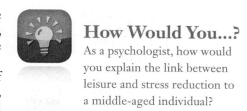

How Would You...?
As a psychologist, how would you explain the link between leisure and stress reduction to a middle-aged individual?

Religion and Meaning in Life

What role does religion play in our development as adults? Is the meaning of life an important theme for many middle-aged adults?

Religion and Adult Lives

In research that was part of the Midlife in the United States Study (MIDUS), more than 70 percent of U.S. middle-aged adults said they are religious and consider spirituality a major part of their lives (Brim, 1999). In thinking about religion and adult development, it is important to consider the role of individual differences. Religion is a powerful influence in some adults' lives, whereas it plays little or no role in others' lives (George, 2009; Sapp, 2010). In a longitudinal study of individuals from their early thirties through their late sixties/early seventies, a significant increase in spirituality occurred between late middle (mid-fifties/early sixties) and late adulthood (Wink & Dillon, 2002) (see Figure 13.4).

Females have consistently shown a stronger interest in religion than males have (Bijur & others, 1993). Compared with men, they participate more in both organized and personal forms of religion, are more likely to believe in a higher power or presence, and are more likely to feel that religion is an important dimension of their lives. In the longitudinal study just described, the spirituality of women increased more than men in the second half of life (Wink & Dillon, 2002).

Religion and Health

What might be some of the effects of religion on physical health? Some cults and religious sects encourage behaviors that are damaging to health, such as ignoring sound medical advice. For individuals in the religious mainstream, however, researchers are increasingly finding positive links between religion and physical health (McCullough & Willoughby, 2009). Researchers have found that religious attendance is linked to a reduction

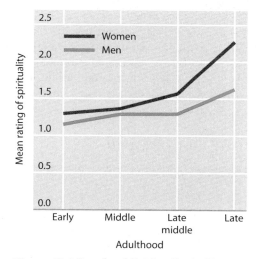

Figure 13.4 Levels of Spirituality in Four Adult Age Periods

In a longitudinal study, the spirituality of individuals in four different adult age periods—early (thirties), middle (forties), late middle (mid-fifties/early sixties), and late (late sixties/early seventies) adulthood—was assessed (Wink & Dillon, 2002). Based on responses to open-ended questions in interviews, the spirituality of the individuals was coded on a five-point scale with 5 being the highest level of spirituality and 1 the lowest.

What roles do religion and spirituality play in the lives of middle-aged adults? Why might religion promote health?

in hypertension (Gillum & Ingram, 2007). And in a recent analysis of a number of studies, adults with a higher level of spirituality/religion had an 18 percent increase in longevity (Lucchetti, Lucchetti, & Koenig, 2011). In this analysis, a high level of spirituality/religion had a stronger link to longevity than 60 percent of 25 other health interventions (such as eating fruits and vegetables and taking statin drugs for cardiovascular disease).

Why might religion promote physical health? There are several possible answers (Hill & Butter, 1995). First, there are *lifestyle issues*—for example, religious individuals have lower drug use than their nonreligious counterparts (Gartner, Larson, & Allen, 1991). Second are *social networks*—the degree to which individuals are connected to others affects their health. Well-connected individuals have fewer health problems (Hill & Pargament, 2003). Religious groups, meetings, and activities provide social connectedness for individuals. A third answer involves *coping with stress*—religion offers a source of comfort and support when individuals are confronted with stressful events. One study revealed that when religion was an important aspect of people's lives, they worried less and were less depressed (Rosmarin, Krumrei, & Andersson, 2009).

Religious counselors often advise people about mental health and coping. To read about the work of one religious counselor, see *Careers in Life-Span Development*.

Meaning in Life

Austrian psychiatrist Viktor Frankl's mother, father, brother, and wife died in the concentration camps and gas chambers in Auschwitz, Poland, during World War II. Frankl survived the concentration camp and went on to write about the search for meaning in life. In his book, *Man's Search for Meaning*, Frankl (1984) emphasized each person's uniqueness and the finiteness of life. He believed that examining the

Careers in life-span development

Gabriel Dy-Liacco, Pastoral Counselor

Gabriel Dy-Liacco is a pastoral counselor at the Pastoral Counseling and Consultation Centers of Greater Washington, D.C. He obtained his Ph.D. in pastoral counseling from Loyola College in Maryland and also has experience as a psychotherapist in various mental health settings, including a substance abuse program, military family center, psychiatric clinic, and community mental health center. As a pastoral counselor, he works with adolescents and adults in the aspects of their life that they show the most concern about—psychological, spiritual, or the interface of both. Having lived in Peru, Japan, and the Philippines, he brings considerable multicultural experi-

ence to the counseling setting. Dr. Dy-Liacco also is a professor in the Graduate School of Psychology and Counseling at Regent University in the Washington, D.C., area.

Pastoral counselors, like Gabriel Dy-Liacco, are trained in both psychology and theology, which enables them to provide clients with psychological and spiritual guidance. Most pastoral counselors have an undergraduate degree and a master's or doctoral degree in theology and/or pastoral counseling. If they have only an advanced theology degree, they also must take a certain amount of pastoral counseling courses. Pastoral counselors usually work in care settings such as hospitals, nursing homes, rehabilitation facilities, psychiatric facilities, and correctional institutions.

finiteness of our existence and the certainty of death adds meaning to life. If life were not finite, said Frankl, we could spend our life doing just about whatever we pleased because our time would be unlimited.

Frankl said that the three most distinct human qualities are spirituality, freedom, and responsibility. Spirituality, in his view, does not have a religious underpinning. Rather, it refers to a human being's uniqueness—to spirit, philosophy, and mind. Frankl proposed that people ask themselves questions about why they exist, what they want from life, and what their lives mean.

It is in middle adulthood that individuals begin to face death more often, especially the deaths of parents and other older relatives. As they become increasingly aware of the diminishing number of years ahead of them, many individuals in middle age begin to ask and evaluate the questions that Frankl proposed. And meaning-making coping is especially helpful in times of chronic stress and loss.

Researchers are increasingly studying the factors involved in a person's exploration of meaning in life and exploring whether developing a sense of meaning in life is linked to positive developmental outcomes (Park, 2010, 2012a, b). In research studies, many individuals state that religion played an important role in increasing their exploration of meaning in life (Krause, 2008, 2009). Studies also suggest that individuals who have found a sense of meaning in life are physically healthier and happier, and experience less depression, than their counterparts who report that they have not discovered meaning in life (Krause, 2009).

Having a sense of meaning in life can lead to clearer guidelines for living one's life and enhanced motivation to take care of oneself and reach goals. A higher level of meaning in life also is linked to a higher level of psychological well-being and physical health (Park, 2012b).

What characterizes the search for meaning in life?

Summary

The Nature of Middle Adulthood

- As more people live to an older age, what we think of as middle age is starting later and lasting longer.

- Middle age involves extensive individual variation. For most people, middle adulthood involves declining physical skills, expanding responsibility, awareness of the young-old polarity, motivation to transmit something meaningful to the next generation, and reaching and maintaining career satisfaction. Increasingly, researchers are distinguishing between early and late midlife.

Physical Development

- The physical changes of midlife are usually gradual. Decline occurs in a number of aspects of physical development.

- In middle adulthood, the frequency of accidents declines and individuals are less susceptible to colds. Stress can be a factor in disease.

- Until recently, cardiovascular disease was the leading cause of death in middle age, but now cancer is the leading cause of death in this age group.

- Most women do not have serious physical or psychological problems related to menopause. Sexual behavior occurs less frequently in middle adulthood than early adulthood.

Cognitive Development

- Horn argued that crystallized intelligence continues to increase in middle adulthood, whereas fluid intelligence declines. Schaie found that declines in cognitive development are less likely to occur when longitudinal rather than cross-sectional studies are conducted. He also revealed that the highest levels of a number of intellectual abilities occur in middle age.
- Working memory declines in late middle age. Memory is more likely to decline in middle age when individuals don't use effective memory strategies. Expertise often increases in middle adulthood.

Careers, Work, and Leisure

- Midlife is often a time to reflect on career progress and prepare for retirement.
- Today's middle-aged workers face a number of challenges.
- We not only need to learn to work well, but also discover how to enjoy leisure.

Religion and Meaning in Life

- The majority of middle-aged adults say that spirituality is a major part of their lives.
- In mainstream religions, religion is positively linked to physical health. Religion can play an important role in coping for some individuals.
- Many middle-aged individuals reflect on life's meaning.

Key Terms

middle adulthood 336
metabolic syndrome 339
climacteric 341

menopause 341
crystallized
    intelligence 343

fluid intelligence 344
working memory 346

leisure 348

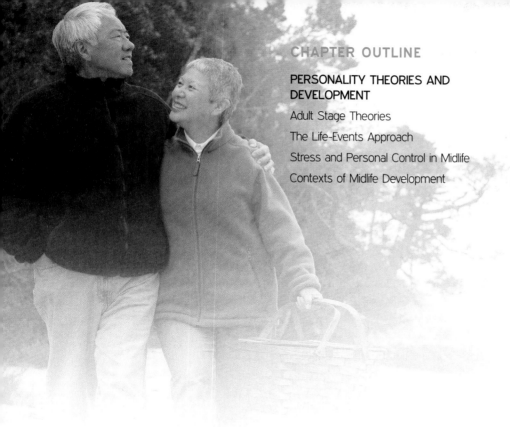

Socioemotional Development in Middle Adulthood

Stories of Life-Span Development: Sarah and Wanda, Middle-Age Variations

Forty-five-year-old Sarah feels tired, depressed, and angry when she looks back on the way her life has gone. She became pregnant when she was 17 and married Ben, the baby's father. They stayed together for three years after their son was born, and then Ben left her for another woman. Sarah went to work as a salesclerk to make ends meet. Eight years later, she married Alan, who had two children of his own from a previous marriage. Sarah stopped working for several years to care for the children. Then, like Ben, Alan started going out on her. She found out about it from a friend. Never-

theless, Sarah stayed with Alan for another year. Finally, he was gone so much that she could not take it anymore and decided to divorce him. Sarah went back to work again as a salesclerk; she has been in the same position for 16 years now. During those 16 years, she has dated a number of men, but the relationships never seemed to work out. Her son never finished high school and has drug problems. Her father died last year, and Sarah is trying to help her mother financially, although she can barely pay her own bills. Sarah looks in the mirror and does not like what she sees. She sees her

past as a shambles, and the future does not look rosy, either.

Forty-five-year-old Wanda feels energetic, happy, and satisfied. As a young woman, she graduated from college and worked for three years as a high school math teacher. She married Andy, who had just finished law school. One year later, they had their first child, Josh. Wanda stayed home with Josh for two years, and then returned to her job as a math teacher. Even during her pregnancy, Wanda stayed active and exercised regularly, playing tennis almost every day. After her pregnancy, she kept up her exercise habits. Wanda and Andy had another child, Wendy. Now, as they move into their middle-age years, their children are both off to college, and Wanda and Andy are enjoying spending more time with each other. Last weekend they visited Josh at his college, and the weekend before they visited Wendy at her college. Wanda continued working as a high school math teacher until six years ago. She had developed computer skills as part of her job and taken some computer courses at a nearby college, doubling up during the summer months. She resigned her math teaching job and took a job with a computer company, where she has already worked her way into management. Wanda looks in the mirror and likes what she sees. She sees her past as enjoyable, although not without hills and valleys, and she looks to the future with zest and enthusiasm.

How Would You...?

As an educator, how would you describe ways in which the profession of teaching might establish generativity for someone in middle adulthood?

As with Sarah and Wanda, there are individual variations in the way people experience middle age. To begin the chapter, we examine personality theories and development in middle age, including ideas about individual variation. Then we turn our attention to how much individuals change or stay the same as they go through the adult years, and finally we explore a number of aspects of close relationships during the middle adulthood years. ■

Personality Theories and Development

What is the best way to conceptualize middle age? Is it a stage or a crisis? How extensively is middle age influenced by life events? Do middle-aged adults experience stress differently from younger and older adults? Is personality linked with contexts such as the point in history in which individuals go through midlife, their culture, and their gender?

Adult Stage Theories

A number of adult stage theories have been proposed and have contributed to the view that midlife brings a crisis in development. Two prominent theories that define stages of adult development are Erik Erikson's life-span view and Daniel Levinson's seasons of a man's life.

Erikson's Stage of Generativity Versus Stagnation

Erikson (1968) proposed that middle-aged adults face a significant issue—generativity versus stagnation, which is the name Erikson gave to the seventh stage in his life-span theory. **Generativity** encompasses adults' desire to leave legacies of themselves to the next generation. Through these legacies adults achieve a kind of immortality. By contrast, **stagnation** (sometimes called "self-absorption") develops when individuals sense that they have done little or nothing for the next generation.

Generative adults commit themselves to the continuation and improvement of society as a whole through their connection to the next generation. Generative adults develop a positive legacy of the self and then offer it as a gift to the next generation (Busch & Hofer, 2012). Middle-aged adults can develop generativity in a number of ways (Kotre, 1984). Through biological generativity, adults have offspring. Through parental generativity, adults nurture and guide children. Through work generativity, adults develop skills that are passed down to others. And through cultural generativity, adults create, renovate, or conserve some aspect of culture that ultimately survives.

generativity Adults' desire to leave legacies of themselves to the next generation; the positive side of Erikson's generativity versus stagnation middle adulthood stage.

stagnation Sometimes called "self-absorption"—develops when individuals sense that they have done little or nothing for the next generation; the negative side of Erikson's generativity versus stagnation middle adulthood stage.

How Would You...?

Through generativity, adults promote and guide the next generation by parenting, teaching, leading, and doing things that benefit the community (Pratt & others, 2008). One of the participants in a study of aging said: "From twenty to thirty I learned how to get along with my wife. From thirty to forty I learned how to be a success at my job, and at forty to fifty I worried less about myself and more about the children" (Vaillant, 2002, p. 114).

Does research support Erikson's theory that generativity is an important dimension of middle age? Yes, it does (McAdams & Cox, 2010; Newton & Stewart, 2012). In one study, Carol Ryff (1984) examined the views of women and men at different ages and found that middle-aged adults especially were concerned about generativity. In a longitudinal study of Smith College women, the desire for generativity increased as the participants aged from their thirties to their fifties (Stewart, Ostrove, & Helson, 2001). And in a recent study, generativity was strongly linked to middle-aged adults' positive social engagement in contexts such as family life and community activities (Cox & others, 2010).

Levinson's Seasons of a Man's Life

In *The Seasons of a Man's Life* (1978), clinical psychologist Daniel Levinson reported the results of extensive interviews with 40 middle-aged men. The interviews were conducted with hourly workers, business executives, academic biologists, and novelists. Levinson bolstered his conclusions with information from the biographies of famous men and the development of memorable characters in literature. Although Levinson's major interest focused on midlife change in men, he described a number of stages and transitions during the period from 17 to 65 years of age, as shown in Figure 14.1. Levinson emphasizes that developmental tasks must be mastered at each stage.

At the end of one's teens, according to Levinson, a transition from dependence to independence should occur. This transition is marked by the formation of a dream—an image of the kind of life the youth wants to have, especially in terms of a career and marriage. Levinson sees the twenties as a *novice phase* of adult development. It is a time of reasonably free experimentation and of testing the dream in the real world. In early adulthood, the two major tasks to be mastered are exploring the possibilities for adult living and developing a stable life structure.

From about age 28 to 33, the man goes through a transition period in which he must face the more serious question of determining his goals. During his thirties, he usually focuses on family and career development. In the later years of this period, he enters a phase of *Becoming One's Own Man* (or BOOM, as Levinson calls it).

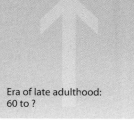

Era of late adulthood: 60 to ?

Late adult transition: Age 60 to 65

Culminating life structure for middle adulthood: 55 to 60

Age 50 transition: 50 to 55

Entry life structure for middle adulthood: 45 to 50

Middle adult transition: Age 40 to 45

Culminating life structure for early adulthood: 33 to 40

Age 30 transition: 28 to 33

Entry life structure for early adulthood: 22 to 28

Early adult transition: Age 17 to 22

Figure 14.1 Levinson's Periods of Adult Development
According to Levinson, adulthood for men has three main stages, which are surrounded by transition periods. Specific tasks and challenges are associated with each stage.

By age 40, he has reached a stable location in his career, has outgrown his earlier, more tenuous attempts at learning to become an adult, and now must look forward to the kind of life he will lead as a middle-aged adult.

According to Levinson, the transition to middle adulthood lasts about five years (ages 40 to 45) and requires the adult male to come to grips with four major conflicts that have existed in his life since adolescence: (1) being young versus being old, (2) being destructive versus being constructive, (3) being masculine versus being feminine, and (4) being attached to others versus being separated from them. Seventy to 80 percent of the men Levinson interviewed found the midlife transition tumultuous and psychologically painful, as many aspects of their lives came into question. According to Levinson, the success of the midlife transition rests on how effectively the individual reduces the polarities and accepts each of them as an integral part of his being.

Because Levinson interviewed middle-aged males, we can consider the data about middle adulthood more valid than the data about early adulthood. When individuals are asked to remember information about earlier parts of their lives, they may distort and forget things. The original Levinson data included no females, although Levinson (1996) reported that his stages, transitions, and the crisis of middle age apply to females as well as males. Levinson's work included no statistical analysis. However, the quality and quantity of the Levinson biographies make them outstanding examples of the clinical tradition.

How Pervasive Are Midlife Crises?

Levinson (1978) views midlife as a crisis, believing that the middle-aged adult is suspended between the past and the future, trying to cope with this gap that threatens life's continuity. George Vaillant (1977) has a different view. Vaillant's study—called the "Grant Study"—involved men who were in their early thirties and in their late forties who initially had been interviewed as undergraduates at Harvard University. He concludes that just as adolescence is a time for detecting parental flaws and discovering the truth about childhood, the forties are a decade of reassessing and recording the truth about the adolescent and adulthood years. However, whereas Levinson sees midlife as a crisis, Vaillant maintains that only a minority of adults experience a midlife crisis.

Today, adult development experts are virtually unanimous in their belief that midlife crises have been exaggerated (Bertrand, Graham, & Lachman, 2013; Brim, Ryff, & Kessler, 2004; Lachman & Kranz, 2010). In sum, the stage theories place too much emphasis on crises in development, especially midlife crises. Also, there often is considerable individual variation in the way people experience the stages, a topic that we turn to next.

The Life-Events Approach

Age-related stages represent one major way to examine adult personality development. A second major way to conceptualize adult personality development is to focus on life events (Luhmann & others, 2012; Schwarzer & Luszczynska, 2013).

In the early version of the life-events approach, life events were viewed as taxing circumstances for individuals, forcing them to change their personality (Holmes & Rahe, 1967). Such events as the death of a spouse, divorce, marriage, and so on were believed to involve varying degrees of stress, and therefore likely to influence the individual's development.

Today's life-events approach is more sophisticated. The **contemporary life-events approach** emphasizes that how life events influence the individual's development depends not only on the life

contemporary life-events approach An approach emphasizing that how a life event influences the individual's development depends not only on the life event but also on mediating factors, the individual's adaptation to the life event, the life-stage context, and the sociohistorical context.

event itself but also on mediating factors (physical health, family supports, for example), the individual's adaptation to the life event (appraisal of the threat, coping strategies, for example), the life-stage context, and the sociohistorical context (see Figure 14.2). For example, if individuals are in poor health and have little family support, life events are likely to be more stressful. Whatever the context or mediating variables, however, one individual may perceive a life event as highly stressful, whereas another individual may perceive the same event as a challenge.

Although the life-events approach is a valuable addition to understanding adult development, it has its drawbacks. One significant drawback is that the life-events approach places too much emphasis on change. Another drawback is its failure to recognize that our daily experiences may be the primary sources of stress in our lives (Almeida & others, 2011). Enduring a boring but tense job, staying in an unsatisfying marriage, or living in poverty do not show up on scales of major life events. Yet the everyday pounding we take from these living conditions can add up to a highly stressful life and eventually lead to illness (McIntosh, Gillanders, & Rodgers, 2010).

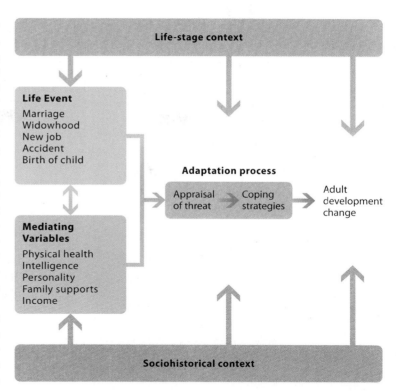

Figure 14.2 A Contemporary Life-Events Framework for Interpreting Adult Developmental Change
According to the contemporary life-events approach, the influence of a life event depends on the event itself, on mediating variables, on the life-stage and sociohistorical context, and on the individual's appraisal of the event and coping strategies.

Stress and Personal Control in Midlife

As we have seen, there is conclusive evidence that midlife is not a time when a majority of adults experience a tumultuous crisis, and when they do experience a midlife crisis, it is often linked to stressful life events. Do middle-aged adults experience stress differently from young adults and older adults? One study using daily diaries over a one-week period found that both young and middle-aged adults had more stressful days than older adults (Almeida & Horn, 2004). In this study, although young adults experienced daily stressors more frequently than middle-aged adults, middle-aged adults experienced more "overload" stressors that involved juggling too many activities at once. In a recent study, healthy older adult women 63 to 93 years of age reported their daily experiences over the course of one week (Charles & others, 2010). In this study, the older the women were, the fewer stressors and less frequent negative emotions they reported.

How Would You...?
As a health-care professional, how would you convince a company that it should sponsor a stress-reduction program for its middle-aged employees?

Developmental Changes in Perceived Personal Control

To what extent do middle-aged adults perceive that they can control what happens to them? Researchers have found that on average a sense of personal control peaks

357

in midlife and then declines (Lachman, 2006). In one study, approximately 80 percent of the young adults (25 to 39 years of age), 71 percent of the middle-aged adults (40 to 59 years of age), and 62 percent of the older adults (60 to 75 years of age) reported that they were often in control of their lives (Lachman & Firth, 2004). However, some aspects of personal control increase with age while others decrease (Lachman, Neupert, & Agrigoroaei, 2011). For example, middle-aged adults have a greater sense of control over their finances, work, and marriage than younger adults but less control over their sex life and their children (Lachman & Firth, 2004). And having a sense of control in middle age is one of the most important modifiable factors in delaying the onset of diseases in middle adulthood and the increasing frequency of diseases in late adulthood (Lachman, Neupert, & Agrigoroaei, 2011).

Stress and Gender

How do women and men differ in the way they experience and respond to stressors?

Women and men differ in the way they experience and respond to stressors (Almeida & others, 2011). Women are more vulnerable to social stressors such as those involving romance, family, and work. For example, women experience higher levels of stress when things go wrong in romantic and marital relationships. Women also are more likely than men to become depressed when they encounter stressful life events such as a divorce or the death of a friend. A recent study of more than 2,800 adults 50 years and older in Taiwan also found that women were more susceptible to depressive symptoms when they felt constant stress from finances, increasing stress from jobs, and fluctuating stress in family relationships (Lin, Hsu, & Chang, 2011).

When men face stress, they are likely to respond in a **fight-or-flight** manner—become aggressive, socially withdraw, or drink alcohol. By contrast, according to Shelley Taylor and her colleagues (2011a, b, c; Taylor & others, 2000), when women experience stress, they are more likely to engage in a **tend-and-befriend** pattern, seeking social alliances with others, especially friends. Taylor argues that when women experience stress an influx of the hormone *oxytocin*, which is linked to nurturing in animals, is released.

Contexts of Midlife Development

The contemporary life-events approach (like Bronfenbrenner's theory, discussed in Chapter 1) highlights the importance of the complex setting of our lives—of everything from our income and family supports to our sociohistorical circumstances. Let's examine how two aspects of the contexts of life influence development during middle adulthood: historical contexts (cohort effects) and culture.

Historical Contexts (Cohort Effects)

Bernice Neugarten (1964) emphasizes the powerful influence of age group or cohort on people's lives. In this view, an individual's values, attitudes, expectations, and behaviors are influenced by the historical time frame in which the person lives. For example, the group of individuals born during the difficult times of the Great Depression may have a different outlook on life from the group born during the optimistic 1950s, says Neugarten.

Neugarten (1986) argues that the social environment of a particular age group can alter its **social clock**—the timetable according to which

fight-or-flight The view that when men experience stress, they are more likely to become aggressive, withdraw from social contact, or drink alcohol.

tend and befriend Taylor's view that when women experience stress, they are more likely to seek social alliances with others, especially female friends.

social clock The timetable according to which individuals are expected to accomplish life's tasks, such as getting married, having children, or establishing a career.

individuals are expected to accomplish life's tasks, such as getting married, having children, or establishing themselves in a career. Social clocks provide guides for our lives; individuals whose lives are not synchronized with these social clocks find life to be more stressful than those who are on schedule, says Neugarten. She argues that today there is much less agreement than in the past on the right age or sequence for the occurrence of major life events such as having children or retiring.

Trying to tease out universal truths and patterns about adult development from one birth cohort is complicated because the findings may not apply to another birth cohort (Schaie, 2010, 2012). Most of the individuals studied by Levinson and Vaillant, for example, were born before and during the Great Depression. What was true for these individuals may not be true for today's 50-year-olds, born in the optimistic aftermath of World War II, or for the post-baby-boom generation as they approach the midlife transition. The midlife men in Levinson's and Vaillant's studies might have been burned out at a premature age rather than being representatives of a normal adult developmental pattern (Rossi, 1989).

Cultural Contexts

In many cultures, especially nonindustrialized cultures, the concept of middle age is not very clear or, in some cases, is absent. It is common in nonindustrialized societies to describe individuals as young or old, but not as middle-aged (Grambs, 1989). Some cultures have no words for "adolescent," "young adult," or "middle-aged adult," but they do have words for other categories.

Gusii dancers perform on habitat day in Nairobi, Kenya. Movement from one status to another in the Gusii culture is due primarily to life events, not age. The Gusii do not have a clearly labeled midlife transition.

What is middle age like for women in other cultures? It depends on the modernity of the culture and the culture's view of gender roles. Some anthropologists believe that when women become middle-aged in nonindustrialized societies they may experience certain advantages (Brown, 1985). First, they are often freed from cumbersome restrictions that were placed on them when they were younger. For example, in middle age they enjoy greater geographical mobility. Child care has ceased or can be delegated, and domestic chores are reduced. They may venture forth from the village for commercial opportunities, visit relatives living at a distance, and attend religious events. Second, with middle age a woman has the right to exercise authority over specified younger kin. Middle-aged women can extract labor from younger family members. The work of middle-aged women tends to be administrative, delegating tasks and making assignments to younger women. Middle-aged women also make important decisions for certain members of the younger generation: what a grandchild is to be named, who is ready to be initiated into adulthood, and who is eligible to marry whom. Third, middle-aged women may become eligible for special statuses, which may provide recognition beyond the household. These statuses include the vocations of midwife, curer, holy woman, and matchmaker.

Stability and Change

Recall from Chapter 1 that questions about stability and change are an important issue in life-span development. One of the main ways that stability and change are assessed is through longitudinal studies that measure the same individuals at different points in their lives.

Longitudinal Studies

We examine three longitudinal studies to help us understand the extent to which there is stability or change in adult personality development: Costa and McCrae's Baltimore Study, the Berkeley Longitudinal Studies, and Vaillant's studies.

Costa and McCrae's Baltimore Study

A major study of adult personality development continues to be conducted by Paul Costa and Robert McCrae (1998; McCrae & Costa, 2006). They focus on what are called the **Big Five factors of personality,** which are openness to experience, conscientiousness, extraversion, agreeableness, and neuroticism (emotional stability); these factors are described in Figure 14.3. (Notice that if you create an acronym from these factor names, you will get the word OCEAN.) A number of research studies point to these factors as important dimensions of personality (Hill & others, 2012; McRae, Gaines, & Wellington, 2013; Roberts, Donnellan, & Hill, 2013).

Using their five-factor personality test, Costa and McCrae (1998, 2000) studied approximately a thousand college-educated men and women aged 20 to 96, assessing the same individuals over many years. Data collection began in the 1950s to mid-1960s and is ongoing. Costa and McCrae concluded that considerable stability across the adult years occurs for the five personality factors.

However, more recent research indicates greater developmental changes in the five personality factors in adulthood (Lucas & Donnellan, 2011; Soto & others, 2011). For example, a recent study found that emotional stability, extraversion, openness, and agreeableness were lower in early adulthood, peaked between 40 and 60 years of age, and decreased in late adulthood, while conscientiousness showed a continuous increase from early adulthood to late adulthood (Specht, Egloff, & Schukle, 2011). Most research studies find that the greatest change occurs in early adulthood (Lucas & Donnellan, 2011; Roberts, Walton, & Viechtbauer, 2006).

Further evidence supporting the importance of the Big Five factors indicates that they are related to major aspects of a person's life such as health, intelligence, and achievement (McRae, Gaines, & Wellington, 2013). The following research reflects these links:

- Across a ten-year period, four of the five Big Five factors (the exception being openness) predicted such self-related health outcomes as physical health, blood pressure, and number of days of limited activity at work or home due to physical health issues (Turiano & others, 2012). Individuals high on neuroticism report more health complaints (Carver & Connor-Smith, 2010).

- One study revealed that openness was related to superior cognitive functioning and IQ across the life span (Sharp & others, 2010).

- A study found that conscientiousness was related to college students' grade point averages (Noftle & Robins, 2007).

The Big Five factors also are related to changing historical circumstances. In a longitudinal study of women in their twenties to their seventies, the Big Five factors were linked to cultural influences, such as changes in the traditional feminine role, the women's movement, and graduate education in careers (George, Helson, & John, 2011).

Openness	**C**onscientiousness	**E**xtraversion	**A**greeableness	**N**euroticism (emotional stability)
• Imaginative or practical	• Organized or disorganized	• Sociable or retiring	• Softhearted or ruthless	• Calm or anxious
• Interested in variety or routine	• Careful or careless	• Fun-loving or somber	• Trusting or suspicious	• Secure or insecure
• Independent or conforming	• Disciplined or impulsive	• Affectionate or reserved	• Helpful or uncooperative	• Self-satisfied or self-pitying

Figure 14.3 The Big Five Factors of Personality
Each of the broad supertraits encompasses more narrow traits and characteristics. Use the acronym OCEAN to remember the Big Five personality factors (openness, conscientiousness, extraversion, agreeableness, neuroticism).

Berkeley Longitudinal Studies

In the Berkeley Longitudinal Studies, more than 500 children and their parents were initially studied in the late 1920s and early 1930s. The book *Present and Past in Middle Life* (Eichorn & others, 1981) profiles these individuals as they became middle-aged. The results from early adolescence through a portion of midlife did not support either extreme in the debate over whether personality is characterized by stability or change. Some characteristics were more stable than others, however. The most stable characteristics were the degree to which individuals were intellectually oriented, self-confident, and open to new experiences. The characteristics that changed the most included the extent to which the individuals were nurturant or hostile and whether they had good self-control or not.

George Vaillant's Studies

Longitudinal studies by George Vaillant explore a question that differs somewhat from the studies described so far: Does personality at middle age predict what a person's life will be like in late adulthood? Vaillant (2002) has conducted three longitudinal studies of adult development and aging: (1) a sample of 268 socially advantaged Harvard graduates born about 1920 (called the Grant Study); (2) a sample of 456 socially disadvantaged inner-city men born about 1930; and (3) a sample of 90 middle-SES, intellectually gifted women born about 1910. These individuals have been assessed numerous times (in most cases, every two years), beginning in the 1920s to 1940s and continuing today for those still living. The main assessments involve extensive interviews with the participants, their parents, and teachers.

Vaillant categorized 75- to 80-year-olds as "happy-well," "sad-sick," and "dead." He used data collected from these individuals when they were 50 years of age to predict which categories they were likely to end up in at 75 to 80 years of age. Alcohol abuse and smoking at age 50 were the best predictors of which individuals would be dead at 75 to 80 years of age. Other factors at age 50 were linked with being in the "happy-well" category at 75 to 80 years of age: getting regular exercise, avoiding being overweight, being well-educated, having a stable marriage, being future-oriented, being thankful and forgiving, empathizing with others, being active with other people, and having good coping skills.

Wealth and income at age 50 were not linked with being in the "happy-well" category at 75 to 80 years of age. Generativity in middle age (defined in this study as "taking care of the next generation") was more strongly related than intimacy to whether individuals would have an enduring and happy marriage at 75 to 80 years of age (Vaillant, 2002).

The results for one of Vaillant's studies, the Grant Study of Harvard men, are shown in Figure 14.4. Note

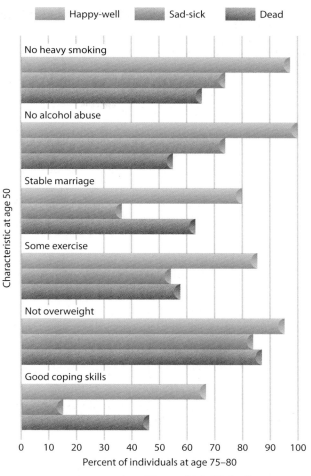

Figure 14.4 Links Between Characteristics at Age 50 and Health and Happiness at Age 75 to 80

In a longitudinal study, the characteristics shown above at age 50 were related to whether individuals were happy-well, sad-sick, or dead at age 75 to 80 (Vaillant, 2002).

How Would You...?

As a health-care professional, how would you use the results of Vaillant's research to advise a middle-aged adult patient who abuses alcohol and smokes?

that when individuals at 50 years of age were not heavy smokers, did not abuse alcohol, had a stable marriage, exercised, maintained a normal weight, and had good coping skills, they were more likely to be alive and happy at 75 to 80 years of age.

Conclusions

What can be concluded about stability and change in personality development during the adult years? Avshalom Caspi and Brent Roberts (2001) concluded that the evidence does not support the view that personality traits become completely fixed at a certain age in adulthood. However, they argue that change is typically limited, and in some cases the changes in personality are small. They also say that age is positively related to stability and that stability peaks in the fifties and sixties. That is, people show greater stability in their personality when they reach midlife than when they were younger adults (Roberts, Donnellan, & Hill, 2013). These findings support what is called a **cumulative personality model** of development, which states that with time and age, people become more adept at interacting with their environment in ways that promote stability of personality.

This does not mean that change is absent throughout midlife. Ample evidence shows that social contexts, new experiences, and sociohistorical changes can affect personality development (Bertrand, Graham, & Lachman, 2013; Mroczek, Spiro, & Griffin, 2006). However, Caspi and Roberts (2001) concluded that as people get older, stability increasingly outweighs change.

In general, changes in personality traits across adulthood also occur in a positive direction. Over time, "people become more confident, warm, responsible, and calm" (Roberts & Mroczek, 2008, p. 33). Such positive changes equate with becoming more socially mature.

In sum, recent research contradicts the old view that stability in personality begins to set in at about 30 years of age (Roberts, Donnellan, & Hill, 2013). Although there are some consistent developmental changes in the personality traits of large numbers of people, at the individual level people can show unique patterns of personality traits—and these patterns often reflect life experiences related to themes of their particular developmental period (Roberts & Mroczek, 2008). For example, researchers have found that individuals who are in a stable marriage and on a solid career track become more socially dominant, conscientious, and emotionally stable as they go through early adulthood (Roberts & Wood, 2006). And, for some of these individuals, there is greater change in their personality traits than for other individuals (McAdams & Olson, 2010; Roberts, Donnellan, & Hill, 2013).

Close Relationships

There is a consensus among middle-aged Americans that a major component of well-being involves positive relationships with others, especially parents, spouse, and offspring (Blieszner & Roberto, 2012; Lachman, 2004). To begin our examination of midlife relationships, let's explore love and marriage in middle-aged adults.

Love and Marriage at Midlife

Remember from Chapter 12 that two major forms of love are romantic love and affectionate love. The fires of romantic love burn strongly in early adulthood. Affectionate, or companionate, love increases during middle adulthood. That is, physical attraction, romance, and passion are more important in new relationships, especially those begun in early adulthood. Security, loyalty, and mutual emotional interest become more important as relationships mature, especially in middle adulthood.

One study revealed that marital satisfaction increased in middle age (Gorchoff, John, & Helson, 2008). Even some marriages that were difficult and rocky during early adulthood turn out to be better adjusted during middle adulthood. Although the partners may have lived through a great deal of turmoil, they eventually discover a deep and solid foundation on which to anchor their relationship. In middle adulthood, the partners may have fewer financial worries, less housework and chores, and more time with each other. Middle-aged partners are more likely to view their marriage as positive if they engage in mutual activities.

What characterizes marriage in middle adulthood?

Most individuals in midlife who are married voice considerable satisfaction with being married. In a large-scale study of individuals in middle adulthood, 72 percent of those who were married said their marriage was either "excellent" or "very good" (Brim, 1999). Possibly by middle age, many of the worst marriages already have dissolved. However, a recent study revealed that married and partnered middle-aged adults were more likely to rate their relationships as more ambivalent or indifferent than their counterparts in late adulthood (Windsor & Butterworth, 2010).

Divorce in middle adulthood may be a more positive experience in some ways, more negative in others, than divorce in early adulthood (Pudrovska, 2009). On the one hand, for mature individuals, the perils of divorce can be fewer and less intense than for younger individuals. They have more resources, and they can use this time as an opportunity to simplify their lives by disposing of possessions, such as a large home, which they no longer need. Their children are adults and may be able to cope with their parents' divorce more effectively than they would have been able to do in childhood or adolescence. The partners may have gained a better understanding of themselves and may be searching for changes that could include the end to an unhappy marriage.

How Would You...?

As a social worker, how would you describe the different reasons for divorce in young and middle-aged couples?

On the other hand, the emotional and time commitment to marriage that has existed for so many years may not be lightly given up. Many midlife individuals perceive a divorce as failing in the best years of their lives. The divorcer might see the situation as an escape from an untenable relationship, but the divorced partner usually sees it as betrayal, the ending of a relationship that had been built up over many years and that involved a great deal of commitment and trust.

A survey by AARP (2004) of 1,148 40- to 79-year-olds who were divorced at least once in their forties, fifties, or sixties found that staying married because of their children was by far the main reason many people took a long time to become divorced. Despite the worry and stress involved in going through a divorce, three in four of the divorcees said they had made the right decision to dissolve their marriage and reported a positive outlook on life. Sixty-six percent of the divorced women said they initiated the divorce, compared with only 41 percent of the divorced men. The divorced women were much more afraid of having financial problems (44 percent) than the divorced men were (11 percent).

What are some ways that divorce might be more positive or more negative in middle adulthood than in early adulthood?

empty nest syndrome A term used to indicate a decrease in marital satisfaction after children leave home.

Following are the main reasons that middle-aged and older adults cited for their divorce:

Main Causes for Women

1. Verbal, physical, or emotional abuse (23 percent)
2. Alcohol or drug abuse (18 percent)
3. Cheating (17 percent)

Main Causes for Men

1. No obvious problems, just fell out of love (17 percent)
2. Cheating (14 percent)
3. Different values, lifestyles (14 percent)

The Empty Nest and Its Refilling

An important event in a family is the launching of a child into adult life. Parents face new adjustments as a result of the child's absence. Students usually think that their parents suffer from their absence. In fact, parents who live vicariously through their children might experience the **empty nest syndrome,** which includes a decline in marital satisfaction after children leave the home. For most parents, however, marital satisfaction does not decline after children have left home. Rather, for most parents marital satisfaction increases during the years after child rearing has ended (Fingerman & Baker, 2006). With their children gone, marital partners have more time to pursue careers and other interests and more time for each other. A recent study revealed that the transition to an empty nest increased marital satisfaction and this increase was linked to an increase in the quality of time—but not the quantity of time—spent with partners (Gorchoff, John, & Helson, 2008).

In today's uncertain economic climate, the refilling of the empty nest is becoming a common occurrence as adult children return to live at home after several years of college, after graduating from college, or to save money after taking a full-time job (Merrill, 2009). Young adults also may move back in with their parents after an unsuccessful career or a divorce. And some individuals don't leave home at all until their middle to late twenties because they cannot financially support themselves. Numerous labels have been applied to these young adults who return to their parents' homes to live, including "boomerang kids" and "B2B" (or Back-to-Bedroom) (Furman, 2005).

The middle generation has always provided support for the younger generation, even after the nest is bare. Through loans and monetary gifts for education, and through emotional support, the middle generation has helped the younger generation. Adult children appreciate the financial and emotional support their parents provide at a time when they often feel considerable stress about their career, work, and lifestyle. And parents feel good that they can provide this support.

However, as with most family living arrangements, there are both pluses and minuses when adult children return to live at home. One of the most common

Doonesbury   BY GARRY TRUDEAU

complaints voiced by both adult children and their parents is a loss of privacy. The adult children complain that their parents restrict their independence, cramp their sex lives, reduce their rock music listening, and treat them as children rather than adults. Parents often complain that their quiet home has become noisy, that they stay up late worrying when their adult children will come home, that meals are difficult to plan because of conflicting schedules, that their relationship as a married couple has been invaded, and that they have to shoulder too much responsibility for their adult children. In sum, when adult children return home to live, a disequilibrium in family life is created, which requires considerable adaptation on the part of parents and their adult children.

What are some strategies that can help parents and their young adult children get along better?

When adult children ask to return home to live, parents and their adult children should agree on the conditions and expectations beforehand. For example, they might discuss and agree on whether young adults will pay rent, wash their own clothes, cook their own meals, do any household chores, pay their phone bills, come and go as they please, be sexually active or drink alcohol at home, and so on. If these conditions aren't negotiated at the beginning, conflict often results because the expectations of parents and young adult children will likely be violated.

How Would You...?

As a psychologist, how would you counsel parents of adult children who return to live at home for a few years following their college graduation?

Sibling Relationships and Friendships

Sibling relationships persist over the entire life span for most adults (Whiteman, McHale, & Soli, 2011). Eighty-five percent of today's adults have at least one living sibling. Sibling relationships in adulthood may be extremely close, apathetic, or highly rivalrous (Bedford, 2009). The majority of sibling relationships in adulthood are close (Cicirelli, 2009). Those siblings who are psychologically close to each other in adulthood tended to be that way in childhood. It is rare for sibling closeness to develop for the first time in adulthood (Dunn, 1984). A recent study revealed that adult siblings often provide practical and emotional support to each other (Voorpostel & Blieszner, 2008). Another study revealed that men who had poor sibling relationships in childhood were more likely to develop depression by age 50 than men who had more positive sibling relationships as children (Waldinger, Vaillant, & Orav, 2007).

Friendships continue to be important in middle adulthood just as they were in early adulthood (Blieszner & Roberto, 2012). It takes time to develop intimate friendships, so friendships that have endured over the adult years are often deeper than those that have just been formed in middle adulthood.

Grandparenting

The increase in longevity is influencing the nature of grandparenting (Monserud, 2011). In 1900 only 4 percent of 10-year-old children had four living grandparents, but in 2000 that figure had risen to more than 40 percent. And in 1990 only about 20 percent of children at 30 years of age had living grandparents, a figure that is projected to increase to 80 percent in 2020 (Hagestad & Uhlenberg, 2007). Further increases in longevity are likely to support this trend in the future, although the current trend toward delayed childbearing is likely to undermine it.

What are some grandparents' roles and styles?

Grandparent Roles

Grandparents play important roles in the lives of many grandchildren (Lumby, 2010; Newton & Stewart, 2012). Many adults become grandparents for the first time during middle age. Researchers have consistently found that grandmothers have more contact with grandchildren than do grandfathers (Watson, Randolph, & Lyons, 2005). Perhaps women tend to define their role as grandmothers as part of their responsibility for maintaining ties between family members across generations. Men may have fewer expectations about the grandfather role and see it as more voluntary.

Three prominent meanings are attached to being a grandparent (Neugarten & Weinstein, 1964). For some older adults, being a grandparent is a source of biological reward and continuity. For others, being a grandparent is a source of emotional self-fulfillment, generating feelings of companionship and satisfaction that may have been missing in earlier adult-child relationships. And for yet others, being a grandparent is a remote role.

The grandparent role may have different functions in different families, in different ethnic groups and cultures, and in different situations (Szinovacz, 2009). For example, in one study of White, African American, and Mexican American grandparents and grandchildren, the Mexican American grandparents saw their grandchildren more frequently, provided more support for the grandchildren and their parents, and had more satisfying relationships with their grandchildren (Bengtson, 1985). And in a study of three generations of families in Chicago, grandmothers had closer relationships with their children and grandchildren and gave more personal advice than grandfathers did (Hagestad, 1985).

The Changing Profile of Grandparents

In 2009, 7.8 million children lived with at least one grandparent, a 64 percent increase since 1981 when 4.7 million children were living with at least one grandparent (U.S. Census Bureau, 2011). Divorce, adolescent pregnancies, and drug use by parents are the main reasons that grandparents are thrust back into the "parenting" role they thought they had shed. A recent study revealed that grandparent involvement was linked with better adjustment when it occurred in single-parent and stepparent families than in two-parent biological families (Attar-Schwartz & others, 2009).

How Would You...?

As a human development and family studies professional, how would you educate parents about the mutual benefits of having grandparents actively involved in their children's lives?

Grandparents who are full-time caregivers for grandchildren are at elevated risk for health problems, depression, and stress (Silverstein, 2009). Caring for grandchildren is linked with these problems in part because full-time grandparent caregivers are often characterized by low-income, minority status and by not being married (Minkler & Fuller-Thompson, 2005). Grandparents who are part-time caregivers are less likely to have the negative health portrait that full-time grandparent caregivers have. In a recent study of part-time grandparent caregivers, few negative effects on grandparents were found (Hughes & others, 2007).

As divorce and remarriage have become more common, a special concern of grandparents is visitation privileges with their grandchildren. In the last 10 to 15 years, more states have passed laws giving grandparents the right to petition a court for visitation privileges with their grandchildren, even if a parent objects. Whether such forced visitation rights for grandparents are in the child's best interest is still being debated.

Intergenerational Relationships

Family is important to most people. When 21,000 adults aged 40 to 79 in 21 countries were asked, "When you think of who you are, you think mainly of _____," 63 percent said "family," 9 percent said "religion," and 8 percent said "work" (HSBC Insurance, 2007). In this study, in all 21 countries, middle-aged and older adults expressed a strong feeling of responsibility between generations in their family, with the strongest intergenerational ties indicated in Saudi Arabia, India, and Turkey. More than 80 percent of the middle-aged and older adults reported that adults have a duty to care for their parents (and parents-in-law) in time of need later in life.

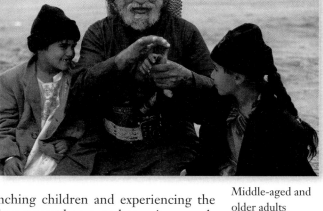

Middle-aged and older adults around the world show a strong sense of family responsibility. A recent study of middle-aged and older adults in 21 countries revealed the strongest intergenerational ties in Saudi Arabia.

Adults in midlife play important roles in the lives of the young and the old (Antonucci, Birditt, & Ajrouch, 2013; Birditt & Wardjiman, 2012; Fingerman & Birditt, 2011). Middle-aged adults share their experience and transmit values to the younger generation. They may be launching children and experiencing the empty nest, adjusting to having grown children return home, or becoming grandparents. They also may be giving or receiving financial assistance, caring for a widowed or sick parent, or adapting to being the oldest generation after both parents have died.

Middle-aged adults have been described as the "sandwich," "squeezed," or "overload" generation because of the responsibilities they have for their adolescent and young adult children on the one hand and their aging parents on the other (Etaugh & Bridges, 2010; Pudrovska, 2009). However, an alternative view is that in the United States, a "sandwich" generation, in which the middle generation cares for both grown children and aging parents simultaneously, occurs less often than a "pivot" generation, in which the middle generation alternates attention between the demands of grown children and aging parents (Birditt & Wardjiman, 2012; Fingerman & Birditt, 2011). By middle age, more than 40 percent of adult children (most of them daughters) provide care for aging parents or parents-in-law (Blieszner & Roberto, 2012; National Alliance for Caregiving, 2009). However, two recent studies revealed that middle-aged parents are more likely to provide support to their grown children than to their parents (Fingerman & others, 2011a, 2012). When middle-aged adults have a parent with a disability, their support for that parent increases (Fingerman & others, 2011b). This support might involve locating a nursing home and monitoring its quality, procuring medical services, arranging public service assistance, and handling finances. In some cases, adult children provide direct assistance with daily living, including such activities as eating, bathing, and dressing. Even less severely impaired older adults may need help with shopping, housework, transportation, home maintenance, and bill paying.

Some researchers have found that relationships between aging parents and their children are often characterized by ambivalence (Birditt, Fingerman, & Zarit, 2010; Birditt & Wardjiman, 2012; Fingerman & Birditt, 2011; Fingerman & others, 2012). Perceptions include love, reciprocal help, and shared values on the positive side and isolation, family conflicts and problems, abuse, neglect, and caregiver stress on the negative side. A recent study, though, revealed that affection and support, reflecting solidarity, were more prevalent than ambivalence in intergenerational relationships (Hogerbrugge & Komter, 2012).

How Would You...?

As a health-care professional, how would you advise a family contemplating the potential challenges of having a middle-aged family member take on primary responsibility for the daily care of a chronically ill parent?

With each new generation, personality characteristics, attitudes, and values are replicated or changed (Antonucci, Birditt, & Ajrouch, 2013). As older family members die, their biological, intellectual, emotional, and personal legacies are carried on in the next generation. Their children become the oldest generation and their grandchildren the second generation. As adult children become middle-aged, they often develop more positive perceptions of their parents (Field, 1999). Both similarity and dissimilarity across generations are found. For example, similarity between parents and an adult child is most noticeable in religion and politics, least in gender roles, lifestyle, and work orientation.

What is the nature of intergenerational relationships?

Several studies provide further evidence of the importance of intergenerational relationships in development. One study found that the motivation of adult children to provide social support to their older parents was linked with earlier family experiences (Silverstein & others, 2002). Children who spent more time in shared activities with their parents and were given more financial support by them earlier in their lives provided more support to their parents when they became older. Another study revealed that children of divorce were disproportionately likely to end their own marriage than were children from intact, never divorced families, although the transmission of divorce across generations has declined in recent years (Wolfinger, 2011).

Gender differences also characterize intergenerational relationships (Etaugh & Bridges, 2010). Women have an especially important role in connecting family relationships across generations. Women's relationships across generations are typically closer than other family bonds (Merrill, 2009). In one study, mothers and their daughters had much closer relationships during their adult years than mothers and sons, fathers and daughters, and fathers and sons (Rossi, 1989). Also in this study, married men were more involved with their wives' kin than with their own. And maternal grandmothers and maternal aunts were cited twice as often as their counterparts on the paternal side of the family as the most important or loved relative. Also, a recent study revealed that mothers' intergenerational ties were more influential for grandparent-grandchild relationships than fathers' were (Monserud, 2008).

Summary

Personality Theories and Development

- Erikson says that the seventh stage of the human life span, generativity versus stagnation, occurs in middle adulthood. Levinson concluded that a majority of Americans, especially men, experience a midlife crisis. Research, though, indicates that midlife crises are not pervasive.

- In the contemporary version of the life-events approach, how life events influence the individual's development depends not only on the life event but also on mediating factors, adaptation to the event, the life-stage context, and the sociohistorical context.

- Young and middle-aged adults experience more stressful days than do older adults, and as adults become older, they report less control over some areas of their lives and more control over other areas.

- Neugarten argues that the social environment of a particular cohort can alter its social clock. Many cultures do not have a clear concept of middle age.

Stability and Change

- In Costa and McCrae's Baltimore Study, the Big Five personality factors showed considerable stability. In the Berkeley Longitudinal Studies, the extremes in the stability-change argument were not supported. George Vaillant's research revealed links between a number of characteristics at age 50 and health and well-being at 75 to 80 years of age.

- Some researchers suggest that stability peaks in the fifties and sixties, others say that it begins to stabilize at about 30, and still others argue that limited personality changes continue during midlife.

Close Relationships

- Affectionate love increases in midlife for many individuals.

- Rather than decreasing marital satisfaction as once thought, the empty nest increases it for most parents. An increasing number of young adults are returning home to live with their middle-aged parents.

- Sibling relationships continue throughout life, and friendships continue to be important in middle age.

- Depending on the family's culture and situation, grandparents assume different roles. The profile of grandparents is changing.

- Family members usually maintain contact across generations. The middle-aged generation plays an important role in linking generations.

Key Terms

generativity 354
stagnation 354
contemporary life-events approach 356

fight-or-flight 358
tend-and-befriend 358

social clock 358
Big Five factors of personality 360

cumulative personality model 362
empty nest syndrome 364

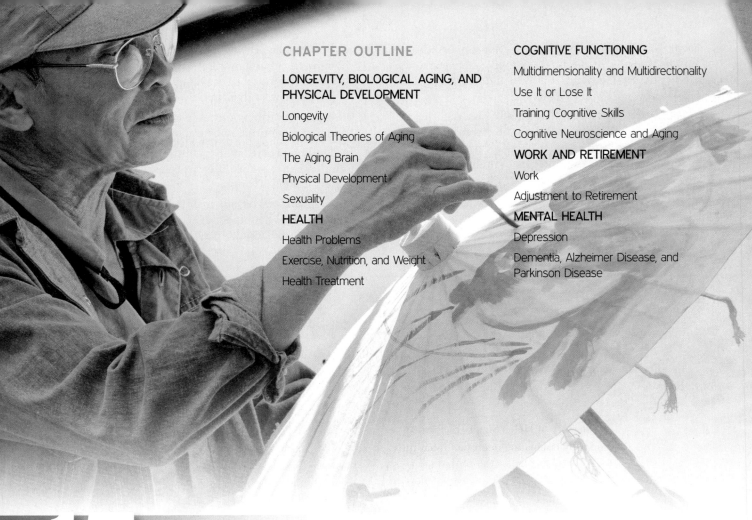

15 Physical and Cognitive Development in Late Adulthood

Stories of Life-Span Development: Learning to Age Successfully

In 2010, 90-year-old Helen Small completed her master's degree at the University of Texas at Dallas. The topic of her master's degree research project was romantic relationships in late adulthood. Helen said that she only interviewed one individual who was older than she was—a 92-year-old man.

I (your author, John Santrock) first met Helen when she took my undergraduate course in life-span development in 2006. After the first test, Helen stopped showing up and I wondered what had happened to her. It turns out that she had broken her shoulder when

she tripped over a curb while hurrying to class. The next semester, she took my class again and did a great job in it, even though the first several months she had to take notes with her left hand (she's right-handed) because of her lingering shoulder problem.

Helen grew up in the Great Depression and first went to college in 1938 at the University of Akron, where she only attended for one year. She got married and her marriage lasted 62 years. After her husband's death, Helen went back to college in 2002, first at Brookhaven Community College and then at

UT-Dallas. When I interviewed her recently, she told me that she had promised her mother that she would finish college. Her most important advice for college students is "Finish college and be persistent. When you make a commitment, always see it through. Don't quit. Go after what you want in life."

Helen not only is cognitively fit, she also is physically fit. She works out three times a week for about an hour each time—aerobically on a treadmill for about 30 minutes and then on six different weight machines.

What struck me most about Helen when she took my undergraduate course in life-span development was how appreciative she was of the opportunity to learn and how passionately she pursued studying and doing well in the course. Helen was quite popular with the younger students in the course and she was a terrific role model for them.

After her graduation, I asked her what she planned to do during the next few years and she responded, "I've got to figure out what I'm going to do with the rest of my life." Helen now comes each semester to my course in life-span development when we are discussing cognitive aging. She wows the class and has been an inspiration to all who come in contact with her.

What has Helen done recently to stay cognitively fit? She has worked as a public ambassador for Dr. Denise Park's Center for Vital Longevity at UT-Dallas and written her first book: *Why Not? My Seventy Year Plan for a College Degree* (Small, 2011). It's a wonderful, motivating invitation to live your life fully and reach your potential no matter what your age.

The story of Helen Small's physical and cognitive well-being in late adulthood raises some truly fascinating questions about life-span development, which we explore in this chapter. They include: Why do we age, and what, if anything, can we do to delay the aging process? What chance do you have of living to be 100? How does the body change in old age? How well do older adults function cognitively? What roles do work and retirement play in older adults' lives? ■

Longevity, Biological Aging, and Physical Development

What do we really know about longevity? What are the current biological theories about why we age? How does our brain change during this part of our life span? What happens to us physically? Does our sexuality change?

Longevity

The United States is no longer a youthful society. As more individuals are living past age 65, the proportion of individuals at different ages has become increasingly similar. Indeed, the concept of a period called "late adulthood," beginning in the sixties or seventies and lasting until death, is a recent one. Before the twentieth century, most individuals died before they reached 65.

Life Span and Life Expectancy

Since the beginning of recorded history, **life span,** the maximum number of years an individual can live, has remained at approximately 120 to 125 years of age. But since 1900 improvements in medicine, nutrition, exercise, and lifestyle have increased our life expectancy an average of 31 additional years.

Recall from Chapter 1 that **life expectancy** is the number of years that the average person born in a particular year will probably live. The

life span The upper boundary of life, which is the maximum number of years an individual can live. The maximum life span of human beings is about 120 to 125 years of age.

life expectancy The number of years that will probably be lived by the average person born in a particular year.

average life expectancy of individuals born today in the United States is 78.3 years (U.S. Census Bureau, 2011). Sixty-five-year-olds in the United States today can expect to live an average of 18.6 more years (19.9 for females, 17.2 for males) (U.S. Census Bureau, 2011). People who are 100 years of age can only expect to live an average of 2.3 years longer (U.S. Census Bureau, 2011).

Differences in Life Expectancy

How does the United States fare in life expectancy, compared with other countries around the world? We do considerably better than some and somewhat worse than others. In 2011, Monaco had the highest estimated life expectancy at birth (90 years), followed by Macau (a region of China near Hong Kong), Japan, and Singapore (84 years) (Central Intelligence Agency, 2012). Of 221 countries, the United States ranked fiftieth at 78 years. The lowest estimated life expectancy in 2011 occurred in the African countries of Chad, Guinea-Bissau, South Africa, and Swaziland (49 years). Differences in life expectancies across countries are due to factors such as health conditions and medical care throughout the life span.

In 2010 the overall life expectancy for women was 80.8 years of age, and for men it was 75.7 years of age (Centers for Disease Control and Prevention, 2012). Beginning in the mid-thirties, women outnumber men; this gap widens during the remainder of the adult years. By the time adults are 75 years of age, more than 61 percent of the population is female; for those 85 and over, the figure is almost 70 percent female. Why can women expect to live longer than men? Social factors such as health attitudes, habits, lifestyles, and occupation are probably important (Saint Onge, 2009). Men are more likely than women to die from most of the leading causes of death in the United States, including cancer of the respiratory system, motor vehicle accidents, cirrhosis of the liver, emphysema, and coronary heart disease (Robine, 2011). These causes of death are associated with lifestyle. For example, the sex difference in deaths due to lung cancer and emphysema occurs because men are heavier smokers than women.

The sex difference in longevity also is influenced by biological factors (Sorensen, 2012). In virtually all species, females outlive males. Women have more resistance to infections and degenerative diseases (Pan & Chang, 2012). For example, the female's estrogen production helps to protect her from arteriosclerosis (hardening of the arteries). And the additional X chromosome that women carry in comparison with men may be associated with the production of more antibodies to fight off disease. The sex difference in mortality is still present in late adulthood but less pronounced than earlier in adulthood, and it is especially linked to the higher level of cardiovascular disease in men than women (Yang & Kozloski, 2011).

Centenarians

In the United States, there were only 15,000 centenarians in 1980, a number that had risen to 55,000 in 2008. It is projected that this number will reach more than 800,000 by 2050.

Many people expect that "the older you get, the sicker you get." However, researchers are finding that is not true for some centenarians (Davinelli, Willcox, & Scapagnini, 2012). A study of 93 centenarians revealed that despite some physical limitations, they had a low rate of age-associated diseases and most had good mental health (Selim & others, 2005). And a recent study of centenarians from 100 to 119 years of age found that the older the age group (110 to 119—referred to as supercentenarians—compared with 100 to 104, for example), the later the onset of diseases such as cancer and cardiovascular disease, as well as functional decline (Andersen & others, 2012). The research just described was conducted as part of the New England Centenarian Study.

What chance do you have of living to be 100? Genes play an important role in surviving to an extreme old age (Anisimov & others, 2012). But there are

Three participants in the New England Centenarian Study: (*Left*) Adelaide Kruger, age 101, watering her flowers; (*middle*) Waldo McBurney, age 104, active beekeeper, gardener, and runner who has earned five gold medals and set international records in track and field events in his age group; (*right*) Daphne Brann, age 110, voting in an election.

additional factors at work such as family history, health (weight, diet, smoking, and exercise), education, personality, and lifestyle (Tabara, Kohara, & Miki, 2012). Remember from Chapter 2 that in the epigenetic approach, there is increasing interest in determining gene x environment (G x E) interactions that influence development (Davinelli, Willcox, & Scapagnini, 2012; Eaton & others, 2012).

Biological Theories of Aging

Even if we stay remarkably healthy, we begin to age at some point. Four biological theories provide intriguing explanations of why we age: evolutionary, cellular clock, free-radical, and hormonal stress.

Evolutionary Theory

In the **evolutionary theory of aging,** natural selection has not eliminated many harmful conditions and nonadaptive characteristics in older adults (Le Couteur & Simpson, 2011; Wensink & others, 2012). Why? Because natural selection is linked to reproductive fitness, which is present only in the earlier part of adulthood. For example, consider Alzheimer disease, an irreversible brain disorder, which does not appear until late middle adulthood or late adulthood. According to evolutionary theory, possibly if Alzheimer disease occurred earlier in development, it might have been eliminated many centuries ago.

Cellular Clock Theory

Cellular clock theory is Leonard Hayflick's (1977) theory that cells can divide a maximum of about 75 to 80 times and that as we age our cells become less capable of dividing. Hayflick found that cells extracted from adults in their fifties to seventies divided fewer than 75 to 80 times. Based on the ways cells divide, Hayflick places the upper limit of human life-span potential at about 120 to 125 years of age.

In the last decade, scientists have tried to fill in a gap in cellular clock theory (Phillips, 2012). Hayflick did not know why cells die. The answer may lie at the tips of chromosomes (Kim & others, 2012).

Each time a cell divides, *telomeres*, which are DNA sequences that cap chromosomes. become shorter and shorter (see Figure 15.1). After about 70 or 80 replications, the telomeres are dramatically reduced, and the cell no longer can reproduce. One study revealed that healthy

evolutionary theory of aging The view that natural selection has not eliminated many harmful conditions and nonadaptive characteristics in older adults.

cellular clock theory Leonard Hayflick's theory that the maximum number of times that human cells can divide is about 75 to 80. As we age, our cells become increasingly less capable of dividing.

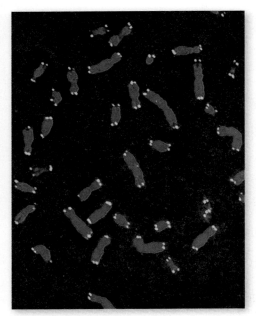

Figure 15.1
Telomeres and Aging
The photograph shows actual telomeres lighting up the tips of chromosomes.

centenarians had longer telomeres than unhealthy centenarians (Terry & others, 2008).

Injecting the enzyme *telomerase* into human cells grown in the laboratory can substantially extend the life of the cells beyond the approximately 70 to 80 normal cell divisions (Aubert & Lansdorp, 2008; Harrison, 2012). However, telomerase is present in approximately 85 to 90 percent of cancerous cells and thus may not produce healthy life extension of cells (Fakhoury, Nimmo, & Autexier, 2007). To capitalize on the high presence of telomerase in cancerous cells, researchers currently are investigating gene therapies that inhibit telomerase and lead to the death of cancerous cells while keeping healthy cells alive (Londono-Vallejo & Wellinger, 2012). A recent focus of these gene therapies is on stem cells and their renewal (Hoffmeyer & others, 2012). Telomeres and telomerase are increasingly thought to be key components of the stem cell regeneration process, providing a possible avenue to restrain cancer and delay aging (Piper & others, 2012; Shay, Reddel, & Wright, 2012).

Free-Radical Theory

A third theory of aging is **free-radical theory,** which states that people age because when cells metabolize energy, the by-products include unstable oxygen molecules known as *free radicals*. The free radicals ricochet around the cells, damaging DNA and other cellular structures (Bachschmid & others, 2012). Overeating is linked with an increase in free radicals, and researchers recently have found that calorie restriction—a diet low in calories but adequate in proteins, vitamins, and minerals—reduces the oxidative damage created by free radicals (Cerqueira & others, 2012). In addition to diet, researchers also are exploring the role that exercise might play in reducing oxidative damage in cells (Muthusamy & others, 2012).

Related to free-radical theory is an emphasis on a decay of *mitochrondria*—tiny bodies within cells that supply essential energy for function, growth, and repair—that is primarily due to oxidative damage and loss of critical micronutrients supplied by the cell (Lee & Wei, 2012). The mitochondrial damage may lead to a range of disorders, including cancer, arthritis, and Alzheimer disease (Eckmann & others, 2012). However, it is not known whether the defects in mitochondria cause aging or merely accompany the aging process (Brand, 2011).

Hormonal Stress Theory

Cellular clock and free radical theories attempt to explain aging at the cellular level. In contrast, **hormonal stress theory** argues that aging in the body's hormonal system can lower resistance to stress and increase the likelihood of disease. Normally, when people experience stressors, the body responds by releasing certain hormones. As people age, the hormones stimulated by stress remain at elevated levels longer than when people were younger (Simm & others, 2008). These prolonged, elevated levels of stress-related hormones are associated with increased risks for many diseases, including cardiovascular disease, cancer, diabetes, and hypertension (Steptoe & Kivimaki, 2012).

Recently, a variation of hormonal stress theory has emphasized the contribution of a decline in immune system functioning with aging (Solana & others, 2012). Aging contributes to immune system deficits that give rise to infectious diseases in older adults (Stowell, Robles, & Kane, 2013). The extended duration of stress and diminished restorative processes in older adults may accelerate the effects of aging on immunity.

free-radical theory A theory of aging proposing that people age because normal cell metabolism produces unstable oxygen molecules known as free radicals. These molecules ricochet around inside cells, damaging DNA and other cellular structures.

hormonal stress theory The theory that aging in the body's hormonal system can lower resilience under stress and increase the likelihood of disease.

Which of these biological theories best explains aging? That question has not yet been answered. It might turn out that more than one or all of these biological processes contribute to aging.

The Aging Brain

How does the brain change during late adulthood? Does it retain plasticity? As we will see, the brain shrinks and slows but still has considerable adaptive ability.

The Shrinking, Slowing Brain

On average, the brain loses 5 to 10 percent of its weight between the ages of 20 and 90. Brain volume also decreases (Fjell & Walhovd, 2010). A recent study found a decrease in total brain volume and volume in key brain structures such as the frontal lobes and hippocampus from 22 to 88 years of age (Sherwood & others, 2011). Another study found that the volume of the brain was 15 percent less in older adults than younger adults (Shan & others, 2005). A recent analysis concluded that in healthy aging the decrease in brain volume is due mainly to shrinkage of neurons, lower numbers of synapses, and reduced length of axons but only to a minor extent by neuron loss (Fjell & Walhovd, 2010).

Some brain areas shrink more than others with aging (Raz & others, 2010). The prefrontal cortex is one area that shrinks, and recent research has linked this shrinkage with a decrease in working memory and other cognitive activities in older adults (Rosano & others, 2012).

A general slowing of function in the brain and spinal cord begins in middle adulthood and accelerates in late adulthood (Rosano & others, 2012). Both physical coordination and intellectual performance are affected. For example, after age 70 many adults no longer show a knee-jerk reflex, and by age 90 most reflexes are much slower (Spence, 1989). Slowing of the brain can impair the performance of older adults on intelligence tests, especially timed tests (Lu & others, 2012).

Aging also has been linked to a decline in the production of some neurotransmitters. Reduction in acetylcholine is linked to a decline in memory loss, especially in Alzheimer disease (Craig, Hong, & McDonald, 2011). Severe reductions in dopamine are involved in a reduction in motor control in Parkinson disease (Ma & others, 2011b).

The Adaptive Brain

The human brain has remarkable repair capability (Vance & others, 2012). Even in late adulthood, the brain loses only a portion of its ability to function, and the activities older adults engage in can still influence the brain's development (Ando, 2012). For example, in a recent fMRI study, higher levels of aerobic fitness were linked with greater volume in the hippocampus, which translates into better memory (Erickson & others, 2011).

Can adults, even aging adults, generate new neurons? Researchers have found that *neurogenesis*, the generation of new neurons, does occur in lower mammalian species, such as mice (Berry & others, 2012). Also, research indicates that exercise and an enriched, complex environment can generate new brain cells in rats and mice, and that stress reduces their survival rate (Salmaso & others, 2012). A recent study revealed that coping with stress stimulated hippocampal neurogenesis in adult monkeys (Lyons & others, 2010). And researchers have discovered that if rats are cognitively challenged to learn something, new brain cells survive longer (Shors, 2009).

It also is now accepted that neurogenesis can occur in human adults (Goritz & Frisen, 2012). However, researchers have documented neurogenesis in only two brain regions: the hippocampus, which is involved in memory, and the olfactory bulb, which is involved in smell (Ming & Song, 2011; Xu & others, 2012). It also is not known what functions these new brain cells perform, and at this point researchers have documented that they last for only several weeks (Nelson, 2008).

Researchers currently are studying factors that might inhibit and promote neurogenesis, including various drugs, stress, and exercise (Gil-Mohapel & others, 2011). They also are examining how the grafting of neural stem cells to various regions of the brain, such as the hippocampus, might increase neurogenesis (Decimo & others, 2012). And increasing attention is being given to the possible role neurogenesis might play in neurodegenerative diseases, such as Alzheimer disease, Parkinson disease, and Huntington disease (Walton & others, 2012; Winner, Kohl, & Gage, 2011).

Dendritic growth can occur in human adults, possibly even in older adults (Eliasieh, Liets, & Chalupa, 2007). Recall from Chapter 3 that dendrites are the receiving portion of the neuron. One study compared the brains of adults at various ages (Coleman, 1986). From the forties through the seventies, the growth of dendrites increased. However, in people in their nineties, dendritic growth no longer occurred.

Changes in lateralization may provide one type of adaptation in aging adults (Cabeza & Dennis, 2011). Recall that lateralization is the specialization of function in one hemisphere of the brain or the other. Using neuroimaging techniques, researchers found that brain activity in the prefrontal cortex is lateralized less in older adults than in younger adults when they are engaging in cognitive tasks (Cabeza, 2002). For example, Figure 15.2 shows that when younger adults are given the task of recognizing words they have previously seen, they process the information primarily in the right hemisphere; older adults are more likely to use both hemispheres (Madden & others, 1999). The decrease in lateralization in older adults might play a compensatory role in the aging brain. That is, using both hemispheres may improve the cognitive functioning of older adults.

How Would You...?

As an educator, how would you use a biological perspective to explain changes in learning as people age?

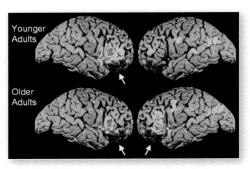

Figure 15.2
The Decrease in Brain Lateralization in Older Adults
Younger adults primarily used the right prefrontal region of the brain (*top left photo*) during a recall memory task, whereas older adults used both the left and right prefrontal regions (*bottom two photos*).

The Nun Study

The Nun Study, directed by David Snowdon, is an intriguing ongoing investigation of aging in 678 nuns, many of whom are from the convent of the Sisters of Notre Dame in Mankato, Minnesota (Snowdon, 2003; Tyas & others, 2007). They lead an intellectually challenging life, and brain researchers conclude that this contributes to their quality of life as older adults and possibly to their longevity. All of the 678 nuns agreed to participate in annual assessments of their cognitive and physical functioning. They also agreed to donate their brains for scientific research when they die, and they are the largest group of brain donors in the world. Examination of the nuns' donated brains, as well as others', has led neuroscientists to believe that the brain has a remarkable capacity to change and grow, even in old age.

In one study of the nuns, idea density, a measure of linguistic ability assessed early in the adult years (age 22), was linked with higher brain weight, fewer incidences of mild cognitive impairment, and fewer characteristics of

Top: Sister Marcella Zachman (*left*) finally stopped teaching at age 97. Now, at 99, she helps ailing nuns exercise their brains by quizzing them on vocabulary or playing a card game called Skip–Bo, at which she deliberately loses. Sister Mary Esther Boor (*right*), also 99 years of age, is a former teacher who stays alert by doing puzzles and volunteering to work the front desk. *Bottom:* A technician holds the brain of a deceased Mankato nun. The nuns donate their brains for research that explores the effects of stimulation on brain growth.

Alzheimer disease in 75- to 95-year-old nuns (Riley & others, 2005). In another study, sisters who had taught for most of their lives showed more moderate declines in intellectual skills than those who had spent most of their lives in service-based tasks, which supports the notion that stimulating the brain with intellectual activity keeps neurons healthy and alive (Snowdon, 2002).

This and other research provide hope that scientists will discover ways to tap into the brain's capacity to adapt in order to prevent and treat brain diseases (Mortimer & others, 2012). For example, scientists might learn more effective ways to improve older adults' cognitive functioning, reduce Alzheimer disease, and help older adults recover from strokes (Bornstein & Poon, 2012; Wang & others, 2012). Even when areas of the brain are permanently damaged by stroke, new message routes can be created to get around the blockage or to resume the function of that area, indicating that the brain does adapt.

Physical Development

Physical decline is inevitable if we manage to live to an old age, but the timing of physical problems related to aging is not uniform. Let's examine some physical changes that occur as we age, including changes in physical appearance and movement, some of the senses, and our circulation and lungs.

Physical Appearance and Movement

In late adulthood, the changes in physical appearance that began occurring during middle age (as discussed in Chapter 13) become more pronounced. Wrinkles and age spots are the most noticeable changes. We also get shorter as we get older. As we saw in Chapter 13, both men and women become shorter in late adulthood because of bone loss in their vertebrae (Hoyer & Roodin, 2009).

Our weight usually drops after we reach 60 years of age. This likely occurs because we lose muscle, which also gives our bodies a "sagging" look (Evans, 2010).

Older adults move slower than young adults, and this slowing occurs for many types of movement with a wide range of difficulty (Davis & others, 2013). Recent research indicates that obesity was linked to mobility limitation in older adults (Vincent, Raiser, & Vincent, 2012). Also, a recent study found that a combined program of physical activity and weight loss helped to preserve mobility in older, obese adults in poor cardiovascular health (Rejeski & others, 2011).

Exercise and appropriate weight lifting can help to reduce the decrease in muscle mass and improve the older person's body appearance. One study revealed that it's not just physical exercise that is linked to preserving older adults' motor functions; in this study, engaging in social activities protected against loss of motor abilities (Buchman & others, 2009).

Sensory Development

Seeing, hearing, and other aspects of sensory functioning are linked with our ability to perform everyday activities, and sensory functioning declines in older adults (Hochberg & others, 2012; Schneider & others, 2011).

Vision In late adulthood, the decline in vision that began for most adults in early or middle adulthood becomes more pronounced (Polat & others, 2012). The eye does not adapt as quickly when moving from a well-lighted place to one of semi-darkness. The tolerance for glare also diminishes. The area of the visual field becomes smaller, and events that occur away from the center of the visual field sometimes are not detected (Scialfa & Kline, 2007). All of these changes can make night driving especially difficult (West & others, 2010).

Recent research has shown that sensory decline in older adults is linked to a decline in cognitive functioning. One study of individuals in their seventies revealed that visual decline was related to slower speed of processing information, which in turn was associated with greater cognitive decline (Clay & others, 2009).

cataracts Involve a thickening of the lens of the eye that causes vision to become cloudy and distorted.

glaucoma Damage to the optic nerve because of the pressure created by a buildup of fluid in the eye.

macular degeneration A disease that involves deterioration of the macula of the retina, which corresponds to the focal center of the visual field.

Color vision also may decline as a result of the yellowing of the lens of the eye (Schieber, 2006). As a result, older adults may have trouble accurately matching closely related colors such as navy socks and black socks.

Depth perception typically declines in late adulthood, which can make it difficult for older adults to determine how close or far away or how high or low something is (Bian & Anderson, 2008). A decline in depth perception can make steps or street curbs difficult to navigate.

Three diseases that can impair the vision of older adults are cataracts, glaucoma, and macular degeneration:

How Would You...?

As a health-care professional, how would you respond to an older adult who shows signs of impaired vision but denies, or is unaware of, the problem?

- **Cataracts** involve a thickening of the lens of the eye that causes vision to become cloudy and distorted (Choi & others, 2012). By age 70, approximately 30 percent of individuals experience a partial loss of vision due to cataracts. Initially, cataracts can be treated by glasses; if they worsen, a simple surgical procedure can replace the natural lenses with artificial ones (Chung & others, 2009).

- **Glaucoma** involves damage to the optic nerve because of the pressure created by a buildup of fluid in the eye (Kokotas & others, 2012). Approximately 1 percent of individuals in their seventies and 10 percent of those in their nineties have glaucoma, which can be treated with eye drops. If left untreated, glaucoma can ultimately destroy a person's vision.

- **Macular degeneration** is a disease that involves deterioration of the *macula* of the retina, which corresponds to the focal center of the visual field. Individuals with macular degeneration may have relatively normal peripheral vision but be unable to see clearly what is right in front of them (Taylor, 2012) (see Figure 15.3). It affects 1 in 25 individuals from age 66 to 74 and 1 in 6 of those age 75 and older. Macular degeneration is difficult to treat and thus is a leading cause of blindness in older adults (Wang & others, 2009). A recent study found that macular degeneration was linked to increased risk of falls in adults 77 years and older (Wood & others, 2011).

Hearing For hearing as for vision, it is important to determine the degree of decline in the aging adult (Pacala & Yeuh, 2012). A recent national survey revealed that 63 percent of adults 70 years and older had a hearing loss, defined as a frequency of more than 25 dB in their better ear (Lin & others, 2011). In this study, hearing aids were used by 40 percent of those with moderate hearing loss. A recent study found that hearing loss was associated with a reduction in cognitive functioning in older adults (Lin, 2011).

Hearing impairment usually does not become much of an impediment until late adulthood, usually due to degeneration of the *cochlea*, the primary neural receptor for hearing in the inner ear (Li-Korotky, 2012). Even in late

Figure 15.3 Macular Degeneration
This simulation of the effect of macular degeneration shows how individuals with this eye disease can see their peripheral field of vision but can't clearly see what is in their central visual field.

adulthood, some, but not all, hearing problems can be corrected with hearing aids (Cook & Hawkins, 2006).

Smell and Taste Most older adults lose some of their sense of smell or taste, or both (Murphy, 2009). These losses often begin around 60 years of age (Hawkes, 2006). A majority of individuals 80 years of age and older experience a significant reduction in smell (Lafreiere & Mann, 2009). Researchers have found that older adults show a greater decline in their sense of smell than in their taste (Schiffman, 2007). Smell and taste decline less in healthy older adults than in their less healthy counterparts.

How Would You...?

As an educator, how would you structure your classroom and plan class activities to accommodate the sensory decline of older adult students?

Touch and Pain Changes in touch and pain are also associated with aging (Pho & others, 2012). For most older adults, a decline in touch sensitivity is not problematic (Hoyer & Roodin, 2009). Older adults are less sensitive to pain and suffer from it less than younger adults (Harkins, Price, & Martinelli, 1986). Although decreased sensitivity to pain can help older adults cope with disease and injury, it can also mask injuries and illnesses that need to be treated.

The Circulatory System and Lungs

Cardiovascular disorders increase in late adulthood (Emery, Anderson, & Goodwin, 2013). Consistent blood pressures above 120/80 should be treated to reduce the risk of heart attack, stroke, or kidney disease. Various drugs, a healthy diet, and exercise can reduce the risk of cardiovascular disease in older adults (Guirado & others, 2012). However, a recent national analysis found that resistant hypertension (hypertension that cannot be controlled with at least four antihypertensive agents) is increasing in the United States, likely because of increases in obesity and in the number of older adults (Roberie & Elliott, 2012). Resistant hypertension is more common in the elderly.

Lung capacity drops 40 percent between the ages of 20 and 80, even without disease (Fozard, 1992). Lungs lose elasticity, the chest shrinks, and the diaphragm weakens (Marek & others, 2011). The good news, though, is that older adults can improve lung functioning with diaphragm-strengthening exercises.

Sleep

Approximately 50 percent of older adults complain of having difficulty sleeping (Neikrug & Ancoli-Israel, 2010). Poor sleep can result in earlier death and is linked to a lower level of cognitive functioning (Naismith, Lewis, & Rogers, 2011). Many of the sleep problems of older adults are associated with health problems (Rothman & Mattson, 2012). A recent study revealed that regular exercise improves the sleep profile of older adults (Lira & others, 2011).

Sexuality

In the absence of two circumstances—disease and the belief that old people are or should be asexual—sexuality can be lifelong (Marshall, 2012). Aging, however, does induce some changes in human sexual performance, more so in the male than in the female (Gray & Garcia, 2012). Orgasm becomes less frequent in males with age, occurring in every second to third attempt rather than every time. More direct stimulation usually is needed to produce an erection.

What are some characteristics of sexuality in older adults? How does sexuality change as older adults go through the late adulthood period?

What are the most common chronic conditions in late adulthood?

One study revealed that many older adults are sexually active as long as they are healthy (Lindau & others, 2007). Sexual activity did decline through the later years of life: 73 percent of 57- to 64-year-olds, 53 percent of 65- to 74-year-olds, and 26 percent of 75- to 85-year-olds reported that they were sexually active. However, with recent advances in erectile dysfunction medications, such as Viagra, an increasing number of older adults, especially the young-old, are able to have an erection (Lowe & Costabile, 2012; Rubio-Aurioles & others, 2012).

Health

What types of health problems do people have in late adulthood, and what can be done to maintain or improve their health and ability to function in everyday life?

Health Problems

As we age, we are more likely to have some disease or illness. The majority of adults still alive at 80 years of age or older have some type of impairment. Chronic diseases (those with a slow onset and a long duration) are rare in early adulthood, increase in middle adulthood, and become more common in late adulthood.

Arthritis is the most common chronic disorder in late adulthood, followed by hypertension. Older women have a higher incidence of arthritis and hypertension and are more likely to have visual problems, but are less likely to have hearing problems, than older men are.

Low income is also strongly related to health problems in late adulthood (Yang & Lee, 2010). Approximately three times as many poor as non-poor older adults report that chronic disorders limit their activities.

Causes of Death in Older Adults

Nearly 60 percent of U.S. adults age 65 to 74 die of cancer or cardiovascular disease (Murphy, Xu, & Kochanek, 2012). As we saw in Chapter 13, "Physical and Cognitive Development in Middle Adulthood," cancer recently replaced cardiovascular disease as the leading cause of death in U.S. middle-aged adults. The same realignment of causes of death has also occurred in 65- to 74-year-olds, with cancer now the leading cause of death in this age group (National Center for Health Statistics, 2010). The decline in cardiovascular disease in middle-aged and older adults is due to improved drugs, a decrease in smoking, better diet, and an increase in exercise. However, in the 75-to-84 and 85-and-over age groups, cardiovascular disease is still the leading cause of death (National Center for Health Statistics, 2010), and the older a person is, the more likely the person will die of cardiovascular disease (National Center for Health Statistics, 2010).

Arthritis

arthritis Inflammation of the joints that is accompanied by pain, stiffness, and movement problems; especially common in older adults.

Arthritis is an inflammation of the joints accompanied by pain, stiffness, and movement problems. This incurable disorder can affect hips, knees, ankles, fingers, and vertebrae. Individuals with arthritis often experience difficulty moving about and performing routine daily activities. Arthritis is especially prevalent in older adults (Davis & others, 2013). Recent studies document the benefits of exercise in older adults with arthritis (Forsyth, Quon, & Konkle, 2011; Semanik, Chang, & Dunlop, 2012).

Osteoporosis

Normal aging brings some loss of bone tissue, but for some individuals loss of bone tissue becomes severe. **Osteoporosis** involves an extensive loss of bone tissue and is the main reason many older adults walk with a marked stoop. Women are especially vulnerable to osteoporosis, which is the leading cause of broken bones in women (Davis & others, 2013; Ragucci & Shrader, 2011). Approximately 80 percent of osteoporosis cases in the United States occur in females, 20 percent in males. Almost two-thirds of women over the age of 60 are affected by osteoporosis. It is more common in non-Latina White, thin, and small-framed women.

How Would You...?

As a health-care professional, how would you educate older adults on the range of chronic diseases that are common for this age group?

Osteoporosis is related to deficiencies in calcium, vitamin D, estrogen, and lack of exercise (Roghani & others, 2012). A program of regular exercise also has the potential to reduce osteoporosis (Iwamoto & others, 2009).

Accidents

Accidents are the sixth leading cause of death among older adults (U.S. Census Bureau, 2011). Falls are the leading cause of injury deaths among adults who are age 65 and older (National Center for Health Statistics, 2012). Each year, approximately 200,000 adults over the age of 65 (most of them women) fracture a hip in a fall. Half of these older adults die within 12 months, frequently from pneumonia. A recent study revealed that participation in an exercise class once a week for three years reduced the fall risk and the number of falling incidents in older adults who were at high risk for falling (Yokoya, Demura, & Sato, 2009).

Exercise, Nutrition, and Weight

Although we may be in the evening of our lives in late adulthood, we are not meant to live out our remaining years passively. Everything we know about older adults suggests they are healthier and happier the more active they are (Freund, Nikitin, & Riediger, 2013; Siegler & others, 2013a, b). Can regular exercise lead to a healthier late adulthood and increase longevity? How does eating a calorie-restricted diet and controlling weight also contribute to living longer?

Exercise

In one study, exercise literally meant a difference in life or death for middle-aged and older adults (Blair, 1990). More than 10,000 men and women were divided into categories of low fitness, medium fitness, and high fitness (Blair & others, 1989). Then they were studied over a period of eight years. As shown in Figure 15.4, sedentary participants (low fitness) were more than twice as likely to die during the eight-year time span of the study as those who were moderately fit and more than three

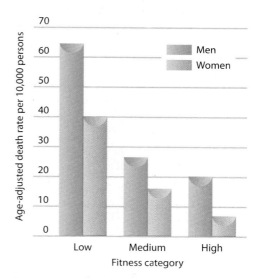

Figure 15.4 Physical Fitness and Mortality
In this study of middle-aged and older adults, being moderately fit or highly fit meant that individuals were less likely to die over a period of eight years than their less fit (sedentary) counterparts (Blair & others, 1989).

times as likely to die as those who were highly fit. The positive effects of being physically fit occurred for both men and women in this study. Also, a recent study of more than 11,000 women found that low cardiorespiratory fitness was a significant predictor of all-cause mortality (Farrell & others, 2010).

Gerontologists increasingly recommend strength training in addition to aerobic activity and stretching for older adults (Geirsdottir & others, 2012). Resistance exercise can preserve and possibly increase muscle mass in older adults (Semanik, Chang, & Dunlop, 2012).

Exercise helps people to live independent lives with dignity in late adulthood (Katzel & Steinbrenner, 2012). At age 80, 90, and even 100, exercise can help prevent older adults from falling down or even being institutionalized (Liao & others, 2011). Exercise increases the information processing skills of older adults (Mortimer & others, 2012). For example, a recent study of older adults revealed that exercise increased the size of the hippocampus and improved memory (Erickson & others, 2011). Exercise is linked to the prevention or delayed onset of chronic diseases, such as cardiovascular disease, type 2 diabetes, and obesity, as well as improvement in the treatment of these diseases (Chae & others, 2012; Ohta & others, 2012).

Exercise is linked to increased longevity. Energy expenditure during exercise of at least 1,000 kcal/week reduces mortality by about 30 percent, while 2,000 kcal/week reduces mortality by about 50 percent (Lee & Skerrett, 2001). A recent study of older adults found that total daily physical activity was linked to increased longevity across a four-year period (Buchman & others, 2012).

Nutrition and Weight

Scientists have accumulated considerable evidence that caloric restriction (CR) in laboratory animals (in most cases rats) can increase the animals' life span (Roth & Polotsky, 2012). Animals fed diets restricted in calories, although adequate in protein, vitamins, and minerals, live as much as 40 percent longer than animals given unlimited access to food (Jolly, 2005). And chronic problems such as cardiovascular, kidney, and liver disease appear at a later age (Han & others, 2012). CR also delays biochemical alterations such as the age-related rise in cholesterol and triglycerides observed in both humans and animals (Fontana, 2009). And recent research indicates that CR may provide neuroprotection for an aging central nervous system (Willette & others, 2012) (see Figure 15.5).

No one knows for certain how CR works to increase the life span of animals. Some scientists say that CR might lower the level of free radicals and reduce oxidative stress in cells (Bloomer & others, 2011). Others argue that CR might trigger a state of emergency called "survival mode" in which the body eliminates all unnecessary functions to focus only on staying alive.

Whether similar very low-calorie diets can stretch the human life span is not known (Stein & others, 2012).

Johnny Kelley, loosening up before one of the many Boston Marathons he ran as an older adult. In 1981, Kelley ran his fiftieth Boston Marathon. In 2000, he was named "Runner of the Century" by *Runner's World Magazine*. At 70 years of age, Kelley was still running approximately 50 miles a week. At that point in his life Kelly said, "I'm afraid to stop running. I feel so good. I want to stay alive." Kelley went on to live 27 more years and died at the age of 97 in 2004.

Figure 15.5 Calorie Restriction in Monkeys Shown here are two male monkeys at the Wisconsin Primate Research Center. Both are 24 years old. The monkey in the top photograph was raised on a calorie-restricted diet, while the monkey in the bottom photograph was raised on a normal diet. Notice that the monkey on the calorie-restricted diet looks younger; he also has lower glucose and insulin levels. The monkey raised on a normal diet has higher triglycerides and more oxidative damage to his cells.

In some instances the animals in these studies ate 40 percent less than normal. In humans, a typical level of calorie restriction involves a 30 percent decrease, which translates into about 1,120 calories a day for the average woman and 1,540 for the average man.

Health Treatment

About 3 percent of adults age 65 and older in the United States reside in a nursing home at some point in their lives. As older adults age, however, their probability of being in a nursing home or other extended-care facility increases. Twenty-three percent of adults aged 85 and older live in nursing homes or other extended-care facilities.

The quality of nursing homes and other extended-care facilities for older adults varies enormously and is a source of national concern (Shah & others, 2012). More than one-third are seriously deficient. They fail federally mandated inspections because they do not meet the minimum standards for physicians, pharmacists, and various rehabilitation specialists (occupational and physical therapists). Further concerns focus on the patient's right to privacy, access to medical information, safety, and lifestyle freedom within the individual's range of mental and physical capabilities.

How Would You...?

As a health-care professional, how would you use your understanding of development in late adulthood to advocate for improved access to quality medical care for older adults?

Because of the inadequate quality and the escalating costs of many nursing homes, many specialists in the health problems of the aged stress that home health care, elder-care centers, and preventive medicine clinics are good alternatives (Berenson & others, 2012). They are potentially less expensive than hospitals and nursing homes. They also are less likely to engender the feelings of depersonalization and dependency that occur so often in residents of institutions. Currently, there is an increased demand for, and a shortage of, home care workers because of the increasing number of older adults and their preference to stay out of nursing homes (Bardach & Rowles, 2012).

In a classic study, Judith Rodin and Ellen Langer (1977) found that an important factor related to health, and even survival, in a nursing home is the patient's feelings of control and self-determination. One group was encouraged to make more day-to-day choices and thus to feel they had more responsibility for control over their lives. They began to decide such matters as what they ate, when their visitors could come, what movies they saw, and who could come to their rooms. Another group in the same nursing home was told by the administrator how caring the nursing home was and how much the staff wanted to help, but these residents were given no added responsibility over their lives. Eighteen months later, the residents who had been given extra responsibility were healthier, happier, and more alert and active than the residents who had not received added responsibility. Even more important was the finding that after 18 months only half as many nursing home residents in the "responsibility" group had died as in the "dependent" group (see Figure 15.6). Perceived control over one's environment, then, can literally be a matter of life or death.

Geriatric nurses can be especially helpful in improving health treatment. To read about the work of one geriatric nurse, see *Careers in Life-Span Development.*

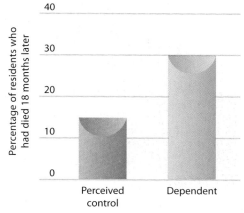

Figure 15.6 Perceived Control and Mortality

In the study by Rodin and Langer (1977), nursing home residents who were encouraged to feel more in control of their lives were more likely to be alive 18 months later than those who were treated to feel more dependent on the nursing home staff.

How Would You...?

As a psychologist, how would you structure the environment of a nursing home to produce maximum health and psychological benefits for the residents?

HEALTH

383

Sarah Kagan, Geriatric Nurse

Sarah Kagan is a professor of nursing at the University of Pennsylvania School of Nursing. She provides nursing consultation to patients, their families, nurses, and physicians regarding the complex needs of older adults related to their hospitalization. She also consults on research and the management of patients who have head and neck cancers. Sarah teaches in the undergraduate nursing program, where she directs a course on "Nursing Care in the Older Adult." In 2003, she was awarded a MacArthur Fellowship for her work in the field of nursing.

In Sarah's own words:

I'm lucky to be doing what I love—caring for older adults and families—and learning from them so that I can share this knowledge and develop or investigate better ways of caring. My special interests in the care of older adults who have cancer allow me the intimate privilege of being with patients at the best and worst times of their lives. That intimacy acts as a beacon—it reminds me of the value I and nursing as a profession contribute to society and the rewards offered in return (Kagan, 2008, p. 1).

Geriatric nurses like Sarah Kagan seek to prevent or intervene in the chronic or acute health problems of older adults. They

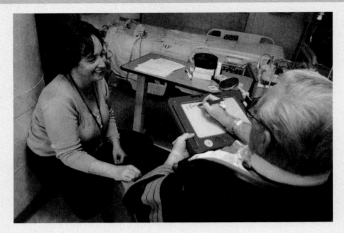

Sarah Kagan with a patient.

may work in hospitals, nursing homes, schools of nursing, or with geriatric medical specialists or psychiatrists in a medical clinic or in private practice. Like pediatric nurses, geriatric nurses take courses in a school of nursing and obtain a degree in nursing, which takes from two to five years. They complete courses in biological sciences, nursing care, and mental health as well as supervised clinical training in geriatric settings. They also may obtain a master's or doctoral degree in their specialty.

Cognitive Functioning

At age 89, the great pianist Arthur Rubinstein gave one of his best performances at New York's Carnegie Hall. When Pablo Casals was 95, a reporter asked him, "Mr. Casals, you are the greatest cellist who ever lived. Why do you still practice six hours a day?" Mr. Casals replied, "Because I feel like I am making progress" (Canfield & Hansen, 1995).

Multidimensionality and Multidirectionality

In thinking about the nature of cognitive change in adulthood, it is important to consider that cognition is a multidimensional concept (Dixon & others, 2013). It is also important to consider that, although some dimensions of cognition might decline as we age, others might remain stable or even improve.

Attention

In Chapter 5, we discussed different types of attention, including selective, divided, and sustained. How do these three types of attention change in older adults?

Selective attention, which consists of focusing on a specific aspect of experience that is relevant while ignoring others that are irrelevant, generally decreases in older adults (Bucur & Madden, 2007; Caban-Holt & others, 2012). *Divided attention* involves concentrating on more than one activity at the same time. When the two competing tasks are reasonably easy, age differences among adults are minimal or nonexistent. However, the more difficult the competing tasks are, the less effectively older adults divide attention than younger adults (Bucur & Madden, 2007). *Sustained attention* is the ability to focus attention on a selected stimulus for a prolong period of time. Researchers have found that older adults often perform as well as middle-aged and younger adults on measures of sustained attention (Berardi, Parasuraman, & Haxby, 2001). However, a recent study of older adults found that the greater the variability in their sustained attention (vigilance), the more likely they were to experience falls (O'Halloran & others, 2012).

Memory

Memory does change during aging, but not all types of memory change with age in the same way (Dixon & others, 2012; Small & others, 2012b). We will begin by exploring possible changes in episodic and semantic memory.

Episodic and Semantic Memory **Episodic memory** is the retention of information about the where and when of life's happenings. For example, what was the color of the walls in your bedroom when you were a child? What did you eat for breakfast this morning?

Younger adults have better episodic memory than older adults have (Talamini & Gorree, 2012). Also, older adults think that they can remember long-ago events better than more recent events. However, researchers consistently have found that the older the memory, the less accurate it is in older adults (Smith, 1996).

Semantic memory is a person's knowledge about the world. It includes a person's fields of expertise, general academic knowledge of the sort learned in school, and "everyday knowledge" about the meanings of words, important places, and common things. Older adults often take longer to retrieve semantic information, but usually they can ultimately retrieve it. However, the ability to retrieve very specific information (such as names) usually declines in older adults (Luo & Craik, 2008). For the most part, episodic memory declines more than semantic memory in older adults (Small & others, 2012b).

Although many aspects of semantic memory are reasonably well preserved in late adulthood, a common memory problem for older adults is the *tip-of-the-tongue (TOT) phenomenon*, in which individuals can't quite retrieve familiar information but have the feeling that they should be able to retrieve it (Bucur & Madden, 2007). Researchers have found that older adults are more likely to experience TOT states than younger adults (Bucur & Madden, 2007). A recent study of older adults found that the errors in memory they reported having in the last 24 hours usually were those involving tip-of-the-tongue (Ossher, Flegal, & Lustig, 2012).

Cognitive Resources: Working Memory and Perceptual Speed Two important cognitive resource mechanisms are working memory and perceptual speed (Salthouse, 2012). Recall from Chapter 13 that *working memory* is closely linked to short-term memory but places more emphasis on memory as a place for mental work (Baddeley, 2007, 2012). Researchers have found declines in working memory during the late adulthood years (Nyberg & others, 2012). A recent study revealed that working memory continued to decline from 65 to 89 years of age (Elliott & others, 2011). Explanation of the decline in working memory in older adults focuses on their less efficient inhibition in preventing irrelevant information from entering working memory and their increased distractibility (Lustig & Hasher, 2009).

Perceptual speed is another cognitive resource that has been studied by researchers on aging. Perceptual speed is the amount of time it takes to perform simple perceptual-motor tasks such as deciding whether pairs of two-digit or two-letter strings are the same, or how long it takes someone to step on the brakes when the car directly ahead stops. Perceptual speed shows considerable decline in late adulthood, and it is strongly linked with decline in working memory (Dirk, 2012; Salthouse, 2012).

episodic memory The retention of information about the where and when of life's happenings.

semantic memory A person's knowledge about the world—including a person's fields of expertise, general academic knowledge of the sort learned in school, and "everyday knowledge."

Explicit and Implicit Memory Researchers also have found that aging is linked with changes in explicit memory (Kim & Giovanello, 2011). **Explicit memory** is memory of facts and experiences that individuals consciously know and can state. Explicit memory also is sometimes called *declarative memory*. Examples of explicit memory include recounting the plot of a movie you have seen or being at a grocery store and remembering what you wanted to buy. **Implicit memory** is memory without conscious recollection; it involves skills and routine procedures that are automatically performed, such as driving a car or typing on a computer keyboard, without having to consciously think about what you are doing. Implicit memory is less likely to be adversely affected by aging than explicit memory (Norman, Holmin, & Bartholomew, 2012).

Noncognitive Factors Health, education, and socioeconomic status (SES) can influence an older adult's performance on memory tasks (Bennett & others, 2012; Freiheit & others, 2012). Although such noncognitive factors as good health are associated with less memory decline in older adults, they do not eliminate memory decline. A recent study revealed that older adults with less education had lower cognitive abilities than those with more education (Lachman & others, 2010). However, for older adults with less education, frequently engaging in cognitive activities improved their episodic memory.

Executive Functioning

We discussed executive functioning in a number of chapters earlier in the text. Recall that *executive functioning* is an umbrella-like concept that consists of a number of higher level cognitive processes linked to the development of the brain's prefrontal cortex. Executive functioning involves managing one's thoughts to engage in goal-directed behavior and to exercise self-control (Diamond, 2013).

How does executive functioning change in late adulthood? Earlier in this chapter, you read that the prefrontal cortex is one area of the brain that shrinks with aging, and recent research has linked this shrinkage with a decrease in working memory and other cognitive activities in older adults (Turner & Spreng, 2012). Older adults also are less effective at engaging in cognitive control than when they were younger (Campbell & others, 2012). For example, in terms of cognitive flexibility, older adults don't perform as well as younger adults at switching back and forth between tasks or mental sets (Luszcz, 2011). And in terms of cognitive inhibition, older adults are less effective than younger adults at inhibiting dominant or automatic responses (Coxon & others, 2012).

Although in general aspects of executive functioning decline in late adulthood, there is considerable variability in executive functioning among older adults. For example, some older adults have a better working memory and are more cognitively flexible than other older adults (Peltz, Gratton, & Fabiani, 2011).

Executive functioning increasingly is thought to not only be involved in cognitive performance but also in regulating emotions,

explicit memory Memory of facts and experiences that individuals consciously know and can state.

implicit memory Memory without conscious recollection; involves skills and routine procedures that are automatically performed.

adapting to life's challenges, responding to motivation, and functioning in society (Luszcz, 2011). Research on these aspects of executive functioning has only recently begun.

Wisdom

Does wisdom, like good wine, improve with age? What is this thing we call "wisdom"? **Wisdom** is expert knowledge about the practical aspects of life that permits excellent judgment about important matters. This practical knowledge involves exceptional insight into human development and interactions, good judgment, and an understanding of how to cope with difficult life problems. Thus, wisdom, more than standard conceptions of intelligence, focuses on life's pragmatic concerns and human conditions (Ferrari & Westsrtate, 2013; Staudinger & Gluck, 2011).

In regard to wisdom, Paul Baltes and his colleagues (2006) have reached the following conclusions: (1) High levels of wisdom are rare. Few people, including older adults, attain a high level of wisdom. That only a small percentage of adults show wisdom supports the contention that it requires experience, practice, or complex skills. (2) Factors other than age are critical for wisdom to develop to a high level. For example, certain life experiences, such as being trained and working in a field involving difficult life problems and having wisdom-enhancing mentors, contribute to higher levels of wisdom. Also, people higher in wisdom have values that are more likely to consider the welfare of others than their own happiness. (3) Personality-related factors, such as openness to experience, generativity, and creativity, are better predictors of wisdom than cognitive factors such as intelligence.

Older adults might not be as quick with their thoughts or behavior as younger people, but wisdom may be an entirely different matter. This older woman shares the wisdom of her experience with a classroom of children. *How is wisdom described by life-span developmentalists?*

Use It or Lose It

Changes in cognitive activity patterns might result in disuse and consequent atrophy of cognitive skills (Hindin & Zelinski, 2012; Marioni & others, 2012). This concept is captured in the concept of "Use it or lose it." The mental activities that likely benefit the maintenance of cognitive skills in older adults are activities such as reading books, doing crossword puzzles, and going to lectures and concerts (Park & Bischof, 2011). In one study, reading daily was linked to reduced mortality in men in their seventies (Jacobs & others, 2008). In another study, 75- to 85-year-olds were assessed for an average of five years (Hall & others, 2009). At the beginning of the research, the older adults indicated how often they participated in six activities on a daily basis: reading, writing, doing crossword puzzles, playing card or board games, having group discussions, and playing music. For each additional activity the older adult engaged in, the onset of rapid memory loss was delayed by 0.18 year. For older adults who participated in 11 activities per week compared with their counterparts who engaged in only 4 activities per week, the point at which accelerated memory decline occurred was delayed by 1.29 years. And in a recent analysis of older adults over a 12-year

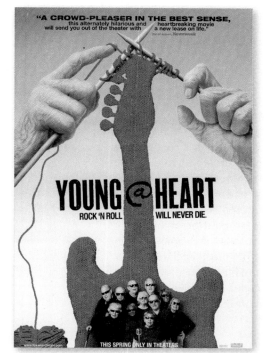

Members of the Young@Heart chorus have an average age of 80. Young@Heart became a hit documentary in 2008. The documentary displays the singing talents, energy, and optimism of a remarkable group of older adults, who clearly are on the "use it" side of "use it or lose it."

period, those who reduced their cognitive lifestyle activities (such as using a computer, playing bridge) subsequently showed declining cognitive functioning in verbal speed, episodic memory, and semantic memory (Small & others, 2012a). The decline in cognitive functioning was linked to subsequent lower engagement in social activities.

Training Cognitive Skills

If older adults are losing cognitive skills, can these skills be regained through training? An increasing number of research studies indicate that they can to a degree (Kramer & Morrow, 2012; Lovden & others, 2012). Two key conclusions can be derived from research in this area: (1) Training can improve the cognitive skills of many older adults, but (2) there is some loss in plasticity in late adulthood, especially in those who are 85 and older (Baltes, Lindenberger, & Staudinger, 2006).

How Would You...?
As a psychologist, how would you design activities and interventions to elicit and maintain cognitive vitality in older adults?

The Stanford Center for Longevity (2011) recently reported on the consensus of a number of leading scientists in the field of aging regarding their views on how successfully the cognitive skills of older adults can be improved. One of their concerns is the misinformation given to the public touting products to improve the functioning of the mind for which there is no scientific support. Nutritional supplements, games, and software products have all been advertised as "magic bullets" to slow the decline of mental functioning and improve the mental ability of older adults. Some of the claims are reasonable but not scientifically tested, while others are unrealistic and implausible. A recent research review of dietary supplements and cognitive aging did indicate that ginkgo biloba was linked with improvements in some aspects of attention in older adults and that omega-3 polyunsaturated fatty acids reduced the risk of age-related cognitive decline (Gorby, Brownawell, & Falk, 2010). In this research review, there was no evidence of cognitive improvements in aging adults who took supplements containing ginseng and glucose. Overall, research has not provided consistent plausible evidence that such dietary supplements can accomplish major cognitive goals in aging adults over the long term. However, some software-based cognitive training games have been found to improve older adults' cognitive functioning (Hertzog & others, 2009). Nonetheless, the training games may improve cognitive skills in a laboratory setting but not generalize to gains in the real world.

Some improvements in the cognitive vitality of older adults can be accomplished through cognitive and physical fitness training (Jak, 2011; Kramer & Morrow, 2012). However, benefits have not been observed in all studies (Salthouse, 2012). Also, it is important to distinguish between short-term improvement and long-term changes when evaluating the benefits of cognitive training in older adults. If older adults' goal is to improve their ability to remember peoples' names at a forthcoming community meeting, research indicates there are good chances that this goal can be accomplished. However, if the goal is to reduce the rate of memory decline over a decade or two in older adults, no intervention has yet been able to document such a result (Stanford Center for Longevity, 2011). Further research is needed to determine more precisely which cognitive improvements occur in older adults (Luszcz, 2011; Salthouse, 2012).

Cognitive Neuroscience and Aging

On several occasions in this chapter, we have noted that certain regions of the brain are involved in links between aging and cognitive functioning. In this section, we further explore the substantial increase in interest in the brain's role in aging and cognitive functioning. The field of *cognitive neuroscience* has emerged as the major discipline that studies links between brain activity and cognitive functioning (Fletcher & Rapp, 2013; Nyberg & others, 2012). This field especially relies on brain imaging techniques, such as fMRI, PET, and DTI (diffusion tensor imaging) to reveal the areas of the brain that are activated when individuals are engaging in certain cognitive activities (Carmichael & Lockhart, 2012; DeCarli & others, 2012). For example, as an older adult is asked to encode and then retrieve verbal materials or images of scenes, the older adult's brain activity will be monitored by an fMRI brain scan.

Changes in the brain can influence cognitive functioning, and changes in cognitive functioning can influence the brain. For example, aging of the brain's prefrontal cortex may produce a decline in working memory (Takeuchi & others, 2012). And, when older adults do not regularly use their working memory (recall the section "Use It or Lose It"), neural connections in the prefrontal lobe may atrophy. Further, cognitive interventions that activate older adults' working memory may increase these neural connections.

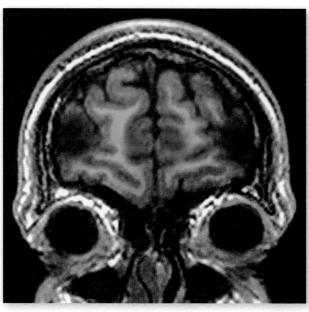

Figure 15.7 The Prefrontal Cortex
Advances in neuroimaging are allowing researchers to make significant progress in connecting changes in the brain with cognitive development. Shown here is an fMRI of the brain's prefrontal cortex. *What links have been found between the prefrontal cortex, aging, and cognitive development?*

Following are some of the results that have been found in cognitive neuroscience studies of aging:

- Neural circuits in specific regions of the brain's prefrontal cortex decline, and this decline is linked to poorer performance by older adults on complex reasoning tasks, working memory, and episodic memory tasks (Grady & others, 2006). (See Figure 15.7.)

- Recall from earlier in the chapter that older adults are more likely than younger adults to use both hemispheres of the brain to compensate for age-related declines in attention, memory, and language (Davis & others, 2012; Dennis & Cabeza, 2008). Two recent neuroimaging studies revealed that better memory performance in older adults was linked to higher levels of activity in both hemispheres of the brain during information processing (Angel & others, 2011; Manenti, Cotelli, & Miniussi, 2011).

- Functioning of the hippocampus declines but to a lesser degree than the functioning of the frontal lobes in older adults. In K. Warner Schaie's (2012) recent research, individuals whose memory and executive functioning declined in middle age had more hippocampal atrophy in late adulthood, but those whose memory and executive functioning improved in middle age did not show a decline in hippocampal functioning in late adulthood.

- Patterns of neural decline with aging are larger for retrieval than encoding (Gutchess & others, 2005).

- Compared with younger adults, older adults often show greater activity in the frontal and parietal lobes of the brain on simple tasks, but as attentional demands increase, older adults display less effective functioning in the frontal and parietal lobes of the brain that involve cognitive control (Campbell & others, 2012).

- Younger adults have better connectivity between brain regions than older adults (Goh, 2011; Waring, Addis, & Kensinger, 2012).

- An increasing number of cognitive and fitness training studies include brain imaging techniques such as fMRI to assess the results of such training on brain functioning (Erickson & others, 2011; Head, Singh, & Bugg, 2012). In one study, older adults who walked one hour a day three days a week for six months showed increased volume in the frontal and temporal lobes of the brain (Colcombe & others, 2006).

Work and Retirement

What percentage of older adults continue to work? How productive are they? Who adjusts best to retirement? These are some of the questions we will examine in this section.

Work

So far in the twenty-first century, the percentage of men over age 65 who are continuing to work full-time is less than it was at the beginning of the twentieth century. The decline from 1900 to the twenty-first century has been as much as 70 percent. An important change in older adults' work patterns is the increase in part-time work after retirement (Hardy, 2006). The percentage of older adults who work part-time post-retirement has steadily increased since the 1960s. Some individuals maintain their productivity throughout their lives, working at least as many hours as younger workers. Older adults are increasingly seeking some type of bridge employment that permits a gradual rather than a sudden movement out of the workforce (Bowen, Noack, & Staudinger, 2011).

Especially important to think about is the large cohort of baby boomers—78 million people—who began to reach traditional retirement age in 2010. Because this cohort is so large, and these are difficult economic times, we are likely to see increasing numbers of older adults who continue to work (Hart, 2007). The aging of the U.S. workforce will continue at least until 2034 when the largest number of the baby boom cohorts has reached 70 (Manton & others, 2007). In 2011 in the United States, the average age of retirement was 64 for men and 62 for women (Munnell, 2011). Older workers have lower rates of absenteeism, fewer accidents, and increased job satisfaction in comparison with their younger counterparts (Warr, 2004). This means that older workers can be of considerable value to a company, above and beyond their cognitive competence. Changes in federal law now allow individuals over the age of 65 to continue working in most jobs.

An increasing number of middle-aged and older adults are embarking on a second or a third career (Feldman, 2007). In some cases, this is an entirely different type of work or a continuation of previous work but at a reduced level. Many older adults also participate in unpaid work as volunteers or as active participants in a voluntary association. These options afford older adults opportunities for productive activity, social interaction, and a positive identity.

Ninety-two-year-old Russell "Bob" Harrell (right) puts in 12-hour days at Sieco Consulting Engineers in Columbus, Indiana. A highway and bridge engineer, he designs and plans roads. James Rice (age 48), a vice president of client services at Sieco, says that Bob wants to learn something new every day and that he has learned many life lessons from being around him. Harrell says he is not planning to retire. *What are some variations in work and retirement in older adults?*

Adjustment to Retirement

In the past, when most people reached an accepted retirement age, such as some point in their sixties, retirement meant a one-way exit from full-time work to full-time leisure (Higo & Williamson, 2009). Leading expert Phyllis Moen (2007) described how today, when people reach their sixties, the life path they follow is less clear: (1) some individuals don't retire, continuing in their career jobs, (2) some retire from their career work and then take up a new and different job, (3) some retire from career jobs but do volunteer work, (4) some retire from a post-retirement job and go on to yet another job, (5) some move in and out of the workforce, so they never really have a "career" job from which they retire, (6) some individuals who are in poor health move to a disability status and eventually into retirement, and (7) some who are laid off define it as "retirement."

Older adults who adjust best to retirement are healthy, have adequate income, are active, are educated, have an extended social network including both friends and family, and usually were satisfied with their lives before they retired (Jokela & others, 2010; Wang, 2012). Older adults who have inadequate income and are in poor health, and who must adjust to other stress that occurs at the same time as retirement, such as the death of a spouse, have the most difficult time adjusting to retirement (Reichstadt & others, 2007). A recent study revealed that a higher level of financial assets and job satisfaction were more strongly linked to men's higher psychological well-being in retirement, while preretirement social contacts were more strongly related to women's psychological well-being in retirement (Kubicek & others, 2010).

The recent economic downturn, high unemployment rate, and potential changes in Social Security and health insurance coverage for retired individuals in the United States have increased the difficulty of saving enough money for retirement (Bosworth, 2012; Kramer, 2012). A 2012 survey indicated that confidence in having enough money to live comfortably in retirement had dropped to 14 percent (Helman, Copeland, & VanDerhei, 2012). In this survey, the percent of workers who reported that they expect to retire after the age of 65 had grown to 37 percent (compared with 11 percent in 1991). With regard to retirement income, the two main worries of individuals as they approach retirement are: (1) drawing retirement income from savings, and (2) paying for health care expenses (Yakoboski, 2011).

What are some keys to adjusting effectively in retirement?

How Would You...?

As a psychologist, how would you assist older adults in making appropriate adjustments and preparations for a psychologically satisfying retirement?

Mental Health

Although a substantial portion of the population can now look forward to a longer life, that life may unfortunately be hampered by a psychological disorder in old age (Knight & Kellough, 2013). This prospect is troubling to individuals and their families, and it is also costly to society. Psychological disorders make individuals increasingly dependent on the help and care of others. The cost of psychological disorders in older adults is estimated at more than $40 billion per year in the United States. More important than the loss in dollars, though, is the loss of human potential and the suffering involved. Although psychological disorders in older adults are a major concern, however, older adults do not have a higher incidence of psychological disorders than younger adults do (Busse & Blazer, 1996).

Depression

Major depression is a mood disorder in which the individual is deeply unhappy, demoralized, self-derogatory, and bored. The person

major depression A mood disorder in which the individual is deeply unhappy, demoralized, self-derogatory, and bored. The person does not feel well, loses stamina easily, has poor appetite, and is listless and unmotivated. Major depression is so widespread that it has been called the "common cold" of psychological disorders.

does not feel well, loses stamina easily, has a poor appetite, and is listless and unmotivated. Major depression has been called the "common cold" of mental disorders. However, a recent review concluded that depression is less common among older adults than younger adults (Fiske, Wetherell, & Gatz, 2009). More than half of the cases of depression in older adults represent the first time in their lives that these individuals have developed depression (Fiske, Wetherell, & Gatz, 2009).

Among the most common predictors of depression in older adults are earlier depressive symptoms, poor health, disability, loss events such as the death of a spouse, and low social support (Ng & others, 2010). Insomnia is often overlooked as a risk factor for depression in older adults (Fiske, Wetherell, & Gatz, 2009). Curtailment of daily activities is a common pathway to late-life depression (Fiske, Wetherell, & Gatz, 2009). Often accompanying this curtailment of activity is an increase in self-critical thinking that exacerbates depression. A recent meta-analysis found that the following living arrangements were linked to risk for depression in older adults: living alone, in a nursing home, or in an institutionalized setting (Xiu-Ying & others, 2012). Depression is a treatable condition, not only in young adults but in older adults as well (Nolen-Hoeksema, 2011; Piazza & Charles, 2012). Combinations of medications and psychotherapy produce significant improvement in almost four out of five older adults with depression (Koenig & Blazer, 1996). Unfortunately, as many as 80 percent of older adults with depressive symptoms receive no treatment at all.

How Would You...?

As a psychologist, how would you advise families who are dealing with an aging parent suffering from depression?

Dementia, Alzheimer Disease, and Parkinson Disease

Among the most debilitating of mental disorders in older adults are the dementias. In recent years, extensive attention has been focused on the most common dementia, Alzheimer disease. Other afflictions common in older adults are multi-infarct dementia and Parkinson disease.

Dementia

Dementia is a global term for any neurological disorder in which the primary symptoms involve a deterioration of mental functioning. Individuals with dementia often lose the ability to care for themselves and may become unable to recognize familiar surroundings and people—including family members (Clare & others, 2012). It is estimated that 23 percent of women and 17 percent of men 85 years and older are at risk for developing dementia (Alzheimer's Association, 2012). However, these estimates may be high because of the Alzheimer's Association's lobbying efforts to increase funding for research and treatment facilities. Dementia is a broad category, and it is important that every effort is made to narrow the older adult's disorder and determine a specific cause of the deteriorating mental functioning.

Alzheimer Disease

One form of dementia is **Alzheimer disease**—a progressive, irreversible brain disorder that is characterized by a gradual deterioration of memory, reasoning, language, and eventually, physical function. In 2012, an estimated 5.4 million adults in the United States had Alzheimer disease, and it is projected that 10 million baby boomers will develop Alzheimer disease in their lifetime (Alzheimer's Association, 2012). Figure 15.8 shows the estimated risks for developing Alzheimer disease at different ages for women and men (Alzheimer's Association, 2010). Women are more likely to develop Alzheimer disease because they live longer than men and their longer life expectancy increases the number of years during which they can develop it. It is estimated that Alzheimer disease triples the

dementia A global term for any neurological disorder in which the primary symptoms involve a deterioration of mental functioning.

Alzheimer disease A progressive, irreversible brain disorder characterized by a gradual deterioration of memory, reasoning, language, and eventually physical function.

health-care costs of Americans 65 years of age and older (Alzheimer's Association, 2010).

Causes and Risk Factors Once destruction of brain tissue occurs from Alzheimer disease, it is unlikely that treatment of the disease will reverse the damage, at least based on the current state of research and the foreseeable future. Alzheimer disease involves a deficiency in the brain messenger chemical *acetylcholine*, which plays an important role in memory (Hunter & others, 2012). Also, as Alzheimer disease progresses, the brain shrinks and deteriorates (see Figure 15.9). This deterioration is characterized by the formation of *amyloid plaques* (dense deposits of protein that accumulate in the blood vessels) and *neurofibrillary tangles* (twisted fibers that build up in neurons) (Luan, Rosales, & Lee, 2012; Hickman & el Khoury, 2012).

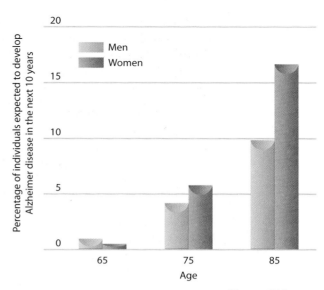

Figure 15.8
Estimated Risks for Developing Alzheimer Disease at Different Ages for Women and Men

There is increasing interest in the role that oxidative stress might play in Alzheimer disease (Gonfloni & others, 2012). Oxidative stress occurs when the body fails to defend itself against free-radical attacks and oxidation. Recall from earlier in the chapter that free-radical theory is a major theory of aging.

Although scientists are not certain what causes Alzheimer disease, age is an important risk factor and genes also are likely to play an important role (Park, Lee, & Han, 2012). The number of individuals with Alzheimer disease doubles for every five years after the age of 65. A gene called *apolipoprotein E* (*ApoE*) is linked to increasing presence of plaques and tangles in the brain (Schellenberg & Montine, 2012). Special attention has focused on an allele (an alternative form of a gene) labeled ApoE4, an allele that is a strong risk factor for Alzheimer disease (Caselli, 2012; Ward & others, 2012). In K. Warner Schaie's (2012) recent research, individuals who had the ApoE4 allele showed more cognitive decline beginning in middle age. A recent study found that the ApoE4 gene creates a cascade of molecular signaling that causes blood vessels to become more porous, allowing toxic substances to leak into the brain and damage neurons (Bell & others, 2012).

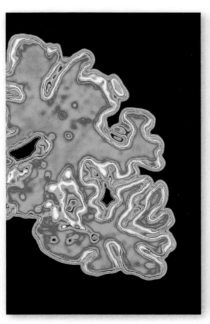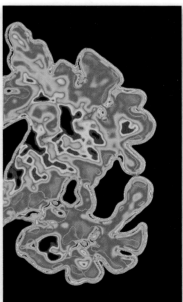

Figure 15.9 **Two Brains: Normal Aging and Alzheimer Disease**
The left photograph shows a slice of a normal aging brain, the right photograph a slice of a brain ravaged by Alzheimer disease. Notice the deterioration and shrinking in the Alzheimer disease brain.

Despite links between the presence of the ApoE4 gene and Alzheimer disease, less than 50 percent of individuals who carry the ApoE4 gene develop dementia in old age. Advances as a result of the Human Genome Project have recently resulted in identification of other genes that are risk factors for Alzheimer disease, although they are not as strongly linked to the disease as the ApoE4 gene (Schellenberg & Montine, 2012).

Although individuals with a family history of Alzheimer disease are at greater risk, the disease is complex and likely to be caused by a number of factors, including lifestyles (Lopez, Becker, & Kuller, 2012). For many years, scientists have known that a healthy diet, exercise, and weight control can lower the risk of cardiovascular disease. Now, they are finding that these healthy lifestyle factors may lower the risk of Alzheimer disease as well (James & Bennett, 2011). One of the best strategies for prevention/intervention in the lives of people who are at risk for Alzheimer's disease is to improve their cardiac functioning through diet, drugs, and exercise (Gelber, Launer, & White, 2012; Wagner & others, 2012).

Mild Cognitive Impairment *Mild cognitive impairment* (*MCI*) represents a transitional state between the cognitive changes of normal aging and very early Alzheimer disease and other dementias. MCI is increasingly recognized as a risk factor for Alzheimer disease. Estimates indicate that as many as 10 to 20 percent of individuals age 65 and older have MCI (Alzheimer's Association, 2012). Some individuals with MCI do not go on to develop Alzheimer disease, but MCI is a risk factor for Alzheimer disease.

How Would You...?

As a health-care professional, how would you respond to an older adult who is concerned that their declining short-term memory is an early symptom of dementia?

Distinguishing between individuals who merely have age-associated declines in memory and those with MCI is difficult, as is predicting which individuals with MCI will subsequently develop Alzheimer disease (Macdonald & others, 2012). One effort in this regard is to have individuals with MCI undergo an fMRI brain scan (Pihlajamaki, Jauhialinen, & Soininen, 2009). If the scan shows that certain brain regions involved in memory are smaller than those of individuals without memory impairments, the individual is more likely to progress to Alzheimer disease (Alzheimer's Association, 2010).

Drug Treatment of Alzheimer Disease Several drugs called cholinerase inhibitors have been approved by the U.S. Food and Drug Administration to treat Alzheimer disease. They are designed to improve memory and other cognitive functions by increasing the level of acetylcholine in the brain (Gil-Bea & others, 2012). Keep in mind, though, that the drugs used to treat Alzheimer disease only slow the downward progression of the disease; they do not treat its cause (Alves & others, 2012). These drugs slow the worsening of Alzheimer symptoms for approximately 6 to 12 months for about 50 percent of the individuals who take them (Alzheimer's Association, 2012). Also, no drugs have yet been approved by the Federal Drug Administration for the treatment of MCI (Alzheimer's Association, 2010).

Caring for Individuals with Alzheimer Disease A special concern is caring for Alzheimer patients (Bursch & Butcher, 2012). Health-care professionals believe that the family can be an important support system for the Alzheimer patient, but this support can have costs for family members, who can become emotionally and physically drained by the extensive care required for a person with Alzheimer disease (Carling-Jenkins & others, 2012). A recent study compared family members' perceptions of caring for someone with Alzheimer disease, cancer, or schizophrenia (Papastavrou & others, 2012). In this study, the highest perceived burden was reported for Alzheimer disease.

Respite care (services that provide temporary relief to those who are caring for individuals with disabilities, illnesses, or the elderly) has been developed to help people who have to meet the day-to-day needs of Alzheimer patients. This type of care provides an important break away from the burden of providing chronic care (de la Cuesta-Benjumea, 2011).

Parkinson Disease Another type of dementia is **Parkinson disease,** a chronic, progressive disease characterized by muscle tremors, slowing of movement, and partial facial paralysis. Parkinson disease is triggered by degeneration of dopamine-producing neurons in the brain (Nishikawa

Parkinson disease A chronic, progressive disease characterized by muscle tremors, slowing of movement, and partial facial paralysis.

& others, 2012). Dopamine is a neurotransmitter that is necessary for normal brain functioning. Why these neurons degenerate is not known.

The main treatment for Parkinson disease involves administering drugs that enhance the effect of dopamine (dopamine agonists) in the disease's earlier stages and later administering the drug L-dopa, which is converted by the brain into dopamine (Reese & others, 2012). However, it is difficult to determine the correct level of dosage of L-dopa and it loses its efficacy over time (Nomoto & others, 2009). Another treatment for advanced Parkinson disease is deep brain stimulation (DBS), which involves implantation of electrodes within the brain (Weaver & others, 2012). The electrodes are then stimulated by a pacemaker-like device. Stem cell transplantation and gene therapy offer hope for treating Parkinson disease (Pardal & Lopez-Barneo, 2012).

Summary

Longevity, Biological Aging, and Physical Development

- Life expectancy has increased dramatically, but life span has not. In the United States, the number of people living to age 100 or older is increasing.

- Four biological theories of aging are evolutionary theory, cellular clock theory, free-radical theory, and hormonal stress theory.

- The aging brain retains considerable plasticity and adaptability.

- Among physical changes that accompany aging are slower movement and the appearance of wrinkled skin and age spots on the skin. There are also declines in perceptual abilities, cardiovascular functioning, and lung capacity. Many older adults' sleep difficulties are linked to health problems.

- Although sexual activity declines in late adulthood, many individuals continue to be sexually active as long as they are healthy.

Health

- The probability of disease or illness increases with age. Chronic disorders, such as arthritis and osteoporosis, become more common in late adulthood. Cancer and cardiovascular disease are the leading causes of death in late adulthood.

- The physical benefits of exercise have been clearly demonstrated in older adults. Leaner adults, especially women, live longer, healthier lives.

- The quality of nursing homes varies enormously. Alternatives include home health care, elder-care centers, and preventive medicine clinics.

Cognitive Functioning

- While older adults are not as adept as middle-aged and younger adults at complicated tasks that involve selective and divided attention, they perform just as well on measures of sustained attention. Some aspects of memory, such as episodic memory, decline in older adults. Components of executive functioning—such as cognitive control and working memory—decline in late adulthood. Wisdom has been proposed to increase in older adults, but researchers have not consistently documented this increase.

- Older adults who engage in cognitive activities, especially challenging ones, have higher cognitive functioning than those who don't use their cognitive skills.

- Cognitive and fitness training can improve some cognitive skills of older adults, but there is some loss of plasticity in late adulthood.

- There has been considerable increased interest in the cognitive neuroscience of aging. A consistent finding is a decline in the functioning of the prefrontal cortex in late adulthood, which is linked to poorer performance in complex reasoning and aspects of memory.

Work and Retirement

- Increasing numbers of older adults engage in part-time work or volunteer work and continue being productive throughout late adulthood.

- Healthy, economically stable, educated, satisfied individuals with an extended social network adjust best to retirement.

Mental Health

- A majority of older adults with depressive symptoms never receive mental health treatment.

- Individuals with dementias, such as Parkinson disease or Alzheimer disease, often lose the ability to care for themselves. Alzheimer disease is by far the most common dementia.

Key Terms

Socioemotional Development in Late Adulthood

16

Stories of Life-Span Development: Bob Cousy, Adapting to Life as an Older Adult

Bob Cousy was a star player on Boston Celtics teams that won numerous National Basketball Association championships. In recognition of his athletic accomplishments, Cousy was honored by ESPN as one of the top 100 athletes of the twentieth century. After he retired from basketball, he became a college basketball coach and then into his seventies was a broadcaster of Boston Celtics basketball games. Now in his eighties, Cousy has retired from broadcasting but continues to play golf and tennis on a regular basis. He has a number of posi-

tive social relationships, including a marriage of more than 50 years, children and grandchildren, and many friends.

For Cousy as for many other famous people, his awards reveal little about his personal life and contributions. Two situations exemplify Cousy's humanitarian efforts to help others (McClellan, 2004). When he played for the Boston Celtics, his African American teammate, Chuck Cooper, was refused a hotel room on a road trip because of his race. Cousy expressed anger to his coach about the situation and then accompanied an

appreciative Cooper on a train back to Boston. In a second example, "Today the Bob Cousy Humanitarian Fund honors individuals who have given their lives to using the game of basketball as a medium to help others" (p. 4). The Humanitarian Fund reflects Cousy's motivation to care for others, be appreciative and give something back, and make the world less self-centered.

Bob Cousy's active, involved life as an older adult reflects some of the themes of socioemotional development in older adults that we discuss in this chapter.

Bob Cousy, as a Boston Celtics star when he was a young adult (*left*) and as an older adult (*right*). *What are some changes he has made in his life as an older adult?*

These themes include the important role that being active plays in life satisfaction, how people adapt to changing skills, and the positive role of close relationships with friends and family in an emotionally fulfilling life.

Our coverage of socioemotional development in late adulthood describes a number of theories about the socioemotional lives of older adults; the older adult's personality and roles in society; the importance of family ties and social relationships; the social contexts of ethnicity, gender, and culture; and the increasing attention focused on elements of successful aging. ■

Theories of Socioemotional Development

In this section, we explore four main theories of socioemotional development that focus on late adulthood: Erikson's theory, activity theory, socioemotional selectivity theory, and selective optimization with compensation theory.

Erikson's Theory

We initially described Erik Erikson's (1968) eight stages of the human life span in Chapter 1, and as we explored different periods of development in this book we examined the stages in more detail. Here we discuss his final stage.

Integrity versus despair is Erikson's eighth and final stage of development, which individuals experience during late adulthood. This stage involves reflecting on the past and either piecing together a positive review or concluding that one's life has not been well spent. Through many different routes, the older adult may have developed a positive outlook in each of the preceding periods. If so, retrospective glances and reminiscences will reveal a picture of a life well spent, and the older adult will be satisfied (integrity). But if the older adult resolved one or more of the earlier stages in a negative way (being socially isolated in early adulthood or stagnating in middle adulthood, for example), retrospective glances about the total worth of his or her life might be negative (despair).

Life review is prominent in Erikson's final stage of integrity versus despair. Life review involves looking back at one's life experiences, evaluating them, interpreting them, and often reinterpreting them (Cappeliez & Robitaille, 2011; Wu & others, 2012). Distinguished aging researcher Robert Butler (2007) argues that the life review is set in motion by looking forward to death. Sometimes the life review proceeds quietly; at other times it is intense, requiring considerable work to achieve some sense of personality integration. The life review may be observed initially in stray and insignificant thoughts about oneself and one's life history. These thoughts may continue to emerge in brief intermittent spurts or become essentially continuous.

When older adults engage in a life review, they may reevaluate previous experiences and their meaning, often with revision or expanded understanding taking place. This reorganization of the past may provide a more valid picture for the individual, providing new and significant meaning to one's life (O'Rourke, Cappeliez, & Claxton,

integrity versus despair Erikson's eighth and final stage of development, which individuals experience in late adulthood. This involves reflecting on the past and either piecing together a positive review or concluding that one's life has not been well spent.

2011; Randall, 2012). A recent study found that a life-review course titled "Looking for Meaning" reduced the depressive symptoms of middle-aged and older adults (Pot & others, 2010).

One aspect of life review involves identifying and reflecting not only on the positive aspects of one's life but also on regrets as part of developing a mature wisdom and self-understanding (Choi & Jun, 2009). The hope is that by examining not only the positive aspects of one's life but also what an individual has regretted doing, a more accurate vision of the complexity of one's life and possibly increased life satisfaction will be attained (King & Hicks, 2007).

Although thinking about regrets can be helpful as part of a life review, however, recent research indicates that it is important for older adults to not dwell on regrets, especially since opportunities to undo regrettable actions decline with age (Suri & Gross, 2012). One study revealed that an important factor in the outlook of older adults who showed a higher level of emotion regulation and successful aging was reduced responsiveness to regrets (Brassen & others, 2012).

What characterizes a life review in late adulthood?

How Would You...?

As a psychologist, how would you explain to an older adult the benefits of engaging in a life review?

In working with older clients, some clinicians use *reminiscence therapy*, which involves discussing past activities and experiences with another individual or group (Cotelli, Manenti, & Zanetti, 2012; Fujiwara & others, 2012). Therapy may include the use of photographs, familiar items, and video/audio recordings. Researchers have found that reminiscence therapy improves the mood of older adults, including those with dementia (Subramaniam & Woods, 2012). A recent meta-analysis of 128 studies found that reminiscence interventions improved older adults' integrity (related to Erikson's integrity versus despair stage) and reduced their depression (Pinquart & Forstmeier, 2012). Smaller effects occurred for purpose in life, preparing for death, mastery, positive well-being, social integration, and cognitive performance. The largest improvements were made for depressive symptoms in depressed individuals and persons with chronic physical disease.

Activity Theory

Activity theory states that the more active and involved older adults are, the more likely they are to be satisfied with their lives. Researchers have found strong support for activity theory, beginning in the 1960s and continuing into the twenty-first century (Neugarten, Havighurst, & Tobin, 1968; Riebe & others, 2005). These researchers have found that when older adults are active, energetic, and productive, they age more successfully and are happier than they are if they disengage from society. A recent study found that older adults were happiest when they combined effortful social, physical, cognitive, and household activities with restful activities (Oerlemans, Bakker, & Veenhoven, 2011).

Activity theory suggests that many individuals will achieve greater life satisfaction if they continue their middle-adulthood roles into late adulthood. If these roles are stripped from them (as in early retirement), it is important for them to find substitute roles that keep them active and involved.

Socioemotional Selectivity Theory

Socioemotional selectivity theory states that older adults become more selective about their social networks. Because they place a high

activity theory Theory that the more active and involved older adults are, the more likely they are to be satisfied with their lives.

socioemotional selectivity theory The theory that older adults become more selective about their social networks. Because they place a high value on emotional satisfaction, older adults often prefer to spend time with familiar individuals with whom they have had rewarding relationships.

value on emotional satisfaction, older adults spend more time with familiar individuals with whom they have had rewarding relationships. Developed by Laura Carstensen (1998, 2006, 2008, 2010), this theory argues that older adults deliberately withdraw from social contact with individuals peripheral to their lives while they maintain or increase contact with close friends and family members with whom they have had enjoyable relationships. This selective narrowing of social interaction maximizes positive emotional experiences and minimizes emotional risks as individuals become older.

Socioemotional selectivity theory challenges the stereotype that the majority of older adults are in emotional despair because of their social isolation (Carstensen & others, 2011). Rather, older adults consciously choose to decrease the total number of their social contacts in favor of spending increased time in emotionally rewarding moments with friends and family. That is, they systematically prune their social networks so that available social partners satisfy their emotional needs.

Is there research evidence to support life-span differences in the composition of social networks? Researchers have found that older adults have far smaller social networks than younger adults (Carstensen & others, 2011; Carstensen & Fried, 2012).

Laura Carstensen (*right*), in a caring relationship with an older woman. Her theory of socioemotional selectivity is gaining recognition as an explanation for changes in social networks as people age.

Socioemotional selectivity theory also focuses on the types of goals that individuals are motivated to achieve (Biggs, Carstensen, & Hogan, 2012). It states that two important classes of goals are (1) knowledge-related and (2) emotion-related (Mikels & others, 2010). This theory emphasizes that the trajectory of motivation for knowledge-related goals starts relatively high in the early years of life, peaking in adolescence and early adulthood and then declining in middle and late adulthood. The emotion-related trajectory is high during infancy and early childhood, declines from middle childhood through early adulthood, and increases in middle and late adulthood.

How Would You...?

As a health-care professional, how would you assess whether an older adult's limited social contacts signal unhealthy social isolation or healthy socioemotional selectivity?

In general, compared with younger adults, the feelings of older adults mellow. Emotional life is on a more even keel, with fewer highs and lows. It may be that although older adults have less extreme joy, they have more contentment, especially when they are connected in positive ways with friends and family. Compared with younger adults, older adults react less strongly to negative circumstances, are better at ignoring irrelevant negative information, and remember more positive than negative information (Mather, 2012).

A recent study revealed that positive emotion increased and negative emotion (except for sadness) decreased from 50 years of age through the mid-eighties (Stone & others, 2010). In this study, a pronounced decline in anger occurred from the early twenties and sadness was essentially unchanged from the early twenties through the mid-eighties. Another recent study found that aging was linked to more positive overall well-being and greater emotional stability (Carstensen & others, 2011). In this study, adults who experienced more positive than negative emotions were more likely to remain alive over a 13-year period. Other research also indicates that happier people live longer (Frey, 2011). In sum, researchers have found that the emotional life of older adults is more positive than stereotypes suggest (Carstensen & Fried, 2012; Wrzus & others, 2012).

How might the brain be involved in the changes that take place in older adults' emotions? Although links between the aging brain and emotion have only just begun to be studied, recent research suggests some possible connections (Samanez-Larkin & Carstensen, 2011). Reduced negative emotion in older adults may be associated with decreased physiological arousal of emotion with aging in the amygdala and autonomic nervous system (Kaszniak & Menchola, 2012). More effective emotion regulation may be related to this reduction in subcortical activation and also to increased activation in the prefrontal cortex (Samanez-Larkin & Carstensen, 2011).

selective optimization with compensation theory The theory that successful aging is related to three main factors: selection, optimization, and compensation.

Selective Optimization with Compensation Theory

Selective optimization with compensation theory states that successful aging is linked with three main factors: selection, optimization, and compensation (SOC). The theory describes how people can produce new resources and allocate them effectively to the tasks they want to master (Baltes, Lindenberger, & Staudinger, 2006; Freund, Nikitin, & Riediger, 2013; Staudinger & Jacobs, 2010). *Selection* is based on the concept that older adults have a reduced capacity and loss of functioning, which require a reduction in performance in most life domains. *Optimization* suggests that it is possible to maintain performance in some areas through continued practice and the use of new technologies. *Compensation* becomes relevant when life tasks require a level of capacity beyond the current level of the older adult's performance potential. Older adults especially need to compensate in circumstances involving high mental or physical demands, such as when thinking about and memorizing new material in a very short period of time, reacting quickly when driving a car, or running fast. When older adults develop an illness, the need for compensation is obvious.

In the view of Paul Baltes and his colleagues (2006), the selection of domains and life priorities is an important aspect of development. Life goals and personal life investments likely vary across the life course for most people. For many individuals, it is not just the sheer attainment of goals, but rather the attainment of *meaningful* goals, that makes life satisfying. In one cross-sectional study, the personal life investments of 25- to 105-year-olds were assessed (Staudinger, 1996) (see Figure 16.1). From 25 to 34 years of age, participants said that they personally invested more time in work, friends, family, and independence, in that order. From 35 to 54 and 55 to 65 years of age, family became more important than friends in terms of their personal investment. Little changed in the rank ordering of persons 70 to 84 years old, but for participants 85 to 105 years old, health became

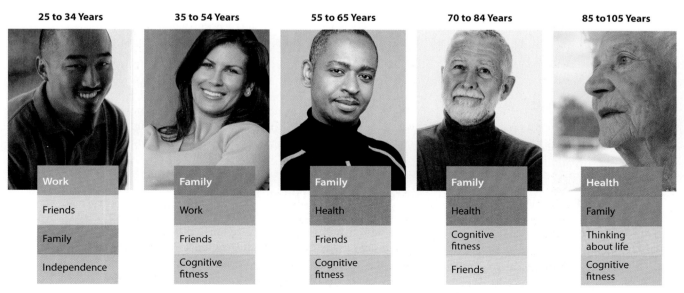

25 to 34 Years	35 to 54 Years	55 to 65 Years	70 to 84 Years	85 to105 Years
Work	Family	Family	Family	Health
Friends	Work	Health	Health	Family
Family	Friends	Friends	Cognitive fitness	Thinking about life
Independence	Cognitive fitness	Cognitive fitness	Friends	Cognitive fitness

Figure 16.1 Degree of Personal Life Investment at Different Points in Life
Shown here are the top four domains of personal life investment at different points in life. The highest degree of investment is listed at the top (for example, work was the highest personal investment from 25 to 34 years of age, family from 35 to 84, and health from 85 to 105).

THEORIES OF SOCIOEMOTIONAL DEVELOPMENT

the most important personal investment. Thinking about life showed up for the first time on the most important list for those who were 85 to 105 years old.

Personality and Society

Is personality linked to mortality in older adults? How are older adults perceived and treated by society?

Personality

We described the Big Five factors of personality in Chapter 14. To remember what the five factors are, you may recall that the first letter of each factor spells OCEAN. Researchers have found that several of the Big Five factors of personality continue to change in late adulthood (Roberts, Donnellan, & Hill, 2013). For example, in one study, older adults were more conscientious and agreeable than middle-aged and younger adults (Allemand, Zimprich, & Hendriks, 2008). Another study examined developmental changes in the components of conscientiousness (Jackson & others, 2009). In this study, the transition into late adulthood was characterized by increases in these aspects of conscientiousness: impulse control, reliability, and conventionality.

Might certain personality traits influence how long older adults live? Researchers have found that some personality traits are associated with the mortality of older adults (Roberts, Donnellan, & Hill, 2013). A longitudinal study of more than 1,200 individuals across seven decades revealed that a higher score on the Big Five personality factor of conscientiousness predicted a lower risk of earlier death from childhood through late adulthood (Martin, Friedman, & Schwartz, 2007). Another study found that two of the Big Five factors were linked to older adults' mortality, with low conscientiousness and high neuroticism predicting earlier death (Wilson & others, 2004). In a five-year longitudinal study, higher levels of conscientiousness, extraversion, and openness were related to a lower risk of earlier death (Iwasa & others, 2008). And in a recent study, a higher level of conscientiousness predicted greater longevity in older adults (Hill & others, 2011).

Following are the results of two other recent studies of the Big Five factors in older adults: In one study, neuroticism was linked to older adults' medication non-adherence across a six-year time frame (Jerant & others, 2011). In another study, elevated neuroticism, lower conscientiousness, and lower openness were related an increased risk of older adults' developing Alzheimer disease across a period of six years (Duberstein & others, 2011).

Older Adults in Society

Does society negatively stereotype older adults? What are some social policy issues in an aging society? What role does technology play in the lives of older adults?

How Would You...?
As a human development and family studies professional, how would you design a public awareness campaign to reduce ageism?

ageism Prejudice against other people because of their age, especially prejudice against older adults.

Stereotyping of Older Adults

Social participation by older adults is often discouraged by **ageism,** which is prejudice against others because of their age, especially prejudice against older adults (Kalache & Blewitt, 2012; Kornadt & Rothermund, 2012). They are often perceived as incapable of thinking clearly, learning new things, enjoying sex, contributing to the community, or holding responsible jobs. Many older adults face painful discrimination and might be too polite and timid to attack it. Because of their age, older adults might not be hired for new jobs or might be eased out of old ones; they might be shunned socially; and they might be edged out of their family life.

Ageism is widespread (Hummert, 2011; Milner, Van Norman, & Milner, 2012). One study found that men were more likely to negatively stereotype older adults than were women (Rupp, Vodanovich, & Crede, 2005). Research indicates that the most frequent form is disrespect for older adults, followed by assumptions about ailments or frailty caused by age (Palmore, 2004). However, the increased number of adults living to an older age has led to active efforts to improve society's image of older adults, obtain better living conditions for older adults, and gain political clout.

Policy Issues in an Aging Society

The aging society and older persons' status in this society raise policy issues about the well-being of older adults (Fisher & others, 2013; Greenlund & others, 2012). These include the status of the economy and income, provision of health care, and eldercare, each of which we consider in turn.

Status of the Economy and Income An important issue involving the economy and aging is the concern that our economy cannot bear the burden of so many older persons, who by reason of their age alone are usually consumers rather than producers. Especially troublesome is the low rate of savings among U.S. adults, which has contributed to the financial problems of older adults in the recent economic downturn (Gould & Hertel-Fernandez, 2010). As indicated in Chapter 15, surveys indicate that Americans' confidence in their ability to retire comfortably has reached all-time lows in recent years (Helman, Copeland, & VanDerhei, 2012).

Of special concern are older adults who are poor. Researchers have found that poverty in late adulthood is linked to an increase in physical and mental health problems (Wight & others, 2009). And one study revealed that low SES increases the risk of earlier death in older adults (Krueger & Chang, 2008).

Census data suggest that the overall number of older people living in poverty has declined since the 1960s, but in 2008, 9.7 percent of older adults in the United States still were living in poverty (U.S. Census Bureau, 2010). In 2008, almost twice as many U.S. women 65 years and older (11.9 percent) lived in poverty as did their male counterparts (U.S. Census Bureau, 2010).

Health Care An aging society also brings with it various problems involving health care (Hellander & Bhargavan, 2012; Siegler & others, 2013a, b). Escalating health-care costs are the focus of considerable concern (Alzheimer's Association, 2012; Fried, Hogan, & Rowe, 2012). Approximately one-third of total health care expenses in the United States involve the care of adults 65 and over, who comprise only 12 percent of the population. The health-care needs of older adults are reflected in Medicare, the program that provides health-care insurance to adults over 65 under the Social Security system (Hansen, 2012). Of interest is the fact that until the Affordable Care Act was recently enacted, the United States was the only developed country that did not have a national health care system.

How Would You...?

As a health-care professional, how would you recommend addressing the medical community's emphasis on "cure" rather than "care" when treating chronic illness in older adults?

A special concern is that while many of the health problems of older adults are chronic rather than acute, the medical system is still based on a "cure" rather than a "care" model. Chronic illness involves long-term, often lifelong conditions and requires long-term, if not life-term, management.

Eldercare Eldercare is the physical and emotional caretaking of older members of the family, whether that care involves day-to-day physical assistance or responsibility for arranging and overseeing such care. An important issue involving eldercare is how it can best

eldercare Physical and emotional caretaking for older members of the family, whether by giving day-to-day physical assistance or by overseeing such care.

be provided (Duxbury, Higgins, & Smart, 2011; Zacher, Jimmieson, & Winter, 2012). When most women were not part of the workforce, they often served as caretakers for the elderly. Now with so many women working outside the home, there is a question of who will replace them as caregivers. An added problem is that many caregivers are in their sixties, and many of them are ill themselves. They may find it especially stressful to be responsible for the care of relatives who are in their eighties or nineties.

Technology The Internet plays an increasingly important role in providing access to information and communication for adults as well as youth (Bers & Kazakoff, 2013). How well are older adults keeping up with changes in technology? Older adults are less likely to have a computer in their home and less likely to use the Internet than younger adults, but older adults are the fastest-growing segment of Internet users (Czaja & others, 2006). Older adults log more time on the Internet (an average of 8.3 hours per week), visit more Web sites, and spend more money on the Internet than their younger adult counterparts. They are especially interested in learning to use e-mail and going online for health information (Westlake & others, 2007). Increasing numbers of older adults use e-mail to communicate with relatives. And a recent study found that frequent computer use was linked to higher performance on cognitive tasks in older adults (Tun & Lachman, 2010). As with children and younger adults, cautions about the accuracy of information on the Internet—especially in areas such as health care—should always be kept in mind (Crabb, Rafie, & Weingardt, 2012; Miller & Bell, 2012).

Are older adults keeping up with changes in technology?

Links between older adults' use of technology and their cognitive development also are being studied. A recent study found that frequent computer use was linked to higher performance on cognitive tasks in older adults (Tun & Lachman, 2010). Researchers also are examining the role that video games might play in maintaining or improving older adults' cognitive skills (Charness, Fox, & Mitchum, 2011; McDougall & House, 2012). For example, a research study found that a lengthy 40-hour video game training program improved older adults' attention and memory skills (Smith & others, 2009). And another study revealed that a brain training game that elderly adults played about 15 minutes a day for four weeks improved their executive functioning and speed of processing information (Nouchi & others, 2012).

Families and Social Relationships

Are the close relationships of older adults different from those of younger adults? What are the lifestyles of older adults like? What characterizes the relationships of older adult parents and their adult children? What do friendships and social networks contribute to the lives of older adults? How might older adults' altruism and volunteerism contribute to positive outcomes?

Lifestyle Diversity

The lifestyles of older adults are changing (Blieszner & Bedford, 2011; Carr & Moorman, 2011). Formerly, the later years of life were likely to consist of marriage for men and widowhood for women. With demographic shifts toward marital dissolution characterized by divorce, one-third of adults can now expect to marry, divorce, and remarry during their lifetime. Let's now explore some of the diverse lifestyles of older adults, beginning with those who are married or partnered.

Married Older Adults

In 2010, 57 percent of U.S. adults over 65 years of age were married (U.S. Census Bureau, 2011). Individuals who are in a marriage or a partnership in late adulthood are usually happier, feel less distressed, and live longer than those who are single (Piazza & Charles, 2012; Strout & Howard, 2012). One study found that older adults were more satisfied with their marriages than were young and middle-aged adults (Bookwala & Jacobs, 2004). Indeed, the majority of older adults evaluate their marriages as happy or very happy (Huyck, 1995). A recent study of octogenarians revealed that marital satisfaction helped to protect their happiness from daily fluctuations in perceived health (Waldinger & Schulz, 2010). Also, a longitudinal study of adults 75 years of age and older revealed that individuals who were married were less likely to die across a span of seven years (Rasulo, Christensen, & Tomassini, 2005).

What are some adaptations that many married older adults need to make?

In late adulthood, married individuals are more likely to find themselves having to care for a sick partner with a limiting health condition (Blieszner & Roberto, 2012). The stress of caring for a spouse who has a chronic disease can place demands on intimacy.

Divorced and Remarried Older Adults

In 2010, 11 percent of women and 9 percent of men 65 years and older in the United States were divorced or separated (U.S. Census Bureau, 2011). Many of these individuals were divorced or separated before they entered late adulthood (Carr & Pudrovska, 2011). The majority of divorced older adults are women, due to their greater longevity, and men are more likely to remarry, thus removing themselves from the pool of divorced older adults (Peek, 2009). Divorce is far less common among older adults than younger adults, likely reflecting cohort effects rather than age effects since divorce was somewhat rare when current cohorts of older adults were young (Peek, 2009).

There are social, financial, and physical consequences of divorce for older adults (Butrica & Smith, 2012; Piazza & Charles, 2012). Divorce can weaken kinship ties when it occurs in later life, especially in the case of older men. Divorced older women are less likely to have adequate financial resources than married older women, and divorce is linked to higher rates of health problems in older adults (Bennett, 2006).

How Would You...?

As a psychologist, how would you assist older adults in coping with the unique challenges faced by divorcées at this age?

Rising divorce rates, increased longevity, and better health have led to an increase in remarriage by older adults (Ganong & Coleman, 2006). What happens when an older adult wants to remarry or does remarry? Researchers have found that some older adults perceive negative social pressure about their decision to remarry (McKain, 1972). These negative sanctions range from raised eyebrows to rejection by adult children (Ganong & Coleman, 2006). However, the majority of adult children support the decision of their older adult parents to remarry.

Adult children can be personally affected by remarriage between older adults. Researchers have found that remarried parents and stepparents provide less support to adult stepchildren than do parents in first marriages (White, 1994).

Cohabiting Older Adults

An increasing number of older adults cohabit (Noel-Miller, 2011). In the middle of the twentieth century, hardly any older adults cohabited. In 2010, 3 percent of older adults were cohabiting (U.S. Census Bureau, 2011). It is expected that the number of cohabiting older adults will increase even further as the large cohort of baby boomers become 65 years of age and older and bring their historically more nontraditional values about love, sex, and relationships to late adulthood. In many cases, the cohabiting is more for companionship than for love. In other cases, such as when one partner faces the potential need for expensive care, a couple may decide to maintain their assets separately and thus not marry. One study found that older adults who cohabited had a more positive, stable relationship than younger adults who cohabited, although cohabiting older adults were less likely to have plans to marry their partner than younger ones were (King & Scott, 2005). Other research also has revealed that middle-aged and older adult cohabiting men and women reported higher levels of depression than their married counterparts (Brown, Bulanda, & Lee, 2005). And a recent study indicated that cohabiting older adults were less likely to receive partner care than married older adults (Noel-Miller, 2011).

Older Adult Parents and Their Adult Children

Approximately 80 percent of older adults have living children, many of whom are middle-aged. About 10 percent of older adults have children who are 65 years or older. Adult children are an important part of the aging parent's social network. Older adults with children have more contacts with relatives than those without children.

Increasingly, diversity characterizes older adult parents and their adult children (Birditt & Wardjiman, 2012). Divorce, cohabitation, and nonmarital childbearing are more common in the history of older adults today than in the past (Carr & Pudrovska, 2011).

Gender plays an important role in relationships involving older adult parents and their children. Adult daughters are more likely than adult sons to be involved in the lives of aging parents. For example, adult daughters are three times more likely than adult sons to give parents assistance with daily living activities (Dwyer & Coward, 1991).

A valuable task that adult children can perform is to coordinate and monitor services for an aging parent (or relative) who becomes disabled (Jones & others, 2011). This might involve locating a nursing home and monitoring its quality, procuring medical services, arranging public service assistance, and handling finances. In some cases, adult children provide direct assistance with daily living, including such activities as eating, bathing, and dressing. Even less severely impaired older adults may need help with shopping, housework, transportation, home maintenance, and bill paying.

How Would You...?

As a human development and family studies professional, how would you characterize the importance of friendships for older adults?

Friendship

In early adulthood, friendship networks expand as new social connections are made away from home. In late adulthood, new friendships are less likely to be forged, although some adults do seek out new friendships, especially following the death of a spouse (Zettel-Watson & Rook, 2009).

Aging expert Laura Carstensen (2006) concluded that people choose close friends over new friends as they grow older. And as

What characterizes friendship in late adulthood?

long as they have several close people in their network, they seem content, says Carstensen.

In one study of 128 married older adults, women were more depressed than men if they did not have a best friend, and women who did have a friend reported lower levels of depression (Antonucci, Lansford, & Akiyama, 2001). Similarly, women who did not have a best friend were less satisfied with life than women who did have a best friend. And a longitudinal study of adults 75 years of age and older revealed that individuals with close ties with friends were less likely to die across a seven-year age span (Rasulo, Christensen, & Tomassini, 2005). The findings were stronger for women than men.

Social Support and Social Integration

Social support and social integration play important roles in the physical and mental health of older adults (Antonucci, Birditt, & Ajrouch, 2013). In the *social convoy* model of social relations, individuals go through life embedded in a personal network of individuals to whom they give, and from whom they receive, social support (Antonucci, Birditt, & Ajrouch, 2013). Social support can help individuals of all ages cope more effectively with life's challenges. For older adults, social support is related to their physical and mental health (Cheng, Lee, & Chow, 2010). It is linked with a reduction in symptoms of disease, with the ability to meet one's own health-care needs, and longevity (Rook & others, 2007). Social support also decreases the probability that an older adult will be institutionalized and is associated with a lower incidence of depression (Heard & others, 2011). Further, a recent study revealed that older adults who experienced a higher level of social support showed later cognitive decline than their counterparts with a lower level of social support (Dickinson & others, 2011).

Social integration also plays an important role in the lives of many older adults (Antonucci, Birditt, & Ajrouch, 2013; Hawkley & Cacioppo, 2013). Remember from our earlier discussion of socioemotional selectivity theory that many older adults choose to have fewer peripheral social contacts and more emotionally positive contacts with friends and family (Carstensen & others, 2011). Thus, a decrease in the overall social activity of many older adults may reflect their greater interest in spending more time in the small circle of friends and families where they are less likely to have negative emotional experiences. A low level of social integration is linked with poorer health and earlier death in older adults (Koropeckyj-Cox, 2009). A recent study revealed that social isolation in late adulthood was associated with higher risks of being inactive, smoking, and engaging in other health-risk behaviors (Shankar & others, 2011). And three recent longitudinal studies found that feelings of loneliness were linked to earlier death (Holwerda & others, 2012; Luo & others, 2012; Perissinotto, Stijacic Cenzer, & Covinsky, 2012).

Researchers have found that older adults tend to report being less lonely than younger adults and less lonely than would be expected based on their circumstances (Schnittker, 2007). Their reports of feeling less lonely than younger adults likely reflect their more selective social networks and greater acceptance of loneliness in their lives (Koropeckyj-Cox, 2009).

Altruism and Volunteerism

A common perception is that older adults need to be given help rather than give help themselves. However, a recent study found that older adults perceived their well-being as better when they provided social support to others than when they received it, except when social support was provided by a spouse or sibling (Thomas, 2010). And a 12-year longitudinal study revealed that older adults who had persistently low or declining feelings of usefulness to others had an increased risk of earlier death (Gruenewald & others, 2009). Further, researchers recently have found that when older adults engage in altruistic behavior and volunteering, they benefit from these activities (Pilkington & others, 2012). A recent analysis concluded that rates of volunteering do not decline significantly until the mid-seventies, and older adults commit more hours than younger volunteers (Morrow-Howell, 2010). Older adults are also more likely than any other age group to volunteer more than 100 hours annually (Burr, 2009).

Researchers also have found that volunteering as an older adult is associated with a number of positive outcomes (Pilkington & others, 2012). For example, a study of 2,000 older adults in Japan revealed that those who gave more assistance to others had better physical health than their elderly counterparts who gave less assistance (Dulin & others, 2012; Krause & others, 1999). Among the reasons for the positive outcomes of volunteering are its provision of constructive activities and productive roles, social integration, and enhanced meaningfulness. However, a recent study revealed that older adults who volunteered for other-oriented reasons had a decreased mortality risk but those who volunteered for self-oriented reasons had a mortality risk similar to that of nonvolunteers (Konrath & others, 2012).

How Would You...?

As an educator, how would you persuade the school board to sponsor a volunteer program to bring older adults into the school system to work with elementary students?

Ninety-eight-year-old volunteer Iva Broadus plays cards with 10-year-old DeAngela Williams in Dallas, Texas. Iva recently was recognized as the oldest volunteer in the Big Sister program in the United States. Iva says that card-playing helps to keep her memory and thinking skills sharp and can help DeAngela's as well.

Ethnicity, Gender, and Culture

How is ethnicity linked to aging? Do gender roles change in late adulthood? What are some of the social aspects of aging in different cultures?

Ethnicity

Of special concern are ethnic minority older adults, especially African Americans and Latinos, who are overrepresented in poverty statistics (Jackson, Govia, & Sellers, 2011). Comparative information about African Americans, Latinos, and non-Latino Whites indicates a possible double jeopardy for elderly ethnic minority individuals. They face problems related to *both* ageism and racism (Hatzfeld, Laveist, & Gaston-Johansson, 2012; Shenson & others, 2012). They also are more likely to have a history of less education, longer periods of unemployment, worse housing conditions, and shorter life expectancies than their older non-Latino White counterparts (Gee, Walsemann, & Brondolo, 2012).

Despite the stress and discrimination older ethnic minority individuals face, many of these older adults have developed coping mechanisms that allow them to survive in the dominant non-Latino White world (Jackson, Govia, & Sellers, 2011). Extension of family networks helps older minority group individuals cope with the bare essentials of living and gives them a sense of being loved. Churches in African American and Latino communities provide avenues for meaningful social participation, feelings of power, and a sense of internal satisfaction (Hill & others, 2005). To read about one individual who is providing help for aging minorities, see *Careers in Life-Span Development.*

Norma Thomas, Social Work Professor and Administrator

Dr. Norma Thomas has worked for more than three decades in the field of aging. She obtained her undergraduate degree in social work from Pennsylvania State University and her doctoral degree in social work from the University of Pennsylvania. Thomas' activities are varied. Earlier in her career, as a social work practitioner, she provided services to older adults of color in an effort to improve their lives. She currently is a professor and academic administrator at Widener University in Chester, Pennsylvania, a fellow of the Institute of Aging at the University of Pennsylvania, and the chief executive officer and co-founder of the Center on Ethnic and Minority Aging (CEMA). CEMA was formed to provide research, consultation, training, and services to benefit aging individuals of color, their families, and their communities. Thomas has created numerous community service events that benefit older adults of color, especially African Americans and Latinos. She has also been a consultant to various national, regional, and state agencies in her effort to improve the lives of aging adults of color.

Norma Thomas.

Gender

Do our gender roles change when we become older adults? Some developmentalists believe there is decreasing femininity in women and decreasing masculinity in men during late adulthood (Gutmann, 1975). The evidence suggests that older men do become more feminine—nurturant, sensitive, and so on—but it appears that older women do not necessarily become more masculine—assertive, dominant, and so on (Turner, 1982). Keep in mind that cohort effects are especially important to consider in areas such as gender roles. As sociohistorical changes take place and are considered more frequently in life-span investigations, what were once perceived to be age effects may turn out to be cohort effects (Schaie, 2012).

A possible double jeopardy also faces many women—the burden of *both* ageism and sexism. The poverty rate for older adult females is almost double that of older adult males.

Not only is it important to be concerned about older women's double jeopardy of ageism and sexism, but special attention also needs to be devoted to female ethnic minority older adults (Jackson, Govia, & Sellers, 2011). They face what could be described as triple jeopardy—ageism, sexism, and racism (Hinze, Lin, & Andersson, 2012).

A special concern is the stress faced by older African American women, many of whom view religion as a source of strength to help them cope. *What are some other characteristics of being female, ethnic, and old?*

Culture

What factors are associated with whether older adults are accorded a position of high status in a culture? Six factors are most likely to predict high status for older adults in a culture (Sangree, 1989):

- Older persons have valuable knowledge.
- Older persons control key family/community resources.

- Older persons are permitted to engage in useful and valued functions as long as possible.
- Age-related role changes involve greater responsibility, authority, and advisory capacity.
- The extended family is a common family arrangement in the culture, and the older person is integrated into the extended family.
- In general, respect for older adults is greater in collectivistic cultures (such as China and Japan) than in individualistic cultures (such as the United States). However, some researchers are finding that this collectivistic/individualistic difference in respect for older adults is not as strong as it used to be and that, in some cases, older adults in individualistic cultures receive considerable respect (Antonucci, Vandewater, & Lansford, 2000).

Cultures vary in the prestige they give to older adults. In the Navajo culture, older adults are especially treated with respect because of their wisdom and extensive life experiences. What are some other factors that are linked with respect for older adults in a culture?

Successful Aging

For too long, the positive dimensions of late adulthood were ignored (Biggs, Carstensen, & Hogan, 2012). Throughout this book, we have called attention to the positive aspects of aging. In fact, examining the positive aspects of aging is an important trend in life-span development and is likely to benefit future generations of older adults (Depp, Vahia, & Jeste, 2012). There are many robust, healthy older adults. With a proper diet, an active lifestyle, mental stimulation and flexibility, positive coping skills, good social relationships and support, and the absence of disease, many abilities can be maintained or in some cases even improved as we get older (Antonucci, Birditt, & Ajrouch, 2013). Even when individuals develop a disease, improvements in medicine mean that increasing numbers of older adults can still lead active, constructive lives (Siegler & others, 2013a, b).

Eighty-one-year-old Warren Buffett, one of the world's richest individuals, continues to have a very active, successful life. He recently donated more than 30 billion dollars to several foundations, with the bulk of the money going to the Bill and Melinda Gates Foundation, which plans to use it to reduce poverty, improve education, and solve health problems.

Being active is especially important to successful aging (Katzel & Steinbrenner, 2012). Older adults who exercise regularly, attend meetings, participate in church activities, and go on trips are more satisfied with their lives than their counterparts who disengage from society (James & others, 2011). Older adults who engage in challenging cognitive activities are more likely to retain their cognitive skills for a longer period of time (Dixon & others, 2013). Older adults who are emotionally selective, optimize their choices, and compensate effectively for losses increase their chances of aging successfully (Carstensen & others, 2011; Freund, Nikitin, & Riediger, 2013). A recent study also found that maximizing psychological resources (such as self-efficacy and optimism) was linked to a higher quality of life in the future (Bowling & Iliffe, 2011). And a very important agenda is to continue improving our understanding of how people can live longer, healthier, more productive and satisfying lives (Beard & others, 2012).

Summary

Theories of Socioemotional Development

- Erikson's eighth stage of development is called integrity versus despair. Life review is an important theme during this stage.

- Older adults who are active are more likely to be satisfied with their lives.

- Older adults are more selective about their social networks than are younger adults. Older adults also experience more positive emotions and less negative emotions than younger adults.

- Successful aging involves selection, optimization, and compensation.

Personality and Society

- Some of the Big Five factors of personality, such as conscientiousness, extraversion, and openness, are linked to well-being and mortality in older adults.

- Ageism, which is prejudice against others because of their age, is widespread. Social policy issues in an aging society include the status of the economy and income, provision of health care, and eldercare. Older adults are the fastest-growing segment of Internet users.

Families and Social Relationships

- Married older adults are often happier than single older adults. Divorce and remarriage present challenges to older adults. An increasing number of older adults cohabit.

- Approximately 80 percent of older adults have adult children who are an important part of their social network.

- Older adults tend to choose long-term friends over new friends.

- Social support is linked to improved physical and mental health in older adults. Older adults who participate in more organizations live longer than their counterparts who have low participation rates.

- Altruism and volunteering are associated with positive benefits for older adults.

Ethnicity, Gender, and Culture

- Aging minorities in the United States face the double burden of ageism and racism.

- There is stronger evidence that men become more feminine (nurturant, sensitive) as older adults than there is that women become more masculine (assertive).

- Factors that predict high status for the elderly across cultures range from value placed on their accumulated knowledge to integration into the extended family.

Successful Aging

- Increasingly, researchers are studying the positive aspects of late adulthood. Factors that are linked with successful aging include an active lifestyle, positive coping skills, good social relationships and support, and the absence of disease.

Key Terms

integrity versus despair 398
activity theory 399
socioemotional selectivity theory 399
selective optimization with compensation theory 401
ageism 402
eldercare 403

17 Death, Dying, and Grieving

Stories of Life-Span Development: Paige Farley-Hackel and Ruth McCourt, 9/11/2001

Paige Farley-Hackel and her best friend Ruth McCourt teamed up to take McCourt's 4-year-old daughter, Juliana, to Disneyland. They were originally booked on the same flight from Boston to Los Angeles, but McCourt decided to use her frequent flyer miles and go on a different airplane. Both their flights exploded 17 minutes apart after terrorists hijacked them, then rammed them into the twin towers of the World Trade Center in New York City on 9/11/2001.

Forty-six-year-old Farley-Hackel was a writer, motivational speaker, and spiritual counselor who lived in Newton, Massachusetts. She was looking forward to the airing of the first few episodes of her new radio program, *Spiritually Speaking*, and wanted to eventually be on *The Oprah Winfrey Show*, said her husband, Allan Hackel. Following 9/11, Oprah televised a memorial tribute to Farley-Hackel, McCourt, and Juliana.

Forty-five-year-old Ruth McCourt was a homemaker from New London, Connecticut, who met Farley-Hackel at a day spa she used to own in Boston.

McCourt gave up the business when she got married, but the friendship between the two women lasted. They often traveled together and shared their passion for reading, cooking, and learning.

In this chapter, we explore many aspects of death and dying. Among the questions that we will ask are: How can death be defined? How is death viewed in other cultures? How do people face their own death? How do people cope with the death of someone they love? ■

Defining Death and Life/Death Issues

Is there one point in the process of dying that is *the* point at which death takes place, or is death a more gradual process? What are some decisions individuals can make about life, death, and health care?

Determining Death

Twenty-five years ago, determining whether someone was dead was simpler than it is today. The end of certain biological functions—such as breathing and blood pressure, and the rigidity of the body (rigor mortis)—were considered to be clear signs of death. In the past several decades, defining death has become more complex (Goswami & others, 2012).

Brain death is a neurological definition of death which states that a person is brain dead when all electrical activity of the brain has ceased for a specified period of time. A flat EEG (electroencephalogram) recording for a specified period of time is one criterion of brain death. The higher portions of the brain often die sooner than the lower portions. Because the brain's lower portions monitor heart-beat and respiration, individuals whose higher brain areas have died may continue to breathe and have a heartbeat (Binderman, Krakauer, & Solomon, 2012). The definition of brain death currently followed by most physicians includes the death of both the higher cortical functions and the lower brain stem functions (Sung & Greer, 2011).

How Would You...?

As a health-care professional, how would you explain "brain death" to the family of an individual who has suffered a severe head injury in an automobile accident?

Some medical experts argue that the criteria for death should include only higher cortical functioning. If the cortical death definition were adopted, then physicians could claim a person is dead who has no cortical functioning, even if the lower brain stem is functioning. Supporters of the cortical death policy argue that the functions we associate with being human, such as intelligence and personality, are located in the higher cortical part of the brain. They believe that when these functions are lost, the "human being" is no longer alive.

Decisions Regarding Life, Death, and Health Care

In cases of catastrophic illness or accidents, patients might not be able to respond adequately to participate in decisions about their medical care. To prepare for this situation, some individuals make choices earlier.

Advance Care Planning

Advance care planning refers to the process of patients thinking about and communicating their preferences regarding end-of-life care (Carr, 2012; Tinetti, 2012). For many patients in a coma, it is not clear what their wishes regarding termination of treatment might be if they still were conscious. Recognizing that some terminally ill patients might prefer to die rather than linger in a painful or vegetative state, the organization "Choice in Dying" created the *living will*, a legal document that reflects the patient's advance care planning.

Physicians' concerns over malpractice suits and the efforts of people who support the living will concept have produced natural death legislation. Laws in all 50 states now accept an *advance directive*, such as a living will. An advance directive states such preferences as whether life-sustaining procedures should or

euthanasia The act of painlessly ending the lives of persons who are suffering from incurable diseases or severe disabilities; sometimes called "mercy killing."

passive euthanasia The withholding of available treatments, such as life-sustaining devices, allowing the person to die.

active euthanasia Death induced deliberately, as by injecting a lethal dose of a drug.

should not be used to prolong the life of an individual when death is imminent (Dunlay & others, 2012). An advance directive must be signed while the individual still is able to think clearly (Spoelhof & Elliott, 2012). A study of end-of-life planning revealed that only 15 percent of patients 18 years of age and older had a living will (Clements, 2009). Almost 90 percent of the patients reported that it was important to discuss health care wishes with their family, but only 60 percent of them had done so.

Recently, Physician Orders for Life-Sustaining Treatment (POLST), a document that is more specific than previous advance directives, was created (Bomba, Kemp, & Black, 2012; Hammes & others, 2012). POLST translates treatment preferences into medical orders such as those involving cardiopulmonary resuscitation, extent of treatment, and artificial nutrition via a tube (Fromme & others, 2012). POLST involves the health care professional and the patient or surrogate in stating the wishes of the patient. POLST is currently available or being considered in 34 states.

How Would You...?
As a social worker, how would you explain to individuals the advantages of engaging in advance care planning?

Euthanasia

Euthanasia ("easy death") is the act of painlessly ending the lives of individuals who are suffering from an incurable disease or severe disability (Augestad & others, 2012). Sometimes euthanasia is called "mercy killing." Distinctions are made between two types of euthanasia: passive and active. **Passive euthanasia** occurs when a person is allowed to die by withholding available treatment, such as withdrawing a life-sustaining device. For example, this might involve turning off a respirator or a heart-lung machine. **Active euthanasia** occurs when death is deliberately induced, as when a lethal dose of a drug is injected.

Technological advances in life-support devices raise the issue of quality of life (Blanker & others, 2012). Nowhere was this more apparent than in the highly publicized case of Terri Schiavo, who suffered severe brain damage related to cardiac arrest and a lack of oxygen to the brain (Givens & Mitchell, 2009). She went into a coma and spent 15 years in a vegetative state. Across the 15 years, the question of whether passive euthanasia should be implemented, or whether she should be kept in the vegetative state with the hope that her condition might change for the better, was debated between family members and eventually at a number of levels in the judicial system. At one point toward the end of her life in early spring 2005, a judge ordered that her feeding tube be removed. However, subsequent appeals led to its reinsertion twice. The feeding tube was removed a third and final time on March 18, 2005, and she died 13 days later. Withholding the life-support system allowed Terri Schiavo to die from passive euthanasia.

Should individuals like Terri Schiavo be kept alive in a vegetative state? The trend is toward acceptance of passive euthanasia in the case of terminally ill patients (Seay, 2011). However, one study revealed that family members were reluctant to have their relatives disconnected from a ventilator but rather wanted an escalation of

Terri Schiavo (*right*) shown with her mother in an undated photo. *What issues did the Terri Schiavo case raise?*

How Would You...?

As a psychologist, how would you counsel the family of a brain-dead patient on the topic of euthanasia when there is no living will or advance directive for guidance?

treatment for them (Sviri & others, 2009). In this study, most of the individuals said that in similar circumstances they would not want to be chronically ventilated or resuscitated.

The most widely publicized cases of active euthanasia involve "assisted suicide." Jack Kevorkian, a Michigan physician, assisted a number of terminally ill patients in ending their lives. After a series of trials, Kevorkian was convicted in the state of Michigan of second-degree murder and served eight years in prison. He was released from prison at age 79 for good behavior in June 2007 and promised not to participate in any further assisted suicides. Kevorkian died recently at the age of 83.

Active euthanasia is a crime in most countries and in all states in the United States except two—Oregon and Washington. In 1994, the state of Oregon passed the Death with Dignity Act, which allows active euthanasia. Through 2001, 91 individuals were known to have died by active euthanasia in Oregon. In January 2006, the U.S. Supreme Court upheld Oregon's active euthanasia law. Active euthanasia is legal in the Netherlands, Belgium, Luxembourg, and Uruguay (Smets & others, 2010; Watson, 2009).

A Dutch study of almost 7,000 dying persons revealed that only 7 percent requested passive or active euthanasia, and of those who requested it, approximately one-third of the requests were granted (Onwuteaka-Philipsen & others, 2010). Also, a recent study found that approximately 50 percent of the requests for euthanasia were granted in Belgium (Van Wesemael & others, 2011). And another study found that in the Netherlands approximately 75 percent of the requests for euthanasia came from cancer patients and the main reason for the requests was pain (van Alphen, Donker, & Marquet, 2010).

Needed: Better Care for Dying Individuals

Too often, death in America is lonely, prolonged, and painful. Scientific advances sometimes have made dying harder by delaying the inevitable. Also, even though painkillers are available, too many people experience severe pain during their last days and months of life. Many health-care professionals have not been trained to provide adequate end-of-life care or to understand its importance.

Care providers are increasingly interested in helping individuals experience a "good death" (Cheng & others, 2012; Lemond & Allen, 2011). One view is that a good death involves physical comfort, support from loved ones, acceptance, and appropriate medical care. For some individuals, a good death involves accepting one's impending death and not feeling like a burden to others (Carr, 2009).

Hospice is a program committed to making the end of life as free from pain, anxiety, and depression as possible (Fauci & others, 2012). Whereas a hospital's goals are to cure illness and prolong life, hospice care emphasizes **palliative care,** which involves reducing pain and suffering and helping individuals die with dignity. Hospice-care professionals work together to treat the dying person's symptoms, make the individual as comfortable as possible, show interest in the person and the person's family, and help them all cope with death (Bull & others, 2012; Junger & others, 2012).

Today more hospice programs are home-based, a blend of institutional and home care designed to humanize the end-of-life experience for the dying person. To read about the work of a home hospice nurse, see *Careers in Life-Span Development.*

How Would You...?

As a human development and family studies professional, how would you advocate for a terminally ill person's desire for hospice care?

hospice A program committed to making the end of life as free from pain, anxiety, and depression as possible. The goals of hospice care contrast with those of a hospital, which are to cure disease and prolong life.

palliative care Emphasized in hospice care; involves reducing pain and suffering and helping individuals die with dignity.

Kathy McLaughlin, Home Hospice Nurse

Kathy McLaughlin is a home hospice nurse in Alexandria, Virginia. She provides care for individuals with terminal cancer, Alzheimer disease, and other diseases. There currently is a shortage of home hospice nurses in the United States.

Kathy says that she has seen too many people dying in pain, away from home, hooked up to needless machines. In her work as a home hospice nurse, she comments, "I know I'm making a difference. I just feel privileged to get the chance to meet this person who is not going to be around much longer. I want to enjoy the moment with this person. And I want them to enjoy the moment. They have great stories. They are better than novels" (McLaughlin, 2003, p. 1).

Kathy McLaughlin with her hospice patient Mary Monteiro.

Hospice nurses, like Kathy McLaughlin, care for terminally ill patients and seek to make their remaining days in life as pain-free and comfortable as possible. They typically spend several hours a day in the terminally ill patient's home, serving not just as a medical caregiver but also as an emotional caregiver. Hospice nurses usually coordinate the patient's care through an advising physician.

Hospice nurses must be registered nurses (RNs) plus be certified for hospice work. Educational requirements are an undergraduate degree in nursing; some hospice nurses also have graduate degrees in nursing. Certification as a hospice nurse requires a current license as an RN, a minimum of two years of experience as an RN in hospice-nursing settings, and passing an exam administered by the National Board for the Certification of Hospice Nurses.

Death and Sociohistorical, Cultural Contexts

Today in the United States, the deaths of older adults account for approximately two-thirds of the 2 million deaths that occur each year. Thus, what we know about death, dying, and grieving mainly is based on information about older adults. Youthful death is far less common. When, where, and how people die have changed historically in the United States. Also, attitudes toward death vary across cultures.

Changing Historical Circumstances

We have already described one of the historical changes involving death—the increasing complexity of determining when someone is truly dead. Another historical change involves the age group in which death most often strikes. Two hundred years ago, almost one of every two children died before the age of 10, and one parent died before children grew up. Today, death occurs most often among older adults (Carr, 2009). In the United States, life expectancy has increased from 47 years for a person born in 1900 to 78 years for someone born today (U.S. Census Bureau, 2008). In 1900, most people died at home, cared for by their family. As our population has aged and become more mobile, growing numbers of older adults die apart from their families (Carr, 2009). In the United States today, more than 80 percent of all deaths occur in institutions or hospitals. The care of a dying older person has shifted away from the family and minimized our exposure to death and its painful surroundings (Gold, 2011).

Death in Different Cultures

Cultural variations characterize the experience of death and attitudes about death (Bruce, 2007). Individuals are more conscious of death in times of war, famine, and plague.

Most societies throughout history have had philosophical or religious beliefs about death, and most societies have a ritual that deals with death (see Figure 17.1). Death may be seen as a punishment for one's sins, an act of atonement, or a judgment of a just God. For some, death means loneliness; for others, death is a quest for happiness. For still others, death represents redemption, a relief from the trials and tribulations of the earthly world. Some embrace death and welcome it; others abhor and fear it. For those who welcome it, death may be seen as the fitting end to a fulfilled life. From this perspective, how we depart from earth is influenced by how we have lived.

In most societies, death is not viewed as the end of existence—although the biological body has died, the spirit is believed to live on (Hedayat, 2006). This religious perspective is favored by most Americans as well. Cultural variations in attitudes toward death include belief in reincarnation, which is an important aspect of the Hindu and Buddhist religions. In the Gond culture of India, death is believed to be caused by magic and demons.

In many ways, we in the United States are death avoiders and death deniers (Norouzieh, 2005). This denial can take many forms: the tendency of the funeral industry to gloss over death and fashion lifelike qualities in the dead; the persistent search for a "fountain of youth"; the rejection and isolation of the aged, who may remind us of death; and the medical community's emphasis on prolonging biological life rather than on diminishing human suffering.

Figure 17.1
A Ritual Associated with Death Family memorial day at the national cemetery in Seoul, South Korea.

Facing One's Own Death

Most dying individuals want an opportunity to make some decisions regarding their own life and death (Kastenbaum, 2012). Some individuals want to complete unfinished business; they want time to resolve problems and conflicts and to put their affairs in order (Emanuel, Bennett, & Richardson, 2007). Might there be a sequence of stages we go through as we face death?

Kübler-Ross' Stages of Dying

Elisabeth Kübler-Ross (1969) divided the behavior and thinking of dying persons into five stages: denial and isolation, anger, bargaining, depression, and acceptance.

Denial and isolation is Kübler-Ross' first stage of dying, in which the person denies that death is really going to take place. The person may say, "No, it can't be me. It's not possible." This is a common reaction to terminal illness. However, denial is usually only a temporary defense. It is eventually replaced with increased awareness when the person is confronted with such matters as financial considerations, unfinished business, and worry about surviving family members.

Anger is Kübler-Ross' second stage of dying, in which the dying person recognizes that denial can no longer be maintained. Denial often gives way to anger, resentment, rage, and envy. The dying person's question is "Why me?" At this point, the person becomes increasingly difficult to care for as anger may become displaced and projected onto physicians, nurses, family members, and even God. The realization of loss is great, and those who symbolize life, energy, and competent functioning are especially salient targets of the dying person's resentment and jealousy.

Bargaining is Kübler-Ross' third stage of dying, in which the person develops the hope that death can somehow be postponed or delayed. Some persons enter into a bargaining or negotiation—often

denial and isolation Kübler-Ross' first stage of dying, in which the dying person denies that she or he is really going to die.

anger Kübler-Ross' second stage of dying, in which the dying person's denial often gives way to anger, resentment, rage, and envy.

bargaining Kübler-Ross' third stage of dying, in which the dying person develops the hope that death can somehow be postponed.

depression Kübler-Ross' fourth stage of dying, in which the dying person comes to accept the certainty of her or his death. A period of depression or preparatory grief may appear.

acceptance Kübler-Ross' fifth stage of dying, in which the dying person develops a sense of peace, an acceptance of her or his fate, and in many cases, a desire to be left alone.

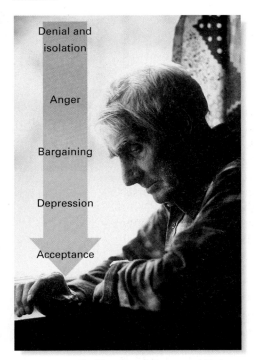

Figure 17.2 Kübler-Ross' Stages of Dying
According to Elisabeth Kübler-Ross, we go through five stages of dying: denial and isolation, anger, bargaining, depression, and acceptance. *Does everyone go through these stages, or go through them in the same order? Explain.*

with God—as they try to delay their death. Psychologically, the person is saying, "Yes, me, but . . ." In exchange for a few more days, weeks, or months of life, the person promises to lead a reformed life dedicated to God or to the service of others.

Depression is Kübler-Ross' fourth stage of dying, in which the dying person comes to accept the certainty of death. At this point, a period of depression or preparatory grief may appear. The dying person may become silent, refuse visitors, and spend much of the time crying or grieving. This behavior is normal and is an effort to disconnect the self from love objects. Attempts to cheer up the dying person at this stage should be discouraged, says Kübler-Ross, because the dying person has a need to contemplate impending death.

Acceptance is Kübler-Ross' fifth stage of dying, in which the person develops a sense of peace, an acceptance of his or her fate, and in many cases, a desire to be left alone. In this stage, feelings and physical pain may be virtually absent. Kübler-Ross describes this fifth stage as the end of the dying struggle, the final resting stage before death. A summary of Kübler-Ross' dying stages is presented in Figure 17.2.

What is the current evaluation of Kübler-Ross' approach? According to Robert Kastenbaum (2009, 2012), there are some problems with Kübler-Ross' approach. For example, the existence of the five-stage sequence has not been demonstrated by either Kübler-Ross or independent research. Also, the stage interpretation neglected the patients' situations, including relationship support, specific effects of illness, family obligations, and the institutional climate in which they were interviewed. However, Kübler-Ross' pioneering efforts were important in calling attention to those who are attempting to cope with life-threatening illnesses. She did much to encourage attention to the quality of life for dying persons and their families.

How Would You...?
As a psychologist, how would you prepare a dying individual for the emotional and psychological stages they may go through as they approach death?

Perceived Control and Denial

Perceived control may work as an adaptive strategy for some older adults who face death. When individuals are led to believe they can influence and control events—such as prolonging their lives—they may become more alert and cheerful. Remember from Chapter 15 that giving nursing home residents options for control improved their attitudes and increased their longevity (Rodin & Langer, 1977).

Denial also may be a fruitful way for some individuals to approach death. It can be adaptive or maladaptive. Denial can be used to avoid the destructive impact of shock by delaying the necessity of dealing with one's death. Denial can insulate the individual from having to cope with intense feelings of anger and hurt; however, if denial keeps us from having a life-saving operation, it clearly is maladaptive. Denial is neither good nor bad; its adaptive qualities need to be evaluated on an individual basis.

How Would You...?
As a human development and family studies professional, how would you advise family members to empower dying loved ones to feel they have more control over the end of their lives?

Coping with the Death of Someone Else

Loss can come in many forms in our lives—divorce, a pet's death, loss of a job, loss of a limb—but no loss is greater than that which comes through the death of someone we love and care for—a parent, sibling, spouse, relative, or friend. In the ratings of life's stresses that require the most adjustment, death of a spouse is given the highest number. How should we communicate with a dying individual? How does grieving help us cope with the death of someone we love? How do we make sense of the world when a loved one has passed away? What are the effects on someone after losing a life partner? And what are some forms of mourning and funeral rites?

Communicating with a Dying Person

Most psychologists believe that it is best for dying individuals to know that they are dying and for significant others to know that their loved one is dying, so they can interact and communicate with each other on the basis of this mutual knowledge (Banja, 2005). What are some of the advantages of this open awareness for the dying individual? First, dying individuals can close their lives in accord with their own ideas about proper dying. Second, they may be able to complete some plans and projects, can make arrangements for survivors, and can participate in decisions about a funeral and burial. Third, dying individuals have the opportunity to reminisce, to converse with others who have been important to them, and to end life conscious of what life has been like. And fourth, dying individuals have more understanding of what is happening within their bodies and what the medical staff is doing for them (Kalish, 1981).

In addition to keeping communication open, what are some suggestions for conversing with a dying individual? Some experts believe that conversation should not focus on mental pathology or preparation for death but instead on strengths of the individual and preparation for the remainder of life. Because external accomplishments are not possible, communication should be directed more at internal growth. Keep in mind also that important support for a dying individual may come not only from mental health professionals but also from nurses, physicians, a spouse, or intimate friends (DeSpelder & Strickland, 2005).

Effective strategies for communicating with a dying person include the following:

1. Establish your presence, be at the same eye level; don't be afraid to touch the dying person—dying individuals are often starved for human touch.

2. Eliminate distractions—for example, ask if it is okay to turn off the TV. Realize that excessive small talk can be a distraction.

3. Dying individuals who are very frail often have little energy. If the dying person you are visiting is very frail, you may want to keep your visit short.

4. Don't insist that the dying person feel acceptance about death if the dying person wants to deny the reality of the situation; on the other hand, don't insist on denial if the dying individual indicates acceptance.

5. Allow the dying person to express guilt or anger; encourage the expression of feelings.

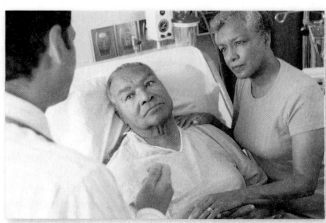

What are some good strategies for communicating with a dying person?

6. Ask the person what the expected outcome for the illness is. Discuss alternatives and unfinished business.

7. Sometimes dying individuals have limited access to other people. Ask the dying person if there is anyone he or she would like to see that you can contact.

8. Encourage the dying individual to reminisce, especially if you have memories in common.

9. Talk with the individual when she or he wishes to talk. If this is impossible, make an appointment for a later time, and keep it.

10. Express your regard for the dying individual. Don't be afraid to express love, and don't be afraid to say good-bye.

Grieving

Grief is a complex emotional state that is an evolving process with multiple dimensions. Our exploration of grief focuses on dimensions of grieving and how coping may vary with the type of death.

Dimensions of Grieving

Grief is the emotional numbness, disbelief, separation anxiety, despair, sadness, and loneliness that accompany the loss of someone we love. An important dimension of grief is pining for the lost person. Pining or yearning reflects an intermittent, recurrent wish or need to recover the lost person. Another important dimension of grief is separation anxiety, which not only includes pining and preoccupation with thoughts of the deceased person but also focuses on places and things associated with the deceased, as well as crying or sighing. Grief may also involve despair and sadness, which include a sense of hopelessness and defeat, depressive symptoms, apathy, loss of meaning for activities that used to involve the person who is gone, and growing desolation (Shear & Skritskaya, 2012).

These feelings occur repeatedly shortly after a loss (Shear, 2012a, b). As time passes, pining and protest over the loss tend to diminish, although episodes of depression and apathy may remain or increase. The sense of separation anxiety and loss may continue to the end of one's life, but most of us emerge from grief's tears, turning our attention once again to productive tasks and regaining a more positive view of life (Lund & others, 2009).

The grieving process is more like a roller-coaster ride than an orderly progression of stages with clear-cut time frames (Wakefield, 2012). The ups and downs of grief often involve rapidly changing emotions, meeting the challenges of learning new skills, detecting personal weaknesses and limitations, creating new patterns of behavior, and forming new friendships and relationships. For most individuals, grief becomes more manageable over time, with fewer abrupt highs and lows. But many grieving spouses report that even though time has brought some healing, they have never gotten over their loss. They have just learned to live with it.

An estimated 80 to 90 percent of survivors experience normal or uncomplicated grief reactions that include sadness and even disbelief or considerable anguish. By six months after their loss, they accept it as a

How Would You...?
As a social worker, how would you respond to bereaved clients who ask, "What is normal grieving?" as they attempt to cope with the death of a loved one?

What are some different types of grieving?

grief The emotional numbness, disbelief, separation anxiety, despair, sadness, and loneliness that accompany the loss of someone we love.

reality, are more optimistic about the future, and function competently in their everyday lives. However, six months after their loss, approximately 10 to 20 percent of survivors have difficulty moving on with their life, feel numb or detached, believe their life is empty without the deceased, and feel that the future has no meaning. This type of grief, which involves enduring despair that is still unresolved over an extended period of time, has been labeled **complicated grief or prolonged grief disorder** by Holly Prigerson and her colleagues (Givens & others, 2011; Morina, von Lersner, & Prigerson, 2011; Prigerson & others, 2011). Prolonged grief usually has negative consequences on physical and mental health (Greer & others, 2011; Wetherell, 2012). A person who loses someone on whom he or she was emotionally dependent is often at greatest risk for developing prolonged grief (Gupta & Bonanno, 2011; Rodriquez Villar & others, 2012). Complicated grief or prolonged grief disorder is now being considered for possible inclusion in DSM-V, the psychiatric classification system of mental health disorders (Bryant, 2012; Shear & others, 2012a, b).

<aside>
complicated grief or prolonged grief disorder Grief that involves enduring despair and is still unresolved over an extended period of time.
</aside>

Recently, there has been a substantial increase in research on complicated grief (Burton & others, 2012). The following studies provide further information about the nature of complicated grief:

- Prolonged grief was more likely to occur when individuals had lost their spouse, lost a loved one unexpectedly, or spent time with the deceased every day in the last week of the person's life (Fujisawa & others, 2010).
- Adults with depression were more likely to also have complicated grief (Sung & others, 2011).
- Complicated grief was more likely to be present in older adults when the grief was in response to the death of a child or a spouse (Newsom & others, 2011).

Another type of grief is *disenfranchised grief*, which describes an individual's grief over a deceased person that is a socially ambiguous loss that can't be openly mourned or supported (Hendry, 2009). Examples of disenfranchised grief include a relationship that isn't socially recognized such as an ex-spouse, a hidden loss such as an abortion, and circumstances of the death that are stigmatized such as death because of AIDS. Disenfranchised grief may intensify an individual's grief because it cannot be publicly acknowledged. This type of grief may be hidden or repressed for many years, only to be reawakened by later deaths.

Coping and Type of Death

The impact of death on surviving individuals is strongly influenced by the circumstances under which the death occurs (Gold, 2011; Kristensen, Weisaeth, & Heir, 2012). Deaths that are sudden, untimely, violent, or traumatic are likely to have more intense and prolonged effects on surviving individuals and make the coping process more difficult for them (Maercker & Lalor, 2012). Such deaths often are accompanied by post-traumatic stress disorder (PTSD) symptoms, such as intrusive thoughts, flashbacks, nightmares, sleep disturbances, problems in concentrating, and others (Nakajima & others, 2012). The death of a child can be especially devastating and extremely difficult for parents (Caeymaex & others, 2012).

Making Sense of the World

One beneficial aspect of grieving is that it stimulates many individuals to try to make sense of their world (Park, 2010, 2012). A common occurrence is to go over again and again all of the events that led up to the death. In the days and weeks after the death, the closest family members share memories with each other, sometimes reminiscing about family experiences.

When a death is caused by an accident or a disaster, the effort to make sense of it is pursued more vigorously. As added pieces of news come trickling in, they are integrated into the puzzle. The bereaved want to put the death into a perspective that they can understand—divine intervention, a curse from a neighboring

These restaurant workers, who lost their jobs on 9/11/01, have made a bittersweet return with a New York restaurant they call their own. Colors, named for the many nationalities and ethnic groups among its owners, is believed to be the city's first cooperative restaurant. World-famous restaurant Windows on the World was destroyed and 73 workers killed when the Twin Towers were destroyed by terrorists. The former Windows survivors at the new venture will split 60 percent of the profits between themselves and donate the rest to a fund to open other cooperative restaurants.

tribe, a logical sequence of cause and effect, or whatever it may be. A study of more than 1,000 college students found that making sense was an important factor in their grieving of a violent loss by accident, homicide, or suicide (Currier, Holland, & Neimeyer, 2006).

Losing a Life Partner

In 2009 in the United States, 13 percent of men and 41 percent of women age 65 and older were widowed (U.S. Census Bureau, 2011). Those left behind after the death of an intimate partner often suffer profound grief and often endure financial loss, loneliness, increased physical illness, and psychological disorders, including depression (Holm & Severinsson, 2012). A recent study of widowed individuals 75 years and older found that loss of a spouse increases the likelihood of psychiatric visits and an earlier death (Moller & others, 2011).

How surviving spouses cope varies considerably (Hahn & others, 2011; Park, 2012). A six-year longitudinal study of individuals 80+ years of age found that the loss of a spouse, especially in men, was related to a lower level of life satisfaction over time (Berg & others, 2009). Another study concluded that chronic grief was more likely to characterize bereaved spouses who were highly dependent on their spouse (Ott & others, 2007). And another study revealed that finding meaning in the death of a spouse was linked to a lower level of anger during bereavement (Kim, 2009).

Many widows are lonely. The poorer and less educated they are, the lonelier they tend to be. The bereaved are also at increased risk for many health problems (Ha & Ingersoll-Dayton, 2011).

For either widows or widowers, social support helps them adjust to the death of a spouse (Ben Zur, 2012; Utz, Caserta, & Lund, 2012). The Widow-to-Widow program, begun in the 1960s, provides support for newly widowed women. Volunteer widows reach out to other widows, introducing them to others who may have similar problems, leading group discussions, and organizing social activities. The program has been adopted by the American Association of Retired Persons and disseminated throughout the United States as the Widowed Persons Service. The model has since been adopted by numerous community organizations to provide support for those going through a difficult transition.

How Would You...?

As a social worker, how would you help a widow or widower to connect with a support group to deal with the death of a loved one?

Forms of Mourning

One decision facing the bereaved is what to do with the body. In the United States, in 2007, 66 percent of corpses were disposed of by burial, 34 percent by cremation—a significant increase from 15 percent in 1985 (Cremation Association of North America, 2012). Projections indicate that by 2015, 44 percent of corpses will be cremated (Cremation Association of North America, 2012). Cremation is more popular in the Pacific region of the United States, less popular in the South. Cremation also is more popular in Canada than in the United States and most popular of all in Japan and many other Asian countries.

The funeral industry has been a target of controversy in recent years. Funeral directors and their supporters argue that the funeral provides a form of closure to the relationship with the deceased, especially when there is an open casket. Their critics claim that funeral directors are just trying to make money and that embalming is grotesque. One way to avoid being exploited during bereavement is to purchase funeral arrangements in advance.

The family and the community have important roles in mourning in some cultures. Two of those cultures are the Amish and traditional Judaism (Worthington, 1989). The Amish are a conservative group with approximately 80,000 members in the United States, Ontario, and several small settlements in South and Central America. The Amish live in a family-oriented society in which family and community support are essential for survival. Today, they live at the same unhurried pace as that of their ancestors, using horses instead of cars and facing death with the same steadfast faith as their forebears. At the time of death, close neighbors assume the responsibility of notifying others of the death. The Amish community handles virtually all aspects of the funeral.

Meeting in a Jewish graveyard.

The funeral service is held in a barn in warmer months and in a house during colder months. Calm acceptance of death, influenced by a deep religious faith, is an integral part of the Amish culture. Following the funeral, a high level of support is given to the bereaved family for at least a year. Visits to the family, special scrapbooks and handmade items for the family, new work projects started for the widow, and quilting days that combine fellowship and productivity are among the supports given to the bereaved family.

We have arrived at the end of this book. Our study of the human life span has been long and complex. You have read about many physical, cognitive, and socioemotional changes that take place from conception through death. This is a good time to reflect on what you have learned. Which theories, studies, and ideas were especially interesting to you? What did you learn about your own development?

I hope this book and course have been a window to the life span of the human species and a window to your own personal journey in life. I wish you all the best in the remaining years of your journey through the human life span.

John W. Santrock

Summary

Defining Death and Life/Death Issues

- Most physicians today agree that the higher and lower portions of the brain must stop functioning in order for an individual to be considered *brain dead*.

- Decisions regarding life, death, and health care can involve a number of circumstances and issues, and individuals can use a living will to make these choices

while they can still think clearly. Hospice care emphasizes reducing pain and suffering rather than prolonging life.

Death and Sociohistorical, Cultural Contexts

- Over the years, the circumstances of when, where, and why people die have changed. Throughout history, most societies have had philosophical or religious beliefs about death, and most societies have rituals that deal with death.

- The United States has been described as a death-denying and death-avoiding culture.

Facing One's Own Death

- Kübler-Ross proposed five stages of facing death, and although her view has been criticized, her efforts were important in calling attention to the experience of coping with life-threatening illness.

- Perceived control over events and denial may work together as an adaptive orientation for a dying individual.

Coping with the Death of Someone Else

- Most psychologists recommend an open communication system with someone who is dying and their significant others.

- Grief is multidimensional and in some cases may last for years. Complicated grief or prolonged grief disorder and disenfranchised grief are especially challenging.

- The grieving process may stimulate individuals to strive to make sense out of the world.

- Usually the most difficult loss is the death of a spouse. The bereaved are at increased risk for health problems.

- Forms of mourning vary across cultures.

Key Terms

brain death 413
euthanasia 414
passive euthanasia 414
active euthanasia 414

hospice 415
palliative care 415
denial and isolation 417
anger 417

bargaining 417
depression 418
acceptance 418
grief 420

complicated grief or prolonged grief disorder 421

Glossary

A

A-not-B error This term is used to describe the tendency of infants to reach where an object was located earlier rather than where the object was last hidden.

acceptance Kübler-Ross' fifth stage of dying, in which the dying person develops a sense of peace, an acceptance of her or his fate, and, in many cases, a desire to be left alone.

accommodation Piagetian concept of adjusting schemes to fit new information and experiences.

active euthanasia Death induced deliberately, as by injecting a lethal dose of a drug.

activity theory The theory that the more active and involved older adults are, the more likely they are to be satisfied with their lives.

adolescent egocentrism The heightened self-consciousness of adolescents.

adoption study A study in which investigators seek to discover whether, in behavior and psychological characteristics, adopted children are more like their adoptive parents, who provided a home environment, or more like their biological parents, who contributed their heredity. Another form of the adoption study compares adoptive and biological siblings.

aerobic exercise Sustained exercise (such as jogging, swimming, or cycling) that stimulates heart and lung activity.

affectionate love In this type of love, also called companionate love, an individual desires to have the other person near and has a deep, caring affection for the other person.

ageism Prejudice against other people because of their age, especially prejudice against older adults.

Alzheimer disease A progressive, irreversible brain disorder characterized by a gradual deterioration of memory, reasoning, language, and eventually physical function.

amygdala The region of the brain that is the seat of emotions.

androgyny The presence of positive masculine and feminine characteristics in the same individual.

anger Kübler-Ross' second stage of dying, in which the dying person's denial often gives way to anger, resentment, rage, and envy.

anger cry A cry similar to the basic cry, with more excess air forced through the vocal cords.

animism The belief that inanimate objects have lifelike qualities and are capable of action.

anorexia nervosa An eating disorder that involves the relentless pursuit of thinness through starvation.

anxious attachment style An attachment style that describes adults who demand closeness, are less trusting, and are more emotional, jealous, and possessive.

Apgar Scale A widely used assessment of the newborn's health at 1 and 5 minutes after birth.

arthritis Inflammation of the joints that is accompanied by pain, stiffness, and movement problems; especially common in older adults.

assimilation Piagetian concept of using existing schemes to deal with new information or experiences.

attachment A close emotional bond between two people.

attention The focusing of mental resources on select information.

attention deficit hyperactivity disorder (ADHD) A disability in which children consistently show one or more of the following characteristics: (1) inattention, (2) hyperactivity, and (3) impulsivity.

authoritarian parenting A restrictive punitive style in which parents exhort the child to follow their directions and to respect work and effort. The authoritarian parent places firm limits and controls on the child and allows little verbal exchange. Authoritarian parenting is associated with children's social incompetence.

authoritative parenting A parenting style in which parents encourage their children to be independent but still place limits and controls on their actions. Extensive verbal give-and-take is allowed, and parents are warm and nurturant toward the child. Authoritative parenting is associated with children's social competence.

autism spectrum disorders (ASD) Also called pervasive developmental disorders, they range from the severe disorder labeled autistic disorder to the milder disorder called Asperger syndrome. These disorders are characterized by problems in social interaction, verbal and nonverbal communication, and repetitive behaviors.

autonomous morality The second stage of moral development in Piaget's theory, displayed by older children (about 10 years of age and older). The child becomes aware that rules and laws are created by people and, in judging an action, one should consider the actor's intentions as well as the consequences.

average children Children who receive an average number of both positive and negative nominations from their peers.

avoidant attachment style An attachment style that describes adults who are hesitant about getting involved in romantic relationships and once in a relationship tend to distance themselves from their partner.

B

bargaining Kübler-Ross' third stage of dying, in which the dying person develops the hope that death can somehow be postponed.

basic cry A rhythmic pattern usually consisting of a cry, a briefer silence, a shorter inspiratory whistle that is higher pitched than the main cry, and then a brief rest before the next cry.

behavioral and social cognitive theories Theories that hold that development can be described in terms of the behaviors learned through interactions with the environment.

behavior genetics The field that seeks to discover the influence of heredity and environment on individual differences in human traits and development.

big five factors of personality Openness to experience, conscientiousness, extraversion, agreeableness, and neuroticism (emotional stability).

biological processes Changes in an individual's physical nature.

brain death A neurological definition of death. A person is brain dead when all electrical activity of the brain has ceased for a specified period of time. A flat EEG recording is one criterion of brain death.

Bronfenbrenner's ecological theory Bronfenbrenner's environmental systems theory that focuses on five environmental systems: microsystem, mesosystem, exosystem, macrosystem, and chronosystem.

bulimia nervosa An eating disorder in which the individual consistently follows a binge-and-purge pattern.

C

care perspective The moral perspective of Carol Gilligan, which views people in terms of their connectedness with others and emphasizes interpersonal communication, relationships with others, and concern for others.

case study An in-depth examination of an individual.

cataracts Involve a thickening of the lens of the eye that causes vision to become cloudy, opaque, and distorted.

cellular clock theory Leonard Hayflick's theory that the maximum number of times that human cells can divide is about 75 to 80. As we age, our cells become increasingly less capable of dividing.

centration The focusing of attention on one characteristic to the exclusion of all others.

cephalocaudal pattern The sequence in which the earliest growth always occurs at the top—the head—with physical growth in size, weight, and feature differentiation gradually working from top to bottom.

child-centered kindergarten Education that involves the whole child by considering both the child's physical, cognitive, and socioemotional development and the child's needs, interests, and learning styles.

child-directed speech Language spoken in a higher pitch than normal with simple words and sentences.

chromosomes Threadlike structures made up of deoxyribonucleic acid, or DNA.

climacteric The midlife transition in which fertility declines.

clique A small group that ranges from 2 to about 12 individuals, averaging about 5 to 6 individuals, and can form because adolescents engage in similar activities.

cognitive processes Changes in an individual's thought, intelligence, and language.

cohort effects Effects that are due to a subject's time of birth or generation but not age.

commitment Marcia's term for the part of identity development in which adolescents show a personal investment in forming an identity.

complicated grief or prolonged grief disorder Grief that involves enduring despair and is still unresolved over an extended period of time.

concepts Cognitive groupings of similar objects, events, people, or ideas.

conservation In Piaget's theory, awareness that altering an object's or a substance's appearance does not change its basic properties.

constructive play Play that combines sensorimotor and repetitive activity with symbolic representation of ideas. Constructive play occurs when children engage in self-regulated creation or construction of a product or a problem solution.

constructivist approach A learner-centered approach that emphasizes the importance of individuals actively constructing their knowledge and understanding with guidance from the teacher.

contemporary life-events approach An approach that emphasizes that how a life event influences the individual's development depends not only on the life event, but also on mediating factors, the individual's adaptation to the life event, the life-stage context, and the sociohistorical context.

context The setting in which development occurs, which is influenced by historical, economic, social, and cultural factors.

continuity-discontinuity issue The debate about the extent to which development involves gradual, cumulative change (continuity) or distinct stages (discontinuity).

controversial children Children who are frequently nominated both as someone's best friend and as being disliked.

conventional reasoning The second, or intermediate, level in Kohlberg's theory of moral development. At this level, individuals abide by certain standards, but they are the standards of others, such as parents or the laws of society.

convergent thinking Thinking that produces one correct answer and is characteristic of the kind of thinking tested by standardized intelligence tests.

core knowledge approach States that infants are born with domain-specific innate knowledge systems.

corpus callosum The location where fibers connect the brain's left and right hemispheres.

correlational research A type of research that focuses on describing the strength of the relation between two or more events or characteristics.

correlation coefficient A number based on statistical analysis that is used to describe the degree of association between two variables.

creative thinking The ability to think in novel and unusual ways and to come up with unique solutions to problems.

crisis Marcia's term for a period of identity development during which the adolescent is exploring alternatives.

critical thinking Thinking reflectively and productively, as well as evaluating the evidence.

cross-cultural studies Comparisons of one culture with one or more other cultures. These provide information on the degree to which children's development is similar, or universal, across cultures, and to the degree to which it is culture-specific.

cross-sectional approach A research strategy in which individuals of different ages are compared at one time.

crowd A larger group structure than a clique, a crowd is usually formed based on reputation, and members may or may not spend much time together.

crystallized intelligence Accumulated information and verbal skills, which increase in middle age, according to Horn.

cultural-familial intellectual disability Intellectual disability characterized by no evidence of organic brain damage, but the individual's IQ generally is between 50 and 70.

culture The behavior patterns, beliefs, and all other products of a group that are passed on from generation to generation.

culture-fair tests Tests of intelligence that are designed to be free of cultural bias.

cumulative personality model States that with time and age, people become more adept at interacting with their environment in ways that promote the stability of personality.

D

date or acquaintance rape Coercive sexual activity directed at someone with whom the perpetrator is at least casually acquainted.

deferred imitation Imitation that occurs after a delay of hours or days.

dementia A global term for any neurological disorder in which the primary symptoms involve a deterioration of mental functioning.

denial and isolation Kübler-Ross' first stage of dying, in which the dying person denies that she or he is really going to die.

depression Kübler-Ross' fourth stage of dying, in which the dying person comes to accept the certainty of her or his death. A period of depression or preparatory grief may appear.

descriptive research Type of research that aims to observe and record behavior.

development The pattern of movement or change that starts at conception and continues through the human life span.

developmental cascade model Involves connections across domains over time that influence developmental pathways and outcomes.

developmentally appropriate practice (DAP) Education that focuses on the typical developmental patterns of children (age appropriateness) and the uniqueness of each child (individual appropriateness).

difficult child A child who tends to react negatively and cry frequently, who engages in irregular daily routines, and who is slow to accept new experiences.

direct instruction approach A structured, teacher-centered approach that is characterized by teacher direction and control, high teacher expectations for students' progress, maximum time spent by students on learning tasks, and efforts by the teacher to keep negative affect to a minimum.

dishabituation Recovery of a habituated response after a change in stimulation.

divergent thinking Thinking that produces many answers to the same question and is characteristic of creativity.

divided attention Concentrating on more than one activity at the same time.

DNA A complex molecule with a double helix shape that contains genetic information.

domain theory of moral development Theory that identifies different domains of social knowledge and reasoning, including moral, social conventional, and personal domains. These domains arise from children's and adolescents' attempts to understand and deal with different forms of social experience.

Down syndrome A chromosomally transmitted form of intellectual disability, caused by the presence of an extra copy of chromosome 21.

dynamic systems theory The perspective on motor development that seeks to explain how motor behaviors are assembled for perceiving and acting.

E

easy child A child who is generally in a positive mood, who quickly establishes regular routines in infancy, and who adapts easily to new experiences.

eclectic theoretical orientation An approach that selects and uses whatever is considered the best in many theories.

ecological view The view that perception functions to bring organisms in contact with the environment and to increase adaptation.

egocentrism The inability to distinguish between one's own perspective and someone else's (salient feature of the first substage of preoperational thought).

elaboration An important strategy that involves engaging in more extensive processing of information.

eldercare Physical and emotional caretaking for older members of the family, whether by giving day-to-day physical assistance or by being responsible for overseeing such care.

embryonic period The period of prenatal development that occurs two to eight weeks after conception. During the embryonic period, the rate of cell differentiation intensifies, support systems for the cells form, and organs appear.

emerging adulthood The transition from adolescence to adulthood (approximately 18 to 25 years of age) that involves experimentation and exploration.

emotion Feeling, or affect, that occurs when a person is in a state or interaction that is important to them. Emotion is characterized by behavior that reflects (expresses) the pleasantness or unpleasantness of the state a person is in or the transactions being experienced.

empty nest syndrome A term used to indicate a decrease in marital satisfaction after children leave home.

epigenetic view Emphasizes that development is the result of an ongoing, bidirectional interchange between heredity and environment.

episodic memory The retention of information about the where and when of life's happenings.

equilibration A mechanism that Piaget proposed to explain how children shift from one stage of thought to the next.

Erikson's theory A psychoanalytic theory in which eight stages of psychosocial development unfold throughout the human life span. Each stage consists of a unique developmental task that confronts individuals with a crisis that must be faced.

ethnic identity An enduring, basic aspect of the self that includes a sense of membership in an ethnic group and the attitudes and feelings related to that membership.

ethnicity A range of characteristics rooted in cultural heritage, including nationality, race, religion, and language.

ethology An approach that stresses that behavior is strongly influenced by biology, tied to evolution, and characterized by critical or sensitive periods.

euthanasia The act of painlessly ending the lives of persons who are suffering from incurable diseases or severe disabilities; sometimes called "mercy killing."

evolutionary psychology Emphasizes the importance of adaptation, reproduction, and "survival of the fittest" in shaping behavior.

evolutionary theory of aging The view that natural selection has not eliminated many harmful conditions and nonadaptive characteristics in older adults.

executive attention Involves action planning, allocating attention to goals, error detection and compensation, monitoring progress on tasks, and dealing with novel or difficult circumstances.

executive functioning An umbrella-like concept that consists of a number of higher level cognitive processes linked to the development of the brain's prefrontal cortex. Executive functioning involves managing one's thoughts to engage in goal-directed behavior and exercise self-control.

experiment A carefully regulated procedure in which one or more of the factors believed to influence the behavior being studied is manipulated and all other factors are held constant. Experimental research permits the determination of cause.

explicit memory Memory of facts and experiences that individuals consciously know and can state.

F

fetal alcohol spectrum disorders (FASD) A cluster of abnormalities that appears in the offspring of mothers who drink alcohol heavily during pregnancy.

fetal period The prenatal period of development that begins two months after conception and lasts for seven months, on the average.

fight-or-flight The view that when men experience stress, they are more likely to become aggressive, withdraw from social contact, or drink alcohol.

fine motor skills Motor skills that involve finely tuned movements, such as finger dexterity.

fluid intelligence The ability to reason abstractly, which steadily declines from middle adulthood on, according to Horn.

free-radical theory A theory of aging that states that people age because inside their cells normal metabolism produces unstable oxygen molecules known as free radicals. These molecules ricochet around inside cells, damaging DNA and other cellular structures.

fuzzy trace theory States that memory is best understood by considering two types of memory representations: (1) verbatim memory trace and (2) gist. In this theory, older children's better memory is attributed to the fuzzy traces created by extracting the gist of information.

G

games Activities engaged in for pleasure that include rules and often competition with one or more individuals.

gender The psychological and sociocultural dimensions of being female or male.

gender identity The sense of being male or female, which most children acquire by the time they are 3 years old.

gender roles Sets of expectations that prescribe how females or males should think, act, and feel.

gender schema theory The theory that gender typing emerges as children gradually develop gender schemas of what is gender-appropriate and gender-inappropriate in their culture.

gender stereotypes Broad categories that reflect our impressions and beliefs about females and males.

generativity Adults' desire to leave legacies of themselves to the next generation; the positive side of Erikson's generativity versus stagnation middle adulthood stage.

genes Units of hereditary information composed of DNA. Genes direct cells to reproduce themselves and manufacture the proteins that maintain life.

gene x environment (g x e) interaction The interaction of a specified measured variation in DNA and a specific measured aspect of the environment.

genotype A person's genetic heritage; the actual genetic material.

germinal period The period of prenatal development that takes place in the first two weeks after conception. It includes the creation of the zygote, continued cell division, and the attachment of the zygote to the uterine wall.

gifted Having above-average intelligence (an IQ of 130 or higher) and/or superior talent for something.

glaucoma Damage to the optic nerve because of the pressure created by a buildup of fluid in the eye.

gonads The sex glands—the testes in males and the ovaries in females.

goodness of fit Refers to the match between a child's temperament and the environmental demands with which the child must cope.

grief The emotional numbness, disbelief, separation anxiety, despair, sadness, and loneliness that accompany the loss of someone we love.

gross motor skills Motor skills that involve large-muscle activities, such as walking.

H

habituation Decreased responsiveness to a stimulus after repeated presentations of the stimulus.

heteronomous morality Kohlberg's first stage in preconventional reasoning in which moral thinking is tied to punishment.

heteronomous morality The first stage of moral development in Piaget's theory, occurring from approximately 4 to 7 years of age. Justice and rules are conceived of as unchangeable properties of the world, removed from the control of people.

hormonal stress theory The theory that aging in the body's hormonal system can lower resilience under stress and increase the likelihood of disease.

hormones Powerful chemical substances secreted by the endocrine glands and carried through the body by the bloodstream.

hospice A program committed to making the end of life as free from pain, anxiety, and depression as possible. The goals of hospice contrast with those of a hospital, which are to cure disease and prolong life.

hypothalamus A structure in the higher portion of the brain that monitors eating and sex.

hypotheses Assertions or predictions, often derived from theories, that can be tested.

hypothetical-deductive reasoning Piaget's formal operational concept that adolescents have the cognitive ability to develop hypotheses, or best guesses, about ways to solve problems.

I

identity achievement Marcia's term for adolescents who have undergone a crisis and have made a commitment.

identity diffusion Marcia's term for adolescents who have not yet experienced a crisis (explored meaningful alternatives) or made any commitments.

identity foreclosure Marcia's term for adolescents who have made a commitment but have not experienced a crisis.

identity moratorium Marcia's term for adolescents who are in the midst of a crisis, but their commitments are either absent or vaguely defined.

imaginary audience Involves adolescents' belief that others are as interested in them as they themselves are; attention-getting behavior motivated by a desire to be noticed, visible, and "on stage."

immanent justice The concept that, if a rule is broken, punishment will be meted out immediately.

implicit memory Memory without conscious recollection; involves skills and routine procedures that are automatically performed.

inclusion Educating a child with special education needs full-time in the regular classroom.

individualism, instrumental purpose, and exchange The second Kohlberg stage of moral development. At this stage, individuals pursue their own interests but also let others do the same.

individualized education plan (IEP) A written statement that spells out a program tailored to a child with a disability.

indulgent parenting A style of parenting in which parents are highly involved with their children but place few demands or controls on them. Indulgent

parenting is associated with children's social incompetence, especially a lack of self-control.

infinite generativity The ability to produce an endless number of meaningful sentences using a finite set of words and rules.

information-processing theory A theory that emphasizes that individuals manipulate information, monitor it, and strategize about it. The processes of memory and thinking are central.

insecure avoidant babies Babies that show insecurity by avoiding the mother.

insecure disorganized babies Babies that show insecurity by being disorganized and disoriented.

insecure resistant babies Babies that often cling to the caregiver, then resist her by fighting against the closeness, perhaps by kicking or pushing away.

integrity versus despair Erikson's eighth and final stage of development, which individuals experience in late adulthood. This involves reflecting on the past and either piecing together a positive review or concluding that one's life has not been well spent.

intellectual disability A condition of limited mental ability in which an individual has a low IQ, usually below 70 on a traditional test of intelligence, and has difficulty adapting to everyday life.

intelligence Problem-solving skills and the ability to learn from, and adapt to, the experiences of everyday life.

intelligence quotient (IQ) A person's mental age divided by chronological age, multiplied by 100.

intermodal perception The ability to relate and integrate information from two or more sensory modalities, such as vision and hearing.

intuitive thought substage Piaget's second substage of preoperational thought, in which children begin to use primitive reasoning and want to know the answers to all sorts of questions (between about 4 and 7 years of age).

J

joint attention Process that occurs when (1) individuals focus on the same object and track each other's behavior, (2) one individual directs another's attention, and (3) reciprocal interaction is present.

justice perspective A moral perspective that focuses on the rights of the individual; individuals independently make moral decisions.

juvenile delinquent An adolescent who breaks the law or engages in behavior that is considered illegal.

L

laboratory A controlled setting in which research can take place.

language A form of communication, whether spoken, written, or signed, that is based on a system of symbols. Language consists of the words used by a community and the rules for varying and combining them.

language acquisition device (LAD) Chomsky's term that describes a biological endowment enabling the child to detect the features and rules of language, including phonology, syntax, and semantics.

lateralization Specialization of function in one hemisphere of the cerebral cortex or the other.

learning disability Describes a child who has difficulty understanding or using spoken or written language or doing mathematics. To be classified as a learning disability, the problem is not primarily the result of visual, hearing, or motor disabilities; intellectual disability; emotional disorders; or due to environmental, cultural, or economic disadvantage.

least restrictive environment (LRE) The concept that a child with a disability should be educated in a setting that is as similar as possible to the one in which children who do not have a disability are educated.

leisure The pleasant times after work when individuals are free to pursue activities and interests of their own choosing.

life expectancy The number of years that will probably be lived by the average person born in a particular year.

life span The upper boundary of life, the maximum number of years an individual can live. The maximum life span of human beings is about 120 to 125 years of age.

life-span perspective The perspective that development is lifelong, multidimensional, multidirectional, plastic, multidisciplinary, and contextual; that it involves growth, maintenance, and regulation; and that it is constructed through biological, sociocultural, and individual factors working together.

longitudinal approach A research strategy in which the same individuals are studied over a period of time, usually several years or more.

long-term memory A relatively permanent type of memory that holds huge amounts of information for a long period of time.

M

macular degeneration A disease that involves deterioration of the macula of the retina, which corresponds to the focal center of the visual field.

major depression A mood disorder in which the individual is deeply unhappy, demoralized, self-derogatory, and bored. The person does not feel well, loses stamina easily, has poor appetite, and is listless and unmotivated. Major depression is so widespread that it has been called the "common cold" of psychological disorders.

meiosis A specialized form of cell division that occurs to form eggs and sperm (or gametes).

memory A central feature of cognitive development, pertaining to all situations in which an individual retains information over time.

menarche A girl's first menstruation.

menopause The complete cessation of a woman's menstruation, which usually occurs in the late forties or early fifties.

mental age (MA) Binet's measure of an individual's level of mental development, compared with that of others.

metabolic syndrome A condition characterized by hypertension, obesity, and insulin resistance. Metabolic syndrome often leads to the development of diabetes and cardiovascular disease.

metacognition Cognition about cognition, or knowing about knowing.

metalinguistic awareness Refers to knowledge about language, such as knowing what a preposition is or the ability to discuss the sounds of a language.

middle adulthood The developmental period beginning at approximately 40 years of age and extending to about 60 to 65 years of age.

mindset The cognitive view that individuals develop for themselves.

mitosis Cellular reproduction in which the cell's nucleus duplicates itself with two new cells being formed, each containing the same DNA as the parent cell, arranged in the same 23 pairs of chromosomes.

Montessori approach An educational philosophy in which children are given considerable freedom and spontaneity in choosing activities and are allowed to move from one activity to another as they desire.

moral development Development that involves thoughts, feelings, and actions regarding rules and conventions about what people should do in their interactions with other people.

morphology Units of meaning involved in word formation.

mutual interpersonal expectations, relationships, and interpersonal conformity Kohlberg's third stage of moral development. At this stage, individuals value trust, caring, and loyalty to others as a basis of moral judgments.

myelination The process by which the axons are covered and insulated with a layer of fat cells, which increases the speed at which information travels through the nervous system.

N

natural childbirth A childbirth method in which no drugs are given to relieve pain or assist in the birth process. The mother and her partner are taught to use breathing methods and relaxation techniques during delivery.

naturalistic observation Observation that occurs in a real-world setting without an attempt to manipulate the situation.

nature-nurture issue The debate about the extent to which development is influenced by nature and by nurture. Nature refers to an organism's biological inheritance, nurture to its environmental experiences.

neglected children Children who are infrequently nominated as a best friend but are not disliked by their peers.

neglectful parenting A style of parenting in which the parent is very uninvolved in the child's life; it is associated with children's social incompetence, especially a lack of self-control.

neo-Piagetians Developmentalists who have elaborated on Piaget's theory, giving more emphasis to how children use attention, memory, and strategies to process information.

neuroconstructivist view Developmental perspective in which biological processes and environmental conditions influence the brain's development; the brain has plasticity and is context dependent; and cognitive development is closely linked with brain development.

neurons Nerve cells that handle information processing at the cellular level in the brain.

nonnormative life events Unusual occurrences that have a major impact on a person's life. The occurrence, pattern, and sequence of these events are not applicable to many individuals.

normal distribution A symmetrical distribution with most scores falling in the middle of the possible range of scores and few scores appearing toward the extremes of the range.

normative age-graded influences Biological and environmental influences that are similar for individuals in a particular age group.

normative history-graded influences Biological and environmental influences that are associated with history. These influences are common to people of a particular generation.

O

object permanence The Piagetian term for understanding that objects and events continue to exist, even when they cannot directly be seen, heard, or touched.

operations In Piaget's theory, internalized reversible sets of actions that allow children to do mentally what they formerly did physically.

organic intellectual disability Intellectual disability that involves some physical damage and is caused by a genetic disorder or brain damage.

organization Piaget's concept of grouping isolated behaviors and thoughts into a higher-order, more smoothly functioning cognitive system.

organogenesis Organ formation that takes place during the first two months of prenatal development.

osteoporosis A chronic condition that involves an extensive loss of bone tissue and is the main reason many older adults walk with a marked stoop. Women are especially vulnerable to osteoporosis.

P

pain cry A sudden appearance of loud crying without preliminary moaning, followed by breath holding.

palliative care Emphasized in hospice care; involves reducing pain and suffering and helping individuals die with dignity.

Parkinson disease A chronic, progressive disease characterized by muscle tremors, slowing of movement, and partial facial paralysis.

passive euthanasia The withholding of available treatments, such as life-sustaining devices, allowing the person to die.

perception The interpretation of what is sensed.

personal fable The part of adolescent egocentrism that involves an adolescent's sense of uniqueness and invincibility (or invulnerability).

perspective taking The social cognitive process involved in assuming the perspective of others and understanding their thoughts and feelings.

phenotype The way an individual's genotype is expressed in observed and measurable characteristics.

phonics approach The idea that reading instruction should teach the basic rules for translating written symbols into sounds.

phonology The sound system of a language, including the sounds used and how they may be combined.

Piaget's theory The theory that children construct their understanding of the world and go through four stages of cognitive development.

pituitary gland An important endocrine gland that controls growth and regulates other glands, including the gonads.

popular children Children who are frequently nominated as a best friend and are rarely disliked by their peers.

postconventional reasoning The highest level in Kohlberg's theory of moral development. At this level, the individual recognizes alternative moral courses, explores the options, and then decides on a personal moral code.

postformal thought Thinking that is reflective, relativistic, and contextual; provisional; realistic; and influenced by emotions.

postpartum period The period after childbirth when the mother adjusts, both physically and psychologically, to the process of childbearing. This period lasts for about six weeks or until her body has completed its adjustment and returned to a near prepregnant state.

practice play Play that involves repetition of behavior when new skills are being learned or when physical or mental mastery and coordination of skills are required for games or sports.

pragmatics The appropriate use of language in different contexts.

preconventional reasoning The lowest level in Kohlberg's theory of moral development. The individual's moral reasoning is controlled primarily by external rewards and punishment.

preoperational stage Piaget's second stage, lasting from about 2 to 7 years of age, during which children begin to represent the world with words, images, and drawings, and symbolic thought goes beyond simple connections of sensory information and physical action; stable concepts are formed, mental reasoning emerges, egocentrism is present, and magical beliefs are constructed.

prepared childbirth Developed by French obstetrician Ferdinand Lamaze, this childbirth strategy is similar to natural childbirth but includes a special breathing technique to control pushing in the final stages of labor and more detailed anatomy and physiology instruction.

pretense/symbolic play Play in which the child transforms the physical environment into a symbol.

Project Head Start A government-funded program that is designed to provide children from low-income families the opportunity to acquire the skills and experiences important for school success.

proximodistal pattern The sequence in which growth starts at the center of the body and moves toward the extremities.

psychoanalytic theories Theories holding that development depends primarily on the unconscious mind and is heavily couched in emotion, that behavior is merely a surface characteristic, that it is important to analyze the symbolic meanings of behavior, and that early experiences are important in development.

psychoanalytic theory of gender A theory deriving from Freud's view that the preschool child develops a sexual attraction to the opposite-sex parent, by approximately 5 or 6 years of age renounces this attraction because of anxious feelings, and subsequently identifies with the same-sex parent, unconsciously adopting the same-sex parent's characteristics.

puberty A period of rapid physical and sexual maturation that occurs mainly during early adolescence.

R

rape Forcible sexual intercourse with a person who does not consent to it.

rapport talk The language of conversation; it is a way of establishing connections and negotiating relationships.

reciprocal socialization Socialization that is bidirectional; children socialize parents, just as parents socialize children.

reflexive smile A smile that does not occur in response to external stimuli. It appears during the first month after birth, usually during sleep.

rejected children Children who are infrequently nominated as a best friend and are actively disliked by their peers.

report talk Talk that is designed to give information and includes public speaking.

rite of passage A ceremony or ritual that marks an individual's transition from one status to another. Most rites of passage focus on the transition to adult status.

romantic love Also called passionate love, or eros; romantic love has strong sexual and infatuation components and often predominates in the early period of a love relationship.

S

scaffolding Parents time interactions so that infants experience turn-taking with the parents.

schemes In Piaget's theory, actions or mental representations that organize knowledge.

secure attachment style An attachment style that describes adults who have positive views of relationships, find it easy to get close to others, and are not overly concerned or stressed out about their romantic relationships.

securely attached babies Babies that use the caregiver as a secure base from which to explore the environment.

selective attention Focusing on a specific aspect of experience that is relevant while ignoring others that are irrelevant.

selective optimization with compensation theory The theory that successful aging is related to three main factors: selection, optimization, and compensation.

self-concept Domain-specific evaluations of the self.

self-efficacy The belief that one can master a situation and produce favorable outcomes.

self-esteem The global evaluative dimension of the self. Self-esteem is also referred to as self-worth or self-image.

self-understanding The child's cognitive representation of self, the substance and content of the child's self-conceptions.

semantic memory A person's knowledge about the world—including a person's fields of expertise, general academic knowledge of the sort learned in school, and "everyday knowledge."

semantics The meaning of words and sentences.

sensation The product of the interaction between information and the sensory receptors—the eyes, ears, tongue, nostrils, and skin.

sensorimotor play Behavior engaged in by infants to derive pleasure from exercising their existing sensorimotor schemes.

sensorimotor stage The first of Piaget's stages, which lasts from birth to about 2 years of age; during this stage infants construct an understanding of the world by coordinating sensory experiences with motoric actions.

separation protest An infant's distressed crying when the caregiver leaves.

seriation The concrete operation that involves ordering stimuli along a quantitative dimension (such as length).

service learning A form of education that promotes social responsibility and service to the community.

sexually transmitted infections (STIs) Infections contracted primarily through sexual contact, including oral-genital and anal-genital contact.

short-term memory The memory component in which individuals retain information for up to 30 seconds, assuming there is no rehearsal of the information.

slow-to-warm-up child A child who has a low activity level, is somewhat negative, and displays a low intensity of mood.

social clock The timetable according to which individuals are expected to accomplish life's tasks, such as getting married, having children, or establishing a career.

social cognitive theory The theory that behavior, environment, and person/cognition factors are important in understanding development.

social cognitive theory of gender A theory that emphasizes that children's gender development occurs through the observation and imitation of gender behavior and through the rewards and punishments children experience for gender-appropriate and gender-inappropriate behavior.

social constructivist approach An approach that emphasizes the social contexts of learning and that knowledge is mutually built and constructed. Vygotsky's theory reflects this approach.

social contract or utility and individual rights The fifth Kohlberg stage. At this stage, individuals reason that values, rights, and principles undergird or transcend the law.

social conventional reasoning Thoughts about social consensus and convention, in contrast with moral reasoning, which stresses ethical issues.

social play Play that involves social interactions with peers.

social policy A national government's course of action designed to promote the welfare of its citizens.

social referencing "Reading" emotional cues in others to help determine how to act in a particular situation.

social role theory A theory that gender differences result from the contrasting roles of men and women.

social smile A smile in response to an external stimulus, which, early in development, typically is a face.

social systems morality The fourth stage in Kohlberg's theory of moral development. Moral judgments are based on understanding the social order, law, justice, and duty.

socioeconomic status (SES) Refers to the conceptual grouping of people with similar occupational, educational, and economic characteristics.

socioemotional processes Changes in an individual's relationships with other people, emotions, and personality.

socioemotional selectivity theory The theory that older adults become more selective about their social networks. Because they place a high value on emotional satisfaction, older adults often spend more time with familiar individuals with whom they have had rewarding relationships.

stability-change issue The debate about the degree to which early traits and characteristics persist through life or change.

stagnation Sometimes called "self-absorption"—develops when individuals sense that they have done little or nothing for the next generation; the negative side of Erikson's generativity versus stagnation middle adulthood stage.

standardized test A test that is given with uniform procedures for administration and scoring.

stranger anxiety An infant's fear and wariness of strangers; it tends to appear in the second half of the first year of life.

Strange Situation An observational measure of infant attachment that requires the infant to move through a series of introductions, separations, and reunions with the caregiver and an adult stranger in a prescribed order.

strategies Consist of deliberate mental activities to improve the processing of information.

sudden infant death syndrome (SIDS) A condition that occurs when an infant stops breathing, usually during the night, and suddenly dies without an apparent cause.

sustained attention Focused and extended engagement with an object, task, event, or other aspect of the environment.

symbolic function substage Piaget's first substage of preoperational thought, in which the child gains the ability to mentally represent an object that is not present (between about 2 and 4 years of age).

syntax The ways words are combined to form acceptable phrases and sentences.

T

telegraphic speech The use of short and precise words without grammatical markers such as articles, auxiliary verbs, and other connectives.

temperament An individual's behavioral style and characteristic way of emotionally responding.

tend and befriend Taylor's view that when women experience stress, they are more likely to seek social alliances with others, especially female friends.

teratogen Any agent that can potentially cause a birth defect or negatively alter cognitive and behavioral outcomes.

theory A coherent set of ideas that helps to explain data and to make predictions.

theory of mind Refers to the awareness of one's own mental processes and the mental processes of others.

thinking Manipulating and transforming information in memory.

top-dog phenomenon   The circumstance of moving from the top position in elementary school to the lowest position in middle or junior high school.

transitivity   The ability to logically combine relations to understand certain conclusions.

triarchic theory of intelligence   Sternberg's theory that intelligence consists of analytical intelligence, creative intelligence, and practical intelligence.

twin study   A study in which the behavioral similarity of identical twins is compared with the behavioral similarity of fraternal twins.

U

universal ethical principles   The sixth and highest stage in Kohlberg's theory of moral development. Individuals develop a moral standard based on universal human rights.

V

visual preference method   A method developed by Fantz to determine whether infants can distinguish one stimulus from another by measuring the length of time they attend to different stimuli.

Vygotsky's theory   A sociocultural cognitive theory that emphasizes how culture and social interaction guide cognitive development.

W

whole-language approach   An approach to reading instruction based on the idea that instruction should parallel children's natural language learning. Reading materials should be whole and meaningful.

wisdom   Expert knowledge about the practical aspects of life that permits excellent judgment about important matters.

working memory   Closely related to short-term memory but places more emphasis on mental work. Working memory is like a mental "workbench" where individuals can manipulate and assemble information when making decisions, solving problems, and comprehending written and spoken language.

Z

zone of proximal development (ZPD)   Vygotsky's term for tasks too difficult for children to master alone but that can be mastered with assistance.

References

A

AAP. (2000). Changing concepts of sudden infant death syndrome. *Pediatrics, 105,* 650–656.

AARP. (2004). *The divorce experience: A study of divorce at midlife and beyond.* Washington, DC: AARP.

Abbott, A. (2003). Restless nights, listless days. *Nature, 425,* 896–898.

Abbott, L. C., & Winzer-Serhan, U. H. (2012). Smoking during pregnancy: Lessons learned from epidemiological studies and experimental studies using animals. *Critical Reviews in Toxicology, 42,* 279–303.

ABC News. (2005, December 12). Larry Page and Sergey Brin. Retrieved September 16, 2007, from http://abcnews.go.com?Entertainment/12/8/05

Accornero, V. H., Anthony, J. C., Morrow, C. E., Xue, L., & Bandstra, E. S. (2006). Prenatal cocaine exposure: An examination of childhood externalizing and internalizing behavior problems at age 7 years. *Epidemiology, Psychiatry, and Society, 15,* 20–29.

Ackerman, J. P., Riggins, T., & Black, M. M. (2010). A review of the effects of prenatal cocaine exposure among school-aged children. *Pediatrics, 125,* 554–565.

Adkins, D. E., Daw, J. K., McClay, J. L., & van den Oord, E. J. (2012). The influence of five monoamine genes on trajectories of depressive symptoms across adolescence and young adulthood. *Development and Psychopathology, 24,* 267–285.

Administration for Children and Families. (2008). *Statistical Fact Sheet Fiscal Year 2008.* Washington, DC: Author.

Adolph, K. E. (1997). Learning in the development of infant locomotion. *Monographs of the Society for Research in Child Development, 62* (3, Serial No. 251).

Adolph, K. E. (2010). Perceptual learning. Retrieved January 10, 2010, from http://www.psych.nyu.edu/adolph/research1.php

Adolph, K. E., & Berger, S. E. (2005). Physical and motor development. In M. H. Bornstein & M. E. Lamb (Eds.), *Developmental psychology* (5th ed.). Mahwah, NJ: Erlbaum.

Adolph, K. E., & Berger, S. E. (2013, in press). Development of the motor system. In H. Pashler, T. Crane, M. Kinsbourne, F. Ferreira, & R. Zemel (Eds.), *The encyclopedia of the mind.* Thousand Oaks, CA: Sage.

Adolph, K. E., & Joh, A. S. (2009). Multiple learning mechanisms in the development of action. In A. Needham & A. Woodward (Eds.), *Learning and the infant mind.* New York: Oxford University Press.

Adolph, K. E., & Robinson, S. R. R. (2013). The road to walking: What learning to walk tells us about development. In P. Zelazo (Ed.) *Oxford handbook of developmental psychology.* New York: Oxford University Press.

Adolph, K. E., & others. (2012, in press). How do you learn to walk? Thousands of steps and dozens of falls per day. *Psychological Science.*

Agency for Healthcare Research and Quality. (2007). *Evidence report/Technology assessment Number 153: Breastfeeding and maternal and infant health outcomes in developed countries.* Rockville, MD: U.S. Department of Health and Human Services.

Agras, W. S., & others. (2004). Report of the National Institutes of Health workshop on overcoming barriers to treatment research in anorexia nervosa. *International Journal of Eating Disorders, 35,* 509–521.

Ahrens, C. E., & Aldana, E. (2012). The ties that bind: Understanding the impact of sexual assault disclosure on survivors' relationships with friends, family, and partners. *Journal of Trauma & Dissociation, 13,* 226–243.

Ailshire, J. A., & Burgard, S. A. (2012). Family relationships and troubled sleep among U.S. adults: Examining the influences of contact frequency and relationship quality. *Journal of Health and Social Behavior, 53,* 248–262.

Ainsworth, M. D. S. (1979). Infant-mother attachment. *American Psychologist, 34,* 932–937.

Akbari, A., & others. (2011). Parity and breastfeeding are preventive measures against breast cancer in Iranian women. *Breast Cancer, 18,* 51–55.

Akhavan, S., & Lundgren, I. (2012). Midwives' experiences of doula support for immigrant women in Sweden—A qualitative study. *Midwifery, 28,* 80–85.

Akhtar, N., & Herold, K. (2008). Pragmatic development. In M. M. Haith & J. B. Benson (Eds.), *Encyclopedia of infant and early childhood development.* Oxford, UK: Elsevier.

Alberga, A. S., & others. (2012). Healthy eating, aerobic and resistance training in youth (HEARTY): Study rationale, design, and methods. *Contemporary Clinical Trials, 33,* 839–847.

Albert, D., & Steinberg, L. (2011a). Judgment and decision making in adolescence. *Journal of Research on Adolescence, 21,* 211–224.

Albert, D., & Steinberg, L. (2011b). Peer influences on adolescent risk behavior. In M. Bardo, D. Fishbein, & R. Milich (Eds.), *Inhibitory control and drug abuse prevention: From research to translation.* New York: Springer.

Alberts, E., Elkind, D., & Ginsberg, S. (2007). The personal fable and risk taking in early adolescence. *Journal of Youth and Adolescence, 36,* 71–76.

Albright, J. A., Stevens, S. A., & Beussman, D. J. (2012). Detecting ketamine in beverage residues: Application in date rape detection. *Drug Testing and Analysis, 4,* 337–341.

Alexander, N., & others. (2012, in press). Interaction of serotonin transporter-linked polymorphic region and environmental adversity: Increased amygdala-hypothalamus connectivity as a potential mechanism linking neural and endocrine hyperreactivity. *Biological Psychiatry.*

Allemand, M., Zimprich, D., & Hendriks, A. A. J. (2008). Age differences in five personality domains across the life span. *Developmental Psychology, 44,* 758–770.

Allen, J. P., & Miga, E. M. (2010). Attachment in adolescence: A move to the level of emotion regulation. *Journal of Social and Personal Relationships, 27,* 226–234.

Allen, J. P., & others. (2009, April). *Portrait of the secure teen as an adult.* Paper presented at the meeting of the Society for Research in Child Development, Denver.

Allen, K., & Diamond, L. M. (2012, in press). Same-sex relationships. In M. Fine & F. Fincham (Eds.), *Family theories.* New York: Routledge.

Allen, T. D. (2013). The work-family role interface: A synthesis of the research from industrial and organizational psychology. In I. B. Weiner & others (Eds.), *Handbook of psychology* (2nd ed., Vol.12). New York: Wiley.

Allor, J., & Al Otaiba, S. A. (2013). In B. G. Cook & M. G. Tankersley (Eds.), *Research-based practices in special education.* Upper Saddle River, NJ: Pearson.

Almeida, D. M., & Horn, M. C. (2004). Is daily life more stressful during middle adulthood? In C. D. Ryff & R. C. Kessler (Eds.), *A portrait of midlife in the United States.* Chicago: University of Chicago Press.

Almeida, D. M., Piazza, J. R., Stawski, R. S., & Klein, L. C. (2011). The speedometer of life: Stress, health, and aging. In K. W. Schaie & S. L. Willis (Eds.), *Handbook of the psychology of aging* (7th ed.). New York: Elsevier.

Alsaker, F. D., & Valanover, S. (2012). The Bernese program against victimization in kindergarten and elementary school. *New Directions in Youth Development, 133,* 15–28.

Alves, L., Correia, A. S., Miguel, R., Alegria, P., & Bugalho, P. (2012, in press). Alzheimer's disease: A clinical practice-oriented review. *Frontiers in Neurology.*

Alzheimer's Association. (2010). 2010 Alzheimer's disease facts and figures. *Alzheimer's Disease & Dementia, 6,* 158–194.

Alzheimer's Association. (2012). 2012 Alzheimer's disease facts and figures. *Alzheimer's Disease and Dementia, 8,* 131–168.

Amato, P. R. (2006). Marital discord, divorce, and children's well-being: Results from a 20-year longitudinal study of two generations. In A. Clarke-Stewart & J. Dunn (Eds.), *Families count.* New York: Cambridge University Press.

Amato, P. R. (2010). Research on divorce: Continuing trends and new developments. *Journal of Marriage and the Family, 72,* 650–666.

Amato, P. R., & Dorius, C. (2010). Fathers, children, and divorce. In M. E. Lamb (Ed.), *The role of the father in child development* (5th ed.) New York: Wiley.

Ambrose, D., Sternberg, R. J., & Sriraman, B. (2012). Considering the effects of dogmatism on giftedness and talent development. In D. Ambrose, R. J. Sternberg, & B. Sriraman (Eds.), *Confronting dogmatism in gifted education.* New York: Taylor & Francis.

Ament, B. H., & others. (2012, in press). Resources as a protective factor for negative outcomes of frailty in elderly people. *Gerontology.*

American Academy of Pediatrics Section on Breastfeeding. (2012). Breastfeeding and the use of human milk. *Pediatrics, 129,* e827–e841.

American Association of University Women. (2006). *Drawing the line: Sexual harassment on campus.* Washington, DC: American Association of University Women.

American Pregnancy Association (2012). *Mercury levels in fish.* Retrieved April 12, 2011, from www.americanpregnancy.org/pregnancyhealth/fishmercury.htm

American Psychological Association (2003). *Psychology: Scientific problem solvers.* Washington, DC: Author.

American Psychological Association (2007). *Stress in America.* Washington, DC: American Psychological Association.

Amsel, E., & Smetana, J. G. (Eds.). (2011). *Adolescent vulnerabilities and opportunities: Constructivist and developmental perspectives.* New York: Cambridge University Press.

Amso, D., & Johnson, S. P. (2010). Building object knowledge from perceptual input. In B. Hood & L. Santos (Eds.), *The origins of object knowledge.* New York: Oxford University Press.

Amstadter, A. B., McCauley, J. L., Ruggiero, K. J., Resnick, H. S., & Kilpatrick, D. G. (2011). Self-rated health in relation to rape and mental health disorders in a national sample of women. *American Journal of Orthopsychiatry, 81,* 202–210.

Amsterdam, B. K. (1968). *Mirror behavior in children under two years of age.* Unpublished doctoral dissertation. University of North Carolina, Chapel Hill.

Anderman, E. M. (2012). Adolescence. In K. L. Harris, S. Graham, & T. Urdan (Eds.), *APA educational psychology handbook.* Washington, DC: American Psychological Association.

Andersen, S. L., Sebastiani, P., Dworkis, D. A., Feldman, L., & Perls, T. T. (2012). Health span approximates life span among many supercentenarians: Compression of morbidity at the approximate limit of life span. *Journals of Gerontology A: Biological Sciences and Medical Sciences, 67A,* 395–405.

Anderson, E., Greene, S. M., Hetherington, E. M., & Clingempeel, W. G. (1999). The dynamics of parental remarriage. In E. M. Hetherington (Ed.), *Coping with divorce, single parenting, and remarriage.* Mahwah, NJ: Erlbaum.

Anderson, E. R., & Greene, S. M. (2011). "My child and I are a package deal": Balancing adult and child concerns in repartnering after divorce. *Journal of Family Psychology, 25,* 741–750.

Anderson, P. J., & others. (2011). Attention problems in a representative sample of extremely preterm/extremely low birth weight children. *Developmental Neuropsychology, 36,* 57–73.

Anderson, S. E., Gooze, R. A., Lemeshow, S., & Whitaker, R. C. (2012). Quality of early maternal-child relationship and risk of adolescent obesity. *Pediatrics, 129,* 132–140.

Andersson, H., & Bergman, L. R. (2011). The role of task persistence in young adolescence for successful educational and occupational attainment in middle adulthood. *Developmental Psychology, 47,* 950–960.

Ando, S. (2012). Neuronal dysfunction with aging and its amelioration. *Proceedings of the Japanese Academy. Series B, Physical and Biological Sciences, 88,* 266–282.

Ang, M., Evans, J. R., & Mehta, J. S. (2012, in press). Manual small incision cataract surgery (MSICS) with posterior chamber intraocular lens versus extracapsular cataract extraction (ECCE) with posterior chamber intraocular lens for age-related cataract. *Cochrane Database of Systematic Reviews, 18,* 4: CD008811.

Angel, L., Fay, S., Bouazzaoui, B., & Isingrini, M. (2011). Two hemispheres for better memory in old age: Role of executive functioning. *Journal of Cognitive Neuroscience, 23,* 3767–3777.

Anisimov, V. N., & others. (2012). The second international conference "Genetics of Aging and Longevity." *Aging, 4,* 305–317.

Anspaugh, D., & Ezell, G. (2013). *Teaching today's health* (10th ed.). Upper Saddle River, NJ: Pearson.

Antonucci, T. C., Lansford, J. E., & Akiyama, H. (2001). The impact of positive and negative aspects of marital relationships and friendships on the well-being of older adults. In J. P. Reinhardt (Ed.), *Negative and positive support.* Mahwah, NJ: Erlbaum.

Antonucci, T. C., Birditt, K. S., & Ajrouch, K. (2013). Social relationships and aging. In I. B. Weiner & others (Eds.), *Handbook of psychology* (2nd ed., Vol. 6). New York: Wiley.

Antonucci, T. C., Vandewater, E. A., & Lansford, J. E. (2000). Adulthood and aging: Social processes and development. In A. Kazdin (Ed.), *Encyclopedia of psychology.* Washington, DC, and New York: American Psychological Association and Oxford University Press.

Apperly, I. A. (2012, in press). EPS prize lecture. "What is theory of mind?": Concepts, cognitive processes, and individual differences. *Quarterly Journal of Experimental Psychology.*

Arbib, M. A. (2012). *How the brain got language.* New York: Oxford University Press.

Ariceli, G., Castro, J., Cesena, J., & Toro, J. (2005). Anorexia nervosa in male adolescents: Body image, eating attitudes, and psychological traits. *Journal of Adolescent Health, 36,* 221–226.

Arnett, J. J. (2004). *Emerging adulthood.* New York: Oxford University Press.

Arnett, J. J. (2006). Emerging adulthood: Understanding the new way of coming of age. In J. J. Arnett & J. L. Tanner (Eds.), *Emerging adults in America.* Washington, DC: American Psychological Association.

Arnett, J. J. (2010). Oh, grow up! Generational grumbling and the new life stage of emerging adulthood—Commentary on Trzesniewski & Donnellan (2010), *Perspectives on Psychological Science, 5,* 89–92.

Arnett, J. J. (Ed.) (2012). *Adolescent psychology around the world.* New York: Psychology Press.

Arnold, A. (2012, April). *Reframing sexual differentiation in the brain.* Paper presented at the Gender Development Research conference, San Francisco.

Aron, A., Aron, E. N., & Coups, E. (2013). *Statistics for psychology* (6th ed.). Upper Saddle River, NJ: Pearson.

Aronson, E. (1986, August). *Teaching students things they think they already know about: The case of prejudice and desegregation.* Paper presented at the meeting of the American Psychological Association, Washington, DC.

Arseth, A., Kroger, J., Martinussen, M., & Marcia, J. E. (2009). Meta-analytic studies of identity status and the relational issues of attachment and intimacy. *Identity, 9,* 1–32.

Arterberry, M. E. (2008). Perceptual development. In M. E. Haith & J. B. Benson (Eds.), *Encyclopedia of infant and early childhood development.* Oxford, UK: Elsevier.

Aslin, R. N. (2012). Infant eyes: A window on cognitive development. *Infancy, 17,* 126–140.

Aslin, R. N., Jusczyk, P. W., & Pisoni, D. B. (1998). Speech and auditory processing during infancy: Constraints on and precursors to language. In W. Damon (Ed.), *Handbook of child psychology* (5th ed., Vol. 2). New York: Wiley.

Aslin, R. N., & Lathrop, A. L. (2008). Visual perception. In M. M. Haith & J. B. Benson (Eds.), *Encyclopedia of infant and early childhood development.* Oxford, UK: Elsevier.

Astell-Burt, T., Maynard, M. J., Lenguerrand, E., & Harding, S. (2012). Racism, ethnic density, and psychological well-being through adolescence: Evidence from Determinants of Adolescent Social Well-Being and Health longitudinal study. *Ethnicity and Health, 17*, 71–87.

Astington, J. W., & Hughes, C. (2013). Theory of mind: Self-reflection and social understanding. In P. D. Zelazo (Ed.), *Oxford handbook of developmental psychology.* New York: Oxford University Press.

Athanasiadis, A. P., & others. (2011). Correlation of 2nd trimester amniotic fluid amino acid profile with gestational age and estimated fetal weight. *Journal of Maternal-Fetal and Neonatal Medicine, 24*, 1033–1038.

Attar-Schwartz, S., Tan, J. P., Buchanan, A., Flouri, E., & Griggs, J. (2009). Grandparenting and adolescent development in two-parent biological, lone-parent, and step-families. *Journal of Family Psychology, 23*, 67–75.

Aubert, G., & Lansdorp, P. M. (2008). Telomeres and aging. *Physiological Review, 88*, 557–579.

Aud, S., & others. (2011). *The condition of education 2011.* Washington, DC: U.S. Department of Education.

Augestad, L. A., Rand-Hendriksen, K., Staverm, K., & Kristiansen, I. S. (2012, in press). Time trade-off and attitudes toward euthanasia: Implications of using 'death' as an anchor in health state valuation. *Quality of Life Research.*

Avent, N. D. (2012). Refining noninvasive prenatal diagnosis with single-molecule next generation sequencing. *Clinical Chemistry, 58*, 657–658.

Avis, N. E., & others. (2009). Longitudinal changes in sexual functioning as women transition through menopause: Results from the Study of Women's Health Across the Nation. *Menopause, 16*, 442–452.

Aylott, M. (2006). The neonatal energy triangle. Part I: Metabolic adaptation. *Pediatric Nursing, 18*, 38–42.

Ayoub, C., Vallotton, C. D., & Mastergeorge, A. M. (2011). Developmental pathways to integrated social skills: The role of parenting and early intervention. *Child Development, 82*, 583–600.

B

Baber, R. (2011). Breast cancer in postmenopausal women after hormone therapy. *JAMA, 305*, 466.

Bachman, J. G., O'Malley, P. M., Schulenberg, J., Johnston, L. D., Bryant, A. L., & Merline, A. C. (2002). *The decline of substance abuse in young adulthood.* Mahwah, NJ: Erlbaum.

Bachman, J. G., O'Malley, P. M., Schulenberg, J. E., Johnston, L. D., Freedman-Doan, P., & Messersmith, E. E. (2008). *The education-drug use connection.* Clifton, NJ: Psychology Press.

Bachrach, R. L., Merrill, J. E., Bytschkow, K. M., & Read, J. P. (2012, in press). Development and initial validation of a measure of motives

for pregaming in college students. *Addictive Behaviors.*

Bachschmid, M. M., & others. (2012, in press). Vascular aging: Chronic oxidative stress and impairment of redox signaling—Consequences for vascular homeostatis and disease. *Annals of Medicine.*

Backhans, M. C., & Hemmingsson, T. (2012). Unemployment and mental health—Who is (not) affected? *European Journal of Public Health, 22*, 429–433.

Baddeley, A. (2007). *Working memory, thought, and action.* New York: Oxford University Press.

Baddeley, A. D. (2012). Working memory: Theories, models, and controversies. *Annual Review of Psychology* (Vol. 63). Palo Alto, CA: Annual Reviews.

Baer, J., & Kaufman, J. C. (2013, in press). *Being creative inside and outside the classroom.* The Netherlands: Sense Publishers.

Bagnato, S. J., & Macy, M. (2012). The authentic alternative for assessment in early childhood intervention. In T. Kehle (Ed.), *Oxford handbook of psychological assessment.* New York: Oxford University Press.

Bahali, K., Akcan, R., Tahiroglu, A. Y., & Avci, A. (2010). Child sexual abuse: Seven years in practice. *Journal of Forensic Science, 55*, 633–636.

Bahrick, L. E. (2010). Intermodal perception and selective attention to intersensory redundancy: Implications for social development and autism. In J. G. Bremner & T. D. Wachs (Eds.), *Wiley-Blackwell handbook of infant development* (2nd ed.). New York: Wiley.

Bahrick, L. E., & Hollich, G. (2008). Intermodal perception. In M. M. Haith & J. B. Benson (Eds.), *Encyclopedia of infant and early childhood development.* Oxford, UK: Elsevier.

Baillargeon, R. (2004). The acquisition of physical knowledge in infancy: A summary in eight lessons. In U. Goswami (Ed.), *Blackwell handbook of childhood cognitive development.* Malden, MA: Blackwell.

Baillargeon, R., & Carey, S. (2012, in press). Core cognition and beyond: The acquisition of physical and numerical knowledge. In S. Pauen & M. Bornstein (Eds.), *Early childhood development and later outcome.* New York: Cambridge University Press.

Baillargeon, R., & others. (2012, in press). Object individuation and physical reasoning in infancy: An integrative account. *Language, Learning, and Development.*

Bakeman, R., & Brown, J. V. (1980). Early interaction: Consequences for social and mental development at three years. *Child Development, 51*, 437–447.

Baker, J. H., Thorton, L. M., Lichtenstein, P., & Bulik, C. M. (2012, in press). Pubertal development predicts eating behaviors in adolescents. *International Journal of Eating Disorders.*

Baker, J. K., Fenning, R. M., & Crnic, K. A. (2011). Emotion socialization by mothers and fathers: Coherence among behaviors and

associations with parent attitudes and children's competence. *Social Development, 20*, 412–430.

Bakermans-Kranenburg, M. J., & van IJzendoorn, M. H. (2011). Differential susceptibility to rearing environment depending on dopamine-related genes: New evidence and a meta-analysis. *Development and Psychopathology, 23*, 39–52.

Baldwin, S. A., Christian, S., Berkeljon, A., & Shadish, W. R. (2012). The effects of family therapies for adolescent delinquency and substance abuse: A meta-analysis. *Journal of Marital and Family Therapy, 38*, 281–304.

Ballard, S. (2011). Blood tests for investigating maternal well-being. 4. When nausea and vomiting in pregnancy becomes pathological: Hyperemesis gravidarum. *Practicing Midwife, 14*, 37–41.

Balsa, A. I., Giuliano, L. M., & French, M. T. (2011). The effects of alcohol use on academic achievement in high school. *Economics of Education Review, 30*, 1–15.

Balsam, K., & Hughes, T. (2013, in press). Sexual orientation, victimization, and hate crimes. In C. J. Patterson & A. R. D'Augelli (Eds.), *Handbook of psychology and sexual orientation.* New York: Oxford University Press.

Baltes, P. B. (1987). Theoretical propositions of life-span developmental psychology: On the dynamics between growth and decline. *Developmental Psychology, 23*, 611–626.

Baltes, P. B. (2003). On the incomplete architecture of human ontogeny: Selection, optimization, and compensation as foundation of developmental theory. In U. M. Staudinger & U. Lindenberger (Eds.), *Understanding human development.* Boston: Kluwer.

Baltes, P. B., Lindenberger, U., & Staudinger, U. (2006). Life span theory in developmental psychology. In W. Damon & R. Lerner (Eds.), *Handbook of child psychology* (6th ed.), New York: Wiley.

Baltes, P. B., Reuter-Lorenz, P., & Rösler, F. (Eds.). (2006). *Lifespan development and the brain.* New York: Cambridge University Press.

Baltes, P. B., & Smith, J. (2003). New frontiers in the future of aging: From successful aging of the young old to the dilemmas of the fourth age. *Gerontology, 49*, 123–135.

Bandura, A. (1986). *Social foundations of thought and action: A social cognitive theory.* Englewood Cliffs, NJ: Prentice Hall.

Bandura, A. (1998, August). *Swimming against the mainstream: Accentuating the positive aspects of humanity.* Paper presented at the meeting of the American Psychological Association, San Francisco.

Bandura, A. (2001). Social cognitive theory. *Annual Review of Psychology.* Palo Alto, CA: Annual Reviews.

Bandura, A. (2004, May). *Toward a psychology of human agency.* Paper presented at the meeting of the American Psychological Society, Chicago.

health) is associated directly with penile-vaginal intercourse, but inversely related to other sexual behavior frequencies. *Journal of Sexual Medicine, 6,* 1947–1954.

Brody, S. (2010). The relative health benefits of different sexual activities. *Journal of Sexual Medicine, 7,* 1336–1361.

Broekhuizen, L. N., & others. (2011). Physical activity, metabolic syndrome, and coronary risk: The EPIC-Norfolk prospective population study. *European Journal of Cardiovascular Prevention and Rehabilitation,18,* 209–217.

Bronfenbrenner, U. (1986). Ecology of the family as a context for human development: Research perspectives. *Developmental Psychology, 22,* 723–742.

Bronfenbrenner, U. (2004). *Making human beings human.* Thousand Oaks, CA: Sage.

Bronfenbrenner, U., & Morris, P. (1998). The ecology of developmental processes. In W. Damon (Ed.). *Handbook of child psychology* (5th ed., Vol. 1). New York: Wiley.

Bronstein, P. (2006). The family environment: Where gender role socialization begins. In J. Worell & C. D. Goodheart (Eds.), *Handbook of girls' and women's psychological health.* New York: Oxford University Press.

Brook, J. S., Brook, D. W., Gordon, A. S., Whiteman, M., & Cohen, P. (1990). The psychological etiology of adolescent drug use: A family interactional approach. *Genetic Psychology Monographs, 116*(2).

Brooker, R. J. (2012). *Genetics* (4th ed.). New York: McGraw-Hill.

Brooks, J. G., & Brooks, M.G. (2001). *The case for constructivist classrooms* (2nd ed.). Upper Saddle River, NJ: Erlbaum.

Brooks-Gunn, J. (2003). Do you believe in magic?: What we can expect from early childhood programs. *Social Policy Report, Society for Research in Child Development, XVII* (No. 1), 1–13.

Brooks-Gunn, J., & Warren, M. P. (1989). The psychological significance of secondary sexual characteristics in 9- to 11-year-old girls. *Child Development 59,* 161–169.

Brotman, L. M., & others. (2012). Early childhood family intervention and long-term obesity prevention among high-risk minority youth. *Pediatrics, 129,* e621–e628.

Brown, B. B. (2011). Popularity in peer group perspective: The role of status in adolescent peer systems. In A. H. N. Cillessen, D. Schwartz, & L. Mayeux (Eds.), *Popularity in the peer system.* New York: Guilford.

Brown, B. B., & Larson, J. (2009). Peer relationships in adolescence. In R. M. Lerner & L. Steinberg (Eds.), *Handbook of adolescent development* (3rd ed.). New York: Wiley.

Brown, B. B., & Larson, R. W. (2002). The kaleidoscope of adolescence: Experiences of the world's youth at the beginning of the 21st century. In B. B. Brown, R. W. Larson, & T. S. Saraswathi (Eds.), *The world's youth.* New York: Cambridge University Press.

Brown, D. (2013, in press). Morphological typology. In J. J. Song (Ed.), *Oxford handbook of linguistic typology.* New York: Oxford University Press.

Brown, J. K. (1985). Introduction. In J. K. Brown & V. Kerns (Eds.), *In her prime: A new view of middle-aged women.* South Hadley, MA: Bergin & Garvey.

Brown, L. D., Feinberg, M., & Kan, M. L. (2012). Predicting engagement in a transition to parenthood program for couples. *Evaluation and Program Planning, 35,* 1–8.

Brown, L. S. (1989). New voices, new visions: Toward a lesbian/gay paradigm for psychology. *Psychology of Women Quarterly, 13,* 445–458.

Brown, R. (1958). *Words and things.* Glencoe, IL: Free Press.

Brown, R. (1973). *A first language: The early stages.* Cambridge, MA: Harvard University Press.

Brown, S. L., Bulanda, J. R., & Lee, G. R. (2005). The significance of nonmarital cohabitation: Marital status and mental health benefits among middle-aged and older adults. *Journals of Gerontology B: Psychological Sciences and Social Sciences, 60,* S21–S29.

Brown, W. H., Pfeiffer, K. A., McIver, K. L., Dowda, M., Addy, C. L., & Pate, R. R. (2009). Social and environmental factors associated with preschoolers' nonsedentary physical activity. *Child Development, 80,* 45–58.

Brownell, C. A., Ramani, G. B., & Zerwas, S. (2006). Becoming a social partner with peers: Cooperation and social understanding in one- and two-year-olds. *Child Development, 77,* 803–821.

Brownell, C., Nichols, S., Svetlova, M., Zerwas, S., & Ramani, G. (2010). The head bone's connected to the neck bone: When do toddlers represent their own body topography? *Child Development, 81,* 797–810.

Bruce, A. (2007). Time(lessness): Buddhist perspectives and end-of-life. *Nursing Philosophy, 8,* 151–157.

Bruchmiller, K., Margraf, J., & Schneider, S. (2012). Is ADHD diagnosed in accord with diagnostic criteria? Overdiagnosis and influence of client gender on diagnosis. *Journal of Consulting and Clinical Psychology, 80,* 128–138.

Bruck, M., & Ceci, S. J. (1999). The suggestibility of children's memory. *Annual Review of Psychology, 50,* 419–439.

Bruck, M., & Ceci, S. J. (2012). Forensic developmental psychology in the courtroom. In D. Faust & M. Ziskin (Eds.), *Coping with psychiatric and psychological testimony.* New York: Cambridge University Press.

Bruine de Bruin, W., Parker, A., & Fischhoff, B. (2007). Can adolescents predict significant events in their lives? *Journal of Adolescent Health, 41,* 208–210.

Brumariu, L. E., & Kerns, K. A. (2010). Parent-child attachment and internalizing symptomatology in childhood and adolescence: A review of empirical findings and

future direction. *Development and Psychopathology, 22,* 177–203.

Brumariu, L. E., Kerns, K. A., & Seibert, A. C. (2012, in press). Mother-child attachment, emotion regulation, and anxiety symptoms in middle childhood. *Personal Relationships.*

Brun, C., & Brock-Utne, J. G. (2012). Paralyzed by beauty. *Journal of Clinical Anesthesia, 24,* 77–78.

Brune, M., & others. (2012). The crisis of psychiatry—insights and prospects from evolutionary theory. *World Psychiatry, 11,* 55–57.

Bryant, D. P., & others. (2013). Instructional practices for improving student outcomes in solving arithmetic combinations. In B. G. Cook & M. G. Tankersley (Eds.), *Research-based practices in special education.* Upper Saddle River, NJ: Pearson.

Bryant, J. B. (2009). Language in social contexts: Communicative competence in the preschool years. In J. Berko Gleason & N. Ratner (Eds.), *The development of language* (7th ed.). Boston: Allyn & Bacon.

Bryant, J. B. (2012). Pragmatic development. In E. L. Bavin (Ed.), *Cambridge handbook of child language.* New York: Cambridge University Press.

Bryant, R. A. (2012). Grief as a psychiatric disorder. *British Journal of Psychiatry, 201,* 9–10.

Brynes, J. P. (2012). How neuroscience contributes to our understanding of learning and development in typically developing and special needs students. In K. R. Harris, S. Graham, & T. Urdan (Eds.), *APA educational psychology handbook.* Washington, DC: American Psychological Association.

Buchanan, S. L., & others. (2012). Trends in morbidity associated with oxytocin use in labor in nulliparas at term. *Australian and New Zealand Journal of Obstetrics and Gynecology, 52,* 173–178.

Buchman, A. S., Boyle, P. A., Wilson, R. S, Fleischman, D. A., Leurgans, S., & Bennett, D. A. (2009). Association between late-life social activity and motor decline in older adults. *Archives of Internal Medicine, 169,* 1139–1146.

Buchman, A. S., Yu, L., Boyle, P. A., Shah, R. C., & Bennett, D. A. (2012). Total daily physical activity and longevity in old age. *Archives of Internal Medicine, 172,* 444–446.

Bucur, B., & Madden, D. J. (2007). Information processing/cognition. In J. E. Birren (Ed.), *Encyclopedia of gerontology* (2nd ed.). San Diego: Academic Press.

Buhl, H. M., & Lanz, M. (2007). Emerging adulthood in Europe: Common traits and variability across five European countries. *Journal of Adolescent Research, 22,* 439–443.

Buhler, E., Bachmann, C., Govert, H., Heinzel-Gutenbrunner, M., & Kamp-Becker, I. (2011). Differential diagnosis of autism spectrum disorder and attention deficit hyperactivity disorder by means of inhibitory control and 'theory of mind.' *Journal of Autism and Developmental Disorders, 41*(12), 1718–1726.

Buhrmester, D. (1998). Need fulfillment, interpersonal competence, and the developmental contexts of early adolescent friendship. In W. M. Bukowski & A. F. Newcomb (Eds.), *The company they keep: Friendship in childhood and adolescence.* New York: Cambridge University Press.

Bukowski, R., & others. (2008, January). *Folic acid and preterm birth.* Paper presented at the meeting of the Society for Maternal-Fetal Medicine, Dallas.

Bukowski, W., & Juang, L. (2012, April). *Gender, culture, and negative experience with peers.* Paper presented at the Gender Development Research Conference, San Francisco.

Bulik, C. M., Berkman, N. D., Brownley, K. A., Sedway, J. A., & Lhor, K. N. (2007). Anorexia nervosa treatment: A systematic review of randomized controlled trials. *International Journal of Eating Disorders, 40,* 310–320.

Bull, J. H., & others. (2012, in press). Demonstration of a sustainable community-based model of care across the palliative continuum. *Journal of Pain and Symptom Management.*

Bullock, C. M., & Beckson, M. (2011). Male victims of sexual assault: Phenomenology, psychology, and physiology. *Journal of American Academy of Psychiatry and the Law, 39,* 197–205.

Bullock, M., & Lutkenhaus, P. (1990). Who am I? Self-understanding in toddlers. *Merrill-Palmer Quarterly, 36,* 217–238.

Bumpus, M. F., Crouter, A. C., & McHale, S. M. (2001). Parental autonomy granting during adolescence: Gender differences in context. *Developmental Psychology, 37,* 163–173.

Bundick, M. J. (2011). The benefits of reflecting on and discussing purpose in life in emerging adulthood. *New Directions in Youth Development, 2011,* 89–103.

Burgess, E. O. (2004). Sexuality in midlife and later life couples. In J. H. Harvey & A. Wetzel (Eds.), *The handbook of sexuality in close relationships.* Mahwah, NJ: Erlbaum.

Burns, C., Dunn, A., Brady, M., Starr, N., & Blosser, C. (2013). *Pediatric primary care* (5th ed.). New York: Elsevier.

Burr, J. (2009). Volunteering, later life. In D. Carr (Ed.), *Encyclopedia of the life course and human development.* Boston: Gale Cengage.

Bursch, H. C., & Butcher, H. K. (2012). Caregivers' deepest feelings in living with Alzheimer's disease: A ricoeurian interpretation of family caregivers' journals. *Research in Gerontological Nursing.*

Burstyn, I., Kuhle, S., Allen, A. C., & Veugelers, P. (2012). The role of maternal smoking in effect of fetal growth restriction on poor scholastic achievement in elementary school. *International Journal of Environmental Research and Public Health, 9,* 408–420.

Burt, K. B., & Paysnick, A. A. (2012). Resilience in the transition to adulthood. *Development and Psychopathology, 24,* 493–505.

Burton, C. L., & others. (2012). Coping flexibility and complicated grief: A comparison of American and Chinese samples. *Depression and Anxiety, 29,* 16–22.

Busch, H., & Hofer, J. (2012). Self-regulation and milestones of adult development: Intimacy and generativity. *Developmental Psychology, 48,* 282–293.

Bushel, P. R., & others. (2012). Population differences in transcript-regulator expression quantitative trait loci. *PLoS One, 7*(3), e34286.

Buss, D. M. (2008). *Evolutionary psychology* (3rd ed.). Boston: Allyn & Bacon.

Buss, D. M. (2012). *Evolutionary psychology* (4th ed.). Boston: Allyn & Bacon.

Busse, E. W., & Blazer, D. G. (1996). *The American Psychiatric Press textbook of geriatric psychiatry* (2nd ed.). Washington, DC: American Psychiatric Press.

Bussey, K., & Bandura, A. (1999). Social cognitive theory of gender development and differentiation. *Psychological Review, 106,* 676–713.

Butler, R. N. (2007). Life review. In J. E. Birren (Ed.), *Encyclopedia of gerontology* (2nd ed.). San Diego: Academic Press.

Butrica, B. A., & Smith, K. E. (2012). The retirement prospects of divorced women. *Social Security Bulletin, 72,* 11–22.

Buzwell, S., & Rosenthal, D. (1996). Constructing a sexual self: Adolescents sexual self-perceptions and sexual risk-taking. *Journal of Research on Adolescence, 6,* 489–513.

Byrd-Bredbenner, C., Moe, G., Beshgetoor, D., & Berning, J. (2013). *Wardlaw's perspectives in nutrition* (9th ed.). New York: McGraw-Hill.

C

Caban-Holt, A., & others. (2012, in press). Age-expanded normative data for the Ruff 2&7 Selective Attention Test: Evaluating cognition in older males. *Clinical Neuropsychology.*

Cabeza, R. (2002). Hemispheric asymmetry reduction in older adults: The HAROLD model. *Psychology and Aging, 17,* 85–100.

Cabeza, R., & Dennis, N. A. (2011). Frontal lobes and aging: Deterioration and compensation. In F. E. M. Craik & T. Salthouse (Eds.), *Handbook of aging and cognition* (3rd ed.). New York: Psychological Press.

Cabrera, N. J., Hofferth, S. L., & Chae, S. (2011). Patterns and predictors of father-infant engagement across race/ethnic groups. *Early Childhood Research Quarterly, 26,* 365–375.

Caddy, S. C., & others. (2011). Pregnancy and neonatal outcomes of women with reactive syphilis serology in Alberta, 2002–2006. *Journal of Obstetrics and Gynecology Canada, 33,* 453–459.

Caeymaex, L., & others. (2012, in press). Perceived role in end-of-life decision making in the NICU affects long-term parental grief response. *Archives of Disease in Childhood. Fetal and Neonatal Edition.*

Calkins, S. D. (2012). Regulatory competence and early disruptive behavior problems: Role of physiological regulation. In S. L. Olson & A. J. Sameroff (Eds.), *Biopsychosocial regulatory processes in the development of childhood behavioral problems.* New York: Cambridge University Press.

Calkins, S. D., & Markovitch, S. (2010). Emotion regulation and executive functioning in early development: Integrating mechanisms of control supporting adaptive functioning. In S. D. Calkins & M. A. Bell (Eds.), *Child development at the intersection of emotion and cognition.* Washington, DC: American Psychological Association.

Callan, J. E. (2001). Gender development: Psychoanalytic perspectives. In J. Worrel (Ed.). *Encyclopedia of women and gender.* San Diego: Academic Press.

Cameron, J. M., Heidelberg, N., Simmons, L., Lyle, S. B., Kathakali, M-V., & Correia, C. (2010). Drinking game participation among undergraduate students attending National Alcohol Screening Day. *Journal of American College Health, 58,* 499–506.

Campbell, I. G., Grimm, K. J., de Bie, E., & Feinberg, I. (2012). Sex, puberty, and the timing of sleep EEG measured in adolescent brain maturation. *Proceedings of the National Academy of Sciences U.S.A., 109,* 5740–5743.

Campbell, K. L., Grady, C. L., Ng, C., & Hasher, L. (2012, in press). Age differences in the frontoparietal cognitive control network: Implications for distractibility. *Neuropsychologia.*

Campbell, L., Campbell, B., & Dickinson, D. (2004). *Teaching and learning through multiple intelligences* (3rd ed.). Boston: Allyn & Bacon.

Campos, J. (2009). Unpublished review of J. W. Santrock's *Life-Span development* (13th ed.). New York: McGraw-Hill.

Canfield, J., & Hansen, M. V. (1995). *A second helping of chicken soup for the soul.* Deerfield Beach, FL: Health Communications.

Capoulade, R., & others. (2012). Impact of metabolic syndrome on progression of aortic stenosis: Influence of age and statin therapy. *Journal of the American College of Cardiology, 60,* 216–223.

Cappeliez, P., & Robitaille, A. (2011). Coping mediates relationships between reminiscence and psychological well-being among older adults. *Aging and Mental Health, 14,* 807–814.

Carl, J. D. (2012). *Short introduction to the U.S. Census.* Upper Saddle River, NJ: Pearson.

Carli, L. L., & Eagly, A. H. (2012). Leadership and gender. In J. Antonakis & D. Day (Eds.), *The nature of leadership* (2nd ed.). Thousand Oaks, CA: Sage.

Carling-Jenkins, R., Torr, J., Iacono, T., & Bigby, C. (2012). Experiences of supporting people with Down syndrome and Alzheimer's disease in aged care and family environments. *Journal of Intellectual and Developmental Disability, 37,* 54–60.

Carlisle, J., Kenney, C., & Vereb, A. (2013). Vocabulary instruction for students with or at risk for learning disabilities: Promising approaches for learning words from text. In B. G. Cook & M. G. Tankersley (Eds.), *Research-based practices in special education*. Upper Saddle River, NJ: Pearson.

Carlson, S. M., & White, R. (2011). *Unpublished research*. Minneapolis: Institute of Child Development, University of Minnesota.

Carlson, S. M., & White, R. (2013, in press). Executive function and imagination. In M. Taylor (Ed.), *Handbook of imagination*. New York: Oxford University Press.

Carlson, S. M., Zelazo, P. D., & Faja, S. (2013). Executive function. In P. D. Zelazo (Ed.), *Oxford handbook of developmental psychology*. New York: Oxford University Press.

Carmichael, O., & Lockhart, S. (2012). The role of diffusion tensor imaging in the study of cognitive aging. *Current Topics in Behavioral Neuroscience, 11*, 289–320.

Carnegie Council on Adolescent Development. (1989). *Turning points: Preparing American youth for the twenty-first century*. New York: Carnegie Foundation.

Carpendale, J. I., & Chandler, M. J. (1996). On the distinction between false belief understanding and subscribing to an interpretive theory of mind. *Child Development, 67*, 1686–1706.

Carpenter, M. (2011). Social cognition and social motivations in infancy. In U. Goswami (Ed.), *Wiley-Blackwell handbook of childhood cognitive development* (2nd ed.). New York: Wiley.

Carr, D. (2009). Death and dying. In D. Carr (Ed.), *Encyclopedia of the life course and human development*. Boston: Gale Cengage.

Carr, D. (2012, in press). "I don't want to die like that. . .": The impact of significant others' death quality on advance care planning. *Gerontologist*.

Carr, D., & Moorman, S. (2011, in press). Social relationships and aging. In R. A. Setterson & J. Angel (Eds.), *Handbook of sociology of aging*. New York: Springer.

Carr, D., & Pudrovska, T. (2011). Divorce and widowhood in later life. In R. Blieszner & V. H. Bedford (Eds.), *Handbook of aging and the family*. Santa Barbara, CA: Praeger.

Carr, R., & Peebles, R. (2012). Developmental considerations of media exposure risk for eating disorders. In J. Lock (Ed.), *Oxford handbook of child and adolescent eating disorders: Developmental perspectives*. New York: Oxford University Press.

Carroll, D., & others. (2011). Low cognitive ability in early adulthood is associated with reduced lung function in middle age: The Vietnam Experience Study. *Thorax, 66*, 884–888.

Carroll, D. J., & others. (2012, in press). How do alternative ways of responding influence 3- and 4-year-olds' performance on tests of executive function and theory of mind? *Journal of Experimental Child Psychology*.

Carroll, J. L. (2013). *Sexuality now* (4th ed.). Boston: Cengage.

Carskadon, M. A. (2006, March). *Too little, too late: Sleep bioregulatory processes across adolescence*. Paper presented at the meeting of the Society for Research on Adolescence, San Francisco.

Carskadon, M. A. (2011a). Sleep in adolescents: The perfect storm. *Pediatric Clinics of North America, 58*, 637–647.

Carskadon, M. A. (2011b). Sleep's effects on cognition and learning in adolescence. *Progress in Brain Research, 190*, 137–143.

Carstensen, L. L. (1998). A life-span approach to social motivation. In J. Heckhausen & C. Dweck (Eds.), *Motivation and self-regulation across the life span*. New York: Cambridge University Press.

Carstensen, L. L. (2006). The influence of a sense of time on human development. *Science, 312*, 1913–1915.

Carstensen, L. L. (2008, May). *Long life in the 21st century*. Paper presented at the meeting of the Association of Psychological Science, Chicago.

Carstensen, L. L. (2010). Social and emotional aging. *Annual Review of Psychology, 2009* (Vol. 61). Palo Alto, CA: Annual Reviews.

Carstensen, L. L. (2011). *A long bright future*. New York: Crown Archetype.

Carstensen, L. L., & Fried, L. P. (2012). The meaning of old age. *Global population aging: Peril or promise?* Geneva, SWIT: World Economic Forum.

Carstensen, L. L., & others. (2011). Emotional experience improves with age: Evidence based on over 10 years of experience sampling. *Psychology & Aging, 26*, 21–33.

Carta, J. J., Greenwood, C., Baggett, K., Buzhardt, J., & Walker, D. (2012). Research-based approaches for individualizing caregiving and educational interventions for infants and toddlers in poverty. In S. L. Odom, E. P. Pungello, & N. Gardner-Neblett (Eds.), *Infants, toddlers, and families in poverty*. New York: Guilford.

Carver, C. S., & Connor-Smith, J. (2010). Personality and coping. *Annual Review of Psychology* (Vol. 61). Palo Alto, CA: Annual Reviews.

Casares, W. N., Lahiff, M., Eskensazi, B., & Halpern-Felsher, B. L. (2010). Unpredicted trajectories: The relationship between race/ethnicity, pregnancy during adolescence, and young women's outcomes. *Journal of Adolescent Health, 47*, 143–160.

Case, R., & Mueller, M. R. (2001). Differentiation, integration, and covariance mapping as fundamental processes in cognitive and neurological growth. In J. L. McClelland & R. S. Slegler (Eds.), *Mechanisms of cognitive development*. Mahwah, NJ: Erlbaum.

Caselli, R. J. (2012, in press). Phenotypic differences between apolipoprotein E genetic subgroups: Research and clinical implications. *Alzheimer's Research and Therapy*.

Casey, B. J., Jones, R. M., & Somerville, L. H. (2011). Braking and accelerating of the adolescent brain. *Journal of Research on Adolescence, 21*, 21–33.

Caspers, K. M., Paradiso, S., Yucuis, R., Troutman, B., Arndt, S., & Philibert, R. (2009). Association between the serontonin transporter promoter polymorphism (5-HTTLPR) and adult unresolved attachment. *Developmental Psychology, 45*, 64–76.

Caspi, A., & Roberts, B. W. (2001). Personality development across the life course; The argument for change and continuity. *Psychological Inquiry, 12*, 49–66.

Caspi, A., & others. (2003). Influence of life stress on depression: Moderation by a polymorphism in the 5-HTT gene. *Science, 301*, 386–389.

Cassidy, J., & others. (2011). Enhancing infant attachment security: An examination of treatment efficacy and differential susceptibility. *Development and Psychopathology, 23*, 131–148.

Catalano, R. F., & others. (2012). Worldwide application of prevention science in adolescent health. *Lancet, 379*, 1653–1664.

Catenacci, V. A., & others. (2008). Physical activity patterns in the National Weight Control Registry. *Obesity, 16*, 153–161.

Cavanagh, S. E. (2009). Puberty. In D. Carr (Ed.), *Encyclopedia of the life course and human development*. Boston: Gale Cengage.

Ceci, S. J., & Gilstrap, L. L. (2000). Determinants of intelligence: Schooling and intelligence. In A. Kazdin (Ed.), *Encyclopedia of Psychology*. Washington, DC, & New York: American Psychological Association and Oxford University Press.

Center for Science in the Public Interest. (2008). *Obesity on the kids' menu at top chains*. Retrieved October 24, 2008, from www.cspinet.org/nes/200808041.html

Center for Survey Research at the University of Connecticut. (2000). *Hours on the job*. Storrs: University of Connecticut, Center for Survey Research.

Centers for Disease Control and Prevention. (2007). *Autism and developmental disabilities monitoring (ADDM) network*. Atlanta: Author.

Centers for Disease Control and Prevention. (2012a). *Birth data*. Atlanta: Author.

Centers for Disease Control and Prevention. (2012b). *Body mass index for children and teens*. Atlanta: Centers for Disease Control and Prevention.

Centers for Disease Control and Prevention. (2012c). *By the numbers full year 2011: Health measures from the National Health Interview Study, January–December 2011*. Atlanta: Author.

Centers for Disease Control and Prevention. (2012d). CDC estimates 1 in 88 children in the United States has been identified as having an autism spectrum disorder. *CDC Division of News & Electronic Media, 404*, 639–3286.

Centers for Disease Control and Prevention. (2012e). *Fast facts: Tobacco.* Retrieved June 8, 2012, from www.cdc.gov/tobacco/data_statistics/fact_sheets/fact_facts/

Centers for Disease Control and Prevention. (2012f). Prepregnancy contraceptive use among teens with unintended pregnancies resulting in live births—Pregnancy Risk Assessment Monitoring System (PRAMS), 2004–2008. *MMWR Morbidity and Morality Weekly Report, 61*(2), 25–29.

Centers for Disease Control and Prevention. (2012g). *Sexually transmitted disease surveillance.* Atlanta, GA: U.S. Department of Health and Human Services.

Central Intelligence Agency. (2012). *The world factbook: Life expectancy at birth.* Washington, DC: CIA.

Cerqueira, F. M., Cunha, F. M., Laurindo, F. R., & Kowaltowski, A. J. (2012). Calorie restriction increases cerebral mitochondrial respiratory capacity in a NO mediated mechanism: Impact on neuronal survival. *Free Radical and Biological Medicine, 52,* 1236–1241.

Chae, J. S., & others. (2012, in press). Supervised exercise program, BMI, and risk of type 2 diabetes in subjects with normal or impaired fasting glucose. *Diabetes Care.*

Chambers, J. A., & Swanson, V. (2012). Stories of weight management: Factors associated with successful and unsuccessful weight maintenance. *British Journal of Health Psychology, 17,* 223–243.

Chandra, A., Mosher, W. D., Copen, C., & Sionean, C. (2011, March 3). Sexual behavior, sexual attraction, and sexual identity in the United States: Data from the 2006–2008 National Survey of Family Growth. *National Health Statistics Reports, 36,* 1–28.

Chang, J. S. (2009). Parental smoking and childhood leukemia. *Methods in Molecular Biology, 472,* 103–137.

Chang, Y. K., Liu, S., Yu, H. H., & Lee, Y. H. (2012). Effect of acute exercise on executive function in children with attention deficit hyperactivity disorder. *Archives of Clinical Neuropsychology, 27,* 225–237.

Chang, Z., Lichtenstein, P., & Larsson, H. (2012). The effects of childhood ADHD symptoms on early-onset substance use: A Swedish twin study. *Journal of Abnormal Child Psychology, 40,* 425–435.

Chao, R. K. (2001). Extending research on the consequences of parenting style for Chinese Americans and European Americans. *Child Development, 72,* 1832–1843.

Chao, R. K. (2005, April). *The importance of Guan in describing control of immigrant Chinese.* Paper presented at the meeting of the Society for Research in Child Development, Atlanta.

Chao, R. K. (2007, March). *Research with Asian Americans: Looking back and moving forward.* Paper presented at the meeting of the Society for Research in Child Development, Boston.

Chao, R. K., & Otsuki-Clutter, M. (2011). Racial and ethnic differences: Sociocultural and contextual explanations. *Journal of Research on Adolescence, 21,* 47–60.

Chao, R. K., & Tseng, V. (2002). Parenting of Asians. In M. H. Bornstein (Ed.), *Handbook of parenting* (2nd ed., Vol. 4). Mahwah, NJ: Erlbaum.

Chaplin, T. M., & others. (2012). Parent-adolescent conflict interactions and adolescent alcohol use. *Addictive Behaviors, 37,* 605–612.

Charles, S. T., & Carstensen, L. L. (2010). Social and emotional aging. In S. Fiske & S. Taylor (Eds.), *Annual Review of Psychology* (Vol. 61). Palo Alto, CA: Annual Reviews.

Charles, S. T., Luong, G., Almeida, D. M., Ryff, C., Sturm, M., & Love, G. (2010). Fewer ups and downs: Daily stressors mediate age differences in negative affect. *Journals of Gerontology B: Psychological Sciences and Social Sciences, 65B,* 279–286.

Charlet, J., Schnekenburger, M., Brown, K. W., & Diederich, M. (2012). DNA demethylation increases sensitivity of neuroblastoma cells to chemotherapeutic drugs. *Biochemical Pharmacology, 83,* 858–865.

Charness, N., Fox, M. C., & Mitchum, A. L. (2011). Life-span cognition and information technology. In K. L. Fingerman, C. A. Berg, J. Smith, & T. C. Antonucci (Eds.), *Handbook of life-span development.* New York: Springer.

Charness, N., & Krampe, R. T. (2008). Expertise and knowledge. In D. F. Alwin & S. M. Hofer (Eds.), *Handbook on cognitive aging.* Thousand Oaks, CA: Sage.

Chen, C., & Stevenson, H. W. (1989). Homework: A cross-cultural comparison. *Child Development, 60,* 551–561.

Chen, J. J., & Brooks-Gunn, J. (2012). Neighborhoods, schools, and achievement. In K. R. Harris, S. Graham, & T. Urdan (Eds.), *APA handbook of educational psychology.* Washington, DC: American Psychological Association.

Chen, K. C., Wang, T. Y., & Chen, C. H. (2012). Associations between HIV and human pathways revealed by protein-protein interactions and correlated gene expression profiles. *PLoS One, 7*(3), e3420.

Chen, X., Hastings, P. D., Rubin, K. H., Chen, H., Cen, G., & Stewart, S. L. (1998). Childrearing attitudes and behavioral inhibition in Chinese and Canadian toddlers: A cross-cultural study. *Developmental Psychology, 34,* 677–686.

Cheng, D., Kettinger, L., Uduhiri, K., & Hurt, L. (2011). Alcohol consumption during pregnancy: Prevalence and provider assessment. *Obstetrics and Gynecology, 117*(2, Pt.2), 212–217.

Cheng, S. T., Lee, C. K., & Chow, P. K. (2010, in press). Social support and psychological well-being of nursing home residents in Hong Kong. *International Geriatrics.*

Cheng, S. Y., & others. (2012, in press). Factors affecting the improvement of quality of dying of terminally ill patients with cancer through palliative care: A 10-year experience. *Journal of Palliative Medicine.*

Cheng, Y., Lou, C., Gao, E., Emerson, M. R., & Zabin, L. S. (2012). The relationship between contact and unmarried adolescents' and young adults' traditional beliefs in three East Asian cities: A cross-cultural analysis. *Journal of Adolescent Health, 50*(Suppl. 3), S4–S11.

Cheong, K. C., & others. (2012, in press). Optimal BMI cut-off values for predicting diabetes, hypertension, and hypercholesterolaemia in a multi-ethnic population. *Public Health Nutrition.*

Cherlin, A. J. (2009). *The marriage-go-round.* New York: Random House.

Cherlin, A. J., & Furstenberg, F. F. (1994). Stepfamilies in the United States: A reconsideration. In J. Blake & J. Hagen (Eds.), *Annual review of sociology.* Palo Alto, CA: Annual Reviews.

Chess, S., & Thomas, A. (1977). Temperamental individuality from childhood to adolescence. *Journal of Child Psychiatry, 16,* 218–226.

Cheung, C., & Pomerantz, E. M. (2012, in press). Why does parental involvement in children's learning enhance children's achievement? The role of parent-oriented motivation. *Journal of Educational Psychology.*

Chi, M. T. (1978). Knowledge structures and memory development. In R. S. Siegler (Ed.), *Children's thinking: What develops?* Hillsdale, NJ: Erlbaum.

Chick, C. F., & Reyna, V. F. (2012). A fuzzy trace theory of adolescent risk taking: Beyond self-control and sensation seeking. In V. F. Reyna & others (Eds.), *The adolescent brain.* Washington, DC: American Psychological Association.

Chiu, R. W., & Lo, Y. M. (2012). Noninvasive prenatal diagnosis empowered by high-throughput sequencing. *Prenatal Diagnosis, 32,* 401–406.

Choi, D., Suramethakul, P., Lindstrom, R. L., & Singh, K. (2012). Glaucoma surgery with and without cataract surgery: Revolution or evolution. *Journal of Cataract and Refractory Surgery, 38,* 1121–1122.

Choi, N. G., & Jun, J. (2009). Life regrets and pride among low-income older adults: Relationships with depressive symptoms, current life stressors, and coping resources. *Aging and Mental Health, 13,* 213–225.

Chomsky, N. (1957). *Syntactic structures.* The Hague: Mouton.

Choudhry, Z., & others. (2012, in press). LPHN3 and attention deficit/hyperactivity disorder: Interaction with maternal stress during pregnancy. *Journal of Child Psychology and Psychiatry.*

Choy, S. C., & Oo, P. S. (2012). Reflective thinking and teaching practices: A precursor for incorporating critical thinking into the classroom? *International Journal of Instruction, 5,* 167–182.

Christenson, S. L., & Thurlow, M. L. (2004). School dropouts: Prevention considerations, interventions, and challenges. *Current Directions in Psychological Science, 13*, 36–39.

Chung, J. K., Park, S. H., Lee, W. J., & Lee, S. J. (2009). Bilateral cataract surgery: A controlled clinical trial. *Japan Journal of Ophthalmology, 53*, 107–113.

Cicchetti, D. (2011). Pathways to resilient functioning in maltreated children: From single to multilevel investigations. In D. Cicchetti & G. I. Roisman (Eds.), *The origins and organization of adaptation and maladaptation: Minnesota Symposia on Child Psychology* (Vol. 36). New York: Wiley.

Cicchetti, D. (2013, in press). Developmental psychopathology. In P. Zelazo (Ed.), *Oxford handbook of developmental psychology.* New York: Oxford University Press.

Cicchetti, D., & Rogosch, F. A. (2012, in press). Neuroendocrine regulation and emotional adaptation in the context of child maltreatment. In T. Dennis, P. Hastings, & K. Buss (Eds.), *Physiological measures of emotion from a developmental perspective: State of the Science. SRCD Monographs in Child Development.* New York: Wiley.

Cicchetti, D., Toth, S. L., Nilsen, W. J., & Manley, J. T. (2013). What do we know and why does it matter? The dissemination of evidence-based interventions for child maltreatment. In H. R. Schaeffer & K. Durkin (Eds.), *Blackwell handbook of developmental psychology in action.* New York: Blackwell.

Cicchetti, D., Toth, S. L., & Rogosch, F. A. (2005). *A prevention program for child maltreatment.* Unpublished manuscript. University of Rochester, Rochester, NY.

Cicirelli, V. (2009). Sibling relationships, later life. In D. Carr (Ed.), *Encyclopedia of the life course and human development.* Boston: Gale Cengage.

Cillessen, A. H. N., & Bellmore, A. D. (2011). Social skills and social competence in interactions with peers. In P. K. Smith & C. H. Hart (Eds.), *Wiley-Blackwell handbook of childhood social development* (2nd ed.). New York: Wiley.

Cillessen, A. H. N., & van den Berg, Y. H. M. (2012). Popularity and school adjustment. In A. M. Ryan & G. W. Ladd (Eds.), *Peer relationships and adjustment at school.* Charlotte, NC: Information Age Publishing.

Citkovitz, C., Schnyer, R. N., & Hoskins, I. A. (2011). Acupuncture during labor: Data are more promising than a recent review suggests. *British Journal of Obstetrics and Gynecology, 118*, 101.

Claes, H. I., & others. (2010). Understanding the effects of sildenafil treatment on erection maintenance and erection hardness. *Journal of Sexual Medicine, 7*(6), 2184–2191.

Clare, L., & others. (2011). Longitudinal trajectories of awareness in early-stage dementia. *Alzheimer Disease and Associated Disorders, 26*, 140–147.

Clark, B. (2008). *Growing up gifted* (7th ed.). Upper Saddle River, NJ: Prentice Hall.

Clark, E. (1993). *The lexicon in acquisition.* New York: Cambridge University Press.

Clark, E. V. (2009). What shapes children's language? Child-directed speech and the process of acquisition. In V. C. M. Gathercole (Ed.), *Routes to Language: Essays in honor of Melissa Bowerman.* New York: Psychology Press.

Clark, E. V. (2012). Lexical meaning. In E. L. Bavin (Ed.), *Cambridge handbook of child language.* New York: Cambridge University Press.

Clarke-Stewart, A. K., & Miner, J. L. (2008). Child and day care, effects of. In M. M. Haith & J. B. Benson (Eds.), *Encyclopedia of infant and early childhood development.* Oxford, UK: Elsevier.

Clay, O. J., & others. (2009). Visual function and cognitive speed of processing mediate age-related decline in memory span and fluid intelligence. *Journal of Aging and Health, 21*, 547–566.

Clearfield, M. W., Diedrich, F. J., Smith, L. B., & Thelen, E. (2006). Young infants reach correctly in A-not-B tasks: On the development of stability and perseveration. *Infant Behavior and Development, 29*, 435–444.

Clements, J. M. (2009). Patient perceptions on the use of advanced directives and life prolonging technology. *American Journal of Hospice and Palliative Care, 26*, 270–276.

Clifton, R. K., Morrongiello, B. A., Kulig, J. W., & Dowd, J. M. (1981). Developmental changes in auditory localization in infancy. In R. N. Aslin, J. R. Alberts, & M. R. Petersen (Eds.), *Development of perception* (Vol. 1). Orlando, FL: Academic Press.

Clifton, R. K., Muir, D. W., Ashmead, D. H., & Clarkson, M. G. (1993). Is visually guided reaching in early infancy a myth? *Child Development, 64*, 1099–1110.

Cluett, E. R., & Burns, E. (2009). Immersion in water in labour and birth. *Cochrane Database of Systematic Reviews*, CD000111.

Cogmed. (2013). *Cogmed: Working memory is the engine of learning.* Upper Saddle River, NJ: Pearson.

Cohen, D. (2012). *How the child's mind develops* (2nd ed.). New York: Psychology Press.

Cohen, F., Kemeny, M. E., Zegans, L. S., Johnson, P., Kearney, K. A., & Stites, D. P. (2007). Immune function declines with unemployment and recovers after stressor termination. *Psychosomatic Medicine, 69*, 225–234.

Cohen, K. M., & Savin-Williams, R. C. (2013, in press). Coming out to self and others: Unfolding of developmental milestones. In P. Levounis, J. Drescher, & M. Barber (Eds.), *Working with lesbian, gay, bisexual, and transgender people: Basic principles and case studies.* Arlington, VA: American Psychiatric Publishing.

Cohen, P. (2012). *In our prime: The invention of middle age.* New York: Scribner.

Cohen, P., Kasen, S., Chen, H., Hartmark, C., & Gordon, K. (2003). Variations in patterns of developmental transitions in the emerging adulthood period. *Developmental Psychology, 39*, 657–669.

Coie, J. (2004). The impact of negative social experiences on the development of antisocial behavior. In J. B. Kupersmidt & K. A. Dodge (Eds.), *Children's peer relations: From development to intervention.* Washington, DC: American Psychological Association.

Colby, A., Koblberg, L., Gibbs, J., & Lieberman, M. (1983). A longitudinal study of moral judgment. *Monographs of the Society for Research in Child Development* (Serial No. 201).

Colcombe, S. J., & others. (2006). Aerobic exercise training increases brain volume in aging humans. *Journals of Gerontology: Medical Sciences, 61A*, 1166–1170.

Cole, P. M., Dennis, T. A., Smith-Simon, K. E., & Cohen, L. H. (2009). Preschoolers' emotion regulation strategy understanding: Relations with maternal socialization and child behavior. *Social Development, 18*(2), 324–352.

Cole, P. M., & Hall, S. E. (2012). Emotion dysregulation as a risk factor for psychopathology. In T. Beauchaine & S. Hinshaw (Eds.), *Developmental Psychopathology.* New York: Wiley.

Cole, P. M., & Tan, P. Z. (2007). Emotion socialization from a cultural perspective. In J. E. Grusec & P. D. Hastings (Eds.), *Handbook of socialization.* New York: Guilford.

Coleman, P. D. (1986, August). *Regulation of dendritic extent: Human aging brain and Alzheimer's disease.* Paper presented at the meeting of the American Psychological Association, Washington, DC.

Coleman-Phox, K., Odouli, R., & Li, D. K. (2008). Use of a fan during sleep and the risk of sudden infant death syndrome. *Archives of Pediatric and Adolescent Medicine, 162*, 963–968.

Collins, C. E., & others. (2011). Parent diet modification, child activity, or both in obese children: An RCT. *Pediatrics, 127*, 619–627.

Collins, J. S., Atkinson, K. K., Dean, J. H., Best, R. G., & Stevenson, R. E. (2011). Long term maintenance of neural tube defects prevention in a high prevalence state. *Journal of Pediatrics. Alcoholism, Clinical and Experimental Research, 159*, 143–149.

Collins, W. A., & van Dulmen, M. (2006). The significance of middle childhood peer competence for work and relationships in early childhood. In A. C. Huston & M. N. Ripke (Eds.), *Developmental contexts in middle childhood.* New York: Cambridge University Press.

Colombo, J., Brez, C., & Curtindale, L. (2013). Infant perception and cognition. In I. B. Weiner & others (Eds.), *Handbook of psychology* (2nd ed., Vol. 6). New York: Wiley.

Colonnesi, C., Stams, G. J., Koster, I., & Noom, M. J. (2010). The relation between pointing and language development: A meta-analysis. *Developmental Review, 30*, 352–366.

Columbo, J., Brez, C., & Curtindale, L. (2013, in press). Infant perception and cognition. In I. B. Weiner & others (Eds.), *Handbook of psychology* (2nd ed., Vol. 6). New York: Wiley.

Comer, J. (1988). Educating poor minority children. *Scientific American, 259*, 42–48.

Comer, J. (2004). *Leave no child behind.* New Haven, CT: Yale University Press.

Comer, J. (2006). Child development: The under-weighted aspect of intelligence. In P. C. Kyllonen, R. D. Roberts, & L. Stankov (Eds.), *Extending intelligence.* Mahwah, NJ: Erlbaum.

Comer, J. (2010). Comer School Development Program. In J. Meece & J. Eccles (Eds.), *Handbook of research on schools, schooling, and human development.* New York: Routledge.

Common Sense Media. (2011). *Zero to eight: Children's media use in America.* Retrieved June 21, 2012, from www.commonsensemedia.org/research

Commoner, B. (2002). Unravelling the DNA myth: The spurious foundation of genetic engineering. *Harper's Magazine, 304*, 39–47.

Conde-Aguedelo, A., Belizan, J. M., & Diaz-Rossello, J. (2011). Kangaroo care to reduce morbidity and mortality in low birth-weight infants. *Cochrane Database of Systematic Reviews, 16*(3) CD002771.

Condition of Education (2012). *Participation in education,* Table A-9-1. Washington, DC: National Center for Education Statistics.

Cong, X., Ludington-Hoe, S. M., & Walsh, S. (2011). Randomized crossover trial of kangaroo care to reduce biobehavioral pain responses in preterm infants: A pilot study. *Biological Research for Nursing, 13*, 204–216.

Conger, R. D., & others. (2012). Resilience and vulnerability of Mexican origin youth and their families: A test of a culturally-informed model of family economic stress. In P. K. Kerig, M. S. Schulz, & S. T. Hauser (Eds.), *Adolescence and beyond.* New York: Oxford University Press.

Connolly, J. A., & McIsaac, C. (2009). Romantic relationships in adolescence. In R. M. Lerner & L. Steinberg (Eds.), *Handbook of adolescent psychology* (3rd ed.), New York: Wiley.

Conry-Murray, C., Kim, J. M., & Turiel, E. (2012, April). *U.S. and Korean children's judgments of gender norm violations.* Paper presented at the Gender Development Research conference, San Francisco.

Cook, E. C., Buehler, C., & Blair, B. L. (2012, in press). Adolescent emotional reactivity across relationship contexts. *Developmental Psychology.*

Cook, J. A., & Hawkins, D. B. (2006). Hearing loss and hearing aid treatment options. Mayo *Clinic Proceedings, 81*, 234–237.

Cooksey, E. C. (2009). Sexual activity, adolescent. In D. Carr (Ed.), *Encyclopedia of the life course and human development.* Boston: Gale Cengage.

Coontz, S. (2005). *Marriage, history.* New York: Penguin.

Cooper, C. (2012). *Intelligence and abilities* (2nd ed.). New York: Psychology Press.

Cooper, C. R. (2011). *Bridging multiple worlds.* New York: Oxford University Press.

Cooper, J. N., & others. (2012, in press). Effects of an intensive weight loss intervention consisting of caloric restriction with or without physical activity on common carotid artery remodeling in seriously obese adults. *Metabolism.*

Copen, C. E., Daniels, K., Vespa, J., & Mosher, W. D. (2012). First marriages in the United States: Data from the 2006–2010 National Survey of Family Growth. *National Health Statistics Reports, 49*, 1–22.

Coplan, R. J., & Arbeau, K. A. (2009). Peer interactions and play in early childhood. In K. H. Rubin, W. M. Bukowski, & B. Laursen (Eds.), *Handbook of peer interactions, relationships, and groups.* New York: Guilford.

Cordier, S. (2008). Evidence for a role of paternal exposure in developmental toxicity. *Basic and Clinical Pharmacology and Toxicology, 102*, 176–181.

Cornew, L., & others. (2012, in press). Atypical social referencing in infant siblings of children with autism spectrum disorders. *Journal of Autism and Developmental Disorders.*

Corsica, J. A., & Perri, M. G. (2013). Obesity. In I. B. Weiner & others (Eds.), *Handbook of psychology* (2nd ed., Vol. 9). New York: Wiley.

Cortes, E., Basra, R., & Kelleher, C. J. (2011). Waterbirth and pelvic floor injury: A retrospective study and postal survey using ICIQ modular long form questionnaires. *European Journal of Obstetrics, Gynecology, and Reproductive Biology, 155*, 27–30.

Cosmides, L. (2013). Evolutionary psychology. *Annual Review of Psychology* (Vol. 6). Palo Alto, CA: Annual Reviews.

Costa, P. T., & McCrae, R. R. (1998). Personality assessment. In H. S. Friedman (Ed.), *Encyclopedia of mental health* (Vol. 3). San Diego: Academic Press.

Costa, P. T., & McCrae, R. R. (2000). Contemporary personality psychology. In C. E. Coffey and J. L. Cummings (Eds.). *Textbook of geriatric neuropsychiatry.* Washington, DC: American Psychiatric Press.

Cote, J., & Bynner, J. M. (2008). Changes in the transition to adulthood in the UK and Canada: The role of structure and aging in emerging adulthood. *Journal of Youth Studies, 11*, 251–258.

Cotelli, M., Manenti, R., & Zanetti, O. (2012). Reminiscence therapy in dementia: A review. *Maturitas, 72*, 203–205.

Courage, M. L., Edison, S. C., & Howe, M. L. (2004). Variability in the early development of visual self-recognition. *Infant Behavior and Development, 27*, 509–532.

Cousineau, T. M., Goldstein, M., & Franco, D. L. (2005). A collaborative approach to nutrition education for college students. *Journal of American College Health, 53*, 79–84.

Cowan, C. P., & Cowan, P. A. (2000). *When partners become parents.* Mahwah, NJ: Erlbaum.

Cowan, P. A., & Cowan, C. P. (2009). How working with couples fosters children's development in M. S. Schulz, P. K. Kerig, M. K. Pruett, & R. D. Parke (Eds.), *Feathering the nest.* Washington, DC: American Psychological Association.

Cowan, P., Cowan, C., Ablow, J., Johnson, V. K., & Measelle, J. (2005). *The family context of parenting in children's adaptation to elementary school.* Mahwah, NJ: Erlbaum.

Cox, K. S., Wilt, J., Olson, B., & McAdams, D. P. (2010). Generativity, the Big Five, and psychosocial adaptation in midlife adults. *Journal of Personality, 78*, 1185–1208.

Coxon, J. P., Van Impe, A., Wenderoth, N., & Swinnen, S. P. (2012). Aging and inhibitory control of action: Cortio-subthalamic connection strength predicts stopping performance. *Journal of Neuroscience, 32*, 8401–8412.

Coyne, S. M., Nelson, D. A., & Underwood, M. K. (2011). Aggression in children. In P. K. Smith & C. H. Hart (Eds.), *Wiley-Blackwell handbook of childhood social development* (2nd ed.). New York: Wiley.

Crabb, R. M., Rafie, S., & Weingardt, K. R. (2012). Health-related Internet use in older primary care patients. *Gerontology, 58*, 161–170.

Craig, L. A., Hong, N. S., & McDonald, R. J. (2011). Revisiting the cholinergic hypothesis in the development of Alzheimer's disease. *Neuroscience and Biobehavioral Reviews, 35*, 1397–1409.

Crain, S. (2012). Sentence scope. In E. L. Bavin (Ed.), *Cambridge handbook of child language.* New York: Cambridge University Press.

Crain, S., & Zhou, P. (2012, in press). Semantics and pragmatics: Acquisition of logical connectives and focus. In C. T. J. Huang & R. Sybesma (Eds.), *Encyclopedia of Chinese language and linguistics.* The Netherlands: Brill.

Crawford, D., & others. (2010). The longitudinal influence of home and neighborhood environments on children's body mass index and physical activity over 5 years: The CLAN study. *International Journal of Obesity, 34*, 1177–1187.

Cremation Association of North America. (2012). *Statistics about cremation trends.* Retrieved July 12, 2012, from www.cremation association/org/Media/Cremation Statistics/tabid/95/Default.aspx

Crijns, H. J., & others. (2012, in press). Prescriptive contraceptive use among isotretinoin users in the Netherlands in comparison with non-users: A drug utilization study. *Pharmacoepidemiology and Drug Safety.*

Crockenberg, S. B. (1986). Are temperamental differences in babies associated with predictable differences in caregiving? In J. V. Lerner & R. M. Lerner (Eds.), *Temperament and social interaction during infancy and childhood.* San Francisco: Jossey-Bass.

Cronk, C. E., & others. (2011). Effects of a culturally tailored intervention on changes in body mass index and health-related quality of life of Latino children and their parents. *American Journal of Health Promotion, 25*, e1–e11.

Crooks, R. L., & Baur, K. (2011). *Our sexuality* (11th ed.). Boston: Cengage.

Crosnoe, R. (2011). *Fitting in, standing out.* New York: Cambridge University Press.

Cross, T. P., Matthews, B., Tommyr, L., Scott, D., & Quimet, C. (2012, in press). Child welfare policy and practice on children's exposure to domestic violence. *Child Abuse and Neglect.*

Crouter, A. C. (2006). Mothers and fathers at work. In A. Clarke-Stewart & J. Dunn (Eds.), *Families count.* New York: Cambridge University Press.

Crowley, K., Callahan, M. A., Tenenbaum, H. R., & Allen, E. (2001). Parents explain more to boys than to girls during shared scientific thinking. *Psychological Science, 12*, 258–261.

Csikszentmihalyi, M. (1995). *Creativity.* New York: HarperCollins.

Csikszentmihalyi, M. (2000). Creativity: An overview. In A. Kazdin (Ed.), *Encyclopedia of psychology.* Washington, DC, & New York: American Psychological Association and Oxford University Press.

Cubbin, C., Brindis, C. D., Jain, S., Santelli, J., & Braveman, P. (2010). Neighborhood poverty, aspirations and expectations, and initiation of sex. *Journal of Adolescent Health, 47*, 399–406.

Cubillo, A., Halari, R., Smith, A., Taylor, E., & Rubia, K. (2012). A review of frontospatial brain abnormalities in children and adults with Attention Deficit Hyperactivity Disorder (ADHD) and new evidence for dysfunction in adults with ADHD during motivation and attention. *Cortex, 48*, 194–215.

Cuevas, K., Swingler, M. M., Bell, M. A., Marcovitch, S., & Calkins, S. D. (2012). Measures of frontal lobe functioning and the emergence of inhibitory control process at 10 months of age. *Developmental Cognitive Neuroscience, 2*, 235–243.

Cummings, E. M., Braungart-Rieker, J. M., & Du Rocher-Schudlich, T. (2013, in press). Emotion and personality development. In I. B. Weiner & others (Eds.), *Handbook of psychology* (2nd ed., Vol. 6). New York: Wiley.

Cummings, E. M., & Davies, P. T. (2010). *Marital conflict and children: An emotional security perspective.* New York: Guilford.

Cummings, E. M., & Merrilees, C. E. (2009, in press). Identifying the dynamic processes underlying links between marital conflict and child adjustment. In M. S. Schulz, P. K. Kerig, M. K. Pruett, & R. D. Parke (Eds.), *Feathering the nest.* Washington, DC: American Psychological Association.

Cunningham, M. (2009). Housework. In D. Carr (Ed.), *Encyclopedia of the life course and human development.* Boston: Gale Cengage.

Cunningham, P. M. (2013). *Phonics they use: Words for reading and writing* (6th ed.). Boston: Allyn & Bacon.

Curran, K., DuCette, J., Eisenstein, J., & Hyman, I. A. (2001, August). *Statistical analysis of the cross-cultural data: The third year.* Paper presented at the meeting of the American Psychological Association, San Francisco, CA.

Currie, C., & others. (2012). Is obesity at individual and national level associated with lower age at menarche? Evidence from 34 countries in the Health Behavior in School-aged Children study. *Journal of Adolescent Health, 50*, 621–626.

Currie, K. D., McKelvie, R. S., & MacDonald, M. J. (2012, in press). Flow-mediated dilation is acutely improved following high-density interval exercise. *Medicine and Science in Sports and Exercise.*

Currier, J. M., Holland, J. M., & Neimeyer, R. A. (2006). Sense-making, grief, and the experience of violent loss: Toward a mediational model. *Death Studies, 30*, 403–428.

Cvencek, D., Meltzoff, A. N., & Greenwald, A. G. (2011). Math-gender stereotypes in elementary school children. *Child Development, 82*, 766–779.

Czaja, S. J., & others. (2006). Factors predicting the use of technology: Findings from the Center for Research and Education on Aging and Technology (CREATE). *Psychology and Aging, 21*, 333–352.

D

da Fonseca, E. B., Bittar, R. E., Damiao, R., & Zugiab, M. (2009). Prematurity prevention: The role of progesterone. *Current Opinion in Obstetrics and Gynecology, 21*, 142–147.

Dahl, R. E. (2004). Adolescent brain development: A period of vulnerability and opportunity. *Annals of the New York Academy of Sciences, 1021*, 1–22.

Dale, P., & Goodman, J. (2004). Commonality and differences in vocabulary growth. In M. Tomasello & D. I. Slobin (Eds.), *Beyond nature-nurture.* Mahwah, NJ: Erlbaum.

Daley, A. J., Macarthur, C., & Winter, H. (2007). The role of exercise in treating postpartum depression: A review of the literature. *Journal of Midwifery & Women's Health, 52*, 56–62.

Dalley, J. W., & Roiser, J. P. (2012, in press). Dopamine, serotonin, and impulsivity. *Neuroscience.*

Damon, W. (2008). *The path to purpose.* New York: Free Press.

Daniels, H. (2011). Vygotsky and psychology. In U. Goswami (Ed.), *Wiley-Blackwell handbook of childhood cognitive development* (2nd ed.). New York: Wiley.

Darcy, E. (2012). Gender issues in child and adolescent eating disorders. In J. Lock (Ed.), *Oxford handbook of child and adolescent eating disorders: Developmental perspectives.* New York: Oxford University Press.

Darwin, C. (1859). *On the origin of species.* London: John Murray.

Dastani, Z., & others. (2012). Novel loci for adiponectin levels and their influence on type 2 diabetes and metabolic traits: A multi-ethnic meta-analysis of 45,891 individuals. *PLoS One, 8*(3), e1002607.

Davidson, M. R., Davidson, M., London, M. L., & Ladewig, P. W. (2012). *Olds' maternal-newborn nursing and women's health across the lifespan: International edition.* (9th ed.). Upper Saddle River, NJ: Pearson.

Davies, G., & others. (2011). Genome-wide association studies establish that human intelligence is highly heritable and polygenic. *Molecular Psychiatry, 16*, 996–1005.

Davies, J., & Brember, I. (1999). Reading and mathematics attainments and self-esteem in years 2 and 6—an eight-year cross-sectional study. *Educational Studies, 25*, 145–157.

Davies, M., Gilston, J., & Rogers, P. (2012, in press). Examining the relationship between male rape myth acceptance, female rape myth acceptance, victim blame, homophobia, gender roles, and ambivalent sexism. *Journal of Interpersonal Violence.*

Davinelli, S., Willcox, D. C., & Scapagnini, G. (2012, in press). Extending healthy aging: Nutrient sensitive pathway and centenarian population. *Immunity and Aging.*

Davis, B. E., Moon, R. Y., Sachs, M. C., & Ottolini, M. C. (1998). Effects of sleep position on infant motor development. *Pediatrics, 102*, 1135–1140.

Davis, K. E., Norris, J., Hessler, D. M., Zawacki, T., Morrison, D. M., & George, W. H. (2010). College women's decision making: Cognitive mediation of alcohol expectancy effects. *Journal of American College Health, 58*, 481–488.

Davis, L., & Keyser, J. (1997). *Becoming the parent you want to be: A sourcebook of strategies for the first five years.* New York: Broadway.

Davis, M. C., Burke, H. M., Zautra, A. J., & Stark, S. (2013). Arthritis and musculo-skeletal conditions. In I. B. Weiner & others (Eds.), *Handbook of psychology* (2nd ed., Vol. 9). New York: Wiley.

Davis, S. W., Kragel, J. E., Madden, D. J., & Cabesa, R. (2012). The architecture of cross-hemispheric communication in the aging brain: Linking behavior to functional and structural connectivity. *Cerebral Cortex, 22*, 232–242.

Day, N. L., Goldschmidt, L., & Thomas, C. A. (2006). Prenatal marijuana exposure contributes to the prediction of marijuana use at age 14. *Addiction, 101*, 1313–1322.

De Decker, E., & others. (2012). Influencing factors of screen time in preschool children: An exploration of parents' perceptions through focus groups in six European countries. *Obesity Reviews, 13* (Suppl. 1), S75–S84.

De Giovanni, N., & Marchetti, D. (2012). Cocaine and its metabolites in the placenta: A systematic review of the literature. *Reproductive Toxicology, 33*, 1–14.

de Haan, M., & Gunnar, M. R. (Eds.) (2009). *Handbook of developmental social neuroscience.* New York: Guilford.

de la Cuesta-Benjumea, C. (2011). Strategies for the relief of burden in advanced dementia care-giving. *Journal of Advanced Nursing, 67,* 1790–1799.

de la Sierra, A., & Barrios, V. (2012, in press). Blood pressure control with angiotensin receptor blocker-based three-drug combinations: Key trials. *Advances in Therapy.*

De Rose, L. M., Shiyko, M. P., Foster, H., & Brooks-Gunn, J. (2011). Associations between menarcheal timing and behavioral developmental trajectories for girls from age 6 to age 15. *Journal of Youth and Adolescence, 40,* 1329–1342.

de Villars, J., & de Villiers, P. (2013). Syntax acquisition. In P. D. Zelazo (Ed.), *Oxford handbook of developmental psychology.* New York: Oxford University Press.

de Wit, L., & others. (2010). Depression and obesity: A meta-analysis of community-based studies. *Psychiatry Research, 178,* 230–235.

Deary, I. J. (2012). Intelligence. *Annual Review of Intelligence* (Vol. 63). Palo Alto, CA: Annual Reviews.

Decarli, C., & others. (2012, in press). Session II: Mechanisms of age-related cognitive change and targets for intervention: Neural circuits, networks, and plasticity. *Journals of Gerontology A: Biological Sciences and Medical Sciences.*

DeCasper, A. J., & Spence, M. J. (1986). Prenatal maternal speech influences newborns' perception of speech sounds. *Infant Behavior and Development, 9,* 133–150.

Decimo, I., Bifari, F., Krampera, M., & Fumagalli, G. (2012). Neural stem cell niches in health and diseases. *Current Pharmaceutical Design, 18,* 1755–1783.

Deeg, D. J. H. (2005). The development of physical and mental health from late midlife to early old age. In S. L. Willis & Martin (Eds.), *Middle adulthood.* Thousand Oaks, CA: Sage.

DeJong, W., DeRicco, B., & Schneider, S. K. (2010). Pregaming: An exploratory study of strategic drinking by college students in Pennsylvania. *Journal of American College Health, 58,* 307–316.

Del Giudice, M. (2011). Sex differences in romantic attachment: A meta-analysis. *Personality and Social Psychology Bulletin, 37,* 193–214.

Demerouti, E. (2012). The spillover and crossover of resources among partners: The role of work-self and family-self facilitation. *Journal of Occupational Health Psychology, 17,* 184–195.

Dempster, F. N. (1981). Memory span: Sources of individual and developmental differences. *Psychological Bulletin, 80,* 63–100.

Denham, S., & others. (2011). Emotions and social development in childhood. In P. K. Smith & C. H. Hart (Eds.), *Wiley-Blackwell handbook of childhood social development* (2nd ed.). New York: Wiley.

Denham, S., & others. (2012, in press). Preschoolers' emotion knowledge: Self-regulatory foundations and predictors of school success. *Cognition and Emotion.*

Denham, S., Warren, H., von Salisch, M., Benga, O., Chin, J-C., & Geangu, E. (2011). Emotions and social development in

childhood. In P. K. Smith & C. H. Hart (Eds.), *Wiley-Blackwell handbook of childhood social development* (2nd ed.). New York: Wiley.

Dennis, N. A., & Cabeza, R. (2008). Neuroimaging of healthy cognitive aging. In F. I. M. Craik & T. A. Salthouse (Eds.). *Handbook of aging and cognition* (3rd ed.). Mahwah, NJ: Erlbaum.

DePaulo, B. (2006). *Singled out.* New York: St. Martin's Press.

DePaulo, B. (2011). Living single: Lightening up those dark, dopey myths. In W. R. Cupach & B. H. Spitzberg (Eds.), *The dark side of close relationships.* New York: Routledge.

Depp, C. A., Vahia, I. V., & Jeste, D. V. (2012). Successful aging. In S. K. Whitbourne & M. J. Sliwinski (Ed.), *Wiley-Blackwell handbook of adult development and aging.* New York: Wiley.

DeSpelder, L. A., & Strickland, A. L. (2005). *The last dance: Encountering death and dying* (6th ed., rev. update). Mountain View, CA: Mayfield.

Devaney, S. A., Palomaki, G. E., Scott, J. A., & Bianchi, D. W. (2011). Noninvasive fetal sex determination using cell-free fetal DNA: A systematic review and meta-analysis. *Journal of the American Medical Association, 306,* 627–636.

DeWall, C. N., Anderson, C. A., & Bushman, B. J. (2013). Aggression. In I. B. Weiner & others (Eds.), *Handbook of psychology* (2nd ed., Vol. 5). New York: Wiley.

DeWall, C. N., & others. (2011). So far away from one's partner, yet so close to romantic alternatives: Avoidant attachment, interest in alternatives, and infidelity. *Journal of Personality and Social Psychology, 101,* 1302–1316.

Di Ciommo, V., Forcella, E., & Cotugno, G. (2012). Living with phenylketonuria from the point of view of children, adolescents, and young adults: A qualitative study. *Journal of Developmental and Behavioral Pediatrics, 33,* 229–235.

Diamond, A. (1985). Development of the ability to use recall to guide action, as indicated by infants' performance on AB. *Child Development, 56,* 866–883.

Diamond, A. (2009). The interplay of biology and the environment broadly defined. *Developmental Psychology, 45,* 1–8.

Diamond, A. (2013). Executive functioning. *Annual Review of Psychology* (Vol. 64). Palo Alto, CA: Annual Reviews.

Diamond, A., Barnett, W. S., Thomas, J., & Munro, S. (2007). Preschool program improves cognitive control. *Science, 318,* 1387–1388.

Diamond, A., Casey, B. J., & Munakata, Y. (2011). *Developmental cognitive neuroscience.* New York: Oxford University Press.

Diamond, A., & Lee, K. (2011). Interventions shown to aid executive function development in children 4 to 12 years old. *Science, 333,* 959–964.

Diamond, L. M. (2013, in press). Concepts of female sexual orientation. In C. Patterson & A. R. D'Augelli (Eds.), *The psychology of sexual orientation.* New York: Cambridge University Press.

Diamond, L. M., & Savin-Williams, R. C. (2011). Same-sex activity in adolescence: Multiple meanings and implications. In R. F. Fassinger & S. L. Morrow (Eds.), *Sex in the margins.* Washington, DC: American Psychological Association.

Diaz-Rico, L. T. (2012). *Course for teaching English Language Learners* (2nd ed.). Boston: Allyn & Bacon.

Dickinson, W. J., & others. (2011). Change in stress and social support as predictors of cognitive decline in older adults with and without depression. *International Journal of Geriatric Psychiatry, 26,* 1267–1274.

Diego, M. A., Field, T., & Hernandez-Reif, M. (2008). Temperature increases in preterm infants during massage therapy. *Infant Behavior and Development, 31,* 149–152.

Diener, E. (2012). *Subjective well-being.* Retrieved April 5, 2012, from http://internal. psychology.illinois.edu/~ediener/SWLS.html

Diener, E., Emmons, R. A., Larson, R. J., & Griffin, S. (1985). The Satisfaction with Life Scale. *Journal of Personality Assessment, 49,* 71–75.

Dilworth-Anderson, P., Pierre, G., & Hilliard, T. S. (2012). Social justice, health disparities, and culture in the care of the elderly. *Journal of Law, Medicine, and Ethics, 40,* 26–32.

Dimmitt, C., & McCormick, C. B. (2012). Metacognition in education. In K. R. Harris, S. Graham, & T. Urdan (Eds.), *Handbook of educational psychology.* Washington, DC: American Psychological Association.

Dirk, J. (2012). Processing speed. In S. K. Whitbourne & M. Sliwinski (Eds.), *Wiley-Blackwell handbook of adulthood and aging.* New York: Wiley.

Dirk, J., & Schmiedek, F. (2012). Processing speed. In S. K. Whitbourne & M. Sliwinski (Eds.), *Wiley-Blackwell handbook of adult development and aging.* New York: Wiley.

Dishion, T. J., & Piehler, T. F. (2009). Deviant by design: Peer contagion in development, interventions, and schools. In K. H. Rubin, W. M. Bukowski, & B. Laursen (Eds.), *Handbook of peer interactions, relationships, and groups.* New York: Guilford.

Diwadkar, V. A., & others. (2012, in press). Differences in cortico-striatal-cerebellar activation during working memory in syndromal and nonsyndromal children with prenatal exposure to alcohol. *Human Brain Mapping.*

Dixon, R. A., McFall, G. P., Whitehead, B. P., & Dolcos, S. (2013, in press). Cognitive development and aging. In I. B. Weiner & others (Eds.), *Handbook of psychology* (2nd ed., Vol. 6). New York: Wiley.

Dixon, R. A., Small, B. J., MacDonald, S. W. S., & McArdle, J. J. (2012). Yes, memory declines with age—but when, how, and why? In M. Naveh Benjamin & N. Ohta (Eds.), *Memory and aging.* New York: Psychology Press.

Dodge, E. (2012). Family evolution and process during the child and adolescent years in eating disorders. In J. Lock (Ed.)., *Oxford handbook of child and adolescent eating disorders: Developmental perspectives.* New York: Oxford University Press.

Dodge, K. A. (1983). Behavioral antecedents of peer social status. *Child Development, 54,* 1386–1399.

Dodge, K. A. (2011a). Context matters in child and family policy. *Child Development, 82,* 433–442.

Dodge, K. A. (2011b). Social information processing models of aggressive behavior. In M. Mikulincer & P. R. Shaver (Eds.), *Understanding and reducing aggression, violence, and their consequences.* Washington, DC: American Psychological Association.

Doherty, M. (2008). *Theory of mind.* Philadelphia: Psychology Press.

Donatelle, R. J. (2013). *Health* (10th ed.). Upper Saddle River, NJ: Pearson.

Dondi, M., Simion, F., & Caltran, G. (1999). Can newborns discriminate between their own cry and the cry of another newborn infant? *Developmental Psychology, 35*(2), 418–426.

Donnerstein, E. (2012). Internet bullying. *Pediatric Clinics of North America, 59,* 623–633.

Doria, E., Buonocore, D., Focarelli, A., & Marzatico, F. (2012, in press). Relationship between human aging muscle and oxidative system pathway. *Oxidative Medicine and Cellular Longevity.*

Doty, R. L., & Shah, M. (2008). Taste and smell. In M. M. Haith & J. B. Benson (Eds.), *Encyclopedia of infant and early childhood development.* Oxford, UK: Elsevier.

Dougall, A. L., & Baum, A. (2012). Health and illness. In A. Baum, T. A. Revenson, & J. Singer (Eds.), *Handbook of health psychology* (2nd ed.). New York: Psychology Press.

Dow, R. S., & Baer, G. T. (2013). *Self-paced phonics* (5th ed.). Boston: Allyn & Bacon.

Dowdy, S., & others. (2012, in press). Empower U: Effectiveness of an adolescent outreach and prevention program with sixth-grade boys and girls: A pilot study. *Journal of Pediatric Nursing.*

Dozier, M., Stovall-McClough, K. C., & Albus, K. E. (2009). Attachment and psychopathology in adulthood. In J. Cassidy & P. R. Shaver (Eds.), *Handbook of attachment* (2nd ed.). New York: Guilford.

Dryfoos, J. G. (1990). *Adolescents at risk: Prevalence or prevention.* New York: Oxford University Press.

Dryfoos, J. G., & Barkin, C. (2006). *Growing up in America today.* New York: Oxford University Press.

Duberstein, P. R., & others. (2011). Personality and risk for Alzheimer's disease in adults 72 years of age and older: A 6-year follow-up. *Psychology and Aging, 26,* 351–362.

Duck, S. (2011). *Rethinking relationships.* Thousand Oaks, CA: Sage.

Dulin, P. L., Gavala, J., Stephens, C., Kostick M., & McDonald, J. (2012, in press). *Volunteering predicts happiness among Maori and non-Maori in the New Zealand Health, Work, and Retirement Study.*

Dulloo, A. G., Jacquet, J., & Montani, J. P. (2012, in press). How dieting makes some fatter: From a perspective of human body composition autoregulation. *Proceedings of the Nutrition Society.*

Duncan, G. J. (2012). Give us this day our daily breadth. *Child Development, 83,* 6–15.

Duncan, G., Magnuson, K., Kalil, A., & Ziol-Guest, K. (2013, in press). *Social indicators research.*

Duncombe, M. E., Havighurst, S. S., Holland, K. A., & Frankling, E. J. (2012, in press). The contribution of parenting practice and parent emotion factors in children at risk for disruptive behavior disorders. *Child Psychiatry and Human Development.*

Dunkel Schetter, C. (2011). Psychological science in the study of pregnancy and birth. *Annual Review of Psychology* (Vol. 62). Palo Alto, CA: Annual Reviews.

Dunlay, S. M., Swetz, K. M., Mueller, P. S., & Roger, V. L. (2012). Advance directives in community patients with heart failure. *Circulation, Cardiovascular Quality and Outcomes, 5,* 283–289.

Dunn, J. (1984). Sibling studies and the developmental impact of critical incidents. In P. B. Baltes & O. G. Brim (Eds.), *Life-span development and behavior* (Vol. 6). Orlando, FL: Academic Press.

Dunn, J. (2007). Siblings and socialization. In J. E. Grusec & P. D. Hastings (Eds.), *Handbook of socialization.* New York: Guilford.

Dunn, J., & Kendrick, C. (1982). *Siblings.* Cambridge, MA: Harvard University Press.

Dunsmore, J. C., Booker, J. A., & Ollendick, T. H. (2012, in press). Parental emotion coaching and child emotion regulation as protective factors for children with oppositional defiant disorder. *Social Development.*

Duriez, B., Luyckx, K., Soenens, B., & Berzonsky, M. (2012). A process-content approach to adolescent identity formation: Examining longitudinal associations between identity styles and goal pursuits. *Journal of Personality, 80,* 135–161.

Durrant, J. E. (2008). Physical punishment, culture, and rights: Current issues for professionals. *Journal of Developmental and Behavioral Pediatrics, 29,* 55–66.

Durrant, R., & Ellis, B. (2013). Evolutionary psychology. In M. Gallagher, R. J. Nelson, I. B. Weiner, & others (Eds.), *Handbook of psychology* (2nd ed., Vol. 3). New York: Wiley.

Durston, S., & others. (2006). A shift from diffuse to focal cortical activity with development. *Developmental Science, 9,* 1–8.

Duxbury, L., Higgins, C., & Smart, R. (2011). Elder care and the impact of caregiver strain on the health of employed caregivers. *Work, 40,* 29–40.

Dvornyk, V., & Waqar-ul-Haq, H. (2012). Genetics of age at menarche: A systematic review. *Human Reproduction Update, 18,* 198–210.

Dweck, C. S. (2006). *Mindset.* New York: Random House.

Dweck, C. S. (2013). Social development. In P. Zelazo (Ed.), *Oxford handbook of developmental psychology.* New York: Oxford University Press.

Dweck, C. S., & Master, A. (2009). Self-theories and motivation: Students' beliefs about intelligence. In K. R. Wentzel & A. Wigfield (Eds.), *Handbook of motivation at school.* New York: Routledge.

Dworkin, S. L., & Santelli, J. (2007). Do abstinence-plus interventions reduce sexual risk behavior among youth? *PLoS Medicine, 4,* 1437–1439.

Dwyer, J. W., & Coward, R. T. (1991). A multivariate comparison of the involvement of adult sons versus daughters in the care of impaired parents. *Journal of Gerontology B: Psychological Sciences and Social Sciences, 46,* S259–S269.

E

Eagly, A. H. (2001). Social role theory of sex differences and similarities. In J. Worrell (Ed.), *Encyclopedia of women and gender.* San Diego: Academic Press.

Eagly, A. H. (2010). Gender roles. In J. Levine & M. Hogg (Eds.), *Encyclopedia of group process and intergroup relations.* Thousand Oaks, CA: Sage.

Eagly, A. H. (2012, in press). Science, feminism, and the investigation of gender. In R.W. Proctor & E. J. Capaldi (Eds.), *Psychology of science: Implicit and explicit reasoning.* New York: Oxford University Press.

Eagly, A. H., & Crowley, M. (1986). Gender and helping: A meta-analytic review of the social psychological literature. *Psychological Bulletin, 108,* 233–256.

Eagly, A. H., & Steffen, V. J. (1986). Gender and aggressive behavior: A meta-analytic review of the social psychological literature. *Psychological Bulletin, 100,* 309–330.

Early Growth Genetics (EGG) Consortium & others. (2012, in press). A genome-wide association meta-analysis identifies new childhood obesity loci. *Nature: Genetics.*

East, P. (2009). Adolescent relationships with siblings. In R. M. Lerner & L. Steinberg (Eds.), *Handbook of adolescent psychology* (3rd ed.). New York: Wiley.

Easterbrooks, M. A., Bartlett, J. D., Beeghly, M., & Thompson, R. A. (2013). Social and emotional development in infancy. In I. B. Weiner & others (Eds.), *Handbook of psychology* (2nd ed., Vol. 6). New York: Wiley.

Eaton, D. K., & others. (2008, June 6). Youth risk surveillance—United States 2007. *MMWR, 57,* 1–131.

Eaton, D. K., & others. (2010, June 4). Youth risk behavior surveillance—United States, 2009. *MMWR Surveillance Summaries, 59*(5), 1–142.

Eaton, D.K., & others (2012). Youth Risk Behavior Surveillance—United States 2011. Atlanta: Centers for Disease Control and Prevention.

Eaton, N. R., & others. (2012). Genes, environment, personality, and successful aging: Toward a comprehensive developmental model in later life. *Journals of Gerontology A: Biological Sciences and Medical Sciences, 67*, 480–488.

Eccles, J. S. (2007). Families, schools, and developing achievement-related motivations and engagement. In J. E. Grusec & P. D. Hastings (Eds.), *Handbook of socialization.* New York: Guilford.

Eccles, J. S., & Roeser, R. W. (2013). Schools as developmental contexts in adolescence. In I. B. Weiner & others (Eds.), *Handbook of psychology* (2nd ed., Vol. 6). New York: Wiley.

Echevarria, J. J., Vogt, M. J., & Short, D. J. (2013). *Making content comprehensible for English learners: The SIOP Model* (4th ed.). Boston: Allyn & Bacon.

Eckerman, C., & Whitehead, H. (1999). How toddler peers generate coordinated action: A cross-cultural exploration. *Early Education & Development, 10*, 241–266.

Eckmann, J., & others. (2012, in press). MITOCHONDRIA: Mitochondrial membranes in aging and neurodegeneration. *International Journal of Biochemistry and Cell Biology.*

Educational Testing Service. (1992, February). *Cross-national comparisons of 9- to 13-year-olds' science and math achievement.* Princeton, NJ: Educational Testing Service.

Edwardson, C. L., & Gorely, T. (2010). Activity-related parenting practices and children's objectively measured physical activity. *Pediatric Exercise Science, 22*, 105–113.

Egli, T., Bland, M. W., Melton, B. F., & Czech, D. R. (2011). Influence of age, sex, and race on college students' exercise motivation of physical activity. *Journal of American College Health, 59*, 399–406.

Eichorn, D. H., Clausen, J. A., Haan, N., Honzik, M. P., & Mussen, P. H. (Eds.). (1981). *Present and past in middle life.* New York: Academic Press.

Eiferman, R. R. (1971). Social play in childhood. In R. Herron & B. Sutton-Smith (Eds.), *Child's play.* New York: Wiley.

Eisenberg, N., Fabes, R. A., & Spinrad, T. L. (2006). Prosocial development. In W. Damon & R. Lerner (Eds.), *Handbook of child psychology* (6th ed.). New York: Wiley.

Eisenberg, N., Morris, A. S., McDaniel, B., & Spinrad, T. L. (2009). Moral cognitions and prosocial responding in adolescence. In R. M. Lerner & L. Steinberg (Eds.), *Handbook of adolescent psychology* (3rd ed.). New York: Wiley.

Eisenberg, N., Spinrad, T. R., & Eggum, N. D. (2010). Emotion-focused self-regulation and its relation to children's maladjustment. *Annual Review of Clinical Psychology* (Vol. 6). Palo Alto, CA: Annual Reviews.

Eisenberg, N., Spinrad, T. L., & Morris, A. S. (2013). Prosocial development. In P. D.

Zelazo (Ed.), *Oxford handbook of developmental psychology.* New York: Oxford University Press.

Eliasieh, K., Liets, L. C., & Chalupa, L. M. (2007). Cellular reorganization in the human retina during normal aging. *Investigative Ophthalmology and Visual Science, 48*, 2824–2830.

Elkind, D. (1976). *Child development and education: A Piagetian perspective.* New York: Oxford University Press.

Elliott, E. M., & others. (2011). Working memory in the oldest-old: Evidence from output serial position curves. *Memory and Cognition, 10*, 20–27.

Elliott, S. N., Kurz, A., & Neergaard, L. (2012). Large-scale assessment for educational accountability. In K. R. Harris, S. Graham, & T. Urdan (Eds.), *APA educational psychology handbook.* Washington, DC: American Psychological Association.

Emanuel, L., Bennett, K., & Richardson, V. E. (2007). The dying role. *Journal of Palliative Medicine, 10*, 159–168.

Emde, R. N., Gaensbauer, T. G., & Harmon, R. J. (1976). Emotional expression in infancy: A biobehavioral study. *Psychological Issues: Monograph Series, 10* (37).

Emery, C. F., Anderson, D. R., & Goodwin, C. L. (2013). Coronary heart disease and hypertension. In I. B. Weiner & others (Eds.), *Handbook of psychology* (2nd ed., Vol. 9). New York: Wiley.

Emes, R. D., & Grant, S. G. N. (2013). Evolution of synapse complexity and diversity. *Annual Review of Neuroscience*, Vol. 35. Palo Alto, CA: Annual Reviews.

Ensor, R., Spencer, D., & Hughes, C. (2011). You feel sad? Emotional understanding mediates effects of verbal ability and mother-child mutuality on prosocial behaviors: Findings from 2 to 4 years. *Social Development, 20*, 93–100.

Erickson, K. I., & others. (2011). Exercise training increases the size of the hippocampus and improves memory. *Proceedings of the National Academy of Sciences U.S.A., 108*, 3017–3022.

Ericsson, K. A., Krampe, R., & Tesch-Romer, C. (1993). The role of deliberate practice in the acquisition of expert performance. *Psychological Review, 100*, 363–406.

Erikson, E. H. (1950). *Childhood and society.* New York: W. W. Norton.

Erikson, E. H. (1968). *Identity: Youth and crisis.* New York: W. W. Norton.

Eriksson, U. J. (2009). Congenital malformations in diabetic pregnancy. *Seminars in Fetal and Neonatal Medicine, 14*, 85–93.

Escobar-Chaves, S. L., & Anderson, C. A. (2008). Media and risky behavior. *Future of Children, 18*, 147–180.

Eshkoli, T., Sheiner, E., Ben-Zvi, Z., & Holcberg, G. (2011). Drug transport across the placenta. *Current Pharmaceutical Biotechnology, 12*, 707–714.

Etaugh, C., & Bridges, J. S. (2010). *Women's lives* (2nd ed.). Boston: Allyn & Bacon.

Evans, G. W., Chen, E., Miller, G., & Seeman, T. (2012). How poverty gets under the skin: A life-course perspective. In V. Maholmes & R. B. King (Eds.), *Oxford handbook of poverty and child development.* New York: Oxford University Press.

Evans, G. W., & English, G. W. (2002). The environment of poverty. *Child Development, 73*, 1238–1248.

Evans, W. J. (2010). Skeletal muscle loss: Cachexia, sarcopenia, and inactivity. *American Journal of Clinical Nutrition, 91*, S1123–S1127.

F

Fabbri, R., & others. (2012, in press). Cryopreservation of ovarian tissue for pediatric patients. *Obstetrics and Gynecology International.*

Fabiano, G. A., Pelham, W. E., Coles, E. K., Gnagy, E. M., Chronis-Tuscano, A., & O'Connor, B. C. (2009). A meta-analysis of behavioral treatments for attention deficit/hyperactivity disorder. *Clinical Psychology Review, 29*, 129–140.

Fabricius, W. V., Braver, S. L., Diaz, P., & Schenck, C. (2010). Custody and parenting time: Links to family relationships and well-being after divorce. In M. E. Lamb (Ed.), *The role of the father in child development* (5th ed.). New York: Wiley.

Fagot, B. I., Rogers, C. S., & Leinbach, M. D. (2000). Theories of gender socialization. In T. Eckes & H. M. Trautner (Eds.), *The developmental social psychology of gender.* Mahwah, NJ: Erlbaum.

Fahey, T. D., Insel, P. M., & Roth, W. T. (2013). *Fit and well* (10th ed.). New York: McGraw-Hill.

Faith, M. S., & others. (2012). Evaluating parents and adult caregivers as "agents of change" for treating obese children: Evidence for parent behavior change strategies and research gaps: A scientific statement from the American Heart Association. *Circulation, 125*, 1186–1207.

Fakhoury, J., Nimmo, G. A., & Autexier, C. (2007). Harnessing telomerase in cancer therapeutics. *Anti-Cancer Agents in Medicinal Chemistry, 7*, 475–483.

Falbo, T., & Poston, D. L. (1993). The academic, personality, and physical outcomes of only children in China. *Child Development, 64*, 18–35.

Falck-Yttere, T., & others. (2012, in press). Gaze performance in children with autism spectrum disorder when observing communicative actions. *Journal of Autism and Developmental Disorders.*

Fall, A. M., & Roberts, G. (2012, in press). High school dropouts: Interactions between social context, self perceptions, school engagement, and student dropout. *Journal of Adolescence.*

Fancy, S. P. J., & others. (2012). Myelin regeneration: A recapitulation of development? *Annual Review of Neuroscience* (Vol. 34). Palo Alto, CA: Annual Reviews.

Fantz, R. L. (1963). *Pattern vision in newborn infants. Science, 140,* 286–297.

Faroogi, A., Hagglof, B., Sedin, G., & Serenius, F. (2011). Impact at 11 years of major neonatal morbidities in children born extremely preterm. *Pediatrics, 127,* e1247–e1257.

Farrell, S. W., Fitzgerald, S. J., McAuley, P., & Barlow, C. E. (2010). Cardiorespiratory fitness, adiposity, and all-cause mortality in women. *Medicine and Science in Sports and Exercise, 42*(11), 2006–2012.

Farrow, C. V. (2012). Do parental feeding practices moderate the relationships between impulsivity and eating in children? *Eating Behavior, 13,* 150–153.

Fasig, L. (2000). Toddlers' understanding of ownership: Implications for self-concept development. *Social Development, 9,* 370–382.

Fatusi, A. O., & Hindin, M. J. (2010). Adolescents and youths in developing countries: Health and development issues in context. *Journal of Adolescence, 33,* 499–508.

Fauci. J., & others. (2012, in press). The utilization of palliative care in gynecologic oncology patients near the end of life. *Gynecologic Oncology.*

Fearon, R. P., & others. (2010). The significance of insecure attachment and disorganization in the development of children's externalizing behavior: A meta-analytic study. *Child Development, 81,* 435–456.

Feeney, S., Moravcik, E., & Nolte, S. (2013). *Who am I in the lives of children?* (9th ed.). Upper Saddle River, NJ: Pearson.

Feil, R., & Fraga, M. F. (2012). Epigenetics and the environment: Emerging patterns and implications. *Nature Reviews: Genetics, 1,* 97–109.

Feinstein, E. E., Richter, L., & Foster, S. E. (2012). Addressing the critical health problem of adolescent substance use through health care, research, and public policy. *Journal of Adolescent Health, 50,* 431–436.

Feldman, D. C. (2007). Career mobility and career stability among order workers. In K. S. Shultz & G. A. Adams (Eds.), *Aging and work in the 21st century.* Mahwah, NJ: Erlbaum.

Feldman, H. D. (2001, April). *Contemporary developmental theories and the concept of talent.* Paper presented at the meeting of the Society for Research in Child Development, Minneapolis.

Ferguson, D. M., Harwood, L. J., & Shannon, F. T. (1987). Breastfeeding and subsequent social adjustment in 6- to 8-year-old children. *Journal of Child Psychology and Psychiatry, 28,* 378–386.

Fernandez, I. D., Su, H., Winters, P. C., & Liang, H. (2010). Association of workplace chronic and acute stressors with employee weight status: Data from worksites in turmoil. *Journal of Occupational and Environmental Medicine, 52* (Suppl. 1), S34–S41.

Fernandez-Martinez, F. J., & others. (2012). Noninvasive fetal sex determination in maternal plasma: A prospective feasibility study. *Genetics in Medicine, 14,* 101–106.

Ferrari, M., & Weststrate, N. (Eds.) (2013, in press). *Personal wisdom.* New York: Springer.

Ferrie, J. E., & others. (2011). Change in sleep duration and cognitive function: Findings from the Whitehall II Study. *Sleep, 34,* 565–573.

Field, D. (1999). A cross-cultural perspective on continuity and change in social relations in old age: Introduction to a special issue. *International Journal of Aging and Human Development, 48,* 257–262.

Field, R. D., England, D. E., Andrews, C. Z., Martin, C. L., & Zosuls, K. M. (2012, April). *"I understand girls but not boys": Assessing gender-based relationship efficacy.* Paper presented at the Gender Development Research conference, San Francisco.

Field, T. M. (2001). Massage therapy facilitates weight gain in preterm infants. *Current Directions in Psychological Science, 10,* 51–55.

Field, T. M. (2007). *The amazing infant.* Malden, MA: Blackwell.

Field, T. M. (2010a). Pregnancy and labor massage. *European Review of Obstetrics and Gynecology, 5,* 177–181.

Field, T. M. (2010b). Postpartum depression effects on early interactions, parenting, and safety practices: A review. *Infant Behavior and Development, 33,* 1–6.

Field, T. M., Diego, M., & Hernandez-Reif, M. (2008). Prematurity and potential predictors. *International Journal of Neuroscience, 118,* 277–289.

Field, T. M., Diego, M., & Hernandez-Reif, M. (2011). Preterm infant massage therapy research: A review. *Infant Behavior and Development, 34,* 383–389.

Field, T. M., Diego, M., Hernandez-Reif, M., Medina, L., Delgado, J., & Hernandez, A. (2012). Yoga and massage therapy reduce prenatal depression and prematurity. *Journal of Bodywork and Movement Therapies, 16,* 204–209.

Field, T. M., Figueiredo, B., Hernandez-Reif, M., Diego, M., Deeds, O., & Ascencio, A. (2008). Massage therapy reduces pain in pregnant women, alleviates prenatal depression in both parents and improves their relationships. *Journal of Bodywork and Movement Therapies, 12,* 146–150.

Field, T. M., Grizzle, N., Scafidi, F., & Schanberg, S. (1996). Massage and relaxation therapies' effects on depressed adolescent mothers. *Adolescence, 31,* 903–911.

Field, T.M., & Hernandez-Reif, M. (2013) Touch and pain perception in infants. In D. Narvaez & others (Eds.), *Evolution, early experience, and development.* New York: Oxford University Press.

Field, T. M., Hernandez-Reif, M., Diego, M., Feijo, L., Vera, Y., & Gil, K. (2004). Massage therapy by parents improves early growth and development. *Infant Behavior & Development, 27,* 435–442.

Field, T. M., & others. (1986). Tactile/kinesthetic stimulation effects on preterm neonates. *Pediatrics, 77,* 654–658.

Finch, C. E. (2009). The neurobiology of middle-age has arrived. *Neurobiology of Aging, 30,* 503–520.

Finger, B., Hans, S. L., Bernstein, V. J., & Cox, S. M. (2009). Parent relationship quality and infant-mother attachment. *Attachment and Human Development, 11,* 285–306.

Fingerhut, A. W., & Peplau, L. A. (2013). Same-sex romantic relationships. In C. J. Patterson & A. R. D'Augelli (Eds.), *Handbook of psychology and sexual orientation.* New York: Oxford University Press.

Fingerman, K. L., & Baker, B. (2006). Socioemotional aspects of aging. In J. Wilmouth & K. Ferraro (Eds.), *Perspectives in Gerontology* (3rd ed.). New York: Springer.

Fingerman, K. L., & Birditt, K. S. (2011). Relationships between adults and their aging parents. In K. W. Schaie & S. L. Willis (Eds.), *Handbook of the psychology of aging* (7th ed.). New York: Elsevier.

Fingerman, K. L., Chan, W., Pitzer, L. M., Birditt, K. S., Franks, M. M., & Zarit, S. (2011a). Who gets what and why: Help middle-aged adults provide to parents and grown children. *Journal, of Gerontology B: Psychological Sciences and Social Sciences, 66,* 87–98.

Fingerman, K. L., Cheng, Y. P., Tighe, L., Birditt, K. S., & Zarit, S. (2011b, in press). Parent-child relationships in young adulthood. In A. Booth & others (Eds.), *Early adulthood in a family context.* New York: Springer.

Fingerman, K. L., Pillemer, K. A., Silverstein, M., & Suitor, J. J. (2012). The Baby Boomers' intergenerational relationships. *Gerontologist, 52,* 199–209.

Finkelstein, E. A., & others. (2012). Obesity and severe obesity forecasts through 2030. *American Journal of Preventive Medicine, 42,* 563–570.

Fischhoff, B., Bruine de Bruin, W., Parker, A. M., Millstein, S. G., & Halpern-Felsher, B. L. (2010). Adolescents' perceived risk of dying. *Journal of Adolescent Health, 46,* 265–269.

Fisher, C. B., Busch-Rossnagel, N. A., Jopp, D. S., & Brown, J. L. (2013, in press). Applied developmental psychology across the life span. In I. B. Weiner & others (Eds.), *Handbook of psychology* (2nd ed., Vol. 6). New York: Wiley.

Fisher, H. L., & others. (2012, in press). Bullying victimization and risk of self-harm in early adolescence: Longitudinal cohort study. *British Medical Journal.*

Fiske, A., Wetherell, J. L., & Gatz, M. (2009). Depression in older adults. *Annual Review of Clinical Psychology* (Vol. 5). Palo Alto, CA: Annual Reviews.

Fitzpatrick, K. K. (2012). Developmental considerations when treating anorexia nervosa in adolescents and young adults. In J. Lock (Ed.), *Oxford handbook of child and adolescent eating disorders: Developmental perspectives.* New York: Oxford University Press.

Fivush, R. (1993). Developmental perspectives on autobiographical recall. In G. S.

Goodman, & B. Bottoms (Eds.). *Child victims and child witnesses: Understanding and improving testimony.* New York: Guilford.

Fivush, R. (2011). The development of autobiographical memory. *Annual Review of Psychology* (Vol. 62). Palo Alto, CA: Annual Reviews.

Fjell, A. M., & Walhovd, K. B. (2010). Structural brain changes in aging: Courses, causes, and consequences. *Reviews in the Neurosciences, 21,* 187–222.

Flavell, J. H. (2004). Theory-of-mind development: Retrospect and prospect. *Merrill-Palmer Quarterly, 50,* 274–290.

Flavell, J. H., Friedrichs, A., & Hoyt, J. (1970). Developmental changes in memorization processes. *Cognitive Psychology, 1,* 324–340.

Flavell, J. H., Green, F. L., & Flavell, E. R. (1995). The development of children's knowledge about attentional focus. *Developmental Psychology, 31,* 706–712.

Flavell, J. H., Green, F. L., & Flavell, E. R. (2000). Development of children's awareness of their own thoughts. *Journal of Cognition and Development, 7,* 97–112.

Fletcher, B. R., & Rapp, P. R. (2013, in press). Normal neurocognitive aging. In I. B. Weiner & others (Eds.), *Handbook of psychology* (2nd ed.). New York: Wiley.

Flint, M. S., Baum, A., Chambers, W. H., & Jenkins, F. J. (2007). Induction of DNA damage, alteration of DNA repair, and transcriptional activation by stress hormones. *Psychoneuroendocrinology, 32,* 470–479.

Flom, R., & Pick, A. D. (2003). Verbal encouragement and joint attention in 18-month-old infants. *Infant Behavior and Development, 26,* 121–134.

Florin, T., & Ludwig, S. (2011). *Netter's pediatrics.* New York: Elsevier.

Florsheim, P., Moore, D., & Edgington, C. (2003). Romantic relationships among pregant and parenting adolescents. In P. Florsheim (Ed.), *Adolescent romantic relations and sexual behavior.* Mahwah, NJ: Erlbaum.

Flouri, E., & Buchanan, A. (2004). Early father's and mother's involvement and child's later educational outcomes. *British Journal of Educational Psychology, 74,* 141–153.

Flynn, J. R. (1999). Searching for justice: The discovery of IQ gains over time. *American Psychologist, 54,* 5–20.

Flynn, J. R. (2007). The history of the American mind in the 20th century: A scenario to explain IQ gains over time and a case for the relevance of g. In P. C. Kyllonen, R. D. Roberts, & L. Stankov (Eds.), *Extending intelligence.* Mahwah, NJ: Erlbaum.

Flynn, J. R. (2011). Secular changes in intelligence. In R. J. Sternberg & S. B. Kaufman (Eds.), *Cambridge handbook of intelligence.* New York: Cambridge University Press.

Flynn, J. R. (2012). *Are we getting smarter?* New York: Cambridge University Press.

Flynn, J. R., & Blair, C. (2013). The history of intelligence: New spectacles for developmental psychology. In P. D. Zelazo (Ed.), *Oxford handbook of developmental psychology.* New York: Oxford University Press.

Fontana, L. (2009). The scientific basis of caloric restriction leading to longer life. *Current Opinion in Gastroenterology, 25,* 144–150.

Forsyth, A. L., Quon, D. V., & Konkle, B. A. (2011, in press). Role of exercise and physical activity on haemophilc arthropathy, fall prevention, and osteoporosis. *Haemophilia.*

Fosco, G. M., Frank, J. L., & Dishion, T. J. (2012). Understanding the influence of deviant peers on problem behavior: Coercion and contagion in peer, family, and school environments. In S. R. Jimerson & others (Eds.), *Handbook of school violence and school safety.* New York: Routledge.

Fosco, G. M., Stormshak, E. A., Dishion, T. J., & Winter, C. E. (2012). Family relationships and parental monitoring during middle school as predictors of early adolescent problem behavior. *Journal of Clinical Child and Adolescent Psychology, 41,* 202–213.

Fox, B. J. (2012). *Word identification strategies* (5th ed.). Boston: Allyn & Bacon.

Fox, M. K., Pac, S., Devancy, B., & Jankowski, L. (2004). Feeding infants and toddlers study: What foods are infants and toddlers eating? *American Dietetic Association Journal, 104* (Suppl.), S22–S30.

Fox, M. K., & others. (2010). Food consumption patterns of young preschoolers: Are they starting off on the right path? *Journal of the American Dietetic Association, 110* (Suppl. 12), S52–S59.

Fox, S. E., Levitt, P., & Nelson, C. A. (2010). How the timing and quality of early experiences influence the development of brain architecture. *Child Development, 81,* 28–40.

Fozard, J. L. (1992, December 6). Commentary in "We can age successfully." *Parade Magazine,* pp. 14–15.

Fraiberg, S. (1959). *The magic years.* New York: Scribner's

Franchak, J. M., Kretch, K. S., Soska, K. C., & Adolph, K. E. (2011). Head-mounted eye-tracking: A new method to describe the visual ecology of infants. *Child Development, 82,* 1738–1750.

Francis, J., Fraser, G., & Marcia, J. E. (1989). *Cognitive and experimental factors in moratorium-achievement (MAMA) cycles.* Unpublished manuscript, Department of Psychology, Simon Fraser University, Burnaby, British Columbia.

Franco, P., & others. (2011). Fewer spontaneous arousals in infants with apparent life threatening event. *Sleep, 34,* 733–743.

Frankl, V. (1984). *Man's search for meaning.* New York: Basic Books.

Frederikse, M., Lu, A., Aylward, E., Barta, P., Sharma, T., & Pearlson, G. (2000). Sex differences in inferior lobule volume in schizophrenia. *American Journal of Psychiatry, 157,* 422–427.

Freiheit, E. A., & others. (2012). A dynamic view of depressive symptoms and neurocognitive change among patients with coronary artery disease. *Archives of General Psychiatry, 69,* 244–255.

Freitag, C. M., Asherson, P., & Hebebrand, J. (2012). Behavioral genetics of childhood disorders. *Current Topics in Behavioral Neuroscience, 12,* 395–428.

Freud, S. (1917). *A general introduction to psychoanalysis.* New York: Washington Square Press.

Freund, A. M., Nikitin, J., & Riediger, M. (2013, in press). Successful aging. In I. B. Weiner & others (Eds.), *Handbook of psychology* (2nd ed., Vol. 6). New York: Wiley.

Frey, B. S. (2011). Happy people live longer. *Science, 331,* 542–543.

Freyer-Adam, J., Gaertner, B., Tobschall, S., & John, U. (2011). Health risk factors and self-rated health among job-seekers. *BMC Public Health, 11,* 659.

Fried, A. L. (2012). Ethnics in psychological research: Guidelines and regulations. In H. Cooper (Ed.), *APA handbook of research methods in psychology.* Washington, DC: American Psychological Association.

Fried, L. P., Hogan, P., & Rowe, J. (2012). Design and operation of health systems in wealthy nations. *Global population aging: Peril or promise?* Geneva, SWIT: World Economic Forum.

Friedman, S. L., Melhuish, E., & Hill, C. (2009). Childcare research at the dawn of a new millennium: An update. In G. Brenner & T. Wachs (Eds.), *Wiley-Blackwell handbook of infant development.* New York: Wiley.

Friend, M. (2011). *Special education* (3rd ed.). Upper Saddle River, NJ: Merrill.

Frisen, A., & Holmqvist, K. (2010). What characterizes early adolescents with a positive body image? A qualitative investigation of Swedish boys and girls. *Body Image, 7,* 205–212.

Frodl, T., & O'Keane, V. (2012, in press). How does the brain deal with cumulative stress? A review with focus on developmental stress, HPA axis function, and hippocampal structure in humans. *Neurobiology of Disease.*

Fromme, E. K., & others. (2012). POLST registry do-not-resuscitate orders and other patient treatment preferences. *JAMA, 307,* 34–35.

Frost, D. M. (2011). Stigma and intimacy in same-sex relationships: A narrative approach. *Journal of Family Psychology, 25,* 1–10.

Fujisawa, D., & others. (2010). Prevalence and determinants of complicated grief in general population. *Journal of Affective Disorders, 127,* 352–358.

Fujiwara, E., & others. (2012). Usefulness of reminiscence therapy for community mental health. *Psychiatry and Clinical Neuroscience, 66,* 74–79.

Fung, C. K. H., & Cheng, D. P. W. (2012). Consensus or disconsensus? Stakeholders' views on the role of play in learning. *Early years: An International Journal of Research and Development, 32,* 17–33.

Fung, H. (2011). Cultural psychological perspectives on social development. In P. K. Smith & C. H. Hart (Eds.), *Wiley-Blackwell handbook of childhood social development* (2nd ed.). New York: Wiley.

Fung, L. K., Quintin, E. M., Haas, B. W., & Reiss, A. L. (2012). Conceptualizing neurodevelopmental disorders through a mechanistic understanding of fragile X syndrome and Williams syndrome. *Current Opinion in Neurology, 25,* 112–124.

Furman, E. (2005). *Boomerang nation.* New York: Fireside.

Furman, W., Low, S., & Ho, M. J. (2009). Romantic experience and psychosocial adjustment in middle adolescence. *Journal of Clinical Child and Adolescent Psychology, 38,* 75–90.

Furstenberg, F. F. (2007). The future of marriage. In A. S. Skolnick & J. H. Skolnick (Eds.), *Family in transition* (14th ed.). Boston: Allyn & Bacon.

Furth, H. G., & Wachs, H. (1975). *Thinking goes to school.* New York: Oxford University Press.

G

Gabbe, S., & others. (Eds.) (2012). *Obstetrics* (6th ed.). New York: Elsevier.

Gadi, R., Amanullah, A., & Figueredo, V. M. (2012, in press). HDL-C: Does it matter? An update on novel HDL-directed pharmaco-therapeutic strategies. *International Journal of Cardiology.*

Gaias, L. M., & others. (2012). Cross-cultural temperamental differences in infants, children, and adults in the United States of America and Finland. *Scandinavian Journal of Psychology, 53,* 119–128.

Gaither, S. E., Pauker, K., & Johnson, S. P. (2012, in press). Biracial and monoracial infant own-race face perception: An eye tracking study. *Developmental Science.*

Galambos, N. L., Howard, A. L., & Maggs, J. L. (2011). Rise and fall of sleep quality with student experiences across the first year of the university. *Journal of Research on Adolescence, 21,* 342–349.

Galinsky, E. (2010). *Mind in the making.* New York: Harper Collins.

Galland, B. C., Taylor, B. J., Edler, D. E., & Herbison, P. (2012). Normal sleep patterns in infants and children: A systematic review of observational studies. *Sleep Medicine Review, 16,* 213–222.

Galloway, J. C., & Thelen, E. (2004). Feet first: Object exploration in young infants. *Infant Behavior & Development, 27,* 107–112.

Ganong, L., & Coleman, M. (2006). Obligations to stepparents acquired in later life: Relationship quality and acuity of needs. *Journals of Gerontology B: Psychological Sciences and Social Sciences, 61,* S80–S88.

Ganong, L., Coleman, M., & Hans, J. (2006). Divorce as prelude to stepfamily living and the consequences of re-divorce. In M. A. Fine & J. H. Harvey (Eds.), *Handbook of divorce and relationship dissolution.* Mahwah, NJ: Erlbaum.

Gao, Z. (2012, in press). Urban Latino school children's physical activity correlates and daily physical activity participation: A social cognitive approach. *Psychology, Health, and Medicine.*

Gardner, H. (1983). *Frames of mind.* New York: Basic Books.

Gardner, H. (1993). *Multiple intelligences.* New York: Basic Books.

Gardner, H. (2002). The pursuit of excellence through education. In M. Ferrari (Ed.), *Learning from extraordinary minds.* Mahwah, NJ: Erlbaum.

Garofalo, R. (2010). Cytokines in human milk. *Journal of Pediatrics, 156* (Suppl. 2), S36–S40.

Gartner, J., Larson, D. B., & Allen, G. D. (1991). Religious commitment and mental health: A review of the empirical literature. *Journal of Psychology and Theology, 19,* 6–25.

Gartstein, M. A., Bridgett, D. J., Young, B. N., Panksepp, J., & Power, T. (2012, in press). Origins of effortful control: Infant and parent contributions. *Infancy.*

Gartstein, M. A., Peleg, Y., Young, B. N., & Slobodskaya, H. R. (2009). Infant temperament in Russia, United States of America, and Israel: Differences and similarities between Russian-speaking families. *Child Psychiatry and Human Development, 40,* 241–256.

Garvey, C. (2000). *Play* (Enlarged ed.). Cambridge, MA: Harvard University Press.

Gates, W. (1998, July 20). Charity begins when I'm ready (interview). *Fortune magazine.*

Gathwala, G., Singh, B., & Singh, J. (2010). Effect of kangaroo care on physical growth, breastfeeding, and its acceptability. *Tropical Doctor, 40,* 199–202.

Gault-Sherman, M. (2012). It's a two-way street: The bidirectional relationship between parenting and delinquency. *Journal of Youth and Adolescence, 41,* 121–145.

Gauvain, M. (2011). Applying the cultural concept to cognitive development. *Journal of Cognition and Development, 12,* 121–133.

Gauvain, M. (2013). Sociocultural contexts of learning. In P. D. Zelazo (Ed.), *Oxford handbook of developmental psychology.* New York: Oxford University Press.

Gauvain, M., & Parke, R. D. (2010). Socialization. In M. H. Bornstein (Ed.), *Handbook of cultural developmental science.* New York: Psychology Press.

Geaghan, S. M. (2012). Fetal laboratory medicine: On the frontier of maternal-fetal medicine. *Clinical Chemistry, 58,* 337–352.

Gee, C. C., Walsemann, K. M., & Brondolo, E. (2012). A life course perspective on how racism may be related to health inequities. *American Journal of Public Health, 102,* 967–974.

Gee, C. L., & Heyman, G. D. (2007). Children's evaluations of other people's self-descriptions. *Social Development, 16,* 800–818.

Geirsdottir, O. G., & others. (2012). Physical function predicts improvement in quality of life in elderly Icelanders after 12 weeks of resistance exercise. *Journal of Nutrition, Health, and Aging, 16,* 62–66.

Geisinger, K. F. (2012). Norm- and criterion-referenced testing. In H. Cooper (Ed.), *APA handbook of research methods in psychology.* Washington, DC: American Psychological Association.

Gelber, R. P., Launer, L. J., & White, L. R. (2012, in press). The Honolulu-Asia Aging Study: Epidemiologic and neuropathogenic research on cognitive impairment. *Current Alzheimer Research.*

Gelman, R. (1969). Conservation acquisition: A problem of learning to attend to relevant attributes. *Journal of Experimental Child Psychology, 7,* 67–87.

Gelman, S. A. (2013). Concepts in development. In P. Zelazo (Ed.), *Oxford handbook of developmental psychology.* New York: Oxford University Press.

Gelman, S. A., & Frazier, B. N. (2012). Development of thinking in children. In K. Holyoak & R. Morrison (Eds.), *Oxford handbook of thinking and reasoning.* New York: Oxford University Press.

Gelman, S. A., & Kalish, C. W. (2006). Conceptual development. In W. Damon & R. Lerner (Eds.), *Handbook of child psychology* (6th ed.). New York: Wiley.

Geng, X., & others. (2012, in press). Quantitative tract-based white matter development from birth to age 2 years. *Neuroimage.*

Gennetian, L. A., & Miller, C. (2002). Children and welfare reform: A view from an experimental welfare reform program in Minnesota. *Child Development, 73,* 601–620.

Gentile, D. A. (2011). The multiple dimensions of video game effects. *Child Development Perspectives, 5,* 75–81.

Georgakilas, A. G. (2011). From chemistry of DNA damage to repair and biological significance. Comprehending the future. *Mutation Research, 711,* 1–2.

George, L. K. (2009). Religiousness and spirituality, later life. In D. Carr (Ed.), *Encyclopedia of the life course and human development.* Boston: Gale Cengage.

George, L. G., Helson, R., & John, O. P. (2011). The "CEO" of women's work lives: How Big Five Conscientiousness, Extraversion, and Openness predict 50 years of work experiences in a changing sociocultural context. *Journal of Personality and Social Psychology, 101*(4), 812–830.

Gershoff, E. T. (2002). Corporal punishment by parents and associated child behaviors and experiences: A meta-analysis and theoretical review. *Psychological Bulletin, 128,* 539–579.

Gershoff, E. T., Lansford, J. E., Sexton, H. R., Davis-Kean, P., & Sameroff, A. (2012). Longitudinal links between spanking and children's externalizing behaviors in a national sample of White, Black, Hispanic, and Asian American families. *Child Development, 83,* 838–843.

Gershoff, E. T., & others. (2010). Parent discipline practices in an international sample: Associations with child behaviors and moderation by perceived normativeness. *Child Development, 81,* 487–502.

Gerstorff, D., & Ram, N. (2012). Late-life: A venue for studying the mechanisms by which contextual factors influence individual development. In S. K. Whitbourne & M. Sliwinski (Eds.), *Wiley-Blackwell handbook of adult development and aging.* New York: Wiley.

Gertner, Y., & Fisher, C. (2012, in press). Predicted errors in children's early sentence comprehension. *Cognition.*

Ghazarian, S., & Roche, K. M. (2010). Social support and low-income, urban mothers: Longitudinal associations with adolescent delinquency *Journal of Youth and Adolescence, 39,*1097–1108.

Ghetti, S., & Alexander, K. W. (2004). "If it happened, I would remember it": Strategic use of event memorability in the rejection of false autobiographical events. *Child Development, 75,* 542–561.

Ghetti, S., & Bauer, P. J. (Eds.) (2012). *Origins and development of recollection.* New York: Oxford University Press.

Ghosh, S., Feingold, E., Chakaborty, S., & Dey, S. K. (2010). Telomere length is associated with types of chromosome 21 nondisjunction: A new insight into the maternal age effect on Down syndrome birth. *Human Genetics, 127,* 403–409.

Gibbons, L., & others. (2012, in press). Inequities in the use of cesarean section deliveries in the world. *American Journal of Obstetrics and Gynecology, 206.*

Gibbs, J. C. (2010). *Moral development and reality* (2nd ed.). Boston: Allyn & Bacon.

Gibbs, J. C., Basinger, K. S., Grime, R. L., & Snarey, J. R. (2007). Moral judgment development across cultures: Revisiting Kohlberg's universality claims. *Developmental Review, 27,* 443–500.

Gibson, E. J. (1969). *Principles of perceptual learning and development.* New York: Appleton-Century-Crofts.

Gibson, E. J. (1989). Exploratory behavior in the development of perceiving, acting, and the acquiring of knowledge. *Annual Review of Psychology* (Vol. 39). Palo Alto, CA: Annual Reviews.

Gibson, E. J. (2001). *Perceiving the affordances.* Mahwah, NJ: Erlbaum.

Gibson, E. J., & Walk, R. D. (1960). The "visual cliff." *Scientific American, 202,* 64–71.

Gibson, E. L., & others. (2012). A narrative review of psychological and educational strategies applied to young children's eating behaviors aimed at reducing obesity risk. *Obesity Reviews, 13*(Suppl. 1), S85–S95.

Gibson, H. J. (2009). Leisure and travel, adulthood. In D. Carr (Ed.), *Encyclopedia of the life course and human development.* Boston: Gale Cengage.

Gibson, J. J. (1966). *The senses considered as perceptual systems.* Boston: Houghton Mifflin.

Gibson, J. J. (1979). *The ecological approach to visual perception.* Boston: Houghton Mifflin.

Giedd, J. N., & others. (2012). Automatic magnetic resonance imaging of the developing child and adolescent brain. In V. F. Reyna & others (Eds.), *The adolescent brain.* Washington, DC: American Psychological Association.

Gil-Bea, F. J., & others. (2012, in press). Cholinergic deactivation exacerbates amyloid pathology and induces hippocampal atrophy in Tg2576 mice. *Neurobiology of Disease.*

Gilliam, M., & others. (2011). Developmental trajectories of the corpus callosum in attention-deficit/hyperactivity disorder. *Biological Psychiatry, 69,* 839–846.

Gillig, P. M., & Sanders, R. D. (2011). Higher cortical functions: Attention and vigilance. *Innovations in Clinical Neuroscience, 8,* 43–46.

Gilligan, C. (1982). *In a different voice.* Cambridge, MA: Harvard University Press.

Gilligan, C. (1996). The centrality of relationships in psychological development: A puzzle, some evidence, and a theory. In G. G. Noam & K. W. Fischer (Eds.), *Development and vulnerability in close relationships.* Hillsdale, NJ: Erlbaum.

Gillum, R. F., & Ingram, D. D. (2007). Frequency of attendance at religious services, hypertension, and blood pressure: The third National Health and Nutrition Examination Survey. *Psychosomatic Medicine, 68,* 382–385.

Gil-Mohapel, J., Simpson, J. M., Titerness, A. K., & Christie, B. R. (2010). Characterization of the neurogenesis quiet zone in the rodent brain: Effects of age and exercise. *European Journal of Neuroscience, 31,* 797–807.

Gilmore, A. K., Granato, H. F., & Lewis, M. A. (2012, in press). The use of drinking and condom-related protective strategies in association with condom use and sex-related alcohol use. *Journal of Sex Research.*

Giorgis, C. (2012). *Literature for young children: Supporting emergent literacy, ages 0-8* (7th ed.). Upper Saddle River, NJ: Pearson.

Giorgis, C., & Glazer, J. (2013). *Literature for young children: Supporting emergent literacy, ages 0–8* (7th ed.). Upper Saddle River, NJ: Pearson.

Giovannini, M., Verduci, E., Salvatici, E., Paci, S., & Riva, E. (2012, in press). Phenylketonuria: Nutritional advances and challenges. *Nutrition and Metabolism.*

Girls, Inc. (1991). *Truth, trusting, and technology: New research on preventing adolescent pregnancy.* Indianapolis: Author.

Givens, J. L., & Mitchell, J. L. (2009). Concerns about end-of-life care and support for euthanasia. *Journal of Pain and Symptom Management, 38,* 167–173.

Givens, J. L., & others. (2011). Grief among family members of nursing home residents with advanced dementia. *American Journal of Geriatric Society, 19,* 543–550.

Glei, D. A. (1999). Measuring contraceptive use patterns among teenage and adult women. *Family Planning Perspectives, 31,* 73–80.

Gluck, M. E., Venti, C. A., Lindsay, R. S., Knowler, W. C., Salbe, A. D., & Krakoff, J. (2009). Maternal influence, not diabetic intrauterine environment, predicts children's energy intake. *Obesity, 17*(4), 772–777.

Goga, A. E., & others. (2012, in press). Infant feeding practices at routine PMTCT site, South Africa: Results of a prospective observational study amongst HIV exposed and unexposed infants—birth to 9 months. *International Breastfeeding Journal.*

Gogtay, N., & Thompson, P. M. (2010). Mapping gray matter development: Implications for typical development and vulnerability to psychopathology. *Brain and Cognition, 72,* 6–15.

Goh, J. O. (2011). Functional dedifferentiation and altered connectivity in older adults: Neural accounts of cognitive aging. *Aging and Disease, 2,* 30–48.

Gold, D. (2011). Death and dying. In R. H. Binstock & L. K. George (Eds.), *Handbook of aging and the social sciences* (7th ed.). New York: Elsevier.

Goldberg, W. A., & Lucas-Thompson, R. (2008). Maternal and paternal employment, effects of. In M. M. Haith & J. B. Benson (Eds.), *Encyclopedia of infant and early childhood development.* Oxford, UK: Elsevier.

Goldenberg, R. L., & Culhane, J. F. (2007). Low birth weight in the United States. *American Journal of Clinical Nutrition, 85*(Suppl.), S584–S590.

Goldfield, B. A., & Snow, C. A. (2009). Individual differences in language development. In J. Berko Gleason & N. Ratner (Eds.), *The development of language* (7th ed.). Boston: Allyn & Bacon.

Goldfield, G. S. (2012). Making access to TV contingent on physical activity: Effects on liking and relative reinforcing value of TV and physical activity in overweight and obese children. *Journal of Behavioral Medicine, 35,* 1–7.

Goldin-Meadow, S. (2012, in press). What modern-day gesture can tell us about language evolution. In K. Gibson & M. Tallerman (Eds.), *Oxford handbook of language evolution.* New York: Oxford University Press.

Goldin-Meadow, S., & Alibali, M. W. A. (2013, in press). Gesture's role in learning and development. In P. Zelazo (Ed.), *Oxford University handbook of developmental psychology.* New York: Oxford University Press.

Goldschmidt, L., Richardson, G. A., Willford, J., & Day, N. L. (2008). Prenatal marijuana exposure and intelligence test performance at age 6. *Journal of the American Academy of Child and Adolescent Psychiatry, 47,* 254–263.

Golley, R. K., & others. (2012, in press). An index measuring adherence to complementary feeding guidelines has convergent validity as a measure of infant diet quality. *Journal of Nutrition.*

Gollnick, D. M., & Chinn, P. C. (2013). *Multicultural education in a pluralistic society* (9th ed.). Boston: Allyn & Bacon.

Golombok, S. (2011a). Children in new family forms. In R. Gross (Ed.), *Psychology* (6th ed.). London: Hodder Education.

Golombok, S. (2011b). Why I study lesbian families. In S. Ellis & others (Eds.), *LGBTQ psychologies*. New York: Cambridge University Press.

Golombok, S., & Tasker, F. (2010). Gay fathers. In M. E. Lamb (Ed.), *The role of the father in child development* (5th ed.). New York: Wiley.

Gomes, R. S., & others. (2011). Primary versus secondary hypertension in children followed up at an outpatient tertiary unit. *Pediatric Nephrology, 26,* 441–447.

Gompel, A., & Santen, R. J. (2012). Hormone therapy and breast cancer risk 10 years after the WHI. *Climacteric, 15,* 241–249.

Goncu, A., & Gauvain, M. (2011). Sociocultural approaches to educational psychology: Theory, research, and application. In K. R. Harris, S. Graham, & T. Urdan (Eds.), *APA educational psychology handbook*. Washington, DC: American Psychological Association.

Gonfloni, S., & others. (2012). Oxidative stress, DNA damage, and c-Abl signaling: At the crossroad in neurodegenerative diseases? *International Journal of Cell Biology.*

Gonsalves, S. (2011). Connecting curriculum with community. *Education Digest, 76*(6), 56–59.

Gonzales, M., Jones, D. J., Kincaid, C. Y., & Cuellar, J. (2012). Neighborhood context and adjustment in African American youths from single mother homes: The intervening role of hopelessness. *Cultural Diversity and Ethnic Minority Psychology, 18,* 109–117.

Goodnough, L. T., & others. (2011). How we treat: Transfusion medicine support of obstetric services. *Transfusion, 204,* e1–e12.

Gopnik, A. (2010). Commentary in E. Galinsky (2010), *Mind in the making*. New York: Harper Collins.

Gorby, H. E., Brownawell, A. M., & Falk, M. C. (2010). Do specific dietary constituents and supplements affect mental energy? Review of the evidence. *Nutrition Reviews, 68,* 697–718.

Gorchoff, S. M., John, O. P., & Helson, R. (2008). Contextualizing change in marital satisfaction during middle age: An 18-year longitudinal study. *Psychological Science, 19,* 1194–1200.

Goritz, C., & Frisen, J. (2012). Neural stem cells and neurogenesis in the adult. *Cell: Stem Cell, 10,* 657–659.

Gorrese, A., & Ruggieri, R. (2012). Peer attachment: A meta-analytic review of gender and age differences and associations with parent attachment. *Journal of Youth and Adolescence, 41,* 650–672.

Goswami, S., & others. (2012, in press). Determination of brain death by apnea test adapted to extracorporeal cardiopulmonary resuscitation. *Journal of Cardiothoracic and Vascular Anesthesia.*

Gottlieb, G. (2007). Probabalistic epigenesis. *Developmental Science, 10,* 1–11.

Gottman, J. M. (2012). *Bringing home baby*. Retrieved on April 27, 2012, from www.bbhonline.org/

Gottman, J. M. (1994). *What predicts divorce?* Mahwah, NJ: Erlbaum.

Gottman, J. M. (2006, April, 29). Secrets of long term love. *New Scientist, 2549,* 40.

Gottman, J. M. (2009). *Research on parenting*. Retrieved December 9, 2009, from http://www.gottman.com/parenting/research

Gottman, J. M. (2011). *The science of trust.* New York: Norton.

Gottman, J. M. (2012). *Research on parenting*. Retrieved June 19, 2012, from www.gottman.com/parenting/research

Gottman, J. M., & Gottman, J. S. (2009). Gottman method of couple therapy. In A. S. Gurman (Ed.), *Clinical handbook of couple therapy* (4th ed.). New York: Guilford.

Gottman, J. M., Gottman, J. S., & Shapiro, A. (2009). A new couples approach to interventions for the transition to parenthood. In M. S. Schulz, P. K. Kerig, M. K. Pruett, & R. D. Parke (Eds.), *Feathering the nest*. Washington, DC: American Psychological Association.

Gottman, J. M., & Parker, J. G. (Eds.). (1987). *Conversations of friends*. New York: Cambridge University Press.

Gottman, J. M., & Silver, N. (2000). *The seven principles for making marriages work*. New York: Crown.

Gouin, K., & others. (2011). Effects of cocaine use during pregnancy on low birth-weight and preterm birth: Systematic and metanalyses. *American Journal of Obstetrics and Gynecology, 204*(4), 1.e1–1.e12.

Gould, E., & Hertel-Fernandez, A. (2010). Early retiree and near-elderly health insurance in a recession. *Journal of Aging and Social Policy, 22,* 172–187.

Gould, S. J. (1981). *The mismeasure of man*. New York: W. W. Norton.

Gouldner, H., & Strong, M. M. (1987). *Speaking of friendship*. New York: Greenwood Press.

Gove, W. R., Style, C. B., & Hughes, M. (1990). The effect of marriage on the well-being of adults. *Journal of Marriage and the Family, 11,* 4–35.

Graber, J. A., Brooks-Gunn, J., & Warren, M. P. (2006). Pubertal effects on adjustment in girls: Moving from demonstrating effects to identifying pathways. *Journal of Youth and Adolescence, 35,* 391–401.

Graber, J. A., & Sontag, L. M. (2009). Internalizing problems during adolescence. In R. M. Lerner & L. Steinberg (Eds.), *Handbook of adolescent psychology* (3rd ed.). New York: Wiley.

Graber, K. C., & Woods, A. M. (2013). *Physical education and activity for elementary classroom teachers*. New York: McGraw-Hill.

Grady, C. L., Springer, M. V., Hongwanishkul, D., McIntosh, A. R., & Winocur, G. (2006). Age-related changes in brain activity across the adult lifespan. *Journal of Cognitive Neuroscience, 18,* 227–241.

Grafenhain, M., Behne, T., Carpenter, M., & Tomasello, M. (2009). Young children's understanding of joint commitments. *Developmental Psychology, 45,* 1430–1443.

Graham, G. M., Holt-Hale, S., & Parker, M. A. (2013). *Children moving* (9th ed.). New York: McGraw-Hill.

Grambs, J. D. (1989). *Women over forty* (rev. ed.). New York: Springer.

Grant, J. (1993). *The state of the world's children*. New York: UNICEF and Oxford University Press.

Grant, N., Wardle, J., & Steptoe, A. (2009). The relationship between life satisfaction and health behavior: A cross-cultural analysis of young adults. *International Journal of Behavioral Medicine, 16,* 259–268.

Graven, S. (2006). Sleep and brain development. *Clinical Perinatology, 33,* 693–706.

Gravetter, R. J., & Forzano, L. B. (2012). *Research methods for the behavioral sciences* (4th ed.). Boston: Cengage.

Gray, P. B., & Garcia, J. R. (2012, in press). *Aging and human sexual behavior: Biocultural perspectives—a mini-review.*

Graziano, A. M., & Raulin, M. L. (2013). *Research methods* (8th ed.). Upper Saddle River, NJ: Pearson.

Gredler, M. E. (2012). Understanding Vygotsky for the classroom: Is it too late? *Educational Psychology Review, 24,* 113–131.

Green, J., Muir, H., & Maher, M. (2011). Child pedestrian casualties and deprivation. *Accidents: Analysis and Prevention, 43,* 714–723.

Green, M. J., Espie, C. A., Hunt, K., & Benzeval, M. (2012). The longitudinal course of insomnia symptoms: Inequalities by sex and occupational class among two different age cohorts followed for 20 years in the west of Scotland. *Sleep, 35,* 815–823.

Greenhaus, J. H. (2013). Career dynamics. In I. B. Weiner & others (Eds.), *Handbook of psychology* (2nd ed., Vol. 12). New York: Wiley.

Greenlund, K. J., & others. (2012, in press). Public health options for improving cardiovascular health among older Americans. *American Journal of Public Health.*

Greer, J. A., & others. (2011). Anxiety disorders in long-term survivors of adult cancers. *Psychosomatics, 52,* 417–423.

Gregorson, M., Kaufman, J. C., & Snyder, H. (Eds.) (2013, in press). *Teaching creatively and teaching creativity*. New York: Springer.

Greif, M. L., & Needham, A. (2012). The development of tool use early in life. In T. McCormack, C. Hoerl, & S. Butterfill (Eds.), *Tool use and causal cognition*. New York: Oxford University Press.

Griffiths, J. D., Marslen-Wilson, W. D., Stamatakis, E. A., & Tyler, L. K. (2012, in press). Functional organization of the neural language system: Dorsal and ventral pathways are critical for syntax. *Cerebral Cortex.*

Grigorenko, E. (2000). Heritability and intelligence. In R. J. Sternberg (Ed.), *Handbook of intelligence*. New York: Cambridge U. Press.

Grigorenko, E. L., Kornilov, S. A., Tan, M., Elliott, J., & Sternberg, R. J. (2012, in press). Gifted identification with Aurora: Widening the spotlight. *Journal of Psychoeducational Assessment*.

Grigorenko, E. L., & Takanishi, R. (Eds.) (2012). *Immigration, diversity, and education*. New York: Routledge.

Gross, L. S. (2013). *Electronic media* (11th ed.). New York: McGraw-Hill.

Gruber, K. J. (2012). A comparative assessment of early adult life status of graduates of the North Carolina adolescent parenting program. *Journal of Child and Adolescent Psychiatric Nursing, 25*, 75–83.

Gruenewald, T. L., Karlamangia, A. S., Greendale, G. A., Singer, B. H., & Seeman, T. E. (2009). Increased mortality risk in older adults with persistently low or declining feelings of usefulness to others. *Journal of Aging and Health, 21*, 398–425.

Grusec, J. E. (2011). Socialization processes in the family: Social and emotional development. *Annual Review of Psychology* (Vol. 62). Palo Alto, CA: Annual Reviews.

Grusec, J. E., Chaparro, M. P., Johnston, M., & Sherman, A. (2013). Social development and social relationships in middle childhood. In I. B. Weiner & others (Eds.), *Handbook of psychology* (2nd ed., Vol. 6). New York: Wiley.

Grusec, J. E., & Sherman, A. (2011). Prosocial behavior. In M. K. Underwood & L. H. Rosen (Eds.), *Social development*. New York: Guilford.

Guerrero, L. K., Andersen, P. A., & Afifi, W. A. (2011). *Close encounters: Communication in relationships* (3rd ed.). Thousand Oaks, CA: Sage.

Guilford, J. P. (1967). *The structure of intellect*. New York: McGraw-Hill.

Guirado, G. N., & others. (2012). Combined exercise training in asymptomatic elderly with controlled hypertension: Effects of functional capacity and cardiac diastolic function. *Medical Science Monitor, 28*, CR461–CR465.

Gunderson, E. A., Ramirez, G., Beilock, S. L., & Levine, S. C. (2012). The role of parents and teachers in the development of gender-related attitudes. *Sex Roles, 66*, 153–166.

Gunnar, M. R., Malone, S., & Fisch, R. O. (1987). The psychobiology of stress and coping in the human neonate: Studies of the adrenocortical activity in response to stress in the first week of life. In T. Field, P. McCabe, & N. Scheiderman (Eds.). *Stress and coping*. Hillsdale, NJ: Erlbaum.

Gunnar, M., & Quevado, K. (2007). The neurobiology of stress and development. *Annual Review of Psychology* (Vol. 58). Palo Alto, CA: Annual Reviews.

Gunning, T. G. (2013). *Creating literacy instruction for all children in grades Pre-K to 4* (2nd ed.). Boston: Allyn & Bacon.

Gupta, S., & Bonanno, G. A. (2011). Complicated grief and deficits in emotional expressive flexibility. *Journal of Abnormal Psychology, 120*, 635–643.

Gur, R. C., & others. (1995). Sex differences in regional cerebral glucose metabolism during a resting state. *Science, 267*, 528–531.

Gurwitch, R. H., Silovksy, J. F., Schultz, S., Kees, M., & Burlingame, S. (2001). *Reactions and guidelines for children following trauma/disaster*. Norman, OK: Department of Pediatrics, University of Oklahoma Health Sciences Center.

Gustafsson, J-E. (2007). Schooling and intelligence. Effects of track of study on level and profile of cognitive abilities. In P. C. Kyllonen, R. D. Roberts, & L. Stankov (Eds.), *Extending intelligence*. Mahwah, NJ: Erlbaum.

Gustafsson, P. E., Persson, M., & Hammarstrom, A. (2011). Life course origins of the metabolic syndrome in middle-aged women and men: The role of socioeconomic status and metabolic risk in adolescence and early adulthood. *Annals of Epidemiology, 21*, 103–110.

Gutchess, A. H., & others. (2005). Aging and the neural correlates of successful picture encoding: Frontal activations compensate for decreased medial-temporal activity. *Journal of Cognitive Neuroscience, 17*, 84–96.

Gutmann, D. L. (1975). Parenthood: A key to the comparative study of the life cycle. In N. Datan & L. Ginsberg (Eds.), *Life-span developmental psychology: Normative life crises*. New York: Academic Press.

Guttmannova, K., & others. (2012). Examining explanatory mechanisms of the effects of early alcohol use on young adult alcohol competence. *Journal of Studies of Alcohol and Drugs, 73*, 379–390.

H

Ha, H. H., & Ingersoll-Dayton, B. (2011). Moderators in the relationship between social contact and psychological distress among widowed adults. *Aging and Mental Health, 15*, 354–363.

Hadwin, J., & Perner, J. (1991). Pleased and surprised: Children's cognitive theory of emotion. *British Journal of Developmental Psychology, 9*, 215–234.

Hagen, J. W., & Lamb-Parker, F. G. (2008). Head Start. In M. M. Haith & J. B. Benson (Eds.), *Encyclopedia of infant and early childhood development*. Oxford, UK: Elsevier.

Hagenauer, M. H., & Lee, T. M. (2012, in press). The neuroendocrine control of the circadian system: Adolescent chronotype. *Frontiers in Neuroendocrinology*.

Hagestad, G. O. (1985). Continuity and connectedness. In V. L. Bengston & J. Robertson (Eds.). *Grandparenthood*. Newbury Park, CA: Sage.

Hagestad, G. O., & Uhlenberg, P. (2007). The impact of demographic changes on relations between age groups and generations: A comparative perspective. In K. W. Schaie & P. Uhlenberg (Eds.), *Demographic changes and the well-being of older persons*. New York: Springer.

Hagman, J. O., & Frank, G. K. W. (2012). Developmental concerns in psychopharmacological treatment of children and adolescents with eating disorders. In J. Lock (Ed.), *Oxford handbook of child and adolescent eating disorders: Developmental perspectives*. New York: Oxford University Press.

Hahn, D. B., Payne, W. A., & Lucas, E. B. (2013). *Focus on health* (11th ed.). New York: McGraw-Hill.

Hahn, E. A., Cichy, K. E., Almeida, D. M., & Haley, W. E. (2011). Time use and well-being in older widows: Adaptation and resilience. *Journal of Women and Aging, 23*, 149–159.

Hahn, W. K. (1987). Cerebral lateralization of function: From infancy through childhood. *Psychological Bulletin, 101*, 376–392.

Hakuta, K. (2001, April). *Key policy milestones and directions in the education of English language learners*. Paper prepared for the Rockefeller Symposium on Educational Equity, Washington, DC.

Hakuta, K. (2005, April.). *Bilingualism at the intersection of research and public policy*. Paper presented at the meeting of the Society for Research in Child Development, Atlanta.

Hakuta, K., Butler, Y. G., & Witt, D. (2000). *How long does it take English learners to attain proficiency?* Berkeley, CA: The University of California Linguistic Minority Research Institute Policy Report 2000–1.

Hall, C. B., Lipton, R. B., Sliwinski, M., Katz, M. J., Derby, C. A., & Verghese, J. (2009). Cognitive activities delay onset of memory decline in persons who develop dementia. *Neurology, 73*, 356–361.

Hall, G. S. (1904). *Adolescence* (Vols. 1 & 2). Englewood Cliffs, NJ: Prentice Hall.

Hall, L. J. (2013). *Autism spectrum disorders* (2nd ed.). Upper Saddle River, NJ: Pearson.

Hallahan, D. P., Kaufmann, J. M., & Pullen, P. C. (2012). *Exceptional learners* (12th ed.). Boston: Allyn & Bacon.

Halonen, J., & Santrock, J. W. (2013). *Your guide to college success* (7th ed.). Boston: Cengage.

Halpern, D. F. (2012). *Sex differences in cognitive abilities* (2nd ed.). New York: Psychology Press.

Halpern, D. F., Benbow, C. P., Geary, D. C., Gur, R. C., Hyde, J. S., & Gernsbacher, M. A. (2007). The science of sex differences in science and mathematics. *Psychological Science in the Public Interest, 8*, 1–51.

Hammes, B. J., & others. (2012). The POLST program: A retrospective review of the demographics of use and outcomes in one community where advance directives are prevalent. *Journal of Palliative Medicine, 15*, 77–85.

Han, W-J. (2009). Maternal employment. In D. Carr (Ed.). *Encyclopedia of the life course and human development*. Boston: Gale Cengage.

..., & others. (2012, in press). Influence ...long-term caloric restriction on myocardial and cardiomycte contractile function and autophagy in mice. *Journal of Nutritional Biochemistry*.

Handrinos, J., Cooper, P., Pauletti, R., & Perry, D. G. (2012, April). *Influences on girls' aggression toward gender-atypical boys*. Paper presented at the Gender Development Research conference, San Francisco.

Hansard, K. (2012). Compassion and empathy—a doula's best friends. *Midwifery Today and International Midwife, 31*, 69.

Hansell, N. K., & others. (2012). Genetic co-morbidity between neuroticism, anxiety/depression, and somatic distress in a sample of adolescent and young adult twins. *Psychological Medicine, 42*, 1249–1260.

Hansen, M. (2012). Confronting costs: Medicaid spending is at the top of many legislative lists. *State Legislatures, 38*, 30–32.

Harden, K. P., & Mendle, J. (2011). Adolescent sexual activity and the development of delinquent behavior: The role of relationship context. *Journal of Youth and Adolescence, 40*, 825–838.

Hardy, M. (2006). Older workers. In R. H. Binstock & L. K. George (Eds.), *Handbook of aging and the social sciences* (6th ed.). San Diego: Academic Press.

Harkins, S. W., Price, D. D., & Martinelli, M. (1986). Effects of age on pain perception. *Journal of Gerontology, 41*, 58–63.

Harkness, S., & Super, E. M. (1995). Culture and parenting. In M. H. Bornstein (Ed.), *Handbook of parenting* (Vol. 3). Hillsdale, NJ: Erlbaum.

Harlow, H. F. (1958). The nature of love *American Psychologist, 13*, 673–685.

Harris, G., Thomas, A., & Booth, D. A. (1990). Development of salt taste in infancy. *Developmental Psychology, 26*, 534–538.

Harris, J., Golinkoff, R. M., & Hirsh-Pasek, K. (2011). Lessons from the crib for the classroom: How children really learn vocabulary. In S. B. Neuman, & D. K. Dickinson (Eds.), *Handbook of early literacy research*. New York: Guilford.

Harris, J. J., & Atwell, D. (2012). The energetics of CNS white matter. *Journal of Neuroscience, 32*, 356–371.

Harris, K. M., Gorden-Larsen, P., Chantala, K., & Udry, J. R. (2006). Longitudinal trends in race/ethnic disparities in leading health indicators from adolescence to young adulthood. *Archives of Pediatric and Adolescent Medicine, 160*, 74–81.

Harris, P. L. (2000). *The work of the imagination*. New York: Oxford University Press.

Harris, P. L. (2006). Social cognition. In W. Damon & R. Lerner (Eds.), *Handbook of child psychology* (6th ed.). New York: Wiley.

Harrison, C. (2012). Aging: Telomerase gene therapy increases longevity. *Nature Reviews/Drug Discovery, 11*, 518.

Hart, B., & Risley, T. R. (1995). *Meaningful differences in the everyday experience of young Americans*. Baltimore: Paul H. Brookes.

Hart, C. H., Yang, C., Charlesworth, R., & Burts, D. C. (2003, April). *Early childhood teachers' curriculum beliefs, classroom practices, and children's outcomes: What are the connections?* Paper presented at the biennial meeting of the Society for Research in Child Development, Tampa, FL.

Hart, D., & Karmel, M. P. (1996). Self-awareness and self-knowledge in humans, great apes, and monkeys. In A. Russori, K. Bard, & S. Parker (Eds.), *Reaching into thought*. New York: Cambridge University Press.

Hart, D., Matsuba, M. K., & Atkins, R. (2008). The moral and civic effects of learning to serve. In L. Nucci & D. Narvaez (Eds.), *Handbook of moral and character education*. Clinton, NJ: Psychology Press.

Hart, K. A. (2007). The aging workforce: implications for health care organizations. *Nursing Economics, 25*, 101–102.

Harter, S. (2006). The self. In W. Damon & R. Lerner (Eds.), *Handbook of child psychology* (6th ed.). New York: Wiley.

Harter, S. (2012). *The construction of the self* (2nd ed.). New York: Wiley.

Hartshorne, H., & May, M. S. (1928–1930). *Moral studies in the nature of character*. New York: Macmillan.

Hartup, W. W. (1983). The peer system. In P. H. Mussen (Ed.), *Handbook of child psychology* (4th ed., Vol. 4). New York: Wiley.

Hartup, W. W. (1996). The company they keep: Friendships and their developmental significance. *Child Development, 67*, 1–13.

Hartup, W. W. (2009). Critical issues and theoretical viewpoints. In K. H. Rubin, W. M. Bukowski, & B. Laursen (Eds.), *Handbook of peer interactions, relationships, and groups*. New York: Guilford.

Hattery, A. J., & Smith, E. (2007). *African American families*. Thousand Oaks, CA: Sage.

Hatzfeld, J. J., Laveist, T. A., & Gaston-Johansson, F. G. (2012, in press). Racial/ethnic disparities in the prevalence of selected chronic diseases among U.S. Air Force members, 2008. *Preventing Chronic Disease*.

Hauck, F. R., & others. (2011). Breastfeeding and reduced risk of sudden infant death syndrome: A meta-analysis. *Pediatrics, 128*, 103–110.

Hauser-Cram, P., & Mitchell, D. B. (2012). Early childhood education. In K. R. Harris, S. Graham, & T. Urdan (Eds.), *Handbook of educational psychology*. Washington, DC: American Psychological Association.

Hawkes, C. (2006). Olfaction in neurogenerative disorder. *Advances in Otorhinollaryngology, 63*, 133–151.

Hawkley, L. C., & Cacioppo, J. T. (2013, in press). Social connection and relationships in successful aging. In J. M. Rippe (Ed.), *Encyclopedia of lifestyle medicine and health*. Thousand Oaks, CA: Sage.

Haydon, A., & Halpern, G. T. (2010). Older romantic partners and depressive symptoms during adolescence. *Journal of Youth and Adolescence, 39*, 1240–1251.

Haydon, A. A., Herring, A. H., Prinstein, M. J., & Halpern, C. T. (2012). Beyond age at first sex: Patterns of emerging sexual behavior in adolescence and young adulthood. *Journal of Adolescent Health, 50*, 456–463.

Hayes, J. R., & Berninger, V. (2013, in press). Cognitive processes in writing: A framework. In B. Arte, J. Dockrell, & V. Berninger (Eds.), *Writing development and instruction in children with hearing, speech, and language disorders*. New York: Oxford University Press.

Hayflick, L. (1977). The cellular basis for biological aging. In C. E. Finch & L. Hayflick (Eds.), *Handbook of the biology of aging*. New York: Van Nostrand.

Hazan, C., & Shaver, P. R. (1987). Romantic love conceptualized as an attachment process. *Journal of Personality and Social Psychology, 52*, 522–524.

Head, D., Singh, T., & Bugg, J. M. (2012). The moderating role of exercise on stress-related effects on the hippocampus and memory in late adulthood. *Neuropsychology, 26*, 133–143.

Heard, E., & others. (2011). Mediating effects of social support on the relationship between perceived stress, depression, and hypertension in African Americans. *Journal of the American Medical Association, 103*, 116–122.

Hebl, M. R., & Avery, D. R. (2013). Diversity in organizations. In I. B. Weiner & others (Eds.), *Handbook of psychology* (2nd ed., Vol.12). New York: Wiley.

Hedayat, K. (2006). When the spirit leaves: Childhood death, grieving, and bereavement in Islam. *Journal of Palliative Medicine, 9*, 1282–1291.

Heiman, G. W. (2013). *Basic statistics for the behavioral sciences* (7th ed.). Boston: Cengage.

Heimann, M., Strid, K., Smith, L., Tjus, T., Ulvund, S. E., & Melzoff, A. N. (2006). Exploring the relation between memory, gestural communication, and the emergence of language in infancy: A longitudinal study. *Infant and Child Development, 15*, 233–249.

Helgeson, V. S. (2012). *Psychology of gender* (4th ed.). Upper Saddle River, NJ: Pearson.

Hellander, I., & Bhargavan, R. (2012). Report from the United States: The U.S. health crsisis deepens amid rising inequality—a review of data, fall 2011. *International Journal of Health Services, 42*, 161–175.

Helman, R., Copeland, C., & VanDerhei, J. (2012). The 2012 Retirement Confidence Survey: Job insecurity, debt weigh on retirement confidence, savings. *EBRI Issue Brief, 369*, 5–32.

Helwig, C. C., & Turiel, E. (2011). Children's social and moral reasoning.

In P. K. Smith & C. H. Hart (Eds.), *Wiley-Blackwell handbook of childhood social development* (2nd ed.). New York: Wiley.

Henderson, V. W. (2011). Gonadal hormones and cognitive aging: A midlife perspective. *Women's Health, 7,* 81–93.

Hendry, C. (2009). Incarceration and the tasks of grief: A narrative review. *Journal of Advanced Nursing, 65,* 270–278.

Henggeler, S. W., & Sheidow, L. J. (2012). Empirically supported family-based treatments for conduct disorder and delinquency in adolescents. *Journal of Marital and Family Therapy, 38,* 30–58.

Henninger, M. L. (2013). *Teaching young children* (5th ed.). Upper Saddle River, NJ: Pearson.

Henretta, J. C. (2010). Lifetime marital history and mortality after age 50. *Journal of Aging and Health, 22*(8), 1198–1212.

Henriksen, T. B., & others. (2004). Alcohol consumption at the time of conception and spontaneous abortion. *American Journal of Epidemiology, 160,* 661–667.

Herbers, J. E., & others. (2011). Direct and indirect effects of parenting on academic functioning of young homeless children. *Early Education and Development, 22,* 77–104.

Herman-Giddens, M. E. (2007). The decline in the age of menarche in the United States: Should we be concerned? *Journal of Adolescent Health, 40,* 201–203.

Herrera, S. G., & Murry, K. G. (2011). *Mastering ESL and bilingual methods* (2nd ed.). Boston: Allyn & Bacon.

Hertenstein, M. J., & Keltner, D. (2011). Gender and the communication of emotion via touch. *Sex Roles, 64,* 70–80.

Hertzog, C., Kramer, A. F., Wilson, R. S., & Lindenberger, U. (2009). Enrichment effects on adult cognitive development. *Psychological Perspectives in the Public Interest, 9,* 1–65.

Hetherington, E. M. (1989). Coping with family transitions: Winners, losers, and survivors. *Child Development, 60,* 1–14.

Hetherington, E. M. (2006). The influence of conflict, marital problem solving, and parenting on children's adjustment in nondivorced, divorced, and remarried families. In A. Clarke-Stewart & J. Dunn (Eds.), *Families count.* New York: Oxford University Press.

Hetherington, E. M., & Kelly, J. (2002). *For better or for worse: Divorce reconsidered.* New York: Norton.

Hetherington, E. M., & Stanley-Hagan, M. (2002). Parenting in divorced and remarried families. In M. H. Bornstein (Ed.), *Handbook of parenting* (2nd ed., Vol. 3). Mahwah, NJ: Erlbaum.

Heude, B., & others. (2012). Pre-pregnancy body mass index and weight gain during pregnancy: Relations with gestational diabetes and hypertension, and birth outcomes. *Maternal and Child Health, 16,* 255–263.

Hewlett, B. S. (1991). *Intimate fathers: The nature and context of Aka Pygmy.* Ann Arbor, MI: University of Michigan Press.

Hewlett, B. S. (2000). Culture, history, and sex: Anthropological perspectives on father involvement. *Marriage and Family Review, 29,* 324–340.

Hewlett, B. S., & MacFarlan, S. J. (2010). Fathers, roles in hunter-gatherer and other small-scale cultures. In M. E. Lamb (Ed.) *The role of the father in child development* (5th ed.). New York: Wiley.

Hickman, S. E., & el Khoury, J. (2012, in press). The neuroimmune system in Alzheimer's disease: The glass is half full. *Journal of Alzheimer's Disease.*

Higginbotham, B., Davis, P., Smith, L., Dansie, L., Skogrand, L., & Reck, K. (2012). Stepfathers and stepfamily education. *Journal of Divorce & Remarriage, 53,* 76–90.

High/Scope Resource. (2005, Spring). The High/Scope Perry Preschool Study and the man who began it. *High/Scope Resource 9.* Ypsilanti, MI: High/Scope Press.

Highfield, R. (2008, April 30). *Harvard's baby brain research lab.* Retrieved January 24, 2009, from www.telegraph.co.uk/scienceand technology/science/sciencenews/3341166/Harvards-baby-brain-research-lab.html

Highhouse, S., & Schmitt, N. (2013). A snapshot in time: Industrial-organizational psychology today. In I. B. Weiner & others (Eds.), *Handbook of psychology* (2nd ed., Vol. 12). New York: Wiley.

Higo, M., & Williamson, J. B. (2009). Retirement. In D. Carr (Ed.), *Encyclopedia of the life course and human development.* Boston: Gale Cengage.

Hildebrandt, T., Bacow, T., Markella, M., & Loeb, K. L. (2012, in press). Anxiety in anorexia nervosa and its management using family-based treatment. *European Eating Disorders Review.*

Hill, C. R., & Stafford, E. P. (1980). Parental care of children: Time diary estimate of quantity, predictability, and variety. *Journal of Human Resources, 15,* 219–239.

Hill, P. C., & Butter, E. M. (1995). The role of religion in promoting physical health. *Journal of Psychology and Christianity, 14,* 141–155.

Hill, P. C., & Pargament, K. I. (2003). Advances in conceptualization and measurement of religion and spirituality: Implications for physical and mental health research. *American Psychologist, 58,* 64–74.

Hill, P. L., Turiano, N. A., Mroczek, D. K., & Roberts, B. W. (2012, in press). Examining concurrent and longitudinal relations between personality traits and social well-being in adulthood. *Social Psychological and Personality Science.*

Hill, P. L., & others. (2011). Conscientiousness and longevity: An examination of possible Mediators. *Health Psychology, 30,* 536–541.

Hill, T. D., Angel, J. L., Ellison, [...], Angel, R. J. (2005). Religious atten[...] mortality: An 8-year follow-up of ol[...] Mexican Americans. *Journals of Geron[...] Psychological Sciences and Social Sciences,* [...] S102–S109.

Hillemeier, M. M., Morgan, P. L., Far[...] G., & Maczuga, S. A. (2012, in press). Q[...] ity disparities in child care for at-risk chil-dren: Comparing Head Start and non-Head Start settings. *Maternal and Child Health Journal.*

Hilliard, L., & Liben, L. (2012, April). *No boys in ballet: Response to gender bias in mother-child conversations.* Paper presented at the Gender Development Research conference, San Francisco.

Hillier, A., & others. (2012, in press). The impact of WIC food package changes on access to healthful food in two low-income neighborhoods. *Journal of Nutrition Education and Behavior.*

Himes, C. L. (2009). Age structure. In D. Carr (Ed.), *Encyclopedia of the life course and human development.* Boston: Gale Cengage.

Hindin, S. B., & Zelinski, E. M. (2012). Extended practice and aerobic exercise interventions benefit untrained cognitive outcomes in older adults: A meta-analysis. *Journal of the American Geriatric Association, 60,* 136–141.

Hindman, A. H., Skibbek, L. E., Miller, A., & Zimmerman, M. (2010). Ecological contexts and early learning: Contributions of child, family, and classroom factors during Head Start to literacy and mathematics growth through first grade. *Early Childhood Research Quarterly, 25,* 235–250.

Hinze, S. W., Lin, J., & Andersson, T. E. (2012). Can we capture the intersections? Older Black women, education, and health. *Women's Health Issues, 22,* e91–e98.

Hipwell, A. E., Keenan, K., Loeber, R., & Battista, D. (2010). Early predictors of intimate sexual behaviors in an urban sample of young girls. *Developmental Psychology, 46,* 366–378.

Hirsch, B. J., & Rapkin, B. D. (1987). The transition to junior high school: A longitudinal study of self-esteem, psychological symptomatology, school life, and social support. *Child Development, 58,* 1235–1243.

Hirsh-Pasek, K., & Golinkoff, R. M. (2013, in press). Early language and literacy: Six principles. In S. Gilford (Ed.), *Head Start teacher's guide.* New York: Teacher's College Press.

Hirsh-Pasek, K., Golinkoff, R. M., Singer, D., & Berk, L. (2009). *A mandate for playful learning in preschool: Presenting the evidence.* New York: Oxford University Press.

Ho, J., Yeh, M., McCabe, K., & Lau, A. (2012). Perceptions of the acceptability of parent training among Chinese immigrant parents: Contributions of cultural factors and clinical need. *Behavior Therapy, 43,* 436–449.

C. G., & ... (2012). Association ...ge-related ...disability. *Science,*

...ck, W. J., & ...he timing hy-...rt disease preven-...rapy: Past, present, ...ctive. *Climacteric, 15,*

...M. (2013). *Biology essentials.* ...McGraw-Hill.

...r, L. (2009). Divorce and separation. ... Carr (Ed.), *Encyclopedia of the life course ...d human development.* Boston: Gale Cengage.

Hofer, A., & others. (2007). Sex differences in brain activation patterns during processing of positively and negatively balanced emotional stimuli. *Psychological Medicine, 37,* 109–119.

Hofer, S. M., Rast, P., & Piccinin, A. M. (2012). Methodological issues in research on adult development and aging. In S. K. Whitbourne & M. J. Sliwinski (Eds.), *Wiley-Blackwell handbook of adult development and aging.* New York: Wiley.

Hoff, E. (2012, in press). Interpreting the early language trajectories of children from low-SES and language minority homes: Implications for closing achievement gaps. *Developmental Psychology.*

Hoff, E., Laursen, B., & Tardif, T. (2002). Socioeconomic status and parenting. In M. H. Bornstein (Ed.), *Handbook of parenting* (2nd ed.). Mahwah, NJ: Erlbaum.

Hoffman, E., & Ewen, D. (2007). Supporting families, nurturing young children. *CLASP Policy Brief No. 9,* 1–11.

Hoffmeyer, K., & others. (2012). Wnt/B-catenin signaling regulates telomerase in stem cells and cancer cells. *Science, 336,* 1549–1554.

Hogan, M. J. (2012). Prosocial effects of media. *Pediatric Clinics of North America, 59,* 635–645.

Hogerbrugge, M. J., & Komter, A. E. (2012). Solidarity and ambivalence: Comparing two perspectives on intergenerational relations using longitudinal panel data. *Journals of Gerontology B: Psychological Sciences and Social Sciences, 67,* 372–383.

Holden, G. W., Vittrup, B., & Rosen, L. H. (2011). Families, parenting, and discipline. In M. K. Underwood & L. H. Rosen (Eds.), *Social development.* New York: Guilford.

Holland, A. S., & Roisman, G. I. (2010). Adult attachment security and young adults' dating relationships over time: Self-reported, observational, and physiological evidence. *Developmental Psychology, 46,* 552–557.

Hollister, M. (2011). Employment stability in the U.S. labor market: Rhetoric versus reality. *Annual Review of Sociology* (Vol. 37). Palo Alto, CA: Annual Reviews.

Holloway, D. (2010). Clinical update on hormone replacement therapy. *British Journal of Nursing, 19,* 496, 498–504.

Holloway, I. W., & others. (2012, in press). Effects of sexual expectancies on early sexualized behavior among urban minority youth. *Journal of the Society for Social Work and Research.*

Holm, A. L., & Severinsson, E. (2012). Systematic review of emotional state and self-management of widows. *Nursing and Health Sciences, 14,* 109–120.

Holman, A., & Sillars, A. (2012). Talk about "hooking up": The influence of college student social networks on nonrelationship sex. *Health Communication, 27,* 205–217.

Holmes, L. B. (2011). Human teratogens: Update 2010. *Birth Defects Research Part A: Clinical and Molecular Teratology, 91,* 1–7.

Holmes, T. H., & Rahe, R. H. (1967). The social readjustment rating scale. *Journal of Psychosomatic Research, 11,* 213–218.

Holsen, I., Carlson Jones, D., & Skogbrott Birkeland, M. (2012). Body image satisfaction among Norwegian adolescents and young adults: A longitudinal study of the influence of interpersonal relationships and BMI. *Body Image, 9,* 201–208.

Holwerda, T. J., & others. (2012). Increased risk of mortality associated with social isolation in older men: Only when feeling lonely? Results from the Amsterdam Study of the Elderly (AMSTEL). *Psychological Medicine, 42,* 843–853.

Hope, D. A. (2009). Contemporary perspectives on lesbian, gay, and bisexual identities: Introduction. *Nebraska Symposium on Motivation, 54,* 1–4.

Horn, J. L., & Donaldson, G. (1980). Cognitive development II: Adulthood development of human abilities. In O. G. Brim & J. Kagan (Eds.), *Constancy and change in human development.* Cambridge, MA: Harvard University Press.

Hornor, G. (2012). Medical evaluation for child physical abuse: What the PNP needs to know. *Journal of Pediatric Health Care, 26,* 163–170.

Horowitz, E. K. (2013). *Becoming a second language teacher* (2nd ed.). Boston: Allyn & Bacon.

Hospital for Sick Children, Dipchard, A., Friedman, J., Gupta, S., Bismilla, Z., & Lam, C. (2010). *The Hospital for Sick Children's handbook of pediatrics* (11th ed.). London: Elsevier.

Houde, O., & others. (2011). Functional magnetic resonance imaging study of Piaget's conservation-of-number task in preschool and school-age children: A neo-Piagetian approach. *Journal of Experimental Child Psychology, 110*(3), 332–346.

Houston, D., Golinkoff, R., Ma, W., & Hirsh-Pasek, I. (2012, in press). Word learning in infant- and adult-directed speech. *Language Learning and Development.*

Howe, G. W., Homberger, A. P., Weihs, K., Moreno, F., & Neiderhiser, J. M. (2012). Higher-order structure in the trajectories of depression and anxiety following sudden involuntary unemployment. *Journal of Abnormal Psychology, 121,* 325–338.

Howe, M. J. A., Davidson, J. W., Moore, D. G., & Sloboda, J. A. (1995). Are there early childhood signs of musical ability? *Psychology of Music, 23,* 162–176.

Howe, N., Ross, H. S., & Recchia, H. (2011). Sibling relations in early and middle childhood. In P. K. Smith & C. H. Hart (Eds.), *Wiley-Blackwell handbook of childhood social development* (2nd ed.). New York: Wiley.

Howell, A., & Evans, G. D. (2011). Hormone replacement therapy and cancer. *Recent Results in Cancer Research, 188,* 115–124.

Howerton, C. L., & Bale, T. L. (2012, in press). Prenatal programming: At the intersection of maternal stress and immune activation. *Hormones and Behavior.*

Hoyer, W. J., & Roodin, P. A. (2009). *Adult development and aging* (6th ed.). New York: McGraw-Hill.

Hoyert, D. (2012). 75 years of mortality in the United States. *NCHS Data Brief, 88,* 1–8.

Hoyt, M. A., & Stanton, A. (2012). Adjustment to chronic illness. In A. Baum, T. A. Revenson, & J. Singer (Eds.), *Handbook of health psychology* (2nd ed.). New York: Psychology Press.

Hrabosky, J. I., Masheb, R. M., White, M. A., & Grilo, C. M. (2007). Overvaluation of shape and weight in binge eating disorder. *Journal of Consulting and Clinical Psychology, 75,* 175–180.

HSBC Insurance. (2007). *The future of retirement: The new old age global report.* London: HSBC.

Huang, J-H., DeJong, W., Towvim, L. G., & Schneider, S. K. (2009). Sociodemographic and psychobehavioral characteristics of U.S. college students who abstain from alcohol. *Journal of American College Health, 57,* 395–410.

Huang, P. M., Smock, P. J., Manning, W. D., & Bergstrom-Lynch, C. A. (2011). He says, she says: Gender and cohabitation. *Journal of Family Issues, 32,* 876–905.

Huberman, H. S., & Mendelsohn, A. L. (2012). Preventive interventions: Parenting and the home environment. In V. Maholmes & R. B. King (Eds.), *Oxford handbook of poverty and child development.* New York: Oxford University Press.

Hudley, C., & Irving, M. (2012). Ethnic and racial identity in childhood and adolescence. In K. R. Harris, S. Graham, & T. Urdan (Eds.), *APA handbook of educational psychology.* Washington, DC: American Psychological Association.

Huerta, M., Cortina, L. M., Pang, J. S., Torges, C. M., & Magley, V. J. (2006). Sex and power in the academy: Modeling sexual harassment in the lives of college women. *Personality and Social Psychology Bulletin, 32,* 616–628.

Huesmann, L. R., Dubow, E. F., Eron, L. D., & Boxer, P. (2006). Middle childhood family-contextual and personal factors as predictors of adult outcomes. In A. G. Huston & M. N. Ripke (Eds.), *Developmental contexts in middle childhood: Bridges to adolescence and adulthood*. New York: Cambridge University Press.

Hughes, J. F., & Rozen, S. (2012). Genomics and genetics of human and primate Y chromosomes. *Annual Review of Genomics and Human Genetics* (Vol. 13). Palo Alto, CA: Annual Reviews.

Hughes, M. E., Waite, L. J., LaPierre, T. A., & Luo, Y. (2007). All in the family: The impact of caring for grandchildren on grandparents' health. *Journals of Gerontology B: Psychological Sciences and Social Sciences, 62*, S108–S119.

Hummert, M. L. (2011). Age stereotypes and aging. In K. W. Schaie & S. L. Willis (Eds.), *Handbook of the psychology of aging* (7th ed.). New York: Elsevier.

Hunter, J. M., & others. (2012). Morphological and pathological evolution of the brain microcirculation in aging and Alzheimer's disease. *PLoS One, 7*(5), e36893.

Hurt, H., Brodsky, N. L., Roth, H., Malmud, F., & Giannetta, J. M. (2005). School performance of children with gestational cocaine exposure. *Neurotoxicology and Teratology, 27*, 203–211.

Hustedt, J. T., Friedman, A. H., & Barnett, W. S. (2012). Investments in early education: Resources at the federal and state levels. In R. C. Pianta (Ed.), *Handbook of early childhood education*. New York: Guilford.

Huston, A. C., & Ripke, N. N. (2006). Experiences in middle and late childhood and children's development. In A. C. Huston & M. N. Ripke (Eds.), *Developmental contexts in middle childhood*. New York: Cambridge University Press.

Huston, T. L., & Holmes, E. K. (2004). Becoming parents. In A. L. Vangelisti (Ed.), *Handbook of family communication*. Mahwah, NJ: Erlbaum.

Hutchinson, S. L., & Nimrod, G. (2012). Leisure as a resource for successful aging by older adults with chronic health conditions. *International Journal of Aging and Human Development, 74*, 41–65.

Huttenlocher, P. R., & Dabholkar, A. S. (1997). Regional differences in synaptogenesis in human cerebral cortex. *Journal of Comparative Neurology, 37*(2), 167–178.

Huyck, M. H. (1995). Marriage and close relationships of the marital kind. In R. Blieszner & V. H. Bedford (Eds.), *Handbook of aging and the family*. Westport, CT: Greenwood Press.

Hwang, S. H., Hwang, J. H., Moon, J. S., & Lee, D. H. (2012). Environmental tobacco smoke and children's health. *Korean Journal of Pediatrics, 55*, 35–41.

Hyde, D. C., & Spelke, E. S. (2012, in press). Spatio-temporal dynamics of numerical processing: An ERP source localization study. *Human Brain Mapping*.

Hyde, J. S. (2005). The gender similarities hypothesis. *America Psychologist, 60*, 581–592.

Hyde, J. S. (2007). *Half the human experience* (6th ed.). Boston: Houghton Mifflin.

Hyde, J. S., & DeLamater, J. D. (2011). *Understanding human sexuality* (11th ed.). New York: McGraw-Hill.

Hyde, J. S., & Else-Quest, N. (2013). *Half the human experience* (8th ed.). Boston: Cengage.

Hyde, J. S., Lindberg, S. M., Linn, M. C., Ellis, A. B., & Williams, C. C. (2008). Gender similarities characterize math performance. *Science, 321*, 494–495.

Hyoun, S. C., Obican, S. G., & Scialli, A. R. (2012). Teratogen update: Methotrexate. *Birth Defects Research A: Clinical and Molecular Teratology, 94*, 187–204.

Hyson, M. C., Copple, C., & Jones, J. (2006). Early childhood development and education. In W. Damon & R. Lerner (Eds.), *Handbook of child psychology* (6th ed.). New York: Wiley.

I

Ibrahim, R., & Eviatar, Z. (2012, in press). The contribution of two hemispheres to lexical decision in different languages. *Behavioral and Brain Functions*.

Ickovics, J. R., & others. (2011). Effects of group prenatal care on psychosocial risk in pregnancy: Results from a randomized controlled trial. *Psychology and Health, 26*, 235–250.

Imdad, A., Sadig, K., & Bhutta, Z. A. (2011). Evidence-based prevention of childhood malnutrition. *Current Opinion in Clinical Nutrition and Metabolic Care, 14*(3), 276–285.

Insel, P. M., & Roth, W. T. (2012). *Connect core concepts in health* (12th ed.). New York: McGraw-Hill.

International Montessori Council. (2006). Larry Page and Sergey Brin, founders of Google.com, credit their Montessori education for much of their success on prime-time television. Retrieved June 24, 2006, from http://www.Montessori.org/enews/Barbara_walters.html

Iovannone, R. (2013). Teaching students with autism spectrum disorders. In B. G. Cook & M. G. Tankerslee (Ed.), *Research based practices in special education*. Upper Saddle River, NJ: Pearson.

Iqbal, M., & others. (2012). Placental drug transporters and their role in fetal protection. *Placenta, 33*, 137–142.

Iruka, I. U., Laforett, D. R., & Odom, E. C. (2012, in press). Examining the validity of the family investment and stress models and relationships to children's school readiness across five cultural groups. *Journal of Family Psychology*.

Isaacs, B. (2012). *Understanding the Montessori approach: Early years education practice*. New York: Routledge.

Issel, L. M., & others. (2011). A review of prenatal home-visiting effectiveness for improving birth outcomes. *Journal of Obstetrics, Gynecologic, and Neonatal Nursing, 40*, 157–165.

Iwamoto, J., Sato, Y., Takeda, T., & Matsumoto, H. (2009). Role of sport and exercise in the maintenance of female bone health. *Journal of Bone and Mineral Metabolism, 27*, 530–537.

Iwasa, H., Masul, Y., Gondo, Y., Inagaki, H., Kawaal, C., & Suzuki, T. (2008). Personality and all-cause mortality among older adults dwelling in a Japanese community: A five-year population-based prospective cohort study. *American Journal of Geriatric Psychiatry, 16*, 399–405.

J

Jackson, J. J., & others. (2009). Not all conscientiousness scales change alike: A multimethod, multisample study of age differences in the facets of conscientiousness. *Journal of Personality and Social Psychology, 96*, 446–459.

Jackson, J. S., Govia, I. O., & Sellers, S. L. (2011). Racial and ethnic influences over the life course. In R. H. Binstock & L. K. George (Eds.), *Handbook of aging and the social sciences* (7th ed.). New York: Elsevier.

Jackson, L. A., & others. (2012). The digital divide. In J. R. Levesque (Ed.), *Encyclopedia of adolescence*. New York: Springer.

Jacobs, J. M., Hammerman-Rozenberg, R., Cohen, A., & Stressman, J. (2008). Reading daily predicts reduced mortality among men from a cohort of community dwelling 70-year-olds. *Journals of Gerontology B: Psychological Sciences and Social Sciences, 63*, S73–S80.

Jacobson, L. A., & others. (2011). Working memory influences processing speed and reading fluency in ADHD. *Child Neuropsychology, 17*, 209–224.

Jaeggi, S. M., Berman, M. G., & Jonides, J. (2009). Training attentional processes. *Trends in Cognitive Science, 37*, 644–654.

Jaffee, S., & Hyde, J. S. (2000). Gender differences in moral orientation: A meta-analysis. *Psychological Bulletin, 126*, 703–726.

Jak, A. J. (2011). The impact of physical and mental activity on cognitive aging. *Current Topics in Behavioral Neurosciences, 10*, 273–291.

James, B. D., & Bennett, D. A. (2011). Smoking in midlife and dementia in old age: Risk across the life course. *Archives of Neurology, 68*, 365–368.

James, B. D., Boyle, P. A., Buchman, A. S., & Bennett, D. A. (2011). Relation of late-life social activity with incident disability among community-dwelling older adults. *Journals of Gerontology A: Biological Sciences and Medical Sciences, 66*, 467–473.

James, J., Ellis, B. J., Scholmer, G. L., & Garber, J. (2012). Sex-specific pathways to early puberty, sexual debut, and sexual risk taking: Tests of an integrated evolutionary-developmental model. *Developmental Psychology, 48,* 687–702.

James, W. (1890/1950). *The principles of psychology.* New York: Dover.

Jansen, J., de Weerth, C., & Riksen-Walraven, J. M. (2008). Breastfeeding and the mother-infant relationship—A review. *Developmental Review, 28,* 503–521.

Janssen, I., & others. (2005). Comparison of overweight and obesity prevalence in school-aged youth from 34 countries and their relationships with physical activity and dietary patterns. *Obesity Reviews, 6,* 123–132.

Jardri, R., & others. (2012). Assessing fetal response to maternal speech using a noninvasive functional brain imaging technique. *International Journal of Developmental Neuroscience, 30,* 159–161.

Javaroni, V., & Neves, M. F. (2012, in press). Erectile dysfunction and hypertension: Impact on cardiovascular risk and treatment. *International Journal of Hypertension.*

Jayson, S. (2006, June 29). The 'millennials' come of age. *USA Today,* pp. 1D–2D.

Jazaieri, H., Goldin, P. R., Werner, K., Ziv, M., & Gross, J. J. (2012, in press). A randomized trial of MBSR versus aerobic exercise for social anxiety disorder. *Journal of Clinical Psychology.*

Jenni, O. G., and Carskadon, M. A. (2007). Sleep behavior and sleep regulation from infancy through adolescence: Normative aspects. In O. G. Jenni and M. A. Carskadon (Eds), *Sleep Medicine Clinics: Sleep in Children and Adolescents.* Philadelphia: W. B. Saunders.

Jerant, A., Chapman, B., Duberstein, P., Robbins, J., & Franks, P. (2011). Personality and medication non-adherence among older adults enrolled in a six-year trial. *British Journal of Health Psychology, 16,* 151–159.

Ji, B. T., & others. (1997). Paternal cigarette smoking and the risk of childhood cancer among offspring of nonsmoking mothers. *Journal of the National Cancer Institute, 89,* 238–244.

Jia, R., & Schoppe-Sullivan, S. J. (2011). Relations between coparenting and father involvement in families with preschool-age children. *Developmental Psychology, 47,* 106–118.

Jiao, S., Ji, G., & Jing, Q. (1996). Cognitive development of Chinese urban only children and children with siblings. *Child Development, 67,* 387–395.

Jin, M. K., Jacobvitz, D., Hagen, N., & Jung, S. H. (2012). Maternal sensitivity and infant attachment security in Korea: Cross-cultural validation of the Strange Situation. *Attachment and Human Development, 14,* 33–44.

Jinyao, Y., & others. (2012, in press). Insecure attachment as a predictor of depressive and anxious symptomatology. *Depression and Anxiety.*

Jitendra, A., & Montague, M. (2013). Strategies for improving student outcomes in mathematical reasoning. In B. G. Cook & M. G. Tankersley (Eds.), *Research-based practices in special education.* Upper Saddle River, NJ: Pearson.

Joel, S., MacDonald, G., & Shimotomai, A. (2011). Conflicting pressures on romantic relationship commitment for anxiously attached individuals. *Journal of Personality, 79,* 51–73.

Joffe, H., & others. (2011). Increased estradiol and improved sleep, but not hot flashes, predict enhanced mood during the menopausal transition. *Journal of Clinical Endocrinology and Metabolism, 90,* E1044–E1054.

Johns Hopkins University. (2006, February 17). Undergraduate honored for launching health program in India. Baltimore: Johns Hopkins University News Releases.

Johnson, A. D., & Brooks-Gunn, J. (2012). Child care and early education for low-income families: Choices and consequences. In V. Maholmes & R. B. King (Eds.), *Oxford handbook of poverty and child development.* New York: Oxford University Press.

Johnson, J. S., & Newport, E. L. (1991). Critical period effects on universal properties of language: The status of subjacency in the acquisition of a second language. *Cognition, 39,* 215–258.

Johnson, L., Giordano, P. C., Manning, W. D., & Longmore, M. A. (2011). Parent-child relations and offending during young adulthood. *Journal of Youth and Adolescence, 40*(7), 786–799.

Johnson, M. (2008, April 30). Commentary in R. Highfield *Harvard's baby brain research lab.* Retrieved January 24, 2008, from www.telegraph.co.uk/scienceandtechnology/science/sciencenews/3341166/Harvards-baby-brain-research-lab.html

Johnson, M. D. (2012). *Human biology* (6th ed.). Upper Saddle River, NJ: Pearson.

Johnson, M. H., & de Haan, M. (2012). *Developmental cognitive neuroscience* (3rd ed.). New York: Wiley-Blackwell.

Johnson, M. H., Grossmann, T., and Cohen-Kadosh, K. (2009). Mapping functional brain development: Building a social brain through Interactive Specialization. *Developmental Psychology, 45,* 151–159.

Johnson, S. P. (2004). Development of perceptual completion in infancy. *Psychological Science, 15,* 769–775.

Johnson, S. P. (2010). Perceptual completion in infancy. In S. P. Johnson (Ed.), *Neoconstructivism: The new science of cognitive development.* New York: Oxford University Press.

Johnson, S. P. (2011). A constructivist view of object perception in infancy. In L. M. Oakes & others (Eds.), *Infant perception and cognition.* New York: Oxford University Press.

Johnson, S. P. (2012, in press). Development of the visual system. In P. Rakic & J. Rubenstein (Eds.), *Developmental neuroscience—Basic and clinical mechanisms.* New York: Oxford University Press.

Johnson, S. P. (2013). Object perception. In P. D. Zelazo (Ed.), *Handbook of developmental psychology.* New York: Oxford University Press.

Johnston, L. D., O'Malley, P. M., Bachman, J. G., & Schulenberg, J. E. (2008b). *Monitoring the Future national survey results on drug use, 1975–2007 (Vol. 2: College students and adults ages 19–45).* Washington, DC: National Institute of Drug Abuse.

Johnston, L. D., O'Malley, P. M., Bachman, J. G., & Schulenberg, J. E. (2011). *Monitoring the Future national survey results on drug use, 1975–2010 (Vol. 2: College students and adults ages 19–50).* Bethesda, MD: National Institute on Drug Abuse.

Johnston, L. D., O'Malley, P. M., Bachman, J. G., & Schulenberg, J. E. (2012). *Monitoring the Future national survey results on adolescent drug use: Overview of key findings, 2011.* Institute for Social Research, University of Michigan, Ann Arbor.

Jokela, M., & others. (2010). From midlife to early old age: Health trajectories associated with retirement. *Epidemiology, 21,* 284–290.

Jolly, C. A. (2005). Diet manipulation and prevention of aging, cancer, and autoimmune disease. *Current Opinions in Clinical Nutrition and Metabolic Care, 8,* 382–387.

Jones, E., & Reynolds, G. (2011). *The play's the thing: Teachers' roles in children's play.* New York: Columbia University Press.

Jones, L., & others. (2012). Pain management for women in labor: An overview of systematic reviews. *Cochrane Database of Systematic Reviews, 14*(3), CD009234.

Jones, M. C. (1965). Psychological correlates of somatic development. *Child Development, 36,* 899–911.

Jones, N. A. (2012). Delayed reactive cries demonstrate emotional and physiological dysregulation in newborns of depressed mothers. *Biological Psychology, 89,* 374–381.

Jones, P. S., & others. (2011). Development of a caregiver empowerment model to promote positive outcomes. *Journal of Family Nursing, 17,* 11–28.

Jonson-Reid, M., Kohl, P. L., & Drake, B. (2012). Child and adolescent outcomes of chronic child maltreatment. *Pediatrics, 129,* 839–845.

Jose, A., O'Leary, K. D., & Moyer, A. (2010). Does premarital cohabitation predict subsequent marital stability and marital quality? A meta-analysis. *Journal of Marriage and the Family, 72,* 105–116.

Joseph, J. (2006). *The missing gene.* New York: Algora.

Jozkowski, K. N., & Sanders, N. A. (2012). Health and sexual outcomes of women who have experienced forced or coercive sex. *Women's Health, 52,* 108–118.

Judd, F. K., Hickey, M., & Bryant, C. (2012). Depression and midlife: Are we overpathologizing the menopause? *Journal of Affective Disorders, 136,* 199–211.

Jung, C. (1933). *Modern man in search of a soul.* New York: Harcourt Brace.

Junger, S., & others. (2012, in press). Consensus building in palliative care: A Europe-wide delphi study on common understandings and conceptual differences. *Journal of Pain and Symptom Management.*

Just, M. A., Keller, T. A., Malave, V. L., Kana, R. K., & Varma, S. (2012). Autism as a neural systems disorder: A theory of frontal-posterior underconnectivity. *Neuroscience and Biobehavioral Reviews, 36,* 1292–1313.

K

Kagan, J. (1987). Perspectives on infancy. In J. D. Osofsky (Ed.), *Handbook on infant development* (2nd ed.). New York: Wiley.

Kagan, J. (2002). Behavioral inhibition as a temperamental category. In R. J. Davidson, K. R. Scherer, & H. H. Goldsmith (Eds.), *Handbook of affective sciences.* New York: Oxford University Press.

Kagan, J. (2010). Emotions and temperament. In M. H. Burnstein (Ed.), *Handbook of cultural developmental science.* New York: Psychology Press.

Kagan, J. (2013). Temperamental contributions to inhibited and uninhibited profiles. In P. D. Zelazo (Ed.), *Oxford handbook of developmental psychology.* New York: Oxford University Press.

Kagan, J. J., Kearsley, R. B., & Zelazo, P. R. (1978). *Infancy: Its place in human development.* Cambridge, MA: Harvard University Press.

Kagan, S. H. (2008). Faculty profile, University of Pennsylvania School of Nursing. Retrieved January 5, 2008, from www.nursing.upenn.edu/faculty/profile.asp

Kahn, J. A., & others. (2008). Patterns and determinants of physical activity in U.S. adolescents. *Journal of Adolescent Health, 42,* 369–377.

Kail, R. V. (2007). Longitudinal evidence that increases in processing speed and working memory enhance children's reasoning. *Psychological Science, 18,* 312–313.

Kalache, A., & Blewitt, R. (2012). Human rights in older age. *Global population aging: Peril or promise?* Geneva, SWIT: World Economic Forum.

Kalder, M., Knoblauch, K., Hrgovic, I., & Munstedt, K. (2011). Use of complementary and alternative medicine during pregnancy and delivery. *Archives of Gynecology and Obstetrics, 283*(3), 475–482.

Kalish, R. A. (1981). *Death, grief, and caring relationships,* Monterey, CA: Brooks/Cole.

Kaplan, H., Gurven, M., & Winking, J. (2009). An evolutionary theory of human life span: Embodied capital and the human adaptive complex. In V. L. Bengtson, D. Gans, N. M. Putney, & M. Silverstein (Eds.), *Handbook of theories of aging* (2nd ed.). New York: Springer.

Karg, K., & Sen, S. (2012, in press). Gene x environment interaction models in psychiatry. *Current Topics in Behavioral Neuroscience.*

Karniol, R., Grosz, E., & Schorr, I. (2003). Caring, gender-role orientation, and volunteering. *Sex Roles, 49,* 11–19.

Karoly, L. A., & Bigelow, J. H. (2005). *The economics of investing in universal preschool education in California.* Santa Monica, CA: RAND Corporation.

Karreman, A., van Tuijl, C., van Aken, M. A., & Dekovic, M. (2008). Parenting, co-parenting, and effortful control in preschoolers. *Journal of Family Psychology, 22,* 30–40.

Kastenbaum, R. J. (2009). *Death, society, and human experience* (10th ed.). Boston: Allyn & Bacon.

Kastenbaum, R. J. (2012). *Death, society, and human experience* (11th ed.). Boston: Allyn & Bacon.

Kaszniak, A.W., & Menchola, M. (2012). Behavioral neuroscience of emotion in aging. *Current Topics in Behavioral Neuroscience, 10,* 51–56.

Katz, L. (1999). Curriculum disputes in early childhood education. *ERIC Clearinghouse on Elementary and Early Childhood Education,* Document EDO-PS-99-13.

Katzel, L. I., & Steinbrenner, G. M. (2012). Physical exercise and health. In S. K. Whibourne & M. J. Sliwinski (Eds.), *Wiley-Blackwell handbook of adult development and aging.* New York: Wiley.

Kauffman, J. M., McGee, K., & Brigham, M. (2004). Enabling or disabling? Observations on changes in special education. *Phi Delta Kappan, 85,* 613–620.

Kaufman, J. C., & Sternberg, R. J. (2013, in press). The creative mind. In C. Jones, M. Lorenzen, & R. F. Proctor (Eds.), *Handbook of psychology: Experimental psychology* (Vol. 4). New York: Wiley.

Kaur, A., & Phadke, S. R. (2012, in press). Analysis of short stature cases referred for genetic evaluation. *Indian Journal of Pediatrics.*

Kawabata, Y., Tseng, W. L., Murray-Close, D., & Crick, N. R. (2012, in press). Developmental trajectories of Chinese children's relational and physical aggression: Associations with social-psychological adjustment problems. *Journal of Abnormal Child Psychology.*

Keating, D. P. (1990). Adolescent thinking. In S. S. Feldman & G. R. Elliott (Eds.), *At the threshold: The developing adolescent.* Cambridge, MA: Harvard University Press.

Keen, R. (2011). The development of problem solving in young children: A critical cognitive skill. *Annual Review of Psychology* (Vol. 62). Palo Alto, CA: Annual Reviews.

Keijsers, L., & Laird, R. D. (2010). Introduction to special issue: Careful conversations: Adolescents managing their parents' access to information. *Journal of Adolescence, 33,* 255–259.

Keller, A., Ford, L., & Meacham, J. (1978). Dimensions of self-concept in preschool children. *Developmental Psychology, 14,* 485–489.

Kelley-Moore, J. (2009). Chronic illness, adulthood and later life. In D. Carr (Ed.), *Encyclopedia of the life course and human development.* Boston: Gale Cengage.

Kelly, J. P., Borchert, J., & Teller, D. Y. (1997). The development of chromatic and achromatic sensitivity in infancy as tested with the sweep VEP. *Vision Research, 37,* 2057–2072.

Kendler, K. S., & others. (2012, in press). Genetic and familial environmental influences on the risk for drug abuse: A national Swedish adoption study. *Archives of General Psychiatry.*

Kendrick, K., Jutengren, G., & Stattin, H. (2012, in press). The protective role of supportive friends against bullying perpetration and victimization. *Journal of Adolescence.*

Kennell, J. H. (2006) Randomized controlled trial of skin-to-skin contact from birth versus conventional incubator for physiological stabilization in 1200g to 2199g newborns. *Acta Paediatica (Swedent), 95,* 15–16.

Kennell, J. H., & McGrath, S. K. (1999). Commentary: Practical and humanistic lessons from the third world for perinatal caregivers everywhere. *Birth, 26,* 9–10.

Kenney, J. (2012). *Loosening the grip: A handbook of alcohol information* (10th ed.). New York: McGraw-Hill.

Kerns, K. A., & Seibert, A. C. (2012, in press). Finding your way through the thicket: Promising approaches to assessing attachment in middle childhood. In E. Waters & B. Vaughn (Eds.), *Measuring attachment.* New York: Guilford.

Kerns, K. A., Siener, S., & Brumariu, L. E. (2011). Mother-child relationships, family context, and child characteristics as predictors of anxiety symptoms in middle childhood. *Development and Psychopathology, 23,* 593–604.

Khan, M. R., Berger, A. T., Wells, B. E., & Cleland, C. M. (2012). Longitudinal associations between adolescent alcohol use and adult sexual risk behavior and sexually transmitted infection in the United States: Assessment of differences by race. *American Journal of Public Health, 102,* 867–876.

Khashan, A. S., Baker, P. N., & Kenny, L. C. (2010). Preterm birth and reduced birthweight in first and second teenage pregnancies: A register-based cohort study. *BMC Pregnancy and Childbirth, 10,* 36.

Kielsmeier, J. (2011). The time is now. *Prevention Researcher, 18,* 3–7.

Kilic, S., & others. (2012, in press). Environmental tobacco smoke exposure during intrauterine period promotes granulosa cell apoptosis: A prospective, randomized study. *Journal of Maternal-Fetal and Neonatal Medicine*.

Kim, S. H. (2009). The influence of finding meaning and worldview of accepting death on anger among bereaved older spouses. *Aging and Mental Health, 13*, 38–45.

Kim, K. H. (2010, May). Unpublished data. School of Education, College of William & Mary, Williamsburg, VA.

Kim, S., & others. (2012). Telomere maintenance genes SIRT1 and XRCC6 impact age-related decline in telomere length but only SIRT1 is associated with human longevity. *Biogerontology, 13*, 119–131.

Kim, S. Y., & Giovanello, K. S. (2011). The effects of attention on age-related relational memory deficits: Evidence from a novel attentional manipulation. *Psychology and Aging, 26*, 678–688.

Kimble, M., Neacsiu, A. D., Flack, W. F., & Horner, J. (2008). Risk of unwanted sex for college women: Evidence for a red zone. *Journal of American College Health, 57*, 331–338.

King, L. A. (2011). *Psychology* (2nd ed.). New York: McGraw-Hill.

King, L. A. (2013). *Experience psychology* (2nd ed.). New York: McGraw-Hill.

King, L. A., & Hicks, J. A. (2007). Whatever happened to "What might have been?" Regrets, happiness, and maturity. *American Psychologist, 62*, 625–636.

King, V., & Scott, M. E. (2005). A comparison of cohabiting relationships among older and younger adults. *Journal of Marriage and the Family, 67*, 271–285.

Kingsmore, S. F., & others. (2012, in press). Next-generation community genetics for low- and middle-income countries. *Genomic Medicine*.

Kini, S., Morrell, D., Thong, K. J., Kopakaki, A., Hillier, S., & Irvine, D. S. (2010). Lack of impact of semen quality on fertilization in assisted conception. *Scottish Medicine, 55*, 20–23.

Kins, E., & Beyers, W. (2010). Failure to launch, failure to achieve criteria for adulthood? *Journal of Adolescent Research, 25*, 743–777.

Kirkham, N. Z., Wagner, J. B., Swan, K. A., & Johnson, S. P. (2012). Sound support: Intermodal information facilitates infants' perception of an occluded trajectory. *Infant Behavior and Development, 35*, 174–178.

Kirkorian, H. L., Anderson, D. R., & Keen, R. (2012). Age differences in online processing of video: An eye movement study. *Child Development, 83*, 497–507.

Kisilevsky, B. S., & others. (2009). Fetal sensitivity to properties of maternal speech and language. *Infant Behavior and Development, 32*, 59–71.

Kitsantas, P., & Gaffney, K. F. (2010). Racial/ethnic disparities in infant mortality. *Journal of Perinatal Medicine, 38*, 87–94.

Kitts, R. L., & Goldman, S. J. (2012). Education and depression. *Child and Adolescent Psychiatry Clinics of North America, 21*, 421–426.

Kitzinger, S. (2011). Human rights and midwifery. *Birth, 38*, 86–87.

Klaus, M., & Kennell, H. H. (1976). *Maternal-infant bonding*. St. Louis: Mosby.

Klinenberg, E. (2012). *Going solo: The extraordinary rise and surprising appeal of living alone*. New York: Penguin.

Klingman, A. (2006). Children and war trauma. In W. Damon & R. Lerner (Eds.), *Handbook of child psychology* (6th ed.). New York: Wiley.

Knight, B. B., & Kellough, J. (2013, in press). Psychotherapy with older adults within a family context. In I. B. Weiner & others (Eds.), *Handbook of psychology* (2nd ed., Vol. 8). New York: Wiley.

Knopik, V. S. (2009). Maternal smoking during pregnancy and child outcomes: Real or spurious effect? *Developmental Neuropsychology, 34*, 1–36.

Knox, M. (2010). On hitting children: A review of corporal punishment in the United States. *Journal of Pediatric Health Care, 24*, 103–107.

Kocer, O., & others. (2011, July 30). Prevalence and predictors of depressive symptoms and wellbeing during and up to nine years after outpatient cardiac rehabilitation. *Swiss Medical Weekly*, p.141.

Kochanek, K. D., & others. (2011). Deaths: Preliminary data 2009. *National Vital Statistics Reports, 59*(4), 1–51.

Koenig, H. G., & Blazer, D. G. (1996). Depression. In J. E. Birren (Ed.), *Encyclopedia of gerontology* (Vol. 1). San Diego: Academic Press.

Kohen, D. E., Lerenthal, T., Dahinten, V. S., & McIntosh, C. N. (2008). Neighborhood disadvantage: Pathways of effects for young children. *Child Development, 79*, 156–169.

Kohlberg, L. (1958). The development of modes of moral thinking and choice in the years 10 to 16. Unpublished doctoral dissertation, University of Chicago.

Kohlberg, L. (1986). A current statement of some theoretical issues. In S. Modgil & C. Modgil (Eds.), *Lawrence Kohlberg*. Philadelphia: Falmer.

Kokkevi, A., & others. (2012, in press). Multiple substance use and self-reported suicide attempts by adolescents in 16 countries. *European Child and Adolescent Psychiatry*.

Kokotas, H., & others. (2012). Biomarkers in primary open angle glaucoma. *Clinical Chemistry and Laboratory Medicine, 29*, 1–13.

Kolialexi, A. (2012). Early non-invasive detection of fetal Y chromosome sequences in maternal plasma using multiplex PCR. *European Journal of Obstetrics, Gynecology, and Reproductive Medicine, 161*, 34–37.

Kolotkin, R. L., Zunker, C., & Ostbye, T. (2012, in press). Sexual functioning and obesity: A review. *Obesity*.

Konrath, S., Fuhrel-Forbis, A., Lou, A., & Brown, S. (2012). Motives for volunteering are associated with mortality risk in older adults. *Health Psychology, 31*, 87–96.

Koo, Y. J., & others. (2012). Pregnancy outcomes according to increasing maternal age. *Taiwan Journal of Obstetrics and Gynecology, 51*, 60–65.

Kopp, F., & Lindenberger, U. (2011). Effects of joint attention on long-term memory in 9-month-old infants: An event-related potentials study. *Developmental Science, 14*, 660–672.

Koren, G., & Nordeng, H. (2012, in press). Antidepressant use during pregnancy: The benefit-risk ratio. *American Journal of Obstetrics and Gynecology*.

Kornadt, A. E., & Rothermund, K. (2012). Internalization of age stereotypes into the self-concept via future self-views: A general model and domain-specific differences. *Psychology and Aging, 27*, 164–172.

Koropeckyj-Cox, T. (2009). Loneliness, later life. In D. Carr (Ed.), *Encyclopedia of the life course and human development*. Boston: Gale Cengage.

Koss, K. J., & others. (2011). Understanding children's emotional processes and behavioral strategies in the context of marital conflict. *Journal of Experimental Child Psychology, 109*, 336–352.

Kostovic, I., Judas, M., & Sedmak, G. (2011). Developmental history of the subplate zone, subplate neurons, and interstitial white matter neurons: Relevance for schizophrenia. *International Journal of Developmental Neuroscience*.

Kotre, J. (1984). *Outliving the self: Generativity and the interpretation of lives*. Baltimore: Johns Hopkins University Press.

Kottak, C. P. (2009). *Cultural anthropology* (13th ed.). New York: McGraw-Hill.

Kottak, C. P., & Kozaitis, K. A. (2012). *On being different* (4th ed.). New York: McGraw-Hill.

Kotter-Gruhn, D., & Smith, J. (2011). When time is running out: Changes in positive future perception and their relationships to changes in well-being in old age. *Psychology and Aging, 26*, 381–387.

Kowalski, R. M., Limber, S. P., & Agatston, P. W. (2012). *Cyberbullying* (2nd ed.). New York: Wiley.

Kozol, J. (2005). *The shame of the nation*. New York: Crown.

Kramer, A. F., & Morrow, D. (2012, in press). Cognitive training and expertise. In D. Park & N. Schwartz (Eds.), *Cognitive aging: A primer*. New York: Psychology Press.

Kramer, L. (2006, July 10). Commentary in "How your siblings make you who you are" by J. Kluger, *Time*, pp. 46–55.

Kramer, L., & Perozynski, L. (1999). Parental beliefs about managing sibling conflict. *Developmental Psychology, 35,* 489–499.

Kramer, L., & Radey, C. (1997). Improving sibling relationships among young children: A social skills training model. *Family Relations, 46,* 237–246.

Kramer, W. E. (2012). Large employers see scenarios under which they could move workers and retirees to exchanges. *Health Affairs, 31,* 299–305.

Krause, N. (2008). The social foundations of religious meaning in life. *Research on Aging, 30*(4), 395–427.

Krause, N. (2009). Deriving a sense of meaning in late life. In V. L. Bengtson, D. Gans, N. M. Putney, & M. Silverstein (Eds.), *Handbook of theories of aging.* New York: Springer.

Krause, N., Ingersoll-Dayton, B., Liang, J., & Sugisawa, H. (1999). Religion social-behavior and health among the Japanese elderly. *Journal of Health and Social Behavior, 40,* 405–421.

Kreutzer, M., Leonard, C., & Flavell, J. H. (1975). An interview study of children's knowledge about memory. *Monographs of the Society for Research in Child Development, 40* (Serial No. 159).

Kriemler, S., & others. (2010). Effect of school based physical activity program (KISS) on fitness and adiposity in primary schoolchildren: Cluster randomized controlled trial. *British Medical Journal, 45,* 923–930.

Kring, A. M. (2000). Gender and anger. In A. H. Fischer (Ed.), *Gender and emotion: Social psychological perspectives.* New York: Cambridge University Press.

Kristensen, P., Weisaeth, L., & Heir, T. (2012). Bereavement and mental health after sudden and violent losses: A review. *Psychiatry, 75,* 76–97.

Kroger, J. (2012). The status of identity developments in identity research. In P. K. Kerig, M. S. Schulz, & S. T. Hauser (Eds.), *Adolescence and beyond.* New York: Oxford University Press.

Kroger, J., Martinussen, M., & Marcia, J. E. (2010). Identity change during adolescence and young adulthood: A meta-analysis. *Journal of Adolescence, 33,* 683–698.

Krueger, J. I., Vohs, K. D., & Baumeister, R. F. (2008). Is the allure of self-esteem a mirage after all? *American Psychologist, 63,* 64.

Krueger, P. M., & Chang, V. W. (2008). Being poor and coping with stress: Health behaviors and the risk of death. *American Journal of Public Health, 98,* 889–896.

Kruger, J., Blanck, H. M., & Gillespie, C. (2006). Dietary and physical activity behaviors among adults successful at weight loss management. *International Journal of Behavioral Nutrition and Physical Activity, 3,* 17.

Kubicek, B., Korunka C., Hoonakker, P., & Raymo, J. M. (2010). Work and family characteristics as predictors of early retirement in men and women. *Research on Aging, 32,* 467–498.

Kübler-Ross, E. (1969). *On death and dying.* New York: Macmillan.

Kuebli, J. (1994, March). Young children's understanding of everyday emotions. *Young Children,* 36–48.

Kuhl, P. K. (2000). A new view of language acquisition. *Proceedings of the National Academy of Science. 97*(22), 11850–11857.

Kuhl, P. K. (2009). Linking infant speech perception to language acquisition: phonetic learning predicts language growth. In J. Colombo, P. McCardle, & L. Freund (Eds.), *Infant pathways to language.* New York: Psychology Press.

Kuhl, P. K. (2011). Social mechanisms in early language acquisition: Understanding integrated brain systems and supporting language. In J. Decety & J. Cacioppo (Eds.), *Handbook of social neuroscience.* New York: Oxford University Press.

Kuhl, P. K. (2012, in press). Language learning and the developing brain: Cross-cultural studies unravel the effects of biology and culture. *Journal of the Acoustical Society of America.*

Kuhl, P. K., & Damasio, A. (2012). Language. In E. R. Kandel & others (Eds.), *Principles of neural science* (5th ed.). New York: McGraw-Hill.

Kuhn, D. (1998). Afterword to Volume 2: Cognition, perception, and language. In W. Damon (Ed.), *Handbook of child psychology* (5th ed., Vol. 2). New York: Wiley.

Kuhn, D. (2009). Adolescent thinking. In R. M. Lerner & L. Steinberg (Eds.), *Handbook of adolescent psychology* (3rd ed.). New York: Wiley.

Kuhn, D. (2011). What is scientific thinking and how does it develop? In U. Goswami (Ed.), *Wiley-Blackwell handbook of childhood cognitive development* (2nd ed.). New York: Wiley.

Kuo, L. J., & Anderson, R. C. (2012). Effects of early bilingualism on learning phonological regularities in a new language. *Journal of Experimental Child Psychology, 111,* 455–467.

Kwan, M. Y., Cairney, J., Faulkner, G. E., & Pullenayegum, E. E. (2012). Physical activity and other health-risk behaviors during the transition into early adulthood: A longitudinal cohort study. *American Journal of Preventive Medicine, 42,* 14–20.

L

Labouvie-Vief, G. (1986, August). *Modes of knowing and life-span cognition.* Paper presented at the meeting of the American Psychological Association, Washington, DC.

Labouvie-Vief, G. (2009). Cognition and equilibrium regulation in development and aging. In V. Bengtson & others (Eds.), *Handbook of theories of aging.* New York: Springer.

Labouvie-Vief, G., Gruhn, D., & Studer, J. (2010). Dynamic integration of emotion and cognition: Equilibrium regulation in development and aging. In M. E. Lamb, A. Freund, & R. M. Lerner (Eds.), *Handbook of life-span development* (Vol. 2). New York: Wiley.

LaBrie, J. W., Hummer, J., Kenney, S., Lac, A., & Pedersen, E. (2011). Identifying factors that increase the likelihood for alcohol-induced blackouts in the prepartying context. *Substance Use and Misuse, 46,* 992–1002.

Lacelle, C., Hebert, M., Lavoie, F., Vitaro, F., & Tremblay, R. E. (2012). Sexual health in women reporting a history of child sexual abuse. *Child Abuse and Neglect, 36,* 247–259.

Lachman, M. E. (2004). Development in midlife. *Annual Review of Psychology* (Vol. 55). Palo Alto, CA: Annual Reviews.

Lachman, M. E. (2006). Perceived control over aging-related declines. *Current Directions in Psychological Science, 15,* 282–286.

Lachman, M. E., Agrigoroaei, S., Murphy, C., & Tun, P. A. (2010). Frequent cognitive activity compensates for education differences in episodic memory. *American Journal of Geriatric Psychiatry, 18,* 4–10.

Lachman, M. E., & Firth, K. M. P. (2004). The adaptive value of feeling in control during midlife. In O. G. Brim, C. D. Ruff, & R. C. Kessler (Eds.), *How healthy are we?* Chicago: University of Chicago Press.

Lachman, M. E., & Kranz, E. (2010). The midlife crisis. In I. Wiener & E. Craighead (Eds.), *The Corsini encyclopedia of psychology* (4th ed.). New York: Wiley.

Lachman, M. E., Maier, H., & Budner, R. (2000). *A portrait of midlife.* Unpublished manuscript, Brandeis University, Waltham, MA.

Lachman, M. E., Neupert, S. D., & Agrigoroaei, S. (2011). The relevance of control beliefs for health and aging. In K. W. Schaie & S. L. Willis (Eds.), *Handbook of the psychology of aging* (7th ed.). New York: Elsevier.

Ladd, G. W., Kochenderfer-Ladd B., Visconti, J., & Ettekal, I. (2012). Classroom peer relations and children's social and scholastic development: Risk factors and resources. In A. M. Ryan & G. W. Ladd (Eds.), *Peer relationships and adjustment at school.* Charlotte, NC: Information Age Publishing.

Laflin, M. T., Wang, J., & Barry, M. (2008). A longitudinal study of adolescent transition from virgin to nonvirgin status. *Journal of Adolescent Health, 42,* 228–236.

Lafreniere, D., & Mann, N. (2009). Anosmia: Loss of smell in the elderly. *Otolaryngologic Clinics of North America, 42,* 123–131.

Laible, D., & Thompson, R. A. (2007). Early socialization: A relationship perspective. In J. E. Grusec & P. D. Hastings (Eds.), *Handbook of socialization.* New York: Guilford.

Laird, R. D., & Marrero, M. D. (2010). Information management and behavior problems: Is concealing misbehavior necessarily a sign of trouble? *Journal of Adolescence, 33,* 297–308.

Lamb, M. E. (1986). *The father's role: Applied perspectives*. New York: Wiley.

Lamb, M. E. (1994). Infant care practices and the application of knowledge. In C. B. Fisher & R. M. Lerner (Eds.), *Applied developmental psychology*. New York: McGraw-Hill.

Lamb, M. E. (2000). The history of research on father involvement: An overview. *Marriage and Family Review, 29*, 23–42.

Lamb, M. E. (2005). Attachments, social networks, and developmental contexts. *Human Development, 48*, 108–112.

Lamb, M. E. (2010). How do fathers influence children's development? In M. E. Lamb (Ed.), *The role of the father in child development* (5th ed.). New York: Wiley.

Lamb, M. E. (2012, in press). Non-parental care and emotional development. In S. Pauen & M. Bornstein (Eds.), *Early childhood development and later outcomes*. New York: Cambridge University Press.

Lamb, M. E., Bornstein, M. H., & Teti, D. M. (2002). *Development in infancy* (4th ed.). Mahwah, NJ: Erlbaum.

Lamb, M. E., & Malloy, L. C. (2013). Child development and the law. In I. B. Weiner & others (Eds.), *Handbook of psychology* (2nd ed., Vol. 6). New York: Wiley.

Lampard, A. M., Byrne, S. M., McLean, N., & Fursland, A. (2012). The Eating Disorder Inventory-2 perfectionism scale: Factor structure and associations with dietary restraint and weight and shape concern in eating disorders. *Eating Behaviors, 13*, 49–53.

Lampl, K. M., & others. (2012, in press). Risk of autism spectrum disorders in low birth weight and small for gestational age infants. *Journal of Pediatrics*.

Lamy, C. (2012). Poverty is a knot, preschool is an untangler. In R.C. Pianta (Ed.), *Handbook of early childhood education*. New York: Guilford.

Lane, H. (1976). *The wild boy of Aveyron*. Cambridge, MA: Harvard University Press.

Langstrom, N., Rahman, Q., Carlstrom, E., & Lichtenstein, P. (2010). Genetic and environmental effects on same-sex sexual behaviour: A population study of twins in Sweden. *Archives of Sexual Behavior, 39*, 75–80.

Lansford, J. E. (2009). Parental divorce and children's adjustment. *Perspectives on Psychological Science, 4*, 140–152.

Lansford, J. E. (2012). Divorce. In R.J. R. Levesque (Ed.), *Encyclopedia of adolescence*. New York: Springer.

Lansford, J. E., & Deater-Deckard, K. (2012, in press). Childrearing discipline and violence in developing countries. *Child Development*.

Lansford, J. E., Wager, L. B., Bates, J. E., Pettit, G. S., & Dodge, K. A. (2012, in press). Forms of spanking and children's externalizing problems. *Family Relations*.

Lansford, J. E., Yu, T., Erath, S. A., Pettit, G. S., Bates, J. E., & Dodge, K. A. (2010).

Developmental precursors of number of sexual partners from ages 16 to 22. *Journal of Research on Adolescence, 20*, 651–677.

Lansford, J. E., & others. (2005). Cultural normativeness as a moderator of the link between physical discipline and children's adjustment: A comparison of China, India, Italy, Kenya, Philippines, and Thailand. *Child Development, 76*, 1234–1246.

Lapsley, D., & Yeager, D. (2013, in press). Moral-character education. In I. B. Weiner & others (Eds.), *Handbook of psychology* (2nd ed., Vol.7). New York: Wiley.

Larson, R. W., Wilson, S., & Rickman, A. (2009). Globalization, societal change, and adolescence across the world. In R. M. Lerner & L. Steinberg (Eds.), *Handbook of adolescent psychology* (3rd ed.). New York: Wiley.

Larson, R. W., & Angus, R. (2011). Adolescents' development of skills for agency in youth programs: Learning to think strategically. *Child Development, 82*, 277–294.

Larson, R. W., & Dawes, N. P. (2013, in press). Cultivating intrinsic motivation in American youth programs. In M. Csikszentmihalyi (Ed.), *Education and youth development in cross-cultural psychology: Contributions from positive psychology*. New York: Springer.

Larzelere, R. E., & Kuhn, B. R. (2005). Comparing child outcomes of physical punishment and alternative disciplinary tactics: A meta-analysis. *Clinical Child and Family Psychology Review, 8*, 1–37.

Laslett, A. M., Room, R., Dietze, P., & Ferris, J. (2012, in press). Alcohol's involvement in recurrent child abuse and neglect cases. *Addiction*.

Lauer, R. H., & Lauer, J. C. (2012). *Marriage and the family* (8th ed.). New York: McGraw-Hill.

Laumann, E. O., Glasser, D. B., Neves, R. C., & Moreira, E. D. (2009). A population-based survey of sexual activity, sexual problems, and associated help-seeking behavior patterns in mature adults in the United States of America. *International Journal of Impotence Research, 21*, 171–178.

Laursen, B., & Pursell, G. (2009). Conflict in peer relationships. In K. H. Rubin, W. M. Bukowski, & B. Laursen (Eds.), *Handbook of peer interactions, relationships, and groups*. New York: Guilford.

Lavner, J. A., & Bradbury, T. N. (2012). Why do even satisfied newlyweds eventually go on to divorce? *Journal of Family Psychology, 26*, 1–10.

Lavoie-Tremblay, M., Leclerc, E., Marchionni, C., & Drevniok, U. (2010). The needs and expectations of generation Y nurses in the workplace. *Journal for Nurses in Staff Development, 26*, 2–8.

Le Couteur, D. G., & Simpson, S. J. (2011). Adaptive senectitude: The prolongevity effects on aging. *Journals of Gerontology A: Biological Sciences and Medical Sciences, 66A*, 179–182.

Leaper, C. (2013). Gender development during childhood. In P. Zelazo (Ed.), *Oxford handbook of developmental psychology*. New York: Oxford University Press.

Leaper, C., & Bigler, R. S. (2011). Gender. In M. H. Underwood & L. H. Rosen (Eds.), *Social development*. New York: Guilford.

Leaper, C., & Smith, T. E. (2004). A meta-analytic review of gender variations in children's language use: Talkativeness, affiliative speech, and assertive speech. *Developmental Psychology, 40*, 993–1027.

Leatherdale, S. T. (2010). Factors associated with communication-based sedentary behaviors among youth: Are talking on the phone, texting, and instant messaging new sedentary behaviors to be concerned about? *Journal of Adolescent Health, 47*, 315–318.

Lebel, C., & others. (2012). Diffusion tensor imaging of white matter tract evolution over the lifespan. *Neuroimage, 60*, 340–352.

Lee, H. C., & Wei, Y. H. (2012). Mitochondria and aging. *Advances in Experimental Medicine and Biology, 942*, 311–327.

Lee, I. M., & Skerrett, P. J. (2001). Physical activity and all-cause mortality: What is the dose-response relation? *Medical Science and Sports Exercise, 33* (6 Suppl.), S459–S471.

Lee, K., Cameron, C. A., Doucette, J., & Talwar, V. (2002). Phantoms and fabrications: Young children's detection of implausible lies. *Child Development, 73*, 1688–1702.

Lee, K. Y., & others. (2011). Effects of combined radiofrequency radiation exposure on the cell cycle and its regulatory proteins. *Bioelectromagnetics, 32*, 169–178.

Lee, L. A., Sbarra, D. A., Mason, A. E., & Law, R. W. (2011). Attachment anxiety, verbal immediacy, and blood pressure: Results from a laboratory-analog study following marital separation. *Personal Relationships, 18*, 285–301.

Lee, Y. S., Turkeltaub, P., Granger, R., & Raizada, R. D. (2012). Categorical speech processing in Broca's area: An fMRI study using multivariate pattern-based analysis. *Journal of Neuroscience, 32*, 3942–3948.

Leedy, P. D., & Ormrod, J. E. (2013). *Practical research* (10th ed.). Upper Saddle River, NJ: Pearson.

Leerkes, E. M., Parade, S. H., & Gudmundson, J. A. (2011, in press). Mothers' emotional reactions to crying pose risk for subsequent attachment insecurity. *Journal of Family Psychology, 25*, 635–643.

Lefkowitz, E. S., & Gillen, M. M. (2006). "Sex is just a normal part of life": Sexuality in emerging adulthood. In J. J. Arnett & J. L. Tanner (Eds.), *Emerging adults in America*. Washington, DC: American Psychological Association.

Lehman, E. B., & others. (2010). Long-term stability of young children's eyewitness accuracy, suggestibility, and resistance to misinformation. *Journal of Applied Developmental Psychology, 31*, 145–154.

Lehman, H. C. (1960). The age decrement in outstanding scientific creativity. *American Psychologist, 15*, 128–134.

Lehr, C. A., Hanson, A., Sinclair, M. F., & Christensen, S. I. (2003). Moving beyond dropout prevention towards school completion. *School Psychology Review, 32*, 342–364.

Lemond, L., & Allen, L. A. (2011). Palliative care and hospice in advanced heart failure. *Progress in Cardiovascular Diseases, 54*, 168–178.

Lemstra, M. E., Nielsen, G., Rogers, M. R., Thompson, A. T., & Moraros, J. S. (2012). Risk indicators and outcomes associated with bullying in youth aged 9-15 years. *Canadian Journal of Public Health, 103*, 9–13.

Lenhart, A., Purcell, K., Smith, A., & Zickuhr, K. (2010, February 3). *Social media and young adults*. Washington, DC: Pew Research Center.

Leonardi-Bee, J. A., Smyth, A. R., Britton, J., & Coleman, T. (2008). Environmental tobacco smoke on fetal health: Systematic review and analysis. *Archives of Disease in Childhood: Fetal and Neonatal Edition, 93*, F351–F361.

Lerner, H. G. (1989). *The dance of intimacy*. New York: Harper & Row.

Lerner, J. V., & others. (2013). Positive youth development: Processes, philosophies, and programs. In I. B. Weiner & others (Eds.), *Handbook of psychology* (2nd ed., Vol. 6). New York: Wiley.

Lerner, J. W., & Johns, B. (2012). *Learning disabilities and related mild disabilities* (12th ed.). Boston: Cengage.

Lerner, R. M., Boyd, M., & Du, D. (2008). Adolescent development. In I. B. Weiner & C. B. Craighead (Eds.). *Encyclopedia of psychology* (4th ed). Hoboken, NJ: Wiley.

Lerner, R. M., Easterbrooks, M. A., & Mistry, J. (2013). Developmental science across the life span: An introduction. In I. B. Weiner & others (Eds.), *Handbook of psychology* (2nd ed., Vol. 6). New York: Wiley.

Lerner-Geva, L., Boyko, V., Blumstein, T., & Benyamini, Y. (2010). The impact of education, cultural background, and lifestyle on symptoms of the menopausal transition: The Women's Health at Midlife Study. *Journal of Women's Health, 19*, 975–985.

Lesley, C. (2005). *Burning fence: A Western memoir of fatherhood*. New York: St. Martin's Press.

Lessow-Hurley, J. (2013). *Foundations of dual language instruction*. (6th ed.). Boston: Allyn & Bacon.

Lester, B. M., & others. (2002). The maternal lifestyle study: Effects of substance exposure during pregnancy on neurodevelopmental outcome in 1-month-old infants. *Pediatrics, 110*, 1182–1192.

Levelt, W. J. M. (1989). *Speaking: From intention to articulation*. Cambridge, MA: MIT Press.

Levine, T. P., & others. (2008). Effects of prenatal cocaine exposure on special education in school-aged children. *Pediatrics, 122*, e83–e91.

Levinson, D. J. (1978). *The seasons of a man's life*. New York: Knopf.

Levinson, D. J. (1996). *Seasons of a woman's life*. New York: Alfred Knopf.

Levinson, P. (2013). *New new media* (2nd ed.). Upper Saddle River, NJ: Pearson.

Lewis, A. C. (2007). Looking beyond NCLB. *Phi Delta Kappan, 88*, 483–484.

Lewis, C., Hill, M., Skirton, H., & Chitty, L. S. (2012, in press). Non-invasive prenatal diagnois for fetal sex determination: Benefits and disadvantages from the service users' perspective. *European Journal of Genetics*.

Lewis, M. (2005). Selfhood. In B. Hopkins (Ed.), *The Cambridge encyclopedia of child development*. Cambridge, UK: Cambridge University Press.

Lewis, M. (2007). Early emotional development. In A. Slater & M. Lewis (Eds.), *Introduction to infant development*. Malden, MA: Blackwell.

Lewis, M. (2010). The emergence of consciousness and its role in human development. In W. F. Overton & R. M. Lerner (Eds.), *Handbook of life-span development* (2nd ed.). New York: Wiley.

Lewis, M., & Brooks-Gunn, J. (1979). *Social cognition and the acquisition of the self*. New York. Plenum.

Lewis, M., Feiring, C., & Rosenthal, S. (2000). Attachment over time. *Child Development, 71*, 707–720.

Lewis, M. A., & others. (2012, in press). Predictors of hooking up sexual behaviors and emotional reactions among U.S. college students. *Archives of Sexual Behavior*.

Lewis, R. (2012). *Human genetics* (10th ed.). New York: McGraw-Hill.

Lhila, A., & Long, S. (2011). What is driving the black-white difference in low birthweight in the U.S.? *Health Economics, 21*, 301–315.

Li, B. J., Jiang, Y. J., Yuan, F., & Ye, H. X. (2010). Exchange transfusion of least incompatible blood for severe hemolytic disease of the newborn due to anti-Rh17. *Transfusion Medicine, 20*, 66–69.

Li, Z., & Heber, D. (2012). Sarcopenic obesity in the elderly and strategies for weight management. *Nutrition Reviews, 70*, 57–64.

Liao, W. C., & others. (2011). Healthy behaviors and onset of functional disability in older adults: Results of a national longitudinal study. *Journal of the American Geriatrics Society, 59*, 200–206.

Liben, L. S. (1995). Psychology meets geography: Exploring the gender gap on the national geography bee. *Psychological Science Agenda, 8*, 8–9.

Libertus, K., & Needham, A. (2010). Teach to reach: The effects of active versus passive reading experiences on action and perception. *Vision Research, 50*, 2750–2757.

Liechty, J. M. (2010). Body image distortion and three types of weight loss behaviors among nonoverweight girls in the United States. *Journal of Adolescent Health, 47*, 176–182.

Liew, J. (2012). Effortful control, executive functions, and education: Bringing self-regulatory and social-emotional competencies to the table. *Child Development Perspectives, 6*, 105, 111.

Li-Korotky, H. S. (2012). Age-related hearing loss: Quality of care for quality of life. *Gerontologist, 52*, 265–271.

Lillard, A. (2006). Pretend play in toddlers. In C. A. Brownell & C. B. Kopp (Eds.), *Socioemotional development in the toddler years*. New York: Oxford University Press.

Lin, F., & others. (2012). Effect of leisure activities on inflammation and cognitive function in an aging sample. *Archives of Gerontology and Geriatrics, 54*, e398–e404.

Lin, F. R. (2011). Hearing loss and cognition among older adults in the United States, *Journals of Gerontology A: Biological Sciences and Medical Sciences, 66*, 1131–1136.

Lin, F. R., Thorpe, R., Gordon-Salant, S., & Ferrucci, L. (2011). Hearing loss prevalence and risk factors among older adults in the United States. *Journals of Gerontology A: Biological Sciences and Medical Sciences*. doi: 10.1093/gerona/glr002

Lin, H. W., Hsu, H. C., & Chang, M. C. (2011). Gender differences in the association between stress trajectories and depressive symptoms among middle aged and older adults in Taiwan. *Journal of Women and Aging, 23*, 233–245.

Lindau, S. T., & Gavrilova, N. (2010). Sex, health, and years of sexually active life gained due to good health: Evidence from two U.S. population based cross sectional surveys of aging. *British Medical Journal, 340*, c810.

Lindau, S. T., Schumm, L. P., Laumann, E. O., Levinson, W., O'Muircheartaigh, C. A., & Waite, L. J. (2007). A study of sexuality and health among older adults in the United States. *New England Journal of Medicine, 357*, 162–174.

Lindberg, S. M., Hyde, J. S., Petersen, J. L., & Lin, M. C. (2010). New trends in gender and mathematics performance: A meta-analysis. *Psychological Bulletin, 136*, 1123–1135.

Lindblad, F., & Hjern, A. (2010). ADHD after fetal exposure to maternal smoking. *Nicotine and Tobacco Research, 12*, 408–415.

Lira, F. S., & others. (2011). Exercise training improves sleep pattern and metabolic profile in elderly people in a time-dependent manner. *Lipids in Health and Disease, 10*, 1–6.

Liu, W. M., & Hernandez, J. (2008). Social class and classism. In N. J. Salkind (Eds.), *Encyclopedia of educational psychology*. Thousand Oaks, CA: Sage.

Livesly, W., & Bromley, D. (1973). *Person perception in childhood and adolescence*. New York: Wiley.

Lock, J. (2012a). Developmental translational research: Adolescence, brain circuitry, cognitive processes, and eating disorders. In J. Lock (Ed.), *Oxford handbook of child and adolescent eating disorders.* New York: Oxford University Press.

Lock, J. (2012b) (Ed.). *Oxford handbook of child and adolescent eating disorders.* New York: Oxford University Press.

Lock, M. (1998). Menopause: Lessons from anthropology. *Psychosomatic Medicine, 60,* 410–419.

Loehlin, J. C. (2010). Is there an active gene-environment correlation in adolescent drinking behavior? *Behavior Genetics, 40*(4), 447–451.

Logan, A. G. (2011). Hypertension in aging patients. *Expert Review of Cardiovascular Therapy, 9,* 113–120.

Logsdon, M. C., Wisner, K., & Hanusa, B. H. (2009). Does maternal role functioning improve with antidepressant treatment in women with postpartum depression? *Journal of Women's Health, 18,* 85–90.

Londono-Vallejo, J. A., & Wellinger, R. J. (2012, in press). Telomeres and telomerase dance to the rhythm of the cell cycle. *Trends in Biochemical Science.*

Lopez, O. L., Becker, J. T., & Kuller, L. H. (2012, in press). Patterns of compensation and vulnerability in normal subjects at risk for Alzheimer's disease. *Journal of Alzheimer's Disease.*

Loponen, M., Hublin, C., Kalimo, R., Manttari, M., & Tenkanen, L. (2010). Joint effect of self-reported sleep problems and three components of the metabolic syndrome on risk of coronary heart disease. *Journal of Psychosomatic Research, 68,* 149–158.

Loprinzi, P. D., & Trost, S. G. (2010). Parental influences on physical activity behavior in preschool children. *Preventive Medicine, 50,* 129–133.

Lorenz, K. Z. (1965). *Evolution and the modification of behavior.* Chicago: University of Press.

Loucks, J., & Sommerville, J. A. (2012). The role of motor experience in understanding action function: The case of precision grip. *Child Development, 83,* 801–809.

Lovden, M., Brehmer, Y., Li, S. C., & Lindenberger, U. (2012, in press). Training-induced compensation versus magnification of individual differences in memory performance. *Frontiers in Human Neuroscience.*

Low, J., & Simpson, S. (2012, in press). Effects of labeling on preschoolers' explicit false belief performance: Outcomes of cognitive flexibility or inhibitory control? *Child Development.*

Lowdermilk, D. L., & Perry (2012). *Maternity and women's health care* (10th ed.). New York: Elsevier.

Lowdermilk, D. L., Perry, S. E., & Cashion, M. C. (2011). *Maternity nursing* (8th ed.). New York: Elsevier.

Lowe, G., & Costabile, R. A. (2012, in press). 10-year analysis of adverse event reports to the Food and Drug Administration for phosphodiesterase type-5 inhibitors. *Journal of Sexual Medicine.*

Lowe, J. R., & others. (2012). Association of maternal interaction with emotional regulation in 4- and 9-month old infants during the Still Face Paradigm. *Infant Behavior and Development, 35,* 295–302.

Lu, C. J., Yu, J. J., & Deng, J. W. (2012). Disease-syndrome combination clinical study of psoriasis: Present status, advantages, and prospects. *China Journal of Integrative Medicine, 18,* 166–171.

Lu, P. H., & others. (2011). Age-related slowing in cognitive processing speed is associated with myelin integrity in a very healthy elderly sample. *Journal of Clinical and Experimental Neuropsychology, 33,* 1059–1068.

Luan, K., Rosales, J. L., & Lee, K. Y. (2012, in press). Viewpoint: Crosstalks between neurofibrillary tangles and amyloid plaque formation. *Aging Research and Review.*

Lucas, P. J., McIntosh, K., Petticrew, M., Roberts, H., & Shiell, A. (2008). Financial benefits for child health and well-being in low income or socially disadvantaged families in developed world countries. *Cochrane Database of Systematic Reviews, 16,* CD006358.

Lucas, R. E., Clark, A. E., Yannis, G., & Diener, E. (2004). Unemployment alters the setpoint for life satisfaction. *Psychological Science, 15,* 8–13.

Lucas, R. E., & Donnellan, M. B. (2011). Personality development across the life span: Longitudinal analyses with a national sample in Germany. *Journal of Personality and Social Psychology, 10,* 847–861.

Lucchetti, G., Lucchetti, A. L., & Koenig, H. G. (2011). Impact of spirituality/religiosity on mortality: Comparison with other health interventions. *Explore, 7,* 234–238.

Lucovnik, M., & others. (2011). Progestin treatment for the prevention of preterm births. *Acta Obstetrica et Gynecologica Scandinavica, 90,* 1057–1069.

Luders, E., & others. (2004). Gender differences in cortical complexity. *Nature Neuroscience, 1,* 799–800.

Luhmann, M., Hofmann, W., Eid, M., & Lucas, R. E. (2012). Subjective well-being and adaptation to life events: A meta-analysis. *Journal of Personality and Social Psychology 102,* 592–615.

Lumby, J. (2010). Grandparents and grandchildren: A grand connection. *International Journal of Evidence Based Healthcare, 8,* 28–31.

Lumeng, J. C., & others. (2012). Observed assertive and intrusive maternal feeding behaviors increase child adiposity. *American Journal of Clinical Nutrition, 95,* 640–647.

Lumpkin, A. (2011). *Introduction to physical education, exercise science, and sports studies* (8th ed.). New York: McGraw-Hill.

Lund, B., & others. (2011). Risk factors for treatment related mortality in childhood acute lymphoblastic leukemia. *Pediatric Blood Cancer, 56,* 551–559.

Lund, D. A., Utz, R., Caserta, M. S., & De Vries, B. (2008–2009). Humor, laughter, and happiness in the lives of recently bereaved spouses. *Omega, 58,* 87–105.

Lund, H. G., Reider, B. D., Whiting, A. B., & Prichard, J. R. (2010). Sleep patterns and predictors of disturbed sleep in a large population of college students. *Journal of Adolescent Health, 46,* 124–132.

Lundin, A., Backhans, M., & Hemmingsson, T. (2012). Unemployment and hospitalization owing to alcohol-related diagnosis among middle-aged men in Sweden. *Alcoholism: Clinical and Experimental Research, 36,* 663–669.

Luo, L., & Craik, F. I. M. (2008). Aging and memory: A cognitive approach. *Canadian Journal of Psychology, 53,* 346–353.

Luo, Y., Hawkley, L. C., Waite, L. J., & Cacioppo, J. T. (2012). Loneliness, health, and mortality in old age: A national longitudinal study. *Social Science and Medicine, 74,* 907–914.

Luria, A., & Herzog, E. (1985, April). *Gender segregation across and within settings.* Paper presented at the biennial meeting of the Society for Research in Child Development, Toronto.

Lusardi, A., Mitchell, O. S., & Curto, V. (2012). *Financial sophistication in the older population.* Retrieved June 12, 2012, from www.pensionresearchcouncil.org/publications/document.php?fi...

Lusis, A. J. (2012). Genetics of atherosclerosis. *Trends in Genetics 28*(6) 267–275.

Lustig, C., & Hasher, L. (2009). Interference. In R. Schulz, L. Noelker, K. Rockwood, & R. Sprott (Eds.), *Encyclopedia of Aging* (4th ed.). New York: Springer Publishing.

Luszcz, M. (2011). Executive functioning and cognitive aging. In K. W. Schaie & S. L. Willis (Eds.), *Handbook of the psychology of aging* (7th ed.). New York: Elsevier.

Lyberg, A., Viken, B., Haruna, M., & Severinsson, E. (2012). Diversity and challenges in the management of maternal care for migrant women. *Journal of Nursing Management, 20,* 287–295.

Lyon, T. D., & Flavell, J. H. (1993). Young children's understanding of forgetting over time. *Child Development, 64,* 789–800.

Lyons, D. M., & others. (2010). Stress coping stimulates hippocampal neurogenesis in adult monkeys. *Proceedings of the National Academy of Sciences U.S.A., 107,* 14823–14827.

Lytle, L. A. (2012, in press). Dealing with the childhood obesity epidemic: A public health approach. *Abdominal Imaging.*

M

Ma, T., & others. (2011a). Amyloid *B*-induced impairments in hippocampal synaptic plasticity are rescued by decreasing mitochondrial superoxide. *Journal of Neuroscience, 31,* 5589–5595.

Ma, Y., Peng, S., Dhawan, V., & Eidelberg, D. (2011b). Dopamine cell transplantation in Parkinson's disease: Challenge and perspective. *British Medical Bulletin, 100,* 173–189.

Maalouf, F. T., & Brent, D. A. (2012). Child and adolescent depression intervention overview: What works for whom and how well? *Child and Adolescent Psychiatry Clinics of North America, 21,* 299–312.

MacArthur, C. A. (2012). Strategies instruction. In K. R. Harris, S. Graham, & T. Urdan (Eds.), *Handbook of educational psychology.* Washington, DC: American Psychological Association.

Maccoby, E. E. (1984). Middle childhood in the context of the family. In *Development During middle childhood.* Washington, DC: National Academy Press.

Maccoby, E. E. (1998). *The two sexes: Growing up apart, coming together.* Cambridge, MA: Harvard University Press.

Maccoby, E. E. (2002). Gender and group processes. *Current Directions in Psychological Science, 11,* 54–58.

Maccoby, E. E., & Martin, J. A. (1983). Socialization in the context of the family: Parent-child interaction. In P. H. Mussen (Ed.), *Handbook of child psychology* (4th ed., Vol. 4). New York: Wiley.

Macdonald, K. E., & others. (2012, in press). The value of hippocampal and temporal horn volume and rates of change in predicting future conversion to Alzheimer's disease. *Alzheimer Disease and Associated Disorders.*

MacDonald, S. W., DeCarlo, C. A., & Dixon, R. A. (2011). Linking biological and cognitive aging: Toward improving characterizations of developmental time. *Journals of Gerontology B: Psychological Sciences and Social Sciences, 66B*(Suppl. 1), i59–i70.

MacEvoy, J. P., & Asher, S. R. (2012). When friends disappoint: Boys' and girls' responses to transgressions of friendship expectations. *Child Development, 83,* 104–119.

MacFarlane, J. A. (1975). Olfaction in the development of social preferences in the human neonate. In *Parent-infant interaction.* Ciba Foundation Symposium No. 33. Amsterdam: Elsevier.

MacGeorge, E. L. (2003). Gender differences in attributions and emotions in helping contexts. *Sex Roles, 48,* 175–182.

Madden, D. J., & others. (1999). Aging and recognition memory: Changes in regional cerebral blood flow associated with components of reaction time distributions. *Journal of Cognitive Neuroscience, II,* 511–520.

Mader, S. S., & Windelspecht, M. (2013). *Biology* (11th ed.). New York: McGraw-Hill.

Madill, A. (2012). Interviews and interviewing techniques. In H. Cooper (Ed.), *APA handbook of research methods in psychology.* Washington, DC: American Psychological Association.

Maercker, A., & Lalor, J. (2012). Diagnostic and clinical considerations in prolonged grief disorder. *Dialogues in Clinical Neuroscience, 14,* 167–176.

Mahn, H., & John-Steiner, V. (2013, in press). Vygotsky and sociocultural approaches to teaching and learning. In I. B. Weiner & others (Eds.), *Handbook of psychology* (2nd ed., Vol. 7). New York: Wiley.

Maholmes, V., & King, R. B. (Eds.) (2012). *Oxford handbook of poverty and child development.* New York: Oxford University Press.

Major Depressive Disorder Working Group of the Psychiatric GWAS Consortium. (2012, in press). A mega-analysis of genome-wide association studies for major depressive disorder. *Molecular Psychiatry.*

Malamitsi-Puchner, A., & Boutskikou, T. (2006). Adolescent pregnancy and perinatal outcome. *Pediatric Endocrinology Review, 3*(Suppl 1), S170–S171.

Malizia, B. A., Hacker, M. R., & Penzias, A. S. (2009). Cumulative live-birth rates after in vitro fertilization. *New England Journal of Medicine, 360,* 236–243.

Malloy, L. C., La Rooy, D. J., Lamb, M. A., & Katz, C. (2012). Developmentally sensitive interviewing for legal purposes. In M. E. Lamb, D. J. La Rooy, L. C. Malloy, & C. Katz (Eds.), *Children's testimony* (2nd ed.). New York: Wiley.

Mandara, J. (2006). The impact of family functioning on African American males' academic achievement: A review and clarification of the empirical literature. *Teachers College Record, 108,* 206–233.

Mandler, J. (2000). Unpublished review of J. W. Santrock's *Life-Span Development* (8th ed.). New York: McGraw-Hill.

Mandler, J. M. (2004). *The foundations of the mind: Origins of conceptual thought.* New York: Oxford University Press.

Mandler, J. M. (2009). Conceptual categorization. In D. H. Rakison & L. M. Oakes (Eds.), *Early category and concept development.* New York: Oxford University Press.

Mandler, J. M., & DeLoach, J. (2012, in press). The beginnings of conceptual development. In S. Pauen & M. Bornstein (Eds.), *Early child development and later outcome.* New York: Cambridge University Press.

Mandler, J. M., & McDonough, L. (1993). Concept formation in infancy. *Cognitive Development, 8,* 291–318.

Manenti, R., Cotelli, M., & Miniussi, C. (2011). Successful physiological aging and episodic memory: A brain stimulation study. *Behavioral Brain Research, 216,* 153–158.

Mann, T., Tomiyama, A. J., Westling, E., Lew, A-M., Samuels, B., & Chatman, J. (2007). Medicare's search for effective obesity treatments. *American Psychologist, 62,* 220–233.

Manning, W. D., & Cohen, J. (2012, in press). Premarital cohabitation and marital dissolution: An examination of recent marriages. *Journal of Marriage and the Family.*

Manton, K. G., Lowrimore, G. R., Ullian, A. D., Gu, X., & Tolley, H. D. (2007). From the cover: Labor force participation and human capital increases in an aging population and implications for U.S. research investment. *Proceedings of the National Academy of Sciences USA, 104,* 10802–10807.

Marcell, J. J. (2003). Sarcopenia: Causes, consequences, and preventions. *Journals of Gerontology A: Biological Sciences and Medical Sciences,* M911–M916.

Marcia, J. E. (1980). Ego identity development. In J. Adelson (Ed.), *Handbook of adolescent psychology.* New York: Wiley.

Marcia, J. E. (1994). The empirical study of ego identity. In H. A. Bosma, T. L. G. Graafsma, H. D. Grotevant, & D. J. De Levita (Eds.), *Identity and development.* Newbury Park, CA: Sage.

Marcia, J. E. (2002). Identity and psychosocial development in adulthood. *Identity: An International Journal of Theory and Research, 2,* 7–28.

Marcotte, T. D., Bekman, N. M., Meyer, R. A., & Brown, S. A. (2012, in press). High-risk driving behaviors among binge drinkers. *American Journal of Drug and Alcohol Abuse.*

Marek, W., & others. (2011). Lung function in our aging population. *European Journal of Medical Research, 16,* 108–114.

Marinkovic, K., & others. (2012). Right hemisphere has the last laugh: Neural dynamics of joke appreciation. *Cognitive, Affective, and Behavioral Neuroscience, 11,* 113–130.

Marioni, R. E., & others. (2012). Active cognitive lifestyle associates with cognitive recovery and a reduced risk of cognitive decline. *Journal of Alzheimer's Disease, 28,* 223–230.

Marsh, H., Ellis, L., & Craven, R. (2002). How do preschool children feel about themselves? Unraveling measurement and multidimensional self-concept structure. *Developmental Psychology, 38,* 376–393.

Marsh, H. W., Martin, A. J., & Xu, M. (2012). Self-concept: Synergy of theory, mind, and application. In K. R. Harris, S. Graham, & T. Urdan (Eds.), *APA educational psychology handbook.* Washington, DC: American Psychological Association.

Marshall, B. L. (2012). Medicalization and the refashioning of age-related limits on sexuality. *Journal of Sexual Research, 49,* 337–343.

Marti, C. N., Stice, E., & Springer, D. W. (2010). Substance use and abuse trajectories across adolescence: A latent trajectory analysis of a community-recruited sample of girls. *Journal of Adolescence, 33,* 449–461.

Martin, C., Darnell, A., Escofet, C., Duran, C., & Perez, V. (2012). Fetal MRI in the evaluation of pulmonary and digestive system pathology. *Insights into Imaging, 3,* 277–293.

Martin, C., & Evaldsson, A-C. (2012). Affordances for participation: Children's appropriation of rules in a Reggio Emilia school. *Mind, Culture, and Activity, 19,* 51–74.

Martin, C. L., & Ruble, D. N. (2010). Patterns of gender development. *Annual Review of Psychology* (Vol. 61). Palo Alto, CA: Annual Reviews.

Martin, J. A., Hamilton, B. E., Menacker, F., Sutton, P. D., & Matthews, T. J. (2005, November 15). Preliminary births for 2004: Infant and maternal health. *Health E-Stats.* Atlanta: National Center for Health Statistics.

Martin, L. R., Friedman, H. S., & Schwartz, J. E. (2007). Personality and mortality risk across the life span: The importance of conscientiousness as a biopsychosocial attribute. *Health Psychology, 26,* 428–436.

Mascalo, M. F., & Fischer, K. (2007). The co-development of self and socio-moral emotions during the toddler years. In C. A. Brownell & C. B. Kopp (Eds.), *Transitions in early development.* New York: Guilford.

Mascalo, M. F., & Fischer, K. W. (2010). The dynamic development of thinking, feeling, and acting over the life span. In W. F. Overton & R. M. Lerner (Eds.), *Handbook of life-span development* (Vol. 1). New York: Wiley.

Mason, L., Harris, K. L., & Graham, S. (2013). Strategies for improving student outcomes in written expression. In B. G. Cook & M. G. Tankersley (Eds.), *Research-based practices in special education.* Upper Saddle River, NJ: Pearson.

Masselli, G., & others. (2011). MR imaging in the evaluation of placental abruption: Correlation with sonographic findings. *Radiology.*

Masten, A. S. (2012). Faculty profile: Ann Masten. *The Institute of Child Development, Further Developments.* Minneapolis: School of Education.

Masten, A. S. (2013). Risk and resilience in development. In P. D. Zelazo (Ed.), *Oxford handbook of developmental psychology.* New York: Oxford University Press.

Masten, A. S., & Narayan, A. J. (2012). Child development in the context of disaster, war, and psychopathology: The legacy of Norman Garmezy. *Annual Review of Psychology* (Vol. 63.) Palo Alto, CA: Annual Reviews.

Masten, A. S., Obradovic, J., & Burt, K. B. (2006). Resilience in emerging adulthood: Developmental perspectives on continuity and transformation. In J. J. Arnett & J. L. Tanner (Eds.), *Emerging adults in America.* Washington, DC: American Psychological Association.

Masten, A. S., & Tellegen, A. (2012). Resilience in developmental psychology: Contributions of the Project Competence Longitudinal Study. *Development and Psychopathology, 24,* 345–361.

Masten, A. S., & others. (2008). School success in motion: Protective factors for academic achievement in homeless and highly mobile children in Minneapolis. *Center for Urban and Regioinal Affairs Reporter, 38,* 3–12.

Match.com. (2011). The Match.com Single in America Study. Retrieved February 7 from http://blog.match.com/singles-study

Match.com. (2012). *Singles in America 2012.* Retrieved June 10, 2012, from http://blog.match.com/singles-in-america/

Mather, M. (2012, in press). The emotion paradox in the human brain. *Annals of the New York Academy of Sciences.*

Matlin, M. W. (2012). *The psychology of women* (7th ed.). Boston: Cengage.

Matlin, S. L., Molock, S. D., & Tebes, J. K. (2011). Suicidality and depression among African American adolescents: The role of family and peer support and community connectedness. *American Journal of Orthopsychiatry, 81,* 108–117.

Matos, A. P., Ferreira, J. A., & Haase, R. F. (2012). Television and aggression: A test of a mediated model with a sample of Portuguese students. *Journal of Social Psychology, 152,* 75–91.

Matsuda, H., Yoshida, M., Wakamatsu, H., & Furuya, K. (2011). Fetal intraperitoneal injection of immunoglobulin diminishes alloimmune hemolysis. *Journal of Perinatology, 31,* 289–292.

Matsumoto, D., & Juang, L. (2012). *Culture and psychology* (5th ed.). Boston: Cengage.

Mattson, S., & Smith, J. E. (2011). *Core curriculum for maternal-newborn nursing* (4th ed.). New York: Elsevier.

Maxson, S. (2013). Behavioral genetics. In I. B. Weiner & others (Eds.), *Handbook of psychology* (2nd ed., Vol. 3). New York: Wiley.

Mayer, K. D., & Zhang, L. (2009). Short- and long-term effects of cocaine abuse during pregnancy on heart development. *Therapeutic Advances in Cardiovascular Disease, 3,* 7–16.

Mayo Clinic. (2012). Pregnancy and fish: *What's safe to eat?* Retrieved March 6, 2011, from www.mayoclinic.com/health/pregnancy-and-fish/PR00158

Mbugua Gitau, G., Liversedge, H., Goffey, D., Hawton, A., Liversedge, N., & Taylor, M. (2009). The influence of maternal age on the outcomes of pregnancy complicated by bleeding at less than 12 weeks. *Acta Obstetricia et Gynecologica Scandinavica, 88,* 116–118.

McAdams, D. P., & Cox, K. S. (2010). Self and identity across the life span. In A. Freund, M. Lambs & R. Lerner (Eds.), *Handbook of life-span development* (Vol. 2). New York: Wiley.

McAdams, D. P., & Olson, B. D. (2010). Personality development: Continuity and change over the life course. *Annual Review of Psychology* (Vol. 61). Palo Alto, CA: Annual Reviews.

McCabe, D. P., & Loaiza, V. M. (2012). Working memory. In S. K. Whitbourne & M. Sliwinski (Eds.), *Wiley-Blackwell handbook of adult development and aging.* New York: Wiley.

McCartney, K. (2003, July 16). Interview with Kathleen McCartney in A. Bucuvalas, "Child care and behavior." *HGSE News,* pp. 1–4. Cambridge, MA: Harvard Graduate School of Education.

McCartney, K., Dearing, E., Taylor, B. A., & Bub, K. L. (2007). Quality child care supports the achievement of low-income children: Direct and indirect pathways through caregiving and the home environment. *Journal of Applied Developmental Psychology, 28,* 411–426.

McClellan, M. D. (2004, February 9). Captain Fantastic: The interview. *Celtic Nation,* pp. 1–9.

McClelland, K., Bowles, J., & Koopman, P. (2012). Male sex determination: Insights into molecular mechanisms. *Asian Journal of Andrology, 14,* 164–171.

McCombs, B. L. (2013, in press). Educational psychology and educational transformation. In I. B. Weiner & others (Eds.), *Handbook of psychology* (2nd ed., Vol. 7). New York: Wiley.

McCormack, L. A., & others. (2011). Weight-related teasing in a racially diverse sample of sixth-grade children. *Journal of the American Dietetic Association, 111,* 431–436.

McCormack, T., Hoerl, C., & Butterfill, C. (2012). *Tool use and causal cognition.* New York: Oxford University Press.

McCormick, C. B., Dimmitt, C., & Sullivan, F. R. (2013, in press). Metacognition, learning, and instruction. In I. B. Weiner & others (Eds.), *Handbook of psychology* (2nd ed., Vol. 7). New York: Wiley.

McCoy, D. C., & Raver, C. C. (2012, in press). Caregiver emotional expressiveness, child emotion regulation, and child behavior problems among Head Start families. *Social Development.*

McCrae, R. R., & Costa, P. T. (2006). Cross-cultural perspectives on adult personality trait development. In D. K. Mroczek & T. D. Little (Eds.). *Handbook of personality development.* Mahwah, NJ: Erlbaum.

McCullough, M. E., & Willoughby, B. L. (2009). Religion, self-regulation, and self-control: Associations, explanations, and implications. *Psychological Bulletin, 135,* 69–93.

McDermott, B. M., & Cobham, V. E. (2012, in press). Family functioning in the aftermath of a disaster. *BMC Psychiatry.*

McDonald, S. D., & others. (2010). Preterm birth and low birth weight among in vitro fertilization twins: A systematic review and meta-analyses. *European Journal of Obstetrics, Gynecology, and Reproductive Biology, 148,* 105–113.

McDougall, S., & House, B. (2012). Brain training in older adults: Evidence of transfer to memory span performance and pseudo-Matthew effects. *Neuropsychology, Development, and Cognitiion B. Aging, Neuroscience, and Cognition, 19,* 195–221.

McElhaney, K. B., & Allen, J. P. (2012). Sociocultural perspectives on adolescent autonomy. In P. K. Kreig, M. S. Schulz, & S. T. Hauser (Eds.), *Adolescence and beyond*. New York: Oxford University Press.

McGarry, J., Kim, H., Sheng, X., Egger, M., & Baksh, L. (2009). Postpartum depression and help seeking behavior. *Journal of Midwifery and Women's Health, 54*, 50–56.

McGee, L. M., & Richgels, D. J. (2012). *Literacy's beginnings* (6th ed.). Boston: Allyn & Bacon.

McGettigan, C., & others. (2012). An application of univariate and multivariate approaches to fMRI to quantifying the hemispheric lateralization of acoustic and linguistic processes. *Journal of Cognitive Neuroscience, 24*, 636–652.

McHale, J., & Sullivan, M. (2008). Family systems. In M. Hersen & A. Gross (Eds.), *Handbook of Clinical Psychology* (Vol. 2). New York: Wiley.

McIntosh, E., Gillanders, D., & Rodgers, S. (2010). Rumination, goal linking, daily hassles, and life events in major depression. *Clinical Psychology and Psychotherapy, 17*, 33–43.

McKain, W. C. (1972). A new look at older marriages. *The Family Coordinator, 21*, 61–69.

McKinney, E., & Murray, S. (2013). *Maternal-child nursing* (4th ed.). New York: Elsevier.

McLaughlin, K. (2003, December 30). Commentary in K. Painter, "Nurse dispenses dignity for dying." *USA Today*, Section D, pp. 1–2.

McLaughlin, K. A., Fox, N. A., Zeanah, C. H., & Nelson, C. A. (2011). Adverse rearing environments and neural development in children: The development of frontal electroencephalogram asymmetry. *Biological Psychiatry, 70*, 1008–1015.

McLean, I. A., Balding, V., & White, C. (2005). Further aspects of male-on-male rape and sexual assault in greater Manchester. *Medical Science and Law, 45*, 225–232.

McLeskey, J. M., Rosenberg, M. S., & Westling, D. L. (2013). *Inclusion* (2nd ed.). Upper Saddle River, NJ: Pearson.

McMahon, E. M., Reulbach, U., Keeley, H., Perry, I. J., & Arensman, E. (2012). Reprint of: Bullying victimization, self-harm, and associated factors in Irish boys. *Social Science and Medicine, 74*, 490–497.

McMillan, J. H., & Wergin, J. F. (2010). *Understanding and evaluating educational research* (4th ed.). Upper Saddle River, NJ: Pearson.

McRae, K., & others. (2012). The development of emotion regulation: An fMRI study of cognitive reappraisal in children, adolescents, and adults. *Social Cognitive and Affective Neuroscience, 7*, 11–22.

McRae, R. R., Gaines, J. F., & Wellington, M. A. (2013). The five-factor model in fact and fiction. In I. B. Weiner & others (Eds.), *Handbook of psychology* (2nd ed., Vol. 5). New York: Wiley.

McWilliams, L. A., & Bailey, S. J. (2010). Association between adult attachment rating and health conditions: Evidence from the National Comorbidity Survey replication. *Health Psychology, 29*, 446–453.

Meade, C. S., Kershaw, T. S., & Ickovics, J. R. (2008). The intergenerational cycle of teenage motherhood: An ecological approach. *Health Psychology, 27*, 419–429.

Meaney, M. J. (2010). Epigenetics and the biological definition of gene x environment interactions. *Child Development, 81*, 41–79.

Meerlo, P., Sgoifo, A., & Suchecki, D. (2008). Restricted and disrupted sleep: Effects on autonomic function, neuroendocrine stress systems, and stress responsivity. *Sleep Medicine Review*.

Mehari, A., & others. (2012). Mortality in adults with sickle-cell disease and pulmonary hypertension. *Journal of the American Medical Association, 307*, 1254–1256.

Mehl, M. R., Vazire, S., Ramirez-Esparza, N., Slatcher, R. B., & Pennebaker, J. W. (2007). Are women really more talkative than men? *Science, 317*, 82.

Meltzoff, A. N. (1988). Infant imitation and memory: Nine-month-old infants in immediate and deferred tests. *Child Development, 59*, 217–225.

Meltzoff, A. N. (2004). Imitation as a mechanism of social cognition: Origins of empathy, theory of mind, and the representation of action. In U. Goswami (Ed.), *Blackwell handbook of childhood cognitive development*. Malden, MA: Blackwell.

Meltzoff, A. N. (2005). Imitation. In B. Hopkins (Ed.), *Cambridge encyclopedia of child development*. Cambridge: Cambridge University Press.

Meltzoff, A. N. (2007). Infants' causal learning. In A. Gopnik & L. Schulz (Eds.), *Causal learning*. New York: Oxford University Press.

Meltzoff, A. N. (2011). Social cognition and the origins of imitation, empathy, and theory of mind. In U. Goswami (Ed.), *Wiley-Blackwell handbook of childhood cognitive development* (2nd ed.). New York: Wiley.

Meltzoff, A. N., & Brooks, R. (2009). Social cognition: The role of gaze following in early word learning. In J. Colombo, P. McCardle, & L. Frend (Eds). *Infant pathways in language*. Clifton, NJ: Psychology Press.

Meltzoff, A. N., & Williamson, R. A. (2013). Imitation: Social, cognitive, and theoretical perspectives. In P. D. Zelazo (Ed.), *Oxford handbook of developmental psychology*. New York: Oxford University Press.

Memari, A., Ziaee, V., Mirfaxeli, F., & Kordi, R. (2012). Investigation of autism comorbidities and associations in a school-based community sample. *Journal of Child and Adolescent Psychiatric Nursing, 25*, 84–90.

Mendez, M. A., & others. (2012, in press). The brain GABA-benzodiazepine receptor alpha-5 subtype in autism spectrum disorder: A pilot [(11)C] Ro15-4513 positron emission tomography study. *Neuropharmacology*.

Menendez, S., Hidalgo, M. V., Jiminez, L., & Moreno, M. C. (2011). Father involvement and marital relationship during transition to parenthood: Differences between dual and single earners. *Spanish Journal of Psychology, 14*, 639–647.

Menn, L., & Stoel-Gammon, C. (2009). Phonological development: Learning sounds and sound patterns. In J. Berko Gleason (Ed.), *The development of language* (7th ed.). Boston: Allyn & Bacon.

Menon, R., & others. (2011). Cigarette smoking induces oxidative stress and atopsis in normal fetal membranes. *Placenta, 32*, 317–322.

Meredith, N. V. (1978). Research between 1960 and 1970 on the standing height of young children in different parts of the world. In H. W. Reece & L. P. Lipsitt (Eds.), *Advances in child development and behavior* (Vol. 12). New York: Academic Press.

Merrill, D. A., & others. (2012). Self-reported memory impairment and brain PET of amyloid and tau in middle-aged and older adults without dementia. *International Psycho-geriatrics, 24*, 1076–1084.

Merrill, D. M. (2009). Parent-child relationships: Later-life. In D. Carr (Ed.), *Encyclopedia of the life course and human development*. Boston: Gale Cengage.

Messiah, S. E., Miller, T. L., Lipshultz, S. E., & Bandstra, E. S. (2011). Potential latent effects of prenatal cocaine exposure on growth and the risk of cardiovascular and metabolic disease in childhood. *Progress in Pediatric Cardiology, 31*, 59–65.

Meyer, S. L., Weible, C. M., & Woeber, K. (2010). Perceptions and practice of water-birth: A survey of Georgia midwives. *Journal of Midwifery and Women's Health, 55*, 55–59.

Michael, R. T., Gagnon, J. H., Laumann, E. O., & Kolata, G. (1994). *Sex in America*. Boston: Little, Brown.

Mikels, J. A., & others. (2010). Following your heart or your head: Focusing on emotions versus information differentially influences the decisions of younger and older adults. *Journal of Experimental Psychology: Applied, 17*, 87–95.

Milburn, N. G., & others. (2012). A family intervention to reduce sexual risk behavior, substance use, and delinquency among newly homeless youth. *Journal of Adolescent Health, 50*, 358–364.

Miller, G. E., & Reynolds, W. M. (2013, in press). Future perspectives in educational psychology. In I. B. Weiner & others (Eds.), *Handbook of psychology* (2nd ed., Vol. 7). New York: Wiley.

Miller, G. T., & Spoolman, S. (2012). *Living in the environment* (17th ed.). Boston: Cengage.

Miller, L. M., & Bell, R. A. (2012). Online health information seeking: The influence of age, information trustworthiness, and search

National Center for Vital Statistics. (2010). Births, marriages, divorces, deaths: Provisional data for November 2009. *National Vital Statistics Reports, 58*(23), 1–5.

National Center on Shaken Baby Syndrome. (2012). *Shaken baby syndrome.* Retrieved April, 20, 2011, from www.dontshake.org/

National Clearinghouse on Child Abuse and Neglect. (2004). *What is child abuse and neglect?* Washington, DC: U.S. Department of Health and Human Services.

National Council on Aging. (2000, March). *Myths and realities survey results.* Washington, DC: Author.

National Human Genome Research Institute. (2012). *Genome-wide association studies.* Retrieved April 11, 2012, from www.genome.gov/20019523

National Institute of Mental Health. (2012). *Autism spectrum disorders (pervasive developmental disorders).* Retrieved May 11, 2012, from www.nimh.nih.gov/Publicat/autism.clm

National Institutes of Health. (2004). *Women's Health Initiative Hormone Therapy Study.* Bethesda, MD: National Institutes of Health.

National Marriage Project (2011). *Unmarried cohabitation.* Retrieved June 9, 2012, from www.stateofouruniions.org/2011/social_indicators.php

National Sleep Foundation. (2006). *Sleep in America poll 2006.* Washington, DC: Author.

National Sleep Foundation. (2007). *Sleep in America poll 2007.* Washington, DC: Author.

National Vital Statistics Reports (2008, June 11). Table 7. Deaths and death rates for the 10 leading causes of death in specified age groups: United States, preliminary 2006. *National Vital Statistics Reports, 56*(16), 30

Navab, A., Gillespie-Lynch, K., Johnson, S. P., Sigman, M., & Hutman, T. (2012, in press). Eye tracking as a measure of responsiveness to joint attention in infants at risk for autism. *Infancy.*

Needham, A., Barrett, T., & Peterman, K. (2002). A pick-me-up for infants' exploratory skills: Early simulated experiences reaching for objects using 'sticky mittens' enhances young infants' object exploration skills. *Infant Behavior and Development, 25,* 279–295.

Negriff, S., Susman, E. J., & Trickett, P. K. (2011). The development pathway from pubertal timing to delinquency and sexual activity from early to late adolescence. *Journal of Youth and Adolescence, 40,* 1343–1356.

Neikrug, A. B., & Ancoli-Israel, S. (2010). Sleep disorders in the older adult: A minireview. *Gerontology, 56,* 181–189.

Nelson, C. A. (2003). Neural development and lifelong plasticity. In R. M. Lerner, F. Jacobs, & D. Wertlieb (Eds.), *Handbook of applied developmental science* (Vol. 1). Thousand Oaks, CA: Sage.

Nelson, C. A. (2008). Unpublished review of J. W. Santrock's *Topical life-span development,* 5th ed. New York: McGraw-Hill.

Nelson, C. A. (2012). Brain development and behavior. In A. M. Rudolph, C. Rudolph, L. First, G. Lister, & A. A. Gersohon (Eds.), *Rudolph's pediatrics* (22nd ed.). New York: McGraw-Hill.

Nelson, C. A. (2013, in press). Neural development and lifelong plasticity. In D. P. Keating (Ed.), *Nature and nurture in early childhood development.* New York: Cambridge University Press.

Nelson, J. A., Leerkes, E. M., O'Brien, M., Calkins, S. D., & Maracovitch, S. (2012). African American and European American mothers' beliefs about negative emotions and emotion socialization practices. *Parenting, 12,* 22–41.

Nelson, J. L., Palonsky, S. B., & McCarthy, M. R. (2013). *Critical issues in education* (8th ed.). New York: McGraw-Hill.

Nelson, L. J., Padilla-Walker, L. M., Carroll, J. S., Madsen, S. D., Barry, C. M., & Badger, S. (2007). "If you want me to treat you like an adult, start acting like one!" Comparing the criteria that emerging adults and their parents have for adulthood. *Journal of Family Psychology, 21,* 665–674.

Nemec, S. F., & others. (2011). Male sexual development in utero: Testicular descent on prenatal MRI. *Ultrasound in Obstetrics and Gynecology, 38,* 688–694.

Neugarten, B. L. (1964). *Personality in middle and late life.* New York: Atherton.

Neugarten, B. L. (1986). The aging society. In A. Pifer & L. Bronte (Eds.), *Our aging society: Paradox and promise.* New York: W. W. Norton.

Neugarten, B. L., Havighurst, R. J., & Tobin, S. S. (1968). Personality and patterns of aging. In B. L. Neugarten (Ed.), *Middle age and aging.* Chicago: University of Chicago Press.

Neugarten, B. L., & Weinstein, K. K. (1964). The changing American grandparent. *Journal of Marriage and the Family, 26,* 199–204.

Neville, H. J. (2006). Different profiles of plasticity within human cognition. In Y. Munakata & M. H. Johnson (Eds.). *Attention and Performance XXI: Processes of change in brain and cognitive development.* Oxford, UK: Oxford University Press.

Newcombe, N. (2008). The development of implicit and explicit memory. In N. Cowan & M. Courage (Eds.), *The development of memory in childhood.* Philadelphia: Psychology Press.

Newman, M. L., Groom, C. J., Handelman, L. D., & Pennebaker, J. W. (2008). *Discourse Perspectives, 45,* 211–236.

Newsom, R. S., Boelen, P. A., Hofman, A., & Tiemeier, H. (2011). The prevalence and characteristics of complicated grief in older adults. *Journal of Affective Disorders, 132,* 231–238.

Newton, A. W., & Vandeven, A. M. (2010). Child abuse and neglect: A worldwide concern. *Current Opinion in Pediatrics, 22,* 226–233.

Newton, N. J., & Stewart, A. J. (2012). Personality development in adulthood. In S. K. Whitbourne & M. Sliwinski (Eds.), *Wiley-Blackwell handbook of adult development and aging.* New York: Wiley.

Nezu, A. M., Raggio, G., Evans, A. N., & Zezu, C. M. (2013, in press). Diabetes mellitus. In I. B. Weiner & others (Eds.), *Handbook of psychology* (2nd ed.,Vol. 9). New York: Wiley.

Ng, T. P., Feng, L., Niti, M., & Yap, K. B. (2010). Low blood pressure and depressive symptoms among Chinese older subjects: A population-based study. *American Journal of Medicine, 123,* 342–349.

Nguyen, T. V., & others. (2012, in press). Testosterone-related cortical maturation across childhood and adolescence. *Cerebral Cortex.*

NICHD. (2012). *SIDS facts.* Retrieved January 8, 2012, from www.nichd.nih/gov/sids

NICHD Early Child Care Research Network. (2001). Nonmaternal care and family factors in early development: An overview of the NICHD study of Early Child Care. *Journal of Applied Developmental Psychology, 22,* 457–492.

NICHD Early Child Care Research Network. (2002). Structure → Process → Outcome: Direct and indirect effects of child care quality on young children's development. *Psychological Science, 13,* 199–206.

NICHD Early Child Care Research Network. (2003). Does amount of time spent in child care predict socioemotional adjustment during the transition to kindergarten? *Child Development, 74,* 976–1005.

NICHD Early Child Care Research Network. (2004). Type of child care and children's development at 54 months. *Early Childhood Research Quarterly, 19,* 203–230.

NICHD Early Child Care Research Network. (2005). *Child care and development.* New York: Guilford.

NICHD Early Child Care Research Network. (2005). Predicting individual differences in attention, memory, and planning in first graders from experiences at home, child care, and school. *Developmental Psychology, 41,* 99–114.

NICHD Early Child Care Research Network. (2006). Infant-mother attachment classification: Risk and protection in relation to changing maternal caregiving quality. *Developmental Psychology, 42,* 38–58.

NICHD Early Child Care Research Network. (2010). Testing a series of causal propositions relating time spent in child care to children's externalizing behavior. *Developmental Psychology, 46*(1), 1–17.

Nielsen, M. B., & Einarsen, S. (2012). Prospective relationships between workplace sexual harassment and psychological distress. *Occupational Medicine, 62,* 226–228.

Nieto, S., & Bode, P. (2012). *Affirming diversity* (6th ed.). Boston: Allyn & Bacon.

Nigro, G., & others. (2011). Role of the infections in recurrent spontaneous abortion. *Journal of Maternal-Fetal and Neonatal Medicine, 24,* 983–989.

Nisbett, R. E. (2003). *The geography of thought.* New York: Free Press.

Nisbett, R. E., & others. (2012, in press). Intelligence: New findings and theoretical developments. *American Psychologist.*

Nishikawa, N., & others. (2012, in press). Co-administration of Doperidone increases plasma Levodopa concentration in patients with Parkinson disease. *Clinical Neuropharmacology.*

Nixon, S. A., Rubincam, C., Casale, M., & Flicker, S. (2011). Is 80% a passing grade? Meanings attached to condom use in an abstinence-plus HIV prevention programme in South Africa. *AIDS Care, 23,* 213–220.

Nodine, P. M., & Hastings-Tolsma, M. (2012). Maternal obesity: Improving pregnancy outcomes. *MCN American Journal of Maternal Child Nursing, 37,* 110–115.

Noel-Miller, C. M. (2011). Partner caregiving in older cohabiting couples. *Journals of Gerontology B: Psychological Sciences and Social Sciences, 66B,* 341–353.

Noftle, E. E., & Robins, R. W. (2007). Personality predictors of academic outcomes: Big Five correlates of GPA and SAT scores. *Journal of Personality and Social Psychology, 93,* 116–130.

Nolen-Hoeksema, S. (2011). *Abnormal psychology* (5th ed.). New York: McGraw-Hill.

Nolen-Hoeksema, S. (2012). Emotion regulation and psychopathology: The role of gender. *Annual Review of Clinical Psychology* (Vol. 8). Palo Alto, CA: Annual Review.

Nomoto, M., & others. (2009). Inter- and intra-individual variation in L-dopa pharmacokinetics in the treatment of Parkinson's disease. *Parkinsonism and Related Disorders, 15*(Suppl. 1), S21–S24.

Norman, J. F., Holmin, J. S., & Bartholomew, A. N. (2011). Visual memories for perceived length are well preserved in older adults. *Vision Research, 51,* 2057–2062.

Norouzieh, K. (2005). Case management of the dying child. *Case Manager, 16,* 54–57.

Nottelmann, E. D., & others. (1987). Gonadal and adrenal hormone correlates of adjustment in early adolescence. In R. M. Lerner & T. T. Foch (Eds.), *Biological-psychological interactions in early adolescence.* Hillsdale, NJ: Erlbaum.

Nouchi, R., & others. (2012). Brain training game improves executive functions and processing speed in the elderly: A randomized controlled trial. *PLoS One, 7(1),* e29676.

Nucci, L. (2006). Education for moral development. In M. Killen & J. Smetana (Eds.), *Handbook of moral development.* Mahwah, NJ: Erlbaum.

Nurmsoo, E., Einav, S., & Hood, B. M. (2012). Best friends: Children use mutual gaze to identify friendship in others. *Developmental Science, 15,* 417–425.

Nyberg, L., & others. (2012). Memory aging and brain maintenance. *Trends in Cognitive Science, 16,* 292–305.

O'Brien, M., & Moss, P. (2010). Fathers, work, and family policies in Europe. In M. E. Lamb (Ed.), *The father's role in child development* (5th ed.). New York: Wiley.

O'Callahan, M., & others. (2013, in press). Coronary heart disease and hypertension. In I. B. Weiner & others (Eds.), *Handbook of psychology* (2nd ed., Vol. 9). New York: Wiley.

O'Connor, D. B., & others. (2011). The relationships between sex hormones and sexual function in middle-aged and older European men. *Journal of Clinical Endocrinology and Metabolism, 96,* E1577–E1587.

O'Donnell, A. M. (2012). Constructivism. In K. R. Harris, S. Graham, & T. Urdan (Eds.), *APA educational psychology handbook.* Washington, DC: American Psychological Association.

O'Halloran, A. M., & others. (2012, in press). Falls and fall efficacy: The role of sustained attention in older adults. *BMC Geriatrics.*

O'Hara, R. E., Gibbons, F. X., Weng, C. Y., Gerrard, M., & Simons, R. L. (2012). Perceived racial discrimination as a barrier to college enrollment for African Americans. *Personality and Social Psychology Bulletin, 38,* 77–89.

O'Rourke, N., Cappeliez, P., & Claxton, A. (2011). Functions of reminiscence and the psychological well-being of young-old and older adults over time. *Aging and Mental Health, 15,* 272–281.

Oakes, L. M. (2012). Advances in eye-tracking in infancy research. *Infancy, 17,* 1–8.

Oates, J., & Abraham, S. (2010). *Llewellyn-Jones fundamentals of obstetrics and gynecology* (9th ed.). New York: Elsevier.

Occupational Outlook Handbook 2010–2011. (2010). Washington, DC: U.S. Department of Labor, Bureau of Labor Statistics.

Occupational Outlook Handbook 2012–2013. (2012). Washington, DC: U.S. Department of Labor, Bureau of Labor Statistics.

OECD. (2010). *Obesity and the economics of prevention—Fit or fat.* Paris: OECD.

Oerlemans, W. G., Bakker, A. B., & Veenhoven, R. (2011). Finding the key to happy aging: A day reconstruction of happiness. *Journals of Gerontology B: Psychological Sciences and Social Sciences, 66B,* 665–674.

Offer, D., Ostrov E., Howard, K.I., & Atkinson, R. (1988). *The teenage world: Adolescents' self-image in ten countries.* New York: Plenum.

Ogden, C. L., Carroll, M. D., Kit, B. K., & Flegal, K. M. (2012, January). Prevalence of obesity in the United States, 2009–2010. *NCHS Data Brief,* No. 82, pp. 1–9. Hyattsville, MD: National Center for Health Statistics.

Ogden, L. G., & others. (2012, in press). Cluster analysis of the National Weight Control Registry to identify distinct subgroups maintaining successful weight loss. *Obesity.*

Ohta, M., Tajiri, Y., Yamato, H., & Ikeda, M. (2012, in press). Effects of exercise therapy alone and in combination with a calcium channel blocker or an angiotensin receptor blocker in hypertensive patients. *Clinical and Experimental Hypertension.*

Olds, D. L., & others. (2004). Effects of home visits by paraprofessionals and nurses: Age four follow-up of a randomized trial. *Pediatrics, 114,* 1560–1568.

Olds, D. L., & others. (2007). Effects of nurse home visiting on maternal and child functioning: Age 9 follow-up of a randomized trial. *Pediatrics, 120,* e832–e845.

Olmstead, S. B., Pasley, K., & Fincham, F. D. (2012, in press). Hooking up and penetrative hookups: Correlates that differentiate college men. *Archives of Sexual Behavior.*

Olszewski-Kubilius, P., & Thomson, D. (2013, in press). Gifted education programs and procedures. In I. B. Weiner & others (Eds.), *Handbook of psychology* (2nd ed., Vol. 7). New York: Wiley.

Olweus, D. (2003). Prevalence estimation of school bullying with the Olweus bully/victim questionnaire. *Aggressive Behavior, 29*(3), 239–269.

Onwudiwe, N. C., Stuart, B., Zuckerman, I. H., & Sorkin, J. D. (2011). Obesity and Medicare expenditure: Accounting for age-related height loss. *Obesity, 19,* 204–211.

Onwuteaka-Philipsen, B. D., Rurup, M. L., Pasman, H. R., & van der Heide, A. (2010). The last phase of life: Who requests and who receives euthanasia or physician-assisted suicide. *Medical Care, 48,* 596–603.

Orbach, Y., Lamb, D., & Pipe, M-E. (2012). A case study of witness consistency and memory recovery across multiple investigative interviews. *Applied Cognitive Psychology, 26,* 118–129.

Ornstein, P., Coffman, J. L., & Grammer, J. K. (2007, April). *Teachers' memory-relevant conversations and children's memory performance.* Paper presented at the biennial meeting of the Society for Research in Child Development, Boston.

Ornstein, P. A., Coffman, J. L., Grammer, J. K., San Souci, P. P., & McCall, L. E. (2010). Linking the classroom context and the development of children's memory skills. In J. Meece & J. Eccles (Eds.), *Handbook of research on schools, schooling, and human development.* New York: Routledge.

Orsi, C. M., Hale, D. E., & Lynch, J. L. (2011). Pediatric obesity epidemiology.

Current Opinion in Endocrinology, Diabetes, and Obesity, 18, 14–22.

Ortigosa Gomez, S., & others. (2011). Use of illicit drugs over gestation and their neonatal impact. Comparison between periods 1982–1988 and 2002–2008. *Medicina Clinica, 136,* 423–430.

Ossher, L., Flegal, K. E., & Lustig, C. (2012, in press). Everyday memory errors in older adults. *Neuropsychology, Development, and Cognition, B. Aging, Neuroscience, and Cognition.*

Ott, C. H., Lueger, R. J., Kelber, S. T., & Prigerson, H. G. (2007). Spousal bereavement in older adults: Common, resilient, and chronic grief with defining characteristics. *Journal of Nervous and Mental Disease, 195,* 332–341.

P

Pacala, J. T., & Yeuh, B. (2012). Hearing defects in the older patient: "I didn't notice anything." *JAMA, 307,* 1185–1194.

Padilla-Walker, L. M., & Coyne, S. M. (2011). "Turn that thing off!" Parent and adolescent predictors of proactive media monitoring. *Journal of Youth and Adolescence, 34,* 705–715.

Painter, A., Williams, A. D., & Burd, L. (2012a). Fetal alcohol spectrum disorders—implications for child neurology, part 1: Prenatal exposure and dosimetry. *Journal of Child Neurology, 27,* 258–263.

Painter, A., Williams, A. D., & Burd, L. (2012b). Fetal alcohol spectrum disorders—implications for child neurology, part 2: Diagnosis and management. *Journal of Child Neurology, 27,* 355–362.

Palmore, E. B. (2004). Research note: Ageism in Canada and the United States. *Journal of Cross Cultural Gerontology, 19,* 41–46.

Pan, B. A., & Uccelli, P. (2009). Semantic development. In J. Berko Gleason & N. B. Rather (Eds.) (2009). *The development of language* (7th ed.). Boston: Allyn & Bacon.

Pan, Z., & Chang, C. (2012). Gender and the regulation of longevity: Implications for autoimmunity. *Autoimmunity Reviews, 11,* A393–A403.

Panigraphy, A., & others (2012). Neuroimaging biomarkers of preterm brain injury: Toward developing the preterm connectome. *Pediatric Radiology, 42, Suppl 1,* S33–S61.

Papastavrou, E., Charlalambous, A., Tsangari, H., & Karayiannis, G. (2012). The burdensome and depressive experience of caring: What cancer, schizophrenia, and Alzheimer's disease caregivers have in common. *Cancer Nursing, 35,* 187–194.

Pardal, R., & Lopez-Barneo, J. (2012). Neural stem cells and transplantation studies in Parkinson's disease. *Advances in Experimental Medicine and Biology, 741,* 206–216.

Parens, E., & Johnston, J. (2009). Facts, values, and attention-deficit hyperactivity disorder (ADHD): An update on the controversies.

Child and Adolescent Psychiatry and Mental Health, 3, 1.

Park, B., Lee, W., & Han, K. (2012). Modeling the interactions of Alzheimer-related genes from the whole brain microarray data and diffusion tensor images of human brain. *BMC Informatics, 13*(Suppl. 7), S10.

Park, C. J., Yelland, G. W., Taffe, J. R., & Gray, K. M. (2012). Morphological and syntactic skills in language samples of preschool aged children with autism: Atypical development? *International Journal of Speech and Language Pathology, 14,* 95–108.

Park, C. L. (2010). Making sense out of the meaning literature: An integrative review of meaning making and its effect on adjustment to stressful life events. *Psychological Bulletin, 136,* 257–301.

Park, C. L. (2012a, in press). Meaning making in cancer survivorship. In P. T. P. Wong (Ed.), *Handbook of meaning* (2nd ed.). Thousand Oaks, CA: Sage.

Park, C. L. (2012b). Meaning, spirituality, and growth: Protective and resilience factors in health and illness. In A. S. Baum, T. A. Revenson, & J. E. Singer (Eds.), *Handbook of health psychology* (2nd ed.). New York: Sage.

Park, D. (2001). Commentary in R. Restak, *The secret life of the brain.* Washington, DC: Joseph Henry Press.

Park, D. C., & Bischof, G. N. (2011). Neuroplasticity, aging, and cognitive function. In K. W. Schaie & S. L. Willis (Eds.), *Handbook of the psychology of aging* (7th ed.). New York: Elsevier.

Park, M. J., Paul Mulye, T., Adams, S. H., Brindis, C. D., & Irwin, C. E. (2006). The health status of young adults in the United States. *Journal of Adolescent Health, 39,* 305–317.

Parkay, F. W. (2013). *Becoming a teacher* (9th ed.). Upper Saddle River, NJ: Pearson.

Parke, R. D., & Clarke-Stewart, A. K. (2011). *Social development.* New York: Wiley.

Parke, R. D., Coltrane, S., & Schofield, T. (2011). The bicultural advantage. In J. Marsh, R. Mendoza-Denton, & J. A. Smith (Eds.), *Are we born racist?* Boston: Beacon Press.

Parkes, K. R. (2006). Physical activity and self-rated health: Interactive effects of activity in work and leisure domains. *British Journal of Health Psychology, 11,* 533–550.

Parra Cardona, J. R., & others. (2012). Culturally adapting an evidence-based parenting intervention for Latino immigrants: The need to integrate fidelity and cultural relevance. *Family Process, 51,* 56–72.

Parrett, A. L., & others. (2011). Adiposity and aerobic fitness are associated with metabolic disease risk in children. *Applied Physiology, Nutrition, and Metabolism, 36,* 72–79.

Pasley, K., & Moorefield, B. S. (2004). Stepfamilies. In M. Coleman & L. Ganong (Eds.), *Handbook of contemporary families.* Thousand Oaks, CA: Sage.

Passini, S. (2012). The delinquency-drug relationship: The influence of social reputation and moral disengagement. *Addictive Behaviors, 37,* 577–579.

Patel, R., & others. (2011). European guidelines for the management of genital herpes, 2010. *International Journal of STD and AIDS, 22,* 1–10.

Patrick, M. E., & Schulenberg, J. E. (2010). Alcohol use and heavy episodic drinking prevalence among national samples of American eighth- and tenth-grade students. *Journal of Studies on Alcohol and Drugs, 71,* 41–45.

Patterson, C., & D'Augelli, A. R. (Eds.) (2013, in press). *The psychology of sexual orientation.* New York: Cambridge University Press.

Patterson, C. J. (2013, in press). Family lives of lesbian and gay adults. In G. W. Peterson & K. R. Bush (Eds.), *Handbook of marriage and the family.* New York: Springer.

Patterson, C. J., & Farr, R. H. (2012, in press). Children of lesbian and gay parents: Reflections on the research-policy interface. In H. R. Schaffer & K. Durkin (Eds.), *Blackwell handbook of developmental psychology in action.* New York: Blackwell.

Patton, G. C., & others. (2011). Overweight and obesity between adolescence and early adulthood: A 10-year prospective study. *Journal of Adolescent Health, 45,* 275–280.

Pauletti, R. E., Menon, M., Menon, M., Tobin, D. D., & Perry, D. G. (2012). Narcissism and adjustment in preadolescence. *Child Development, 83,* 831–837.

Paulhus, D. L. (2008). Birth order. In M. M. Haith & J. B. Benson (Eds.), *Encyclopedia of infant and early childhood development.* Oxford, UK: Elsevier.

Paus, T., & others. (2007). Morphological properties of the action-observation cortical network in adolescents with low and high resistance to peer influence. *Social Neuroscience 3*(3), 303–316.

Payer, L. (1991). The menopause in various cultures. In H. Burger & M. Boulet (Eds.), *A portrait of the menopause.* Park Ridge, NJ: Parthenon.

Pea, R., & others. (2012). Media use, face-to-face communication, media multitasking, and social well-being among 8- to 12-year-old girls. *Developmental Psychology, 48,* 327–336.

Pedersen, W., & Mastekaasa, A. (2011). Conduct disorder symptoms and subsequent pregnancy, child-birth, and abortion: A population-based longitudinal study of adolescents. *Journal of Adolescence, 34,* 1025–1033.

Peek, M. K. (2009). Marriage in later life. In D. Carr (Ed.), *Encyclopedia of the life course and human development.* Boston: Gale Cengage.

Peets, K., Hodges, E. V. E., & Salmivalli, C. (2011). Actualization of social cognitions into aggressive behavior toward disliked targets. *Social Development, 20,* 233–250.

Pelaez, M., Virues-Ortega, J., & Gewirtz, J. L. (2012). Acquisition of social referencing via discrimination training in infants. *Journal of Applied Behavior Analysis, 45,* 23–36.

Pellegrini, A. (2013). Play. In P. D. Zelazo (Ed.), *Oxford handbook of developmental psychology.* New York: Oxford University Press.

Pellicano, E. (2010). Individual differences in executive function and central coherence predict developmental changes in theory of mind in autism. *Developmental Psychology, 46,* 530–544.

Peltz, C. B., Gratton, G., & Fabiani, M. (2011). Age-related changes in electrophysiological and neuropsychological indices of working memory, attention control, and cognitive flexibility. *Frontiers in Psychology, 2,* 190.

Peltzer-Karpf, A. (2012). The dynamic matching of neural and cognitive growth cycles. *Nonlinear Dynamics, Psychology, and Life Sciences, 16,* 61–78.

Penela, E. C., & others. (2012, in press). Maternal caregiving moderates the relation between temperamental fear and social behavior with peers. *Infancy.*

Pennell, A., Salo-Coombs, V., Hering, A., Spielman, F., & Fecho, K. (2011). Anesthesia and analgesia-related preferences and outcomes of women who have birth plans. *Journal of Midwifery and Women's Health, 56,* 376–381.

Perissinotto, C. M., Stijacic Cenzer, I., & Covinsky, K. E. (2012, in press). Loneliness in older persons: A predictor of functional decline and death loneliness in older persons. *Archives of Internal Medicine.*

Perry, N. B., Nelson, J. A., Leerkes, E. M., O'Brien, M., Calkins, S. D., & Maracovitch, S. (2012, in press). The relation between maternal emotional support and child physiological regulation across the preschool years. *Developmental Psychobiology.*

Persson, K. E., Fridlund, B., Kvist, L. J., & Dykes, A .K. (2011). Mothers' sense of security in the first postnatal week: Interview study. *Journal of Advanced Nursing, 67,* 105–116.

Peskin, H. (1967). Pubertal onset and ego functioning. *Journal of Abnormal Psychology, 72,* 1–15.

Peters, K. F., & Petrill, S. A. (2011). Comparison of background, needs, and expectations for genetic counseling of adults with experience with Down syndrome, Marfan syndrome, and neurofibromatosis. *American Journal of Medical Genetics A, 155,* 684–696.

Petersen, I. T., & others. (2012, in press). Interaction between serotonin transporter polymorphism (5-HTTLPR) and stressful life events in adolescents' trajectories of anxious/depressed symptoms. *Developmental Psychology.*

Petersen, J. L., & Hyde, J. S. (2010). A meta-analytic review of research on gender differences in sexuality, 1973–2007. *Psychological Bulletin, 136,* 21–38.

Petrick-Steward, E. (2012). *Beginning writers in the zone of proximal development.* New York: Psychology Press.

Pew Research Center. (2010a). *The decline of marriage and rise of new families.* Washington, DC: Author.

Pew Research Center. (2010b). *Millennials: Confident, connected, open to change.* Washington, DC: Pew Research Center.

Pew Research Center. (2011, December). *Barely half of U.S. adults are married—a record low.* Washington, DC: Pew Research Center.

Pfeifer, J. H., & Blakemore, S. J. (2012). Adolescent social cognitive and affective neuroscience: Past, present, and future. *Social Cognitive and Affective Neuroscience, 7,* 1–10.

Philip, R. C., & others. (2012). A systematic review and meta-analysis of the fMRI investigation of autism spectrum disorders. *Neuroscience and Biobehavioral Reviews, 36,* 901–942.

Phillips, M. I. (2012, in press). Gene, stem cell, and future therapies for orphan diseases. *Clinical Pharmacology and Therapeutics.*

Phinney, J. S. (2008). Bridging identities and disciplines: Advances and challenges in understanding multiple identities. In M. Azmitia, M. Syed, & K. Radmacher (Eds.), *The intersections of personal and social identities. New Directions for Child and Adolescent Development, 120,* 97–109.

Phinney, J. S., & Ong, A. D. (2007). Ethnic identity in immigrant families. In J. E. Lansford, K. Deater-Deckard, & M. H. Bornstein (Eds.), *Immigrant families in contemporary society.* New York: Guilford.

Pho, A. T., & others. (2012, in press). Nursing strategies for promoting and maintaining function among community-living older adults: The CAPABLE intervention. *Geriatric Nursing.*

Piaget, J. (1932). *The moral judgment of the child.* New York: Harcourt Brace Jovanovich.

Piaget, J. (1952). *The origins of intelligence in children.* (M. Cook, Trans.). New York: International Universities Press.

Piaget, J. (1954). *The construction of reality in the child.* New York: Basic Books.

Piaget, J. (1962). *Play, dreams, and imitation.* New York. W.W. Norton.

Piaget, J., & Inhelder, B. (1969). *The child's conception of space* (F. J. Langdon & J. L. Lunger, Trans.). New York: W. W. Norton.

Piazza, J. R., & Charles, S. T. (2012). Affective disorders and age: The view through a developmental lens. In S. K. Whitbourne & M. J. Sliwinski (Eds.), *Wiley-Blackwell handbook of adult development and aging.* New York: Wiley.

Pietilainen, K. H., Saarni, S. E., Kaprio, J., & Rissanen, A. (2012). Does dieting make you fat? A twin study. *International Journal of Obesity, 36,* 456–464.

Pihlajamaki, M., Jauhialinen, A. M., & Soininen, H. (2009). Structural and functional fMRI in mild cognitive impairment. *Current Alzheimer Research, 6,* 179–185.

Piko, B. F., & Balazs, M. A. (2012). Authoritative parenting style and adolescent smoking and drinking. *Addictive Behaviors, 37,* 353–356.

Pilkington, P. D., Windsor, T. D., & Crisp, D. A. (2012). Volunteering and subjective well-being in midlife and older adults: The role of supportive social networks. *Journals of Gerontology B: Psychological Sciences and Social Sciences, 67,* 249–260.

Pines, A., Sturdee, D. W., & Maclennan, A. H. (2012). Quality of life and the role of menopausal hormone therapy. *Climacteric, 15,* 213–216.

Pinquart, M., & Frostmeier, S. (2012). Effects of reminiscence interventions on psychosocial outcomes: A meta-analysis. *Aging and Mental Health, 16,* 541–558.

Pinsker, J. E. (2012, in press). Turner syndrome: Updating the paradigm of clinical care. *Journal of Clinical and Endocrinology and Metabolism.*

Piper, B. J., & others. (2011). Abnormalities in parentally rated executive function in methamphetamine/polysubstance exposed children. *Pharmacology, Biochemistry, and Behavior, 98,* 432–439.

Piper, S. L., & others. (2012, in press). Inducible immortality in hTERT-human mesenchymal stem cells. *Journal of Orthopedic Research.*

Pipp, S. L., Fischer, K. W., & Jennings, S. L. (1987). The acquisition of self and mother knowledge in infancy. *Developmental Psychology, 23,* 86–96.

Pitkänen, T., Lyyra, A. L., & Pulkkinen, L. (2005). Age of onset of drinking and the use of alcohol in adulthood: A follow-up study from age 8–42 for females and males. *Addiction, 100,* 652–661.

Plener, P. L., Singer, H., & Goldbeck, L. (2011). Traumatic events and suicidality in a German adolescent community sample. *Journal of Traumatic Stress, 24,* 121–124.

Plomin, R. (2012, in press). Child development and molecular genetics: 14 years later. *Child Development.*

Plomin, R., DeFries, J. C., McClearn, G. E., & McGuffin, P. (2009). *Behavioral genetics* (5th ed.). New York: W. H. Freeman.

Plucker, J. (2010, July 19). Commentary in P. Bronson & A. Merryman, The creativity crisis. *Newsweek,* pp. 45–46.

Pluess, M., & Belsky, J. (2009). Differential susceptibility to rearing experience: The case of child care. *Journal of Child Psychology and Psychiatry, 50,* 396–404.

Polat, U., & others. (2012, in press). Training the brain to overcome the effect of aging on the human eye. *Scientific Reports.*

Pollack, W. (1999). *Real boys.* New York: Owl Books.

Polo-Kantola, P. (2011). Sleep problems in midlife and beyond. *Maturitas, 68,* 224–232.

Pomerantz, E. M., Cheung, C. S., & Qin, L. (2012). Relatedness between children and parents: Implications for motivation. In R. Ryan (Ed.), *Oxford handbook of motivation*. New York: Oxford University Press.

Pomerantz, E. M., Kim, E. M., & Cheung, C. S. (2012). Parents' involvement in children's learning. In K. R. Harris & others (Eds.), *APA educational psychology handbook*. Washington, DC: American Psychological Association.

Poorthuis, A. M., & others. (2012, in press). Prosocial tendencies predict friendship quality, but not for popular children. *Journal of Experimental Child Psychology.*

Popenoe, D. (2009). *The state of our unions 2008. Updates of social indicators: Tables and charts.* Piscataway, NJ: The National Marriage Project.

Popham, W. J. (2011). *Classroom assessment* (6th ed.). Boston: Allyn & Bacon.

Posner, M. I., & Rothbart, M. K. (2007). *Educating the human brain*. Washington, DC: American Psychological Association.

Postert, C., Dannlowski, U., Muller, J. M., & Konrad, C. (2012). Beyond the blues: Cross-cultural phenomenology of depressed mood. *Psychopathology, 45*, 185–192.

Poston, L., & others. (2011). Obesity in pregnancy: Implications for the mother and lifelong health of the child. A consensus statement. *Pediatric Research, 69*, 175–180.

Pot, A. M., & others. (2010). The impact of life review on depression in older adults: A randomized controlled trial. *International Psychogeriatrics, 22*, 572–581.

Potochnick, S., Perreira, K. M., & Fuligni, A. (2012). Fitting in: The roles of social acceptance and discrimination in shaping the daily psychological well-being of Latino youth. *Social Science Quarterly, 93*, 173–190.

Power, T. G. (2011). Social play. In P. K. Smith & C. H. Hart (Eds.), *Wiley-Blackwell handbook of childhood social development* (2nd ed.). New York: Wiley.

Prabhakar, H. (2007). Hopkins interactive guest blog: The public health experience at Johns Hopkins. Retrieved January 31, 2008, from http://hopkins.typepad.com/guest/2007/03/the_public_heal.html

Prameela, K. K. (2011). Breastfeeding—antiviral potential and relevance to the influenza virus pandemic. *Medical Journal of Malaysia, 66*, 166–169.

Pratt, M. W., Norris, J. E., Hebblethwaite, S., & Arnold, M. O. (2008). International transmission of values: Family generality and adolescents' narratives of parent and grandparent value teaching. *Journal of Personality, 76*, 171–198.

Preer, G., Sorrentino, D., & Newton, A.W. (2012). Child abuse pediatrics: Prevention, evaluation, and treatment. *Current Opinion in Pediatrics, 24*, 266–273.

Pressley, M. (2007). Achieving best practices. In L. B. Bambrell, L. M. Morrow, & M. Pressley (Eds.), *Best practices in literacy instruction*. New York: Guilford.

Pressley, M. (2007). An interview with Michael Pressley by Terri Flowerday and Michael Shaughnessy. *Educational Psychology Review, 19*, 1–12.

Prigerson, H. G., & others. (2011). Prolonged grief disorder: Psychometric validation of criteria for proposed for DSM-V and ICD-11. *PLOS Medicine, 6*(8), e1000121.

Prinstein, M. J., & Dodge, K. A. (2008). Current issues in peer influence. In M. J. Prinstein & K. A. Dodge (Eds.), *Understanding peer influence in children and adolescents*. New York: Guilford.

Prinstein, M. J., Rancourt, D., Guerry, J. D., & Browne, C. B. (2009). Peer reputations and psychological adjustment. In K. H. Rubin, W. M. Bukowksi, & B. Laursen (Eds.), *Handbook of peer interactions, relationships, and groups*. New York: Guilford.

Pruden, S., Goksun, T., Roseberry, S., Hirsh-Pasek, K., & Golinkoff, R. M. (2012, in press). Infant categorization of path relations during dynamic events. *Child Development.*

Pudrovska, T. (2009). Midlife crises and transitions. In D. Carr (Ed.), *Encyclopedia of the life course and human development*. Boston: Gale Cengage.

Pufal, M. A., & others. (2012, in press). Prevalence of overweight children of obese patients: A dietary overview. *Obesity Surgery.*

Puma, M., & others. (2010). *Head Start impact study. Final report.* Washington, DC: Administration for Children & Families.

Purper-Ouakil, D., & others. (2011). Neurobiology of attention deficit/hyperactivity disorder. *Pediatric Research, 69*, 69R–76R.

Putallaz, M., Grimes, C. L., Foster, K. J., Kupersmidt, J. B., Clie, J. D., & Dearing, K. (2007). Overt and relational aggression and victimization: Multiple perspectives within the school setting. *Journal of School Psychology, 45*, 523–547.

Puzzanchera, C., & Sickmund, M. (2008, July). *Juvenile court statistics 2005*. Pittsburgh: National Center for Juvenile Justice.

Q

Quinn, P. C., Anzures, G., Lee, K., Pascalis, O., Slater, A., & Tanaka, J. W. (2013, in press). On the developmental origins of differential responding to social category information. In M. R. Banaji & S. A. Gelman (Eds.), *Navigating the social world*. New York: Oxford University Press.

R

Rachner, T. D., Khosia, S., & Hofbauer, L. C. (2011). Osteoporosis: Now and the future. *Lancet, 377*, 1276–1287.

Ragucci, K. R., & Shrader, S. P. (2011). Osteoporosis treatment: An evidence-based approach. *Journal of Gerontological Nursing, 37*, 17–22.

Raikes, H., & others. (2006). Mother-child bookreading in low-income families: Correlates and outcomes during the first three years of life. *Child Development, 77*, 924–953.

Raj, T., & others. (2012). Alzheimer disease susceptibility loci: Evidence for a protein network under natural selection. *American Journal of Human Genetics, 90*, 720–726.

Rajaraman, P., & others. (2011). Early life exposure to diagnostic radiation and ultrasound scans and risk of childhood cancer: Case-control study. *British Medical Journal, 342*, d472.

Rakison, D. H., & Lawson, C. A. (2013). Categorization. In P. D. Zelazo (Ed.), *Oxford handbook of developmental psychology*. New York: Oxford University Press.

Rakoczy, H. (2012). Do infants have a theory of mind? *British Journal of Developmental Psychology, 30*, 59–74.

Ramsdell, H. L., Oller, D. K., Buder, E. H., Ethington, C. A., & Chorna, L. (2012, in press). Identification of prelinguistic phonological categories. *Journal of Speech, Language, and Hearing Research.*

Randall, W. L. (2012, in press). The importance of being ironic: Narrative openness and personal resilience in later life. *Gerontologist.*

Rasmussen, S. A. (2012). Human teratogens update 2011: Can we ensure safety during pregnancy? *Birth Defects Research A: Clinical and Molecular Teratology, 94*, 123–128.

Rasulo, D., Christensen, K., & Tomassini, C. (2005). The influence of social relations on mortality in later life: A study on elderly Danish twins. *Gerontologist, 45*, 601–608.

Rathunde, K., & Csikszentmihalyi, M. (2006). The developing person: An experiential perspective. In W. Damon & R. Lerner (Eds.), *Handbook of child psychology* (6th ed.). New York: Wiley.

Raver, C. C., & others. (2011). CSRP's impact on low-income preschoolers preacademic skills: Self-regulation as a mediating mechanism. *Child Development, 82*, 362–378.

Raver, C. C., & others. (2012, in press). Testing models of children's self-regulation within educational contexts: Implications for measurement. *Advances in Child Development and Behavior.*

Raz, N., Ghisletta, P., Rodrique, K. M., Kennedy, K. M., & Lindenberger, U. (2010). Trajectories of brain imaging in middle-aged and older adults: Regional and individual differences. *Neuroimage, 51*(2), 501–511.

Read, J. P., Merrill, J. E., & Bytschkow, K. (2010). Before the party starts: Risk factors and reasons for "pregaming" in college students. *Journal of American College Health, 58*, 461–472.

Realini, J. P., Buzi, R. S., Smith, P. B., & Martinez, M. (2010). Evaluation of "big decisions": An abstinence-plus sexuality. *Journal of Sex and Marital Therapy, 36*, 313–326.

Reef, S. E., & others. (2011). Progress toward control of rubella and prevention of congenital rubella syndrome—worldwide, 2009. *Journal of Infectious Diseases, 204*(Suppl. 1), S24–S27.

Reese, J. P., & others. (2012). Pharmacoeconomic considerations in treating patients with advanced Parkinson's disease. *Expert Opinion in Pharmacotherapy, 13*, 939–958.

Reeve, C. L., & Charles, J. E. (2008). Survey of opinions on the primacy of g and social consequences of ability testing: A comparison of expert and non-expert views. *Intelligence, 36*, 681–688.

Regalado, M., Sareen, H., Inkelas, M., Wissow, L. S., & Halfon, N. (2004). Parents' discipline of young children: Results from the National Survey of Early Childhood Health. *Pediatrics, 113*, 1952–1958.

Regev, R. H., & others. (2003). Excess mortality and morbidity among small-for-gestational-age premature infants: A population based study. *Journal of Pediatrics, 143*, 186–191.

Reichstadt, L., Depp, C. A., Palinkas, L. A., Folsom, D. P., & Jeste, D. V. (2007). Building blocks of successful aging: A focus group study of older adults' perceived contributors to successful aging. *American Journal of Geriatric Psychiatry, 15*, 194–201.

Reijmerink, N. E., & others. (2011). Toll-like receptors and microbial exposure: Gene-gene and gene-environment interaction in the development of atopy. *European Respiratory Journal, 38*, 833–840.

Reindollar, R. H., & Goldman, M. B. (2012). Gonadotropin therapy: A 20th century relic. *Fertility and Sterility, 97*, 813–818.

Reinhold, S. (2010). Reassessing the link between marital cohabitation and marital instability. *Demography, 47*, 719–733.

Rejeski, W. J., & others. (2011). Translating weight loss and physical activity into the community to preserve mobility in older, obese adults in poor cardiovascular health. *Archives of Internal Medicine, 171*(10), 880–886.

Rendall, M. S., Weden, M. M., Faveault, M. M., & Waldron, H. (2011). The protective effect of marriage for survival: A review and update. *Demography, 48*, 481–506.

Rende, R. (2012, in press). Behavioral resilience in the post-genomic era: Emerging models linking genes with environment. *Frontiers in Human Neuroscience.*

Repetti, R., Flook, L., & Sperling, J. (2011). Family influences in development across the life span. In K. L. Fingerman, C. A. Berg, J. Smith, & T. C. Antonucci (Eds.), *Handbook of life-span development.* New York: Springer.

Reproductive Endocrinology and Infertility Committee & others. (2012). Advanced reproductive age and fertility. *Journal of Obstetrics and Gynecology Canada.*

Resick, P. A., & others. (2012). Long-term consequences of cognitive-behavioral treatments for posttraumatic stress disorder among female rape survivors. *Journal of Consulting and Clinical Psychology, 80*, 201–210.

Reutzel, D. R., & Cooter, R. B. (2012). *Teaching children to read* (6th ed.). Boston: Allyn & Bacon.

Reutzel, D. R., & Cooter, R. B. (2013). *Essentials of teaching children to read* (3rd ed.). Boston: Allyn & Bacon.

Rey-Lopez, J. P., Vinente-Rodriguez, G., Biosca, M., & Moreno, L. A. (2008). Sedentary behavior and obesity development in children and adolescents. *Nutrition, Metabolism, and Cardiovascular Diseases, 18*, 241–252.

Reyna, V. F., Chapman, S. B., Dougherty, M. R., & Confrey, J. (Eds.) (2012). *The adolescent brain.* Washington, DC: American Psychological Association.

Reyna, V. F., & Rivers, S. E. (2008). Current theories of risk and rational decision making. *Developmental Review, 28*, 1–11.

Rhoades, G. K., Stanley, S. M., & Markham, H. J. (2009). The pre-engagement cohabitation effect: A replication and extension of previous findings. *Journal of Family Psychology, 23*, 107–111.

Rhoades, G. K., Stanley, S. M., & Markham, H. J. (2012). The impact of transition to cohabitation on relationship functioning: Cross-sectional and longitudinal findings. *Journal of Family Psychology, 26*, 348–358.

Richards, J. E. (2010). Infant attention, arousal, and the brain. In L. Oakes, C. Cashon, M. Casasola, & D. Rakison (Eds.), *Infant perception and cognition.* New York: Oxford University Press.

Richardson, C. R., Faulkner, G., McDevitt, J., Skrinar, G. S., Hutchinson, D. S., & Piette, J. D. (2005). Integrating physical activity into mental health services for persons with serious mental illness. *Psychiatric Services, 56*, 324–331.

Richardson, G. A., Goldschmidt, L., Leech, S., & Willford, J. (2011). Prenatal cocaine exposure: Effects on mother- and teacher-rated behavior problems and growth in school-aged children. *Neurotoxicology and Teratology, 33*, 69–77.

Richardson, G. A., Goldschmidt, L., & Willford, J. (2008). The effects of prenatal cocaine use on infant development. *Neurotoxicology and Teratology, 30*, 96–106.

Rideout, V., Foehr, U. G., & Roberts, D. P. (2010). *Generation M: Media in the lives of 8- to 18-year-olds.* Menlo Park, CA: Kaiser Family Foundation.

Riebe, D., & others. (2005). Physical activity, physical function, and stages of change in older adults. *American Journal of Health Behavior, 29*, 70–80.

Riesch, S. K., & others. (2012, in press). Modifiable family factors among treatment-seeking families of children with high body mass index: Report of a pilot study. *Journal of Pediatric Health Care.*

Riggins, T. (2012, in press). Building blocks of recollection. In S. Ghetti & P. J. Bauer (Eds.), *Origins and development of recollection.* New York: Oxford University Press.

Riley, K. P., Snowdon, D. A., Derosiers, M. F., & Markesbery, W. R. (2005). Early life linguistic ability, late life cognitive function, and neuropathology: Findings from the Nun Study. *Neurobiology of Aging, 26*, 341–347.

Riley, M., & Bluhm, B. (2012). High blood pressure in children and adolescents. *American Family Physician, 85*, 693–700.

Rimsza, M. E., & Kirk, G.M. (2005). Common medical problems of the college student. *Pediatric Clinics of North America, 52*, 9–24.

Rizzo, M. S. (1999, May 8). Genetic counseling combines science with a human touch. *Kansas City Star*, p. 3.

Robbers, S., & others. (2012, in press). Childhood problem behavior and parental divorce: Evidence for gene-environment interaction. *Social Psychiatry and Psychiatric Epidemiology.*

Roberie, D. R., & Elliott, W. J. (2012). What is the prevalence of resistant hypertension in the United States? *Current Opinion in Cardiology, 27*, 386–391.

Roberts, B. W., Donnellan, M. B., & Hill, P. L. (2013, in press). Personality trait development in adulthood: Findings and implications. In I. B. Weiner & others (Eds.), *Handbook of psychology* (2nd ed., Vol. 5). New York: Wiley.

Roberts, B. W., & Mroczek, D. (2008). Personality trait change in adulthood. *Current Directions in Psychological Science, 17*, 31–35.

Roberts, B. W., Walton, K. E., & Viechtbauer, W. (2006). Patterns of mean-level change in personality traits across the life course. A meta-analysis of longitudinal studies. *Psychological Bulletin, 132*, 1–25.

Roberts, B. W., & Wood, D. (2006). Personality development in the context of the Neo-Socioanalytic Model of personality. In D. Mroczek & T. Little (Eds.), *Handbook of personality development.* Mahwah, NJ: Erlbaum.

Roberts, D. F., & Foehr, U. G. (2008). Trends in media use. *Future of Children, 18*(1). 11–37.

Roberts, M. E., & others. (2012). From racial discrimination to risky sex: Prospective relations involving peers and parents. *Developmental Psychology, 48*, 89–102.

Robine, J. M. (2011). The weaker sex. *Aging: Clinical and Experimental Research, 23*, 80–83.

Robinson-Riegler, B., & Robinson-Riegler, G. L. (2012). *Cognitive psychology* (3rd ed.). Upper Saddle River, NJ: Pearson.

Robledo-Colonia, A. F., & others. (2012). Aerobic exercise training during pregnancy reduces symptoms in nulliparous women: A randomized trial. *Journal of Physiotherapy, 58*, 9–15.

Rochlen, A. B., McKelley, R. A., Suizzo, M-A., & Scaringi, V. (2008). Predictors of relationship satisfaction, psychological well-being, and life-satisfaction among stay-at-home fathers. *Psychology of Men and Masculinity, 9,* 17–28.

Rode, S. S., Chang, P., Fisch, R. O., & Sroufe, L. A. (1981). Attachment patterns of infants separated at birth. *Developmental Psychology, 17,* 188–191.

Rodin, J., & Langer, E. J. (1977). Long-term effects of a control-relevant intervention with the institutionalized aged. *Journal of Personality and Social Psychology, 35,* 397–402.

Rodkin, P. C., & Ryan, A. M. (2012). Child and adolescent peer relationships in educational context. In K. R. Harris, S. Graham, & T. Urdan (Eds.), *APA handbook of educational psychology.* Washington, DC: American Psychological Association.

Rodriquez Villar, S., & others. (2012). Prolonged grief disorder in the next of kin of adult patients who die during or after admission to intensive care. *Chest, 141,* 1635–1636.

Roelfs, D. J., Shor, E., Davidson, K. W., & Schwartz, J. E. (2011). Losing life and livelihood: A systematic review and meta-analysis of unemployment and all-cause mortality. *Social Science & Medicine, 72,* 840–854.

Roese, N. J., & Summerville, A. (2005). What we regret most ... and why. *Personality and Social Psychology Bulletin, 31,* 1273–1285.

Rogers, L. O., Zosuals, K. M., Halilm, M. L., Ruble, D., Hughes, D., & Fuligni, A. (2012). Meaning making in middle childhood: An exploration of the meaning of ethnic identity. *Cultural Diversity and Ethnic Minority Psychology, 18,* 99–108.

Roghani, T., & others. (2012, in press). Effects of short-term aerobic exercise with and without external loading on bone metabolism and balance in postmenopausal women with osteoporosis. *Rheumatology International.*

Roisman, G. I., & Groh, A.M. (2011). Attachment theory and research in developmental psychology: An overview and appreciative critique. In M. K. Underwood & L. H. Rosen (Eds.), *Social development.* New York: Wiley.

Roland, E., & Midthassel, U. V. (2012). *The Zero Program. New Directions in Youth Development, 133,* 29–39.

Rolland, Y., & others. (2011). Treatment strategies for sarcopenia and frailty. *Medical Clinics of North America, 95,* 427–438.

Ronninger, M., & others. (2012). Interaction analysis between HLA-DRB1 shared epitope alleles and MHC class II transactivator CIITA gene with regard to risk of rheumatoid arthritis. *PLoS One, 7*(3), e32861.

Rook, K. S., Mavandadi, S., Sorkin, D. H., & Zettel, L. A. (2007). Optimizing social relationships as a resource for health and well-being in later life. In C. M. Aldwin, C. L. Park, & A. Spiro (Eds.), *Handbook of health psychology and aging.* New York: Guilford.

Roring, R. W., Hines, F. G., & Charness, N. (2007). Age differences in identifying words in synthetic speech. *Human Factors, 49,* 25–31.

Rosano, C., & others. (2012). Slower gait, slower information processing, and smaller prefrontal area in older adults. *Age and Aging, 41,* 58–64.

Rose, A. J., & others. (2012). How girls and boys expect disclosure about problems will make them feel: Implications for friendship. *Child Development, 83,* 844–863.

Rosengard, C. (2009). Confronting the intendedness of adolescent rapid repeat pregnancy. *Journal of Adolescent Health, 44,* 5–6.

Rosenstein, D., & Oster, H. (1988). Differential facial responses to four basic tastes in newborns. *Child Development, 59,* 1555–1568.

Rosmarin, D. H., Krumrei, E. J., & Andersson, G. (2009). Religion as a predictor of psychological distress in two religious communities. *Cognitive Behavior Therapy, 38,* 54–64.

Rosnow, R. L., & Rosenthal, R. (2013). *Beginning psychological research* (7th ed.). Boston: Cengage.

Ross, J. L., & others. (2012). Behavioral and social phenotypes in boys with 47, XYY syndrome or 47, XXY Klinefelter syndrome. *Pediatrics, 129,* 769–778.

Rossi, A. S. (1989). A life-course approach to gender, aging, and intergenerational relations. In K. W. Schaie & C. Schooler (Eds.), *Social structure and aging.* Hillsdale, NJ: Erlbaum.

Rostosky, S. S., Riggle, E. D., Horner, S. G., Denton, F. N., & Huellemeier, J. D. (2010). Lesbian, gay and bisexual individuals' psychological reactions to amendments denying access to civil marriage. *American Journal of Orthopsychiatry, 80,* 302–310.

Rote, W. M., & others. (2012). Associations between observed mother-adolescent interactions and adolescent information management. *Journal of Research on Adolescence, 22,* 206–214.

Roth, J., Brooks-Gunn, J., Murray, L., & Foster, W. (1998). Promoting healthy adolescents: Synthesis of youth development program evaluations. *Journal of Research on Adolescence, 8,* 423–459.

Roth, L. W., & Polotsky, A. J. (2012). Can we live longer by eating less? A review of caloric restriction and longevity. *Maturitas, 71,* 315–319.

Rothbart, M. K. (2011). *Becoming who we are.* New York: Guilford Press.

Rothbart, M. K., & Bates, J. E. (2006). Temperament. In W. Damon & R. Lerner (Eds.), *Handbook of child psychology* (6th ed.). New York: Wiley.

Rothbaum, F., Poll, M., Azuma, H., Miyake, K., & Welsz, J. (2000). The development of close relationships in Japan and the United States: Paths of symbiotic harmony and generative tension. *Child Development, 71,* 1121–1142.

Rothman, S. M., & Mattson, M. P. (2012, in press). Sleep disturbances in Alzheimer's and Parkinson's diseases. *Neuromolecular Medicine.*

Rousssotte, F. F. (2011). Abnormal brain activation during working memory in children with prenatal exposure to drugs of abuse: The effects of methamphetamine, alcohol, and polydrug exposure. *NeuroImage, 54,* 3067–3075.

Rovee-Collier, C. (1987). Learning and memory in children. In J. D. Osofsky (Ed.), *Handbook of infant development* (2nd ed.). New York: Wiley.

Rovee-Collier, C. (2008). The development of infant memory. In N. Cowan & M. Courage (Eds.), *The development of memory in infancy and childhood* (2nd ed.). Philadelphia: Psychology Press.

Rovee-Collier, C., & Barr, R. (2010). Infant learning and memory. In U. J. G. Bremner & T. D. Wachs (Ed.), *Wiley-Blackwell handbook of infant development* (2nd ed.). New York: Wiley.

Roza, S. J., & others. (2010). Maternal folic acid supplement use in early pregnancy and child behavioral problems: The Generation R study. *British Journal of Nutrition, 103,* 445–452.

Rubin, K. H., Bowker, J. C., McDonald, K. L., & Menzer, M. (2013). Peer relationships in childhood. In P. D. Zelazo (Ed.), *Oxford handbook of developmental psychology.* New York: Oxford University Press.

Rubin, K. H., Bukowski, W., & Parker, J. G. (1998). Peer interactions, relationships, and groups. In N. Eisenberg (Ed.), *Handbook of child psychology* (5th ed., Vol. 3). New York: Wiley.

Rubin, K. H., Bukowski, W., & Parker, J. G. (2006). Peer interactions, relationships, and groups. In W. Damon & R. Lerner (Eds.), *Handbook of child psychology* (6th ed.). New York: Wiley.

Rubin, K. H., Coplan, R. J., Bowker, J. C., & Menzer, M. (2011). Social withdrawal and shyness. In P. K. Smith & C. H. Hart (Eds.), *Wiley-Blackwell handbook of childhood social development* (2nd ed.). New York: Wiley.

Rubio-Aurioles, E., & others. (2012, in press). A randomized open-label trial with a cross-over comparison of sexual self-confidence and other treatment outcomes following tadalafil once a day vs. tadalafil or sildenafil on-demand in men with erectile dysfunction. *Journal of Sexual Medicine.*

Ruble, D. (1983). The development of social comparison processes and their role in achievement-related self-socialization. In E. Higgins, D. Ruble, & W. Hartup (Eds.), *Social cognitive development: A social-cultural perspective.* New York: Cambridge University Press.

Ruchat, S. M., & others. (2012, in press). Nutrition and exercise reduce excessive weight gain in normal-weight pregnant women. *Medicine and Science in Sports and Exercise.*

Rudang, R., Mellstrom, D., Clark, E., Ohlsson, C., & Lorentzon, M. (2012). Advancing maternal age is associated with lower bone mineral density in young adult male offspring. *Osteoporosis International, 23*, 475–482.

Rueda, M. R., Posner, M. I., & Rothbart, M. K. (2005). The development of executive attention: Contributions to the emergence of self-regulation. *Developmental Neuropsychology, 28*, 573–594.

Ruffman, T., Slade, L., & Crowe, E. (2002). The relation between children's and mothers' mental state language and theory-of-mind understanding. *Child Development, 73*, 734–751.

Ruiter, M., & others. (2012, June 11). *Short sleep predicts stroke symptoms in persons of normal weight.* Paper presented at the annual meeting of the Associated Professional Sleep Societies (APSS), Boston.

Rutter, M. (2013, in press). Biological and experiential influences on psychological development. In D. P. Keating (Ed.), *Nature and nurture in early childhood development.* New York: Cambridge University Press.

Rumberger, R. W. (1983). Dropping out of high school: The influence of race, sex, and family background. *American Educational Research Journal, 20*, 199–220.

Rumberger, R. W. (1995). Dropping out of middle school: A multilevel analysis of students and schools. *American Education Research Journal, 3*, 583–625.

Runquist, J. (2007). Persevering through postpartum fatigue. *Journal of Obstetric, Gynecologic, and Neonatal Nursing, 36*, 28–37.

Rupp, D. E., Vodanovich, S. J., & Crede, M. (2005). The multidimensional nature of ageism: Construct validity and group differences. *Journal of Social Psychology, 145*, 335–362.

Russell, M., & Airasian, P. W. (2012). *Classroom assessment* (7th ed.). New York: McGraw-Hill.

Russell, S. T., Crockett, L. J., & Chao, R. K. (2010). *Asian American parenting and parent-adolescent relationships.* New York: Springer.

Rutherford, M. D., & Przednowek, M. (2012). Fathers show modifications of infant-directed action similar to that of mothers. *Journal of Experimental Child Psychology, 111*, 367–378.

Ryff, C. D. (1984). Personality development from the inside: The subjective experience of change in adulthood and aging. In P. B. Baltes & O. G. Brim (Eds.), *Life-span development and behavior.* New York: Academic Press.

S

Saarni, C. (1999). *The development of emotional competence.* New York: Guilford.

Saarni, C., Campos, J., Camras, L. A., & Witherington, D. (2006). Emotional development. In W. Damon & R. Lerner (Eds.), *Handbook of child psychology* (6th ed.). New York: Wiley.

Sabbagh, M. A., Xu, F., Carlson, S. M., Moses, L. J., & Lee, K. (2006). The development of executive functioning and theory of mind: A comparison of Chinese and U.S. preschoolers. *Psychological Science, 17*, 74–81.

Sadeh, A. (2008). Sleep. In M. M. Haith & J. B. Benson (Eds.), *Encyclopedia of infant and early childhood development.* Oxford, UK: Elsevier.

Sadker, D. M., & Zittleman, K. (2012). *Teachers, schools, and society* (3rd ed.). New York: McGraw-Hill.

Saffran, J. R., Werker, J. F., & Werner, L. A. (2006). The infant's auditory world: Hearing, speech, and the beginnings of language. In W. Damon & R. Lerner (Eds.), *Handbook of child psychology* (6th ed.). New York: Wiley.

Sagiv, S. K., Epstein, J. N., Bellinger, D. C., & Korrick, S. A. (2012, in press). Pre- and postnatal risk factors for ADHD in a nonclinical pediatric population. *Journal of Attention Disorders.*

Saifer, S. (2007, August 29). *Tools of the Mind—A Vygotskian-inspired early childhood curriculum.* Paper presented at the 17th Annual Conference of the European Early Childhood Education Research Assocation, Prague.

Saint Onge, J. M. (2009). Mortality. In D. Carr (Ed.), *Encyclopedia of the life course and human development.* Boston: Gale Cengage.

Sakuma, I. (2012, in press). What type of statin and what level of low-density lipoprotein cholesterol should be appropriate for secondary prevention for Japanese patients with coronary artery disease? *Circulation Journal.*

Sales, J. M., Brown, J. L., Vissman, A. T., & Diclemente, R. J. (2012). The association between alcohol use and sexual risk behaviors among African American women across three developmental periods: A review. *Current Drug Abuse Reviews, 5*, 117–128.

Salloum, A., & Overstreet, S. (2012). Grief and trauma intervention for children after disaster: Exploring coping skills versus trauma narration. *Behavior Research and Therapy, 50*, 169–179.

Salmaso, N., & others. (2012). Environmental enrichment increases the GFAP+ stem cell pool and reverses hypoxia-induced cognitive deficits in juvenile mice. *Journal of Neuroscience, 32*, 8930–8939.

Salmivalli, C., Garandeau, C. F., & Veenstra, R. (2012). KiVa Anti-Bullying Program: Implications for school adjustment. In A. M. Ryan & G. W. Ladd (Eds.), *Peer relationships and adjustment at school.* Charlotte, NC: Information Age Publishing.

Salmivalli, C., Peets, K., & Hodges, E. V. E. (2011). Bullying. In P. K. Smith & C. H. Hart (Eds.), *Wiley-Blackwell handbook of childhood social development* (2nd ed.). New York: Wiley.

Salthouse, T. A. (2009). When does age-related cognitive decline begin? *Neurobiology of Aging, 30*, 507–514.

Salthouse, T. A. (2012). Consequences of age-related cognitive declines. *Annual Review of Psychology* (Vol. 63). Palo Alto, CA: Annual Reviews.

Salthouse, T. A. (2013, in press). Executive functioning. In D. C. Park & N. Schwartz (Eds.), *Cognitive aging* (2nd ed.). New York: Psychology Press.

Salthouse, T. A., & Skovronek, E. (1992). Within-context assessment of working memory. *Journal of Gerontology, 47*, P110–P117.

Salvatore, J. E., Kuo, S. I., Steele, R. D., Simpson, J. A., & Collins, W. A. (2011). Recovering from conflict in romantic relationships: A developmental perspective. *Psychological Science, 22*, 376–383.

Samanez-Larkin, G. R., & Carstensen, L. L. (2011). Socioemotional functioning and the aging brain. In J. Decety & J. T. Cacioppo (Eds.), *Handbook of social neuroscience.* New York: Oxford University Press.

Sameroff, A. J. (2009). The transactional model. In A. J. Sameroff (Ed.), *The transactional model of development: How children and contexts shape each other.* Washington, DC: American Psychological Association.

Sameroff, A. J. (2012, in press). Conceptual issues in studying the development of self-regulation. In S. L. Olson & A. J. Sameroff (Eds.), *Biopsychosocial regulatory processes in the development of childhood behavioral problems.* New York: Cambridge University Press.

Sanders, E. (2008). Medial art and play therapy with accident survivors. In C. A. Malchiodi (Ed.), *Creative interventions with traumatized children.* New York: Guilford.

Sangree, W. H. (1989). Age and power: Life-course trajectories and age structuring of power relations in East and West Africa. In D. I. Kertzer & K. W. Schaie (Eds.), *Age structuring in comparative perspective.* Hillsdale, NJ: Erlbaum.

Sanson, A., & Rothbart, M. K. (1995). Child temperament and parenting. In M. H. Bornstein (Ed.), *Handbook of parenting* (Vol. 4). Hillsdale, NJ: Erlbaum.

Sapp, S. (2010). What have religion and spirituality to do with aging? Three approaches. *Gerontologist, 50*, 271–275.

Sasson, N. J., & Elison, J. T. (2012, in press). Eye tracking in young children with autism. *Journal of Visualized Experiments.*

Saunders, N. R., Liddelow, S. A., & Dziegielewska, K. M. (2012, in press). Barrier mechanisms in the developing brain. *Frontiers in Pharmacology.*

Savin-Williams, R. C. (2013, in press). The new sexual-minority teenager. In J. S. Kaufman & D. A. Powell (Eds.), *Sexual identities.* Thousand Oaks, CA: Sage.

Scafidi, F., & Field, T. M. (1996). Massage therapy improves behavior in neonates born to HIV-positive mothers. *Journal of Pediatric Psychology, 21*, 889–897.

Society for Research in Child Development, 38 (Serial No. 152).

Shor, E., Roelfs, D. J., Bugyi, P., & Schwartz, J. E. (2012). Meta-analysis of

Scarr, S. (1993). Biological and cultural diversity: The legacy of Darwin for development. children: The role of parental smoking. *Circulation, 123*, 292–298.

Simpkin, P., & Bolding, A. (2004). Update on nonpharmacological approaches to relieve labor pain and prevent suffering. *Journal of Midwifery and Women's Health, 49*, 489–504.

Simpkins, S. D., Delgado, M. Y., Price, C. D., Quach, A., & Starbuck, E. (2012, in press). Socioeconomic status, ethnicity, culture, and immigration: Examining the potential mechanisms underlying Mexican-origin adolescents' organized activity participation. *Developmental Psychology.*

Simpkins, S. D., Fredricks, J. A., Davis-Kean, P. E., & Eccles, J. S. (2006). Healthy mind, healthy habits: The influence of activity involvement in middle childhood. In A. C. Huston & M. N. Ripke (Eds.), *Developmental contexts in middle childhood.* New York: Cambridge University Press.

Simpson, J. A., Collins, W. A., Tran, S., & Haydon, K. C. (2007). Attachment and the experience and expression of emotions in romantic relationships: A developmental perspective. *Journal of Personality and Social Psychology, 92*, 355–367.

Singer, D., Golinkoff, R. M., & Hirsh-Pasek, K. (Eds.) (2006). *Play = learning: How play motivates and enhances children's cognitive and social-emotional growth.* New York: Oxford University Press.

Sinnott, J. D. (2003). Postformal thought and adult development: Living in balance. In J. Demick & C. Andreoletti (Eds.), *Handbook of adult development.* New York: Kluwer.

Sirsch, U., Dreher, E., Mayr, E., & Willinger, U. (2009). What does it take to be an adult in Australia? Views of adulthood in Australian adolescents, emerging adults and adults. *Journal of Adolescent Research, 24*, 275–292.

Sisson, S. B., Broyles, S. T., Baker, B. L., & Katzmarzyk, P. T. (2010). Screen time, physical activity, and overweight in U.S. youth: National Survey of Children's Health 2003. *Journal of Adolescent Health, 47*, 309–311.

Skinner, B. F. (1938). *The behavior of organisms: An experimental analysis.* New York: Appleton-Century-Crofts.

Skinner, B. F. (1957). *Verbal behavior.* New York: Appleton-Century-Crofts.

Slatcher, R. B., & Trentacosta, C. J. (2012, in press). Influences of parent and child negative emotionality on young children's everyday behaviors. *Emotion.*

Slater, A. M. (2012). Imitation in infancy: Revisiting Meltzoff & Moore's study. In A. M. Slater & P. C. Quinn (Eds.), *Developmental psychology: Revisiting the classic studies.* Thousand Oaks, CA: Sage.

Slater, A. M., Bremner, J. G., Johnson, S. P., & Hayes, R. (2011). The role of perceptual processes in infant addition/subtraction events. In L. M. Oakes, C. H. Cashon, M. Casasola, & D. H Rakison (Eds.), *Early perceptual and cognitive development.* New York: Oxford University Press.

Slater, A. M., Field, T., & Hernandez-Reif, M. (2007). The development of the senses. In A. Slater & M. Lewis (Eds.), *Introduction to infant development* (2nd ed.). New York: Oxford University Press.

Slavin, R. E. (2012). Classroom applications of cooperative learning. In K. R. Harris, S. Graham, & T. Urdan (Eds.), *APA educational psychology handbook.* Washington, DC: American Psychological Association.

Slavin, R. E. (2013). Cooperative learning and achievement: Theory and research. In I. B. Weiner & others (Eds.), *Handbook of psychology* (2nd ed., Vol. 7). New York: Wiley.

Sleet, D. A., & Mercy, J. A. (2003). Promotion of safety, security, and well-being. In M. H. Bornstein, L. Davidson, C. L. M. Keyes, & K. A. Moore (Eds.), *Well-being.* Mahwah, NJ: Erlbaum.

Sliwinski, M. J. (2011). Approaches to modeling intraindividual and interindividual facets of change for developmental research. In K. L. Fingerman, C. A. Berg, J. Smith, & T. C. Antonucci (Eds.), *Handbook of life-span development.* New York: Springer.

Slobin, D. (1972, July). Children and language: They learn the same way all around the world. *Psychology Today*, 71–76.

Slomko, H., Heo, H. J., & Einstein, F. H. (2012). Minireview: Epigenetics of obesity and diabetes in humans. *Endocrinology, 15*, 1025–1030.

Small, B. J., Dixon, R. A., McArdle, J. J., & Grimm, K. J. (2012a). Do changes in lifestyle engagement moderate cognitive decline in normal aging? Evidence from the Victoria Longitudinal Study. *Neuropsychology, 26*, 144–155.

Small, B. J., Rawson, K. S., Eisel, S., & McEvoy, C. L. (2012b). Memory and aging. In S. K. Whitbourne & M. Sliwinski (Eds.), *Wiley-Blackwell handbook of adulthood and aging.* New York: Wiley.

Small, H. (2011). *Why not? My seventy year plan for a college degree.* Franklin, TN: Carpenter's Son Publishing.

Smetana, J. G. (2010). The role of trust in adolescent-parent relationships: To trust is to tell you. In K. Rotenberg (Ed.), *Trust and trustworthiness during childhood and adolescence.* New York: Cambridge University Press.

Smetana, J. G. (2011a). *Adolescents, families, and social development: How adolescents construct their worlds.* New York: Wiley-Blackwell.

Smetana, J. G. (2011b). Adolescents' social reasoning and relationships with parents: Conflicts and coordinations within and across domains. In E. Amsel & J. Smetana (Eds.), *Adolescent vulnerabilities and opportunities: Constructivist and developmental perspectives.* New York: Cambridge University Press.

Smetana, J. G. (2013) Moral development: The social domain theory view. In P.D. Zelazo (Ed.), *Oxford handbook of developmental psychology.* New York: Oxford University Press.

Schneider, J. M., & others. (2011). Dual sensory impairment in older age. *Journal of negative psychosocial functioning. Journal of Youth and Adolescence, 40*, 839–859.

Smets, T., & others. (2010). Euthanasia in patients dying at home in Belgium: Interview study on adherence to legal standards. *British Journal of General Practice, 60*, e163–e170.

Smith, A. D. (1996). Memory. In J. E. Birren (Ed.), *Encyclopedia of gerontology* (Vol. 2). San Diego: Academic Press.

Smith, C. A., Collins, C. T., Crowther, C. A., & Levett, K. M. (2011, July 6). Acupuncture or acupressure for pain management of labor. *Cochrane Database of Systematic Reviews, 7.* CD009232.

Smith, C. A., Levett, K. M., Collins, C. T., & Jones, L. (2012). Massage, reflexology, and other manual methods for pain management. *Cochrane Database of Systematic Reviews, 15*(2), CD009290.

Smith, G. E., & others. (2009). A cognitive training program based on principles of brain plasticity: Results from the improvement in memory with plasticity-based adaptive cognitive training (IMPACT) study. *Journal of the American Geriatrics Society, 57*, 594–603.

Smith, J. B. (2009). High school organization. In D. Carr (Ed.), *Encyclopedia of the life course and human development.* Boston: Gale Cengage.

Smith, L. E., & Howard, K. S. (2008). Continuity of paternal social support and depressive symptoms among new mothers. *Journal of Family Psychology, 22*, 763–773.

Smith, P. H., Hornish, G. G., Leonard, K. E., & Cornelius, J. R. (2012, in press). Women ending marriage to a problem drinking partner decrease their own risk for problem drinking. *Addiction.*

Smith, R. A., & Davis, S. F. (2013). *Psychologist as detective* (6th ed.). Upper Saddle River, NJ: Pearson.

Smith, R. L., Rose, A. J., & Schwartz-Mette, R. A. (2010). Relational and overt aggression in childhood and adolescence: Clarifying mean-level gender differences and associations with peer acceptance. *Social Development, 19*, 243–269.

Smith, T. E. C., Polloway, E. A., Patton, J. R., & Dowdy, C. A. (2012). *Teaching students with special needs in inclusive settings* (6th ed.). Upper Saddle River, NJ: Pearson.

Smoreda, Z., & Licoppe, C. (2000). Gender-specific use of the domestic telephone. *Social Psychology Quarterly, 63*, 238–252.

Snarey, J. (1987, June). A question of morality. *Psychology Today*, pp. 6–8.

Snel, M., & others. (2012). Effects of adding exercise to a 16-week very low-calorie diet in obese, insulin-dependent type 2 diabetes mellitus patients. *Journal of Clinical Endocrinology and Metabolism.*

Snow, C. E., & Kang, J. Y. (2006). Becoming bilingual, biliterate, and bicultural. In W. Damon & R. Lerner (Eds.), *Handbook of child psychology* (6th ed.). New York: Wiley.

Snowdon, D. A. (2002). *Aging with grace: What the Nun Study teaches us about leading* *longer, healthier, and more meaningful lives.* New York: Bantam.

Snowdon, D. A. (2003). Healthy aging and dementia: Findings from the Nun Study. *Annals of Internal Medicine, 139,* 450–454.

Snyder, J. A., Scherer, H. L., & Fisher, B. S. (2012). Social organization and social ties: Their effects on sexual harassment victimization in the workplace. *Work, 42,* 137–150.

Soares, N. S., & Patel, D. R. (2012). Office screening and early identification of children with autism. *Pediatric Clinics of North America, 59,* 89–102.

Soerensen, M. (2012). Genetic variation and human longevity. *Danish Medical Journal, 59,* B4454.

Soerensen, M., & others. (2012, in press). Human longevity and variation in GH/IGF-1/insulin signaling, DNA damage signaling and repair and pro/antioxidant pathway genes: Cross sectional and longitudinal studies. *Experimental Gerontology.*

Sokol, B. W., Snjezana, H., & Muller, U. (2010). Social understanding and self-regulation: From perspective-taking to theory-of-mind. In B. Sokol, U. Muller, J. Carpendale, A. Young, & G. Iarocci (Eds.), *Self- and social-regulation.* New York: Oxford University Press.

Solana, R., & others. (2012, in press). Innate immunosenescence: Effect of aging on cells and receptors of the innate immune system in humans. *Seminars in Immunology.*

Solmeyer, A. R., McHale, S. M., Killoren, S. E., & Updegraff, K. A. (2011). Coparenting around siblings' differential treatment in Mexican-origin families. *Developmental Psychology, 25,* 251–260.

Sophian, C. (1985). Perseveration and infants' search: A comparison of two-and three-location tasks. *Developmental Psychology, 21,* 187–194.

Soto, C. J., John, O. P., Gosling, S. D., & Potter, J. (2011). Age differences in personality traits from 10 to 65: Big Five domains and facets in a large cross-sectional sample. *Journal of Personality and Social Psychology, 100,* 333–348.

South, M., & Isaacs, D. (2013). *Practical pediatrics.* New York: Elsevier.

Spangler, G., Johann, M., Ronai, Z., & Zimmermann, P. (2009). Genetic and environmental influence on attachment disorganization. *Journal of Child Psychology and Psychiatry, 50,* 952–961.

Specht, J., Egloff, B., & Schukle, S. C. (2011). Stability and change of personality across the life course: The impact of age and major life events on mean-level and rank-order stability of the Big Five. *Journal of Personality and Social Psychology, 101*(4), 862–882.

Spelke, E. S. (2004). Core knowledge. In N. Kanwisher & J. Duncan (Eds.), *Attention and Performance: Functional neuroimaging of visual cognition* (Vol. 20, pp. 29–56). Oxford, UK: Oxford University Press.

Spelke, E. S. (2011). Natural number and natural geometry. In E. Brannon & S. Dehaene (Eds.), *Space, time, and number in the brain.* New York: Oxford University Press.

Spelke, E. S., & Owsley, C. J. (1979). Intermodal exploration and knowledge in infancy. *Infant Behavior and Development, 2,* 13–28.

Spence, A. P. (1989). *Biology of human aging.* Englewood Cliffs, NJ: Prentice Hall.

Spence, J. T., & Helmreich, R. (1978). *Masculinity and femininity: Their psychological dimensions.* Austin: University of Texas Press.

Spieker, S. J., & others. (2012). Relational aggression in middle childhood: Predictors and adolescent outcomes. *Social Development, 21,* 354–375.

Spielmann, G., & others. (2011). Aerobic fitness is associated with lower proportions of senescent blood T cells in man. *Brain, Behavior, and Immunity, 25,* 1121–1129.

Spoelhof, G. D., & Elliott, B. (2012). Implementing advance directives in office practice. *American Family Physician, 85,* 461–466.

Spohn, C., & Tellis, K. (2012). The criminal justice system's response to sexual violence. *Violence Against Women, 18,* 169–192.

Spring, J. (2013). *Deculturalization and the struggle for equality* (7th ed.). New York: McGraw-Hill.

Squires, J., Pribble, L., Chen, C-I., & Pomes, M. (2013, in press). Early childhood education: Improving outcomes for young children and families. In I. B. Weiner & others (Eds.), *Handbook of psychology* (2nd ed., Vol. 7). New York: Wiley.

Sroufe, L. A., Coffino, B., & Carlson, E. A. (2010). Conceptualizing the role of early experience: Lessons from the Minnesota longitudinal study. *Developmental Review, 30,* 36–51.

Sroufe, L. A., Egeland, B., Carlson, E., & Collins, W. A. (2005). The place of early attachment in developmental context. In K. E. Grossman, K. Krossman, & E. Waters (Eds.), *The power of longitudinal attachment research: From infancy and childhood to adulthood.* New York: Guilford.

Sroufe, L. A., Waters, E., & Matas, L. (1974). Contextual determinants of infant affectional response. In M. Lewis & L. Rosenblum (Eds.), *Origins of fear.* New York: Wiley.

Stanford Center for Longevity. (2011). *Experts consensus on brain health.* Retrieved April 30, 2011, from http://longevity.stanford.edu/my mind/cognitiveagingstatement

Stanovich, K. E., West, R. F., & Toplak, M. E. (2012). Judgment and decision making in adolescence: Separating intelligence from rationality. In V. F. Reyna (Ed.), *The adolescent brain.* Washington, DC: American Psychological Association.

Starr, C. (2011). *Biology* (8th ed.). Boston: Cengage.

Starr, C., Taggart, R., Evers, C., & Starr, L. (2013). *Evolution of life* (13th ed.). Boston: Cengage.

Starr, L. R., & Davila, J. (2009). Clarifying co-rumination: Associations with internalizing symptoms and romantic involvement among adolescent girls. *Journal of Adolescence, 32,* 19–37.

Starr, L. R., & others. (2012, in press). Love hurts (in more ways than one): Specificity of psychological symptoms as predictors and consequences of romantic activity among early adolescent girls. *Journal of Clinical Psychology.*

Staszewski, J. (Ed.) (2013, in press). *Expertise and skill acquisition: The impact of William C. Chase.* New York: Taylor & Francis.

Staudinger, U. M. (1996). Psychologische Produktivitat und Selbstenfaltung im Alter. In M. M. Baltes & L. Montada (Eds.), *Produktives Leben im Alter.* Frankfurt: Campus.

Staudinger, U. M., & Gluck, J. (2011). Psychological wisdom research. *Annual Review of Psychology* (Vol. 62). Palo Alto, CA: Annual Reviews.

Staudinger, U. M., & Jacobs, C. B. (2010). Life-span perspectives on positive personality development in adulthood and old age. In R. M. Lerner, W. F. Overton, A. M. Freund, & M. E. Lamb (Eds.), *Handbook of life-span development.* New York: Wiley.

Steel, A. J., & Sutcliffe, A. (2010). Long-term health implications for children conceived by IVF/ ICSI. *Human Fertility, 12,* 21–27.

Steele, J., Waters, E., Crowell, J., & Treboux, D. (1998, June). *Self-report measures of attachment: Secure bonds to other attachment measures and attachment theory.* Paper presented at the meeting of the International Society for the Study of Personal Relationships, Saratoga Springs, NY.

Stein, P. K., & others. (2012, in press). Caloric restriction may reverse age-related autonomic decline in humans. *Aging Cell.*

Steinberg, L. (2012, in press). Adolescent risk-taking: A social neuroscience perspective. In E. Amsel & J. Smetana (Eds.), *Adolescent vulnerabilities and opportunities: Constructivist developmental perspectives.* New York: Cambridge University Press.

Steinberg, L. (2013, in press). How should the science of adolescent brain development inform legal policy? In J. Bhabha (Ed.), *Coming of age: A new framework for adolescent rights.* Philadelphia: University of Pennsylvania Press.

Steinberg, L., & Collins, W. A. (2011). Psychosocial development and behavior. In M. Fisher & others (Eds.), *Textbook of adolescent health care.* Elk Grove Village, IL: American Academy of Pediatrics.

Steinberg, L. D., & Silk, J. S. (2002). Parenting adolescents. In M. Bornstein (Ed.), *Handbook of parenting* (2nd ed., Vol. I). Mahwah, NJ: Erlbaum.

Cengage.

Szinovacz, M.E. (2011). Introduction: The aging workforce: Challenges for societies, employers, and older workers. *Journal of Aging and Social Policy, 23,* 95–100.

Szwedo, D. E., Mikami, A. Y., & Allen, J. P. (2011). Qualities of peer relations on social networking websites: Predictions from negative mother-teen interactions. *Journal of Research on Adolescence, 21,* 595–607.

social psychology. Thousand Oaks, CA: Sage.

Taylor, S. E., & others. (2000). Biobehavioral responses to stress in females: Tend-and-befriend, not fight-or-flight. *Psychological Review, 107,* 411–429.

te Velde, S. J., & others. (2012). Energy balance-related behaviors associated with overweight and obesity in preschool children: A systematic review of prospective studies. *Obesity Reviews, 13* (Suppl. 1), S56–S74.

(Eds.), *Handbook of child psychology* (6th ed.). New York: Wiley.

Thompson, R. A. (2011). The emotionate child. In D. Cicchetti & G.I. Roissman (Eds.), *The origins and organization of adaptation and maladaptation. Minnesota Symposium on Child Psychology* (Vol. 36). New York: Wiley.

Thompson, R. A. (2012, in press). Whither the preoperational child? Toward a life-span moral development theory. *Child Development.*

Steiner, J. E. (1979). Human facial expressions in response to taste and smell stimulation. In H. Reese & L. Lipsitt (Eds.), *Advances in Child Development and Behavior, 13,* 257–295.

Steiner, N. J., Sheldrick, R. C., Gotthelf, D., & Perrin, E. C. (2011). Computer-based attention training in schools for children with attention deficit hyperactivity disorder: A preliminary trial. *Clinical Pediatrics, 50*(7), 615–622.

the world by the year 2000: In C. A. Nelson (Ed.), *Basic and applied perspectives on learning, cognition, and development.* Minneapolis: University of Minnesota Press.

Stevenson, H. W. (2000). Middle childhood: Education and schooling. In A. Kazdin (Ed.), *Encyclopedia of psychology.* Washington, DC, & New York: American Psychological Association and Oxford University Press.

Stevenson, H. W., Hofer, B. K., & Randel, B. (1999). *Middle childhood: Education and*

Stone, H. F., Zhu, Z., Thach, T. Q., & Ruegg, C. L. (2011). Characterization of diffusion and duration of action of a new botulinum toxin type A formulation. *Toxicon, 58,* 159–167.

Stowell, J. R., Robles, T., & Kane, H. S. (2013, in press). Psychoneuroimmunology: Mechanisms, individual differences, and interventions. In I. B. Weiner & others (Eds.), *Handbook of psychology* (2nd ed., Vol. 9). New York: Wiley.

Thompson, R. A. (2013). Attachment and its development: Precis and prospect. In P. Zelazo (Ed.), *Oxford handbook of developmental psychology.* New York: Oxford University Press.

Thompson, R. A. (2013b, in press). Interpersonal relations. In A. Ben-Arieh, I. Frones, F. Cases, & J. Korbin (Eds.), *Handbook of child well-being.* New York: Springer.

Thompson, R. A. (2013c, in press). Relationships, regulation, and development. In R. M. Lerner (Ed.), *Handbook of child psychology* (7th ed.). New York: Wiley.

Thompson, R. A. (2013d, in press). Socialization of emotion regulation in the family. In J. Gross (Ed.), *Handbook of emotion regulation* (2nd ed.). New York: Guilford.

Thompson, R. A., & Murachver, T. (2001). Predicting gender from electronic discourse. *British Journal of Social Psychology, 40,* 193–208.

Thompson, R. A., & Virmani, E. A. (2010). Self and personality. In M. H. Bornstein (Ed.), *Handbook of cultural developmental science.* New York: Psychology Press.

Thorton, A., & Camburn, D. (1989). Religious participation and sexual behavior and attitudes. *Journal of Marriage and the Family, 49,* 117–128.

Tikotzky, L., & Shaashua, L. (2012). Infant sleep and early parental sleep-related cognitions predict sleep in pre-school children. *Sleep Medicine, 13,* 185–192.

Tincoff, R., & Jusczyk, P. W. (2012, in press). Six-month-olds comprehend words that refer to parts of the body. *Infancy.*

Tinetti, M. E. (2012). The retreat from advanced care planning. *JAMA, 307,* 915–916.

To, W. W. (2012) Prenatal diagnosis and assessment of facial clefts: Where are we now? Hong Kong Medical Journal, 18, 146–152.

Tobler, A. L., & Komro, K. A. (2010). Trajectories of parental monitoring and communication and effects on drug use among urban young adolescents. *Journal of Adolescent Health, 46,* 560–568.

Tolani, N., & Brooks-Gunn, J. (2008). Family support, international trends. In M. M. Haith & J. B. Benson (Eds.), *Encyclopedia of infant and early childhood development.* Oxford, UK: Elsevier.

Tolou-Shams, M., Hadley, W., Conrad, S. M., & Brown, L. K. (2012). The role of family affect in juvenile drug court offenders' substance use and HIV risk. *Journal of Child and Family Studies, 21,* 449–456.

Toma, C., & others. (2012, in press). Neurotransmitter systems and neurotrophic factors in autism: Association study of 37 genes suggests involvement of DDC. *World Journal of Biology.*

Tomasello, M. (2006). Acquiring linguistic constructions. In W. Damon & R. Lerner (Eds.), *Handbook of child psychology* (6th ed.). New York: Wiley.

Tomasello, M. (2011). Language development. In U. Goswami (Ed.), *Wiley-Blackwell handbook of childhood cognitive development* (2nd ed.). New York: Wiley.

Tomasello, M., & Hamann, K. (2012). Collaboration in young children. *Quarterly Journal of Experimental Psychology, 65,* 1–12.

Tompkins, G. E. (2013). *Language arts* (8th ed.). Boston: Allyn & Bacon.

Tortora, G. J., Funke, B. R., & Case, C. L. (2013). *Microbiology* (11th ed.). Upper Saddle River, NJ: Pearson.

Trasande, L., & Elbel, B. (2012). The economic burden placed on healthcare systems by childhood obesity. *Expert review of Pharmacoeconomics and Outcomes, 12,* 39–45.

Trasande, L., & others. (2010). Translating knowledge about environmental health to practitioners: Are we doing enough? *Mount Sinai Journal of Medicine, 77,* 114–123.

Trehub, S. E., Schneider, B. A., Thorpe, L. A., & Judge, P. (1991). Observational measures of auditory sensitivity in early infancy. *Developmental Psychology, 27,* 40–49.

Tremblay, M. S., & others. (2012). Canadian sedentary behavior guidelines for the early years (0–4 years). *Applied Physiology, Nutrition, and Metabolism, 37,* 370–380.

Trickett, P. K., Negriff, S., Ji, J., & Perkins, M. (2011). Child maltreatment and adolescent development. *Journal of Research on Adolescence, 21,* 3–20.

Triulzi, F., Manganaro, L., & Volpe, P. (2011). Fetal magnetic resonance imaging: indications, study protocols, and safety. *La Radiologia Medica, 116,* 337–350.

Trommsdorff, G. (2012). A social change and human development perspective on the value of children. In S. Bekman & A. Aksu-Koc (Eds.), *Perspectives on human development, families, and culture.* New York: Cambridge University Press.

Trost, S. G., Fees, B., & Dzewaltowski, D. (2008). Feasibility and efficacy of "move and learn" physical activity curriculum in preschool children. *Journal of Physical Activity and Health, 5,* 88–103.

Tucker, J. S., & others. (2012). Resisting smoking when a best friend smokes: Do intrapersonal and contextual factors matter? *Journal of Research on Adolescence, 22,* 113–122.

Tull, M. T., Weiss, N. H., Adams, C. E., & Gratz, K. L. (2012, in press). The contribution of emotion regulation difficulties to risky sexual behavior within a sample of patients in residential substance abuse treatment. *Addictive Behaviors.*

Tun, P. A., & Lachman, M. E. (2010). The association between computer use and cognition across adulthood: Use it so you won't lose it? *Psychology and Aging, 25*(3), 560–568.

Turiano, N. A., Pitzer, L., Armour, C., Karlamangia, A., Ryff, C. D., & Mroczek, D. K. (2012). Personality trait level and change as predictors of health outcomes: Findings of a national study of Americans (MIDUS). *Journals of Gerontology B: Psychological Sciences and Social Sciences, 67,* 4–12.

Turkeltaub, P. E., Gareau, L., Flowers, D. L., Zeffiro, T. A., & Eden, G. F. (2003). Development of neural mechanisms for reading. *Nature Neuroscience, 6,* 767–773.

Turnbull, A., Rutherford-Turnbull, H., Wehmeyer, M. L., & Shogren, K. A. (2013). *Exceptional lives* (7th ed.). Upper Saddle River, NJ: Pearson.

Turner, B. F. (1982). Sex-related differences in aging. In B. B. Wolman (Ed.). *Handbook of developmental psychology.* Englewood Cliffs, NJ: Prentice Hall.

Turner, G. R., & Spreng, R. N. (2012, in press). Executive functions and neurocognitive aging: Dissociable patterns of brain activity. *Neurobiology of Aging.*

Turner, H. A., & others. (2012). Family context, victimization, and child trauma symptoms: Variations in safe, stable, and nurturing relationships during early and middle childhood. *American Journal of Orthopsychiatry, 82,* 209–219.

Tyas, S. L., & others. (2007). Transitions to mild cognitive impairments, dementia, and death: Findings from the Nun Study. *American Journal of Epidemiology, 165,* 1231–1238.

U

Uher, R., & Rutter, M. (2012). Classification of feeding and eating disorders: Review of evidence and proposals for ICD-11. *World Psychiatry, 11,* 80–92.

Umana-Taylor, A. J., Wong, J. J., Gonzalez, N. A., & Dumka, L. E. (2012, in press). Ethnic identity and gender as moderators of the association between discrimination and academic adjustment among Mexican-origin adolescents. *Journal of Adolescence.*

UNAIDS. (2011). *AIDS at 30: Nations at a crossroads.* Geneva, SWIT: United Nations.

Underwood, M. K. (2011). Aggression. In M. K. Underwood & L. H. Rosen (Eds.), *Social development.* New York: Wiley.

Underwood, M. K., & others. (2012). The BlackBerry project: Capturing the content of adolescents' text messaging. *Developmental Psychology, 48,* 295–302.

UNICEF. (2004). *The state of the world's children 2004.* Geneva, SWIT: UNICEF.

UNICEF. (2007). *The state of the world's children 2007.* Geneva, SWIT: UNICEF

UNICEF. (2012). *The state of the world's children 2012.* Geneva, SWIT: UNICEF.

UNICEF. (2013). *The state of the world's children 2013.* Geneva, SWIT: UNICEF.

United Nations. (2002). *Improving the quality of life of girls.* New York: United Nations.

Updegraff, K. A., Kim, J-Y., Killoren, S. E., & Thayer, S. M. (2010). Mexican American parents' involvement in adolescents' peer relationships: Exploring the role of culture and adolescents' peer experiences. *Journal of Research on Adolescence, 20,* 65–87.

Urdan, T. (2012). Factors affecting the motivation and achievement of immigrant students. In K. R. Harris, S. Graham, & T. Urdan (Eds.), *APA handbook of educational psychology*. Washington, DC: American Psychological Association.

Ursache, A., Blair, C., & Raver, C. C. (2012). The promotion of self-regulation as a means of enhancing school readiness and early achievement in children at risk for school failure. *Child Development Perspectives, 6*, 122–128.

U.S. Census Bureau. (2008). *Death statistics.* Washington, DC: U.S. Census Bureau.

U.S. Census Bureau. (2010a). *People.* Washington DC: U.S. Department of Labor.

U.S. Census Bureau. (2010b). *Statistical abstracts of the United States.* Washington, DC: U.S. Government Printing Office.

U.S. Census Bureau. (2011a). *Births, deaths, marriages, divorces: Life expectancy.* Table 102. Author: U.S. Department of Labor.

U.S. Census Bureau (2011b). Census Bureau reports 64 percent increase in the number of children living with a grandparent over the last two decades. Retrieved September 2, 2011, from www.census.gov/prod/2011pubs/p.70-126.pdf

U.S. Census Bureau. (2011c, September). Income, poverty, and health insurance coverage in the United States: 2010. *Current Population Survey, Annual Social and Economic Supplement,* P60-239.

U.S. Census Bureau. (2011d, May 8). *Mother's day: May 8, 2011.* Retrieved August 28, 2011, from www.census.gov/newsroom/releases/archives/facts_for_features_special_editions/cb

U.S. Census Bureau. (2011e). *People.* Washington, DC: U.S. Department of Labor.

U.S. Census Bureau. (2012). *The 2012 statistical abstract.* Washington, DC: U.S. Department of Labor.

U.S. Center for Health Statistics. (2011). *Births.* Atlanta: Centers for Disease Control and Prevention.

U.S. Department of Energy. (2001). *The human genome project.* Washington. DC: U.S. Department of Energy.

U.S. Department of Health and Human Services. (2010). *Child maltreatment 2009.* Washington, DC: Author.

U.S. Department of Health and Human Services. (2012). *Folic acid.* Retrieved June 12, 2012, from www.cdc.gov/ncbddd/folicacid/

Utz, R. L., Caserta, M., & Lund, D. (2012). Grief, depressive symptoms, and physical health among recently bereaved spouses. *Gerontologist, 52*, 460–471.

V

Vacca, J. A., Vacca, R. T., Gove, M. K., Burkey, L. C., Lenhart, L. A., & McKeon, C. A. (2012). *Reading and learning to read* (8th ed.). Boston: Allyn & Bacon.

Vaillant, G. E. (1977). *Adaptation to life.* Boston: Little, Brown.

Vaillant, G. E. (2002). *Aging well.* Boston: Little, Brown.

Vaish, A., Carpenter, M., & Tomasello, M. (2010). Young children selectively avoid helping people with harmful intentions. *Child Development, 81*, 1661–1669.

Valenzuela, C. F., Morton, R. A., Diaz, M. R., & Topper, L. (2012, in press). Does moderate drinking harm the fetal brain? Insights from animal models. *Trends in Neuroscience.*

Valkenburg, P. M., & Peter, J. (2011). On-line communication among adolescents: An integrated model of its attraction, opportunities, and risks. *Journal of Adolescent Health, 48*, 121–127.

van Alphen, J. E., Donker, G. A., & Marquet, R. L. (2010). Requests for euthanasia in general practice before and after implementation of the Dutch Euthanasia Act. *British Journal of General Practice, 60*, 263–267.

Van Beveren, T. T. (2012, January). *Personal conversation.* Richardson, TX: Department of Psychology, University of Texas at Dallas.

van Harmelen, A. L., & others. (2010). Child abuse and negative explicit and automatic self-associations: The cognitive scars of emotional maltreatment. *Behavior Research and Therapy, 48*, 486–494.

Van Norstrand, D.W., & others. (2012). Connexin43 mutation causes heterogeneous gap junction loss and sudden infant death. *Circulation, 125*, 474–481.

Van Ryzin, M. J., Carlson, E. A., & Sroufe, L. A. (2011). Attachment discontinuity in a high-risk sample. *Attachment and Human Development, 13*, 381–401.

Van Ryzin, M. J., & Dishion, T. J. (2012, in press). The impact of a family-centered intervention on the ecology of adolescent antisocial behavior: Modeling developmental sequelae and trajectories during adolescence. *Development and Psychopathology.*

Van Wesemael, Y., & others. (2011). Process and outcomes of euthanasia requests under the Belgian Act on Euthanasia: A nationwide survey. *Journal of Pain and Symptom Management, 42*, 721–733.

Vance, D. E., & others. (2012). Neuroplasticity and successful cognitive aging: A brief overview for nursing. *Journal of Neuroscience Nursing, 44*, 218–227.

Vandell, D. L., & others. (2010). Do effects of early childcare extend to age 15 years? From the NICHD Study of Early Child Care and Youth Development. *Child Development, 81*, 737–756.

Vanhalst, J., Luyckx, K., Raes, F., & Goossens, L. (2012). Loneliness and depression symptoms: The mediating and moderating role of uncontrollable ruminative thoughts. *Journal of Psychology, 146*, 259–276.

VanKim, N. A., & Laska, M. N. (2012, in press). Socioeconomic disparities in emerging adult weight and weight behaviors. *American Journal of Health Behavior.*

Vasquez, M. J., & Berg, O. R. (2012). The Baby-Friendly journey in a U.S. public hospital. *Journal of Perinatal and Neonatal Nursing, 26*, 37–46.

Vaughan Van Hecke, A., & others. (2012). Infant responding to joint attention, executive processes, and self-regulation in preschool children. *Infant Development and Behavior, 35*, 303–311.

Vazsonyi, A. T., & Huang, L. (2010). Where self-control comes from: On the development of self-control and its relationship to deviance over time. *Developmental Psychology, 46*, 245–257.

Velez, C. E., Wolchik, S. A., Tein, J. Y., & Sandler, I. (2011). Protecting children from the consequences of divorce: A longitudinal study of the effects of parenting on children's coping responses. *Child Development, 82*, 244–257.

Venners, S. A., & others. (2004). Paternal smoking and pregnancy loss: A prospective study using a biomarker of pregnancy. *American Journal of Epidemiology, 159*, 993–1001.

Ventura, S. J., & Hamilton, B. E. (2011, February). U.S. teenage birth rate resumes decline. *NCHS Data Brief, 58*, 1–3.

Verster, J. C., van Duin, D., Volkerts, E. R., Schreueder, A. H., & Verbaten, M. N. (2002). Alcohol hangover effects on memory-functioning and vigilance performance after an evening of binge drinking. *Neuropsychopharmacology, 28*, 740–746.

Vesco, K. K., & others. (2012, in press). Healthy Moms, a randomized trial to promote and evaluate weight maintenance among obese pregnant women: Study design and rationale. *Contemporary Clinical Trials.*

Viachantoni, A. (2012, in press). Financial inequality and gender in older people. *Maturitas.*

Villanueva, C. M., & Buriel, R. (2010). Speaking on behalf of others: A qualitative study of the perceptions and feelings of adolescent Latina language brokers. *Journal of Social Issues, 66*, 197–210.

Vincent, H. K., Raiser, S. N., & Vincent, K. R. (2012). The aging musculoskeletal system and obesity-related considerations with exercise. *Aging Research and Reviews, 11*, 361–373.

Vinik, J., Almas, A., & Grusec, J. (2011). Mothers' knowledge of what distresses and comforts their children predicts children's coping, empathy, and prosocial behavior. *Parenting: Science and Practice, 11*, 56–71.

Vitaro, F., Boivin, M., & Bukowski, W. M. (2009). The role of friendship in child and adolescent psychological development. In K. H. Rubin, W. M. Bukowski, & B. Laursen (Eds.), *Handbook of peer interaction, relationships, and groups.* New York: Guilford.

Vittrup, B., Holden, G. W., & Buck, M. (2006). Attitudes predict the use of physical punishment: A prospective study of the emergence of disciplinary practices. *Pediatrics, 117*, 2055–2064.

Volbrecht, M. M., & Goldsmith, H. H. (2010). Early temperamental and family predictors of shyness and anxiety. *Developmental Psychology, 46,* 1192–1205.

Von Polier, G. G., Vioet, T. D., & Herpertz-Dahlmann, B. (2012). ADHD and delinquency—A developmental perspective. *Behavioral Sciences and the Law, 30,* 121–139.

Vong, K-I. (2012). Play—A multimodal manifestation in kindergarten education in China. *Early Years: An International Journal of Research and Development, 32*(1), 35–48.

Voorpostel, M., & Blieszner, R. (2008). Intergenerational solidarity and support between adult siblings. *Journal of Marriage and the Family, 70,* 157–167.

Votavova, H., & others. (2012, in press). Deregulation of gene expression induced by environmental tobacco smoke exposure in pregnancy. *Nicotine and Tobacco Research.*

Votruba-Drzal, E., Coley, R. L., & Chase-Lansdale, P. L. (2004). Child care and low-income children's development: Direct and moderated effects. *Child Development, 75,* 296–312.

Vrangalova, Z., & Savin-Williams, R. C. (2013). Mostly heterosexual and mostly gay/lesbian: New sexual orientation identities and the sexual orientation continuum. *Archives of Sexual Behavior.*

Vreeman, R. C., & Carroll, A. E. (2007). A systematic review of school-based interventions to prevent bullying. *Archives of Pediatric and Adolescent Medicine, 161,* 78–88.

Vurpillot, E. (1968). The development of scanning strategies and their relation to visual differentiation. *Journal of Experimental Child Psychology, 6,* 632–650.

Vygotsky, L. S. (1962). *Thought and language.* Cambridge, MA: MIT Press.

W

Waasdorp, T. E., Bradshaw, C. P., & Leaf, P. J. (2012). The impact of schoolwide positive behavioral interventions and supports on bullying and peer rejection: A randomized controlled effectiveness trial. *Archives of Pediatric and Adolescent Medicine, 166,* 149–156.

Wachs, T. D., & Bates, J. E. (2010). Temperament. In J. G. Bremner & T. D. Wachs (Eds.), *Wiley-Blackwell handbook of infant development* (2nd ed.). New York: Wiley.

Waddell, L. (2012). The power of vitamins. *Journal of Family Health Care, 22,* 16–20, 22–25.

Wagner, G., & others. (2012). Antihypertensive treatment and risk of dementia: A retrospective database study. *International Journal of Clinical Pharmacology and Therapy, 50,* 195–201.

Wagner, L., & Hoff, E. (2013). Language development. In I. B. Weiner & others (Eds.), *Handbook of psychology* (2nd ed.). New York: Wiley.

Waite, L. J. (2009). Marriage. In D. Carr (Ed.), *Encyclopedia of the life course and human development.* Boston: Gale Cengage.

Wakefield, J. D. (2012). Should prolonged grief be reclassified as a mental disorder in DSM-5?: Reconsidering the empirical and conceptual arguments for complicated grief disorder. *Journal of Nervous and Mental Disease, 200,* 499–511.

Waldinger, R. J., & Schulz, M. C. (2010). What's love got to do with it? Social functioning, perceived health, and daily happiness in married octogenarians. *Psychology and Aging, 25,* 422–431.

Waldinger, R. J., Vaillant, G. E., & Orav, E. J. (2007). Childhood sibling relationships as a predictor of major depression in adulthood: A 30-year prospective study. *American Journal of Psychiatry, 164,* 949–954.

Waldron, J. J., & Dieser, R. B. (2010). Perspectives of fitness and health in college men and women. *Journal of College Student Development, 51,* 65–78.

Walker, L. (1982). The sequentiality of Kohlberg's stages of moral development. *Child Development, 53,* 1130–1136.

Walker, L. J. (2004). Progress and prospects in the psychology of moral development. *Merrill-Palmer Quarterly, 50,* 546–557.

Walker, L. J., & Frimer, J. A. (2011). The science of moral development. In M. K. Underwood & L. Rosen (Eds.), *Social development.* New York: Guilford.

Waller, E. M., & Rose, A. J. (2010). Adjustment trade-offs of co-rumination in mother-adolescent relationships. *Journal of Adolescence, 33,* 487–497.

Wallin, K., & others. (2012, in press). Midlife rheumatoid arthritis increases the risk of cognitive impairment two decades later: A population-based study. *Journal of Alzheimer's Disease.*

Walsh, R. (2011). Lifestyle and mental health. *American Psychologist, 66*(7), 579–592.

Walton, N. M., & others. (2012). Adult neurogenesis transiently generates oxidative stress. *PLoS One, 7*(4), e35264.

Wang, H., & others. (2012). Blood folate is associated with asymptomatic or partially symptomatic Alzheimer's disease in the Nun Study. *Journal of Alzheimer's Disease, 28,* 637–645.

Wang, M. (2012). Retirement: An adult development perspective. In S. K. Whitbourne & M. J. Sliwinski (Eds.), *Wiley-Blackwell handbook of adult development and aging.* New York: Wiley.

Wang, M., Zang, M., Chen, X., & Zhang, H. (2009). Detecting genes and gene-gene interactions for age-related macular degeneration with a forest-based approach. *Statistics in Biopharmaceutical Research, 1,* 424–440.

Wang, N., & others. (2012). Effects of television viewing on body fatness among Chinese children and adolescents. *Chinese Medical Journal, 125,* 1500–1503.

Ward, A., & others. (2012). Prevalence of apolipoprotein E4 genotype and homozygotes (APOEe4/4) among patients diagnosed with Alzheimer's disease: A systematic review and meta-analysis. *Neuroepidemiology.*

Wardlaw, G. M., & Smith, A. M. (2012). *Contemporary nutrition: A functional approach* (2nd ed.). New York: McGraw-Hill.

Waring, J. D., Addis, D. R., & Kensinger, E. A. (2012, in press). Effects of aging on neural connectivity underlying selective memory for emotional scenes. *Neurobiology of Aging.*

Warr, P. (2004). Work, well-being, and mental health. In J. Baring, E. K. Kelloway, & M. R. Frone (Eds.), *Handbook of work stress.* Thousand Oaks, CA: Sage.

Warren, M. P. (2007). Historical perspectives on postmenopausal hormone therapy: Defining the right dose and duration. *Mayo Clinic Proceedings, 82,* 219–226.

Watamura, S. E., Phillips, D. A., Morrissey, D. A., McCartney, T. W., & Bub, K. (2011). Double jeopardy: Poorer social-emotional outcomes for children in the NICHD SECCYD who experience home and child-care environments that convey risk. *Child Development, 82,* 48–65.

Waterman, A. S. (1985). Identity in the context of adolescent psychology. In A. S. Waterman (Ed.), *Identity in adolescence: Processes and contents.* San Francisco: Jossey-Bass.

Waterman, A. S. (1992). Identity as an aspect of optimal psychological functioning. In G. R. Adams, T. P. Gullotta, & R. Montemayor (Eds.), *Adolescent identity formation.* Thousand Oaks, CA: Sage.

Watson, D. (2012). Objective tests as instruments of psychological theory and research. In H. Cooper (Ed.), *APA handbook of research methods in psychology.* Washington, DC: American Psychological Association.

Watson, J. A., Randolph, S. M., & Lyons, J. L. (2005). African-American grandmothers as health educators in the family. *International Journal of Aging and Human Development, 60,* 343–356.

Watson, R. (2009). Luxembourg is to allow euthanasia from 1 April. *British Medical Journal, 338,* 1248.

Watts, C., & Zimmerman, C. (2002). Violence against women: Global scope and magnitude. *Lancet, 359,* 1232–1237.

Waugh, C. K., & Gronlund, N. E. (2013). *Assessment of student achievement* (10th ed.). Upper Saddle River, NJ: Pearson.

Waxman, S., & Goswami, U. (2012). Acquiring language: Learning the spoken and written word. In S. Pauen & M. Bornstein (Eds.), *Early child development and later outcome.* New York: Cambridge University Press.

Way, N., & Silverman, L. R. (2012). The quality of friendships across adolescence: Patterns across context, culture, and age. In P. K. Kerig, M. S. Schulz, & S. T. Hauser (Eds.), *Adolescence and beyond.* New York: Oxford University Press.

Wayne, A. (2011). Commentary in interview: Childhood cancers in transition. Retrieved April 12, 2011, from http://home.ccr.cancer. gov/connections/2010/Vol4_No2/clinic2.asp

Weaver, F. M., & others. (2012). Randomized trial of deep brain stimulation for Parkinson disease: Thirty-six-month outcomes. *Neurology, 79,* 55–65.

Webb, L. D., Metha, A., & Jordan, K. F. (2013). *Foundations of American education* (7th ed.). Upper Saddle River, NJ: Pearson.

Webster, N. S., & Worrell, F. C. (2008). Academically talented students' attitudes toward service in the community. *Gifted Child Quarterly, 52,* 170–179.

Wechsler, H., Davenport, A., Sowdall, G., Moetykens, B., & Castillo, S. (1994). Health and behavioral consequences of binge drinking in college. *Journal of the American Medical Association, 272,* 1672–1677.

Weikert, D. P. (1993). Long-term positive effects in the Perry Preschool Head Start Program. Unpublished data, High Scope Foundation, Ypsilanti, MI.

Weinraub, M., & others. (2012, in press). Patterns of developmental change in infants' nighttime sleep awakenings from 6 through 36 months of age. *Developmental Psychology.*

Weir, J. M., Zakama, A., & Rao, U. (2012). Developmental risk I: Depression and the developing brain. *Child and Adolescent Psychiatric Clinics of North America, 21,* 237–249.

Welch, K. J. (2012). *Family life now census update* (2nd ed.). Upper Saddle River, NJ: Pearson.

Wellman, H. M. (2011). Developing a theory of mind. In U. Goswami (Ed.), *Wiley-Blackwell handbook of childhood cognitive development* (2nd ed.). New York: Wiley.

Wellman, H. M., Cross, D., & Watson, J. (2001). Meta-analysis of theory-of-mind development: The truth about false belief. *Child Development, 72,* 655–684.

Wells, E. M., & others. (2011). Body burdens of mercury, lead, selenium, and copper among Baltimore newborns. *Environmental Research, 111,* 411–417.

Wenger, N. S., & others. (2003). The quality of medical care provided to vulnerable community-dwelling older patients. *Annals of Internal Medicine, 139,* 740–747.

Wensink, M. J., van Heemst, D., Rozing, M. P., & Westendorp, R. G. (2012). The maintenance gap: A new theoretical perspective on the evolutionary theory of aging. *Biogerontology, 13,* 197–201.

Wentzel, K. R. (2013). School adjustment. In I. B. Weiner & others (Eds.), *Handbook of psychology* (2nd ed., Vol. 7). New York: Wiley.

Wentzel, K. R., & Asher, S. R. (1995). The academic lives of neglected, rejected, popular and controversial children. *Child Development, 66,* 754–763.

Wentzel, K. R., Barry, C. M., & Caldwell, K. A. (2004). Friendships in middle schools: Influences on motivation and school adjustment. *Journal of Educational Psychology, 96,* 195–203.

Wertsch, J. V. (2007). Mediation. In H. Daniels, J. Wertsch, & M. Cole (Eds.), *The Cambridge companion to Vygotsky.* New York: Cambridge University Press.

West, S. K., & others. (2010). Older drivers and failure to stop at red lights. *Journals of Gerontology A: Biological Sciences and Medical Sciences, 65A,* 179–183.

Westerhof, G. J. (2009). Age identity. In D. Carr (Ed.), *Encyclopedia of the life course and human development.* Boston: Gale Cengage.

Westerman, G., Thomas, M. S. C., & Karmiloff-Smith, A. (2011). Neuroconstructivism. In U. Goswami (Ed.), *Wiley-Blackwell handbook of childhood cognitive development* (2nd ed.). New York: Wiley.

Westlake, C., Evangelista, L. S., Stromberg, A., Ter-Galstanyan, A., Vazirani, S., & Dracup, K. (2007). Evaluation of a web-based education and counseling pilot for older heart failure patients. *Progress in Cardiovascular Nursing, 22,* 20–26.

Wetherell, J. L. (2012). Complicated grief therapy as a new treatment approach. *Dialogues in Clinical Neuroscience, 14,* 159–166.

Whaley, L. (2013, in press). Syntactic typology. In J. J. Song (Ed.), *Oxford handbook of linguistic typology.* New York: Oxford University Press.

Whaley, S. E., Jiang, L., Gomez, J., & Jenks, E. (2011). Literacy promotion for families participating in the Women, Infants, and Children program. *Pediatrics, 127,* 454–461.

Whaley, S. E., Ritchie, L. D., Spector, P., & Gomez, J. (2012, in press). Revised WIC food package improves diets of WIC families. *Journal of Nutrition and Education Behavior.*

Wheeler, A., & others. (2011). Caucasian infants scan own- and other-race faces differently. *PLoS One, 6,* e18621.

Whitbourne, S. K., & Sliwinski, M. (Eds.). (2012). *Wiley-Blackwell handbook of adulthood and aging.* New York: Wiley.

White, B. A., & Kistner, J. A. (2011). Biased self-perceptions, peer rejection, and aggression in children. *Journal of Abnormal Child Psychology, 39,* 645–656.

White, J. W. (2001). Aggression and gender. In J. Worell (Ed.), *Encyclopedia of gender and women.* San Diego: Academic Press.

White, L. (1994). Stepfamilies over the life course: Social support. In A. Booth and J. Dunne (Eds.), *Stepfamilies: Who benefits and who does not.* Hillsdale, NJ: Erlbaum.

Whitehead, B. D., & Popenoe, D. (2003). *The state of our Unions.* Piscataway, NJ: The National Marriage Project, Rutgers University.

Whiteman, S. D., McHale, S. M., & Soli, A. (2011). Theoretical perspectives on sibling relationships. *Journal of Family Theory and Review, 3,* 124–139.

WIC New York. (2011). *The new look of the women, infants, and children (WIC) program.* Retrieved July 30, 2009, from www.health. state.ny.us/prevention/nutrition/wic/the_ new_look_of_wic.htm

Widman, L., & McNulty, J. K. (2010). Sexual narcissism and the prepetration of sexual aggression. *Archives of Sexual Behavior, 39,* 939–946.

Widom, C. S., Czaja, S. J., Bentley, T., & Johnson, M. S. (2012, in press). A prospective investigation of physical health outcomes in abused and neglected children: New findings from a 30-year follow-up. *American Journal of Public Health.*

Widom, C. S., & Nikulina, V. (2012). Long-term consequences of child neglect in low-income families. In V. Maholmes & R. B. King (Eds.), *Oxford handbook of poverty and child development.* New York: Oxford University Press.

Wiesel, A., & others. (2011). Maternal occupational exposure to ionizing radiation and birth defects. *Radiation and Environmental Biophysics, 50,* 325–328.

Wight, G., Cummings, J. R., Karlamangia, A. S., & Aneshensei, C. S. (2009). Urban neighborhood context and change in depressive symptoms in late life. *Journals of Gerontology B: Psychological Sciences and Social Sciences, 64,* 247–251.

Wilcox, S., Sharpe, P. A., Parra-Medina, D., Granner, M., & Hutto, B. (2011). A randomized trial of a diet and exercise intervention for overweight and obese women from economically disadvantaged neighborhoods: Sisters Taking Action for Real Success (STARS). *Contemporary Clinical Trials, 32*(6), 931–945.

Willett, W. (2013, in press). The current evidence on healthy eating. *Annual Review of Nutrition* (Vol. 34). Palo Alto, CA: Annual Reviews.

Willette, A. A., & others. (2012). Calorie restriction reduces the influence of glucoregulatory dysfunction on regional brain volume in aged rhesus monkeys. *Diabetes, 61,* 1036–1042.

Williams, N. M., & others. (2012). Genome-wide analysis of copy number variants in attention deficit hyperactivity disorder: The role of rare variants and duplications at 15q13.3. *American Journal of Psychiatry, 169,* 195–204.

Willis, S. L., & Martin, M. (2005). Preface. In S. L. Willis & M. Martin (Eds.), *Middle adulthood.* Thousand Oaks, CA: Sage.

Willoughby, V., Heger, A., Rogers, C., & Sathyavagiswaran, L. (2012). Sexual assault documentation program. *American Journal of Forensic Medicine and Pathology, 33,* 22–25.

Wilson, D., & Hockenberry, M. (2012). *Wong's clinical manual of pediatric nursing* (7th ed.). New York: Elsevier.

Wilson, K. R., Havighurst, S. S., & Harley, A. E. (2012). Tuning in to kids: An effectiveness trial of a parenting program targeting emotion socialization of preschoolers. *Journal of Family Psychology, 26,* 56–65.

Wilson, R. S., Mendes de Leon, C. F., Bienas, J. L., Evans, D. A., & Bennett, D. A. (2004). Personality and mortality in old age. *Journals of Gerontology B: Psychological Sciences and Social Sciences, 59,* P110–P116.

Windle, M. (2012). Longitudinal data analysis. In H. Cooper (Ed.), *APA handbook of research methods in psychology.* Washington, DC: American Psychological Association.

Windle, W. F. (1940). *Physiology of the humantus.* Philadelphia: W. B. Saunders.

Windsor, T. D., & Butterworth, P. (2010). Supportive, aversive, ambivalent, and indifferent partner evaluations in midlife and young-old adulthood. *Journals of Gerontology B: Psychological Sciences and Social Sciences, 65B,* 287–295.

Wink, P., & Dillon, M. (2002). Spiritual development across the adult life course: Findings from a longitudinal study. *Journal of Adult Development, 9,* 79–94.

Winner, B., Kohl, Z., & Gage, F. H. (2011). Neurodegenerative disease and adult neurogenesis. *European Journal of Neuroscience, 33,* 1139–1151.

Winner, E. (1996). *Gifted children: Myths and realities.* New York: Basic Books.

Winner, E. (2009). Toward broadening our understanding of giftedness: The spatial domain. In F. D. Horowitz, R. F. Subotnik, & D. J. Matthews (Eds.), *The development of giftedness and talent across the life span.* Washington, DC: American Psychological Association.

Winsler, A., Carlton, M. P., & Barry, M. J. (2000). Age-related changes in preschool children's systematic use of private speech in a natural setting. *Journal of Child Language, 27,* 665–687.

Winsper, C., Lereya, T., Zanarini, M., & Wolke, D. (2012). Involvement in bullying and suicide-related behavior at 11 years: A prospective birth cohort study. *Journal of the Academy of Child and Adolescent Psychiatry, 51,* 271–282.

Wise, P. M. (2006). Aging of the female reproductive system. In E. J. Masoro & S. N. Austad (Eds.), *Handbook of the biology of aging* (6th ed.). San Diego: Academic Press.

Witherington, D. C., Campos, J. J., Harriger, J. A., Bryan, C., & Margett, T. E. (2010). Emotion and its development in infancy. In J. G. Bremner & T. D. Wachs (Eds.), *Wiley-Blackwell handbook of infant development* (2nd ed.). New York: Wiley.

Witkin, H. A., & others. (1976). Criminality in XYY and XXY men. *Science, 193,* 547–555.

Witte, R. (2012). *Classroom assessment for teachers.* New York: McGraw-Hill.

Wittig, S. L., & Spatz, D. L. (2008). Induced lactation: Gaining a better understanding. *MCN, The Journal of Maternal Child Nursing, 33,* 76–81.

Wittmeier, K. D., Mollard, R. C., & Kriellaars, D. J. (2008). Physical activity intensity and risk of overweight and adiposity in children. *Obesity, 16,* 415–420.

Woelders, L. C. S., Larsen, J. K., Scholte, R., Cillessen, T., & Engles, R. C. M. E. (2011). Friendship group influences on body dissatisfaction and dieting among adolescent girls: A prospective study. *Journal of Adolescent Health, 47,* 456–462.

Wolfinger, N. H. (2011). More evidence for trends in the intergenerational transmission of divorce: A completed cohort approach using data from the general social survey. *Demography, 48,* 581–592.

Wolitzky-Taylor, K. B., & others. (2011). Reporting rape in a national sample of college women. *American Journal of College Health, 59,* 582–587.

Wolke, D., Schreier, A., Zanarini, M. C., & Winsper, C. (2012, in press). Bullied by peers in childhood and borderline personality symptoms at 11 years of age: A prospective study. *Journal of Child Psychology and Psychiatry.*

Wood, A., & others. (2011). Retinal and choroidal thickness in early age-related macular degeneration. *American Journal of Ophthalmology, 152,* 1030–1038.

Wood, J. T. (2012, in press). *Gendered lives* (10th ed.) Boston: Cengage.

Woolett, L. A. (2011). Review: Transport of maternal cholesterol to the fetal circulation. *Placenta, 32*(Suppl. 2), S18–S21.

Worthington, E. L. (1989). Religious faith across the life span: Implications for counseling and research. *Counseling Psychologist, 17,* 555–612.

Wright, R. O., & Christiani, D. (2010, in press). Gene-environment interaction and children's health and development. *Current Opinion in Pediatrics.*

Wright, R. H., Mindel, C. H., Tran, T. V., & Habenstein, R. W. (2012). *Ethnic families in America* (5th ed.). Upper Saddle River, NJ: Pearson.

Wrzus, C., Hanel, M., Wagner, J., & Neyer, F. J. (2012, in press). Social network changes and life events across the life span: A meta-analysis. *Psychological Bulletin.*

Wu, L. F., Chuo, L. J., & Wu, S. T. (2012). The effect of group instrumental reminiscence therapy in older single veterans who live in a veterans home in Taiwan. *International Journal of Geriatric Psychiatry, 27,* 107–108.

Wu, T., Gao, X., Chen, M., & van Dam, R. M. (2009). Long-term effectiveness of diet-plus-exercise interventions vs. diet-only interventions for weight loss: A metaanalysis. *Obesity, 10,* 313–323.

Wu, Z. C., Yu, J. T., Li, Y., & Tan, L. (2012). Clusterin in Alzheimer's disease. *Advances in Clinical Chemistry, 56,* 155–173.

Wuest, D. A., & Fisette, J. L. (2012). *Foundations of physical education, exercise science, and sports* (17th ed.). New York: McGraw-Hill.

X

Xiao, Y., & others. (2012, in press). Systematic identification of functional modules related to heart failure with different etiologies. *Gene.*

Xiu-Ying, H., & others. (2012). Living arrangements and risk for late life depression: A meta-analysis of published literature. *International Journal of Psychiatry in Medicine, 43,* 19–34.

Xu, H., & others. (2012, in press). The function of BMP4 during neurogenesis in the adult hippocampus in Alzheimer's disease. *Aging Research and Reviews.*

Xu, L., & others. (2011). Parental overweight/obesity, social factors, and child overweight/obesity at 7 years of age. *Pediatric International, 53,* 826–831.

Xue, F., Holzman, C., Rahbar, M. H., Trosko, K., & Fischer, L. (2007). Maternal fish consumption, mercury levels, and risk of preterm delivery. *Environmental Health Perspectives, 115,* 42–47.

Y

Yakoboski, P. J. (2011). Worries and plans as individuals approach retirement. *Benefits Quarterly, 27,* 34–37.

Yang, X. P., & Reckelhoff, J. F. (2011). Estrogen, hormonal replacement therapy, and cardiovascular disease. *Current Opinion in Nephrology and Hypertension, 20,* 133–138.

Yang, Y. (2008). Social inequalities in happiness in the United States, 1972–2004: An age-period-cohort analysis. *American Sociological Review, 73,* 204–226.

Yang, Y., & Kozloski, M. (2011). Sex differences in age trajectories of physiological dysregulation: Inflammation, metabolic syndrome, and allostatic load. *Journals of Gerontology A: Biological Sciences and Medical Sciences, 66A,* 493–500.

Yang, Y., & Lee, L. C. (2010). Dynamics and heterogeneity in the process of human frailty and aging: Evidence from the U.S. older adult population. *Journals of Gerontology B: Psychological Sciences and Social Sciences, 65B,* 246–255.

Yarber, W., Sayad, B., & Strong, B. (2013). *Human sexuality* (8th ed.). New York: McGraw-Hill.

Yassin, A. A., Akhras, F., El-Sakka, A. I., & Saad, F. (2011). Cardiovascular diseases and erectile dysfunction: The two faces of the coin on androgen deficiency. *Andrologia, 43,* 1–8.

Yates, D. (2012, in press). Neurogenetics: Unraveling the genetics of autism. *Nature Reviews: Neuroscience.*

Yi, O., & others. (2012). Association between environmental tobacco smoke exposure of children and parental socioeconomic status: A cross-sectional study in Korea. *Nicotine and Tobacco Research, 14,* 607–615.

Yiallourou, S. R., Sands, S. A., Walker, A. M., & Horne, R. S. (2011). Baroreflex sensitivity during sleep in infants: Impact of sleeping position and sleep state. *Sleep, 34,* 725–732.

Yin, R. K. (2012). Case study methods. In H. Cooper (Ed.), *APA handbook of research methods in psychology.* Washington, DC: American Psychological Association.

Yokoya, T., Demura, S., & Sato, S. (2009). Three-year follow-up of the fall risk and physical function characteristics of the elderly participating in a community exercise class. *Journal of Physiological Anthropology, 28,* 55–62.

Yolton, K., & others. (2010). Associations between secondhand smoke and exposure and sleep patterns in children. *Pediatrics, 125,* e261–e268.

Yoshikawa, H. (2011). *Immigrants raising citizens: Undocumented parents and their young children.* New York: Russell Sage.

Young, K. T. (1990). American conceptions of infant development from 1955 to 1984: What the experts are telling parents. *Child Development, 61,* 17–28.

Youth Risk Behavior Survey. (2011). *Trends in the prevalence of suicide-related behaviors National YRB: 1991–2011.* Retrieved June 6, 2012, from www.cdc.gov/yrbss

Yu, C. Y., & others. (2012, in press). Prenatal predictors for father-infant attachment after childbirth. *Journal of Clinical Nursing.*

Yudof, M. G., Levin, B., Moran, R., & Ryan, J. M. (2012). *Educational policy and the law* (5th ed.). Boston: Cengage.

Z

Zacher, H., Jimmieson, N. L., & Winter, G. (2012). Eldercare demands, mental health, and work performance: The moderating role of satisfaction with eldercare tasks. *Journal of Occupational Health Psychology.*

Zaff, J. F., Hart, D., Flanagan, C., Youniss, J., & Levin, P. (2010). Developing civic engagement within a civic context. In M. E. Lamb, A. M. Freund, & R. M. Lerner (Eds.), *Handbook of life-span development* (Vol. 2). New York: Wiley.

Zannas, A. S., & others. (2012, in press). Stressful life events, perceived stress, and 12-month course of geriatric depression: Direct effects and moderation by the 5-HTTLPR and COMT Val158Met polymorphisms. *Stress.*

Zeiders, K. H., Roosa, M. W., & Tein, J. Y. (2011). Family structure and family processes in Mexican-American families. *Family Process, 50,* 77–91.

Zeifman, D., & Hazan, C. (2008). Pair bonds as attachments: Reevaluating the evidence. In J. Cassidy & P. R. Shaver (Eds.), *Handbook of attachment* (2nd ed.). New York: Guilford.

Zeisel, S. H. (2011). The supply of choline is important for fetal progenitor cells. *Seminars in Cell and Developmental Biology, 22,* 624–628.

Zelazo, P. D., & Muller, U. (2011). Executive function in typical and atypical children. In U. Goswami (Ed.), *Wiley-Blackwell handbook of childhood cognitive development* (2nd ed.). New York: Wiley.

Zeskind, P. S., Klein, L., & Marshall, T. R. (1992). Adults' perceptions of experimental modifications of durations and expiratory sounds in infant crying. *Developmental Psychology, 28,* 1153–1162.

Zettel-Watson, L., & Rook, K. S. (2009). Friendship, later life. In D. Carr (Ed.). *Encyclopedia of the life course and human development.* Boston: Gale Cengage.

Zhai, F., Raver, C. C., & Jones, S. (2012, in press). Quality of subsequent schools and impacts of early interventions: Evidence from a randomized controlled trial in Head Start settings. *Children and Youth Services Review.*

Zhang, L.-F., & Sternberg, R. J. (2012, in press). Learning in cross-cultural perspective. In T. Husen & T. N. Postelwaite (Eds.), *International encyclopedia of education* (3rd ed.). New York: Elsevier.

Zhou, Q., Chen, S. H., & Main, A. (2012). Commonalities and differences in the research on children's effortful control and executive function: A call for an integrated model of self-regulation. *Child Development Perspectives, 6,* 112–121.

Zielinski, D. S. (2009). Child maltreatment and adult socioeconomic well-being. *Child Abuse and Neglect, 33,* 666–678.

Ziemer, C. J., Plumert, J. M., & Pick, A. D. (2012, in press). To grasp or not to grasp: Infants' actions toward objects and pictures. *Infancy.*

Zigler, E. F., Gilliam, W. S., & Barnett, W. S. (Eds.). (2011). *The pre-K debates: Controversies and Issues.* Baltimore: Brookes.

Zigler, E. F., Gilliam, W. S., & Jones, S. M. (2006). *A vision for universal preschool education.* New York: Cambridge. University Press.

Zigler, E. F., & Styfco, S. J. (1994). Head Start: Criticisms in a constructive context. *American Psychologist, 49,* 127–132.

Zigler, E. F., & Styfco, S. J. (2010). *The hidden history of Head Start.* New York: Oxford University Press.

Zimmer-Gembeck, M. J., & Helfand, M. (2008). Ten years of longitudinal research on U.S. adolescent sexual behavior: Developmental correlates of sexual intercourse, and the importance of age, gender, and ethnic background. *Developmental Review, 28,* 153–224.

Zimmerman, F. J., Ortiz, S. E., Christakis, D. A., & Elkun, D. (2012). The value of social-cognitive theory to reducing preschool TV viewing: A pilot randomized trial. *Preventive Medicine, 54,* 212–218.

Zotter, H., & Pichler, G. (2012, in press). Breast feeding is associated with decreased risk of sudden infant death syndrome. *Evidence Based Medicine.*

Zozuls, K., Martin, C., England, D., Andrews, N., & Borders, A. (2012, April). *"I don't want to talk to them because I don't know how to": The role of relationship efficacy in children's gender-related intergroup processes.* Paper presented at the Gender Development Research conference, San Francisco.

Zugazaga Cortazar, A., & Martin Martinez, C. (2012, in press). Usefulness of magnetic resonance imaging in the prenatal study of malformations of the face and neck. *Radiologia.*

Credits

Photo Credits

Contents

Page vii (left): © Keren Su/China Span/Getty Images; p. vii (top right): © Harry Bartlett/Taxi/Getty Images; p. vii (middle right): © Chris Windsor/Digital Vision/Getty Images RF; p. vii (bottom right): © Peter Dazeley/Photographer's Choice/Getty Images; p. viii: © Dorling Kindersley/Getty Images; p. ix (top): © John Carter/Photo Researchers; p. ix (bottom): © RubberBall Productions/Getty Images RF.

Chapter 1

Opener: © Julie Habel/age fotostock; p. 2 (Kaczynski adult): © Seanna O'Sullivan Photography; p. 2 (Kaczynski teen): ©WBBM-TV/AFP/Getty Images; p. 2 (Walker adult): © AP Wide World Photos; p. 2 (Walker child): Courtesy of Alice Walker; 1.1: © iStockphoto.com/leezsnow; p. 5: © Adam Hunger/Reuters/Landov; p. 6: Courtesy of Luis Vargas; p. 7: © Nancy Agostini; p. 8: © Naser Siddique/UNICEF Bangladesh; p. 12(a): © Jay Syverson/Corbis; p. 12(b): © Owaki-Kulla/Corbis; p. 17: © Sarah Putman; 1.8 (left to right): © Stockbyte/Getty Images RF; © BananaStock/PunchStock RF; © image100/Corbis RF; © RF/Corbis; p. 18: © Yves de Braine/Black Star/Stock Photo; p. 19: © A.R. Lauria/Dr. Michael Cole, Laboratory of Human Cognition, University of California, San Diego; p. 20: © Linda A. Cicero/Stanford News Service; p. 22: © Nina Leen/Time & Life Pictures/Getty Images; p. 23: Courtesy of Urie Bronfenbrenner; p. 25: © Philadelphia Inquirer/MCT/Landov Images; p. 26: © Bettmann/Corbis; 1.12: © Digital Vision/PunchStock RF; p. 30: © Inti St. Clair/Digital Vision/Getty Images RF.

Chapter 2

Opener: © Alamy Images RF; p. 34: © Enrico Ferorelli Enterprises; 2.1: ©Photodisc/Getty Images RF; p. 36: © David Wilkie; p. 38: © Rick Rickman; 2.3: © Custom Medical Stock Photo; p. 42 (top): © Joel Gordon Photography; p. 42 (bottom): From R. Simensen and R. Curtis Rogers, "Fragile X Syndrome" in *American Family Physician*, 39(5): 186, May 1989 © American Academy of Family Physicians; p. 43: © Andrew Eccles/August Images; p. 44: Courtesy of Holly Ishamel; p. 45: © RF/Corbis; 2.8 (top to bottom): © Last Refuge, Ltd./PhotoTakeUSA.com; © Neil_Bromhall/Photo Researchers, Inc.; © Brand X Pictures/PunchStock RF; 2.9: © Lennart Nilsson/Scanpix Sweden AB; 2.10: © Larry Berman; p. 54: Courtesy of Ann Streissguth; p. 55: © John Chiasson; p. 58: © Betty Press/Woodfin Camp & Associates; p. 59: © Ryan Pyle/Ryan Pyle/Corbis; p. 60: © Mark Randall/Sun Sentinel. All Rights Reserved; p. 61 (top): © Southern Illinois University School of Medicine; p. 61 (bottom): © RF/Corbis; p. 63: Dr. Holly Beckwith; p. 64: Courtesy of Linda Pugh; p. 65: © AP Wide World Photos; p. 66 (top): © iStockphoto.com/casenbina; p. 66 (bottom): Courtesy of Dr. Tiffany Field; p. 68: © Howard Grey/Getty Images RF.

Chapter 3

Opener: © Harry Bartlett/Taxi/Getty Images; p. 72 (left): © Wendy Stone/Corbis; p. 72 (right): © Dave Bartruff/Corbis; 3.2: © ER Productions/Getty Images RF; 3.6(a): © David Grugin Productions, Inc. Reprinted by permission; 3.6(b): Image courtesy of Dana Boatman, Ph.D., Department of Neurology, John Hopkins University, reprinted with permission from *The Secret Life of the Brain*, Joseph Henry Press; p. 78: © Maria Teijeiro/Cultura/Getty Images RF; p. 79: © Blend Images/Getty Images RF; p. 80: Courtesy Brazelton Touchpoints Center; p. 81: Courtesy of Esther Thelen; 3.8: © Dr. Karen Adolph, New York University; 3.9 (left to right): © Barbara Penoyar/Getty Images RF; © Digital Vision/Getty Images RF; © Image Source/Getty Images RF; © Titus/Getty Images RF; © Digital Vision RF; © BananaStock/Getty Images RF; © Corbis/PictureQuest RF; © BrandX/Punchstock RF; 3.10: Courtesy Amy Needham, Duke University; 3.11: © David Linton; 3.12: Image courtesy of Dr. Karen E. Adolph; 3.13: © Kevin Peterson/Getty Images/Simulation by Vischeck RF; 3.15: © Mark Richards/PhotoEdit; 3.16: Rosenstein, D. & Oster, H. (1988) Differential facial responses to four basic tastes in newborns. *Child Development*, 59, p. 1561; p. 92: © Dorling Kindersley/Getty Images; p. 93: © Laura Dwight/Corbis; 3.17: © Doug Goodman/Photo Researchers; p. 95: © Joe McNally; 3.18: Courtesy of Dr. Carolyn Rovee-Collier; 3.19: © Andrew Meltzoff; 3.21: From Jean Mandler, University of California, San Diego. Reprinted by permission of Oxford University Press, Inc.; 3.22: © 2003 University of Washington, Institute for Learning and Brain Sciences (I-LABS); p. 102: © ABPL Image Library/Animals Animals/Earth Scenes; p. 105: © John Carter/Photo Researchers.

Chapter 4.

Opener: © Rick Gomez/Corbis; p. 109: © Jose Luis Pelaez Inc./Getty Images RF; 4.1 (left to right): © BananaStock/PictureQuest RF; © The McGraw-Hill Companies, Inc./Jill Braaten, photographer; © David Sacks/Getty Images; © Getty Images RF; p. 111: © Andy Cox/Stone/Getty Images; p. 114-115: © Tom Merton/Getty Images RF; p. 116: © Corbis/age fotostock RF; 4.3: © Digital Vision/Getty Images RF; 4.4: Courtesy Celia A. Brownell, University of Pittsburgh; 4.5 © Martin Rogers/Stock Boston; p. 122: © George Doyle/Stockbyte/Getty Images RF; p. 123: © Penny Tweedie/Stone/Getty Images; 4.6: © Photodisc/Getty Images RF; p. 125: © BananaStock/PictureQuest RF; p. 126 (left): © BrandX/Punchstock RF; p. 126 (right): © Jessie Jean/Taxi/Getty Images; p. 127: Courtesy of Dr. Barry Hewlett; p. 128: © Lawrence Schwartzwald; p. 129: Courtesy of Wanda Mitchell; p. 130: © Reena Rose Sibayan/The Jersey Journal /Landov Images.

Chapter 5

Opener: © Ariel Skelley/Blend Images/Getty Images RF; p. 134 (top): © Ruby Washington/The New York Times/Redux Pictures; p. 134 (bottom): © DK Stock/Robert Glenn; p. 136: © C Squared Studios/Getty Images RF; p. 137: © Lilian Perez/Corbis; p. 138: © RubberBall Productions/Getty Images RF; p. 139: © AP Wide World Photos; 5.4: © Paul Fusco/Magnum Photos; 5.6: © Jose Luis Pelaez, Inc./Blend Images/Getty Images RF; p. 145: © BananaStock/PunchStock RF; 5.7 (left): © A.R. Lauria/Dr. Michael Cole, Laboratory of Human Cognition, University of California, San Diego; 5.7 (right): © Bettmann/Corbis; p. 148: © BananaStock/PunchStock RF; p. 149: © 2012 www.polychromemedia/jameskamp; 5.9: Photo by Dawn Villella, Courtesy of Stephanie Carlson; p. 151: Courtesy of Helen Hadani; p. 152: © Joe Baker, Images.com/Corbis; p. 156: © James Leynse/Corbis; p. 158: Courtesy of Yolanda Garcia; p. 159: © Ronnie Kaufman/The Stock Market/Corbis.

Chapter 6

Opener: © Topic Photo Agency IN/age fotostock; p. 164 (top): © Kevin Dodge/Corbis; p. 164 (bottom): © RF/Corbis; p. 166: © Dann Tardif/LWA/Corbis; p. 168: © Yves De Braine/Black Star/Stock Photo; p. 170: © Getty Images RF; 6.2: © Ariel Skelley/Corbis; p. 174: © Jose Luis Pelaez, Inc./Corbis; p. 175: Courtesy of Darla Botkin; p. 176: © Joshua Gunter/The Plain Dealer/Landov Images; p. 178 (top right): © RubberBall Productions/Getty Images RF; p. 178 (bottom left): © Image Source/Getty Images RF; p. 179: © Keith Brofsky/Photodisc/Getty Images RF; p. 181: © Image Source/PunchStock RF; p. 182: © 2009 Jupiterimages Corporation RF; p. 183: © Bill Aron/PhotoEdit; p. 184: © Fotosearch/PhotoLibrary RF; p. 186: © Dann Tardif/LWA/Corbis; p. 187 (top): Courtesy of Dr. Kathy Hirsh-Pasek; p. 187 (bottom): © Jekaterina Nikitina/Flickr/Getty Images.

Figure 2.9: From John Santrock, *Child Development*, 10th ed. Copyright © 2004 The McGraw-Hill Companies, Inc. Reproduced with permission by The McGraw-Hill Companies.

Figure 3.1: From John Santrock, *Children*, 9th ed. Copyright © 2007 The McGraw-Hill Companies, Inc. Reproduced with permission by The McGraw-Hill Companies.

Figure 3.3: From John Santrock, *Child Development*, 10th ed. Copyright © 2004 The McGraw-Hill Companies, Inc. Reproduced with permission by The McGraw-Hill Companies.

Figure 3.5: From John Santrock, *A Topical Approach to Life-Span Development*. Copyright ©2002 The McGraw-Hill Companies, Inc. Reproduced with permission by The McGraw-Hill Companies.

Figure 3.7: From John Santrock, *Children*, 5th ed. Copyright © 1997 The McGraw-Hill Companies, Inc. Reproduced with permission by The McGraw-Hill Companies.

Figure 3.20: From *Learning and the Infant Mind* edited by Woodward and Needham (2009). Table 1, p. 12. © 2005 by Amanda Woodward and Amy Needham. By permission of Oxford University Press, Inc.

Figure 3.23: From John Santrock, *Children*, 9th ed. Copyright © 2007 The McGraw-Hill Companies, Inc. Reproduced with permission by The McGraw-Hill Companies.

Figure 3.24: From John Santrock, *Children*, 9th ed. Copyright © 2007 The McGraw-Hill Companies, Inc. Reproduced with permission by The McGraw-Hill Companies.

Figure 3.25: From John Santrock, *Child Development*, 10th ed. Copyright © 2004 The McGraw-Hill Companies, Inc. Reproduced with permission by The McGraw-Hill Companies.

Figure 4.3: From John Santrock, *Life-Span Development*, 4th ed. Copyright © 1992 The McGraw-Hill Companies, Inc. Reproduced with permission by The McGraw-Hill Companies.

Figure 4.6: From Jay Belsky, "Early Human Experiences: A Family Perspective," in *Developmental Psychology*, Vol. 17, pp. 3–23. Copyright © 1981 by the American Psychological Association.

Figure 4.9: Reprinted from *Encyclopedia of Infant and Early Childhood Development*, Vol. I, A. Clarke-Steward and J.L. Miner, "Child and Day Care, Effects of," p. 269. Copyright © 2008 with permission from Elsevier.

Figure 5.1: From John Santrock, *Children*, 9th ed. Copyright © 2007 The McGraw-Hill Companies, Inc. Reproduced with permission by The McGraw-Hill Companies.

Figure 5.2: From *Well Being* by M.H. Bornstein et al. (eds.). Copyright 2003 by Taylor & Francis Group, LLC—Books. Reproduced with permission of Taylor & Francis Group LLC—Books in the format Textbook via Copyright Clearance Center.

Figure 5.3: From John Santrock, *Psychology*, 7th ed. Copyright © 2003 The McGraw-Hill Companies, Inc. Reproduced with permission by The McGraw-Hill Companies.

Figure 5.11: Courtesy of Jean Berko Gleason.

Ch. 5, p. 141: (The devl and the babe ghoste) From Jean Berko Gleason, *The Development of Language*, 3/e. Published by Allyn and Bacon, Boston MA. Reprinted with permission by Maryanne Wolf, Ph.D., Tufts University.

Ch. 6, pp. 157–168: Text excerpts from Craig Lesley, *Burning Fence: A Western Memoir of Fatherhood*, pp. 8–10, St. Martin's Press. Copyright © 2005 Craig Lesley. Reprinted by permission from St. Martin's Press, LLC.

Figure 6.1: From John Santrock, *Child Development*, 10th ed. Copyright © 2004 The McGraw-Hill Companies, Inc. Reproduced with permission by The McGraw-Hill Companies.

Figure 6.3: From John Santrock, *Life-Span Development*, 13th ed. Copyright © 2011 The McGraw-Hill Companies, Inc. Reproduced with permission by The McGraw-Hill Companies.

Figure 7.2: From John Santrock, *Children*, 9th ed. Copyright © 2007 The McGraw-Hill Companies, Inc. Reproduced with permission by The McGraw-Hill Companies.

Figure 7.9: From "The Rise in IQ Scores from 1932 to 1997" from "The Increase in IQ Scores from 1932 to 1997" by Ulric Neisser. Reprinted by permission.

Figure 8.2: From Colby et al., "A Longitudinal Study of Moral Judgment," *Monographs of the Society for Research in Child Development*, Serial No. 201. Reprinted with permission by Blackwell Publishing, Ltd.

Figure 8.3: Reproduced by special permission of the Publisher, Mind Garden, Inc., www.mindgarden.com from the Bem Sex Role Inventory by Sandra Bem. Copyright © 1978, 1981 by Consulting Psychologists Press, Inc. Further reproduction is prohibited without the Publisher's written consent.

Figure 8.5: From Stevenson, Lee, & Stigler, 1986, Figure 6. "Mathematics Achievement of Chinese, Japanese and American Children," *Science*, Vol. 231, pp. 693–699. Reprinted with permission from AAAS.

Figure 10.3: From John Santrock, *Child Development*, 11th ed. Copyright © 2007 The McGraw-Hill Companies, Inc. Reproduced with permission by The McGraw-Hill Companies.

Figure 11.1: Reprinted from *Journal of Adolescent Health* 39, Park et al., "The Health Status of Young Adults . . ." pp. 305–317. Elsevier Science. Copyright 2006, with permission from Elsevier.

Figure 11.3: Centers for Disease Control and Prevention (2006). Based on data collected in the 2005 National Health Interview Study.

Figure 11.5: From *Sex in America* by Robert T. Michael, John H. Gagnon, Edward O. Laumann, and Gina Kolata. Copyright © 1994 by CSG Enterprises, Inc. Edward O. Laumann, Robert T. Michael, and Gina Kolata. By permission of Little, Brown and Company.

Figure 11.6: From John Santrock, *Children*, 9th ed. Copyright © 2007 The McGraw-Hill Companies, Inc. Reproduced with permission by The McGraw-Hill Companies.

Figure 12.3: From Popenoe, David and Barbara DaFoe Whitehead. *The State of Our Unions: The Social Health of Marriage in America, 2005*, copyright 2005 by The National Projects at Rutgers University.

Ch. 13, p. 347: "Time in a Bottle." Words and Music by Jim Croce. Copyright © 1972 Denjac Music Company. © Renewed 2000 and assigned to Croce Publishing in the U.S.A. All Rights outside the U.S.A. administered by Denjac Music Company. All Rights Reserved. Used by permission.

Figure 13.1: From John Santrock, *Life-Span Development*, 11th ed. Copyright © 2008 The McGraw-Hill Companies, Inc. Reproduced with permission by The McGraw-Hill Companies.

Figure 13.2: From *Developmental Influences on Adult Development* by Schaie (2005). Figure 5.7a, p. 127. © 2005 by Oxford University Press, Inc. By permission of Oxford University Press, Inc.

Figure 13.3: From John Santrock, *Life-Span Development*, 11th ed. Copyright © 2008 The McGraw-Hill Companies, Inc. Reproduced with permission by The McGraw-Hill Companies.

Figure 13.4: From John Santrock, *Life-Span Development*, 11th ed. Copyright © 2008 The McGraw-Hill Companies, Inc. Reproduced with permission by The McGraw-Hill Companies.

Figure 14.1: From John Santrock, *Life-Span Development*, 11th ed. Copyright © 2008 The McGraw-Hill Companies, Inc. Reproduced with permission by The McGraw-Hill Companies.

Figure 14.2: From John Santrock, *Life-Span Development*, 11th ed. Copyright © 2008 The McGraw-Hill Companies, Inc. Reproduced with permission by The McGraw-Hill Companies.

Figure 14.3: From John Santrock, *Psychology*, 7th ed. Copyright © 2003 The McGraw-Hill Companies, Inc. Reproduced with permission by The McGraw-Hill Companies.

Name Index

subject Index

SUBJECT INDEX